# Sailing Skills
# and Seamanship

A fleet of two-person sailing dinghies races on a windless afternoon. The last-place crew is using their weight to heel the boat and, they hope, catch whatever breeze comes along. The crew just ahead of them senses a whiff of breeze from behind and has responded by winging out their jib opposite the mainsail. Until the wind fills in, no one is going anywhere fast. (PHOTO BY ED SWEENEY)

# Sailing Skills and Seamanship

## SIXTH EDITION

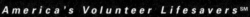

**United States Coast Guard Auxiliary**
*America's Volunteer Lifesavers*℠

International Marine / McGraw-Hill
Camden, Maine • New York • Chicago • San Francisco • Lisbon • London • Madrid • Mexico City •
Milan • New Delhi • San Juan • Seoul • Singapore • Sydney • Toronto

**The McGraw·Hill Companies**

1 2 3 4 5 6 7 8 9 0  QPD  QPD  9 8

*Library of Congress Cataloging-in-Publication Data*

United States Coast Guard Auxiliary.
  Sailing skills and seamanship / United States Coast Guard Auxiliary. — 6th ed.
      p.        cm.
  Rev. ed. of : Sailing and seamanship.
  Includes index.
  ISBN-13: 978-0-07-147029-2 (pbk. : alk. paper)
  ISBN-10: 0-07-147029-8 (pbk. : alk. paper)
  1.  Sailing. 2.  Seamanship.  I. United States Coast Guard Auxiliary. II. Sailing and Seamanship.
  GV811.S2552 2007
  797.1'24—dc22                    2007019528

ISBN 978-0-07-147029-2
MHID 0-07-147029-8

Questions regarding the content of this book should be addressed to
International Marine
P.O. Box 220
Camden, ME  04843
www.internationalmarine.com

Questions regarding the ordering of this book should be addressed to
The McGraw-Hill Companies
Customer Service Department
P.O. Box 547
Blacklick, OH  43004
Retail customers: 1-800-262-4729
Bookstores: 1-800-722-4726

The sixth edition of *Sailing Skills and Seamanship* has been edited and revised by Paul DeVita, Branch Chief—Course Management, USCGAUX.

The following Coast Guard Auxiliary members have also contributed time, talents, and efforts to *Sailing Skills and Seamanship*, sixth edition:
Henry Foglino, Division Chief, Course Management, USCGAUX
Anne Lockwood, Deputy Chief—Education, USCGAUX
Robin Freeman, Department Chief—Education, USCGAUX
Robert J. Dennis, Division Chief—Imagery and Multimedia, USCGAUX
Martin L. Phillips, Executive Director, Coast Guard Auxiliary Association Inc.
Peter J. Urgola, Department Chief—Vessel Exam, USCGAUX
W. James Montz, USCGAUX
Carla Kiwior, Branch Chief—Imagery, USCGAUX
USCGAUX Photo Corps, Department of Public Affairs, USCGAUX

Unless otherwise credited, illustrations by Joseph Comeau.

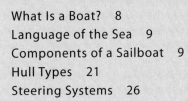
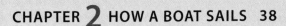

## CHAPTER 10 SAILING SAFETY 227

# Part Two: More Sailing Skills

## CHAPTER 11 MORE ON SAIL TRIM AND BOAT HANDLING 249

## CHAPTER 12 INTRODUCTION TO NAVIGATION 269

## CHAPTER 13 ENGINES FOR SAILBOATS 307

## CHAPTER 14 LINES AND KNOTS FOR YOUR BOAT 333

Dear Fellow Boater,

The mission of the United States Coast Guard Auxiliary, the uniformed volunteer component of the U.S. Coast Guard, is to assist the Coast Guard in the performance of its civil functions—particularly the promotion of recreational boating safety. The United States Coast Guard Auxiliary does this through its public education, vessel examination, and operations programs.

This book is the text for one of the core public education courses taught by the United States Coast Guard Auxiliary—Sailing Skills and Seamanship (SS&S). This course is a key component of a well-developed educational program that reaches from preschool through adulthood. The United States Coast Guard Auxiliary Public Education Program is the most comprehensive program available to today's pleasure boaters.

The sixth edition of the SS&S text continues our tradition of providing courses for quality classroom education to boaters. The SS&S course is approved by the National Association of State Boating Law Administrators. Information contained herein is consistent with current knowledge and with federal regulations in effect at the time of printing. Your instructor will present supplementary material on applicable state regulations. Many insurance companies provide discounts to graduates of the SS&S course.

This text has been prepared at no cost to the United States government. Members of the United States Coast Guard Auxiliary, America's Volunteer Lifesavers$^{SM}$, teach this course. United States Coast Guard Auxiliary members are a well-prepared, experienced group of volunteers dedicated to saving lives by promoting recreational boating safety. Their pay is the satisfaction of doing a good job and knowing they have helped other people have safe and enjoyable boating experiences.

I hope that you find this course both stimulating and enjoyable. Let me also urge you to take other Coast Guard Auxiliary courses and to consider supporting and even joining the U.S. Coast Guard Auxiliary.

Sincerely,

Steven M. Budar
National Commodore

# Welcome Aboard!

THE BOOK YOU ARE ABOUT TO READ is designed to help you become a better recreational sailor. Through it, we hope to teach you the knowledge and skills you need to sail safely. With this knowledge, you can avoid problems and enhance your enjoyment of on-the-water activities. We also want to raise your awareness of what bad things might happen to you or others, so that these things can be prevented.

Some sailors say that the worst day on the water is better than the best day ashore. The purpose of this book is to help ensure that the memories you carry with you when you return to the dock are great ones. (PHOTO BY BOB DENNIS)

# The Need for Safety on the Water

When you take appropriate precautions, being on the water is not only a wonderful experience but a safe one too—safer, for example, than driving a car. But boating accidents do occur, and sometimes they involve injury, financial loss, and occasionally even death. Considering the small amount of time we actually spend on the water, injury and death rates exceed those of many hazardous occupations.

Fortunately, injury and death rates are declining. This has resulted, in part, from the efforts of the United States Coast Guard, the Coast Guard Auxiliary, the United States Power Squadrons, and state and local agencies. They have been effective in preventing boating accidents and in saving lives.

# Promoting Boating Safety

Among the factors that account for improved boating safety are improved boater safety education, expanded law enforcement, safer boats, and greater awareness of the roles of alcohol and drugs in boating accidents. The purpose of this book is to promote safe boating.

# Sailing Skills and Seamanship

This book uses a timeline approach—a logical sequence for your introduction to the sport that begins with thinking about sailing and buying a boat through equipping it and using it safely and legally. The timeline should be clear from the chapter descriptions given below. Part One, Basic Skills and Seamanship (Chapters 1 through 10), introduces the basics of sailing, seamanship, the Rules of the Road, and safety on the water. In Part Two, More Sailing Skills (Chapters 11 through 16), we delve into topics you'll want to explore after your initial sailing experiences.

Each chapter has been written to help you achieve important goals. The chapter objectives are stated at the outset, and there are practice questions at the end of each chapter to confirm your understanding. (State and local boating information is not included because of the large variation of requirements between the states. State regulations are available from the National Association of State Boating Law Administrators [NASBLA] at www.nasbla.org.)

Although the chapters are designed to be read in sequence, this is certainly not mandatory. Some readers, for example, might prefer to skip Chapter 1—a survey of sailboat components and types—and begin instead with Chapters 2 through 4 in order to get out on the water that much quicker. There's nothing at all wrong with that approach, though we suspect that such a reader will return to Chapter 1 for the answers to questions that arise along the way. Here's how the book is organized:

## PART ONE: BASIC SKILLS AND SEAMANSHIP

*CHAPTER 1, ABOUT SAILBOATS,* provides an overview of the common sailboat types, from sailing dinghies and open daysailers with daggerboards or centerboards to much larger keelboats with cabins and accommodations for cruising. It also describes the common sailboat rig types together with their advantages and disadvantages. The chapter introduces the rich language of sailing and provides some guidance on selecting and purchasing a boat.

*CHAPTER 2, HOW A BOAT SAILS,* explores the miraculous harnessing of the wind by sails to produce motion through the water. We'll see that the aerodynamics of a sail have something in common with an airplane wing, but a sail—the shape of which is flexible and changes over time and in response to changing conditions—is more complex than a wing. We'll examine the sleight of hand that enables a sailboat to make progress in the direction from which the wind is blowing, and we'll explain how changing the shape of a sail can affect the sailboat's efficiency.

*CHAPTER 3, BASIC SAILBOAT MANEUVERING,* covers the fundamentals of making a sailboat do what you want it to do. When you're harnessing the wind, it isn't always possible simply to point the boat where you want to go and go there. Sometimes you have to proceed by indirection, and each time you alter course you'll have to adjust your sails. We'll cover tacking, jibing, and sailing a course—the "blocking and tackling" of sailing—so that you'll know what to expect before you raise the sails, cast off the docklines, and head out there.

**CHAPTER 4, RIGGING AND BOAT HANDLING,** gets us underway. We rig and hoist the sails, leave the dock or mooring, learn a little more about controlling the sails, and return to the mooring or dock after enjoying our sail. We also learn how to anchor and how to recover an anchor.

**CHAPTER 5, EQUIPMENT FOR YOUR BOAT,** shows you what to have on board to satisfy legal requirements. You will also learn what other equipment to carry for your safety and convenience. And you will learn how to find out if your boat and its equipment meet safety and legal requirements.

**CHAPTER 6, TRAILERING YOUR SAILBOAT,** provides the information you need to get a trailerable sailboat safely and legally from your home to where you want to launch it. It also describes launch ramp procedures—including how to back up with a trailer—and shows you how to launch and recover your boat with a minimum of fuss. Finally, this chapter includes some pointers for storing a boat on a trailer to protect it from the weather and from theft.

**CHAPTER 7, YOUR "HIGHWAY" SIGNS,** teaches you about the aids to navigation provided by federal, state, and local authorities. Knowing about these aids will help you have a safe voyage, and knowing how to locate them on a chart will help you keep track of where you are. These aids to navigation and the Navigation Rules in Chapter 8 are important guides when you sail.

**CHAPTER 8, THE RULES OF THE NAUTICAL ROAD,** describes the Navigation Rules that govern the conduct of your vessel while it is on the water.

Sailing is a sport for all ages and budgets. Freedom, adventure, self-reliance, harmony, contentment—these are all words used by sailors when asked to describe what they value most about sailing, and you can experience any one of these sensations as readily on a small daysailer as on a big cruising sailboat. (PHOTO BY BOB DENNIS)

These traffic rules help prevent boat collisions, and knowledge of the rules will help you have safe and enjoyable sailing experiences. The proper boat lighting, sound signals, and distress signals are also covered.

**CHAPTER 9, INLAND BOATING,** concentrates on such questions as: What special knowledge do you need to boat safely on rivers, lakes, and canals? What do you need to know to operate safely around dams? What procedures should you use in locks? The use of river charts, which differ in their symbology from coastal charts, is also explained.

**CHAPTER 10, SAILING SAFETY,** considers a variety of safety concerns, including what causes small boat accidents and how to avoid them. The pre-

A sturdy cruising cutter under a full press of sail. The projecting bow platform on this traditional-looking boat provides a landing for the forwardmost headsail and is reminiscent of the bowsprits that were once commonplace on sailing craft. The wire stay from the end of the bow platform to the stem of the hull is called a bobstay, and the strut that bisects the bobstay is called a dolphin striker. You can sail your entire life without encountering a boat that has these parts. (PHOTO BY ALFRED GALE)

vention of cold-water immersion and carbon monoxide poisoning are also explained, and good sources of weather information are provided.

## PART TWO: MORE SAILING SKILLS

**CHAPTER 11, MORE ON SAIL TRIM AND BOAT HANDLING,** describes how to tune a sailboat's rigging for best performance and explores some nuances of mainsail trim not covered in earlier chapters. In this chapter we also examine sail selection and boat handling in light airs, including the setting and trimming of a spinnaker. Finally, this chapter describes how to manage your boat in heavy weather, including reefing the sails and preventing and recovering from gear breakage, a knockdown, or a capsize.

**CHAPTER 12, INTRODUCTION TO NAVIGATION,** teaches you the basics of how to get from where you are to where you want to be. You will learn how to read a chart, plot a course, and measure your voyage progress.

**CHAPTER 13, ENGINES FOR SAILBOATS,** covers what a sailor should know about his or her outboard or inboard engine, including its maintenance and operation.

**CHAPTER 14, LINES AND KNOTS FOR YOUR BOAT,** shows you how to tie and when to use the most important knots, and also tells you what you need to know about the proper handling of ropes and lines.

**CHAPTER 15, WEATHER AND SAILING,** tells you where to find weather reports and forecasts and how to interpret and refine them using your own deck-level observations of wind, clouds, and barometer. The goal is to provide you with the knowledge you need to make informed go, no-go decisions prior to leaving the dock and throughout your voyage.

**CHAPTER 16, YOUR BOAT'S RADIO,** describes the use of marine radios and introduces the proper phraseology and etiquette for radio communications. You will also find insights for purchasing an appropriate radio for your applications.

The Auxiliary's goal is to help you become a better recreational boater. We wish you safe and happy boating!

# Basic Skills and Seamanship

This contemporary fiberglass sloop is set up for cruising convenience, with its primary anchor stowed on a bow roller, its roller-furling headsail that can be conveniently roller-reefed when the wind comes up, its radar antenna (two-thirds of the way up the mast) for navigating and collision avoidance, and its cockpit awning to provide shelter from sun and rain.
(PHOTO BY FRED SCHLACTER)

# About Sailboats

**The objectives of this chapter are to describe:**

- Parts of a sailboat in proper language.
- Sailboat hull types and rigs.
- The variety of sailboats available to match your needs.
- How boats are built.
- How to get information on possible defects in a vessel.
- Considerations in a contract to purchase a boat.

SAILBOATS AND POWERBOATS together make up the world of recreational boating. The two differ considerably, not only in their appearance and locomotive power, but also in the ways people use them. Sailboats don't make very good fishing platforms, and you can't water-ski behind one, but they bring you closer to nature, to the

Quiet anchorages like this one in Penobscot Bay, Maine, await the cruising sailor. (PHOTO BY STEPHEN GROSS)

wind and the waves. They challenge a skipper's skill and judgment. They require greater effort than most powerboats, but the rewards are often proportional to the effort expended.

To many people, the thrill of getting there, the ability to master the elements, is more important than the destination itself. These are the folks we see sailing in local waters week after week while their powerboating friends head off to new and exotic destinations. At the other extreme, we find that most around-the-world cruises are carried out in sailboats, which are more seakindly, less noisy, and not completely dependent on refueling facilities. There is room for all kinds of recreational boating on our increasingly crowded waterways, but only if all boaters respect both the interests and the rights of others.

Although there are literally hundreds of types of sailboats afloat today, all sailboats are basically similar. In this book, we will concentrate on the more common types, but the principles that apply to them will generally hold true for exotic or unusual craft as well.

# What Is a Boat?

A boat is anything used for transportation on the water. Huck Finn's raft was a boat. A seaplane is a boat when it is on the water. Canoes, kayaks, rowboats, and other small craft are boats. Boats range in size from personal watercraft (PWC) to large ships, and they might have deep or shallow hulls; flat, round, or V-shaped bottom sections; and tall or short cabin sides and superstructures. They can be slender or stout, and they might have one, two, or even three hulls. They vary, too, in the materials from which they're built. As defined by the Federal Boat Safety Act of 1971, all boats are vessels, but a vessel is not a boat (and therefore exempt from certain commercial safety regulations) unless it was manufactured or is engaged primarily for noncommercial use or is engaged in carrying six or fewer passengers for hire.

# Language of the Sea

Newcomers to any subject usually must learn a new vocabulary, and boating is no exception. The language of mariners has been developing for many centuries. It has the virtues of utility, economy, and an exactitude you need when talking about boats and boating.

As we introduce terms, we will usually define them for you. You can also find some of them in the Glossary at the back of the book. If you do not find a word listed in the Glossary, look for it in the Index. The first time we define a technical term, we will print it in **red**.

Some nautical terms have found their way into our everyday vocabulary. The term "blue Monday" came to us from England. The British Navy disciplined sailors on Mondays for infractions over the preceding week. The punishment consisted of lashes with a cat-o'-nine tails, or whip. No wonder Monday was blue. When not in use, the cat stayed in a sack. Of course, the cat was "out of the bag" when used.

Other terms came from Norway. Sailboats are steered by *rudders*. On an ancient sailing boat, the rudder was to the right of center at the rear, or *stern*, of the vessel. There it was protected from damage when the ship was in port. The *tiller*, which turned the rudder, was kept under the helmsman's right arm.

In Norway, the rudder was a "stjorn" board or steering board. *Stjorn*, when pronounced, sounds like "starn." So the right side of a vessel when looking *forward* became known as the "stjorn board" or *starboard* side (Figure 1-1).

When a vessel came into port, it was with its left side next to the wharf. This was the side most visible to the helmsman. It was also the side for the "load board." No wonder the left side of the vessel became known as the *larboard* side. "Larboard" and "starboard" are more exact terms than "left" and "right" since they do not change if you are facing forward or *aft*.

Because larboard and starboard sound somewhat alike, they are easily confused. Thus, larboard was changed to *port*. This was a logical choice, as this was the side of a vessel next to the wharf when the vessel was in port. Larger vessels load through *ports*, or openings, in their sides.

Remnants of ancient boats made of large, hollowed-out tree trunks or *keels* still exist. These unstable vessels took on water easily. Although they

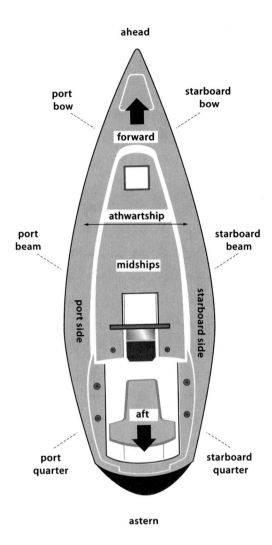

**Figure 1-1.** Directions and locations on a boat.

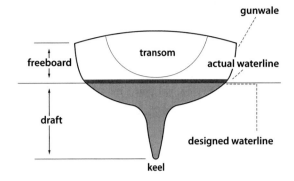

**Figure 1-2.** Some terms used to describe a boat.

# Components of a Sailboat

Once you become accustomed to using sailors' terminology, it will come naturally. It's a lot easier in the long run to have at your command a word like *halyard*, for instance, than to grope for the approximate equivalent in everyday English: a rope or wire that raises and lowers a sail.

There are two basic parts of any sailboat—the hull (or hulls) and the rig. A sailboat *hull* is simply the load-carrying part of the vessel. Besides supporting the crew, their equipment, the engine (if any), and the mast and sails, the hull has other functional requirements. It must move efficiently through the water in the direction the boat is steered while at the same time resisting forces that attempt to push it in other directions. Meanwhile, it must stay reasonably upright, opposing the pressure of the wind on the sails.

The *rig* is the collective term for the various elements that form a sailboat's power system. There are basically three interacting parts—the spars (see below), the rigging, and the sails.

## THE HULL

Many sailboat terms are so much a part of the language that you'll find you know them already. Others are less well known. We covered bow, stern, port, and starboard above. Now let's run through a few others that pertain to the hull.

didn't sink, they were of little value when slightly submerged in rough or icy water.

Planks were added later, and the trunk became but one part of the vessel. The name keel remained, however. The body of the vessel, formed by the keel and the planks together, became known as the *hull*.

The aft terminus of many boats is a flat, vertical surface extending from one side of the vessel to the other. This part of a boat became known as a *transom*, from the Latin root "trans," meaning across (Figure 1-2).

The *bow* is the forwardmost portion of a vessel. This term came from the Norwegian word "bov," meaning shoulder, and pronounced "bow." You can almost see the shoulder of a boat pushing its way through the water.

If you were to measure the length of a boat along its deck from bow to stern (but not including a bowsprit or stern sprit, if either were present), the dimension would be labeled as *length overall*. When the dimensions of a sailboat appear in magazines or sales literature, this term is frequently abbreviated LOA (Figure 1-3). *Length at the waterline* (for more, see below) is called LWL for short. The width of the hull at the widest point is her *beam*, and the depth of water required to float her is known as the boat's *draft*. Many sailboats have retractable bottom appendages called *centerboards* (which retract by pivoting sternward) or *daggerboards* (which retract straight upward), so in this case two drafts may be listed—one with *board up* and one with *board down* (Figure 1-4, and see page 23).

The *waterline* is the line of intersection of the water surface with the boat's hull. A stripe painted along and above the waterline when the boat is

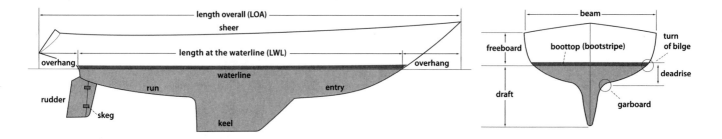

**Figure 1-3.** Characteristics of a sailboat hull.

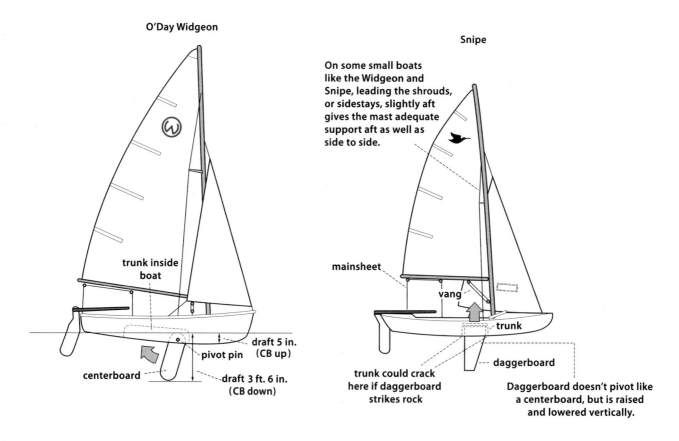

**Figure 1-4.** Small open sailboats frequently have centerboards (left) or daggerboards (right) rather than fixed keels, as discussed later in this chapter.

floating upright is called the ***boottop*** or ***bootstripe*** (see Figure 1-3). It serves as a useful reference to determine if the boat has been properly loaded. When the boottop shows clearly around the hull

and is parallel with the water surface, the boat is said to be correctly trimmed. If the hull is down by the bow or stern, or tipped to one side or the other, or too high or low in the water, she's out of trim (Figure 1-5).

Very small sailboats may be completely open (Figure 1-6). Most boats, however, have a covering, the ***deck***, over the forward part of the hull (Figure 1-7), and in many craft there are side decks as well. The deck keeps rain and spray out of the hull, provides a place to attach hardware, and helps keep the mast in place (Figure 1-8). The cutout tub in

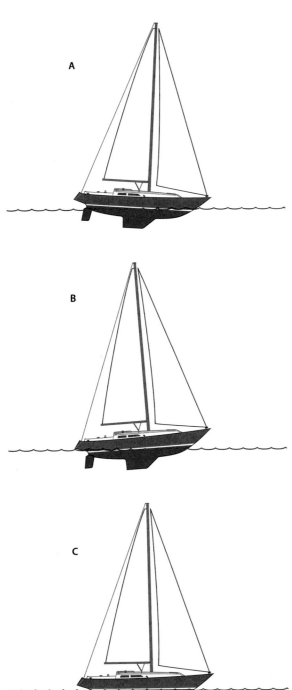

**Figure 1-6.** The Laser sailing dinghy is a 13-foot, 10-inch Olympic-class boat that was introduced in 1970. Like a Snipe, this small open boat has a daggerboard, which makes it ideal for sailing off the beach. A Laser is fast enough to get up on the surface of the water and *plane* over it rather than plowing through it, and sailing one is a wet but exhilarating experience for adults as well as kids. The boat is raced solo but can be sailed by two. (REPRINTED WITH PERMISSION FROM *YOUR FIRST SAILBOAT* BY DANIEL SPURR)

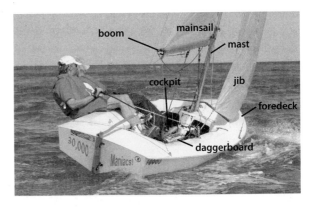

**Figure 1-7.** The Snipe was designed for plywood construction in 1931, but today is manufactured in fiberglass. Note the foredeck, through which the mast passes. The skipper and crew are hiked out to counter the heeling force of the wind in the sails, and their feet are tucked under a hiking strap on the cockpit sole. This is athletic sailing! (REPRINTED WITH PERMISSION FROM *YOUR FIRST SAILBOAT* BY DANIEL SPURR)

**Figure 1-5.** Hull trim. Boat A has too much weight forward and is down by the bow. Boat B has too much weight aft and is down by the stern. Boat C is properly trimmed fore and aft and is also resting on her designed waterline, a sign that she is neither overloaded nor insufficiently ballasted.

the center of the deck, from which the skipper steers and the crew operates the boat, is the *cockpit*. There's frequently a raised lip around the edge of the cockpit—the *coaming*—that serves to deflect water.

The floor of the cockpit is called the cockpit *sole*. In a contemporary fiberglass boat the decks, the cockpit tub and sole, and the cabin sides and

**Figure 1-8.** Like the Laser and Snipe, the J/24 is a one-design—meaning that multiple copies have been produced in fiberglass from the manufacturer's molds. Unlike the Laser or Snipe, it is also a *keelboat*—meaning that it has a fixed keel rather than a daggerboard or centerboard—and it is among the world's most popular one-design keelboats. This boat is fully decked, and the mast passes through the cabin top and steps atop the keel. The crew is on the rail to keep the boat more level (and therefore faster) while racing, but at other times the ballast on the bottom of the keel suffices to counter the heeling force of the wind. Note that these crewmembers don't have to hike out as the crew of the Snipe do. (PHOTO BY DANIEL FORSTER, REPRINTED WITH PERMISSION FROM *YOUR FIRST SAILBOAT* BY DANIEL SPURR)

top (if the boat has a cabin) are frequently molded as one large piece, which is then bonded to the hull mold. In wooden boats, however, all these parts are hand built. Like other walk-on surfaces aboard, the sole should be **nonskid** (Figure 1-9). A nonskid effect can be achieved using paint with sand in it, or, in a fiberglass boat, with a molded-in pattern. If your boat doesn't have nonskid where it's needed, you can buy, at most boating supply stores, waterproof tape with a slightly abrasive surface. It's a good investment in safety. Some wooden boats and older fiberglass boats have a grate of interlocked wood strips (usually teak) on the cockpit sole to provide good footing while keeping shoes dry.

Most hardware on a sailboat is connected with handling the sails, but some pertains to the hull itself. Even the smallest boat should have a **cleat** or eye bolt at bow and stern for attaching mooring or towing lines. Cleats may be wood, metal, or plastic, but they should be bolted through the deck and preferably through a backing plate under the deck as well (Figure 1-10). More and more fiberglass sailboats—especially smaller, more open ones—have built-in flotation between the outer skin of the hull and the inner skin, called the *liner*. This flotation (as in Figure 1-10) is usually in the form of rigid plastic foam, inserted in sufficient quantity to keep the water-filled boat plus her crew afloat.

Some small sailboats have *self-bailers* built into the after end of the cockpit. These are one-way valves that operate to expel bilge water from the

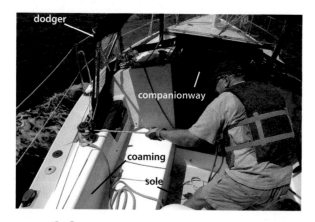

**Figure 1-9. Left:** This view into the cockpit of a 30-foot fiberglass keelboat gives a feel for the enhanced comfort and security a somewhat larger sailboat can provide. A canvas dodger over the *companionway* (the cabin entrance) provides shelter from sun and wind, while the deep cockpit tub and elevated coaming keep the crew safe and comparatively dry. (PHOTO BY BOB DENNIS) **Right:** The nonskid pattern on the cabin top of this cruising sailboat is clearly visible. (PHOTO BY DON LINDBERG)

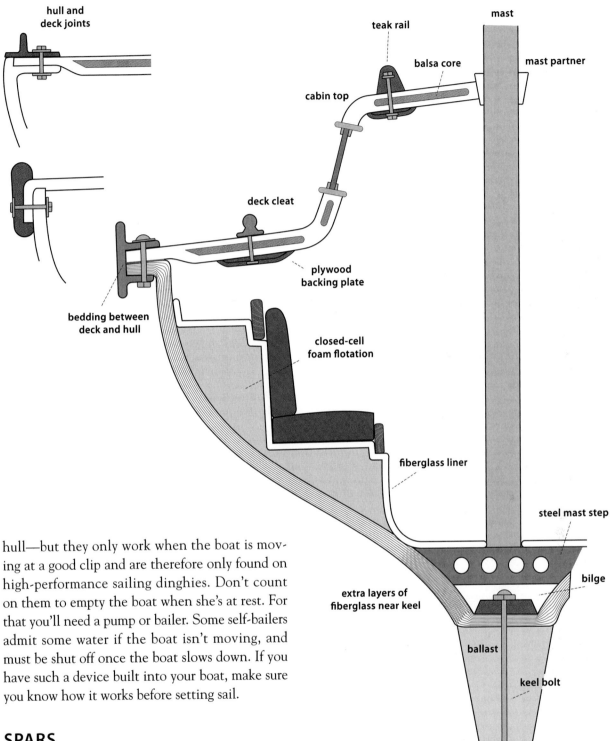

hull—but they only work when the boat is moving at a good clip and are therefore only found on high-performance sailing dinghies. Don't count on them to empty the boat when she's at rest. For that you'll need a pump or bailer. Some self-bailers admit some water if the boat isn't moving, and must be shut off once the boat slows down. If you have such a device built into your boat, make sure you know how it works before setting sail.

## SPARS

*Spar* is the general term for the rigid members that support and extend the sails. The primary spar is the *mast*, a vertical member that holds the sails up. Most boats also have a *boom*, which holds out the *foot*, or bottom, of the sail at right angles to the mast. The mast and boom are joined by a kind of

**Figure 1-10.** Cross section of a keel sailboat, showing three alternative ways for a fiberglass deck to be mated with a fiberglass hull. On this boat the mast passes through the cabin top and is stepped in the bilge. Note the backing plate for the through-bolted deck cleat.

universal joint called a *gooseneck*, which allows the boom to pivot up, down, or sideways (Figure 1-11).

There are other types of spars—gaffs, yards, and spinnaker poles, to name the most common—but they are restricted to specialized boat types or advanced forms of sailing, and will be dealt with later.

Spars were traditionally fashioned from wood, but the strength, light weight, and durability of aluminum have made it the most popular spar material for contemporary sailboats. On some smaller boats where bending spars are useful, fiberglass spars, rather like oversize fishing poles, are occasionally seen. Carbon fiber, which is even lighter and stronger than aluminum, is sometimes used on high-performance sailboats when cost is no object. Some older boats and ones of traditional appearance still retain wood spars, either hollow sections glued together or solid pieces of timber.

Whatever the construction material, all spars have much the same kinds of fittings attached to them. As we shall see in a later chapter, it's important not only to extend a sail but also to vary the tension along its edges, thereby controlling and optimizing its shape. Sail control fittings on the spars

perform this function. Once we've had a chance to consider how sails are shaped and how they are fastened to spars, we can consider the various types of fittings and how they work.

The mast fits into or onto a *mast step*, or socket, which is shaped so that the spar's *heel*, or base, cannot slide off (see Figure 1-10). In most boats the step is cast metal (though it may be wood in a wooden boat) and is mounted in a reinforced area of the boat's bilge. In some boats, however, the mast is stepped on deck, making it much easier to raise and lower at the beginning and end of the sailing season. If the boat is trailered and the mast must be raised and lowered frequently, it will often be stepped in a pivot fitting called a *tabernacle*. Any deck-stepped mast must be supported by a compression strut or other substantial reinforcing structure beneath it to transfer rigging loads from the deck or cabin top to the boat's hull and keel.

When the mast is stepped in the bilge, it passes through a tight-fitting hole in the deck or, in some small open boats, through a hole in a forward seat. Often, in larger boats, the mast passes through the cabin roof, where a reinforcing collar called the *mast partner* is placed to help take the strain of

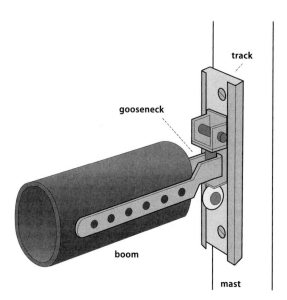
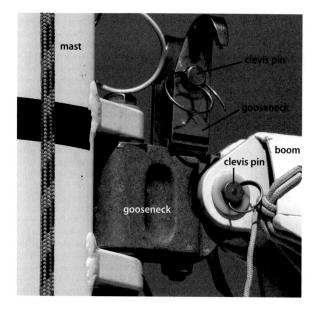

**Figure 1-11.** A gooseneck fitting is designed to allow the boom to pivot up and down as well as side to side. As with so many items of sailboat hardware, it can take a variety of forms and still fulfill this basic function. The illustration shows a simple gooseneck such as you might encounter on a small keelboat or large dinghy. The photo shows a heavier-duty gooseneck on a cruising sailboat. The boom in the photo can pivot in the vertical plane around the clevis pin that attaches it to the gooseneck, while the gooseneck itself pivots side to side around the vertical pin that attaches it to the mast. The forward lower corner of the mainsail will be attached to the clevis pin that runs between the two horns projecting upward from the gooseneck. (PHOTO BY NORMA LOCOCO)

the spar. On some small boats, this arrangement alone provides sufficient support for the mast, but on most boats a certain amount of rigging, varying with the size of boat, is necessary to keep the mast up and straight.

# STANDING AND RUNNING RIGGING

There are two types of rigging—standing and running. *Standing rigging* stays put; it supports the mast under tension. *Running rigging* requires frequent adjustment; it runs through **blocks** (the nautical term for pulleys) to raise, lower, ease out, or trim in the sails.

## Standing Rigging

The standing rigging of the average sailboat is not complicated. Its purpose is to keep the mast upright and straight. Remember also that any pull on the mast from one direction must be matched from the opposite side if the spar is to remain in position and *in column* (i.e., undistorted). A *backstay* keeps the mast from falling forward over the bow, while one or more *forestays* keep the mast from falling over the stern. A forestay that runs from the very bow of the boat to a position at or near the top of the mast is also called a *headstay*. On some boats an *inner forestay*, or *babystay*, runs from a point on the foredeck midway between the bow and the mast to a landing point some two-thirds of the way up the mast, permitting a smaller jib to be flown in strong winds (Figure 1-12).

If a backstay landing on the middle of the boat's transom would interfere with the tiller and rudder, the backstay might be offset slightly to one side or the other, or it might be split into two lower legs, one leading to the boat's starboard quarter and one to its port quarter.

When, for reasons of design, the forestay doesn't end near the masthead, aftward tension to balance the forestay is provided by a pair of *running backstays*, one on each side of the boat (Figure 1-13). Each running backstay ends in a rope tackle, and only the *windward* one (the one on the side over which the wind is blowing) is set up. The one to *leeward* is left slack so as not to interfere with the mainsail.

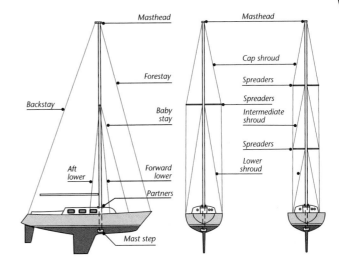

**Figure 1-12.** A typical keelboat rig. Note that the forestay runs all the way to the masthead, making this a *masthead rig*. This boat has a babystay, from which a smaller jib can be flown. The stern view at right shows what is probably a larger boat with two sets of spreaders and intermediate shrouds. Most boats less than 32 to 35 feet long have only a single set of spreaders. (REPRINTED WITH PERMISSION FROM *HOW BOAT THINGS WORK* BY CHARLIE WING)

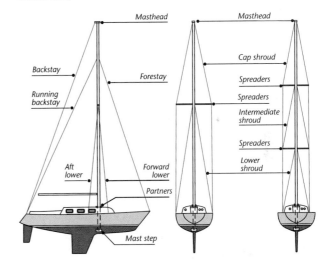

**Figure 1-13.** On this boat with a *fractional rig*, the forestay lands well below the masthead, and its tension is opposed by a pair of running backstays to keep the mast in column. The advantage of this rig is that it permits the masthead to be bent backward by means of an adjustable backstay, thus changing the shape of the mainsail to match wind conditions. (REPRINTED WITH PERMISSION FROM *HOW BOAT THINGS WORK* BY CHARLIE WING)

A mast is kept from falling to the side by standing rigging called *shrouds*. On small boats there is usually only one set, running from the side of the hull up to the masthead. Sometimes, to make a more mechanically effective lead of the shrouds to the masthead, a pair of horizontal spars called *spreaders* are fitted about two-thirds of the way up the mast. The spreader, as its name suggests, simply widens the angle at which the wire reaches the masthead, giving a more effective sideways angle of pull.

The shrouds that run over spreaders to the masthead are called *upper shrouds*, or just *uppers*, or sometimes *cap shrouds*. Other shrouds run from the sides of the hull to the mast just beneath the intersection of the spreaders; these are *lower shrouds* or *lowers*. There may be one or two pairs of them. On some boats, an inner forestay does the same job as the pair of forward lowers.

Shrouds and stays are normally made of stiff stranded wire rope, generally stainless steel. Since it's necessary to balance the stresses of the various pieces of standing rigging against their opposite numbers, adjustable fittings are provided at the bottom end of each stay and shroud. The most common fit-

ting for this job, called a *turnbuckle*, is usually cast in bronze or stainless steel (Figure 1-14). It allows for a limited adjustment of wire tension, a process called tuning, dealt with in more detail in Chapter 11.

The turnbuckles are in turn fitted to *toggles*, small castings that allow the turnbuckle to lie in the same straight line as the stay or shroud to which it is fitted. And many toggles, in turn, are secured to *chainplates*—heavy metal straps bolted and/or fiberglassed to the hull or its principal bulkheads (partitions).

## Running Rigging

While standing rigging is almost invariably wire, running rigging may be wire or rope or a combination of the two. The two most common types of running rigging are *halyards*, which raise and lower the sails, and *sheets* (ropes), which control the set of a sail in order to use the wind most efficiently (Figure 1-15). There are other kinds of running rigging, but they are specialized in nature, to be discussed in Chapter 11.

Each sail has at least one halyard, which normally takes its name from the sail it raises. Because rope stretches, halyards are frequently half rope

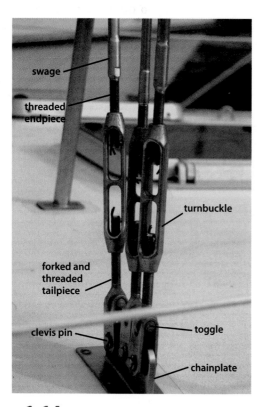

**Figure 1-14.** In this view aft on a sailboat's starboard side, we see the turnbuckles for (right to left) the starboard forward lower shroud, the starboard upper shroud, and the starboard after lower shroud. The wire rope shrouds terminate in the swaged end fittings at the top of the photo. The chainplates are substantially reinforced and anchored belowdecks to handle the rigging loads. (PHOTO BY DON LINDBERG)

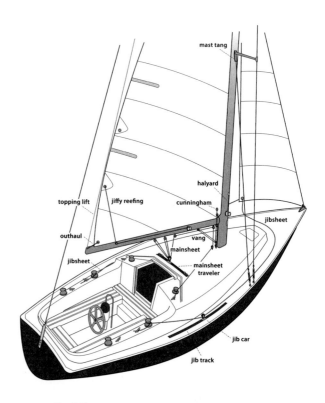

**Figure 1-15.** The principal running rigging.

and half wire, so that when the sail is fully raised, all the tension is taken by nonstretching wire. The sheets, too, are named by the sail they control—most commonly the *mainsheet* and *jibsheets*—and are normally Dacron rope, which stretches less than nylon. The type of wire used for halyards is quite flexible, and different in construction, if not in material, from the wire used for stays and shrouds. Rigging materials are discussed further in Chapter 4.

Halyards run either through blocks set into the top of the mast (Figure 1-16), or through blocks attached partway up the mast, depending on how high the sail is to be raised. (Note that the rolling part of a block is called a *sheave*, and sailors often

use the terms block and sheave interchangeably.) Most halyards on smaller sailboats terminate at cleats on the mast itself, but in larger sailboats they are often led through blocks at the base of the mast and from there back to the cockpit, so that the crew can raise and lower the sails without having to leave the cockpit. In many cases (especially aboard larger craft) the halyard is led around a winch—mounted either on the mast or on the cabin top near the cockpit—to increase the tension on the halyard and, by extension, on the sail it is hoisting.

A sheet normally runs from the after corner, or *clew*, of the sail it controls, or (in the case of the mainsheet) from the mainsail boom down to the cockpit area. Mechanical advantage of the sheets may be increased by the use of winches or block-and-tackle systems as required. The end of a sheet is made fast to a cleat. While the traditional, anvil-shaped cleats are often seen, more and more skippers are turning to one or another style of quick-release **cam** or **jam cleats**. In these devices, the rope is simply led through a gripping pair of jaws that hold it fast until it is forcibly released by a crewmember (see Figure 4-11). The attachment is as secure as a cleated line, and a great deal quicker both to make fast and to let free, and in smaller boats quick release of a sheet may be the difference between capsizing and staying upright.

A third type of running rigging is the *topping lift*, which is used to support the boom when its sail is not raised. The topping lift usually runs from the masthead to the aft end of the boom.

## SAILS

All this structure—spars, standing and running rigging—exists to make the sails function efficiently. Today's sailboats use triangular sails flown in a fore-and-aft plane in what is variously known as a *jib-headed*, *marconi*, or *Bermudan* rig. When sailboats functioned as fishing craft or ferries, the sails employed in everyday business were known as the *working sails*. Now that we use our boats for cruising and racing, we often call our smaller, stronger cruising sails **working sails** to distinguish them from larger, more expensive **racing sails**.

The most common sailboat type is the *sloop*—a

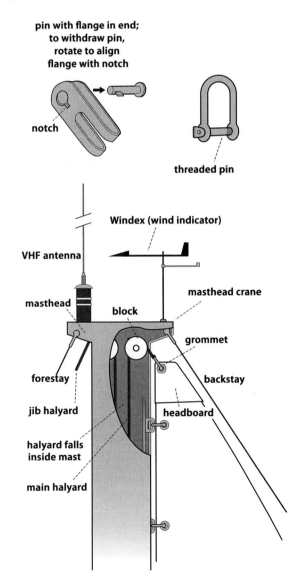

**pin with flange in end; to withdraw pin, rotate to align flange with notch**

notch

threaded pin

Windex (wind indicator)

VHF antenna

masthead crane

masthead

block

grommet

forestay

backstay

jib halyard

headboard

halyard falls inside mast

main halyard

**Figure 1-16.** Masthead halyard blocks. This boat is likely a keelboat at least 22 to 24 feet long. A smaller sailboat does not normally require a masthead crane as shown here.

vessel with a single mast and two sails, one set ahead of the mast and one behind. The sail behind the mast is the *mainsail*, usually shortened to *main*, and the sail in front is the *jib* (Figure 1-17).

A triangular sail has three corners—the *head*, at the top; the *tack*, at the forward lower corner; and the *clew*, at the after lower corner. The sail's leading edge is the *luff*, its lower edge is its *foot*, and its after edge is the *leech*. Each sail is formed from a number of cloths—called *panels*—that are sewn together in one of several patterns. A sail, unlike a flag, is a three-dimensional airfoil—more complex than an airplane wing due to the sail's flexibility—and the cloth panels are sewn to create this airfoil, the shape of which can be altered with sail controls to make the sail flatter for fresh winds or fuller for light winds. The sail's edges are reinforced with rope or extra thicknesses of cloth.

A mainsail is attached to the mast along its luff and to the boom along its foot. The luff and foot are fitted with **slides**, which ride along external tracks on the mast and boom; or with **slugs**, which fit a groove recessed into the mast or boom; or with

a **bolt rope**, which fits inside the mast and boom grooves (Figure 1-18 and Figures 4-4 and 4-6). Sometimes—especially on small open daysailers—the foot of the mainsail is loose, attached to the boom only at its clew and tack.

The mainsail's leech is its free edge, and it is normally supported and extended by wood or plastic strips, called **battens**, which are set into pockets at right angles to the leech. These supports enable the leech to be cut in a convex curve, called the **roach**, for greater sail area and more power (see Figure 1-17). Without battens to stiffen it, the roach would be limp and curled, failing to assume its airfoil shape.

At each corner of the sail is a **cringle**, a circular metal reinforcement for attaching hardware: the halyard is made fast to the head cringle (or the opening in the headboard); the **gooseneck** is fitted to the tack cringle; and the **outhaul**, a carriage riding on the boom to extend the foot of the sail aft, is fitted to the clew cringle (Figure 1-19).

The jib is a somewhat simpler sail to describe: it too has a luff, foot, and leech, along with cringles in its three reinforced corners to accept hardware (Figure 1-20). The luff is **hanked**, or snapped, along the forestay, while the leech and the foot fly free. The jib tack fastens with a shackle to the tack fitting, which very likely also anchors the lower end of the forestay, and the jib's head takes the halyard shackle. The jib clew cringle accepts the jibsheets—usually a pair of lines that lead aft to winches or cleats on either side of the cockpit. Some jibs have a boom, in which case a single jibsheet leading from mid-boom (usually with a small tackle for additional leverage) can trim the sail on either side of the boat. Such jibs are called *self-tending*. Most jibs, however, have no boom, so that the jibsheets must lead from the clew; in consequence, each time the jib moves from one side of the boat to the other, one jibsheet must be cast off and the other (the one on the side the jib moves to) must be trimmed in.

Today's sails are nearly all made from synthetic fabric. Polyester (commonly marketed under the trade name Dacron) stretches less than nylon and is used for mainsails and jibs, while nylon is used for specialized sails (such as spinnakers and light-air drifters) in which slight shape deformation is no problem. Dacron sails require little or no care com-

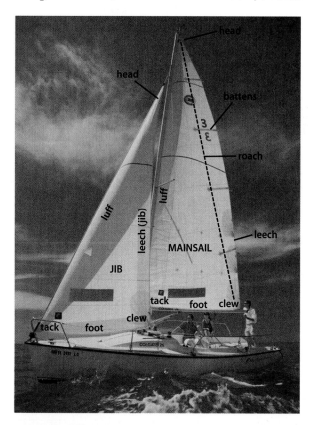

**Figure 1-17.** A sloop-rigged sailboat with the parts of the sails identified. (REPRINTED WITH PERMISSION FROM *FAST TRACK TO CRUISING* BY STEVE AND DORIS COLGATE)

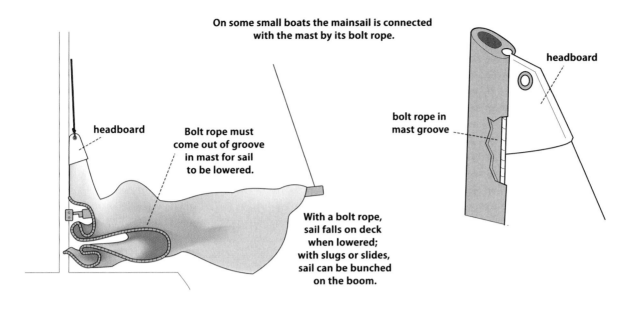

On some small boats the mainsail is connected with the mast by its bolt rope.

headboard

Bolt rope must come out of groove in mast for sail to be lowered.

With a bolt rope, sail falls on deck when lowered; with slugs or slides, sail can be bunched on the boom.

headboard

bolt rope in mast groove

Other boats—including almost all above 20 feet long or so— attach the mainsail to the mast with slides or slugs.

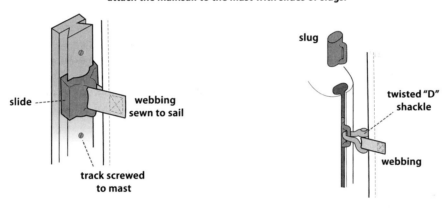

slide

webbing sewn to sail

track screwed to mast

slug

twisted "D" shackle

webbing

**Figure 1-18.** The three common methods of attaching the mainsail to the mast and boom.

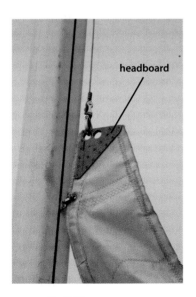

headboard

halyard

mast

tack grommet (cringle)

gooseneck

boom

reefing lines

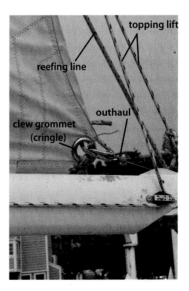

topping lift

reefing line

clew grommet (cringle)

outhaul

**Figure 1-19. Left to right:** The head, tack, and clew of a mainsail, showing its reinforcements and hardware. (PHOTOS BY BOB DENNIS)

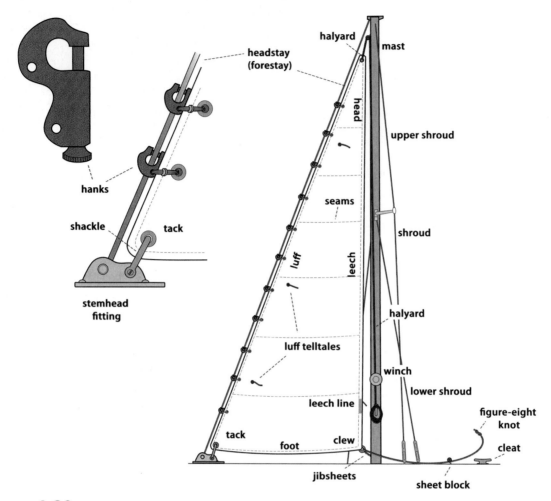

**Figure 1-20.** The parts of a jib.

pared with their cotton predecessors: if you sail on salt water, simply rinse the salt out of them from time to time. If possible, dry the sails before stowing them in their bags for prolonged periods to avoid mildew (which will not affect Dacron except to make unsightly stains on its surface). Sails should be stowed neatly after each excursion, either furled (on the boom) with a sail cover, or folded in a sail-bag. (See Chapter 4 for more on furling sails.) Like all artificial fibers, Dacron is sensitive to ultraviolet radiation and will weaken if exposed to prolonged sunlight. Increasingly, sails used for racing are being constructed from high-tech, highly stable Mylar and Kevlar fabrics (Figure 1-21). These materials are considerably more expensive and harder to care for than Dacron.

**Figure 1-21.** The sails on this J/133 are made of a Kevlar/Mylar laminate, reinforced with carbon fiber tapes (the black lines). (PHOTO BY HOWARD MCMICHAEL, COURTESY UK-HALSEY SAIL-MAKERS)

# Hull Types

As sailboat designers are painfully aware, the hull characteristics that keep a sailboat upright, moving efficiently, and responsive to its helm are sometimes in mutual opposition. It can be a tricky job to reconcile them. All boats, sail or power, are compromises, but sailing craft embody more trade-offs in their design than powerboats. Most modern sailboats give nearly equal attention to stability, load-carrying ability, and a speedy hull, with perhaps a slight tilt toward one factor or another, depending on the designer's special aims. As you get into the nearly "pure" racing sailboats, speed-producing elements are emphasized to the detriment of other factors. Cruising sailboats tend to be designed for comfort and cabin amenities instead of speed.

Not so long ago, when nearly all boats were built of wood, the most obvious basic distinction between hull types was that of shape: hard chine versus round bottom. Round or at least curved bottoms have been the traditional hull shape for centuries. They move easily through the water, but their construction in wood planking requires both time and skill, and as the cost of workmanship became a larger and larger factor in boatbuilding expense, round-bottom wooden boats became increasingly costly.

By contrast, flat-bottom boats are easy to build, even for amateurs. With the advent of sheet plywood, flat-bottom craft became outstandingly inexpensive, but their tendency to pound in even a slightly choppy sea caused designers to give them a mildly V-shaped bottom. The *chine*—or intersection between side and bottom—remained hard, or abrupt, giving the hull type its name. The Snipe pictured in Figure 1-7 is a hard-chine boat. Though built of fiberglass now, the first Snipes were built from plywood in the early 1930s. The same is true of the Lightning (Figure 1-22), which dates back to 1938. Hard-chine craft sail well as long as they remain upright, and they have considerable *initial stability*: they resist tipping easily (Figure 1-23). A round-bottom boat, in contrast, tips more readily in a light breeze but may very well have greater *ultimate stability*—resistance to capsize—than a hard-chine boat.

**Figure 1-22.** Developed in 1938, the 19-foot Lightning is still one of America's top racing and daysailing one-designs. Her hard chine (just visible at the bottom of the photo) and ballasted 130-pound centerboard give her the stability of a small keelboat with the ability to plane in the right conditions. (REPRINTED WITH PERMISSION FROM *YOUR FIRST SAILBOAT* BY DANIEL SPURR)

With the advent of fiberglass-molded hulls, it became as easy to produce a curved hull as a flat one. More important, fiberglass engineering makes use of curvature in strengthening the hull. Given the great predominance of fiberglass boats today, most hulls are more or less curved, and the hard chine has been considerably modified.

**Figure 1-23.** These two sprit-rigged sailing prams are built from plywood with hard chines. The Optimist class of prams, which are very much like these, are raced by kids worldwide. (COURTESY NATIONAL MARINE MANUFACTURERS ASSOCIATION)

**Figure 1-24. Left:** This fishing vessel in St. John's, Newfoundland, shows how much water a displacement vessel pushes aside at cruising speed. Any further incremental speed increase is gained only at the cost of greatly increased fuel consumption. The bow wave is clearly visible, and the stern wave has migrated most of the way back to the transom. **Right:** This keel sailboat is also a displacement hull. (PHOTOS BY JIM BARTLETT, COURTESY NATIONAL MARINE MANUFACTURERS ASSOCIATION)

## DISPLACEMENT VS. PLANING HULLS

Sailboats can have displacement hulls or planing hulls. A **displacement hull** must always push through the water, while a **planing hull**, when moving fast enough and with the right weight distribution, can ride on top of it.

Any floating object at rest displaces an amount of water equal to its own weight. If you could freeze the water around and below a floating vessel, then remove the boat without cracking the ice, then fill the hole left behind with water, the water in the hole would equal the boat's weight.

As a boat begins to move, it must push aside the water ahead while the water behind rushes in to fill the space vacated by the hull. This sounds like a process that requires a lot of effort, and it is. What's more, a boat that can only move by displacing its own weight in water is restricted to a relatively low top speed.

Displacement boats generally cannot go faster than a certain speed, which is closely related to the boat's waterline length. You can figure your boat's maximum displacement speed—called its *hull speed*—quite easily: take the square root of the boat's length at the waterline (its LWL) in feet, and

multiply it by 1.34 to find the boat's approximate maximum speed in nautical miles per hour. (A nautical mile is approximately 6,080 feet, as opposed to 5,280 feet for a statute, or land, mile. Thus, a nautical mile is about 1.15 statute miles. A speed of 1 nautical mile per hour is called 1 knot.)

It doesn't matter if the boat in question is propelled by oars, sails, or engine, nor does it matter how much power is applied; unless the boat can escape from displacement-type movement through the water, it cannot increase its speed much above 1.34 x the square root of its waterline length. A displacement boat that is 16 feet long at the waterline cannot go much faster than 5.36 knots. A considerably larger boat, 25 feet on the waterline, will only go about 6.7 knots.

A displacement sailboat won't even go this fast most of the time. A boat that can average a speed in knots equal to the square root of its waterline length in feet—4 knots for a 16-foot boat—is doing very well. What's holding the boat back is both friction from the water and the waves caused by the boat's motion through the water. These speed-reducing waves are not the familiar, V-shaped swells that form the boat's wake. In addition to its wake, a boat forms two waves—one near the bow and one at some distance back toward the stern—

the crests of which are at right angles to the hull (Figure 1-24). As the boat gathers speed, the stern wave drops farther aft, until at hull speed the boat is virtually suspended between the two. The only way to escape is for the boat to receive enough additional propulsive force to ride up and over the bow wave and then move over, instead of through, the water, rather like a ski moving on snow. This kind of motion, very familiar to powerboat people, is called *planing*. While there are practical limits to speed in a boat, there is no theoretical maximum speed for a planing hull.

The main requirements for a hull capable of planing are fairly obvious. The hull must be fairly shallow in cross-sectional shape, able to move easily over the water rather than through it—like the Laser in Figure 1-6, the Snipe in Figure 1-7, and the Lightning in Figure 1-22. It cannot carry great loads, and it requires sufficient power—whether in engine or sail area—to get it up and over the watery "hump" between displacement and planing modes.

Boats that aren't designed to plane have deeper, fuller shapes. They can carry greater loads relative to the size of the boat, and the power required is less—because more power will not move them faster than hull speed. To counterbalance the weight of masts and sails, displacement hulls frequently have a weighted appendage called a *keel*, which we'll discuss next. When deep-keeled displacement boats are overpowered either by wind or by surfing ahead of large waves, steering becomes erratic or difficult, larger bow and secondary waves are formed, and the hull actually tends to ride relatively lower in the water. Planing boats seldom have deep keels, and they must achieve stability either through hull shape or through the use of the crew as counterweights, as in Figures 1-7 and 1-22.

## KEELS AND CENTERBOARDS

Sailboat hulls are designed to pursue a straight-ahead course with as little disturbance of the water as possible. And yet, even as the boat is moving forward, wind pressure on the sails is attempting to push it sideways through the water. This lateral or sideways movement, called **leeway**, is partially (but never completely) counteracted by the hull shape. When the boat is moving in the direction the wind blows it is moving to **leeward** (pronounced "loo • ard").

The hull protuberance or appendage that minimizes leeway is called a **keel**, **centerboard**, or **daggerboard**, depending upon which is used in the design of the boat. This fin-shaped feature in the bottom of the hull allows forward movement while maximizing the hull's lateral resistance. A keel is normally fixed in place—bolted or molded to the hull—while a centerboard or daggerboard, as mentioned above, can be raised and lowered through a slot in the hull bottom. Within the hull, a centerboard is housed in a structure called the **centerboard trunk**.

### Fixed Keel

A keel (Figure 1-25) has no moving parts, hence nothing to break or jam. A lead keel bolted to the bottom of a boat's hull is also soft enough to absorb the sudden jolt of a grounding on rock or coral without damaging the hull. But keels have their disadvantages, too. Lead is an expensive metal, and the depth of a keel may add so much to a boat's draft that she is excluded from many shallow-water sailing areas. In addition, a boat with a fixed keel is difficult to launch from a highway trailer and will probably never have the potential for planing.

The keel is usually weighted, or *ballasted*, while most centerboards are not. While many boards are metal and quite heavy, their weight relative to the boat's displacement is small. A keel, however, may contain an amount of weight—usually in the form of lead ballast—equal to half the boat's total displacement. This much weight is there for a reason. While the shape of the keel prevents or at least minimizes leeway, its weight enhances the boat's stability by counterbalancing the heeling force of the wind on the sails and the weight of the mast, rigging, and sails. Since *Australia II* won the America's Cup in 1983, the *wing keel*—a keel with horizontal winglets at its lower end—has been incorporated in a number of production sailboats. A wing keel provides as much resistance to leeway as a standard keel of deeper draft.

### Swing Keel

Some designers have produced swing-keel boats; in these, the weighted keel can be partially retracted

**Figure 1-25. Left:** This sailboat on a trailer shows a fixed fin keel. The spade rudder (at left in the photo) is well separated from the keel. This configuration—which is common on modern fiberglass sailboats—makes the boat responsive to its rudder and also reduces underwater surface area, thus reducing skin friction and increasing speed under sail. (PHOTO BY NORMA LOCOCO) **Middle:** A more traditional full-keel configuration, in which the keel extends well aft and the rudder hangs off the back end of the keel, gives protection to the rudder and provides a well-mannered boat that holds its course well even if it isn't quick to respond to its helm (especially under reverse engine power). (PHOTO BY MOLLY MULHERN) **Right:** This deep, narrow fin keel with a ballasted bulb on its tip is designed for speed and performance, not for leisurely daysailing or cruising. The trailer probably had to be custom-built. (PHOTO BY NORMA LOCOCO)

into the hull or locked in the fully lowered position. These often look similar to a heavy centerboard, as described below. For many people, a swing keel makes a good compromise, offering some of the ballast stability of a fixed keel along with most of the trailerability of a centerboard boat.

## Centerboard and Daggerboard

When shallow draft is critical, a centerboard or daggerboard boat (see Figure 1-4) is the first choice. A centerboard pivots around a pin in its forward corner and thus can be fully raised or lowered. It can also be partly raised, which moves the boat's center of lateral resistance aft and, as we shall see, has an important effect on the boat's sailing ability under certain conditions. A centerboard does have several drawbacks, however; for one thing, it is easily damaged if the boat should hit an underwater obstruction. Although the centerboard will sometimes pivot up into its trunk when it hits something, it is more likely to splinter or crack (if wood), bend and jam in the trunk (if metal), or exert a sudden strain on the trunk and the hull, which can lead to a serious leak.

Centerboard trunk leaks are not as common in fiberglass boats as they were in wooden craft, but they still happen, and they are still among the most stubborn defects to repair.

Finally, a centerboard has the disadvantage of taking up space in the boat (Figure 1-26). Although some centerboard trunks don't protrude much above the floorboards, they are still visible, and it's difficult to use that area of the cockpit or cabin for anything else. Some high trunks require bracing to the sides of the hull. It's sometimes possible to make these braces into seats, but for the most part a centerboard trunk is an obstruction in an already crowded area.

The most popular alternative to a centerboard in small open sailboats is a daggerboard, which, as mentioned earlier, slides up and down in its trunk instead of pivoting. Simpler than a centerboard, it requires no *pendant*, or line, to raise and lower it. Its cheapness and simplicity have made it a standard installation on smaller boats, where a handle fixed to the top makes lifting easier. The problem with a daggerboard is that, since it's not pivoted, it must extend above the top of its trunk when raised. This has two implications. First, the trunk cannot be capped at the top, which allows water to splash into the cockpit. Second, when fully raised the dagger greatly interferes with operations in the cockpit and may get in the way of maneuvering. Although a centerboard may pivot upward out of harm's way if a submerged object is struck, a daggerboard almost certainly cannot slide upward and is thus considerably more vulnerable.

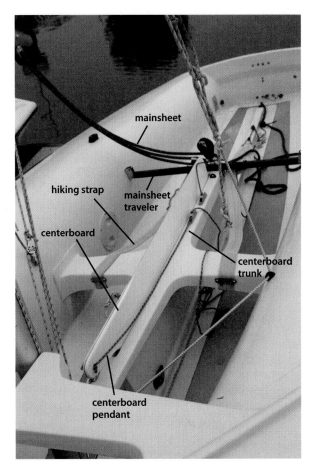

**Figure 1-26.** A view aft in the cockpit of a sailing dinghy. The centerboard is raised in its trunk, and the pendant with which the board is raised and lowered is clearly visible. When the crew need to hike out to windward to counteract the heeling force of the wind, they hook their feet beneath the hiking strap. Note that the tiller and rudder have not yet been attached. (PHOTO BY BOB DENNIS)

***USING A CENTERBOARD OR DAGGERBOARD.*** One advantage of both the centerboard and the daggerboard over a fixed keel is that they can be raised or lowered to varying heights to counter the effects of leeway while minimizing underwater hull resistance. A racing skipper knows that the board is not needed to resist leeway when running downwind, and raising the board at such times will make the boat faster. This same skipper will have to drop the board upon turning upwind, however, in order to minimize leeway.

***CARE OF A CENTERBOARD OR DAGGERBOARD.*** As either the centerboard or daggerboard is adjustable, care should be taken to make sure that it can be raised or lowered with ease. Occasionally on wooden boats a tight-fitting board or the trunk itself will swell or expand when the boat is left in the water for a period of time. This swelling usually results in damage to the trunk itself as well as extreme difficulty in raising or lowering the board when required.

Centerboard boats that must be left in the water require attention to prevent the centerboard from being jammed in the trunk by marine growth. In addition to regular haulouts and bottom painting, preventive measures might include underwater hull cleaning or brushing and movement of the centerboard through constant or routine use.

***CENTERBOARDS AND DAGGERBOARDS ON MULTI-HULLS.*** Most trailerable *catamarans* (two-hulled boats) do not have a centerboard in either hull, depending instead on their relatively deep underwater hull profiles to resist leeway (Figure 1-27). Large

**Figure 1-27. Left:** The Hobie 16 catamaran has no centerboard or daggerboard, making it an ideal boat for sailing off the beach. Speeds of 15 to 20 knots are not uncommon, but wear a bathing suit or wet suit because you will get wet! (COURTESY HOBIE CAT) **Right:** The 20-foot Tornado catamaran, with its twin centerboards, is capable of reaching 30 knots. This Olympic-class sailboat is said to be the fastest production catamaran in the world. In this photo the windward centerboard is raised. (PHOTO BY DANIEL FORSTER, REPRINTED WITH PERMISSION FROM *YOUR FIRST SAILBOAT* BY DANIEL SPURR)

**Figure 1-28.** The Corsair F-27 trimaran has a single centerboard in its center hull and can reach speeds in excess of 20 knots. The outer hulls, or amas, are designed to fold into the main hull for trailering, at which point the boat is a road-legal 8 feet, 5 inches wide. (REPRINTED WITH PERMISSION FROM *YOUR FIRST SAILBOAT* BY DANIEL SPURR)

catamarans that must be kept in the water will often have either a keel or centerboard in each hull, but these can be unballasted since the twin-hull design provides great initial stability.

*Trimarans* (three-hulled boats) will have either a centerboard or a keel in the center hull, which might be either ballasted or unballasted, depending upon the size of the hull and the speeds for which the craft is designed. Trailerable trimarans will usually have an unballasted centerboard (Figure 1-28).

## Twin Keels

Twin keels, also called bilge keels, are popular in some shallow-water areas or areas subject to extreme ranges in tide, such as the estuaries of Great Britain. These stubby keels—one on either side of the boat—allow a boat to stand upright on a tidal flat in an area where the water drains away completely at low tide. The keels are not particularly efficient, and a boat with twin keels is not fast.

# Steering Systems

Most people, even if they've never seen a boat, are aware that it is steered by means of a rudder. A ***rudder*** is a fin located toward the stern of the boat. On small craft, it's usually hung from the transom as in Figure 1-7. As it pivots from side to side, the rudder thrusts one face or the other into the water streaming past the moving boat. The pressure of water on the rudder blade then turns the boat by pushing the stern away from the side toward which the rudder is turned.

On most smaller sailboats, the rudder is worked by a simple lever called a ***tiller***, which makes it possible to turn even a fairly large rudder on a fast-moving boat without too much effort. On larger craft steering wheels are quite common, since these provide even more mechanical advantage than do tillers while permitting the rudder to be mounted under the boat rather than on the transom (Figures 1-29 and 1-30). A steering wheel on a boat works in the same manner as the one on your car: turning the wheel to the right causes the boat to turn to starboard, and vice versa.

**Figure 1-29.** A wheel-steered cruising sailboat. On a boat like this the rudder is mounted under the boat. This boat is sailing on a *reach*, with the sails eased out and the waves rolling in gently from the side rather than slapping the bow. Reaching is often called "sailing free," and that describes it pretty well. (PHOTO BY BOB DENNIS)

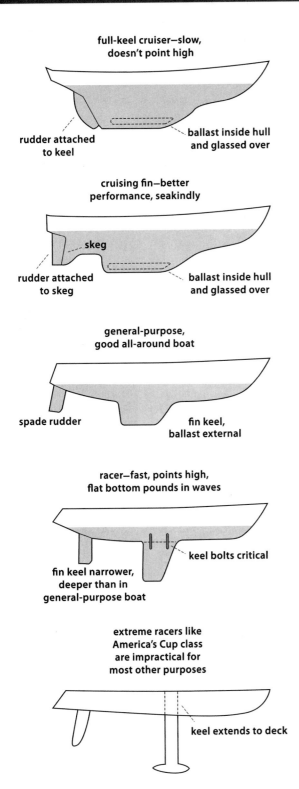

full-keel cruiser—slow,
doesn't point high

rudder attached
to keel

ballast inside hull
and glassed over

cruising fin—better
performance, seakindly

skeg

rudder attached
to skeg

ballast inside hull
and glassed over

general-purpose,
good all-around boat

spade rudder

fin keel,
ballast external

racer—fast, points high,
flat bottom pounds in waves

keel bolts critical

fin keel narrower,
deeper than in
general-purpose boat

extreme racers like
America's Cup class
are impractical for
most other purposes

keel extends to deck

**Figure 1-30.** A range of keel and rudder configurations for wheel-steered boats.

A tiller, on the other hand, operates in reverse: pushing the tiller to port causes the rudder to swing to starboard, and that in turn pushes the stern to port. As the stern swings to port, the boat pivots around its keel or centerboard, and the bow swings to starboard. Thus, you move the tiller toward the side opposite your intended turn. It takes beginning sailors a little while to get used to this fact of tiller steering, but it soon becomes natural.

When steering a boat with a tiller, remember that the boat pivots like a weather vane around a point somewhere near amidships. A boat is quite unlike a car, which follows its front wheels through a turn. A boat turning is more like a car skidding in that the bow describes a small circle while the stern swings in a wider circle outside it. This means that careless skippers frequently hit docks and other boats with their own boats' sterns when turning sharply.

Second, bear in mind that a rudder cannot function unless water is moving past it. For this reason a boat must gain speed before it can be steered—unless, of course, it's anchored in a place where water is running swiftly past the hull while the boat is standing still, as in a river.

Third, a rudder pushed too hard to one side or the other acts more like a brake than a turning force. With the face of the rudder nearly at right angles to the moving water, the boat's tendency is simply to slow down and even become unmanageable. One of the first things to learn about any boat is how far the tiller must be put over to one side in order to make the boat turn. It is far less than you might think.

# Other Rigs

The sailboats we have been describing thus far have a single mast with a triangular mainsail and jib. This is called a **sloop rig**, and a boat so rigged is called a **sloop**. The conventional sloop rig is the most efficient, the cheapest to make (if you include the cost of the rig), and the easiest to handle. Modern sloops generally perform better upwind than any of the other rigs. The marconi sloop rig is therefore by far the most common, but you will see many other rig types on the water.

In the early years of the 20th century, before aluminum spars and stainless steel shrouds and stays made tall masts practical, most sailboats were **gaff-rigged**. A gaff mainsail has four sides and is supported by a spar, called the *gaff*, across the top of the sail. It provides a great deal of sail area close to the water, but the rigging is more complicated and requires two main halyards, one at each upper corner.

A gaff-rigged sail is demonstrably less efficient than a marconi or Bermudan sail most of the time, but many people have an affection for gaff sails because of their traditional appearance. Gaffs are still popular among working sailboats such as the Newfoundland fishing schooner, a tribute to the usefulness of the rig. A sloop with a gaff mainsail has, of course, a jib of normal shape.

On some small sailboats, the tall mast required for an effective Bermudan rig may be a danger at anchor, when the weight of the spar can cause the boat to tip over or capsize. Shorter masts also are more convenient to carry on a car top and to rig before each sail. Such short masts are usually combined with an upper spar that allows the head of the mainsail to be raised above the top of the mast. The upper spar is called a gaff on a gunter-rigged boat and a yard on a lateen, lug, or sprit-rigged boat (Figure 1-31; see also Figure 1-23). The most common of these rigs, the lateen, is found on the Sunfish (Figure 1-32) and similar boats, which are easy to sail, fast, portable, and fairly inexpensive.

Another sail variation, common but not exclusive to smaller sailboats, is the **loose-footed mainsail.** Unlike the lug sail, the more common loose-footed

**Figure 1-32.** The Sunfish, designed in 1948 and produced in fiberglass since 1959, may be the most popular sailboat ever built. Note the lateen rig. (REPRINTED WITH PERMISSION FROM *YOUR FIRST SAILBOAT* BY DANIEL SPURR)

**Figure 1-33.** The Mistral is an Olympic-class sailboard. Note the wishboom, which the sailor is gripping. There is no rudder. To steer, the sailor pivots the sail forward or aft, and the mast is mounted on a universal joint to permit this. (PHOTO BY DANIEL FORSTER, REPRINTED WITH PERMISSION FROM *YOUR FIRST SAILBOAT* BY DANIEL SPURR)

mainsail has a boom but is attached to it only at its tack and clew, which permits the sail to assume its proper shape over more of its total area. A sailboard, which is neither a surfboard nor a sailboat but a hybrid of the two, has a loose-footed main controlled by a wishbone boom (Figure 1-33).

## SINGLE-MASTED BOATS

There are three different single-masted sailboat rigs. The mast on a catboat is set quite near the forward end of its waterline. Small catboats are the simplest of all boats to sail because they have only one sail to worry about. Consequently, a large number of small boats are **cat-rigged;** they make popular beginners' sailboats, providing all the

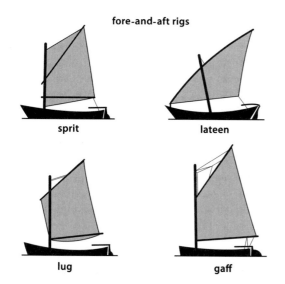

**fore-and-aft rigs**

sprit

lateen

lug

gaff

**Figure 1-31.** The lateen, sprit, lug, and gaff rigs. When the yard on a lug rig approaches the vertical at full hoist, the rig is called a gunter. In a sliding gunter rig, the heel of the yard slides on the mast.

thrills of sailing with a minimum of sail setting problems. Catboats such as the 14-foot Laser (see Figure 1-6), a planing sailboat that weighs only 130 pounds, are extremely popular for both daysailing and racing and are capable of speeds as high as 15 knots in strong winds.

The catboat rig is less attractive for larger boats because the boat's balance, which is discussed in Chapter 11, cannot be maintained when the mainsail is reefed (reduced in size) in heavy weather. Furthermore, large catboat mainsails (especially those over 400 square feet or so) become difficult to handle without specialized sail-control gear. On the other hand, small sails yield less drive per unit area than large sails, so all other things being equal, catboats with their single sails are more efficient than rigs that distribute the same sail area among two or three sails.

We have already discussed the sloop rig, both masthead and fractional. The jibs on fractional rigs are usually smaller than the mainsail even if they overlap the mast. On most masthead rigs, however, the jibs overlap the mast considerably, contain more square footage than the mainsail, and are trimmed far aft. Overlapping jibs are commonly known as *genoa jibs* (Figure 1-34).

**Figure 1-34.** The genoa jib on this sloop-rigged boat is mounted on a roller furler, making it easier to handle, as will be discussed in Chapter 4. (PHOTO BY BOB DENNIS)

The third single-masted rig is the *cutter*, with its mast stepped anywhere from 40% to 50% of the deck length back from the bow. A cutter normally sets three sails: the mainsail, which is smaller than the one on a sloop of comparable size; the forestaysail (staysail for short), which is often set on a boom so that it is self-tending; and outside and forward of the staysail, the jib, which is often a high-cut sail set on a *tack pendant*, a length of wire running from the jib tack to the deck.

A cutter has several advantages over a sloop. It provides a greater choice of sail configurations for the cruising sailor. In stormy weather, the jib can be dropped or roller furled and the boat sailed with main and staysail. To tack this abbreviated rig, you simply put the tiller over—each of the two boomed sails is self-tending. In light weather, the cutter can drop its staysail and set from the jibstay a truly immense drifter or reaching jib.

The disadvantages of the cutter rig are its extra cost and the greater number of parts that can break or go awry.

The distinction between sloop and cutter has become more and more blurred in recent years, especially as roller-furling systems have improved. We'll discuss roller furling in Chapter 4. Suffice it to say here that sloop-rigged boats with inner forestays from which a smaller headsail can be set are now common on the water. What makes this configuration more feasible is that the larger jib can be rolled up around the headstay when tacking, then unrolled on the other tack. This prevents it from wrapping itself around the inner forestay when tacking.

## MULTI-MASTED RIGS

As sailboats get larger, the sail area necessary to drive them at hull speed increases. Because of handling limitations on the size of an individual sail, the rigs have to be divided to carry the necessary sail area. Today, ease in sail handling has introduced divided rigs to sailboats somewhat smaller than the divided rigs found on older working boats (Figure 1-35). Most pleasure boats are limited to two masts, although working schooners in the last century carried up to seven masts.

The most common two-masted yachts are ketches and yawls. According to the classic defini-

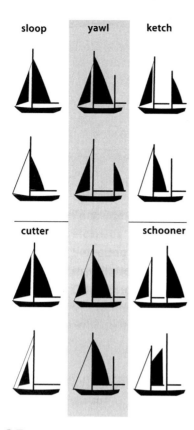

sloop | yawl | ketch

cutter | schooner

**Figure 1-35.** This illustration showing how the sail plans of a sloop, cutter, ketch, yawl, and schooner might be reduced as the wind increases demonstrates how the sail-handling options increase with a divided rig.

tions, a *ketch* is a two-masted sailing vessel in which the forward mast, called the *mainmast*, is the larger, and the after mast, the *mizzen*, is stepped forward of the rudderpost.

A *yawl* is also two-masted, but its mainmast is comparatively larger than that of a ketch and its mizzen comparatively smaller. The mizzenmast of a yawl is stepped aft of the rudderpost.

While these definitions are accurate as far as they go, they are not terribly helpful in distinguishing a ketch from a yawl at a distance, or in suggesting why these are really two quite different types of boats.

## Ketch

A ketch is a two-masted boat in which the combined sail area of the jib and mizzen is approximately equal to the area of the mainsail; in modern ketches, the jib is usually somewhat larger than the mizzen. The rig came about because, beyond a certain point, a sail becomes too big for one

person to handle, even with mechanical aids like winches. Dividing the sail area makes for less aerodynamic efficiency but easier handling, which is why a ketch is usually a cruising boat, and is seldom seen in lengths under about 30 feet. When *running* (sailing with the wind from behind), a ketch's mizzen will often blanket the mainsail unless it can be set on the opposite side of the boat.

## Yawl

A yawl, on the other hand, is really a sloop with a small balancing sail set well aft. The mizzen contributes little power, and is often not set when the boat is sailing upwind, but when the boat is sailing downwind the mizzen does make it faster. Until recent decades many yawls raced; indeed, the rig was developed in part as a way to gain extra sail area without incurring a penalty in handicapped racing. Off the wind, both ketch and yawl can set a *mizzen staysail*, a large, light-air sail that is set flying from the mizzen masthead and sheeted to the end of the mizzen boom. The staysail's tack is on deck, more or less amidships at the foot of the mainmast; thus the sail is often as large as the mainsail, and far easier to control than a spinnaker, as it is entirely within the boat.

Without real power in its mizzen, however, the yawl rig is a hybrid with more disadvantages than advantages; it lacks the ketch's evenly divided sail area and the sloop's windward efficiency. Thus, yawls are less common today than they were a generation ago.

## Schooner

The schooner is a rig associated with America, although it did not originate on this side of the Atlantic. Most *schooners* today—the few remaining—are two-masted vessels of some size with the mainmast aft and the smaller foremast forward. A three-masted schooner's masts, proceeding from front to rear, are the fore, main, and mizzen. The schooner is a complex and inefficient rig except off the wind, and the mainmast usually winds up blocking the cabin. Its proponents argue that a schooner is the fastest of rigs on a *reach* (with the wind blowing more or less perpendicular to the boat's course), which may or may not be true, and that the rig is easy to handle when shorthanded.

Most schooners are gaff-rigged on the main and foremasts, though some have marconi mainsails and gaff foresails, and other arrangements are possible. Off the wind, a schooner may set a big fisherman staysail in the space between fore and main. No matter how inefficient she may be compared to a modern sloop, a schooner driving along on a reach is a splendid sight.

# Boatbuilding Materials

The first boats were built of wood. Today, boatbuilders use fiberglass, aluminum, steel, wood with epoxy, and combinations of these materials in addition to wood.

## STEEL

Steel is an ideal material for shipbuilding. Unfortunately, steel-hulled boats less than 30 to 35 feet long are too heavy for economical operation, but when speed can be sacrificed for strength, steel is an excellent building material, producing a boat that will withstand collisions and groundings to an extraordinary degree. Because steel does not lend itself to production boatbuilding, steel sailboats are built either in an owner's backyard or by professionals on a custom, or "one-off," basis. Still, you can always find steel sailboats scattered on the world's oceans, with many of the boats making extraordinary voyages through reef- and ice-strewn waters.

## ALUMINUM

Aluminum hulls are lighter than steel hulls and can take the hard knocks of groundings and ice floes almost as well. Aluminum is also easier to work than steel. Thus it is not surprising that many custom voyaging and ocean-racing sailboats have been built of aluminum (Figure 1-36). Aluminum has the disadvantage of transmitting noise and heat (or cold) through the hull with great efficiency. Thorough insulation—often foam—is necessary to reduce interior noise and condensation.

**Figure 1-36.** *Hawk* is a 47-foot aluminum sloop designed for ocean voyaging in any latitude. (COURTESY BETH LEONARD, AUTHOR OF *BLUE HORIZONS* AND *THE VOYAGER'S HANDBOOK*)

Another disadvantage of aluminum is that it is easily corroded by **electrolysis**, a serious consideration for boats moored in salt water. Boats moored in salt water usually have their bottoms painted with **antifouling paint** to reduce plant and animal growth. Most of these paints contain copper. In salt water, copper and aluminum set up an electrolytic action, and the aluminum quickly corrodes. Tin-based antifouling paints, which do not interact as readily with aluminum, were once used on aluminum hulls but the U.S. Environmental Protection Agency has determined that the tin is poisonous to marine life, so such paints are now banned.

There are presently two alternatives for protecting aluminum. One is to use a layer of nonmetallic paint between the hull and the antifouling bottom paint, which works fine unless a scratch exposes the aluminum hull. The other alternative is to use a polymer antifouling paint, which is expensive and difficult to apply.

## WOOD

Wood, once the primary choice of boatbuilders, is used much less frequently today. This is not because wood is an undesirable construction material; many people would not trade their wooden boats for any other. Wood is attractive and, if properly maintained, lasts a long time. Good wood for boat construction is expensive, however, and demands considerable attention. Owners of traditional plank-on-frame wooden boats spend many hours each year getting them ready for launching. Wood needs scraping, sanding, and repainting annually, and the underwater seams of wooden boats need periodic **caulking** to make them watertight.

These drawbacks have been overcome with newer methods that use wood in combination with reinforcing resins and fabrics to eliminate caulked seams, increase longevity, and reduce maintenance while retaining the distinctive beauty of a wooden boat. In stitch-and-glue boatbuilding, for example, hull panels are cut to prescribed measurements from marine plywood sheets, laid down over temporary station molds cut to the cross-sectional shapes of the boat at various points along its centerline, and then stitched together where their edges meet using temporary wire stitches. The stitches hold the hull together long enough for these joints to be permanently glued with rock-solid epoxy fillets; then the entire structure is covered with fiberglass, Dynel, or another fabric laid in place with epoxy or fiberglass resin. This technique is not only user-friendly for home builders, but it also makes a handsome, long-lasting boat.

Another popular technique—especially suited to canoes and kayaks built in a home workshop—creates a boat from narrow strips of wood coated and attached with epoxy resin. The boats are beautiful and amazingly durable and maintenance free, and the skills required are well within reach of an enthusiastic amateur builder (Figure 1-37).

While methods like these have spurred a renewal of amateur wooden boat building, they are not suitable for commercial production of boats. In production boatbuilding, fiberglass predominates.

## FIBERGLASS

For commercial boatbuilding, fiberglass is the material of choice. Fiberglass boats account, in large part, for the rapidly growing popularity of recreational boating. Our nation's waterways abound with fiberglass boats of every description, both power and sail, and when you're in the market for a sailboat, you can almost always find a used fiberglass sailboat that will meet your needs for a very reasonable cost. Your first sailboat should probably be fiberglass.

Fiberglass is relatively inexpensive and can easily be formed into complex shapes and curves (Figure 1-38). It's ideal for production boatbuilding because a single hull mold can be used to build dozens or even hundreds of copies of the same hull. Furthermore, fiberglass is easily repaired when damaged, lasts seemingly indefinitely, and most importantly for the average boatowner, is easily maintained, requiring much less effort and time than wood. Less time spent on maintenance means more time on the water.

Fiberglass, or more properly, glass-reinforced plastic (GRP), does have disadvantages. It is heavy, for one thing; fiberglass with the strength of steel weighs more than steel. Today's more carefully engineered boats are a lot lighter than the fiberglass boats of 30 to 40 years ago, however, simply be-

**Figure 1-37.** A strip-built tandem canoe, suitable for home construction. The method can be used for small sailboats as well. (COURTESY NICK SCHADE)

**Figure 1-38.** A fiberglass boat under construction. (COURTESY NATIONAL MARINE MANUFACTURERS ASSOCIATION)

cause early fiberglass boats were built to wooden boat thicknesses (in the absence of better guidance) and thus were way overbuilt. Also, although the glass will not burn, the resins that bind it together will.

## How Fiberglass Boats Are Built

To build a production run of fiberglass hulls, the builder needs a mold in which the fiberglass materials can be shaped and adhered. The first step, therefore, is to construct a plug in the shape of the hull, and then form a mold over the plug. Imagine carving the shape of the hull from a huge block of wood; if you could do this, you would be creating a plug. The surface of the plug must be flawless so that the inner surface of the female mold formed over the plug will also be flawlessly smooth. When the fiberglass mold has cured and been properly stiffened on the outside, the plug is removed from the mold, which is then ready for building a series of hulls.

Each hull is built from the outside in within the female mold. The gelcoat is sprayed over the mold surface first, which gives the vessel its color and finished, mirror-smooth outer surface. Then follow layers of fiberglass mat (or chopped fiberglass strands sprayed from a hand-operated gun) alternated with layers of finely woven fiberglass cloth and/or coarse woven roving, until the desired thickness of the hull is reached.

The strength and durability of the hull will depend on what fiberglass materials and resins are used, how they are combined, how many layers are laid down, and how much quality control is exercised throughout. When hull thickness is built up in part with chopped strands sprayed from a chopper gun (which mixes the strands with resin as it sprays), the gun operator must be careful to keep the fiber-to-resin ratio at optimal levels—neither resin starved nor too resin rich. Ask the dealer if the boat you're looking at incorporates chopped strand. If it does, ask what kind of quality control the builder exercises.

A builder will also typically make a hull thicker near the keel and in high-stress areas, and may use special, directionally reinforced materials locally to impart particular strength. After the hull is laminated and cured, it is strengthened with stiffeners,

stringers, and other members. Then decks, cabins, and superstructure are added; usually these too are fiberglass, and in production boatbuilding these so-called parts are likewise laminated in molds.

## Variations on the Method

Over time, variations on the fundamental method have evolved. In one, known as **sandwich construction**, a core material (usually balsa wood) is sandwiched on either side by layers of fiberglass impregnated with resin. Other core materials are sometimes used, such as Airex foam or other formed plastics. Sandwich construction provides a boat that is strong and buoyant. Should leaks develop in the fiberglass and water reach a balsa core, however, rot will occur.

In another variation called a **matched-die process**, male and female molds, usually made of metal, are clamped together with a fiberglass-and-resin laminate between them. By applying the correct pressure and heat, the hull is made uniform throughout.

The international demand for environmental and worker safety, along with the need for more efficient manufacturing, has resulted in another

### Boatbuilding Materials

#### Steel

- Strong and heavy
- Better for large boats than small
- Must be painted to avoid rust

#### Aluminum

- Lightweight
- Relatively inexpensive
- Rather noisy
- Can take hard knocks
- Vulnerable to electrolysis in salt water

#### Fiberglass

- Today's most popular boatbuilding material
- Strong and heavy
- Easily molded
- Easily repaired
- Relatively easy to maintain

new process for producing fiberglass products in the marine and aircraft industry called the **Seeman Composite Resin Infusion Molding Process**, or SCRIMP. This process, like the matched-die process, requires a male and female mold between which the fiberglass or other filler material is encapsulated. Then resin is injected with a vacuum assist to ensure that unwanted encapsulated gases are removed. This is an environmentally clean process and results in a laminate with no voids. This process can be used to produce aircraft and even small submarines as well as boats, and is finding increasing favor, in large part because of its environmental benefits.

### General Considerations

Fiberglass boats are strong, and since most production-line boats are built of fiberglass, they dominate the market. A fiberglass hull lasts indefinitely—longer, usually, than the engine that powers it and the gear it carries—so the used-boat market is also dominated by fiberglass. For these reasons, as well as for economy and ease of maintenance, your first boat is likely to be fiberglass—along with your second boat and most boats thereafter. The quality of workmanship is not always obvious in a fiberglass boat, so the reputation of the builder should be one important guide for you. Ask around, and browse boat sites on the Internet.

Fiberglass is heavier than water and a fiberglass boat filled with water will sink unless it has built-in flotation. Powerboats less than 20 feet long are legally required to have sufficient built-in flotation to keep a portion of the boat above water even when the boat is flooded. There is no such legal requirement for sailboats, but some small sailboats are nevertheless built with this feature. (This would not be feasible on larger boats; however, they are less vulnerable to swamping.) Sometimes the flotation is in the form of a sealed compartment; sometimes it is Styrofoam or another closed-cell foam.

You can find out more about the boat you wish to buy by reading the literature published by its manufacturer. How complete is the information? Reputable manufacturers want you to know what you are buying, and are usually proud of their quality control programs, which are critical in this industry. If you can visit the manufacturing plant, arrange for a tour. Most factories will be glad to show you boats in various stages of construction.

# Marine Surveyors

Marine surveyors make boats their specialty, serving much the same function that home appraisers serve ashore. If you are planning to buy a used boat, it is a good idea to hire a surveyor. The surveyor will assess the boat's condition and tell you what the boat needs to bring it to good working condition. He or she will also appraise the boat's value based on condition, builder's reputation, and the local market for the kind of boat in question, so that you can judge the fairness of the asking price. Finally, a surveyor can help you judge to what extent the money you save by buying old versus new will be consumed by the repairs and upgrades you might have to make. With a little knowledge and care you can eliminate many boats from consideration without the expense of a professional survey, but when you get ready to make an offer, you're well advised to get a professional second opinion. Sometimes a surveyor will also suggest that you hire a mechanic to compression-test and otherwise evaluate the boat's engine or engines.

# Buying a Boat

When you are buying a boat—new or used—there is no substitute for a written sales agreement that clearly states your intent and that of the seller. This should prevent unpleasant surprises. The sales contract should state the price, delivery date, and method of payment, and should also include an inventory of the boat's equipment and a detailed description of the overall condition of the boat. Any refundable deposit you make should be noted, along with possible limitations on the refund. If a loan is involved, the contract should state whether the sale is subject to the availability of the loan.

The contract should also stipulate that the sale is subject to a satisfactory marine survey. As a buyer, you should take a sea trial, but have the survey done on land. Problems noted during the trial run and the survey should be addressed in the contract. If the boat is not being sold "as is," the contract should say so. It should also state whether the seller is responsible for correcting problems or defects and if so, what the time limit is for making such corrections. The length of time for discovering and correcting new problems after the purchase date should be included as well.

Even if you are having the boat surveyed, you should ask probing questions about its prior use, maintenance record, and history of problems. Has it had any blistering? Has it had accidental damage? What is its present condition? The seller should be completely honest, but again beware!

Finally, make certain that you have all of the boat's papers. You will need them for state registration or for new documentation with the Coast Guard, as you'll see in Chapter 5.

As a buyer, you should realize that you do not have any rights under the seller's insurance. Arrange to have your own insurance in place at the closing date.

# Practice Questions

**IMPORTANT BOATING TERMS**
In the following exercise, match the words in the column on the left with the definitions in the column on the right. In the blank space to the left of each term, write the letter of the item that best matches it. Do not use an item in the right-hand column more than once.

| THE ITEMS | | THE RESPONSES |
|---|---|---|
| 1. _____ | stern | a. controls the rudder |
| 2. _____ | keel | b. a boat that has no headsails |
| 3. _____ | marconi | c. a piece of hardware on which to secure lines |
| 4. _____ | centerboard | d. a fixed fin under the hull |
| 5. _____ | Dacron | e. a two-masted boat with the mainmast forward |
| 6. _____ | tiller | f. a long-lasting boatbuilding material |
| 7. _____ | catboat | g. a low-stretch polyester used in sails and lines |
| 8. _____ | ketch | h. a rig that includes a triangular mainsail, also known as Bermudan |
| 9. _____ | fiberglass | i. the back end of a boat |
| 10. _____ | cleat | j. a pivoting fin under the hull |

# Multiple-Choice Items

In the following items, choose the best response:

**1-1.** "Starboard" is derived from

a. sideboard
b. cardboard
c. farboard
d. larboard

**1-2.** The mast and boom are joined with a

a. spinnaker
b. socket
c. gooseneck
d. wire

**1-3.** The two types of rigging are

a. standing and running
b. stationary and floating
c. light and heavy
d. upper and lower

**1-4.** Shrouds are adjusted with

a. bolts
b. chainplates
c. halyards
d. turnbuckles

**1-5.** A sloop has

a. two masts and two sails
b. one mast and two sails
c. one mast and one sail
d. two masts and three sails

**1-6.** Each corner of a sail is reinforced with a

a. fold
b. leech
c. halyard
d. cringle

**1-7.** Dacron sails

a. are subject to much deformation
b. have little stretch
c. are vulnerable to salt water
d. are the latest innovation for racing

**1-8.** Hard-chine boats

a. initially resist tipping
b. move through the water more easily than round-bottom boats
c. are more difficult to construct
d. are very expensive

**1-9.** Fiberglass boats are

a. stronger than steel, pound for pound
b. weaker than steel, pound for pound
c. difficult to repair
d. not the most popular hull

**1-10.** The waterline of a boat is measured

a. at the stern
b. at the bow
c. where water meets the hull surface
d. by the mast

**1-11.** The deck cutout area where the crew operates is called the

a. berth
b. galley
c. foredeck
d. cockpit

**1-12.** The most popular spar material is

a. wood
b. steel
c. aluminum
d. fiberglass

**1-13.** A planing hull

a. displaces less water when at rest
b. always has a fixed keel
c. displaces less water when on plane
d. is limited in top speed

**1-14.** A displacement hull is

a. limited in top speed
b. unlimited in top speed
c. easy to plane
d. usually light weight

**1-15.** A fixed keel

a. makes a boat immune from heeling
b. is ideal for trailering
c. usually carries ballast for stability
d. is light weight

**1-16.** A leeboard is mounted

a. at the bow
b. at the stern
c. externally on one or both sides
d. inside the hull

# Multiple-Choice Items (continued)

**1-17.** A sailboat is steered with its

    a. daggerboard
    b. centerboard
    c. keel
    d. rudder

**1-18.** A catboat design

    a. has no jib
    b. is always two-masted
    c. is faster than a sloop
    d. is often chosen for large boats

**1-19.** A ketch is generally

    a. more suited to cruising than racing
    b. faster than a sloop
    c. a racing boat
    d. less than 30 feet long

**1-20.** A yawl is configured

    a. without a forward mast
    b. usually as a racing boat
    c. with the mizzen aft of the rudderpost
    d. with a single mast

**1-21.** A schooner has

    a. one mast
    b. no mizzenmast
    c. two or more masts
    d. no foremast

**1-22.** The gelcoat on a fiberglass hull is

    a. applied to the outside surface
    b. applied to the inside surface
    c. mixed with the resin
    d. mixed with the fiberglass cloth

**1-23.** Sailboats requiring flotation are

    a. none
    b. over 20 feet
    c. under 20 feet
    d. over 40 feet

**1-24.** Having a boat checked for value and condition is called a

    a. marine survey
    b. marine check
    c. vessel examination
    d. vessel check

# How a Boat Sails

## The objectives of this chapter are to describe:

- How to read the wind.
- How to judge which directions you can sail in and which you can't.
- The points of sailing—running, close hauled, and reaching—and how to trim the sails for each.
- How the mainsail and jib convert wind to forward propulsion, and how to adjust their shapes to make them more efficient.
- How to respond when the wind gets a little stronger.

It's the sails—and wind—that provide a sailboat's power. Shown here is CHN 95, the China team's entrant in the 2007 America's Cup races. (PHOTO BY DANIEL FORSTER, COURTESY UK-HALSEY SAILMAKERS)

A SAILBOAT'S RIG is its engine, and its fuel is the wind. As with any useful engine, the power the rig transmits to the boat can be controlled. We do this by altering the position of the sail(s) relative to the wind's direction.

The sheets control the sails, and as we trim or ease a sheet, we move the sail closer to or farther from the boat's fore-and-aft centerline. If the boat maintains a steady course while we're trimming or easing, we are also changing the sail's angle of attack to the approaching wind. We can produce the same effect by leaving the sails unchanged while we change the direction, or **heading**, of our boat. In effect, we have two throttles with which to control the transmission of wind power through the rig to our hull.

As we look further into how wind is transformed into boat motion, try to remember these two throttles. If at any time you feel that the wind is **overpowering**, or overwhelming, your boat, you can **depower** the boat—i.e., reduce its angle of heel and, if you wish, slow it down—either by easing the sheets or by heading closer to the wind. In a real emergency you can do both.

# Reading the Wind

When you stand on a pier and feel the breeze on your face, what you're sensing is the **true wind**—air in motion. With a little experience, you'll learn to tell how strongly the wind is blowing and from what direction. (Wind directions are always given in relation to where the wind is blowing **from**: thus, a north wind is blowing from north to south.)

A moving vehicle, whether on land or sea, creates a "wind" of its own as it moves through the air. This is called **wind of motion**. Suppose, for example, that you're in a powerboat on a day when no true wind is blowing at all, and you're cruising north at 10 knots. If you raise your head above the windshield, you'll feel a "north wind" of that same strength—10 nautical miles per hour—blowing straight at you. This is the boat's wind of motion.

Now take the example one step further: Again you're in a boat moving north at 10 knots, but this time there is a true wind blowing from the north at 5 knots. What you feel in the boat is a 15-knot wind from the north—the combination of your boat's wind of motion and the true wind. This combination is called **apparent wind**: the wind experienced by an observer in motion.

Sometimes the apparent wind is less than either of its two components: Imagine that you're still in your boat, moving north at 5 knots into a north wind that's blowing at 7 knots. The apparent wind is thus 12 knots from the north (Figure 2-1). Now you turn your boat 180° and head south at 5 knots, with the same 7-knot wind now blowing from directly astern. Your apparent wind is now 7 knots **minus** 5 knots, or a mere 2 knots from the north.

The apparent wind is easy to calculate when the wind is from directly ahead or astern, but it becomes more complicated when the wind is blowing from either side of the boat, as in Figure 2-2. In this situation, if we know the true wind's speed and direction (which we can observe before we set out or by stopping momentarily) and the boat's speed and direction, we can (in theory) figure out the apparent wind by use of a **vector diagram**, as in Figure 2-3.

In practice, you won't need to calculate the apparent wind, because apparent wind is what you observe and experience while your boat is in motion and what your instruments measure. If your boat carries a **wind vane indicator** (see below), it points into the apparent wind, not the true. If your boat has an **anemometer**, it measures apparent wind strength, not true wind strength. You could resolve the vector diagram in reverse to find the true wind, but why bother? All you have to know is the concept of apparent wind and its implications for sail-

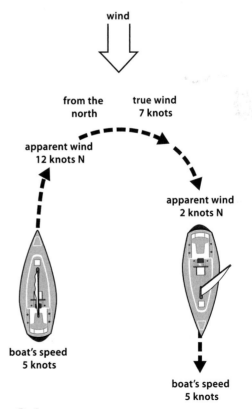

**Figure 2-1.** The relation between boat speed and apparent wind when the boat is traveling directly into or away from the true wind.

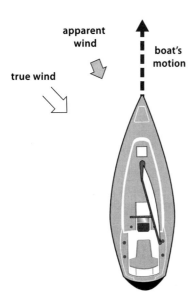

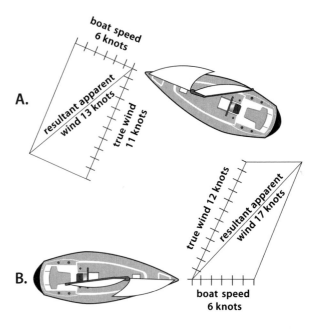

**Figure 2-2.** When the true wind is blowing from one side or the other of the boat's heading, the apparent wind will be from somewhere between the true wind and the boat's heading.

ing, because it's the apparent wind that you steer by and trim your sails to. Sailors who don't consider the distinction between true and apparent wind can get an unpleasant surprise when, after sailing with the wind for some time, they suddenly head their boat into the breeze—only to find that what appeared a gentle zephyr when heading downwind is quite blustery when going the other way.

To keep track of wind direction, most skippers use a **wind vane** (a rigid, pivoting vane analogous to a weather vane ashore), one or more **telltales** (lengths of yarn, ribbons, or strips of fabric tied to shrouds), or both. A wind vane should be located where it can easily be seen and where the wind hitting it will not have been deflected by sails or rigging, which makes the masthead an ideal spot (Figure 2-4). In larger boats the wind at the top of the mast may be blowing in a slightly different direction from the breeze at deck level, however, so larger sailboats often have telltales tied or taped to the upper shrouds about 5 or 6 feet above the deck (Figure 2-5), and perhaps another telltale on the backstay to sense a wind from astern.

On cruising sailboats, where the mast may be 30, 40, or even 50 or more feet high, an electronic device at the masthead may measure both wind

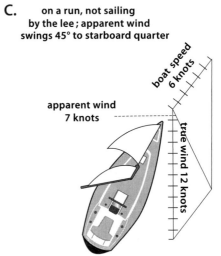

**Figure 2-3.** If you know the true wind and your boat's speed and heading, you can calculate the apparent wind by means of a vector diagram. Using any arbitrary measure (say, ¼ inch) to represent 1 knot, construct a vector to represent the true wind and a vector to represent your boat's motion. Considering these two vectors as two sides of a rectangle, complete the other two sides, then draw the rectangle's diagonal back to your boat. The length and direction of that diagonal represent the strength and direction of the apparent wind. No one bothers to do this in practice, but an understanding of how it works will help you on the water. There are three general cases: **A.** When the true wind is blowing from directly abeam—i.e., perpendicular to the boat's heading—the apparent wind will be stronger than the true wind. **B.** The same is true—but the effect is even more dramatic—when the true wind is from forward of the beam. **C.** When the true wind is from aft of the beam, the apparent wind will be weaker than the true wind.

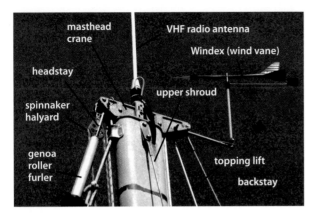

**Figure 2-4.** A Windex wind indicator on a masthead tells the helmsman where the apparent wind is coming from. (PHOTO BY NORMA LOCOCO)

**Figure 2-5.** Telltales in the luff of the jib (see also Figure 2-14) let you judge sail trim and air flow, while those on the shrouds are reliable apparent wind indicators. (REPRINTED WITH PERMISSION FROM *FAST TRACK TO CRUISING* BY STEVE AND DORIS COLGATE)

direction and speed and supply a readout to a pair of instrument dials in the cockpit. On small boats such instrumentation may be convenient, but it's not really necessary.

# Points of Sailing: Running

It's easy to visualize a sailboat moving with the wind behind it—being pushed *downwind*. When the wind is more or less directly astern of a boat, she is said to be *running*. For most efficient sailing, the mainsail and jib should be as square to the wind as possible. In practice it will not be possible to get the mainsail square to the wind without having it chafe against the shrouds and/or spreader, so just ease it as much as you can.

On a run, the mainsail is likely to *blanket* the jib, depriving it of wind, if both sails are extended to the same side of the boat. The jib then collapses or flops about ineffectually, which often fools a beginning sailor into trimming the jib in a mistaken belief that it is luffing (see below for a discussion of luffing). But trimming will not help in this instance. What will help is to set the sails *wing and wing*—with the main fully out on one side of the boat and the jib out on the other (Figure 2-6).

A boat sailing directly before the wind can be difficult to steer, responding sluggishly to her rudder. In addition, overtaking seas may throw the stern sideways, and the wind direction is constantly oscillating by small degrees. All things considered, it's possible for the wind to get behind the fully extended mainsail and blow it—boom and all—across the boat to fully extended on the other side. This is called an *accidental jibe*, and it can cause injury or put serious strains on the rigging. A *preventer*—a line leading from the main boom to a belay point forward of it—will help prevent an accidental jibe but must be watched carefully (see Chapter 11).

A simpler, more common way to prevent an accidental jibe—especially on very windy days—is to avoid sailing directly downwind. Instead, cheat a little to one side so that the wind comes from the *quarter*—the corner of the transom—that is opposite the side on which the mainsail is set. On this heading, the mainsail will be reasonably efficient and you should still be able to set the jib on the opposite side, though you may require a portable spar called a whisker pole to keep it extended and filled. A **whisker pole** (see Figure 2-6) is a light aluminum tube with a snap hook at one end and a narrow prong at the other. The snap hook clips to an eye on the forward side of the mast, while the prong goes through the jib clew cringle. When the jibsheet is trimmed in, the pole acts like a boom.

It takes a good deal of practice to sail a boat wing and wing, and at first it will seem like it's more trouble than it's worth. If your boat has a small jib, it may indeed be too much effort to bother winging it out, so concentrate at least for the time being on sailing with the main alone.

Try to keep the mainsail at right angles to the apparent wind—or as close as your shrouds and spreaders will permit—watching either the telltale on the backstay or the masthead vane. To adjust the angle at which the wind strikes the sail, you can either turn the boat or play the mainsheet in and out. Many experienced sailors never cleat the mainsheet at all, and certainly—at least on a small boat—the sheet should always be ready to let run, to spill the wind from the sail in a hurry. At the same time, it's tiring and dull to have to hold a

**Figure 2-6.** These small boats heading downwind are sailing wing and wing, with their jibs swung out opposite their mainsails. Note how a whisker pole keeps the jib extended to the wind. Note too that the main halyard of the closer boat has been eased, introducing wrinkles in the luff of the mainsail—all in an effort to make the main slightly fuller and more powerful and produce a tiny increment of additional speed. No one out for a lazy sail would bother with such adjustments—these boats must be racing! (PHOTO BY BOB DENNIS)

piece of line all day. A quick-release cleat (see Chapter 14) works very well and is quite safe.

# Points of Sailing: Close Hauled

We can see how a boat can sail before the wind—the boat is simply pushed from behind—but it's harder to understand how a boat moved by the wind can sail into the direction from which the wind is blowing. Yet modern, well-designed sailboats sail to within 40° of the true wind, and even old-fashioned, gaff-rigged boats can sail to within about 50° of the wind. We usually say that the average boat can sail to within approximately 45° of the **wind's eye**—the direction from which the true wind is blowing—at which point the boat's angle with the apparent wind might be 30° or even less.

That means, of course, that a sailboat skipper in a reasonably good boat has a choice of headings covering 270° of the conventional 360° true-wind circle (Figure 2-7). This is a major improvement over the square-rigged sailing vessels in the age of sail. They were restricted to a mere 200° or so—not enough to make any reliable progress to windward.

A sailboat heading at approximately 45° to the true wind is said to be sailing **close hauled** (Figure 2-8). She may also be referred to as sailing **upwind** or **on the wind, beating to windward**, or simply **beating**. All these terms mean the same thing: the boat referred to is sailing as close to the source of the wind as she efficiently can.

How is it done? Essentially, a sail on a boat going to windward is an airfoil, although one that in practice is more complex and variable than an airplane wing. As mentioned in Chapter 1, a sail has a three-dimensional shape built into it. For reasons that remain difficult to summarize, the flow of air over the **leeward**, convex surface of the sail (the side away from the wind) is accelerated much like the flow of air over the upper side of an aircraft wing.

To simplify what's happening, we can picture air being split by a sail (or wing). Part of the air passes closely over each side of the airfoil, and because the air passing over the leeward side of the sail (the upper side of a wing) is moving faster than

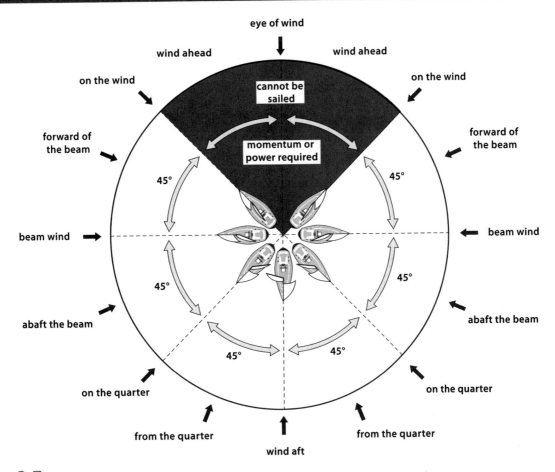

**Figure 2-7.** The true-wind circle.

**Figure 2-8.** These boats are sailing close hauled in a fresh, "rail-down" breeze. Their sails are trimmed close to their centerlines, and their crews are enjoying a great ride. These traditional one-designs date from the first half of the twentieth century, when large mainsails, small jibs, and long bow and stern overhangs were the norm. Such boats remain fast, well mannered, and a lot of fun to sail. (PHOTO BY BILL MORRIS)

the flow on the opposite side, it creates a negative pressure, or **lift**, which is everywhere perpendicular to the sail or wing surface. At this point the sail-wing analogy becomes less intuitive. It is easy to picture how lift on a wing's upper surface tends to move the wing upward, but it's less clear how lift on a sail's leeward side can move a boat forward.

This is where the sail's **belly**, or draft, becomes critical. When a boat is sailing to windward, the lift developed by the wind on the sails can be resolved into two components (Figure 2-9)—a forward force

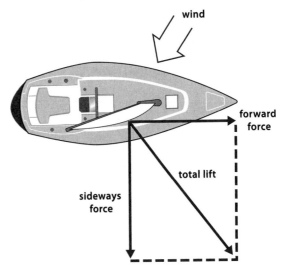

**Figure 2-9.** The lift generated by a sail can be resolved into two components.

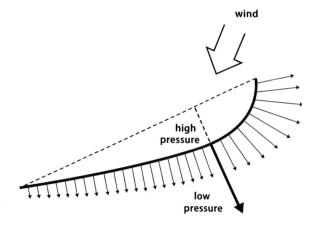

**Figure 2-10.** Only the lift from the forward one-quarter of the sail generates a useful forward component. The goal of sail trim and sail design is to maximize that forward component near the sail's luff.

that propels the boat, and a sideways force that both pushes the boat to leeward and causes it to tip or **heel**. As can be seen in Figure 2-10, the lift generated over the after three-quarters of the sail is useless, serving only to heel the boat. It is only the lift generated in the forward quarter of the sail—along the luff and a relatively small distance back—that drives the boat forward. Thus, when sailing close hauled, the after three-quarters of the sail function merely to create the circulation that results in the needed lift being generated in the forward quarter. One goal of your sail trimming and sail shaping (which we'll discuss in Chapter 11) is to maximize this useful component of lift, and this is also why a fairly pronounced curve is cut into the luff of a mainsail or jib.

Even so, the heeling/sideways component of lift would overwhelm the forward component, leaving a boat unable to make progress to windward, were it not counteracted by other factors. Heeling can be controlled by hull shape, by a ballast keel, by crew weight, or by sail trim. And hull shape, whether the boat has a keel or centerboard, is so designed that **leeway**, or sideways motion, is strongly resisted even as forward motion meets minimal resistance.

## FUNCTION OF A CLOSE-HAULED JIB

Thanks to great refinements in hull and sail design, today's sailboats move to windward very efficiently,

all things considered. Both sails function in this process, but the jib—if it is a large one, as many are today—contributes more lift, or drive, than does the main. Lift over the mainsail surface is degraded by turbulence caused by the mast, while air striking the jib luff is only mildly disturbed by the forestay, jib hanks, or roller-furler foil. Further, the apparent wind bends as it approaches your sails (Figure 2-11), giving the jib a more favorable angle of attack than the main. This, too, permits the jib to generate a larger forward lift component.

Not only does the jib provide its own lift to windward, it also helps funnel wind across the leeward surface of the mainsail. This creates a **slot effect**, which accelerates the wind over the main and thus makes its lift more effective (Figure 2-12).

If lift is to be created, air must flow smoothly over the surfaces of the sail, with as little turbulence as possible. In order for smooth flow to occur, the sail must be set at the proper angle to the wind. If the angle of attack—i.e., the angle at which the wind hits the sail's leading edge—is much too small, the sail will **luff**, or shiver, along its

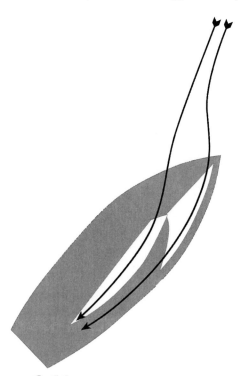

**Figure 2-11.** The apparent wind bends as it approaches your sails, giving the jib a more favorable wind angle than the main. This permits the jib to be eased out relative to the main, enabling it to generate greater forward lift. (REPRINTED WITH PERMISSION FROM *SAIL TRIM AND RIG TUNING: A CAPTAIN'S QUICK GUIDE* BY BILL GLADSTONE)

leading edge; a luffing sail is an obvious warning that the sail is set too close to the wind (Figure 2-13). It is possible, however, to sail with enough wind in the sails to fill them, yet at an incorrect angle, so that lift isn't nearly as great as it should be. Until fairly recently, it was hard to sail to windward efficiently, and most people took many hours of practice to develop a **feel** for when the boat was moving most efficiently to windward. Fortunately such a feel, while useful in getting the last ounce of drive from a boat, is no longer necessary. A person at the helm can now **see** how the wind is moving over the sails of his or her boat. Simply thread two or three pieces of knitting yarn, in a color that contrasts with the sail, through the jib luff at evenly spaced intervals of height. These *telltales*, sometimes called *woolies*, *streamers*, or *wind tallies*, should be 4 to 6 inches back from the jib luff. They should be long enough—6 inches or so on either side of the sail—to hang freely, yet not so long that they catch in seams or get snagged when the sail is bagged or set (Figure 2-14).

When sailing to windward, trim the jib all the way in (being careful, however, not to press it against the leeward spreader tip or the leeward shrouds) and hold the sheet while edging the boat up into the wind. (On a larger boat you will need two or three turns of the jibsheet around a winch to hold it comfortably.) As the jib approaches its optimum angle

**Figure 2-13.** This boat is turning into the wind to begin a tack (see Chapter 3), causing both its mainsail and jib to begin luffing. More commonly, the luffing you will want to correct with sail trim will look more subtle than this and will be confined to the forward sections of the sails. (PHOTO BY BOB DENNIS)

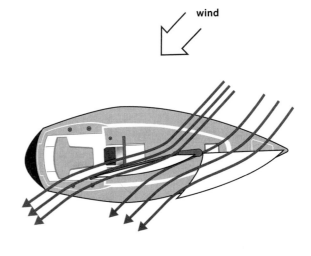

**Figure 2-12. Left:** The slot between the jib and mainsail is clearly visible in this photo. (REPRINTED WITH PERMISSION FROM *FAST TRACK TO CRUISING* BY STEVE AND DORIS COLGATE) **Right:** The slot effect causes an acceleration of flow.

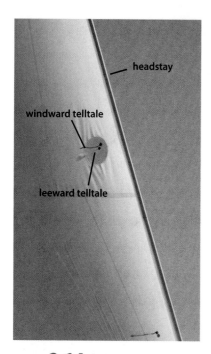

**Figure 2-14.** **Left:** The telltales on this well-trimmed jib are streaming aft in unison. The leeward telltale of the upper pair is visible, and it too is streaming aft, a sign that the sail is pulling with maximum efficiency. **Right:** Another view of the same jib. The foot of the jib is eased away from the leeward shrouds, which means that the boat is on a close reach rather than close hauled. Note the uncluttered side deck with nonskid surface and sturdy lifelines for crew safety. (PHOTOS BY BOB DENNIS)

with the wind, both the windward and leeward telltales will stream back horizontally across the sail. If the boat is too close to the wind, the windward streamers (those on the concave side of the sail) will begin to lift and twirl, graphically indicating the air turbulence around them. When the boat heads too far off the wind for the set of the jib, the leeward streamers will begin to twirl (Figure 2-15).

For most vessels, there is an area of 2° to 5° of heading wherein the sail trim is good enough that the windward telltales stream aft horizontally and the leeward telltales just barely lift off the sail surface. As a general rule, the leeward telltale can be seen through the sail fabric, at least in sunlight, but many people have a sailmaker put a small, clear plastic window in the sail where the key jib telltale—about one-third of the luff length up from the deck—is located.

Having trimmed the jib for maximum efficiency, you can then proceed to do the same with the mainsail. As you trim it in, the sail will fill, the luffing in its forward sections will decrease, and unless the wind is very light you will feel a surge of power being transmitted to the hull. As the boom nears the boat's fore-and-aft centerline, you will reach a point where further trimming pulls the

boom more down than in, putting tension on the leech of the sail. Some leech tension is good, but too much is not, and the correct amount depends in large part on wind strength. At this point you should be guided by the telltales sewn into the edge of the leech, assuming your mainsail has these (and most do). The telltales will stream back from the leech when the air flow off the leech is smooth (Figure 2-16). When the flow around the leech separates and gets turbulent, the sail is stalled, and the telltales will collapse and disappear behind the leech. At this point you'll know you've trimmed too far. Essentially, you want to trim far enough to make the sail's forward sections stop luffing, but not so far as to stall the leech. When the sail's upper batten is more or less parallel with the boom, and the leech telltales stream aft with only an occasional stall, you have things about right.

On most boats, it should be possible to trim each sail until both are drawing properly, but on some modern boats with very large jibs, when the jib is trimmed properly, air will flow off its leeward side with such velocity that it will interfere with the mainsail, causing a mild luffing referred to as **backwind**. There is usually no good solution to this problem, but in many cases the jib is so much more

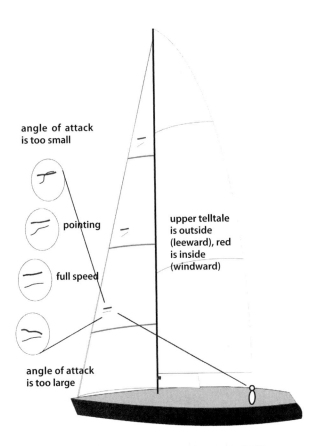

**Figure 2-16.** The telltales in the leech of the mainsail stream aft from the leech when the sail is drawing well, as it is here. When the telltales collapse and drop to leeward of the leech, the sail is overtrimmed to the point of stalling the flow of air off the leech. (PHOTO BY BILL MORRIS)

**Figure 2-15.** In this illustration, the windward telltale of each pair is red. When the jib is trimmed for maximum efficiency, both telltales stream aft. When the leeward telltale lifts (bottom inset), either the sail is trimmed too tightly or the boat is not heading as close to the wind as it should be for maximum efficiency. When the windward telltale lifts (top inset), either the sail needs to be trimmed in or the boat is heading slightly too close to the wind. The windward telltale will lift only slightly (second inset from top) when the helmsman is pointing as *high* (close into the wind) as possible while still maintaining speed. This is the way to gain the maximum distance to windward while sailing close hauled. (REPRINTED WITH PERMISSION FROM *SAIL TRIM AND RIG TUNING: A CAPTAIN'S QUICK GUIDE* BY BILL GLADSTONE)

effective in moving the boat upwind that it doesn't seem to matter.

When sailing to windward, the fact of ever-changing wind direction becomes quite apparent. Although in many parts of the country the prevailing summer breeze seems to blow from the same direction for days at a time, in fact its actual direction will oscillate constantly a few degrees to either side of its average direction. These shifts aren't noticeable to most people, but to sailors trying to urge their craft to windward, they can be crucial. Called *playing the puffs*, the helmsman's technique of responding with the tiller to each slight wind shift

can make a dramatic difference to a boat's progress over a reasonable distance.

# Points of Sailing: Reaching

A boat may be said to be sailing close hauled when it is within perhaps 5° of pointing as close to the wind as it can. Likewise, a boat is running when the wind is blowing from anywhere within a 10° to 15° arc dead astern. Thus, close-hauled sailing occupies a mere 10° or so of the available 270° of the wind circle through which a boat can sail, while running occupies another 25° or 30° (Figure 2-17). The remaining 235° consists of various types of reaching.

Almost beating is known as *close reaching*. The wind's action on the sails is much as it is when sailing close hauled—most of the force moving the boat is aerodynamic lift, with perhaps a little more push than when beating. Close reaching is slightly faster than beating—because of the extra push—

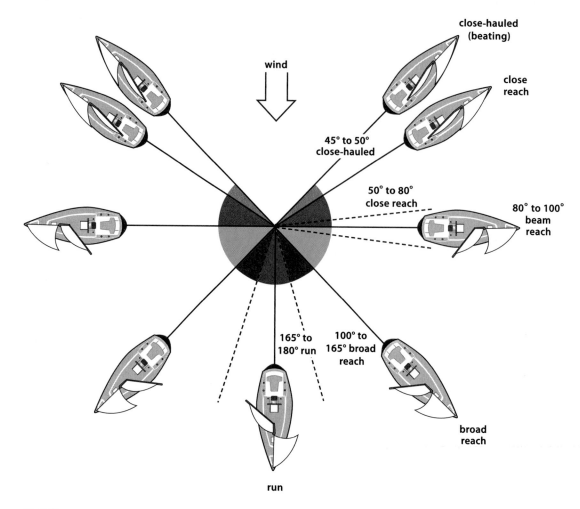

**Figure 2-17.** The points of sailing.

and there's a slight degree of extra flexibility in boat control, too. Because the boat is not already sailing as close to the wind as it can, the person steering may head into the wind a trifle (called *heading up*, as opposed to turning away from the wind, which is *falling off*), trimming in the sheets for the new heading as the boat turns. The telltales are used in a close reach just about the same as in beating, and they should be just as helpful.

As the boat's bow turns farther away from the wind, she approaches a *beam reach*, with the apparent wind blowing over the boat more or less at right angles. A beam reach combines excellent lift over the leeward side of the sail with good thrust on the windward side. For this reason, beam reaching is usually a boat's fastest point of sailing. It also offers maximum maneuverability and is probably the safest point of sailing for a beginner.

The telltales should be reasonably effective on a beam reach—at least the ones on the leeward

side of the jib. If you are in doubt about your sail trim, try the old trick of letting the sails out until they begin to luff just a little, then trimming them back in until the luffing stops, then trimming them just a hair more. This rule-of-thumb system should leave you with the sails drawing effectively.

As the wind moves aft from a beam reach, the boat is said to be on a *broad reach*. Probably the telltales will cease to be effective, as the force moving the boat is mostly thrust from astern, with just a little lift remaining over the leeward side of the sail. Broad reaching is safe, reasonably fast in any kind of wind, and quite exhilarating. The only common mistake new sailors make is failing to let out the sails far enough. Trimmed in, the sails seem to be catching more wind; the boat heels and appears to be roaring along. In fact, however, *easing* (letting out) the sheets a bit may bring the boat back up on her feet, and while she may not appear to be going as fast, she will really be moving more swiftly. The proper way to trim sails for broad reaching is the luff-and-let-out system described above. A **log** or **knotmeter** will help you determine if your boat is moving at her best.

The differences between beating, close reaching, and broad reaching—the three types of reaching—are not instantly apparent, nor do they matter a great deal in practice. The important thing to learn is proper sail trim for each heading, and for this the concepts of beating, reaching, and running are useful.

Perhaps the best way to test sail trim is to get another boat identical to yours and sail the same courses, with each skipper varying sail trim, one at a time. The most effective trim for every major heading will soon become apparent, and it will soon become second nature. Another good way to learn sail trim is to sail with someone who knows your kind of boat. Don't be afraid to ask questions about the best practices. Most sailors are happy to impart what they know, and your only problem may be absorbing more information than you really need.

These explanations of the points of sailing will become intuitive very quickly once you get a wheel or tiller in your hand. Also, a very small sailboat makes the best "teacher" because it responds so quickly to changes in sail trim and heading. When you are overtrimmed, undertrimmed, or headed too close into the wind, a small boat will let you know almost instantly, whereas a big keelboat with all its momentum responds much more slowly.

# Sail Shape

The curvature that gives your sail its aerodynamic shape is built into the sail by the sailmaker. While all the seams between the sail's panels **look** parallel when your sail is set, each panel is cut with curved edges where the seams will be. When the panels are sewn together, these curves give the sail **belly**, or **draft**.

Today, sailmakers can use a computer to determine how much draft to build into a sail so as to optimize its efficiency over an expected range of wind speeds. The relationship between the depth of the draft at a given height and the straight-line distance between the luff and leech of the sail at that height is called the sail's **camber ratio**, or sim-

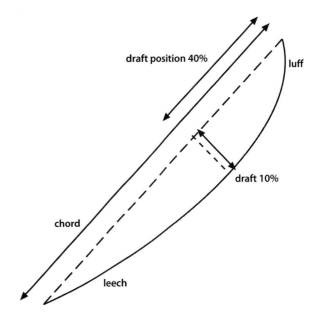

**Figure 2-18.** Here the maximum draft, or camber, is 10% of the straight-line distance from luff to leech (known as the *chord length*), and the point of maximum draft, known as the *draft position*, is 40% of the chord length aft of the luff. A mainsail with a maximum draft of 10% is a flat sail, whereas one with 15% is full. Headsails carry a bit more draft than mains—say, 12% to 20%. (REPRINTED WITH PERMISSION FROM *SAIL TRIM AND RIG TUNING: A CAPTAIN'S QUICK GUIDE* BY BILL GLADSTONE)

ply its **camber**. The greater the camber, the more belly there is in the sail (Figure 2-18).

Sails cut for light-wind use have larger camber ratios. Increasing the sail's depth of draft increases the velocity difference between the air flowing over the windward and leeward surfaces, and that velocity difference determines the sail's lift, or power.

In the days of cotton sails, serious sailboat skippers often bought a new set of sails every spring. Those sails were usually heavy-weather sails—that is, they had a small camber. The more these sails were used in strong winds, the more the cloth stretched. By the following spring those cotton sails had stretched enough to become light-air sails, and the skipper bought another set of heavy-weather sails.

Today, sail material is much more durable and many more sailcloth weights are available. Serious sailors buy sails of different weights for different wind conditions, each with an appropriate camber. With care, sails will last for several seasons.

But what about the ordinary, budget-minded sailor who would like to get by with one set of sails? Sailmakers try to meet the average sailor's needs by designing a set of sails that match the average wind conditions in the sailor's home waters. These sails are at peak efficiency only when the wind blows at average conditions; at wind speeds near the average, the average skipper can't tell the difference. When the wind speed drops considerably, the skipper's boat won't be as fast as if it were rigged with light-air sails, and in heavier-than-average winds, the sails will overpower the boat more often. In very heavy winds, the sails may be permanently stretched or ripped.

# Sail Adjustments

You can control the shape of your sails within limits to increase their aerodynamic efficiency. We will touch on a few major principles here so you will know what to look for.

For windward work, the point of maximum draft (the deepest part of the curve in the sail) should be located 33% to 40% aft of a jib's luff (Figure 2-19) and about 40% to 45% of the way back on a mainsail. If an overlapping jib is causing a big backwind bubble near the luff of your mainsail, moving the draft farther back (as much as 55% from the main's luff) may cure this. The maximum

draft location on a catboat's mainsail should be located as in a jib, some 40% aft of the luff.

You can control the draft of any sail by changing the luff tension. More tension pulls more cloth out of the central area of the sail, reducing its camber and moving the deepest draft location forward. Consequently, if the wind increases and moves the draft aft (because of sail stretch), you can reduce excessive heeling and increase the sail's forward drive by tightening the halyard or downhaul.

The tension along the boom controls the draft in the lower part of the main; reducing foot tension by easing the outhaul will increase the draft in that area, making the sail more powerful.

As already indicated, mainsheet tension controls the shape of the main's leech. If the sheet is too tight, the leech will flatten and curl to windward, increasing the draft in the after part of the sail and moving the deepest draft location aft. Slacking the sheet tension allows the end of the boom to rise and the leech to fall off to leeward, reducing the draft and moving it forward. Further loosening the sheet will allow the main to twist, causing the top of the sail to luff before the bottom does. This can be considered a safety measure when the wind is a little too strong for comfort, but under normal conditions the leech should not twist in either direction.

Since the jibsheets control both foot and leech tension on your jib, you can't change one without affecting the other. Consequently, the best you can do is to move your **jibsheet lead** (the turning block on deck through which the jibsheet passes) until the whole jib luffs at once (Figure 2-20). If the block is too far forward, the lower part of the jib will luff first; if it is too far aft, the upper part of the jib will luff first. Don't forget that if you then change the jib's luff tension, you will move the jib clew in relation to the jib block. You should reposition the jibsheet blocks and retrim the jibsheet. Generally, if the leech is almost touching the spreader while the foot is almost touching the shroud at the turnbuckle, the lead is set correctly.

After you sail your boat for a while, you will most likely adjust your jib first when you are sailing to windward because the jib's trim has so much effect on the set of your mainsail. When you sail off the wind, on a broad reach or run, you will find the

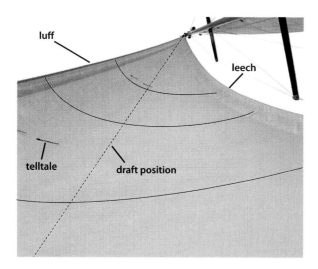

**Figure 2-19.** The location of maximum draft has been superimposed with a dashed line on this well-set jib. Note that the panel seams provide your best visual guide to draft depth and location, and the seams are often sewn in a contrasting thread color for this very reason. (REPRINTED WITH PERMISSION FROM *SAIL TRIM AND RIG TUNING: A CAPTAIN'S QUICK GUIDE* BY BILL GLADSTONE)

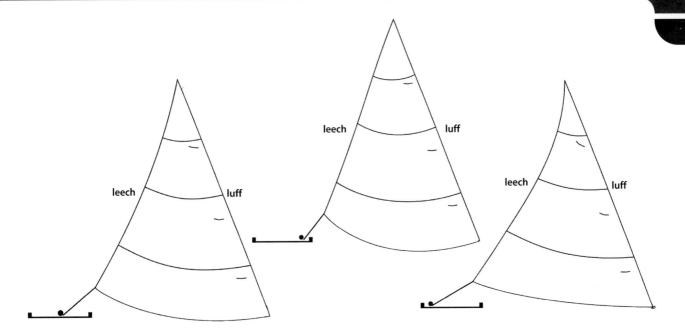

**Figure 2-20.** Jibsheet lead positions. **Left:** The initial lead position should be set so that your genoa shape matches your mainsail shape and the upper telltales break just before the lowers. **Middle:** If you need more power in light wind or to punch through a choppy sea, try moving the lead forward, which will make the sail fuller. This will also tighten the leech, however, so you'll probably have to ease the jibsheet a few inches when close hauled to "open" the leech and restore a smooth flow of air across it. **Right:** When you want to flatten the jib to reduce its power in a strong wind, or to point higher in flat seas when the added power of a full sail isn't needed, try moving the lead aft from its initial position. This will both flatten the sail and loosen its leech, allowing the sail to twist and spill excess wind from its upper portions. (REPRINTED WITH PERMISSION FROM *SAIL TRIM AND RIG TUNING: A CAPTAIN'S QUICK GUIDE* BY BILL GLADSTONE)

sail's aerodynamics are not as important. In fact, on a run, you can reduce all the edge tensions so that you don't reduce the sail area due to tension curl. Your mainsail's leech may still give you a little problem if it spills air. A properly rigged boom vang (see Chapter 11) will keep your leech firm.

# When the Wind Picks Up

All these sail adjustments can be pretty confusing to a beginner. The time you will most want to remember them is when you go for an afternoon sail and the wind picks up unexpectedly. While a sail in a good breeze can be quite exhilarating, if you are constantly being overpowered it can be irritating or even frightening. So let's review what you can do when it's not breezy enough to shorten sail (which we'll cover in Chapter 11) and you want to move faster upwind rather than just heel over more. When the wind increases:

- Tension the jib halyard to flatten the jib and move its draft forward.
- Move the jib lead aft to get the jib drawing properly again.
- Tighten the downhaul or main halyard to flatten the mainsail and move its draft forward.
- Tighten the outhaul to reduce the draft in the lower portions of the mainsail.
- Check to see if your main is being backwinded; if it is, try moving your traveler a bit more to windward or easing out your jib. On the other hand, a backwind bubble is preferable to the excessive heeling that too much mainsail trim would cause.
- If your main still luffs near the top of your mast, trim your mainsheet further. On the other hand, easing the sheet will allow the sail to twist and spill wind from its upper portions. Don't be afraid to experiment. When you must choose between a flogging mainsail and excessive heeling, it's time to reduce sail, as we'll see in Chapter 11.

## Practice Questions

### IMPORTANT BOATING TERMS

In the following exercise, match the words in the column on the left with the definitions in the column on the right. In the blank space to the left of each term, write the letter of the item that best matches it. Do not use an item in the right-hand column more than once.

| THE ITEMS | THE RESPONSES |
|---|---|
| 1. _____ apparent wind | a. sailing between close hauled and running |
| 2. _____ telltale | b. heading more away from the wind |
| 3. _____ jibsheet leads | c. sailing with the wind |
| 4. _____ running | d. heading as close to the wind as possible |
| 5. _____ close hauled | e. a wind streamer |
| 6. _____ luffing | f. heading closer into the wind |
| 7. _____ reaching | g. sails fluttering, shivering, failing to fill with wind |
| 8. _____ belly | h. camber |
| 9. _____ falling off | i. deck-mounted blocks that ride on tracks and can be moved forward or aft according to wind conditions |
| 10. _____ heading up | j. the combination of true wind and the boat's motion |

## Multiple-Choice Items

In the following items, choose the best response:

**2-1.** A sail can be stopped from luffing by

a. trimming the sail
b. heading more away from the wind
c. both a and b
d. neither a nor b

**2-2.** Sensing the wind on your face helps you

a. read the direction of the wind
b. judge the intensity of the wind
c. sense both direction and intensity
d. none of the above

**2-3.** Under power on a calm day, the wind you feel is

a. the wind of motion
b. the forecast wind
c. the wind vector
d. none of the above

**2-4.** Under sail on a windy day, the breeze you feel is

a. the wind of motion
b. the forecast wind
c. the apparent wind
d. none of the above

**2-5.** The sails are trimmed according to

a. the true wind
b. the compass
c. the apparent wind
d. none of the above

**2-6.** The function of a shroud telltale is to indicate

a. boat speed
b. apparent wind direction
c. boat course

# Multiple-Choice Items (continued)

d. true wind direction

**2-7.** The function of a masthead wind vane is

    a. to show apparent wind direction, much like a shroud telltale
    b. to show true wind direction
    c. to show the boat's heading
    d. none of the above

**2-8.** When a sail is blanketed, it is

    a. being protected
    b. being blocked from the wind
    c. in calm winds
    d. in strong winds

**2-9.** The function of telltales in the luff of the jib is to

    a. show you when the jib is overtrimmed for the present course
    b. show you when you need to trim the jib or head down
    c. neither a nor b
    d. both a and b

**2-10.** Moving the jib leads forward will

    a. tighten the leech of the jib
    b. loosen the foot of the jib
    c. increase the jib's camber
    d. all of the above

**2-11.** The telltales on the leech of the mainsail collapse when

    a. you are reaching
    b. the sail is stalled
    c. the jib is luffing
    d. it's time to tack

**2-12.** The point of sailing between close hauled and a beam reach is

    a. a close reach
    b. a broad reach
    c. tacking
    d. none of the above

**2-13.** On a moving boat, the apparent wind is always

    a. aft of the true wind
    b. weaker than the true wind
    c. forward of the true wind
    d. stronger than the true wind

**2-14.** Luffing sails indicate that the boat is

    a. heading too far off the wind for its sail trim
    b. on a proper course for its sail trim
    c. heading too high for its sail trim
    d. none of the above

**2-15.** When the helmsman plays the puffs, he is

    a. ignoring the signs of wind changes
    b. constantly changing the jib trim
    c. making slight course changes to correct for small shifts in wind direction and velocity
    d. constantly changing the mainsail trim

**2-16.** The sail with the greater apparent wind angle when close hauled is

    a. the mainsail
    b. the jib
    c. sometimes a, sometimes b
    d. neither a nor b

**2-17.** The proper trim on both the jib and the mainsail affects

    a. boat performance
    b. the slot effect
    c. boat speed
    d. all of the above

**2-18.** Excessive heeling could indicate

    a. too little sail
    b. too much sail
    c. the centerboard is not adjusted properly
    d. none of the above

**2-19.** Production-built sails are designed for

    a. light-weather conditions
    b. heavy-weather conditions
    c. heavy abuse
    d. average weather conditions

**2-20.** A sail with deep draft or camber is good for

    a. heavy-wind sailing
    b. light-wind sailing
    c. running
    d. reaching

(continued on next page)

## Multiple-Choice Items (continued)

**2-21.** The camber or draft of a sail is also called its

    a. length
    b. width
    c. efficiency
    d. belly

**2-22.** A boat on a reach is

    a. probably on its safest point of sail
    b. on its fastest course
    c. easy to control
    d. all of the above

**2-23.** A mainsail can be made flatter in strong winds with the

    a. main halyard
    b. outhaul and downhaul
    c. boom vang
    d. all of the above

**2-24.** If the jib leech is not quite touching the spreader while the foot is not quite touching the leeward shrouds, the jibsheet leads are

    a. set correctly
    b. too far aft
    c. too far forward
    d. none of the above

# Basic Sailboat Maneuvering

## The objectives of this chapter are to describe:

- What it means to be "on a tack."
- How to get from one tack to the other by tacking.
- How to switch tacks by jibing instead of tacking, and how to control a jibe to keep it safe.
- How to use these maneuvers to reach any destination—even one that's straight into the wind.
- How to reduce your boat's angle of heel and how to improve your boat handling.

I N THE PREVIOUS chapter we considered the three major points of sailing—close hauled, reaching, and running—and the subdivisions of reaching. In a modern fore-and-aft-rigged boat, in which the sails at rest lie along the boat's centerline, the wind can blow on either side of the sails. When the breeze is coming over the boat's starboard side and the main boom is extended out to port, we say the boat is sailing on **starboard tack**. When the wind is coming over the boat's port side and the sail is set to starboard, she is said to be on **port tack** (Figure 3-1). When the boat is running before the wind and the sails are set wing and wing as described in the previous chapter, the position of the mainsail determines her tack. If the mainsail is set to starboard, the boat is considered to be on port tack even if the jib is set to port.

Any description of how a boat is sailing includes both her **point of sailing** and her **tack**: A boat might be said to be "close hauled on starboard tack," for instance (Figure 3-2), or "reaching on port tack." It's important to know which tack your boat is on, as well as which tack nearby boats are on, because this determines what is required by the nautical Rules of the Road when you meet another boat. When two boats *cross tacks* (i.e., converge under sail), the boat on starboard tack is the **stand-on boat** and should hold its course, while the boat on port tack is the

**Figure 3-2.** The Colgate 26 is a fast and wholesome sloop-rigged fiberglass sailboat. Here, a Colgate 26 is hard on the wind, or close hauled, on starboard tack. (REPRINTED WITH PERMISSION FROM *FAST TRACK TO CRUISING* BY STEVE AND DORIS COLGATE)

*give-way boat* and should alter course as necessary to prevent a collision. (The Rules of the Road are covered in Chapter 8.) If the boats are competing in a regatta, the internationally sanctioned racing rules apply, and the starboard-tack boat has right of way over the port-tack boat.

# Tacking and Jibing

Look again at the wind circle in Figures 2-7 and 3-1. Clearly a sailboat must be able to get from port tack to starboard tack. A boat that could sail only on port tack would be confined to destinations between 45° and 180° from the wind, while a boat confined to starboard tack could sail only 180° to 315° from the wind. Neither boat could return to its starting point unless or until the wind shifted radically.

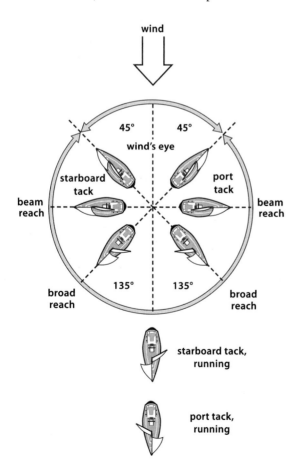

**Figure 3-1.** Starboard versus port tack.

The need to change tacks from time to time is addressed by the two most basic maneuvers of sailing: **tacking** and **jibing**. Because tacking is the more important of the two maneuvers, we'll examine it in detail first.

## TACKING

*Tacking* (also called *coming about* or *going about*) can be defined as turning a boat's bow through the wind's eye from close hauled on one tack to close hauled on the other (Figure 3-3). As the bow turns through the wind's eye, the sails will luff and flog. Far from drawing or helping the boat move through the turn, they will only cause drag until the turn is

complete and they are trimmed to the new close-hauled course.

It's important, therefore, to execute the tacking maneuver as smoothly as possible in order to carry the boat's momentum through the turn. At the same time, if the tiller is pushed too far over, the rudder acts as a brake, which also cuts down on the boat's forward speed. Thus, a well-executed tack is a compromise between a turn that's too slow, causing air drag, and one that's too abrupt, causing water drag.

Let's run through a tack to see how it works (Figure 3-4). Assume a small boat with a mainsail and jib, handled by a crew of two. One of the two is the skipper, usually whoever is steering. The important thing is to make sure that there's only one

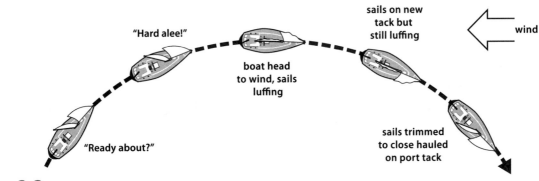

**Figure 3-3.** Tacking.

**Figure 3-4.** Tacking a small sailboat—in this case a 420 (a popular one-design sailing dinghy)—from starboard to port tack with a two-person crew. **1.** The skipper tells the crew to prepare to come about. In a breeze this light, it will be important to execute the tack smoothly so as to carry the boat's momentum through the turn. **2.** The skipper says "Hard alee!" and pushes the tiller to leeward. (Note that the skipper is using a tiller extension, called a hiking stick, which enables him to hike out to windward in a fresh breeze to counteract the wind's heeling force.) **3.** Here the boat's bow has turned past head to wind. The sails are luffing (though it's hardly noticeable in a breeze this light), and the crew releases the port-side jibsheet and prepares to trim the jib on the starboard side. **4.** The tack is completed and the crew has trimmed the jib to the new leeward side. In a fresher breeze the skipper would already have moved to the new windward side, but in a breeze this light he remains to leeward to help the sails fill on the new tack. **5.** The boat has gathered way and the skipper has moved to windward. The crew is in the center of the boat, ready to shift his weight either way as needed to balance the boat. (PHOTOS BY BOB DENNIS)

skipper. You can discuss a sailboat maneuver before or after you do it, but never during the action itself. To do so is just asking for trouble.

The skipper decides when to tack. The reason may be a wind shift (that is, a change in wind direction), another boat in your way, or simply a desire to change course. Having decided to come about, the skipper says, "Stand by to come about." This is a warning to prepare to change tacks. The skipper must be sure the boat is moving at a good, steady speed while close hauled, and be ready to re-

lease the mainsheet if necessary (it shouldn't be, but the skipper should be prepared); the crew normally handles the jibsheet. For reasons explained below, the crew must uncleat but not release the cleated end of the sheet so it's ready to let go.

When the skipper sees that preparations are in hand, the command "Ready about," short for "Get ready to come about," is given. The actual maneuver follows the command "Hard alee" or "Helm alee." These words signify that the rudder has been turned to windward (which means pushing the

**Figure 3-5.** Tacking a larger keelboat is much the same, but with a few new twists. The boat may be wheel-steered (as this one is) and will carry more momentum through the tack. This boat has a big genoa jib that overlaps the mainsail (see Chapter 1), and that complicates things a bit. A sail like this is too big to trim without the assistance of a winch. **1.** The boat is close hauled on port tack. **2.** The tack has been initiated and the crew has cast off the starboard jibsheet and thrown the turns off the starboard-side winch. **3.** The boat is head to wind, and the crew is keeping the slack out of the port-side jibsheet while making sure the starboard-side jibsheet is free to run out and does not snag anything. **4.** The boat has turned past head to wind. The crew is still recovering the slack on the port-side jibsheet, but the bulk of the trimming must be delayed until the genoa clears the port-side shrouds. At this point, though, the crew should wrap at least one or two turns of the sheet around the port-side winch, because they won't want to be without mechanical advantage when that big sail fills with wind! **5.** The genoa is free of the shrouds, and the crew is trimming furiously, knowing that further trim will come a lot harder once the sail fills. **6.** The boat has already started picking up speed on its new tack, but the jib is still luffing and will have to come in a little more. (PHOTOS BY BOB DENNIS)

tiller to leeward if the boat is tiller-steered) to direct the boat to pass through the eye of the wind to the other tack.

Unless the jib is self-tending (see below and Chapter 1), there will be two jibsheets, one leading to either side of the cockpit from the clew of the jib. Only one—the leeward one—is in use, or *working*, at any given time; the other is slack, or *lazy*. When the boat is on starboard tack, the jib is trimmed to the port side of the boat with the corresponding jibsheet, and vice versa. When the boat tacks, the crew must release the working sheet that is about to become lazy, then quickly trim in the lazy sheet that will now be working. The trick is to accomplish this before the sail fills with wind, at which point trimming becomes much harder. (Some jibs, as we saw in Chapter 1, have a boom— the **club** or **jibboom**—and sheet like a mainsail; these jibs are known as *self-tending* because they sheet themselves properly on the opposite tack.)

The maneuver should be swift enough that the boat is still moving easily ahead as she turns. As the bow comes up more and more into the wind, the sails will begin to flutter, or luff—first the jib, then the main. As soon as the jib luffs, but not before, the crew should let go the held sheet and grasp the other one, taking in the slack without forcing the sail to set on the other side of the boat.

As the bow swings into the eye of the wind— known as **head to wind**—the sails will luff straight down the boat's centerline. Then, as the bow continues its turn, the sails will begin to fill out on the other side. As the jib luffs over the deck, the crew takes in the sheet on that side until the luffing diminishes and the sail begins to draw (Figure 3-5). It's not usually necessary to tend the mainsheet— the mainsail will fill and adjust itself. (The only exception is on a sailboat where, for reasons of sail shape, the mainsheet lead is shifted to the windward end of the sheet traveler on each new tack as in Figure 3-6—but that's an optional nuance that need not concern us here.)

When the boat has made a complete turn of 90° from its original close-hauled heading, the sails should both be trimmed to approximately the mirror-image position on the new tack from where they were on the old. The boat now settles down and begins to gain speed. As it does so, make final adjustments as necessary to the jib and mainsail trim.

## Skillful Tacking

The skipper should put the tiller (or wheel) only as far over as is necessary to turn smoothly and fast, without unnecessary braking. This amount of helm will depend on the boat and the conditions and can only be discovered with practice. Generally

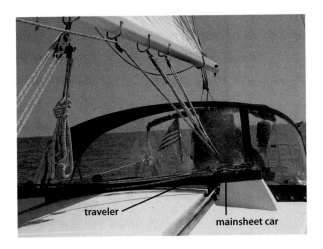

**Figure 3-6.** The mainsheet on most sailboats rides on a traveler car, and on this boat the car position can be controlled from the cockpit. **Left:** For the best possible mainsail trim when close hauled, it may be advantageous to haul the mainsheet car to windward, thus bringing the end of the boom closer to the boat's centerline. If so, the crew does this last when tacking, after trimming and making fast the jibsheet. **Right:** On the other hand, unless you're looking for that last tenth of a knot of speed, you might just leave the car centered, as here. Then you won't have to touch it when you tack. (PHOTOS BY BOB DENNIS)

speaking, a heavy, narrow keelboat carries more momentum and requires less rudder action than does a light, wide centerboard hull, which loses speed dramatically as it turns into the wind.

In the course of tacking, the crew should avoid pulling the jib across to the other side of the boat prematurely—that is, before the boat has turned past the head-to-wind position. Doing so only causes the sail to *backwind*—to take the breeze on its forward side, braking the boat's forward motion and turning the bow back to the old tack. The crew should, when using a relatively small jib, simply allow the jib to luff across the boat on its own, easing out the old working sheet and taking in the slack from the new one to prevent loose line from flapping on the foredeck or getting tangled.

While most boats tack through 85° to 95°, remember the effect of apparent wind, as noted in Chapter 2: Just before tacking, with the boat moving well close hauled, the apparent wind will probably be about 25° off the windward bow. When the tack is completed and the boat begins to move off on its new heading, the apparent wind will probably be more like 40° off the new windward bow because the boat is moving slowly. As the boat gains speed, the apparent wind direction will move forward.

This means that initially the crew need not trim the jib as closely on the new tack as it was trimmed on the old. Then, as the boat regains its speed, the jib will have to come in a little to account for the changing apparent wind.

## Caught In Irons

It sometimes happens, especially in small, light boats, that a vessel will get halfway through a tack and stall with its bow facing directly into the wind. This is called *being in irons*, and it happens to everyone from time to time. It usually happens because the boat wasn't moving fast enough when the tack was begun, or because the skipper tried to tack from a reaching point of sailing without edging up to close hauled first. Sometimes you can get into irons on a very windy day if a wave slaps your bow as you're turning the boat, stopping you cold. Sometimes when there's very little wind, the boat will simply not tack at all.

To avoid getting into irons, make sure—especially if you're unfamiliar with the boat—that

you're moving fast and smoothly before trying to tack. Many skippers will *fall off*—deliberately head the bow 5° or so away from the wind—and pick up a bit of extra speed before coming about.

On very windy days, when there are steep, short waves, put the helm over more abruptly and a bit farther than usual. The idea is to get the bow through the wind's eye, even at a sacrifice of forward speed, before the boat's momentum is stopped by wind or wave.

On very calm days, put the helm over gently, not quite so much as usual, and let the boat ease through the turn. In this case, you're trying to maintain all the momentum you can, at some cost in turning speed.

Most boats will come about from a close reach, but many cannot tack from a beam reach even if the sails are trimmed in during the turn. Better to trim in the sails slowly while heading up to a proper close-hauled heading, then make your tack from there.

Every boat tacks slightly differently from every other boat, and learning how to handle a new craft is just a matter of time and practice. A racing crew will spend hours tacking a new boat over and over again, until the skipper and crew have the maneuver down pat and know just what to expect.

But even top skippers can make a mistake. Sooner or later you'll be in the embarrassing position of finding yourself stalled—dead in the water, with the sails luffing helplessly down the boat's centerline. You're in irons.

## Getting Out of Irons

Getting out of irons isn't particularly difficult. There are several methods; how you do it depends on what kind of boat you're sailing.

If your boat is light, just release the sheets, pull up the centerboard (if there is one), and wait. In a short time, the boat should swing broadside to the wind with the sails luffing out to leeward (Figure 3-7). Drop the board, sheet in the sails, and sail off.

Another method is to *back the jib* (Figure 3-8). Have the crew hold the jib clew out to one side of the boat while you (the skipper) turn the rudder to that same side (which means putting the tiller over to the opposite side). Your boat will slip backward, and her bow will swing away from the

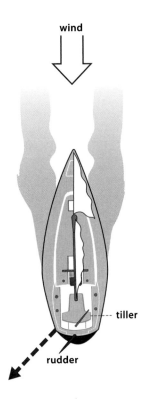

**Figure 3-7.** Drifting backward to get out of irons. With the rudder to port, the bow will fall off to starboard.

**Figure 3-8.** Backing the jib to get out of irons. This boat's bow has fallen off to port, away from the backed jib. (REPRINTED WITH PERMISSION FROM *FAST TRACK TO CRUISING* BY STEVE AND DORIS COLGATE)

side to which the jib is extended. Once you're beam to the wind, you can straighten the rudder, sheet in both sails, and sail off. On a boat with no jib you can back the mainsail instead. This may cause the boat to move straight backward until you put the tiller over. Small catamarans go into irons more easily than other boats and will often begin to sail in reverse almost immediately afterward. Just wait for the boat to pick up a knot or so of speed, then put the tiller over while letting the sheet run.

There are only a couple of things to keep in mind when getting out of irons. First, before taking action, consider which direction you'll want to be heading after you get out of irons. If you back the jib, the bow will wind up headed in the opposite direction. Plan ahead.

In heavy winds, if you take the sheet in too quickly, the sudden wind pressure may spill or heel the boat before it can get going. Better to sheet in just enough to let the boat gain headway, then complete the sheeting operation when you're moving well.

Generally speaking, the heavier the boat, the more positive action will be required to get out of irons. As keelboats are normally heavier than centerboard boats of the same length, they'll need the "jib" backed and the rudder hard over to get out of irons, while a centerboard boat may respond to rudder action alone. This is another of the things you'll have to learn about how your boat reacts.

## JIBING

If a boat is running before the wind on starboard tack, with the main boom fully extended to port, and she changes course only slightly to bring the wind over the port quarter, the main boom will swing across the boat to the starboard side, and the vessel will then be on port tack. The boat has just *jibed*.

Speaking more generally, a jibe—pronounced "jib"—occurs whenever you turn the stern through the eye of the wind in order to bring the breeze onto the other side of the sail. Jibing is the downwind equivalent of tacking, a way to get from port to starboard tack or vice versa. Suppose you are broad reaching on port tack along the shore of an island that is to starboard. You reach the end of the island and wish to alter course 45° to starboard, but doing so will take you from port tack to starboard. You could tack, but that would require a turn of 235° to port—you'd have to slowly round up to close hauled on port tack while trimming the sails, then tack to close hauled on starboard tack, then ease the sheets as you turned offwind, finally reaching your new course. Turning to starboard is clearly the preferred option, but it requires you to jibe.

Many boats sail faster on a broad reach than on a run, so they **tack downwind**, using a series of jibes, first to one side, then to the other, and arrive where they're going faster than if they had sailed the shorter straight-line course.

The essential difference between tacking and jibing is the wind direction relative to the sail. When you tack, the wind rotates around the *luff*, the controlled edge of the sail; when you jibe, the wind rotates around the *leech*, the free edge of the sail. Thus, when you're **tacking**, the sail flutters across the boat with no wind filling it until you sheet in on the new tack. When you **jibe**, on the other hand, the sail always has wind filling it, except for the split second when it is swinging over the boat's centerline.

This means that jibing is potentially hazardous—a less controlled, more violent maneuver than tacking. This does **not** mean you should be afraid to jibe your boat; a good sailor tacks or jibes with equal confidence as the situation demands. Until you can do the same, you're not handling your boat well.

Jibing may require a bit more maneuvering room than tacking, especially when you're jibing a small boat in a stiff breeze. While a tack is a predictable evolution, a fast jibe may result in a sudden burst of speed or a moment's out-of-control stagger. Allow enough room to cope.

The operation itself is simple. Let's assume the same kind of small sloop we had when discussing tacking, with a crew of two (Figure 3-9). To jibe you'll need to put the boat on a run. If you're running wing and wing with a whisker pole extending the jib, remove the pole and stow it out of the way. The jib may or may not remain full, but the jib at the moment is not important. Forget it. The mainsail gets your principal consideration.

The boat is now running, main boom fully extended. The skipper calls out "Stand by to jibe,"

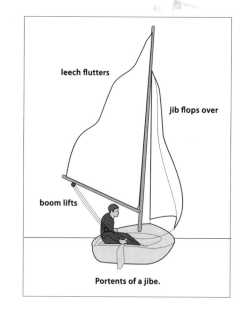

leech flutters

jib flops over

boom lifts

Portents of a jibe.

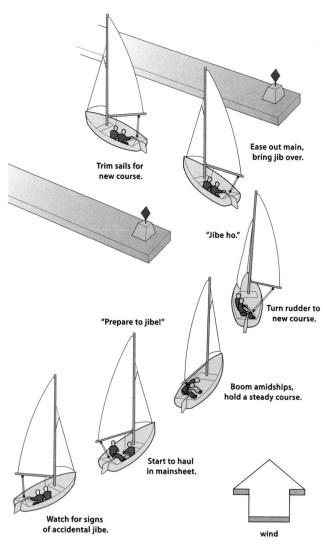

Trim sails for new course.

Ease out main, bring jib over.

"Jibe ho."

Turn rudder to new course.

"Prepare to jibe!"

Boom amidships, hold a steady course.

Start to haul in mainsheet.

Watch for signs of accidental jibe.

wind

**Figure 3-9.** Jibing.

or words to that effect. The crew may handle the mainsheet or the skipper may hold it, according to preference. The skipper then calls "Ready to jibe" as a final warning to the crew, at which point the sheet handler begins to take in the mainsheet. With the command "Jibe ho," the skipper turns the rudder toward the desired direction of the turn (which means turning a tiller **away from** the desired direction), and the mainsheet handler continues trimming.

When the tiller is put over, the boat's stern begins to swing into the wind, and a moment later the main boom will move across, its speed depending largely on the strength of the wind and the control of the sheet handler. In a perfectly timed and controlled jibe, the sheet handler will have trimmed the main boom close to the boat's centerline just as the stern is swinging through the wind. If the main isn't yet all the way in, the helmsman would do well to pause the turn momentarily with the stern pointing into the wind while the trimmer catches up. This way, when the wind moves around the leech of the main and comes to bear on its opposite side, it scarcely moves the boom at all. When the boom crosses the centerline, the sheet handler lets the mainsheet run but keeps some tension on it. This can be accomplished by running the line under the horn of a cleat for friction or simply by employing hand pressure. Let out the sheet in a controlled run as the boat continues its turn, then gradually increase resistance, finally snubbing the sheet so as to stop the boom short of the lee shrouds. Settle down on the new course, then adjust sail trim to the optimum. It's as simple as that.

In light winds, it won't be necessary to take in the main very much before jibing, and in very light zephyrs the crew may have to push the boom across by hand.

### Uncontrolled Jibes

The important aspect of jibing is control: Never allow the boom to swing across without controlling the sheet. In a brisk wind aboard a small boat, the force of an uncontrolled boom hitting the shrouds can snap a shroud, bend the boom, or capsize the boat. There is also the risk of the boom hitting a crewmember. If your boat has a single backstay, the boom can swing up as it moves across out of control and snag on the backstay, which could break the backstay or capsize the boat. If you lose your backstay, the mast might break.

Wear gloves when handling sheets. Some sailors prefer fingerless mitts (it's the palms that need protection) made of chamois or some similar material. Others buy cheap cotton painters' gloves in a hardware store.

One of the dangers of running is that you are not aware of the true wind strength. When heading downwind, your boat's speed is subtracted from the true wind speed, and the apparent wind you feel may be much less than the true wind, which may slam the boom across with quite a crash if you're not ready for it.

Finally, watch your head and those of your crew. The boom doesn't shout a warning as it swings across the cockpit, and more than one sailor has incurred a painful or even serious whack on the head from an accidental or uncontrolled jibe.

# Sailing a Course

Any boat moving from point to point over the water can be said to be *sailing a course*. Some of the time nothing more is involved than heading directly toward your objective on a *straight-line*, or *rhumb-line course*, but frequently things are somewhat more complicated.

If, for instance, the objective is directly upwind, it is impossible to sail directly to it. The way to work a sailboat to windward involves a series of tacks, so that the boat zigzags its way to its ultimate destination (Figure 3-10). When it's necessary to sail a set of tacks to a windward mark, it's usually a good idea to choose a mark that is within sight. If the destination itself is out of range, intermediate marks may be chosen, preferably ones that appear on nautical charts of the area. (A global positioning system [GPS] receiver offers a great way to maintain a good course when the destination is out of sight. See Chapter 12.)

In sailing an upwind course, you have to decide whether to sail long or short tacks to either side of the straight-line course to the objective. There is no right way to do it. Time spent tacking is time lost, and

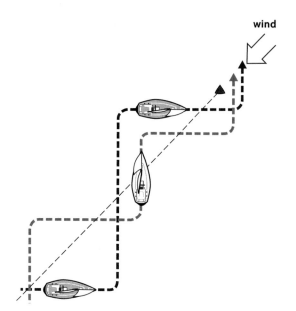

**Figure 3-10.** Two boats sailing a course upwind. One sails longer legs than the other, but they both arrive at the same place.

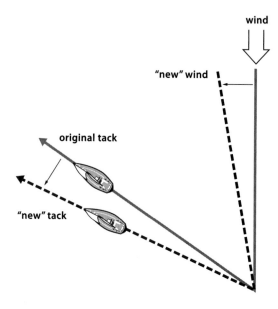

**Figure 3-11.** This 10° wind shift is a header on starboard tack, but it will be a lift on port tack.

all other things being equal, it takes more time to reach an objective with many short tacks than with a few long tacks. On the other hand, it is easier to keep track of your direction and position when short-tacking than when making long tacks well away from the base course, and staying close to the intended course with short tacks will also minimize the negative impacts of any adverse wind shifts.

For example, let's say you are tacking toward a mark directly upwind on starboard tack and the wind shifts 10° to port. This means that, to hold the same course relative to the wind while remaining on starboard tack, the boat will have to head 10° away from your objective (Figure 3-11). This wind shift is called a **header**. But if you tack over to port, it will be possible to sail 10° closer than the former best course. A wind change in your favor is known as a **lift** and enables you to sail closer to your objective than anticipated. A header on one tack is a lift on the other, so racing sailors frequently tack on every header during a windward leg of a race.

Most boats are substantially faster on a broad reach than when running, so you might reach a downwind destination faster by jibing back and forth between a series of broad reaches than you could by sailing the rhumb line. The boat type and the wind strength will have a great deal to do with deciding whether this tactic, known as **tacking**

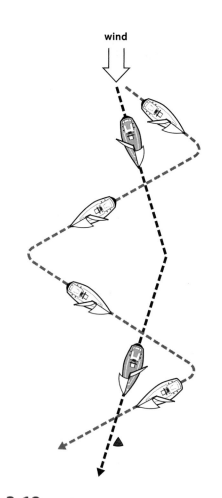

**Figure 3-12.** Two boats tacking downwind. One sails faster than the other with a higher jibing angle but has to travel farther.

*downwind*, is a good one (Figure 3-12). When racing sailors turn from a run to a broad reach, they call it **hardening up** or **heating up**, and they frequently carry expensive electronic performance instruments (or inexpensive plastic slide rules) that read out the advantages and disadvantages of tacking downwind, revealing how much faster you must sail to make up the extra distance of an indirect course.

Normally, the way to change direction when running is to jibe, but sometimes, especially in rough weather, a controlled jibe may be rather tricky, and the skipper may elect to sail a series of broad reaching headings, coming about each time the course is changed. This tactic keeps the wind relatively safely on the quarter, where a sudden wind shift is not likely to cause an unexpected jibe.

It is hard to tack directly from a broad reach, especially in a choppy sea, because most boats lose too much speed in a turn that great to carry their momentum through the eye of the wind to the other tack. It is usually necessary to round up toward the wind slowly until the boat is sailing a very close reach, with the sails properly trimmed, then come about from there. Instead of settling down on the opposite close reach, simply keep the boat turning until the new downwind course is reached. It's a safe and only moderately inefficient way to handle a boat in heavy winds and seas.

A boat beating to windward or sailing a close reach makes a certain amount of **leeway**—the sideways slippage caused by wind pressure—which hull design alone cannot cancel out. The maximum amount of leeway under sail is made by a centerboard boat close hauled with the board fully raised. Try this with your own boat or a friend's. Put her on a close-hauled heading with the board down, sailing right at some mark. Even better, try to line up a *range*—two marks in line. Sail toward it and see how your boat slides gently off to leeward. Now pull the board all the way up and see how much your leeway increases (Figure 3-13). The difference will be dramatic. (Note: Not all centerboard boats are designed to sail close hauled with the board up without capsizing!)

When you're sailing downwind, raising the centerboard makes your boat faster. When you're close hauled, you need the board all the way down

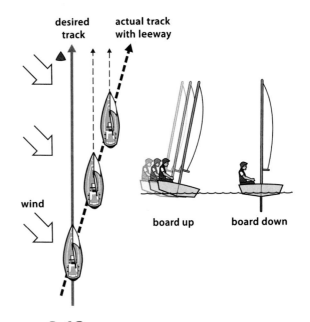

**Figure 3-13.** Leeway affects all sailboats but is most noticeable on a centerboard or daggerboard boat when the board is not all the way down.

to reduce leeway. Every skipper should have a pretty accurate idea of how much leeway his or her boat will make close hauled, close reaching, and beam reaching with the board all the way down, halfway down, and fully raised. After a while this becomes instinctive, but it takes practice.

When sailing toward a windward mark, the final tack is the crucial one. If, after making this tack, you find yourself heading straight for your goal (allowing for leeway), then you have **fetched the mark** and you are sailing down the *layline*, which is the course line you need to reach. If, after you've come about, you find you don't have to sail a close-hauled course to make your target, you've **overstood** and should have tacked sooner. Far more common, however, is the problem of falling short, when you tack too soon for the final leg and then find that another tack will be required (Figure 3-14).

The temptation is to come about as soon as the mark is at 90° to your present heading. Theoretically that should put you on a course directly toward it, but your leeway will make you fall short. In addition, knowing exactly when the mark is at 90°, or directly **abeam**, is tricky. More often than not, wishful thinking will cause you to tack too soon. Be sure you have reached the layline before you tack. It is better to hold on another 30 seconds

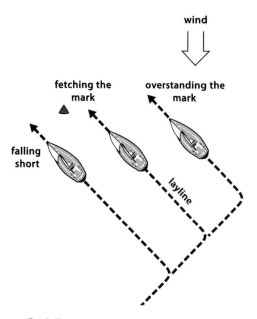

**Figure 3-14.** Fetching a windward mark. Here the mark is a buoy, but it could just as easily be a point of land, a harbor entrance, or any other destination.

**Figure 3-15.** The helmsperson in this 470, a two-person Olympic-class dinghy, is hiking out with her feet hooked under a hiking strap, while the crew is suspended over the water on a trapeze. Both are dressed appropriately for the wet ride a high-performance dinghy like this can offer. (PHOTO BY DANIEL FORSTER, REPRINTED WITH PERMISSION FROM *YOUR FIRST SAILBOAT* BY DANIEL SPURR)

and overstand a bit than to have to make two quick additional tacks.

# Stability and Angle of Heel

A sailboat normally heels in response to wind pressure, and we have seen (Chapter 1) how the degree of heeling is partly controlled by hull shape and partly by ballast. Another important factor is the disposition of crew weight. Even in a stiff wind, a small boat that's dramatically heeled can be brought closer to level by the crew *hiking out* to windward. In bigger boats hiking means sitting and sprawling along the windward gunwale, and it isn't necessary in a keelboat unless the skipper is looking for just a little more sail-carrying ability and speed. But most up-to-date small sailboats have **hiking straps** built in along their cockpit soles. The crew hooks his or her feet under the straps, with his bottom on the gunwale, allowing the entire upper body to lean out to windward as a living counterbalance. This is athletic sailing—like doing a hundred crunches or so. On some high-performance boats the crew stands on the windward gunwale,

**Figure 3-16.** This heeled boat is presenting an oblique sail plan to the wind. This lessens the wind's force in the sails and helps to limit further heeling. If the boat heels much more than this, it will not be at its fastest. (PHOTO BY BILL MORRIS)

with his bottom supported by a wire, or trapeze, hung from the masthead, and arches back to windward. This is the most exciting use of human ballast possible, but it's not for beginners (Figure 3-15).

There are times when a boat should heel and times it shouldn't, and the degree of heel is also a variable. Within limits, heeling is a safety factor. When a sudden gust of wind strikes a boat's sails, and the boat heels, not only does the heeling action absorb some of the wind's force (which would otherwise damage the rig), but the sails of a heeled boat present considerably less wind resistance than those of an upright craft. In effect, the more a boat heels, the more wind it **spills** from the tops of its sails, and this self-correcting mechanism tends to limit further heeling. On the other hand, an excessively heeled boat offers a distorted underwater shape and becomes less efficient (Figure 3-16).

On days of very light breeze, there may not be enough wind to make the sails assume a proper airfoil shape. The cloth just hangs there. But seating the crew to leeward so as to heel the boat 5° or so may induce the sails to sag into their proper shapes (Figure 3-17).

On some boats with long bow and stern overhangs, heeling will effectively lengthen the waterline (Figure 3-18). This means that the boat's potential speed, which is related to waterline length (see Chapter 1), increases somewhat. And some sailboats can be heeled slightly to leeward in faint breezes to reduce the amount of hull surface in contact with the water and thus lessen the friction impeding the boat's movement.

Finally, some boats have a more effective underwater shape when slightly heeled, but this is generally true of older craft such as those pictured in Figure 2-8. Today's high-performance sailboats are almost always at their best when sailed flat or very nearly so. In almost no case is a boat's performance going to improve beyond 20° of heel, and in most boats performance will deteriorate badly above 25° or so.

**Figure 3-17.** Sea Scout Mariners Shaun Poestridge and Jim Parsons are sitting to leeward in a light air—what sailors call a ghosting breeze—to keep the sails at their proper attitude and in their proper shape to catch what little breeze there is. (PHOTO BY BOB DENNIS)

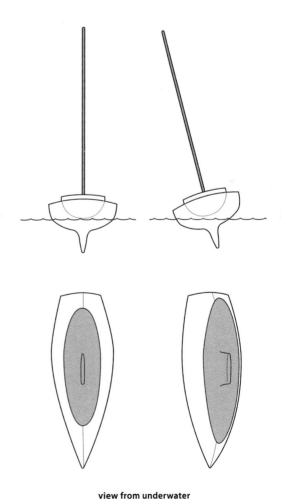

**view from underwater**

**Figure 3-18.** When a boat has bow and stern overhangs, its sailing waterline gets longer as the boat heels (right).

Boats have two kinds of stability: initial and ultimate. ***Initial stability*** is a boat's tendency to resist the first few degrees of heeling, whereas ***ultimate stability*** is the boat's ability to resist capsize. Round-bottom keelboats have relatively little initial stability. They heel easily at first, but only to a point. Once the counterbalancing effect of the ballast

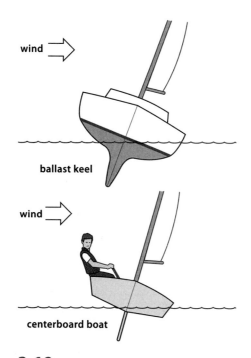

**Figure 3-19.** A round-bottom keelboat (top) is initially *tender* and will tip easily up to the point shown here. Further heeling is resisted more and more strongly, however, as the keel ballast comes into play. By contrast, a hard-chine boat with a centerboard or daggerboard is quite stiff up to the point shown here, but gets more and more tender at steeper angles of heel.

keel comes into play, a round-bottom boat will be very hard to heel any further. It has good ultimate stability (Figure 3-19).

Almost the opposite is true of hard-chine centerboard boats. Such a boat has high initial stability and is very steady at first, but once heeled more than a few degrees, its stability suddenly begins to lessen, until at some point it's easier for the hull to keep going over than to right itself. Such a boat has good initial stability but poor ultimate stability.

The most extreme case is that of a ***multihull***—e.g., a catamaran (with two hulls) or a trimaran (with three). Because of hull shape, these boats have tremendous initial stability, and a catamaran will seldom heel more than 5° or a trimaran more than 10° to 15° (Figure 3-20). But once the windward hull of a catamaran leaves the water, stability is on the point of evaporating, and a cat, once capsized, will tend to turn completely upside down. A trimaran is more stable than a cat with one hull out of the water, but again, if sufficient force is applied to flip her, she will settle in a completely upside-down position. Both cats and tris are normally without ballast and have daggerboards, so there is no counterbalancing weight to bring them back up.

Each type of hull has its advantages and drawbacks. There is no "perfect" hull for all conditions, and in choosing a boat you must aim for that compromise between stability and other attributes (such as speed and maneuverability) that best meets your preferences and the demands of your local waters.

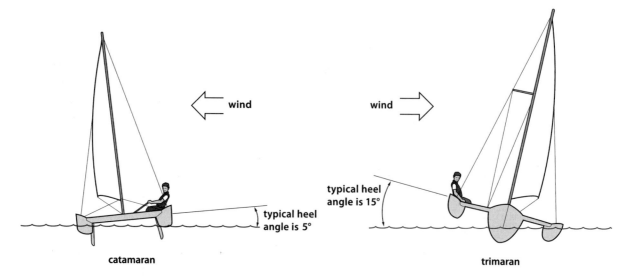

**Figure 3-20.** Catamarans and trimarans both have tremendous initial stability but very little ultimate stability.

# Knowing Your Boat

Practice is the key to good boat handling. New sailors tend to sail erratically until they develop a feel for their tiller and their boat's motion. We have already seen that the relationship of the sails to the wind's direction is the secret of making a boat move well, as opposed to just making it move. You must concentrate on maintaining that relationship, keeping your boat **in the groove**, in spite of other distractions. It's easy to lose your orientation to the wind when you take your eyes off your sails to look at another boat or to chat with your crew. You can easily head up or bear off unknowingly until you develop enough awareness to know when a change in course has changed your boat's angle of heel.

Small changes in wind direction or wind speed while sailing close hauled or reaching also give novices problems. Unless you are careful, you will tend to oversteer to account for these variations. Such changes can usually be felt through your tiller unless you have a strong *weather helm*, which is simply the tendency of a boat when left to its own devices to round up into the wind. Weather helm results from the **center of effort** of the sail plan relative to the **center of lateral resistance** of the boat's underwater profile, and some weather helm is good. It's better, after all, to have an unattended sailboat round up into the wind, sails luffing, than to head away from the wind and jibe. Too much weather helm is bad, however. It forces you to turn the rudder to leeward in order to travel straight ahead, and that slows the boat.

Let's assume your boat has a good, moderate weather helm. Here's how it works: When you get hit by a gust of wind, your boat begins to heel over and the weather helm increases. You should learn to let the tiller pull your hand slightly to leeward to head up a little in a puff, thus depowering the sails; if you push your tiller, you will head up too far and too fast, slowing your boat. A drop in tiller pressure usually means that the apparent wind direction has shifted forward, either because of a true wind direction change or a lower true wind speed. Of course, if you hang onto your tiller as if it were going to run away, you won't feel any subtle changes in tiller pressure.

The tendency to oversteer while sailing before the wind is even greater. The tiller has less sensitivity, the apparent wind is less and seems to shift around more, and the seas tend to push your boat's stern off course. When you find yourself using your tiller like a saw to keep a steady course on a run, try holding your tiller amidships to see what your boat will do. It takes a certain amount of determination to reduce your steering efforts, and you can never eliminate them entirely, but you may be surprised at how well your boat will stay on course when you stop fighting it.

Oversteering slows your boat; your rudder acts like a brake anytime it is turned from your boat's centerline. Try steering your boat through a series of abrupt turns on a broad reach in light air to see just how much braking effect your rudder has.

There are several games you can play to get to know your boat better. They all require practice and plenty of sea room the first few times you try them. For instance, you can bring your boat slowly into the wind, let your jibsheets fly, and see what your boat does after it loses headway. It may fall off the wind and, because the mainsheet is still secured, the mainsail will fill and the boat will sail off. Or your boat may fall astern (move backward). If this happens, try to put your boat on the tack of your choice, port or starboard. Remember, since your boat is moving backward, you should turn your rudder in the direction you want your stern to go. If you want the bow to fall off to starboard, push your tiller to starboard to turn your rudder and your stern to port. Keep trying this until you are sure that you can make your boat fall off on whichever tack you choose.

There are a couple of variations to this game. You can try backing your boat straight backward. If this proves difficult, try holding your jib aback (as in Figure 3-8) and steering straight back, then try the same thing with your main. Eventually, you will know all about backing your boat, assuming it can be done. You will know how much rudder you need to apply, the right time to put your rudder over after your boat starts backing, and when to straighten your rudder as your mainsail fills and your boat starts forward. You will, in effect, know if you can get out of irons without backing a sail, and how efficiently you can get out of irons backing either your main or your jib.

The next game is most suited to test the balance of a small cruising sailboat. When sailing on a close reach, tack your boat without trimming or letting go either your jib- or mainsheets. Once you have put your rudder over, hold it there so that your boat continues to circle. This game should be played in moderate air. You can start this maneuver farther and farther off the wind until you can no longer put your bow through the eye of the wind. Many boats, having made it through the first tack, will continue to jibe and tack as long as you hold the rudder over in the same position.

You can also use this game to decide how best to **heave-to**, or stop your boat without mooring it. The conventional method of heaving-to is to bring your boat close to the wind, trim your jib and mainsail tight, then tack without releasing your jibsheet (Figure 3-21). The object is to wind up on the new tack with your jib sheeted close on the windward side, your mainsail sheeted close on the leeward side, and your tiller secured to leeward. Your rudder and mainsail are supposed to head your boat into the wind, while your jib forces your boat off the wind, resulting in a scalloped course through the water at a slow speed with the mainsail alternately luffing and filling. As we can deduce from the previous game, many modern boats do not lie as calmly as we might like. Some boats begin to swoop vigorously, moving considerable distances, and many boats begin to sail around in a circle.

If your boat doesn't want to heave-to in the conventional manner, you can try the following: trim your jib to weather until its clew is at your mast, ease your mainsheet until it lies at a 45° angle to your boat's centerline, then lash the tiller or wheel so the rudder is all the way over (heading your boat into the wind).

Very few modern sloops will heave-to successfully. Sailing adventure books tell of adventurers riding out a storm hove-to, but that is not your average recreational sailor's cup of tea. The ability to stop your boat at sea does have advantages, however, if you need to recover a man overboard, sort out your navigational problems, get in out of the rain, or just eat a peaceful meal.

**Lying-to** is a variant of heaving-to. If you free all your sheets and lash your tiller to leeward, you will lie more or less beam-to the wind with all sails luff-

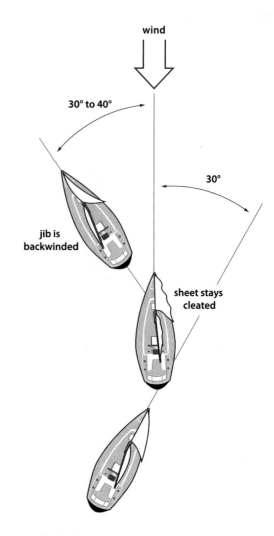

**Figure 3-21.** Heaving-to.

ing to leeward. This results in considerable strain on your nerves, sails, and rigging in any but the lightest breeze, but lying-to does reduce leeway and is a handy maneuver if you need to stop alongside something in the water—such as your hat!

Many sailboats will lie-to under bare poles—that is, they will lie beam-to the wind with no sails up if their tillers are lashed to leeward. Their rate of drift is reduced considerably from that of an uncontrolled sailboat hull, which normally drifts with its bow downwind at about 135° to the wind direction. This has at least two implications: If your motor stops, you can cut your rate of drift by lashing your tiller hard over while you work on your problem (you can also put your sail up and have complete control over your boat while your crew works on the motor); or you can direct your downwind drift. In effect, you may be able to "sail" downwind with bare poles, sometimes at angles of up to 30° to 45° either side of directly downwind.

As you gain confidence you will think of other games that will increase your ability to handle your boat. The more you experiment, the more confidence you will gain in both your boat and yourself.

Develop the habit of wearing a *personal flotation device* (PFD), commonly known as a **life jacket**.

Modern PFDs are streamlined and comfortable and will not hamper your movements—see Chapter 5. There is a need for safety **and** unrestricted movement, especially in adverse conditions. And remember to let your crew try these maneuvers too; after all, sailing is supposed to be fun for everyone on the boat—and someday your life may depend on your crew's seamanship—and their wearing of PFDs.

# Practice Questions

## IMPORTANT BOATING TERMS
In the following exercise, match the words in the column on the left with the definitions in the column on the right. In the blank space to the left of each term, write the letter of the item that best matches it. Do not use an item in the right-hand column more than once.

| THE ITEMS | THE RESPONSES |
|---|---|
| 1. _____ running | a. hold your course |
| 2. _____ stand-on | b. switch tacks by turning the stern through the wind |
| 3. _____ jibe | c. sailed past the layline on the opposite tack |
| 4. _____ reaching | d. stuck head to wind |
| 5. _____ close hauled | e. sailing as close to the wind as possible |
| 6. _____ overstood | f. sailing with the wind |
| 7. _____ in irons | g. a point of sailing between running and close hauled |
| 8. _____ lift | h. jib and main set on opposite sides downwind |
| 9. _____ wing and wing | i. reaching a windward objective on the current tack |
| 10. _____ fetching | j. a wind shift that allows you to point closer to an objective to windward |

# Multiple-Choice Items

In the following items, choose the best response:

**3-1.** If you are the stand-on vessel, you

  a. must maintain course and speed
  b. must yield
  c. must stand still
  d. have the choice to yield

**3-2.** If a boat is running, it is sailing

  a. against the wind
  b. with the wind
  c. across the wind
  d. fast

**(continued on next page)**

# Multiple-Choice Items (continued)

**3-3.** The term "tacking" means

a. coming about
b. filling the sails on the opposite side of the boat
c. turning the bow through the wind
d. all of the above

**3-4.** If your skipper says "Stand by to come about," you

a. are executing a tack
b. are about to execute a tack
c. have completed a tack
d. are not executing a tack

**3-5.** "Ready about" means that you

a. should cancel preparations to tack
b. should actually execute the tack
c. should get ready to execute the tack
d. are not executing a tack

**3-6.** "Hard alee" means that you should

a. cancel the tack
b. get ready to execute the tack
c. prepare for the tack
d. actually execute the tack

**3-7.** As a boat gathers speed after a tack, the apparent wind will

a. move aft
b. move forward
c. decrease
d. remain unchanged

**3-8.** When tacking from a broad reach, you should

a. leave the sheets alone
b. trim in sails gradually
c. ease sheets gradually
d. ease the main only

**3-9.** Jibing is

a. moving the stern through the eye of the wind
b. the downwind equivalent of a tack
c. potentially more hazardous than a tack
d. all of the above

**3-10.** An uncontrolled jibe in a stiff wind can

a. snap a shroud or backstay
b. bend the boom
c. capsize the boat
d. all of the above

**3-11.** The term "header" means the wind has

a. shifted aft
b. subsided
c. shifted forward
d. gotten stronger

**3-12.** Leeway

a. is caused by improper sail trim
b. is limited by a centerboard or keel
c. can be eliminated by sail trim
d. none of the above

**3-13.** The crew of a small centerboard sailboat may use a trapeze to

a. limit the degree of heeling
b. limit the luffing in a sail
c. limit boat speed in a harbor
d. trim the jibsheets

**3-14.** Pronounced heeling in a fresh breeze

a. usually improves performance
b. usually adversely affects performance
c. has little effect on performance
d. none of the above

**3-15.** A hull's initial and ultimate stability indicate

a. its speed potential in high winds
b. how high into the wind it can point
c. its ability to resist heeling and capsize, respectively
d. its ability to recover from capsize

**3-16.** A catamaran or trimaran will

a. right itself after a capsize
b. tend to turn upside down when capsized
c. right itself with minimal effort from capsize
d. heel easily in moderate winds

**3-17.** A rhumb-line course is the

a. straight-line compass course to your destination
b. course that the boat is on at the moment
c. average course maintained on the current tack
d. average of the courses maintained on both tacks when tacking upwind

# Multiple-Choice Items (continued)

**3-18.** Be cautious in heavy winds about

    a. sheeting in too slowly after a tack
    b. sheeting in too quickly after a tack
    c. lowering the centerboard too quickly
    d. raising the centerboard too slowly

**3-19.** Executing a tack from a broad reach

    a. cannot be done in many boats
    b. is easily done on all boats
    c. is dangerous
    d. is recommended

**3-20.** Turning the tiller too far during a tack

    a. causes a braking action
    b. causes the boat to speed up
    c. has no consequences
    d. causes the tack to occur too fast

**3-21.** Raising a centerboard partway may increase your speed without degrading your stability or increasing your leeway when you're

    a. sailing in a heavy breeze
    b. sailing off the wind
    c. sailing in a light breeze
    d. sailing to windward

**3-22.** A boat on a port tack

    a. carries its boom on the starboard side
    b. has the right of way over a starboard-tack boat
    c. carries its boom on the port side
    d. is faster than a boat on a starboard tack

**3-23.** The eye of the wind is the

    a. direction from which the wind is blowing
    b. direction toward which the wind is blowing
    c. tendency of the wind to split around the luff of the sail
    d. point at which you can tack and fetch your objective

**3-24.** The principal danger of a jibe is

    a. capsize
    b. loss of speed
    c. a violent swing of the boom
    d. stretching of the sheets

# Rigging and Boat Handling

A Hinckley Pilot sloop headed out of Rockland, Maine, on a cruise Down East. (PHOTO BY STEPHEN GROSS)

**The objectives of this chapter are to describe:**

- How to prepare your boat for sailing.
- How to depart from and return to a dock, mooring, or beach.
- The characteristics and limitations of anchors.
- How to anchor safely.

AS ANCHORAGES BECOME more crowded and marinas more costly, sailors have turned increasingly to trailering their sailboats (see Chapter 6). But even if you keep your boat at a pier or mooring, you'll find it helpful to know how to set up the rigging from scratch—a task well within the capabilities of any skipper of a boat under about 25 feet long.

# Stepping the Mast

The difficulty of setting up the mast depends on two things: the size and weight of the spar, and the manner in which it's stepped in the boat. In Chapter 1 we considered both keel-stepped and deck-stepped masts. The heel of a keel-stepped mast fits into or around a socket that sits atop the boat's keel or in its bilge. Such a mast may first lead through a **mast partner**—a hole in the deck or a seat—which helps brace the mast both athwartships and fore and aft.

On small, trailerable cruisers and other boats in which the mast is too heavy to treat casually and yet must be raised and lowered frequently, the mast may step on deck in a hinged fitting, which allows it to be raised and lowered quite easily (Figure 4-1). Regardless of the exact configuration, however, stepping the mast should offer no problems if a few orderly steps are followed.

First, select a good location for mast stepping. If your boat is small and lacks floorboards, or if its hull is thin enough that it flexes under your weight, then you will have to launch it before clambering around inside the hull while stepping the mast. Make sure the boat is tied securely to a float or pier so it won't shift underneath you as you step aboard with the spar on your shoulder. Step into the middle of the boat, and keep your weight as low as possible. If you step the mast while the boat is still on its trailer, as many do, first check to be sure that there are no overhead power lines either near you or between you and the launch ramp. A significant number of sailors have been electrocuted when their metal spars or standing rigging came in contact with uninsulated wiring. Before raising the mast, check all parts of the rig, particularly those that will be inaccessible once the mast is up. Make sure the halyards are free to run and lead to the proper sides of the mast. Have your cotter and/or clevis pins ready to use (Figure 4-2), along with any necessary tools.

If you haven't done so already, tie off the stays, shrouds, and halyards against the mast. The easiest way to do this is first to set the spar on two or

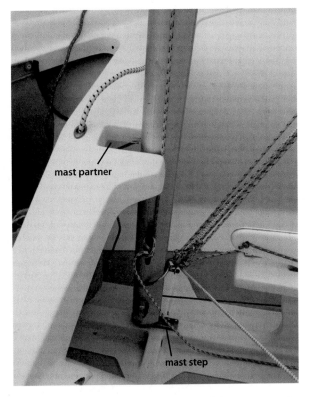

**Figure 4-1.** **Left:** This deck-stepped mast on a centerboard daysailer is raised or lowered by pivoting it around the mast step pin. **Right:** This sailing dinghy mast steps atop a reinforced fiberglass base on the cockpit sole and is supported at deck level by a mast partner that is really just a slot in a thwart. Note that the mast step allows the butt of the mast to be moved forward or aft in order to change mast rake, which alters weather helm and sail shape. (PHOTOS BY BOB DENNIS)

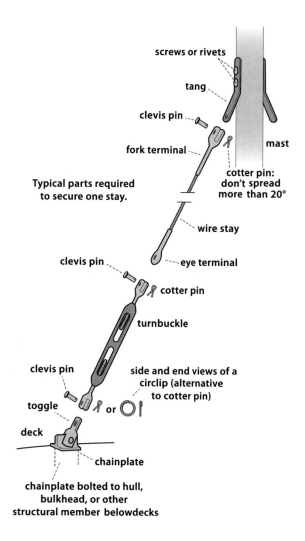

screws or rivets

tang

clevis pin

fork terminal

mast

**Typical parts required
to secure one stay.**

cotter pin:
don't spread
more than 20°

wire stay

clevis pin

eye terminal

cotter pin

turnbuckle

clevis pin

side and end views of a
circlip (alternative
to cotter pin)

toggle

or

deck

chainplate

**chainplate bolted to hull,
bulkhead, or other
structural member belowdecks**

**Figure 4-2.** The typical parts required to secure a stay.

three sawhorses for support. No tie should be higher up the mast than you can reach while standing on the deck after the spar is stepped, for obvious reasons.

For masts that are deck-stepped in a hinged fitting, you may now place the mast foot in the hinge and secure it. If there's no way to secure the foot, or if the spar must first be guided through a deck hole, at least two people will be required to step even a rather small mast—one to locate the foot and the other to raise the spar.

Walk slowly and carefully forward, watching where you put your feet, and raise the mast to the vertical. At this point, one person will have to steady the mast (unless the deck-level support is enough to hold it upright) while another quickly *makes fast* (secures or fastens) the key pieces of **standing rigging**. These are the fore- and backstays

and the upper shrouds, both port and starboard (see Figures 1-12 and 1-13). Once these turnbuckles are attached to the proper chainplates (see Figures 14-12 and 14-42) and taken up enough to hold the mast reasonably steady, it's no longer necessary for anyone to hold the spar erect. For heavier masts, the shrouds and backstay should be loosened but attached to the chainplates prior to raising the mast. This makes it easier to keep the mast vertical while attaching the forestay. We'll have more to say about stepping a heavier mast in Chapter 6.

Make fast the remaining shrouds to their chainplates and be sure the halyards are free to run without being tangled in the rigging or the mast hardware. Although actual **tuning** of the standing rigging is a matter of trial and error, initial tensioning is no great problem. Masthead shrouds and stays should be quite taut—enough so that they vibrate when plucked—while those that run partway up the mast should be tight enough not to flop to and fro but not as tight as the uppers. Once you're sailing, you'll know soon enough if your turnbuckles need adjusting, so for the moment don't overdo.

Rig tuning is covered in Chapter 11. What's important for the moment is to have the mast standing straight in the boat. Sight over the bow to make sure the spar isn't tipped to one side or the other, and sight from the side to determine that the amount of fore-and-aft tilt, known as *rake*, is proper. On most boats, the mast is designed to rake slightly aft—2° to 5° at most. If yours is a class or production boat, other skippers or the manufacturer's literature will tell you what degree of rake works best for your boat. Lacking this information, try a slight tilt aft—enough so that the main halyard, if allowed to swing free from the masthead, will touch the deck about 6 inches aft of the mast step for a 20-foot spar. Mast rake affects the action of your boat when you let the tiller go. The farther aft the mast is raked, the more the boat wants to head into the wind. As mentioned in Chapter 3, this is called **weather helm**, and a certain amount of it is highly desirable as a safety measure. Too much weather helm, however, both tires the helmsman and slows the boat.

With the mast in place, you can attach the boom to the gooseneck track or fixed fitting, whichever your boat is equipped with (see Figure 1-11). Attach the mainsheet to the boom and deck fittings (see Figure 1-15), making sure the line is free to run through its blocks. If your boat has a *topping lift*—a light line or wire running from the masthead to the outer end of the boom—make it fast. The topping lift holds the boom off the deck when the sail isn't up.

Now set up the rudder and tiller, if they're not already attached. On some sailing dinghies, the mainsheet block travels from one side of the boat to the other by riding on a rope or wire **bridle** rather than the fixed **traveler** used on larger boats. The bridle often straddles the tiller with its ends secured to the stern quarters (Figure 4-3). If your boat is set up in this fashion, you must be certain that the tiller is in fact under the traveler. Quite frequently the rudder of a dinghy like this will attach permanently to the tiller via a hinged fitting, and the entire rudder-tiller assembly is stowed in the boat when not in use. In this case you must work the assembly under the mainsheet bridle before dropping the pins, or *pintles*, on the forward edge of the rudder into the corresponding sockets, or **gudgeons**, on the transom of the boat. If these fittings allow, the rudder should be locked in so it cannot float free.

If you have a tilt-up rudder and the boat is not yet launched, be sure that the rudder is in the "up" position. Many boats with heavy centerboards are trailered with the board resting on a crossbeam of the trailer to take the strain off the centerboard lifting mechanism. Before launching, check to make sure the board is fully retracted and the pendant is tied off. Otherwise, the board will almost certainly jam in the trailer frame and make it impossible to launch the boat. Once afloat, however, the centerboard or daggerboard should be lowered.

# Making Sail

Before attaching the sails to the spars and forestay, head the boat more or less into the wind so that the sails, once hoisted, will luff freely. Ideally, a boat should be swinging free at a mooring when making sail, but in many cases you'll be at a pier or float

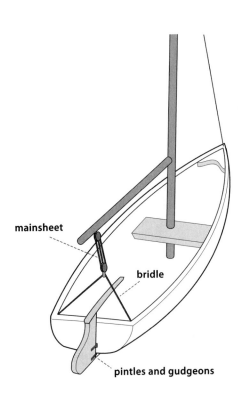

**Figure 4-3.** **Left:** On many sailing dinghies the mainsheet rides on a bridle over the tiller, as shown here. **Right:** A rudder being fitted to a 420 sailing dinghy. Two pins, or pintles, on the forward edge of the rudder drop into corresponding sockets, or gudgeons, on the transom of the boat. (PHOTO BY BOB DENNIS)

and will not be able to head the boat directly into the wind. Do the best you can, and that will be good enough.

## ATTACHING THE SAILS

Work with the mainsail first. Usually, you'll have to take the sail out of the bag and find the *clew*—the lower aft corner (see Figure 1-19). Arrange the sail so the *foot*, from clew to tack, is untwisted. Feed the sail onto (or into, depending on the attachments) the boom track, pulling the foot along the boom until the clew can be made fast to the **outhaul** (see Figure 1-19). Next, fasten the tack cringle to the gooseneck fitting. Then, pull the outhaul toward the outer end of the boom until the sail's foot is taut (Figure 4-4).

Insert the battens in the **batten pockets** (Figure 4-5). Old-fashioned pockets had small grommets at the outer end, corresponding to a hole in the end of the batten. A light line secured the batten in its pocket. Nowadays, however, most sailmakers use a batten pocket that requires no tying. Battens should fit snugly into their pockets, but not so tightly that they stretch the fabric. Remember that the thinned-down end of a wood or fiberglass

batten goes into the pocket first. It might seem that just the opposite would be true, but consider that a batten's job is to support the roach of the sail and to impart an even curve, hence the more easily bendable thin edge should be farther forward in the sail, where the curvature is greater.

If your mainsail luff is fitted with slides (for an exterior track) or slugs (for a recessed track), you can slide these fittings onto or into the track as in Figure 4-6. There's nearly always a gate fitting at the bottom of the track to lock the stack of slides or slugs in place until the sail is raised. If, however, you have a mainsail with a roped luff in place of these fittings, you won't be able to slide this into the mast groove until you raise the sail.

Last, make the halyard fast to the sail's head cringle as in Figure 4-6. Most halyards have a shackle or other piece of hardware for this purpose, but on a small boat it's really not necessary. A **bowline** (see Figures 14-31 and 14-32) will serve just as well. When a shackle is used, however, it should be one with a positive lock rather than a quick-release mechanism. A positive lock is provided by a threaded or flanged pin (Figure 4-7). Before making fast the halyard, sight up along it to make sure that it isn't twisted or snagged.

**Figure 4-4.** **Bending on a mainsail:** Attaching the foot of the sail to the boom. **Left:** The bolt rope along the foot of the mainsail is fed into the groove in the boom, starting with the clew. Some boats have slugs instead of a bolt rope sewn into the foot of the sail, and in other cases the main boom has an external track instead of an internal groove, but the operation is always more or less the same. **Right:** The tack of the mainsail has been secured and the crew is stretching the clew taut. To see how the clew outhaul is rigged on this boat, see the photo in Figure 4-3. The sails would not be raised prior to launching the boat, nor would the jib be raised prior to the mainsail, if the wind were blowing. (PHOTOS BY BOB DENNIS)

**Figure 4-5.** **Bending on a mainsail:** Inserting the battens.
(PHOTO BY DON LINDBERG)

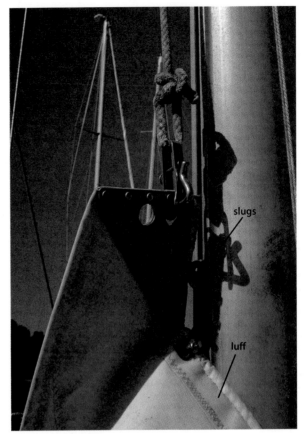

**Figure 4-6.** **Bending on a mainsail:** Attaching the luff of the sail to the mast. This cruising sailboat's mainsail has slugs attached to its luff, and these are fed into the mast groove as the sail is raised. The mast-groove opening will then be sealed with a gate or setscrew so that when the sail is lowered again, the luff will remain attached to the mast while the sail is stowed on the boom. On small boats, however, the mainsail is removed from the mast and boom after each use. (PHOTO BY DON LINDBERG)

If your boat only has a mainsail, you're now ready to hoist it and go. But we're assuming that your boat has a sloop rig and that you have yet to deal with the jib. (In practice, one crewmember may attach the main while the other handles the jib.) Bundle the mainsail loosely atop the boom (see Figure 14-7) and wrap it in place with a couple of **sail stops**—lengths of sail fabric or rubberized shock cord (the latter is recommended) that are carried for just this purpose.

Generally speaking, you can attach the jib to the forestay right from the sailbag provided you were careful to fold and bag the sail so that its tack cringle is right on top. Shackle or snap the tack in place (Figure 4-8), then work up the luff of the jib

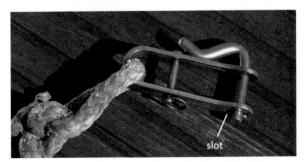

**Figure 4-7.** A main halyard shackle needs a positive lock. The two types in common use are a threaded-pin shackle and a shackle with a flanged pin like the one shown here. The flange is lined up with the corresponding slot when closing the shackle, then rotated away from the slot to hold the shackle closed. (PHOTOS BY DON LINDBERG)

**Figure 4-8. Bending on a jib:** Sea Scout Mariner Shaun Poestridge shackles the tack of the jib to his 420's stemhead fitting. He has shackled the jib halyard temporarily to the stemhead so it will be right at hand when he's ready for it. (PHOTO BY BOB DENNIS)

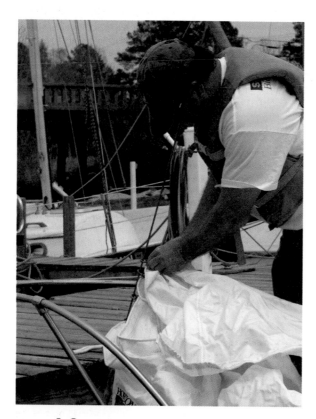

**Figure 4-9. Bending on a jib:** Attaching the hanks to the forestay. (PHOTO BY DON LINDBERG)

snap by snap to the head (Figure 4-9; see also Figure 1-20). As you do so, it may help to run the luff through your hands to keep the edge from being twisted in the process of attachment. When you're done, check that all the jib snap jaws are facing the same way. Virtually all American sailmakers sew on jib snaps (also called hanks) so their openings face to port. Some hanks have spring-loaded gates that you fold inward to open, but the most common type has a spring-loaded piston that you retract to open.

When you get all the hanks in place up to the sail's head, make fast the jib halyard with a bowline or shackle. Unlike a mainsail halyard shackle, a jib halyard shackle is customarily of the quick-release snap-shackle type (Figure 4-10). These won't open accidentally as long as the halyard is under steady tension.

The jibsheets are another story. Remember that they're nearly always doubled, with one sheet running to one side of the mast and cockpit and the other to the other side. There are several ways to attach the sheets to the clew of the jib:

## Splices

A *splice* is a permanent way of making an eye at the end of a line or attaching two lines together. It will never work free when properly done, no matter how briskly the sail luffs or flutters. A good eye splice is not heavy, so two of them (one for each sheet) won't weigh down the clew of the jib, nor will they hurt as much as snap shackles if you are walloped by a flogging jib while trying to gather it in and lower it

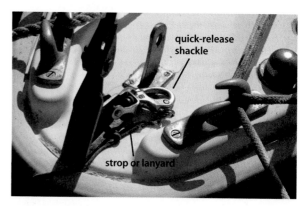

**Figure 4-10.** A quick-release shackle. Yanking on the strop or lanyard will open the shackle. This one is used to secure the tack of the jib, but they are often used on jib halyards as well. (PHOTO BY BOB DENNIS)

on a windy day. On the other hand, a splice can't be undone, so if you have more than one jib, you'll need more than one set of jibsheets, which is a nuisance as well as being expensive. Splicing also takes a little time, especially when you're splicing the double-braid line that is often used for sheets. For splicing three-strand line, see Figure 14-34; for splicing double-braid line, see Figure 14-36.

## Knots

There's no reason you can't tie each part of the jibsheet to the jib clew cringle using a **bowline** (see Figures 14-31 and 14-32). This good knot is easy to tie, once you get the hang of it, and is also easy to untie. Normally, it will not shake itself loose except if badly tied and repeatedly shaken. Two bowlines, however, will weigh down the jib clew in light breezes and will also offer potential snags when tacking. Still, all in all, bowlines are probably the best way to attach jibsheets.

## Snap Shackles

For those who prefer or require a quick release, a snap shackle into whose ring both jibsheets are spliced is often the answer (see Figure 4-10). Stainless steel or bronze snap shackles are relatively light and streamlined, but they are also expensive. Although they have been carefully engineered so as not to pop open unbidden, they nevertheless do so from time to time, and it can be very difficult to capture the wildly flapping clew of a big jib on a windy day. In addition, the hardware can be dangerous or damaging even if it doesn't snap open. More than a few sailors have received bloody noses from being whacked across the face by an untamed shackle.

## HOISTING SAIL

When hoisting sail, you should double-check three things. First, be sure the boat is facing as nearly into the wind as possible. Second, check again before putting tension on a halyard to see that it's free and untangled aloft. And third, be sure that the mainsheet and jibsheet are ready to run free, so that neither sail will fill with wind and start your boat sailing before you're ready. When you're underway you want your sails drawing smartly and powerfully, but until then you want them luffing!

Raise the mainsail first, hoisting it quickly and smoothly. Once the mainsail is raised, your boat will act like a weather vane if it is on a mooring and the main happens to catch any wind. If your boat has a sliding gooseneck, release the downhaul line, allowing the boom to rise so that the sail can be raised without resistance all the way to the masthead. (On many boats there is a band of dark paint or tape near the masthead; when the head of the sail reaches the band, the sail is at full hoist.) On some smaller boats, a halyard lock engages to hold the sail fully raised, but on most boats you'll have to secure the halyard by fastening it on a **horn cleat** (see Figure 14-38) or capturing it in a **cam cleat** (see Figure 14-41) or **clutch stopper** (Figure 4-11). Put tension on the downhaul until the sail's luff is approximately as taut as the foot, then secure the downhaul line.

For rigs without a downhaul, you will have to raise the sail **and** tension the luff with the halyard. If this is the case, you will probably find a mainsail halyard winch to help you get the halyard tension you need. Traditionally this winch is fitted to the

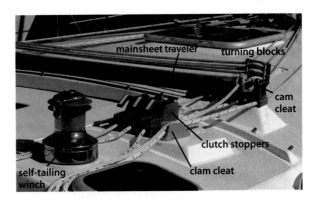

**Figure 4-11.** On contemporary keelboats, it is common to see halyards, reefing lines, the mainsheet, and the mainsheet traveler adjusting lines leading aft along the cabin top so that crew can make adjustments from the safety of the cockpit. This bank of three clutch stoppers to starboard of a cruising boat's companionway probably includes one for the main halyard, which runs aft from a turning block at the base of the mast (just visible at top right) and through another turning block under the mainsheet traveler. The self-tailing winch can be used with any of the three clutch stoppers or with the line secured in the clam cleat, which might be a spinnaker pole topping lift. Closing the lever on top of a clutch stopper "clutches" a line; raising the lever releases it. Whenever a line is under tension, you should take up the tension on the winch before you trip the stopper. Often the clutch stoppers are labeled to help the crew keep track of which line does what. (PHOTO BY DON LINDBERG)

starboard side of the mast, but increasingly on modern keelboats it is mounted on the cabin top, just forward of the cockpit, and the halyard leads through a turning block at the mast partner and then aft over the cabin top to the winch. This configuration allows the sail to be raised and lowered from the cockpit. By taking four or five turns of the halyard wire around the winch drum, then turning the winch, you can increase tension on the main-

sail luff. When the sail shows vertical creases along the luff, it's properly taut; if the creases do not disappear when the sail is full and drawing, the halyard may be overly taut.

The *tail* of the halyard—a length of line about equal to the height of the mast—must now be coiled and stowed where it cannot get free, but where it can be freed and released on a moment's notice (see Figure 14-13).

# Roller-Furling Headsails

Once considered a novelty, roller-furling headsails have become the norm on cruising sailboats due to their enormous convenience. A roller-furling headsail is attached to a luff foil (usually an aluminum extrusion), which in turn slips over the headstay. At the top and bottom of the stay are bearings that allow the luff foil to rotate, and as it does so the sail either rolls up or unrolls around the foil. A control line (also called a furling line) leads aft to the cockpit from a furling drum beneath the bottom bearing, and when the crew wants to roll up the sail they ease off the sheet tension while pulling on the furling line (Figure 4-12). When the sail is all rolled up around the headstay, they simply cleat the furling line. When they want to set the headsail, they have only to uncleat the furling line and let it run free while pulling in the port or starboard headsail sheet—it's as easy as that.

What makes a roller-furling headsail even more attractive is that you can roll it partway up to reduce the size of the sail when the wind gets stronger. This is the equivalent of replacing a big jib with a smaller one, but it's a lot less work and does not require leaving the cockpit.

Roller-furling headsails are not as aerodynamically efficient as hanked-on headsails—especially when partially furled—and thus are rarely found on racing sailboats, which have plenty of crew and which value speed above convenience. But roller furlers are a great convenience on shorthanded cruising sailboats (Figure 4-13).

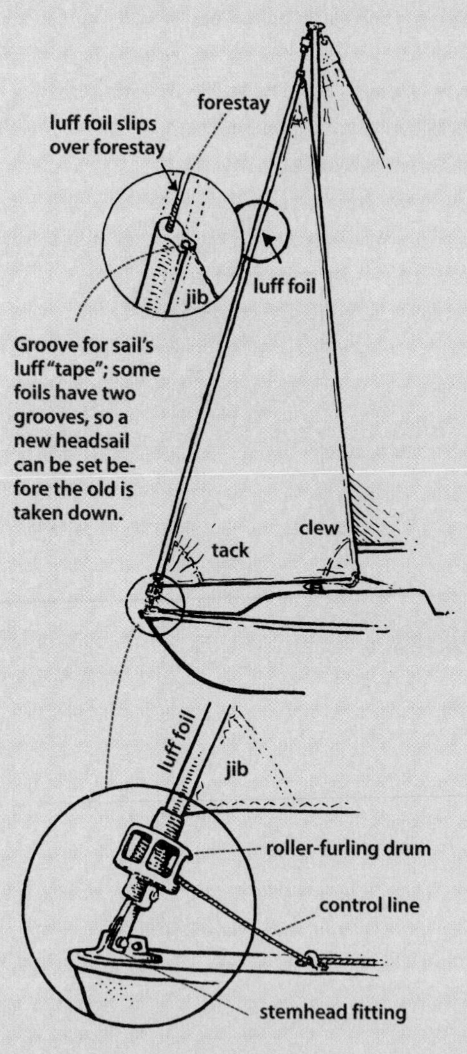

luff foil slips over forestay

forestay

Groove for sail's luff "tape"; some foils have two grooves, so a new headsail can be set before the old is taken down.

jib

luff foil

tack

clew

luff foil

jib

roller-furling drum

control line

stemhead fitting

**Figure 4-12.** A roller-furling headsail. (ILLUSTRATION BY CHRISTOPHER HOYT, REPRINTED WITH PERMISSION FROM *YOUR FIRST SAILBOAT* BY DANIEL SPURR)

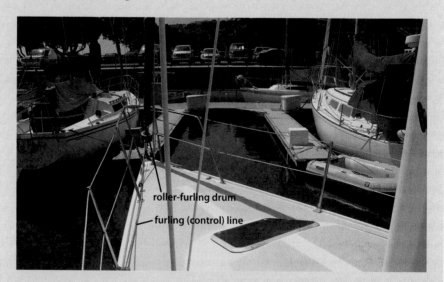

roller-furling drum

furling (control) line

**Figure 4-13.** As this boat returns to its slip, its roller-furled headsail is clearly visible forward. Note that the leech of this headsail is covered with a dark, UV-resistant fabric to keep the sun from degrading it while it's furled. Note too that the boats to port and starboard likewise have roller-furled headsails. (PHOTO BY BOB DENNIS)

With the mainsail raised, it's time to raise the jib—or is it? On some boats and in some circumstances, it may be preferable to clear the dock or mooring or even the anchorage before you raise the jib. How windy is it? How big is your jib, and how much does it impede your view ahead when raised? How well does your boat sail under mainsail alone? How uncluttered and uncomplicated is your departure lane from the dock or mooring? Indeed, skippers of keelboats with auxiliary engines frequently prefer to leave the dock or mooring under engine power—with neither sail hoisted—raising their sails only upon reaching more open water. But these judgments will come naturally to you with just a little experience.

For now, let's assume that you're sailing a small boat with a small jib that adds maneuverability without detracting much from your view ahead. The wind is light to moderate, and it makes sense to hoist the jib before leaving the mooring or dock. Once again, check that the boat is more or less head to wind, the halyard is free of wraps or snags aloft, and the sheets are free to run. On nearly all boats, the jib luff should be as taut as you can get it, but no tauter than the forestay itself. Boats over about 16 or 17 feet usually have a jib halyard winch mounted on the port side of the mast or cabin top, but few craft have jib tack downhauls because of the difficulty of fitting such a piece of gear so close to the deck. Remember which side of the mast each halyard runs down—starboard for the main and port for the jib. This is a near-universal tradition; when you go aboard an unfamiliar boat, you can assume with some confidence that the halyard on the port side of the mainmast raises the jib, and vice versa.

If a boat flies more than one jib at a time, both headsail halyards lead down to port, and if she is gaff-rigged, the two mainsail halyards—**peak** and **throat**—both lead to starboard.

With the jib fully raised, you are ready to go sailing. Now the fun begins!

# Sailing Away

The most important part of getting a sailboat underway is planning ahead, and conversely, the easiest way to get into trouble is to get underway before you look around. You might be leaving from a mooring, a dock, or the beach, so we'll look at all three separately.

## LEAVING A MOORING

A *permanent mooring* is a **ground tackle system** (see below) designed to remain in place for whole seasons at a time (Figure 4-14). Mooring anchors are generally **cast-iron mushroom anchors**, so named because of their appearance. Mushrooms are too heavy and do not dig in fast enough to be used for temporary anchoring, but they excel as long-term moorings on soft bottoms. The longer a mushroom sits on a mud or soft silt, clay, or sand bottom, the deeper it sinks and the more steadfastly it holds. A well-dug-in mushroom will resist pulls from any side.

A variety of other anchors are used for permanent moorings, including drums filled with concrete, scrap engine blocks, and what have you. Some of these provide unreliable holding. Check carefully before you entrust your boat to a questionable mooring. Normal mooring rigs today employ a heavy mushroom (see Table 4-1) shackled to a length of chain approximately equal in length to three times the high-water depth in the anchorage. At the water surface is a buoy, to which is attached the *mooring pendant* (usually pronounced and sometimes spelled "pennant"), a heavy nylon rope with a large eye spliced in its foredeck end. You'll want a sturdy, reinforced mooring buoy capable of taking the strain of the boat from above and the weight of the chain below. Sometimes a small pickup buoy is lashed to the eye splice in the pendant so that the crewmember on the bow can see and grab the pendant more easily.

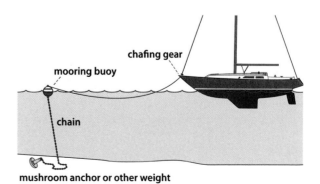

**Figure 4-14.** A typical mooring rig.

### TABLE 4-1 Mooring Rig Sizes

| Boat Length (ft.) | Anchor Weight (lbs.) | Chain Diameter (in.) | Shackle Size (in.) | Pendant Diameter (in.) |
|---|---|---|---|---|
| < 16 | 75 | 3/16 | 1/4 | 3/8 |
| 17–20 | 100 | 1/4 | 5/16 | 7/16 |
| 21–25 | 150 | 5/16 | 3/8 | 1/2 |
| 26–30 | 200 | 3/8 | 1/2 | 5/8 |
| 30–40 | 250–300 | 7/16 | 1/2 | 3/4 |

# Before You Go

## Check Major Systems

A "pre-underway" checklist will ensure that your boat's systems are running smoothly before you go. Don't leave the dock only to discover that your steering doesn't work. If you're leaving the dock under power, take the time to start the engine and check the steering and gears, cooling water flow, oil, and electrical systems. Also check all through-hull fittings. Like a pilot making preflight checks, you should inspect your boat and its systems before every trip.

## Check the Weather

Before you cast off, get an up-to-date marine weather forecast and be guided by it. When stormy weather or rough water is predicted, you may want to cancel your sail. Always load the boat according to the weather conditions you expect to meet.

The most readily accessible and accurate forecasts are those given by the National Weather Service (NWS), a division of the National Oceanic and Atmospheric Administration (NOAA). You can get these on your VHF-FM radio (see Chapter 16), where they are broadcast on a continuous basis and updated as new information is received. Listen to them from time to time as you sail to see if there have been adverse developments. These predictions are also available online at www.nws.noaa.gov, and local newspapers and radio and television broadcasters develop their own local forecasts from NOAA data.

## Required Equipment

Have you brought all the equipment on board that the Coast Guard requires, and any additional equipment you need (see Chapter 5)? This may include electronic equipment such as a global positioning system (GPS) receiver and a VHF-FM radio. Do you have your anchor and enough line? In an emergency you may have to anchor in deeper water than you anticipated. Do you have a whistle or horn aboard?

## Brief Your Crew and Guests

Your passengers and crew should be familiar with your boat and its safety equipment. Show them how to start and stop the engine (if your boat has one) and how to operate the radio. Everyone on board should be wearing a PFD, as described in Chapter 5. Passengers should also be informed of the location of flares and first-aid kits, anchoring procedures (as discussed later in this chapter), rough-weather procedures (Chapter 11), line handling (Chapter 14), and emergency boat operations. Show them where the fire extinguishers are kept and how to operate them. Also let them know that no trash is to be thrown overboard.

## Routine Maintenance

Routine maintenance of your boat and systems will save time and money on repairs later. See Appendix I for a sample preventive maintenance checklist you can modify for your boat.

A mooring is typically easier to leave than a dock or beach, since the boat can (at least in theory) sail off on any heading permitted by the wind direction. In practice, of course, this is seldom true. You must take into account other boats, both anchored and moving, structures such as piers and aids to navigation, and nearby water depths and shorelines.

The wise skipper will also consider that things may not proceed according to plan. If you're counting on leaving a mooring or dock on port tack and then tacking quickly to starboard, bear in mind that your boat may get into irons if you haven't gathered sufficient speed before attempting to tack. Or an unseen boat or swimmer may suddenly appear from behind another vessel, throwing off your calculations. Here are some important things to remember when getting underway:

1. A sailboat cannot be steered until the sails are drawing and the boat is moving; therefore, only the lightest craft will be able to maneuver as soon as they cast off, or when the line holding them to the mooring buoy or pier is released.

2. When casting off from a buoy, your boat will be effectively in irons—headed into the wind with its sails luffing. So your first tactics will be the same as those noted in Chapter 3 for getting out of irons.

3. Remember to allow the boat to fall back from its mooring buoy a few feet before backing the jib, especially in a quick, lightweight boat (Figure 4-15). Otherwise you run the risk of taking off and overrunning the buoy or snagging the mooring line (which is usually permanently attached to the buoy).

4. Alternatively, if your boat is light (less than, say, 25 feet long or 4,000 pounds of displacement) and the breeze is light to moderate, you can generate enough forward motion for steerageway by having a crewmember walk the mooring pendant from bow to stern after untying it from the bow cleat. If you want to leave on starboard tack, have the mooring line walked aft on the starboard side while you turn the rudder to port. Doing so will start the boat moving forward and turning in the desired direction.

5. Plan on sailing off on a beam or close reach if possible, as you'll then have the greatest maneuverability. If the harbor is crowded, however, don't be ashamed to paddle or motor to open water before making sail. Every small sailboat should have a pair of paddles, and boats too large to be moved efficiently with paddles or oars should have an outboard or inboard engine.

A boat on a mooring will point into the wind unless swung in another direction by a current. This is unlikely unless the wind is light, the current is strong, and the boat is a keelboat with a substantial underwater profile, but in extreme cases the boat might even be forced to ride stern-to the breeze. In this case, you can lead the mooring line around to the stern, allowing the boat to swing end for end so her bow is into the wind, or (in a light

**Figure 4-15.** Sailing away from a mooring. **1.** The foredeck crew drops the pendant. **2.** The crew backs the jib *toward* the buoy to push the boat's bow *away* from the buoy. **3, 4.** As the mainsail fills and the boat gathers way, the crew releases the jib to leeward and prepares to trim it. (PHOTOS BY BOB DENNIS)

breeze) you can make sail and head off in the normal way, except that the wind will push you forward instead of backward after casting off. Alternatively, you can hoist only the jib and let it stream out over the bow. Cast off, sheet in the jib, and sail downwind until you are clear of the anchorage area. Then head up into the wind and raise the mainsail. Most boats will sail reasonably well under either the jib or the mainsail, and many skippers use only one sail when the wind is strong.

## LEAVING A DOCK

Sailing away from a pier or float should not be too difficult if you're able to orient your boat more or less head to wind. After hoisting one or both sails, release the bow line first, let the bow swing away, then cast off the stern line. (If necessary, have a crewmember on board push the bow away from the pier with a boathook.) Trim the sheets and sail off (Figure 4-16).

If no side of the pier offers you a more or less head-to-wind berth with clear water immediately to seaward, you'll just have to paddle or motor out to clear water before raising sail. It may be annoying, but it's a lot less embarrassing than being pinned helplessly against the float with your sails raised and no way to get off.

## LEAVING A BEACH

If you're sailing off a beach, one crewmember will usually have to stand about waist deep in the water holding the boat in place until all is ready for sailing (Figure 4-17). Unless your boat is extremely maneuverable, don't try to stay a bit drier by sailing out of shallow water with the centerboard or daggerboard raised. When setting out from a standstill, the board should be completely lowered.

# Under Sail

Once you're away from the mooring or pier, proceed on your chosen point of sailing as described in Chapter 3. In Chapter 2 we mentioned the effect on the shape of the jib produced by adjusting the jibsheet leads. In order for the jib to set optimally when filled with wind, the sheet leads should be properly adjusted for wind strength on any boat that permits such adjustment. If the boat you're sailing has track-mounted jibsheet lead blocks as in Figure 1-15, you can make this adjustment as described in Figure 2-20.

It is rarely necessary to adjust the shrouds and stays while sailing. On boats that remain in the water throughout the sailing season, this is usually done only once—at the beginning of the season. If you've just launched the boat and stepped the mast, however, you may want to be sure your boat's rig is properly tuned. A somewhat out-of-tune rig is not dangerous but does reduce a boat's performance. If you wish to check this, refer to Chapter 11 for guidelines.

**Figure 4-16.** Sailing away from a dock or pier. **1.** With the bow heading into the wind, the sails are set and luffing. The crew pushes the bow away from the dock. **2.** To help the bow fall off the wind, the crew keeps the jib sheeted temporarily to windward. Meanwhile the helmsman trims the mainsail in order to start sailing. **3.** With the turn completed, the crew trims the jib to leeward and the boat begins to gather way. (PHOTOS BY BOB DENNIS)

**Figure 4-17.** Sailing away from a beach is a lot easier when the wind is blowing off or along the beach, as in this sequence. **1.** With sails raised and the bow pointing toward deeper water, the helmsman (in this case, perhaps the crewmember wearing long pants rather than shorts!) climbs aboard first. The kick-up rudder of this 420 is raised, and so is the centerboard, so the boat floats in just a few inches of water. **2.** In slightly deeper water, with the rudder partially lowered, the crew steps on board. **3.** With sails full and the rudder lowered, the crew trims the jib and prepares to lower the centerboard. Both boys should sit or crouch to lower their center of gravity. Standing in a small boat is never advisable unless necessary for the maneuver at hand. (PHOTOS BY BOB DENNIS)

# Returning to Port

Heading back to a beach, pier, or mooring is really just the reverse of sailing away, with a few necessary exceptions. As always, the first item of importance is to plan your maneuvers in advance. The best tactics when returning to an anchorage call for retaining as much maneuverability as you can consistent with reduced speed in case something does go wrong.

The instructions that follow assume that you're returning under sail. Skippers of larger boats frequently lower their sails in clear water and return to port under power, which gives them greater control and greater flexibility of approach, simplifying matters. Should you choose to do this, we offer only one precaution: Keep your sails ready to hoist quickly until you're securely docked or moored. That way, if your engine should fail close to shore or other boats, your "backup power supply" will be only a minute or two away.

## RETURNING TO A MOORING

Until you are familiar with your anchorage, it may help to sail up to your buoy a few times from different directions without trying to pick it up. This will not only provide good information on the best paths among other moored or anchored boats, it will also help you plan what to do should you sail

## Running Aground

It has been said that there are two types of boaters: those who have run aground and those who haven't . . . yet. Running aground can pose a potentially serious threat to the integrity of your boat and to the health of you and your passengers. The best way to avoid running aground is to be familiar with your boating area, monitor the water depth, obey channel markers, and be aware of the changing tides. If you do run aground, make sure all passengers are wearing a PFD. There are several things you can do that may free your boat, but do so **ONLY** after checking for leaks and making sure you aren't taking on water:

- If your boat has a centerboard or daggerboard, try raising the board to reduce the boat's draft. If your boat has a keel, have your crew move to the bow of the boat. This may reduce your boat's draft enough to free you. If there is shallower water to leeward, however, you will want to drop the sails and get an anchor out to windward before attempting this, since otherwise you will simply be blown into shallower water.
- Try rocking the boat back and forth.
- If the water is shallow, wade out to deeper water with an anchor and rode. Once you've set the anchor and are back aboard the boat, pull on the anchor rode to free yourself. If you're towing a dinghy when you run aground, you can row the anchor out to deeper water.
- Hail for assistance on your VHF radio.

up to the mooring and miss picking it up—something that happens to all sailors sooner or later.

If the spacing of other boats allows, try to approach the mooring buoy on a close reach, which will give you good speed with good maneuverability and control. Make your approach—other conditions permitting—on whichever tack will allow you to fall away from the wind safely if you miss the buoy. You probably won't have enough momentum left to come about, but you should, by the time you know whether you'll make the buoy or not, have speed enough to head the bow away from the wind and sail away to make another approach.

If your boat handles reasonably well under mainsail alone, it's often a good idea to lower, remove, and bag the jib before making your final approach to the buoy. This procedure will give you a far better view ahead in a crowded anchorage, and it will also provide an unobstructed foredeck for the crewmember who must grab the mooring line or buoy. If your boat has a centerboard or daggerboard, it should be fully lowered for maximum maneuverability when making the final approach. At some point between one and three boat lengths from the mooring, head right into the wind and coast up to the buoy with the sail luffing and the sheet (or sheets) uncleated. Ideally, the boat should stop dead in the water with the mooring buoy in easy reach (Figure 4-18).

It sounds hard, but you may be surprised how easy it becomes once you're used to your boat and familiar with her *carry*—the amount of distance she requires to lose momentum when headed into the

wind from a close-hauled course. In addition, you can fudge a little just before the final approach by slacking the sheets and letting the sail luff if you're moving too fast, or heading off to gain a little speed.

What is tricky, however, is getting the mooring line aboard and made fast before the boat begins to move off in a new direction. Unlike an automobile, a boat won't stand still while you figure out a new approach to that parking spot. If you miss the mooring, you've got to be ready to do something else right away. Usually the safest tactic is simply to sail clear, get your crew and gear sorted out, and start over from scratch. Trying to make a missed approach into a good one almost never works, and you're far better off to sail clear while you have the momentum and the room, then try again. Sailing, unlike golf, places no limits on the permissible number of "mulligans."

The above remarks are predicated on usual mooring conditions, in which the wind is the dominant factor. As in leaving a mooring, you may sometimes find that a tidal or river current is the dominant influence and runs contrary to the wind. When this happens, you may have to sail downwind to the mooring, in which case it may be easier to do so under jib alone, especially if that sail is smaller than the main.

## RETURNING TO A PIER

Landing on a pier involves much the same considerations as rounding up to a mooring, with the drawbacks being that only three sides of the pier, at

**Figure 4-18.** Picking up a mooring. **1.** The approach is made under mainsail alone. Ideally both crew should be sitting, kneeling, or crouching to keep their weight low, and if the wind were any stronger they undoubtedly would be. **2.** The final approach is made with the boat's bow into the wind and the mainsail luffing. This mooring has no pendant, so the crew must provide one. The crew will make the boat fast to the mooring while the helmsman lowers the mainsail. (PHOTOS BY BOB DENNIS)

most, will be accessible (Figure 4-19). Also, a pier or even a float is much more likely to damage a boat in case of collision than a buoy is. If you're new to sailing, it's probably not a good idea to sail into a slip or up to a pier unless the final approach can be made almost directly into the wind. When the pier is downwind, it's far safer to lower the sails offshore and paddle or motor in (Figure 4-20).

When you're landing on a pier, have your docking lines—or at least your bow and stern lines—ready in advance. Brief your crew on their tasks, and have someone aboard the boat ready to fend off. In small boats up to 16 feet or so, it's practical to sit on deck and fend off with your feet—which should be protected with boat shoes. Fending off this way in large boats can be dangerous, however. Instead, deploy fenders along the side of the boat toward the dock and let these do the fending off—they will absorb much more shock than a crewmember can, and do it better (Figure 4-21). In any case, it's much more seamanlike to sacrifice a piece of gear than to risk injuring a crewmember. The anxious crew stationed at the bow may want to jump off the boat and onto the dock, bow line in hand, even before the boat is alongside, but this too is dangerous and should be discouraged. No one should leave the boat until they can step comfortably onto the dock. Likewise, no one should try to stop any boat's momentum with an arm or a leg while standing up.

**Figure 4-20.** Approaching a slip like this downwind under sail would be asking for trouble! (PHOTO BY BOB DENNIS)

When sailing in a crowded harbor, be ready for sudden wind shifts that may be caused by large buildings ashore, high piers, or even anchored boats. It often pays to sail close by your intended pier without committing yourself to the final approach, then return (if all is well) for the actual maneuver.

## RETURNING TO A BEACH

Many small boats are advertised as being capable of sailing "right up on the beach." With some (a Hobie cat, for example) this may be true, but for most, a beaching at speed is an invitation to a wrenched rudder, a broken daggerboard or centerboard, or perhaps a personal injury. If surf conditions allow, it

**Figure 4-19.** Landing on a dock or pier. **1.** The jib is lowered and the boat approaches the dock under mainsail alone. **2.** Nearing the dock, the skipper lets the mainsail luff and starts rounding into the wind while the crew prepares to fend off. (If this were a larger cruising sailboat the crew would hang fenders over the side of the boat toward the dock.) (PHOTOS BY BOB DENNIS)

**Figure 4-21.** In calm conditions, this cruising sailboat is approaching a dock under sail rather than power. This boat handles well under jib alone, and the roller-furling jib can be rolled up in just a few seconds once the docklines are ashore. Fenders are deployed amidships, and more will be added forward and aft of amidships once the boat is docked. (PHOTO BY BOB DENNIS)

is far better to sail in close to the beach until the water is about waist deep, then round up into the wind while one crewmember goes overboard to hold a bow line. The person going over the side should be wearing a PFD and sneakers, and should know how to swim in case the water is more than waist deep.

If you must sail onto a beach, do so only when you have an accurate idea of how steeply the shore shelves. Pull the centerboard or daggerboard all the way up (don't expect it to pop up by itself), and be prepared to flip up the rudder the instant before the boat touches shore or the second you feel the rudder blade touch bottom, whichever happens first. A kick-up rudder is a great advantage when sailing onto a beach.

## PUTTING THE BOAT TO BED

When returning from a sail, head into the wind before dropping your sails, and lower the jib first (unless you choose to approach a mooring or dock under jib alone), then the main. To drop a sail, first *capsize* the halyard coil on deck—i.e., turn it upside down so it's free to run when uncleated. One crewmember should tend the halyard to prevent snags and to make sure the end doesn't snake up the mast out of reach.

If you're in a hurry, you can simply stuff the jib into its bag with the tack fitting accessible at the top. This will do little harm to the sail. It's better practice, however, to take the sail ashore and lay it out flat, then **flake** it from foot to head and loosely roll the flaked sail before bagging it (Figure 4-22). This will prevent wrinkles in the sail fabric and, more important, will keep the artificial fibers from cracking, as they can if the sail is jammed forcibly into its bag.

On most small boats the mainsail, too, should be folded and bagged (after the battens are removed, of course) in the same manner as the jib. On many larger boats, however, the main is furled on the boom and left there. This is perfectly acceptable and should do the sail no harm provided that you slack off the outhaul, furl the sail properly, and protect it from the sun's ultraviolet rays with a sail cover.

Furling is easy enough to do. As the sail is lowered, try to drop it slightly to one side of the boom. After detaching and securing the halyard, pull a large flake of sail out from the foot to form a semi-bag, then flake out the rest of the main into the receptacle thus formed (Figure 4-23). The resulting bundle will be tighter and neater if you tug the leech of the sail aft every now and then while you work. Roll the bundle tightly on top of the boom in a smooth, sausage-shaped form and secure it in place with sail ties—three should be enough for the average sail, but it's always a good idea to have one extra.

## LAST THOUGHTS ON MOORING AND DOCKING MANEUVERS

All maneuvers with a sailboat require practice to perfect. A boat's behavior in a 5-knot breeze may differ markedly from its behavior when facing 10- or 15-knot winds. One of the best ways to practice your approaches to a mooring or pier in a range of conditions is to anchor an inflated air mattress or plastic detergent bottle in unobstructed water and practice making landings alongside from every possible sailing direction. With a full afternoon's experience in hand, you'll be far more confident, and rightly so. And don't forget to change places with your crew from time to time. Not only will you have a happier and more satisfied sailing companion if you share the tiller, but you'll also have a

**Figure 4-22.** Flaking a jib. **1.** The folding can be done on board, but it's easier when the sail can be laid out on a flat surface ashore. Here the crew begins by folding the tack toward the head so as to make a right triangle for subsequent flaking. **2.** A crewmember at the luff and one at the leech start flaking from foot to head. Each flake, or fold, is 20 to 30 inches wide or so, depending on the diameter of the sailbag in which the sail will be stowed. **3.** As the flaking continues, the head is pulled toward the work site. When the flaking is done, the crew at the leech will roll or fold the flaked "sausage" toward the crew at the luff. Then the sail will be ready to bag. (PHOTOS BY DON LINDBERG)

**Figure 4-23.** Furling a mainsail. One way to do this is to roll the belly, or bunt, of the sail into itself, pulling the leech aft from time to time to keep the gathered roll evenly distributed atop the boom. On this boat, however, the sail is flaked atop the boom much as the jib is flaked in Figure 4-22. **1.** Sea Scout Mariners Serena White and Cortland Brailsford finish flaking the mainsail. **2.** Sail ties, or gaskets (often made of webbing), hold the flaked sail in place. **3.** If the boat will be left for awhile, a sail cover will protect the mainsail from the sun's UV rays. (PHOTOS BY BOB DENNIS)

crewmember who knows much better what the skipper's problems are—just as you'll better appreciate what the crew can and cannot do.

# Anchoring

We've talked about leaving and returning to port— your launch site or your home dock or mooring—but what if you want to stop somewhere along your journey for an island picnic, an overnight stay in a distant anchorage, or some other reason? Or what if

the wind dies, your engine won't start, and the current is sweeping you toward shore? Situations like these often call for anchoring, an art that every skipper should master. You need this ability not just for protection, but also for the enjoyment of boating.

## EQUIPMENT

Anchoring equipment is called *ground tackle*—the same term that we applied to a permanent mooring earlier in this chapter. The kind of ground tackle a boat should carry depends on several factors, including the type, weight, and length of your vessel. Also important are the characteristics of the bottom sediment and the depth of the water in which you will anchor, as well as the strengths of the wind and current. To be adequate, your ground tackle must hold your boat securely under the most adverse conditions.

## Anchor Rode

The *rode* of an anchor is its line and chain. An effective combination consists of 12 to 20 feet or more of heavy chain, a shackle, a thimble, and a nylon line (Figure 4-24). The chain helps the rode lie flat on the bottom, thus enabling the anchor to dig in. It also protects the line against chafing on rocky bottoms.

The *shackle* is a U-shaped piece of hardware, commonly made of galvanized steel, with a pin or bolt across its open end. It connects the chain to the line. Secure the pin or bolt with a length of wire so it won't work loose, causing you to lose your anchor.

The *thimble* is a horse collar–shaped metal or plastic device that is inserted in the eye splice at the end of the anchor line. Its outer surface has a shallow, U-shaped cross section so that the eye splice will not slip off it. The thimble keeps the eye splice from chafing on the shackle.

Nylon makes an excellent anchor line because of its elasticity, which eases the shock of the boat's movements on the anchor. The anchor chain serves the same purpose. As your boat surges, the chain rises and falls, thus easing the strain on the anchor.

## Types of Anchors

There are several types of anchors, and the choice of one over another depends mainly on the type of bottom in which you will anchor (Figure 4-25). Some have greater holding power than others.

**DANFORTH.** By far the most popular anchor for small sailboats is the Danforth (Figure 4-26). This is a lightweight anchor with long, narrow, twin flukes that pivot about the stock and dig into the bottom when the anchor is pulled by the rode. It stows easily in an anchor locker, which is the biggest reason for its dominance in small boats. Once firmly set this anchor style has excellent holding power relative to its weight, but a Danforth anchor will often fail to set on a grassy bottom be-

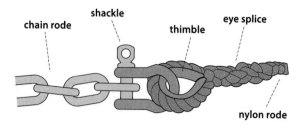

**Figure 4-24.** A combination of chain and nylon rode is a popular choice for anchor ground tackle. The chain at the anchor end of the rode resists chafe on the bottom and provides a more nearly horizontal lead from the anchor, enabling the anchor to dig into the bottom more firmly. The nylon rode acts as a shock absorber and is lighter and easier to handle than chain. The connection between the two is best made with a shackle through a thimbled eye splice in the nylon rode, with the thimble protecting the nylon from chafe.

cause the flukes slide across the grass rather than digging in. The anchor works well in mud and sand but may get hung up on a rocky bottom.

To attach a **trip line** to a Danforth, drill a hole in the crown, tie one end of the line there, and place a small buoy on the surface end of the line. If the flukes snag on a cable or rock, you can retrieve the anchor with this line.

Alternatively, you can shackle the anchor chain itself to a hole in the crown, then lash it to the anchor ring with a relatively weak line. If the anchor hangs up, tie off the anchor rode to a cleat or bitt and power ahead slowly, being careful not to foul the line in your prop. When you have gone far enough, the line fastening the anchor chain to the ring will break. Going farther forward will usually pull the anchor loose.

In one modified Danforth design, the anchor has a slotted shank containing a movable ring to

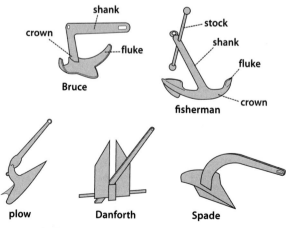

**Figure 4-25.** The most common anchor types.

which the anchor chain attaches. If the anchor hangs up, running back across it with a slack rode will usually pull the ring down to the crown, and a slight pull will then free it.

Anchoring with this modified Danforth requires some care. As you lower the anchor, keep the rode taut, and when the anchor hits bottom, back the boat down while keeping slight pressure on the rode until the anchor digs in. If you don't follow this procedure, the ring may slide to the crown and cause the anchor to skip across the bottom instead of digging in.

Other Danforth-style anchors include the ultra-lightweight Fortress (which can be disassembled for storage) and the West Marine Performance.

**PLOW.** The plow style of anchor takes its name from the shape of its fluke, which resembles a plow. The fluke digs in quickly and deeply in response to a pull on the anchor line. This is an efficient anchor but clumsy to handle and stow, and is used most often on large boats, where it stows outboard, on an anchor platform or bow roller.

One of the first plow anchors was the CQR, and it remains immensely popular on sailboats large enough to stow it on a bow roller. The CQR is distinguished by its hinged shank. The Delta anchor (Figure 4-27) is a fixed-shank version of the CQR and is also very popular, though it can be awkward to stow even on a bow roller. A new generation of plow anchors, now gaining increasing acceptance, features innovations such as ballasted tips and concave blades to permit more efficient setting and holding with lighter overall weight than their predecessors. These new models include the Spade, the Manson Supreme, and others.

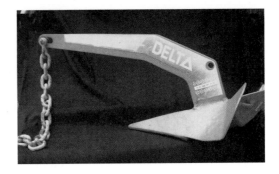

**Figure 4-27.** A Delta anchor

**CLAW.** Like the plow anchor, a claw anchor is a good all-around choice for a primary anchor on any boat big enough to stow it on a bow roller. Among claw anchors, the Bruce (see Figure 4-25) rivals the CQR as an all-time sailors' favorite.

**FISHERMAN.** This is the classic anchor depicted in nautical gifts and sailors' tattoos (see Figure 4-25). Its curved flukes will hold in rocks and thick weed as well as or perhaps better than any other style, but it's much less efficient in mud, sand, or silt than a plow, claw, or Danforth, and needs to be much heavier as a result. It is also awkward to handle and stow, and has fallen from favor as a result.

**MUSHROOM.** Mushroom anchors gradually dig deeply into a mud bottom, and when embedded, they have tremendous holding power, as noted earlier when we discussed permanent moorings. They do not, however, provide the instant holding power of other anchor types, and are therefore less appropriate for anchoring than for mooring. Small mushroom anchors like the one in Figure 4-28 are used

**Figure 4-28.** Small mushroom anchors like this one are sometimes used by anglers, but larger mushrooms are used mainly for permanent moorings, as they must sink into the sediment before they are effective.

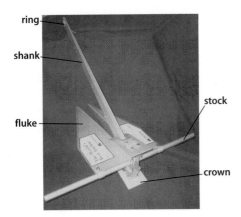

ring
shank
fluke
stock
crown

**Figure 4-26.** A Danforth anchor.

by recreational fishermen when angling, but should not be used to secure a boat left unattended. They do not work well in grassy and rocky bottoms.

***GRAPNEL.*** A grapnel anchor has a straight shank with four or five curved, claw-like arms and no stock (Figure 4-29). This anchor lacks the strength for regular use on a boat of any size, but on a small boat you can use it to anchor above rocks, the idea being to hook one or more of the arms under a rock. It's a good idea to tie a buoyed trip line to one of the arms at the crown, so that you can retrieve the anchor when (not if) it hangs up under a rock.

## YOUR BOAT'S ANCHORS

Your boat should carry at least two anchors. One anchor may be small and light for easy handling. Use this **lunch hook** in good weather, when anchoring in protected areas, or for short stops while fishing. The second anchor should be larger and heavier for overnight anchoring or for use when the smaller anchor might drag.

Cruisers should consider carrying a third anchor as well, for use in heavy weather. Use this

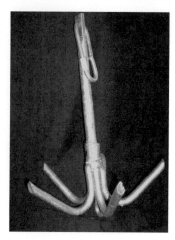

**Figure 4-29.** A grapnel anchor is of limited use for anchoring but is sometimes handy for recovering lost rope or chain from the sea bottom.

storm anchor in winds of 30 knots (34 miles per hour) or higher.

Tables 4-2 and 4-3 provide guidance for selecting your anchors and rodes. In addition, marine dealers and some marine catalogs provide tables and formulas to guide you in the selection of anchors, chain, and lines appropriate for the size of your vessel.

| TABLE 4-2 | Recommended Minimum Primary and Secondary Anchor Sizes for Sail or Power (pounds) | | | | | | |
|---|---|---|---|---|---|---|---|
| Boat Length (ft.) | Delta | CQR | Spade (steel/alum.) | West Marine Performance | Fortress (alum.) | Danforth Deepset | Bruce (claw) |
| 20–25 | 14 | 25 | 22/10 | 6 | 4 | 5 | 11 |
| 25–30 | 22 | 25 | 33/15 | 14 | 7 | 8.5 | 11 |
| 30–35 | 22 | 35 | 33/15 | 14 | 10 | 8.5 | 16 |
| 35–40 | 35 | 35 | 44/20 | 25 | 15 | 13 | 22 |
| 40–45 | 44 | 45 | 44/20 | 40 | 15 | 20 | 33 |

REPRINTED WITH PERMISSION FROM *ANCHORING: A CAPTAIN'S QUICK GUIDE* BY PETER NIELSEN

| TABLE 4-3 | Recommended Rode Sizes | | |
|---|---|---|---|
| Boat LOA (ft.) | Nylon Rode Diameter | Chain Diameter by Type | Weight (all-nylon/all-chain/all high-test chain) (lbs. per 100 ft.) |
| up to 25 | 3/8 in./9 mm | 3/16 in. proof coil | 3.5/50 |
| 27–31 | 7/16 in./11 mm | 1/4 in. proof coil/BBB | 5/76–81 |
| 32–36 | 1/2 in./12 mm | 5/16 in. proof coil/BBB, 1/4 in. high-test | 6.5/115–120/70 |
| 37–44 | 9/16 in./14 mm | 3/8 in. proof coil/BBB, 5/16 in. high-test | 8.2/166–173/106 |
| 45–50 | 5/8 in./16 mm | 3/8 in. proof coil/BBB/high-test | 10.5/166–173/154 |
| 51–62 | 3/4 in./18 mm | 3/8 in. proof coil/BBB/high-test | 14.5/166–173/154 |

REPRINTED WITH PERMISSION FROM *ANCHORING: A CAPTAIN'S QUICK GUIDE* BY PETER NIELSEN

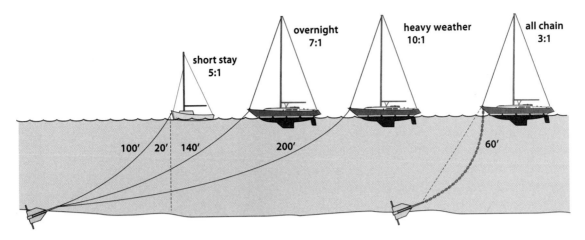

short stay
5:1

overnight
7:1

heavy weather
10:1

all chain
3:1

100' 20' 140'     200'     60'

**Figure 4-30.** Be sure to pay out sufficient scope on your anchor rode. Boats using an all-chain rode can pay out less scope, but all-chain rodes are usually too heavy for small boats to carry.

## ANCHOR RODE SCOPE

An anchor holds best when the pull of its rode is as nearly horizontal as possible. For this reason, holding power increases as you increase the length of the rode (Figure 4-30). The *scope* of an anchor rode is the ratio of its length to the vertical distance from your bow chock to the seabed (i.e., the depth of the water plus the distance from the water surface to the bow chock).

Normally, a scope of 7:1 is adequate for holding a boat. Thus, if the water is 10 feet deep and your bow chock is 4 feet above the water, you need an anchor rode of 98 feet. This means you need a lot of line even for a small boat in calm weather and seas. Remember, too, to account for tidal variations when determining how much scope you will need.

A scope of 5:1 is marginal, and a scope of 3:1 is poor unless the weather is excellent and the bottom is good for anchoring. A 3:1 scope may be enough if you have stopped to eat or to fish and you are not leaving the boat, but you should still watch your anchor at all times with this scope.

When anchoring in heavy weather, you should have a scope of at least 10:1, preferably with a good length of stout chain leading from the anchor. You also should maintain an anchor watch in stormy weather.

## ANCHORING TECHNIQUES

The first step in anchoring is to check the nature of the bottom and its depth. If you can't do this visu-

ally, look at the chart. It may note the bottom type—whether sand, rocks, clay, or mud. You can also tell the type of bottom and its depth by using a **lead** (pronounced "led") **line**, which is simply a light line with depth indicators (frequently bits of cloth sewn into the line at 6-foot, or 1-fathom, intervals) and a weight at its end. The end of the weight will usually be hollowed out, and if you place tallow, wax, chewing gum, or bedding compound in the hollow before **casting the lead**, you'll bring up a sample of the bottom when you retrieve it. Not many boats carry lead lines in this age of electronic depth sounders, but they remain highly useful tools, and they rarely break!

When anchoring, be certain that you have tied the end of the rode securely to the boat. In larger boats it is usually secured below the deck in the chain locker.

If the anchorage you select is pleasant and well protected—perhaps with convenient access to a town, restaurant, or other shoreside attractions—it also is likely to be popular and therefore crowded. If you arrive late in the day, a first glance may convince you that there is no room left to anchor, and you may be right. Don't be hasty, though. If your boat is small and floats in very little water, you may find a site close to shore that won't interfere with other boats.

Having chosen a site, note the position of nearby boats to determine where your boat will settle after it falls back on its anchor in response to wind and current. Make sure your anchor rode will not cross the rodes of other boats, and that you will not be within uncomfortable swinging distance of nearby boats. A boat at anchor will swing in accordance to the current, the wind, or both, and different kinds of boats will react differently to these forces. Deep-draft keelboats, with a great deal of underbody, will often swing according to the current, while shallow center-boarders will respond primarily to wind pressure. When wind and current are in different directions, this can cause problems for dissimilar boats anchored close together, as they may swing into each other.

If the bottom is satisfactory and the water is not too deep or shallow, head your boat into the wind or current, moving very slowly toward your chosen site. Go far enough beyond the site to allow for the anchor rode length, then stop your forward movement and have someone lower the anchor (he or she shouldn't drop or throw it), being careful not to stand on or get caught in the rode. If the boat does not drift astern of its own volition, gently reverse the engine (if you have one) to keep the boat on course. After about one-third of the planned scope is paid out, the line should be temporarily secured to determine whether the anchor is holding. Then the remainder of the rode should be paid out and secured.

An anchor rode should never be tied off to the side or only the stern of your boat. Side or stern anchoring may be convenient but is also dangerous. Large wakes or waves could swamp the boat when you are anchored from the side or stern rather than the bow, and in a current, the stern could be pushed under by the force of the moving water. A secondary anchor from the stern, on the other hand, is sometimes required in very crowded anchorages where there is no room for the boat to swing.

By keeping a hand on the line as it is paid out, you can tell if the anchor has dug in. When it vibrates, the anchor is sliding across the bottom. When it digs in and then skips, or when it just skips, pay out more rode until the anchor digs in firmly. You will feel a definite halt in the drift of the boat when it digs in. When there is a current or a breeze, you will see the bow turn into it. After you have a good bite on your anchor, turn off the engine.

When you have finished anchoring, take sights on two or three stationary objects onshore (Figure 4-31), lining them up with more distant objects be-

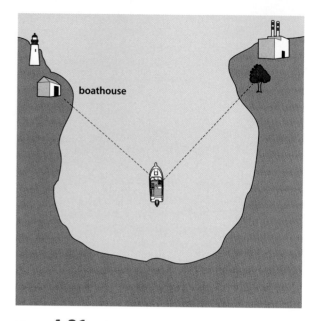

**Figure 4-31.** After anchoring, establish ranges onshore to keep track of your position. As long as the boathouse remains in front of the lighthouse on one shore, and the tree remains in front of the power plant on the other, this boat has not dragged its anchor.

hind them. A church steeple rising up behind a red barn, for example, makes a good sight. Should your anchor drag, you can tell by checking these *ranges*. Most GPS receivers also have an anchor alarm feature that notes your anchored position and sounds an alarm if you drift from this location.

Anchors hold best in mud, clay, or sandy mud. While hard sand is good with some anchors, soft, loose sand is poor, and in soft mud your anchor may not hold at all. Rocks can give good holding power but may hold your anchor permanently!

Avoid anchoring in grassy areas and coral reefs, both of which are habitats for immature marine life. If you anchor in seagrass, you uproot it, and obviously, you should not damage a coral reef.

Be careful how much line you pay out. If the wind or the tide changes, will you swing into another boat, a buoy, a wharf, or onto the shore? If wind or sea conditions deteriorate, check your position frequently to see that you are not dragging anchor. If you are, let out more line. When this is not practical, **weigh** (raise) anchor and set it again in a better location. Be mindful of the change in direction of a tidal current. When the current reverses, your anchor may become fouled in its own rode or may lose its hold on the bottom.

Should your boat lose power in shallow water or a narrow channel, lower your anchor immediately. It may keep you from going aground.

## WEIGHING ANCHOR

When ready to depart an anchorage, go through your departure checklist, then start the engine and make sure it is operating properly. If you're weighing anchor under power, power ahead slowly to a position directly above the anchor, taking up the rode as you proceed. (If you're leaving the anchorage under sail, you can accomplish the same thing by pulling in the anchor line scope hand over hand until you're directly over the anchor.) Usually, the anchor will break free of the bottom when you are over it. It can then be raised and stored.

If the anchor does not break free, it is probably fouled. Take in as much line as possible, and then make the rode fast to a bow bitt or bow cleat and power or sail your boat slowly in circles with the line taut, which will hopefully break out the anchor.

# Practice Questions

## IMPORTANT BOATING TERMS

In the following exercise, match the words in the column on the left with the definitions in the column on the right. In the blank space to the left of each term, write the letter of the item that best matches it. Do not use an item in the right-hand column more than once.

| THE ITEMS | | THE RESPONSES |
|---|---|---|
| 1. _____ pintles | a. | quick-release shackles that are often used on a jib halyard, but not a main halyard |
| 2. _____ rake | b. | the pins on the forward edge of a removable rudder |
| 3. _____ hanks | c. | an anchor with pivoting flukes |
| 4. _____ snap shackles | d. | fittings that connect many jibs to the headstay |
| 5. _____ mushroom anchor | e. | a common choice for use as a permanent mooring |
| 6. _____ Danforth | f. | the fore-and-aft tilt of a mast |
| 7. _____ rode | g. | usually the ideal orientation for leaving or making the final approach to a mooring or dock |
| 8. _____ head to wind | h. | the best point of sailing for maximum control, ideal for the initial approach to a mooring |
| 9. _____ scope | i. | the ratio of the length of deployed anchor rode to the vertical distance from foredeck to seabed |
| 10. _____ close hauled | j. | the chain, line, or combination of the two that connects an anchor to a boat |

# Multiple-Choice Items

In the following items, choose the best response:

4-1. Prior to stepping the mast you should

a. check for overhead power lines
b. make sure halyards are free
c. make sure the mast is oriented correctly
d. all of the above

4-2. Mast rake is

a. a side tilt
b. a forward/backward tilt
c. side bending
d. mast twisting

4-3. The topping lift

a. holds the mast down
b. secures the mast
c. holds up the aft end of the boom when the sail is down
d. prevents the boom from swinging

4-4. When hoisting sails, head the boat

a. with the wind
b. into the wind
c. with the wind over the side
d. away from the dock

4-5. To attach the mainsail to the boom, first find the sail's

a. clew
b. head
c. tack
d. leech

4-6. Battens in modern boats are secured with

a. clips
b. tie strings
c. cringles
d. a snug fit in their pockets

4-7. The order in raising sails is usually raising

a. them together
b. the jib first
c. the main first
d. the jib partially

4-8. The main halyard typically leads down the

a. port side of the mast
b. starboard side of the mast
c. front of the mast
d. aft side of the mast

4-9. The ideal point of sailing for lowering sails is

a. a reach
b. close hauled
c. a run
d. heading into the wind

4-10. The usual order in which sails are lowered on a sloop is

a. the reverse of the order in which they are raised
b. both sails are lowered together
c. mainsail first
d. none of the above

4-11. A mooring anchor is typically a

a. Danforth
b. fisherman
c. mushroom
d. plow

4-12. A mooring buoy is typically connected to its anchor with a

a. heavy shackle
b. nylon pendant
c. chain
d. polypropylene rope

4-13. The point of an anchor that digs into the seabed is called a

a. shank
b. stock
c. fluke
d. pin

4-14. Ground tackle is the

a. anchor and anchor rode
b. anchor chain, but not the nylon line
c. anchor and anchor chain, but not the nylon line
d. anchor line

4-15. The usual anchor rode scope for average conditions is

a. 4:1
b. 10:1
c. 7:1
d. 20:1

# Multiple-Choice Items (continued)

**4-16.** When preparing to anchor, in most cases you should head

    a. into the wind
    b. away from other boats
    c. across the wind
    d. toward the nearest shore

**4-17.** When anchoring on a rocky bottom, you might want to use

    a. an anchor dip hook
    b. a trip line
    c. an anchor remover
    d. an anchor retriever

**4-18.** When you approach a mooring too fast, the best response is to

    a. have your crew grab the mooring buoy and hold it at all costs
    b. back the jib
    c. start your engine and slam it into reverse
    d. resume sailing and circle around for another approach

**4-19.** When you leave a mooring or dock under sail, you should

    a. tack as soon as you are clear
    b. get onto a run as soon as possible
    c. have enough clear water ahead so you can gather speed and steerageway before having to tack or turn sharply
    d. keep the sails luffing

**4-20.** When sailing off a beach, you should

    a. get all crew on board and tell them to "ooch" in unison to slide the boat into the water
    b. have one or two crew in the water pushing the boat off the beach until you can get the daggerboard or centerboard at least partially down
    c. get a tow into deep water from a passing powerboat
    d. any of the above

**4-21.** What point of sailing is best for approaching a mooring?

    a. a close reach
    b. close hauled
    c. a run
    d. a broad reach

**4-22.** If you can feel the anchor line vibrating in your hand, it is probably

    a. dragging
    b. setting itself more firmly
    c. about to break
    d. none of the above

**4-23.** One way to free your boat after a grounding is to

    a. raise the centerboard
    b. move crew to the bow
    c. rock the boat
    d. all of the above

**4-24.** Taking two or three sights on objects ashore when you first anchor is a good way to

    a. familiarize yourself with an anchorage
    b. judge your speed
    c. tell if your anchor is dragging
    d. decide where to anchor

# Equipment for Your Boat

IN 1971 CONGRESS ordered the U.S. Coast Guard to improve recreational boating safety. In response, the Coast Guard drew up a set of regulations known as the Federal Boat Safety Act. This act governs boating safety regulations in the United States and its territories.

**The objectives of this chapter are to describe:**

● The safety equipment your boat must have.

● Additional recommended safety equipment to have on board.

Besides these federal regulations, there are state and local laws you must follow that sometimes exceed the Coast Guard requirements. This chapter discusses only the federal laws. If you're using this book in conjunction with a Coast Guard Auxiliary class, your instructors will cover state and local laws. As with other laws, "Ignorance of the boating laws is no excuse."

The rules fall into two categories: regulations for your boat, and regulations for equipment on your boat. Note that a personal watercraft (PWC) is a motor vessel governed by these laws and regulations, just like any other motor vessel.

# Requirements for Your Boat

Most powerboats and sailboats with auxiliary power must be registered in their state of principal use. Some states exempt documented boats (see below), and some exempt dinghies with small motors (less than 10 horsepower) when these are used solely for transportation to and from a larger registered boat. But with these two exceptions, you can be fairly certain that a boat with an outboard or inboard engine—whether kept on fresh or salt water—must be registered in the state where you use it most. In most states rowboats, canoes, and small sailboats without engines need not be registered.

## DOCUMENTING OF VESSELS

A recreational vessel of 5 or more net tons may be *documented* as a yacht with the U.S. Coast Guard. Assuming your boat is less than 79 feet long, you can calculate its possible eligibility for documentation by multiplying its length on deck by its maximum breadth and then by its depth of hull (from the deck amidships to the bottom of the hull, excluding the keel), with all measurements in feet. Divide that result by 100 and multiply it by 0.67 for a powerboat (or 0.5 for a sailboat) to get an estimate of your boat's gross tonnage, then multiply gross tonnage by 0.8 (or by 0.9 for a sailboat with an auxiliary engine) to get net tonnage. If the result is 5 or more net tons, your boat is probably eligible for documentation.

Documentation is a form of national registration, and as such is highly regulated. It is comparable to recording the sale of real estate property, and the record includes a history of all title transfers for the vessel and may include critical associated documentation. Documentation often permits preferential status for obtaining mortgages. The vessel owner must be a U.S. citizen, a partnership of U.S. citizens, or a corporation controlled by U.S. citizens. The captain and other officers must also be U.S. citizens, though the crew need not be. In foreign ports, the vessel is considered part of the United States. The original documentation papers must be carried aboard the vessel.

A documented boat need not display registration numbers, though most states will still require state registration.

## REGISTRATION OF BOATS

If your sailboat has outboard or inboard engine power and is not documented, it will need to be registered. (If it has no engine or is documented, check state regulations.) Registering a boat is comparable to registering a motor vehicle. A boat used in multiple states should be registered in the state of principal use. When you change from one state to another, you get a 60-day grace period before you must register in the new state, during which time the original registration document must remain with the boat.

## NUMBERING OF VESSELS

You will find a registration number on the registration certificate you receive from your town office or similar authorized registration site. The "number" is, in fact, a sequence of two letters, up to four numerals, and one or two more letters. The first two letters are the code for the state of registration. Unless your boat is documented, you must paint or permanently attach this number to both sides of the forward half of your boat, favoring the bow end. Do not display any other number there (Figure 5-1).

The registration number must be clearly visible. It must not be placed on the obscured underside of a flared bow—i.e., one that, when viewed from ahead, has a pronounced outward curve between the waterline and the deck. If the number

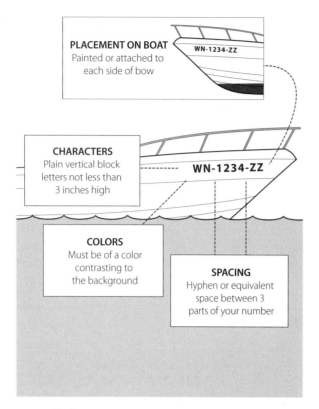

**Figure 5-1.** The proper display of a boat's registration number.

will not fit properly directly on the hull, affix it to a plate or to a forward portion of the superstructure (cabin).

The letters and numbers must be plain vertical block characters and must read from left to right. Use a space or a hyphen to separate the prefix and suffix letters from the numerals. The color of the characters must contrast with that of the background, and they must be at least 3 inches high.

In some states the registration is good for only 1 year, and in others, it is good for as long as 3 years. Renew your registration before it expires. At that time you will receive a new decal or decals, which should be placed within 6 inches of the registration number and as required by state law, after removing the old decals. Some states require that you show only the current decal or decals. If your vessel is moored, it must have a current decal even if it is not in use.

If your boat is lost, destroyed, abandoned, stolen, or transferred, you must inform the issuing authority. You should also notify the issuing authority as soon as possible if you lose your certificate of number or change your address.

## Sales and Transfers

Your registration number is not transferable to another boat. The number stays with the boat unless the boat is registered with another state.

## HULL IDENTIFICATION NUMBER

A *hull identification number* (HIN) is like the vehicle identification number (VIN) on your car. Boats built between November 1, 1972, and July 31, 1984, have HINs like those shown in Figure 5-2A. The letter M in Figure 5-2A means the optional method for showing the date of certification was used. The last four characters show the model year and month when construction started. In the illustration, the 73 means 1973. Model years began in August, which is an A; E stands for December.

Since August 1, 1984, a new format has been used (Figure 5-2B). The first three characters are the manufacturer's ID, and the next five characters are the hull serial number. The ninth character shows the month construction began. In this system, A stands for January. The tenth character is the last digit of the year of manufacture, and the last two characters are the model year.

Your boat's HIN must appear in two places. If the boat has a transom, the primary location is on its starboard side within 2 inches of its top. If it does not have a transom or if it is not practical to use the transom, the number is on the starboard side, within 1 foot of the stern and within 2 inches of the top of the hull side. On pontoon boats, it is on the aft crossbeam within 1 foot of the starboard hull attachment. The secondary location is in an unexposed location determined by the manufacturer. This will be somewhere in the boat's interior or under a fitting or item of hardware.

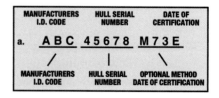

**Figure 5-2A.** Hull identification numbers on boats manufactured between November 1, 1972, and July 31, 1984, look like this.

**Figure 5-2B.** Hull identification numbers on boats manufactured since August 1984 have this format.

## LENGTH OF BOATS

For some purposes, boats are classed by length. Each class has its own requirement for safety equipment.

Manufacturers may measure a boat's length in several ways for marketing purposes. Officially, however, your boat is measured along a straight line from its bow to its stern, parallel to its keel (Figure 5-3), and the length does not include *bowsprits*, *boomkins*, or *pulpits*, rudders, brackets, outboard motors, outdrives, diving platforms, or other hull attachments.

Manufacturers must put *capacity plates* on most monohull recreational motorboats less than 20 feet long, but sailboats (even those with outboard engines), canoes, kayaks, and inflatable boats are exempt. Outboard motorboats must display the maximum permitted engine horsepower on their capacity plates (Figure 5-4), but inboards and stern drives need not (Figure 5-5). Plates must also show the allowable maximum combined weight of the people on board and the allowable maximum combined weight of people, motors, and gear.

The capacity plate must be placed where it is clearly visible to the operator when getting underway. This information serves to remind you of the capacity of your boat under normal circumstances. You should ask yourself, "Is my boat loaded above its recommended capacity?" and, "Is my boat overloaded for the present sea and wind conditions?" If you are stopped by a legal authority, you may be cited if you are overloaded.

There are also capacity limits on PWCs. Those limits should be obtained from the manufacturer if a capacity plate is not on the PWC.

Since your small sailboat need not carry a capacity plate, you will have to exercise good judgment so as not to overload. We return to this topic in Chapter 10.

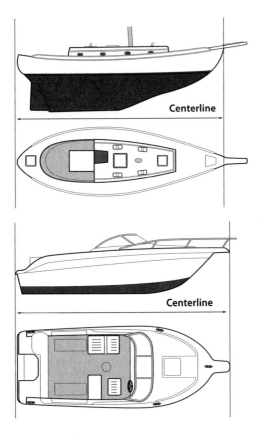

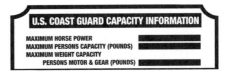

**Figure 5-4.** A capacity plate for an outboard-powered motorboat less than 20 feet long. (Outboard-powered sailboats less than 20 feet long are exempt from this requirement.)

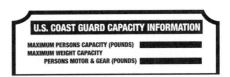

**Figure 5-3.** Length overall, also known as length on deck, includes a bow platform that is a molded part of the boat (bottom) but does not include a bowsprit (top) or a bow pulpit.

**Figure 5-5.** Capacity plate for an inboard or stern-drive boat less than 20 feet long.

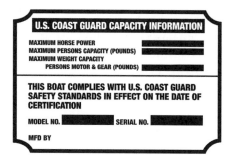

**Figure 5-6.** The manufacturer must also affix a compliance plate on any motorboat less than 20 feet long.

**Figure 5-7.** A combination capacity and compliance plate.

**Figure 5-8.** This boat was destroyed by an electrical fire that started near the batteries and battery charger. (REPRINTED WITH PERMISSION FROM *SEAWORTHY: ESSENTIAL LESSONS FROM BOATU.S.'S 20-YEAR CASE FILE OF THINGS GONE WRONG* BY ROBERT A. ADRIANCE)

## MANUFACTURER'S CERTIFICATE OF COMPLIANCE

Manufacturers are required to put a **compliance plate** on a motorboat less than 20 feet long (Figure 5-6) that says, "This boat [or equipment] complies with U.S. Coast Guard Safety Standards in effect on the date of certification." Letters and numbers can be no less than ⅛ inch high. The manufacturer may combine capacity and compliance plates as shown in Figure 5-7.

# Fire Prevention and Detection

### YOUR BOAT'S VENTILATION

"A cup of gasoline spilled in the bilge has the potential explosive power of 15 sticks of dynamite!" This statement, commonly repeated more than 20 years ago, may be an exaggeration, but it illustrates an important fact. Gasoline fumes in the bilge of a boat are highly explosive and a serious danger. They are heavier than air and will stay in the bilge until vented out.

Because of this danger, Coast Guard regulations require ventilation on many powerboats, on sailboats with gasoline-powered inboard auxiliary engines, and on all boats with permanently installed gasoline generators. There are several ways to supply fresh air to engine and gasoline tank compartments to remove dangerous vapors. Whatever the choice, it must meet Coast Guard standards.

The discussion below does not deal with all regulations, nor does it cover all recreational boats. It deals only with the following:

1. boats built after July 31, 1980
2. vessels made or used for noncommercial purposes
3. vessels leased, rented, or chartered for non-commercial use
4. boats carrying six or fewer passengers for hire

The regulations do not apply to diesel-powered boats, nor do they apply to outboard-powered sailboats without permanently installed fuel tanks. Nevertheless, if you carry a portable gas tank or propane stove fuel aboard your sailboat, you'd do well to observe these precautions.

### General Precautions

Ventilation systems will not remove raw gasoline leaking from tanks or fuel lines. If you smell gasoline fumes, you may need immediate repairs. The best device for sensing gasoline fumes is your nose. **Use it!** If you smell gasoline in an engine compartment or elsewhere, **don't start your engine**. The smaller the compartment, the less gasoline it takes to make an explosive mixture.

## VENTILATION SYSTEMS

A ventilation system is required in an enclosed compartment with a permanently installed gasoline engine that has a cranking motor (see Figures 5-9 and 5-12). A compartment is exempt if its engine is open to the atmosphere.

Table 5-1 on page 106 lists the ventilation requirements for a variety of boat configurations.

To be "open," a boat must meet certain conditions. Engine and fuel tank compartments and long, narrow compartments that join them are to be "open to the atmosphere," which means that at least 15 square inches of open area for each cubic foot of net compartment volume must be open to the atmosphere. Also, there should be no long unventilated spaces open to engine and fuel tank compartments into which flames could extend.

There are two types of ventilation systems. One is *natural ventilation*, in which air circulates through closed spaces due to the boat's motion. The other is *powered ventilation*, in which air is circulated by a motor-driven fan or fans.

## Natural Ventilation System Requirements

Natural ventilation is required for each enclosed compartment that includes one or more of the following (refer to Table 5-1):

- a permanently installed gasoline engine
- a sufficiently large opening between it and a compartment that requires ventilation
- a permanently installed fuel tank and an electrical part that is not ignition-protected against producing sparks
- a fuel tank that vents into it
- a nonmetallic fuel tank that exceeds technical requirements for permeability (some plastic tanks "bleed" excessively)

Gasoline tanks with a capacity of less than 7 gallons may be called **portable**. Tanks larger than 7 gallons may sometimes be called portable, but the Coast Guard considers them permanent and requires

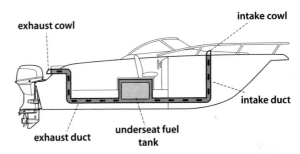

**Figure 5-10.** An example of natural ventilation through a fuel tank compartment.

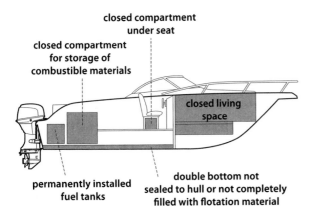

**Figure 5-9.** A boat with one or more enclosed spaces like these must carry at least one fire extinguisher (see page 107). In addition, this boat requires a ventilation system because of its permanent fuel tank in a closed compartment.

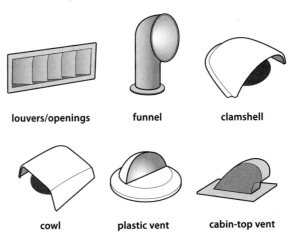

**Figure 5-11.** A natural ventilation system requires an air intake opening like one of these.

**WARNING** *Play it safe: Keep your boat free of explosive vapors. Always sniff the bilge to detect gasoline vapors. On a PWC, remove the seat to check for fuel leaks from the tank, fuel lines, and carburetor.*

**WARNING** *Inspect ducts frequently. Ducts can come loose and plastic ducts can break.*

that they be permanently secured before a boat can be awarded its safety decal.

A natural ventilation system has an air supply from outside the boat (Figure 5-10) or from a ventilated compartment or a compartment open to the atmosphere. Intake openings are required (Figure 5-11), and intake ducts may also be required to direct the air to appropriate compartments.

The system must have an exhaust duct that starts in the lower third of the compartment and opens into another ventilated compartment or into the atmosphere.

Each air supply opening, exhaust opening, and duct, where present, must be above the usual level of the bilge water. Openings should be at least 3 square inches in area or 2 inches in diameter and placed so that exhaust gases do not enter the fresh-air intake, any cabin, or other enclosed nonventilated space. The carbon monoxide gas in exhaust gases is deadly.

Intake and exhaust openings have to be covered by *cowls* or similar devices to keep out rainwater and water from breaking seas. Most

| TABLE 5-1 | **Ventilation for Powerboats** (Vessels built after July 31, 1980) | |
|---|---|---|
| **Type of Boat** | **Powered Ventilation** | **Natural Ventilation** |
| Open boat | No | No |
| Open boat with portable tank | No | No |
| Portable tank in enclosed compartment | No | Yes* |
| Permanent tank vented to outside | No | No |
| Permanent tank and engine compartment | Yes | Yes |
| Permanent tank and engine compartments** | | |
| Tank compartment | No | No*** |
| Engine compartment | Yes | Yes |

   * Assumes that portable tanks are not vented to the outside.
  ** Assumes that permanently installed tanks are vented to the outside.
 *** If electrical components are present, they must be ignition-protected.

often, intake cowls face forward and exhaust openings face aft, but on boats built after March 1987, intake cowls may face in any direction. Forward-facing intake cowls capture the flow of air when the boat is moving or at anchor, since most boats face into the wind when anchored.

## *Powered Ventilation System Requirements*

Powered ventilation systems must meet the standards of a natural system, but also have one or more exhaust blowers (Figure 5-12). The blower duct can serve as the exhaust duct for natural ventilation if fan blades do not obstruct the airflow when not powered.

Openings in engine compartments for carburetion do not count toward satisfying ventilation system requirements.

**WARNING LABEL.** On boats with powered ventilation, a warning label must be mounted near each ignition switch, in plain view of the operator. It should include at least the information in the warning opposite.

## BACKFIRE FLAME ARRESTERS

Gasoline engines other than outboards must have an acceptable means of controlling backfires, which occur when flames from an engine exit through the carburetor instead of the exhaust system. A backfire control keeps these flames from entering the engine compartment.

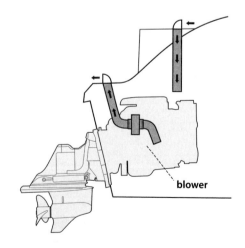

**Figure 5-12.** A powered ventilation system requires a blower in the exhaust duct.

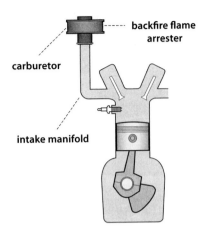

**Figure 5-13.** This simplified schematic (not to scale) shows the location of a backfire flame arrester over a carburetor.

> **WARNING** *Gas vapors can explode. Before starting engine, operate blower for 4 minutes and check engine compartment bilge for gas vapors.*

The usual (though not the only) method of controlling backfires is by fitting a backfire flame arrester (Figure 5-13) to the carburetor. A flame arrester works by rapidly dissipating the heat of the flame, thus keeping the flame out of the engine compartment. An acceptable backfire flame arrester will bear either a Coast Guard approval number, a notice of compliance with Underwriters Laboratories standard UL 1111, or a label stating that it complies with the Society of Automotive Engineers (SAE) standard J1928.

To be effective, flame arresters must be free of oil, grease, and dirt and should therefore be cleaned periodically with grease-dissolving detergent. Otherwise, backfire flame arresters do not need servicing or replacing.

## CARBON MONOXIDE

Carbon monoxide poisoning is a rapidly increasing risk as more and more boatowners are using gasoline generators to power air conditioners. The generator exhaust is commonly located in the transom, which on most powerboats is a popular area for congregating, swimming, and socializing. Houseboats, in particular, experience this problem due to frequent use of air-conditioning while people are socializing and swimming.

When there is a space between the stern and the swim platform, fumes are funneled up and accumulate, possibly resulting in injury and death. Propulsion engines provide another source of carbon monoxide, one to which all boats are subject.

The best solution for this problem is to turn off all engines when activities are in progress at the stern of the boat. Carbon monoxide dangers are discussed in Chapter 10.

# Your Boat's Equipment

Coast Guard regulations require that your boat have certain equipment aboard (see chart next page). These requirements are minimums and should be exceeded whenever possible.

## FIRE EXTINGUISHERS

If your boat includes one or more of the following, you must have at least one fire extinguisher aboard (see Table 5-2 and Figure 5-9):

1. inboard or stern-drive engine(s)
2. closed compartments under *thwarts* and seats where portable fuel tanks can be stored
3. double bottoms not sealed together or not completely filled with flotation materials
4. enclosed living spaces
5. closed stowage compartments in which combustible or flammable materials are stored
6. permanently installed fuel tanks
7. a length of 26 feet or more

Thus, a 24-foot sailboat with an auxiliary outboard engine does not require a fire extinguisher if it is open, but does if it has an enclosed living space.

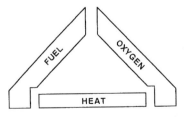

**Figure 5-14.** Removing one element of a fire will suppress it. (REPRINTED WITH PERMISSION FROM *SMALL BOAT SEAMANSHIP MANUAL*)

## Coast Guard Equipment Requirements: Quick Reference Chart

| <16 | 16<26 | 26<40 | 40<65 | Equipment | Requirement |
|---|---|---|---|---|---|
| X | X | X | X | Certificate of Number (State Registration) | All undocumented vessels equipped with propulsion machinery must be State registered. Certificate of Number must be on board when vessel is in use. Note: some States require all vessels to be registered. |
| X | X | X | X | State Numbering | (a) Plain Block letters/numbers not less than 3 inches in height must be affixed on each side of the forward half of the vessel (Contrasting color to boat exterior). (b) State validation sticker must be affixed within six inches of the registration number |
| | X | X | X | Certificate of Documentation | Applies only to "Documented" vessels: (a) Original and current certificate must be on board. (b) Vessel name/hailing port marked on exterior part of hull—letters not less than 4 inches in height. (c) Official Number permanently affixed on interior structure—numbers not less than 3 inches in height. |
| X | X | X | X | Life Jackets (PFDs) | (a) One Type I, II, III, or V wearable PFD for each person on board. (must be USCG approved) |
| | X | X | X | | (b) In addition to paragraph (a), must carry One Type IV (throwable) PFD. |
| X | | | | Visual Distress Signal (VDS) | (a) One electric distress light or Three combination (day/night) red flares. Note: only required to be carried on board when operating between sunset and sunrise. |
| | X | X | X | | (b) One orange distress flag or One electric distress light—or—Three handheld or floating orange smoke signals and One electric distress light—or—Three combination (day/night) red flares: handheld, meteor or parachute type. |
| X | X | | | Fire Extinguishers | (a) One B-I (when enclosed compartment) |
| | | X | | | (b) One B-II or Two B-I.    Note: fixed system equals One B-I |
| | | | X | | (c) One B-II and One B-I or Three B-I.    Note: fixed system equals One B-I or Two B-II |
| X | X | X | X | Ventilation | (a) All vessels built after 25 April 1940 that use gasoline as their fuel with enclosed engine and/or fuel tank compartments must have natural ventilation (at least two ducts fitted with cowls). (b) In addition to paragraph (a), a vessel built after 31 July 1980 must have rated power exhaust blower. |
| X | X | X | | Sound Producing Devices | (a) A vessel of less than 39.4 ft. must, at a minimum, have some means of making an efficient sound signal (i.e. handheld air horn, athletic whistle—Human voice/sound not acceptable). |
| | | X | X | | (b) A vessel 39.4 ft. (12 meters) or greater, must have a sound signaling appliance capable of producing an efficient sound signal, audible for $1/2$ mile with a 4 to 6 seconds duration. In addition, must carry a bell with a clapper (bell size not less than 7.9"—based on the diameter of the mouth) |
| X | X | X | X | Backfire Flame Arrester | Required on gasoline engines installed after 25 April 1940, except outboard motors |
| X | X | X | X | Navigational Lights | Required to be displayed from sunset to sunrise and in or near areas of reduced visibility. |
| | | X | X | Oil Pollution Placard | (a) Placard must be at least 5 by 8 inches, made of durable material. (b) Placard must be posted in the machinery space or at the bilge station. |
| | | X | X | Garbage Placard | (a) Placard must be at least 4 by 9 inches, made of durable material. (b) Displayed in a conspicuous place notifying all on board the discharge restrictions. |
| X | X | X | X | Marine Sanitation Device | If installed toilet: Vessel must have an operable MSD Type I, II, or III. |
| | | X | X | Navigation Rules (Inland Only) | The operator of a vessel 39.4 ft (12 meters) or greater must have on board a copy of these rules. |

*(Column headers: Vessel Length (in feet): <16 | 16<26 | 26<40 | 40<65; Equipment; Requirement)*

## Types of Fires

Fire extinguishers have labels that tell the types of fires for which they are designed. There are three common classes of fires:

- Class A fires are in ordinary combustible materials such as paper or wood.
- Class B fires involve gasoline, oil, or grease.
- Class C fires are electrical.

The extinguishers on boats must be for Class B fires. Never use water on Class B or Class C fires since it spreads Class B fires, and could cause you to be electrocuted if used on a Class C fire.

## Sizes of Extinguishers

Fire extinguishers are also classed by the amount of material they contain. Table 5-3 lists the types of Class B extinguishers and their contents.

## Contents of Extinguishers

Fire extinguishers use a variety of materials (Figure 5-15). Those used on boats usually contain dry chem-

**Figure 5-15.** Left to right: Dry chemical, carbon dioxide, and Halon fire extinguishers. For reasons explained in the text, dry chemical extinguishers are the most popular type on recreational boats. (PHOTO BY NORMA LOCOCO)

| TABLE 5-2 | Required Fire Extinguishers | |
|---|---|---|
| Minimum number of hand-portable fire extinguishers on a boat with and without a fixed extinguishing system | | |
| Length of Vessel | No Fixed System in Machinery Space | Fixed System in Machinery Space |
| Less than 26 ft. | 1 B-I | none |
| 26 ft. to under 40 ft. | 2 B-Is or 1 B-II | 1 B-I |
| 40 ft. to 65 ft. | 3 B-Is or 1 B-I and 1 B-II | 2 B-Is or 1 B-II |

icals, aqueous foam, or carbon dioxide ($CO_2$). Dry chemical extinguishers, which contain chemical powders such as sodium bicarbonate, or baking soda, are the most frequently used extinguishers on recreational boats because they are reasonably inexpensive, convenient, and will put out Class A, B, and C fires.

Carbon dioxide extinguishers leave no residue when discharged and will not damage an engine, and they are therefore sometimes used in an engine compartment's fixed extinguishing system. Portable $CO_2$ extinguishers are not often found on boats, however, in part because $CO_2$ is colorless and odorless when released from an extinguisher. It is not poisonous, but caution must be used when entering compartments filled with it since it keeps oxygen from reaching your lungs and is lethal in fire-killing concentrations. If you are in a compartment with a high concentration of $CO_2$, you will experience no difficulty breathing, but the air you breathe will not contain enough oxygen to support life. Unconsciousness or death can result.

Aqueous foam extinguishers are rarely used because they leave a hard-to-clean residue when discharged and can damage an engine when discharged in the engine compartment.

## Halon and FE-241 Extinguishers

Until 1994, Halon gas was commonly used both in portable extinguishers and in fixed or built-in automatic fire extinguishing systems. Although Halon has excellent firefighting properties, it is thought to deplete the earth's ozone layer and has not been manufactured in the United States since January 1, 1994. In the mid- to late-90s, Halon extinguishers could still be refilled from existing stocks of the gas, but this is no longer possible in most cases. When you dispose of an old Halon extinguisher, take it to a recovery station rather than releasing the gas into the atmosphere.

Alternative gases such as FE-241 have replaced Halon. While appropriate for an engine compartment, FE-241 is toxic and should therefore not be used in occupied spaces.

## Obsolete Extinguishers

Some other extinguishers also require caution. Carbon tetrachloride extinguishers have been outlawed for years, so you are unlikely to encounter one of these. If you do, however, it should be safely disposed of. In contact with a flame, it produces phosgene, a poisonous gas used in World War I.

Some obsolete hand-portable extinguishers must be inverted to be activated and are either ineffective on boat fires or dangerous to use. They include soda-acid, foam, and cartridge-operated

| TABLE 5-3 | Class B Fire Extinguishers | | | | |
|---|---|---|---|---|---|
| Coast Guard Classification (type-size) | Underwriters Laboratories Listing | Aqueous Foam (gals.) | Carbon Dioxide (lbs.) | Dry Chemical (lbs.) | FE-241 (lbs.) |
| B-I | 5B | 1.25 | 4 | 2 | 5 |
| B-II | 10B | 2.5 | 15 | 10 | 10 |

water extinguishers. Neither the soda-acid nor cartridge-operated ones should be used on gasoline, oil, or grease fires, such as occur on boats, because they contain water. All are potentially dangerous; if their discharge hoses are blocked, they may explode. Dispose of them safely.

## Fire Extinguisher Approval

Fire extinguishers must be Coast Guard–approved and in serviceable condition. Look for the approval number on the nameplate and information such as the following on the label: "Marine Type USCG Approved, Size . . ., Type . . ., 162.208/."

## Care and Treatment

Make certain your extinguishers are stowed in their service locations and are not damaged. Replace cracked or broken hoses and be sure nozzles are free of obstructions such as wasps and other insects that sometimes nest inside and render the nozzles inoperable.

Check extinguishers frequently for proper pressure, and check the locking pin with its sealing wire to ensure that it hasn't been used since charging. Don't test an extinguisher by operating it since its valves will not reseat properly, and the remaining gas will leak out. When this happens, the extinguisher is useless.

Weigh and tag carbon dioxide, Halon, or FE-241 extinguishers twice a year (Figure 5-16). If their weight loss exceeds 10% of the weight of the charge, recharge them. You should also check to see that

**Figure 5-16.** A fire extinguisher should carry a tag showing all inspection and service dates. (PHOTO BY NORMA LOCOCO)

they have not been used. They should be inspected by a qualified person every 6 months, and should carry tags showing all inspection and service dates.

If your dry chemical extinguisher has a pressure indicator, check it frequently. Check the nozzle to see if there is powder in it; if there is or if there is low pressure in the nozzle, replace it or have it serviced. The quality and serviceability of extinguishers varies greatly, so the decision to service or replace them is often best made by a professional.

Occasionally invert your dry chemical extinguisher and hit the base with the palm of your hand. The chemical in these extinguishers packs and cakes due to the boat's vibration and pounding, and while there is a difference of opinion about whether hitting the base helps, it can't hurt. Sometimes the gauge will stick in the full position and give a false reading and jarring the extinguisher will often dislodge the stuck indicator. Caking of the chemical powder is a major cause of failure of dry chemical extinguishers. If you hear a thud when tilting the extinguisher back and forth, suspect caking. Carry spare extinguishers in excess of the minimum requirement.

If you have guests aboard, make certain they know where the extinguishers are and how to use them.

## Using a Fire Extinguisher

A fire extinguisher usually has a metal or plastic locking pin or loop to prevent accidental discharge. If you need to use your extinguisher, take it from its bracket, remove the pin or loop, and point the nozzle at the base of the flames. Now squeeze the handle and discharge the extinguisher's contents while sweeping from side to side (Figure 5-17). Recharge or replace a used extinguisher as soon as possible after use.

If you are using a Halon, FE-241, or $CO_2$ extinguisher, keep your hands away from the discharge, as the rapidly expanding gas will freeze them. If the fire extinguisher has a horn, hold it by its handle.

## Legal Requirements for Extinguishers

Carry fire extinguishers as defined by Coast Guard regulations. They must be readily accessible in a

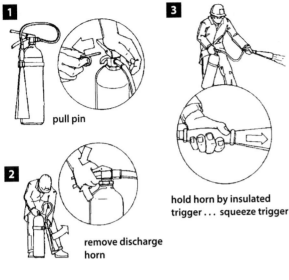

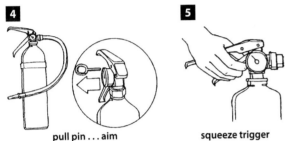

**Figure 5-17.** How to use a $CO_2$ **(1, 2, 3)** or dry chemical **(4, 5)** extinguisher. (REPRINTED WITH PERMISSION FROM *SMALL BOAT SEAMANSHIP MANUAL*)

secure location, and it is recommended that they be attached to the boat. As summarized in Table 5-2 above, a boat less than 26 feet long is required to have at least one approved, hand-portable, Type B-I extinguisher aboard unless the boat either (1) has an approved fixed fire extinguishing system (Figure 5-18), or (2) is propelled by an outboard motor or motors and does not meet any of the criteria listed at the beginning of this section. It's a good idea to carry a portable extinguisher even when not required. If a nearby boat catches fire, or if a fire occurs at a fuel dock, you'll be glad you have it.

A boat 26 feet to under 40 feet long must have at least two Type B-I Coast Guard–approved hand-portable extinguishers or one approved Type B-II. If you have an approved fixed fire extinguishing system, only one Type B-I is required.

A boat 40 to 65 feet long must have at least three approved portable Type B-Is or at least one Type B-I plus one Type B-II. If the boat has an approved fixed fire extinguishing system, two Type B-Is or one Type B-II extinguisher is required.

## WARNING SYSTEM

Various devices such as fire, smoke, gasoline fumes, and carbon monoxide detectors are available to alert you to danger. If your boat has a galley, it should have a smoke detector. Where possible, use wired detectors because household batteries often corrode rapidly on a boat.

You can't see, smell, or taste carbon monoxide gas, but it is lethal. There are many ways in which carbon monoxide can enter your boat, and as little as 1 part in 10,000 parts of air can bring on a headache. The symptoms of carbon monoxide poisoning—headaches, dizziness, and nausea—are like seasickness. By the time you realize what is happening to you, it may be too late to take action. If your boat has enclosed living spaces, protect yourself with a carbon monoxide detector.

| ✓ WHICH EXTINGUISHER TO USE | |
| --- | --- |
| **TYPES OF FIRES** | **APPROPRIATE EXTINGUISHER** |
| CLASS A—Ordinary Combustible Material (such as Paper and Wood) | Water, Halon or FE-241, Carbon Dioxide, Dry Chemical |
| CLASS B—Gasoline, Diesel Fuel, Oil, Grease | Halon or FE-241, Carbon Dioxide, Dry Chemical (NOT WATER) |
| CLASS C—Electrical | Halon or FE-241, Carbon Dioxide, Dry Chemical (NOT WATER) |
| Boats with Motors | Must use a CLASS B Extinguisher |

## PERSONAL FLOTATION DEVICES

*Personal flotation devices* (PFDs) are commonly called life preservers or life jackets and are available in a variety of types and sizes according to intended use. The term "approved PFD" as used here refers to a PFD type that is approved for a given application. Additionally, each individual PFD must bear a label stating that it is approved by the U.S. Coast Guard.

### PFD Characteristics

The most common PFDs are inherently buoyant and do not require inflation. They have been in use for a long time. The relatively new inflatable PFDs, however, are convenient and comfortable to wear. No PFD should be stuffed into storage and forgotten, but inflatable PFDs have mechanisms that require even more regular inspection.

Three inflatable systems are approved by the Coast Guard. One, called a manual inflatable, allows inflation by pulling a lanyard. Another, called a manual inflatable with automatic backup, is inflated the same way but also has a backup automatic inflation system that activates if the PFD becomes wet. A third, called a hybrid, has a small amount of built-in buoyancy that is augmented by a manual or automatic inflatable device. Hybrids are no longer generally available but are still usable if they are serviceable and armed correctly.

All inflatables have an additional backup inflation capability that requires the wearer to blow into a tube. More details are given under the sections on Type III and Type V PFDs below. It's likely that in the near future there will be more inflatable design improvements.

## Types of PFDs

**TYPE I PFDs.** This type is also called an offshore life jacket and will turn most unconscious people to a faceup position (Figure 5-19). These PFDs come in both inherently buoyant (foam-filled) and inflatable models. The adult size in the inherently buoyant models has at least 22 pounds of buoyancy, while the child's size has at least 11 pounds. An adult inflatable generates up to 34 pounds of buoyancy at maximum inflation.

Type I life jackets are bulkier and less comfortable than other types, although the inflatable mod-

**Inherently Buoyant**                 **Hybrid**

**Figure 5-19.** Type I PFDs. (COURTESY PERSONAL FLOTATION DEVICE MANUFACTURERS ASSOCIATION)

### Inherently Buoyant (Primarily Foam)

▌The *most* reliable

▌Adult, Youth, Child, and Infant sizes

▌For swimmers & non-swimmers

▌Wearable & throwable styles

▌Some designed for water sports

| Minimum Buoyancy | | |
| --- | --- | --- |
| Wearable Size | Type | Inherent Buoyancy (Foam) |
| Adult | I | 22 lb. |
| | II & III | 15.5 lb. |
| | V | 15.5 to 22 lb. |
| Youth | II & III | 11 lb. |
| | V | 11 to 15.5 lb. |
| Child and Infant | II | 7 lb. |
| Throwable:<br>Cushion | IV | 20 lb. |
| Ring Buoy | | 16.5 & 32 lb. |

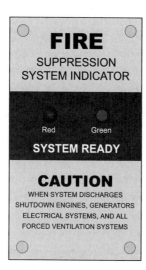

**FIRE**
SUPPRESSION
SYSTEM INDICATOR

Red        Green

**SYSTEM READY**

**CAUTION**
WHEN SYSTEM DISCHARGES
SHUTDOWN ENGINES, GENERATORS
ELECTRICAL SYSTEMS, AND ALL
FORCED VENTILATION SYSTEMS

**Figure 5-18.** A fixed fire-suppression system should have a status light like this one near the helm.

els are quite comfortable when not inflated. Type Is keep an individual afloat for extended periods when rescue is delayed, and are therefore especially appropriate for offshore use. Because of their buoyancy, they will support individuals higher in the water; thus, they are excellent in rough water.

***TYPE II PFDs.*** This type, also called a near-shore buoyant vest, comes in both inherently buoyant and inflatable models (Figure 5-20). Inherently buoyant Type IIs will turn some unconscious individuals to a faceup position, while inflatable models do this as well as Type I foam PFDs do.

While Type IIs are more comfortable than Type Is, they provide less buoyancy. Adult foam models have 15.5 pounds of buoyancy, youth models have 11 pounds, and infant models have 7 pounds (Figure 5-21). Adult inflatable models offer up to 34 pounds of buoyancy, on a par with Type I inflatables.

Type IIs are recommended for inshore and inland cruising on calm waters where the chances of fast rescue are high.

***TYPE III PFDs.*** A Type III is also called a flotation aid (Figures 5-21 and 5-22), and it too comes in inherently buoyant and inflatable models. The foam vest has the same minimum buoyancy as Type II PFDs, but Type IIIs are designed so that their wearers must turn themselves upright and may have to tilt their heads back to avoid being rolled facedown.

Type IIIs are designed for conscious individuals in calm inland waters where the chance of

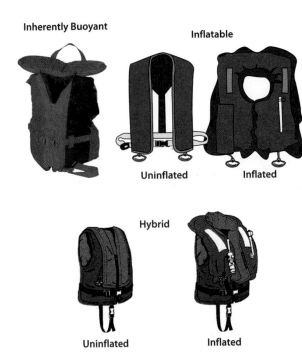

**Inherently Buoyant**

**Inflatable**

Uninflated     Inflated

**Hybrid**

Uninflated     Inflated

**Figure 5-20.** Type II PFDs. (COURTESY PERSONAL FLOTATION DEVICE MANUFACTURERS ASSOCIATION)

**Inflatable**

❙ The most compact
❙ Sizes only for adults
❙ Only recommended for swimmers
❙ Wearable styles only
❙ Some with the best in-water performance

| Minimum Buoyancy | | |
|---|---|---|
| Wearable Size | Type | Inflatable Buoyancy |
| Adult | I & II | 34 lb. |
| | III | 22.5 lb. |
| | V | 22.5 to 34 lb. |

**Figure 5-21. Top:** These kids are wearing inherently buoyant Type III PFDs, while the adult is wearing a Type III inflatable. **Bottom:** The driver is wearing a Type II inflatable vest. Note the lanyard on his wrist. This leads to a kill switch, which would cut the engine should he be thrown from his helm position. In the stern, a child wearing a Type III inherently buoyant PFD sits between two adults wearing Type III inflatable vests. (COURTESY U.S. COAST GUARD OFFICE OF BOATING SAFETY)

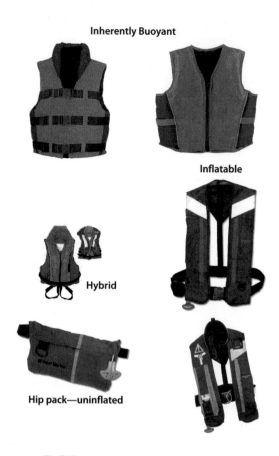

**Figure 5-22.** Type III PFDs. (COURTESY PERSONAL FLOTATION DEVICE MANUFACTURERS ASSOCIATION AND WEST MARINE)

### Hybrid (Foam & Inflation)

▌ Reliable

▌ Adult, Youth, and Child sizes

▌ For swimmers & non-swimmers

▌ Wearable styles only

▌ Some designed for water sports

| Minimum Buoyancy | | | |
|---|---|---|---|
| Wearable Size | Type | Inherent Buoyancy | Inflated Total Buoyancy |
| Adult | II & III | 10 lb. | 22 lb. |
|  | V | 7.5 lb. | 22 lb. |
| Youth | II & III | 9 lb. | 15 lb. |
|  | V | 7.5 lb. | 15 lb. |
| Child | II | 7 lb. | 12 lb. |

quick rescue is high. They come in many colors and styles, such as fishing vests and float coats, and are comfortable to wear. Freedom of movement is one of their strong points, which makes them attractive to sport users.

**Figure 5-23.** Type IV PFDs. (COURTESY PERSONAL FLOTATION DEVICE MANUFACTURERS ASSOCIATION)

**TYPE IV PFDs.** A Type IV, also called a throwable device (Figure 5-23), is designed to be thrown to someone in the water who can hold onto it until rescued. This type, which should not be worn, includes rings, horseshoe buoys, and buoyant cushions. There are no inflatable Type IVs.

Most throwables have handles or grab lines for the person in the water to hold on to. In addition, while not a requirement, it is a good idea to attach about 60 feet of polypropylene line (which floats) to the throwable to better assist the user in retrieving the device and also assist the rescuer in retrieving the user. If your boat is 16 feet or more in length and is not a canoe or kayak, you must have at least one Type IV aboard.

Be careful when throwing the device so that you don't hit and possibly injure the intended receiver.

**TYPE V PFDs.** This type, also called a special-use device, is intended for special activities and may be carried instead of another PFD only if used according to the approval conditions on its label (Figure 5-24). The performance of these devices is marked on their labels. If the label says the PFD is "approved only when worn," the device must be worn except in enclosed spaces (i.e., the boat's cabin) and used in accordance with the approval label.

Some Type Vs offer hypothermia protection. The wide range of varieties includes deck suits, work vests, and windsurfing vests.

## Legal Requirements

A Coast Guard–approved PFD must show the manufacturer's name and approval number. Most are marked as Type I, II, III, IV, or V. You are required to carry at least one wearable PFD of suitable size for each person on board your boat.

1. approved for the activity the vessel is engaged in

2. approved as a substitute for a PFD of the type required on the vessel

3. used as required on the label

4. used in accordance with any requirements in its owner's manual, if the approval label makes reference to such a manual

You are required to keep your PFDs readily accessible. Type IV devices must be immediately at hand so that you can reach out and get them when needed.

Coast Guard–approved inflatable PFDs are authorized only for people at least 16 years old, and it is recommended that nonswimmers wear inherently buoyant PFDs at all times while on board.

## General Considerations

The proper use of a PFD requires the wearer to know how it will perform. You can gain this knowledge only through experience, and a good place to practice donning a PFD is in a swimming pool.

Each person on your boat should be assigned a PFD. To ensure the proper fit of a PFD, have the wearer put it on and adjust the straps as necessary until it feels snug. Have the wearer raise his or her arms above their head and then cinch the upper straps of the PFD firmly. A properly fitted PFD will not ride higher than the ears or mouth of the wearer. Note that it is very difficult to adjust the straps while in the water. *Note: This fitting procedure is not applicable to inflatable PFDs, which should have their retaining straps adjusted loosely to allow for the inflation of the devices.*

It is wise to follow this advice even if the water is calm and you intend to boat near shore. Most drownings occur in inland waters within a few feet of safety, and most victims have PFDs available but fail to wear them.

Storing PFDs in your cabin in the plastic covers they came wrapped in assures that they will stay clean and unfaded, but this is no way to carry them when you are on the water. A PFD must be readily accessible and adjusted to fit its wearer if it's going to be useful. You can't spend time hunting for it or learning how to put it on in an emergency situation.

**Figure 5-24. Top:** A canoeist wearing an inflatable vest. If this is a Type III, the paddler must pull the lanyard to inflate it. If it's a Type V, it will inflate automatically (with manual backup), providing Type II protection. (COURTESY U.S. COAST GUARD OFFICE OF BOATING SAFETY) **Bottom:** This work vest and immersion suit are two examples of Type V special-purpose configurations. (COURTESY PERSONAL FLOTATION DEVICE MANUFACTURERS ASSOCIATION)

If a person elects to wear a Type V PFD with a "required to be worn" label only at selected times, he or she must have another Type I, II, or III PFD aboard to meet the boat's PFD count requirement. Type Vs don't count toward the requirement when not worn or when worn for other than the labeled use.

If your vessel is 16 feet or more long and is not a canoe or a kayak, you must also have at least one Type IV PFD on board. These requirements apply to all recreational vessels that are propelled or controlled by machinery, sails, oars, paddles, poles, or another vessel. Sailboards are not required by federal law to carry PFDs, but some states require them.

You can substitute an older Type V hybrid for any required Type I, II, or III PFD provided that its approval label shows that it is all of the following:

There is no substitute for the experience of entering the water while wearing a PFD. Children, especially, need practice. If possible, give your guests this experience. Advise them to keep their arms to their sides when jumping in, in order to keep the PFD from riding up. Then let them jump in and see how the PFD responds. Is it adjusted so it does not ride up? Is it properly sized? Are all the straps snug? Does a child's PFD fit properly, with proper adjustments?

Nonswimmers, children, and the elderly and handicapped should always wear PFDs on a boat, and many states require this. In hazardous waters, rough weather, and at night everyone aboard should wear one. Indeed, it is highly recommended that all passengers wear PFDs at all times. Coast Guard members always wear PFDs on the water, even when it is calm.

Inspect your lifesaving equipment from time to time, and leave any questionable or unsatisfactory equipment ashore. An emergency is no time to conduct an inspection.

## Care of Life Jackets

Given reasonable care, PFDs last many years. Thoroughly dry them before putting them away in a well-ventilated place. Avoid the bottoms of lockers and deck storage boxes where moisture may collect, and air and dry them frequently no matter where they are stored.

PFDs should not be tossed about or used as *fenders* or cushions. Many contain kapok or fibrous glass material enclosed in plastic bags, which can rupture and become unserviceable. Squeeze your life jacket gently. Does air leak out? If so, water can leak in, rendering the jacket unsafe to use. Cut it up so no one will use it, and throw it away.

The covers of some PFDs are made of nylon or polyester, which, like many other plastics, will break down after extended exposure to the ultraviolet light in sunlight. This process may be more rapid when the materials are dyed with bright dyes such as neon shades.

Rips and badly faded fabric are clues that the covering of your PFD is deteriorating. A simple test is to pinch the fabric between your thumbs and forefingers and then try to tear it. If it can be torn, it should definitely be destroyed and discarded.

The condition of the straps and hardware used to secure a PFD to a person is also an important consideration. A PFD that cannot be securely fastened is of little value to a person in the water. If any of the metal or plastic hardware or the webbing or straps on a PFD are broken, deformed, ripped, or separated from their attachment points, discard it.

## Special Care for Inflatable PFDs

Inflatables require more care than foam-filled PFDs. Users should follow the manufacturer's recommendations. Check to ensure that the green indicator is showing green, and manually inflate the air bladder periodically.

## SOUND-PRODUCING DEVICES

All boats, including PWC, are required to carry some means of making an efficient sound signal. A device for making the whistle or horn noises required by the Navigation Rules must be capable of a 4-second blast that is audible for at least ½ mile. Athletic whistles are not acceptable on boats 12 meters (39 feet) or longer and should be used with caution (Figure 5-25). When wet, some of them come apart and lose their "peas," rendering them useless. Consider attaching a whistle to each PFD.

If your vessel is 12 to 20 meters (39 to 65 feet) long and operating on inland waters (see Chapter 8) both a power whistle (or power horn) and a bell are required on board. The bell must be in operating condition and have a minimum diameter of at least 200 mm (7.9 inches) at its mouth.

**Figure 5-25.** Acceptable sound-signal devices include a bell, a compressed-air horn, a power horn, and a whistle. A boat more than 39 feet long needs both a horn and a bell under the Inland Rules (see Chapter 8).

| TABLE 5-4 | Visual Distress Signals | |
|---|---|---|
| **Pyrotechnic Visual Distress Signals** | | |
| CG Approval Number | Description | Use |
| 160.021 | Handheld flare | Day/night |
| 160.022 | Floating orange smoke | Day only |
| 160.024 | Pistol parachute red flare | Day/night |
| 160.036 | Handheld parachute red flare | Day/night |
| 160.037 | Handheld orange smoke | Day only |
| 160.057 | Floating orange smoke | Day only |
| 160.066 | Red aerial pyrotechnic flare | Day/night |
| **Nonpyrotechnic Visual Distress Signals** | | |
| 160.072 | Orange flag | Day only |
| 161.013 | Electric distress light | Night only |

## VISUAL DISTRESS SIGNALS

*Visual distress signals* (VDS) attract attention to your vessel if you need help. They also help to guide searchers in search-and-rescue situations. Be sure you have the right kinds, and use them properly.

It is illegal to fire flares in a nonemergency unless authorized by the Coast Guard. False distress signals cost the Coast Guard and its Auxiliary many wasted hours in fruitless searches each year. If you signal a distress with flares and subsequently receive the necessary help, please let the Coast Guard or the appropriate search-and-rescue (SAR) agency know so that the distress report can be canceled.

Recreational boats less than 16 feet long are required to carry VDS only when operating on coastal waters between sunset and sunrise. (Coastal waters include oceans and gulfs and the bays or sounds that empty into them; the Great Lakes and their contiguous bays and sounds; and rivers that are more than 2 miles across at their mouths, upstream to where they narrow to 2 miles.) All pyrotechnic VDS must be Coast Guard–approved, readily accessible, serviceable, and within their stamped expiration dates.

Recreational boats 16 feet or longer must carry VDS at all times on coastal waters, day or night, and the same requirement applies to boats carrying six or fewer passengers for hire. Open sailboats less than 26 feet long without engines are exempt

in the daytime, as are manually propelled boats. Also exempt are boats in organized races, regattas, parades, and other such events. Boats owned in the United States and operating on the high seas must be equipped with VDS.

A wide variety of signaling devices meet Coast Guard regulations (Figure 5-26). If you choose pyrotechnic devices, a minimum of three are required. Any combination can be carried, as long as it adds up to at least three signals for day use and at least three signals for night use. Three day/night signals meet both requirements. If possible, carry more than the legal requirement. These devices are listed in Table 5-4.

Flying the American flag upside down is a commonly recognized distress signal, although it is not recognized in Coast Guard regulations. In an emergency, your efforts would probably be better used in more effective signaling methods.

### Types of VDS

All VDS must be Coast Guard–approved, in good serviceable condition, within their stamped expiration dates, and readily accessible to meet federal carriage requirements.

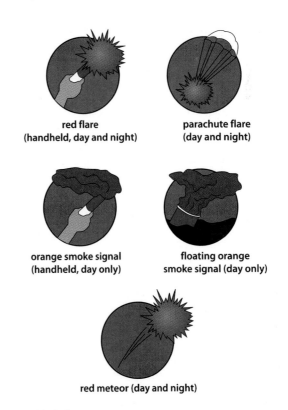

red flare
(handheld, day and night)

parachute flare
(day and night)

orange smoke signal
(handheld, day only)

floating orange
smoke signal (day only)

red meteor (day and night)

**Figure 5-26.** Pyrotechnic distress signals.

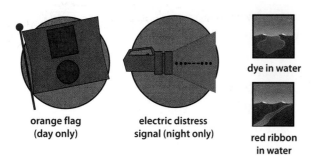

**Figure 5-27.** Nonpyrotechnic distress signals.

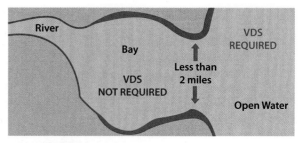

**Figure 5-28.** All boats operating on coastal waters, territorial seas, or the Great Lakes must carry visual distress signals. This requirement also applies on any waterway directly connected with these waters, but only to the point, proceeding inland, where the connecting waterway narrows to less than 2 miles wide.

***DAYTIME NONPYROTECHNIC SIGNALS.*** A bright orange flag with a black square above a black circle is the simplest daytime VDS (Figure 5-27), plus it has the advantage of being a continuous signal.

A mirror, while not an approved device, can be used to good advantage on sunny days. Mirrors can attract the attention of other boaters and of aircraft from great distances and are available with holes in their centers to aid in aiming. In the absence of a mirror, any shiny object such as a CD can be used.

When another boat is in sight, an effective VDS is to extend your arms from your sides and move them slowly up and down. Don't do it too fast or observers may think you are just being friendly. This simple gesture is seldom misunderstood and requires no equipment.

***DAYTIME PYROTECHNIC DEVICES.*** Orange smoke is a useful daytime signal. Handheld or floating smoke flares are very effective in attracting attention from aircraft (Figure 5-26). Smoke flares don't last long and are not effective in high wind or poor visibility, however. As with other pyrotechnic devices, use them only when you know there is a possibility that someone will see the display.

To ensure that they remain usable, keep smoke flares in airtight containers and store them in dry places. If the striker is damp, dry it out before trying to ignite the device. Some pyrotechnic devices require a forceful strike to ignite them.

***NIGHTTIME NONPYROTECHNIC SIGNALS.*** An electric distress light is available (Figure 5-27) that automatically flashes the international Morse code SOS distress signal (• • • – – – • • •). Flashed four to six times a minute, it is an unmistakable VDS. The label must show that it is approved by the Coast Guard. Check the batteries to make sure they haven't expired.

Under the Inland Rules, a high-intensity white light flashing fifty to seventy times per minute is a distress signal (Figure 5-28). Therefore, use strobe lights on inland waters only for distress signals.

***NIGHTTIME PYROTECHNIC DEVICES.*** Aerial and handheld flares can be used at night or in the daytime. Obviously, they are more effective at night.

Currently, the serviceable life of a pyrotechnic device is rated at 42 months from its date of manufacture. Since pyrotechnic devices are expensive, look at their dates before you buy them and choose ones with as much time remaining as possible.

Like smoke flares, aerial and handheld flares may fail to work if they have been damaged or abused. They will not function if they are or have been wet and should therefore be stored in dry, airtight containers in dry but readily accessible places.

Aerial VDS, depending on their type and the conditions in which they are used, may not go very high. Again, use them only when there is a good chance they will be seen.

A serious disadvantage of aerial flares is that most burn for less than 10 seconds. Even parachute flares usually burn for less than 45 seconds.

If you use a VDS in an emergency, do so carefully, even when it is a marine flare designed to lessen risk. Hold handheld flares over the side of the boat and never use a road hazard flare because it can easily start a fire.

**WARNING** *All handheld pyrotechnic devices may produce hot ashes or slag when burning. Hold them over the side of your boat so that they do not burn your hand or drip into your boat.*

Give aerial flares the same respect as firearms, since they are firearms. Never point them at another person, and don't allow children to play with or around them. When you fire one, face away from the wind and aim it downwind and upward at an angle of about 60° to the horizon. If there is a strong wind, aim it somewhat more vertically, but never fire it straight up. Before you discharge a flare pistol, check for overhead obstructions that could be damaged by the flare or that might redirect it to strike something.

## Disposal of VDS

Keep outdated flares when you get new ones. They do not meet legal requirements, but you might need them sometime, and they usually work after their expiration dates. Since it is illegal to fire a VDS on federal navigable waters unless an emergency exists, do not try to dispose of a flare that way. Many states have similar laws. Each state has its own regulations for disposing of unwanted VDS.

## MARINE SANITATION DEVICES

All recreational boats with installed toilets must also have an operable marine sanitation device (MSD) that is certified by the Coast Guard. Type I and Type II MSDs are flow-through devices, the most common of which are called macerator-chlorinators. These grind up solids, disinfect the resultant waste, and discharge the treated effluent overboard. Type II MSDs meet more stringent bacterial coliform counts and are rarely installed in small craft. Type I MSDs—the kind you are more likely to see on a boat—are certified to meet a looser bacterial standard. Some bodies of water are designated no-discharge zones by state or federal statute, and it is illegal to discharge even treated waste into such waters, so know your local regulations.

Type III-A MSDs are the portable toilets such as Porta-Potties, ubiquitous on small boats, that treat waste with disinfectant and hold it for later

removal at an approved land site or mobile pumpout facility (Figure 5-29). Type III-B MSDs are the holding tanks common on somewhat larger boats. Many boatowners install a Y-valve between the toilet and the holding tank, which permits the option of pumping waste overboard when in unrestricted waters (which generally means more than 12 miles offshore in ocean waters). Such a Y-valve must be locked in the closed position by means of a padlock, wire, or other approved method whenever the boat is in restricted waters.

Contact the state marine police to learn the locations of pumpout stations near you. Discharge regulations for garbage are covered in Appendix A.

## EMERGENCY POSITION-INDICATING RADIO BEACON

An emergency position-indicating radio beacon (EPIRB) is a small (about 6 to 20 inches high), battery-powered radio transmitter that is activated either by immersion in water or by a manual switch (Figure 5-30). It requires no license. You should buy an EPIRB that transmits on 406.025 MHz (commonly called 406s).

Recreational boats are not required to carry EPIRBs; some commercial and fishing vessels must have them if they operate beyond the 3-mile limit, however, and vessels carrying six or fewer passengers for hire must have EPIRBs under some circumstances when operating beyond the 3-mile limit.

**Figure 5-29.** Look for this symbol to locate a marine toilet pumpout station.

**Figure 5-30.** A 406 MHz EPIRB.

Some EPIRBs contain a 121.5 MHz frequency, which was intended to be monitored by commercial aircraft. But its use by recreational boaters is prohibited by the U.S. Coast Guard as of 2007. The Coast Guard highly recommends that recreational vessels carry 406s, whose signals can be received worldwide by satellites. When a satellite receives a 406 signal, it records the signal and retransmits it to the first land-based receiving station the satellite passes over. A 406's signal can be pinpointed anywhere on the earth's surface to within 3 nautical miles on the first pass and within 1 mile on the third.

Newer 406 signals are uniquely coded for each unit. The individual information is recorded in National Oceanic and Atmospheric Administration (NOAA) computers; it aids in search-and-rescue efforts by identifying your vessel's characteristics and also helps reduce false alarms.

Too often, EPIRBs are turned on during designated test periods and then are not turned off. When you test your 406, be certain that it is in the "test" mode.

If you buy a new or used 406 EPIRB (or change your boat, address, or telephone number), you must register it with NOAA. To request and submit 406 MHz EPIRB registration forms, go to www.beaconregistration.noaa.gov. You can also write to SARSAT Beacon Registration, NSDF, E/SP3, 4231 Suitland Road, Suitland, MD 20746; send a fax to 301-817-4565; or call 888-212-7283 or 301-817-4515.

The biggest drawback of an EPIRB is its cost, which can be $600 or more for a 406. They are, however, available for leasing. If you are thinking of buying an EPIRB, be sure it has been approved by the Federal Communications Commission (FCC).

## EQUIPMENT NOT REQUIRED BUT RECOMMENDED

Although not required by law, there is other equipment that is good to have aboard.

### Second Means of Propulsion

All boats less than 16 feet long should carry a second means of propulsion. A paddle or oar can come in handy on a small sailboat. If you carry a spare motor, it should have its own fuel tank and starting power, and if you use an electric trolling motor, it should have its own battery.

### Dewatering Devices

All boats should carry at least one effective manual dewatering device such as a bucket, can, scoop, or hand-operated pump in addition to any installed electric bilge pump. If your battery "goes dead" it will not operate your electric pump.

### First-Aid Kit

Your first-aid kit should contain items such as adhesive bandages, gauze, adhesive tape, antiseptic ointment, and aspirin. Check the kit from time to time and replace anything that is outdated. It is also to your advantage to know how to use your kit, and you should consider taking a recognized first-aid course.

### Anchors

Anchors are recommended for all boats, although they are not required by the U.S. Coast Guard. Choose one of suitable size for your boat, or better still, have two anchors of different sizes. Use the smaller one—your "lunch hook"—in calm water or when anchoring for a short time such as to fish or eat. Use the larger one when the water is rougher or for overnight anchoring. See Chapter 4 for more on anchors and anchoring.

Carry enough anchor line of suitable size for your boat and the waters in which you will operate. If your engine fails, the first thing to do is lower your anchor. This is good advice both in shallow water where you may be driven aground by the wind or water and in windy weather or rough water. The anchor will usually hold the bow into the waves.

### VHF-FM Radio

Your best means of summoning help in an emergency or in case of a breakdown is a VHF-FM radio, which you can use to get advice or assistance from the Coast Guard (Figure 5-31). In the event of a serious illness or injury aboard your boat, the Coast Guard can have emergency medical equipment meet you ashore. Chapter 16 covers marine communications in greater depth.

**A REMINDER** *This lesson covers only the federal regulations with which you must comply. You must also comply with all applicable state and local laws and regulations. Your instructor will distribute state and local information.*

## Tools and Spare Parts

Carry a few tools and some spare parts, and learn how to make minor repairs. Many search-and-rescue cases are caused by minor breakdowns that boat operators could have repaired. If your engine is a stern drive or inboard, carry spare belts and impellers and the tools to install them.

# Legal Considerations

Boating entails a number of legal considerations, most of which involve nothing more than common sense and courtesy. All of them have been enacted to protect you, other people, or the environment. Some have already been mentioned; others are discussed in Appendix A. Please take the time to inform yourself of your responsibilities to the environment in which you operate your boat and the other boaters you meet.

**Figure 5-31.** A VHF radio can help avoid collisions like this one, but the first line of defense is a proper lookout and a working knowledge of the nautical Rules of the Road (see Chapter 8). (REPRINTED WITH PERMISSION FROM *SEAWORTHY: ESSENTIAL LESSONS FROM BOAT U.S.'S 20-YEAR CASE FILE OF THINGS GONE WRONG* BY ROBERT A. ADRIANCE)

## Practice Questions

**IMPORTANT BOATING TERMS**
In the following exercise, match the words in the column on the left with the definitions in the column on the right. In the blank space to the left of each term, write the letter of the item that best matches it. Do not use an item in the right-hand column more than once.

| THE ITEMS | | THE RESPONSES |
|---|---|---|
| 1. _____ | Vessel Safety Check | a. Type IV life jacket |
| 2. _____ | not inherently buoyant | b. flares, for example |
| 3. _____ | sound signal | c. all vessels must have the means to make |
| 4. _____ | marine sanitation device | d. it's on the transom |
| 5. _____ | throwable PFD | e. Type II life jacket |
| 6. _____ | VDS | f. an inflatable life jacket |
| 7. _____ | HIN | g. national registration |
| 8. _____ | near-shore buoyant vest | h. free; made by the Coast Guard Auxiliary |
| 9. _____ | offshore life jacket | i. Type I life jacket |
| 10. _____ | documentation | j. required on installed toilets that do not have holding tanks |

# Multiple-Choice Items

In the following items, choose the best response:

**5-1.** A boat's length is measured in a straight line from its bow to its stern and includes

a. bowsprits
b. boomkins
c. pulpits
d. none of the above

**5-2.** If your sailboat has an auxiliary inboard or outboard engine, you must register it in

a. the state where you keep it
b. the state of principal use
c. either the state where you keep it or the state of principal use
d. registration is not required

**5-3.** The registration number of a boat

a. may be transferred to a new replacement boat
b. may not be transferred to a new boat-owner
c. will stay with the boat unless the principal state of use is changed
d. may be changed if the number on the boat is damaged

**5-4.** When purchasing a USCG-approved PFD you should select it based on

a. cost and style
b. use, type, and size
c. the swimming ability of the user
d. color and flexibility

**5-5.** The letters and numbers you use to put your registration number on the bow of the vessel must

a. be at least 3 inches high
b. contrast in color with the hull
c. be plain block letters
d. all of the above

**5-6.** Many small powerboats and some sailboats display a capacity plate where it is clearly visible to the operator. It specifies the recommended

a. maximum speed
b. maximum fuel capacity
c. maximum weight-carrying capacity, among other things
d. minimum engine oil capacity

**5-7.** As their active extinguishing agent, marine-type fire extinguishers usually use

a. water
b. dry chemical
c. carbon tetrachloride
d. soda acid

**5-8.** Most auxiliary-powered sailboats in use on federal waters must be

a. seaworthy
b. properly equipped with an anchor
c. registered or documented
d. operated by licensed skippers

**5-9.** A Class B fire involves

a. paper and wood
b. gasoline, oil, or grease
c. any combustible
d. electrical

**5-10.** One serious disadvantage of aerial flares is that they

a. are so bright they can blind the operator
b. can be seen from long distances
c. have an expiration date
d. burn for only a short time

**5-11.** In order to meet federal boating law requirements, life jackets must be approved by the

a. American Red Cross
b. Underwriters Laboratories
c. U.S. Coast Guard
d. Marine Underwriters

**5-12.** At least one approved life jacket must be aboard each vessel for each

a. person on board
b. available seat
c. paying customer
d. occupied bunk or berth

**5-13.** Even if your flares are within their dates of expiration, they may not function if they have been

a. wet
b. stored in an airtight container

## Multiple-Choice Items (continued)

c. previously used
d. kept aboard the boat in case of emergency

**5-14.** Which of the following equipment is not required by law but is recommended by the U.S. Coast Guard Auxiliary?

a. life jackets
b. a backfire flame arrester
c. a sound-producing device
d. an anchor

**5-15.** Exhaust and air supply ducts must be above

a. the gunwales
b. the bilge
c. the usual level of water in the bilge
d. the engine

**5-16.** Halon extinguishers

a. require an indicator in the engine compartment
b. are no longer manufactured
c. are environmentally friendly
d. have a disagreeable odor

**5-17.** How many minutes should you operate a ventilation blower before starting a gasoline-powered inboard?

a. 2
b. 4
c. 6
d. 7

**5-18.** The most usual means of preventing fires and explosions from gas-engine backfires is a Coast Guard–approved

a. fire extinguisher
b. life jacket
c. gasoline vapor detector
d. backfire flame arrester

**5-19.** Never test your extinguisher by

a. filling it
b. weighing it
c. firing it
d. shaking it

**5-20.** Which type of life jacket affords the greatest protection for its wearer?

a. Type I
b. Type II
c. Type III
d. Type IV

**5-21.** Sailboats less than 26 feet long with enclosed living spaces must have at least

a. one semi-portable Class B extinguisher
b. at least one approved hand-portable Type B-I extinguisher
c. at least one soda-acid extinguisher
d. at least two approved hand-portable Type B-I extinguishers

**5-22.** Type III life jackets are designed for

a. calm, inland water
b. offshore use
c. near-shore use
d. vessels carrying paid passengers

**5-23.** Although not legally required, the Coast Guard Auxiliary recommends that you have which of the following equipment aboard in addition to other equipment?

a. a second means of propulsion
b. a first-aid kit
c. an anchor
d. all of the above

**5-24.** When using a fire extinguisher, you should first remove the pin or loop and

a. shake the container
b. position yourself directly in front of the flames
c. point the nozzle at the base of the flames
d. work from the top of the flames to the base of the fire

**5-25.** It is important to maintain and regularly inspect PFDs for

a. ripped and badly faded fabric
b. straps and hardware that cannot be secured
c. air that leaks out when the PFD is squeezed
d. all of the above

# Trailering Your Sailboat

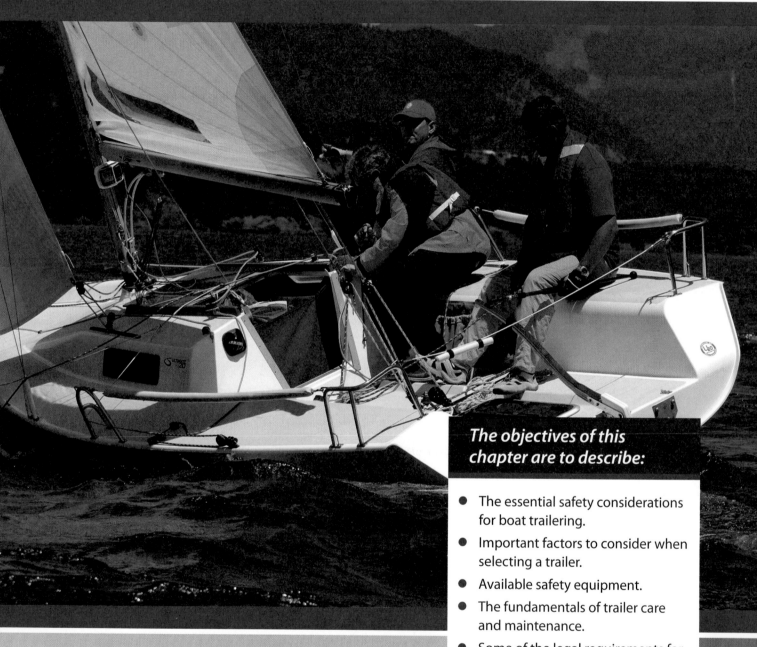

Trailer boats come in all shapes and sizes, like this Ultimate 20. (PHOTO BY DAVID KENNEDY, COURTESY ULTIMATE 20)

CHAPTER 1 SURVEYED the great variety of sailboats, Chapter 5 offered guidance on how to equip a boat, and Chapters 2, 3, and 4 covered the basics of sailing. In this chapter you will learn how to get a trailerable boat to where you will use it.

The place where you keep your boat may limit its use. The average small sailing cruiser

## The objectives of this chapter are to describe:

- The essential safety considerations for boat trailering.
- Important factors to consider when selecting a trailer.
- Available safety equipment.
- The fundamentals of trailer care and maintenance.
- Some of the legal requirements for trailering.
- How to ready a boat and trailer for traveling.
- Considerations for storing a boat and trailer.
- Preventing theft.
- The importance of filing and canceling a float plan.

goes about 4 knots (4.6 miles per hour). On a week-end cruise, with two days of sailing and 5 or 6 hours underway each day, your cruising range is limited to 25 miles or so.

If you dock your boat in a marina for the summer, you probably will cruise in the immediate area of the marina. But you may not be able to find space in a convenient marina, and even if you can, its hours may not be convenient for you or the price of storage may be beyond your means. So where does this leave you?

Trailering a boat has its good and bad points. If your boat is trailerable, you can start your vacation many miles from your usual cruising area and then visit places you don't normally see, while avoiding the costs and hazards of marinas. At season's end, you can store your boat at home and work on it at your convenience through the winter months.

This scenario also has a negative side, and the potential inconveniences of trailering are many. This chapter deals with the most common ones. Once you're comfortable with trailering, however, the good points outweigh the bad, which is why boat trailering has become increasingly popular in recent years. More than 95% of the recreational boats in the United States are trailerable.

# Legal Considerations

There are several legal considerations that affect boat trailering.

## WIDTH

One of the few absolute limits for trailering a boat is its width. Without a special permit, the widest boat you can trailer on many state roads is 8 feet. On interstate highways, some access roads, some state roads, and federally supported highways with 12-foot-wide lanes, the maximum width is 8.5 feet. These widths include both the boat and the trailer.

This width limitation indirectly limits the length of your boat. Practically speaking, a trailerable sailboat with an 8-foot beam is unlikely to be longer than 25 feet. Boats with unusual hull shapes, and especially multihulls, can pose special prob-

lems. Some trimarans are designed with folding *amas* (the outer hulls) to make them trailerable.

## BRAKES

Legal requirements for brakes vary from state to state. Most states require brakes on a trailer if it is designed for a *gross vehicle weight rating* (GVWR—the weight of the trailer and its load) of 3,000 or more pounds. In a few states that requirement is relaxed to 4,000 pounds or higher, and in others it's more stringent—1,500 or 2,000 pounds. The American Boat and Yacht Council recommends trailer brakes for a trailer with a GVWR of 1,500 or more pounds, and this conservative standard is our recommendation as well.

The typical 25-foot trailerable sailboat weighs in excess of 3,000 pounds unloaded; its gear and provisions can easily weigh a few hundred pounds, and a trailer big enough to carry a boat that heavy can easily weigh upward of a half ton. When you put all that together, it's easy to see that the GVWR of such a boat might be 5,000 pounds or more. Stated another way, some boats are more trailerable than others.

Even an 18- or 19-foot trailerable sailboat designed and equipped for overnight cruising is likely to weigh 1,600 to 1,900 pounds, with a GVWR on its trailer of more than 2,500 pounds. It's important to be realistic when you consider how much boat your vehicle can tow, and what you will need to do to be "street legal." We'll talk more about tow vehicle and trailer considerations later in this chapter.

There are three legal brake systems: electric, hydraulic (surge), and air. The trailer's brakes should activate automatically when the car's brakes are applied, and should continue to operate even if the trailer separates from your car. Since electric brakes have long been considered vulnerable to immersion of the trailer's wheels, hydraulic surge brakes are by far the most popular.

Surge brakes work from the trailer's momentum (Figures 6-1 and 6-2). When you apply your car's brakes, the trailer surges forward, depressing a piston in a hydraulic cylinder in its tongue and thereby activating its brakes through a closed hydraulic system. Part of the beauty of this system

## 2006 Towing Laws*

| State | Max. Towing Speed | Max. Trailer Length | Max. Trailer Width | Max. Trailer Height | Max. Overall Length | Weight Requiring Trailer Brakes |
|---|---|---|---|---|---|---|
| Alabama | 70 | 40' | 8' | 13'6" | 57' | 3,000 |
| Alaska | 55 | 40' | 8'6" | 14' | 75' | 5,000 |
| Arizona | 55 | 40' | 8' | 13'6" | 65' | 3,000 |
| Arkansas | 65 | 53'6" | 8'6" | 13'6" | 65' | 3,000 |
| California | 55 | 40' | 8'6" | 14' | 65' | 1,500 |
| Colorado | 65 | 45' | 8'6" | 14'6" | 70' | 3,000 |
| Connecticut | 65 | 45' | 8'6" | 13'6" | 60' | 3,000 |
| Delaware | 55 | 40' | 8'6" | 13'6" | 70' | 4,000 |
| Dist. of Columbia | 55 | 60' | 8' | 13' | 55' | 3,000 |
| Florida | 65 | 40' | 8'6" | 13'6" | 65' | 3,000 |
| Georgia | 55 | N/A | 8'6" | 13'6" | 60' | 3,000 |
| Hawaii | 55 | 40' | 9' | 14' | 65' | 3,000 |
| Idaho | 65 | 48' | 8'6" | 14' | 75' | 1,500 |
| Illinois | 55 | 60' | 8' | 13'6" | 65' | 3,000 |
| Indiana | 55 | 40' | 8'6" | 13'6" | 65' | 3,000 |
| Iowa | 65 | 48' | 8' | 14' | 70' | 3,000 |
| Kansas | 55 | 45' | 8'6" | 14' | 65' | N/A |
| Kentucky | 65 | N/A | 8' | 13'6" | 65' | N/A |
| Louisiana | 70 | 40' | 8' | 13'6" | 70' | 3,000 |
| Maine | 55 | 48' | 8'6" | 13'6" | 65' | 3,000 |
| Maryland | 65 | 40' | 8'6" | 13'6" | 55' | 3,000 |
| Massachusetts | 65 | 40' | 8'6" | 13'6" | 65' | N/A |
| Michigan | 55 | 45' | 8'6" | 13'6" | 65' | 3,000 |
| Minnesota | 70 | 45' | 8'6" | 13'6" | 60' | 3,000 |
| Mississippi | 55 | 40' | 8'6" | 13'6" | 53' | 2,000 |
| Missouri | 70 | N/A | 8' | 13'6" | 55' | N/A |
| Montana | 65 | N/A | 8'6" | 14' | 65' | 3,000 |
| Nebraska | 65 | 40' | 8'6" | 14'6" | 65' | 3,000 |
| Nevada | 65 | N/A | 8' | 14' | 70' | 3,000 |
| New Hampshire | 55 | 48' | 8'6" | 13'6" | N/A | N/A |
| New Jersey | 65 | 40' | 8'6" | 13'6" | 50' | N/A |
| New Mexico | 75 | 40' | 8'6" | 14' | 75' | 3,000 |
| New York | 65 | 48' | 8' | 13'6" | 65' | 3,000 |
| North Carolina | 55 | 35' | 8' | 13'6" | 60' | 4,000 |
| North Dakota | 70 | 53' | 8'6" | 14' | 75' | N/A |
| Ohio | 55 | 40' | 8'6" | 13'6" | 65' | 2,000 |
| Oklahoma | 65 | 40' | 8'6" | 13'6" | 65' | 3,000 |
| Oregon | 55 | 45' | 8'6" | 14' | 65' | N/A |
| Pennsylvania | 55 | 53' | 8'6" | 13'6" | 60' | 3,000 |
| Rhode Island | 65 | 48'6" | 8'6" | 13'6" | 60' | 4,000 |
| South Carolina | 55 | 48' | 8'6" | 13'6" | N/A | 3,000 |
| South Dakota | 65 | 53' | 8'6" | 14' | 80' | 3,000 |
| Tennessee | 70 | 48' | 8'6" | 13'6" | 65' | 3,000 |
| Texas | 70 | N/A | 8'6" | 13'6" | 65' | 4,500 |
| Utah | 65 | 40' | 8'6" | 14' | 65' | N/A |
| Vermont | 65 | 45' | 8'6" | 13'6" | 65' | 3,000 |
| Virginia | 55 | 45' | 8'6" | 13'6" | 65' | 3,000 |
| Washington | 60 | 48' | 8'6" | 14' | 60' | 3,000 |
| West Virginia | 65 | 40' | 8' | 13'6" | 75' | 3,000 |
| Wisconsin | 65 | 48' | 8'6" | 13'6" | 60' | 3,000 |
| Wyoming | 65 | 45' | 8'6" | 14' | 65' | N/A |

*Subject to change: check with your state or search online for updates.
SOURCE: *AAA DIGEST OF MOTOR LAWS*

**Figure 6-1.** A surge brake actuator mounted on a trailer tongue. Note that the light breakaway chain exiting the trailer coupling contains less slack than the heavier, crisscrossed safety chains beneath it. Should the trailer jump off the hitch, the breakaway chain will activate the trailer's brakes before the safety chains come taut. (PHOTO BY BOB DENNIS)

is that the braking response of the trailer is automatically proportional to the intensity of braking in the tow vehicle. If you have surge brakes, make sure the emergency brake cable that exits from the trailer's coupler is fastened by means of its S-hook to the tow vehicle or the hitch. That way, if the trailer breaks loose, this lightweight cable (sometimes it's a light chain rather than a cable) will come taut and engage the trailer brakes.

The problem with hydraulic surge brakes is that they are more often than not incompatible with a weight-distribution hitch (discussed later in this chapter). In order to derive the benefits of a weight-distribution hitch, you would probably need a trailer with electric brakes, which are activated by the tow vehicle's 12-volt system. The

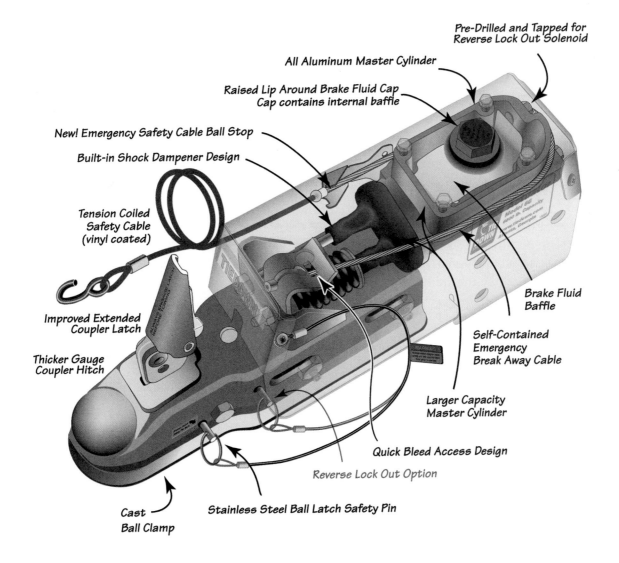

Pre-Drilled and Tapped for
Reverse Lock Out Solenoid

All Aluminum Master Cylinder

Raised Lip Around Brake Fluid Cap
Cap contains internal baffle

New! Emergency Safety Cable Ball Stop

Built-in Shock Dampener Design

Tension Coiled
Safety Cable
(vinyl coated)

Improved Extended
Coupler Latch

Thicker Gauge
Coupler Hitch

Brake Fluid
Baffle

Self-Contained
Emergency
Break Away Cable

Larger Capacity
Master Cylinder

Quick Bleed Access Design

Reverse Lock Out Option

Cast
Ball Clamp

Stainless Steel Ball Latch Safety Pin

**Figure 6-2.** Cutaway view of a surge brake actuator. (COURTESY TIE-DOWN ENGINEERING)

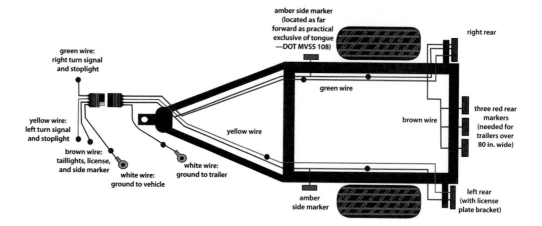

amber side marker
(located as far
forward as practical
exclusive of tongue
—DOT MVSS 108)

right rear

green wire:
right turn signal
and stoplight

green wire

three red rear
markers
(needed for
trailers over
80 in. wide)

brown wire

yellow wire:
left turn signal
and stoplight

yellow wire

brown wire:
taillights, license,
and side marker

white wire:
ground to trailer

white wire:
ground to vehicle

amber
side marker

left rear
(with license
plate bracket)

**Figure 6-3.** Typical trailer wiring setup. (COURTESY CEQUENT TOWING PRODUCTS)

good news is that more marine trailers are likely to be equipped with electric brakes in the future, now that brake manufacturers have overcome some of the problems of corroded wiring, solenoids, and connections that haunted the electric brakes of 20 years ago. Perhaps in another 10 or 20 years electric brakes will dominate boat trailers, enabling boaters to enjoy the benefits of load-equalizing hitches and antisway bars. As of this writing, however, the vast majority of boat trailers utilize hydraulic surge brakes.

## LIGHTS

Lights may be required on trailers in your state. Some states do not require trailer lights if the taillights, stoplights, and turn signals of the tow vehicle are not obscured by the trailer or the boat. Other states require trailers to have sidelights, taillights, stoplights, and turn signals under all conditions (Figure 6-3). Check with your automobile registration authority.

Pay special attention to the plug and socket that connect the car's lighting system to the trailer (Figure 6-4). The wiring should be under no stress, or tension, and should be as weatherproof as possible. It should not sag or loop so it can catch on anything, nor drag along the road. Use stranded wire because it reduces vibration damage. A good ground is necessary, so a ground wire may be needed between the car and trailer. The most frequent cause of trailer light failure is a poor ground.

You may want to add reflectors and taillights on your boat or trailer beyond those required by law since they increase safety at night. A heavy-duty flasher to control the turn signals when towing is also better than a normal flasher, which operates too fast under a heavy electrical load. If you have a heavy-duty flasher, though, you will not know if you have a burned-out turn signal bulb since the flash inside the car will continue to show. So check your bulbs from time to time. Flashers are easy to install.

A vehicle with separate turn signals and brake lights needs an adapter to match the car's lights to the trailer.

**Figure 6-4.** A four-prong harness connects the trailer's wiring with the vehicle's electrical system. The green wire from the vehicle feeds the trailer's right turn signal and brake lights, the yellow wire feeds the left turn signal and brake lights; the brown wire feeds the taillights; and the white wire is the ground. (PHOTO BY BOB DENNIS)

**Figure 6-5.** This extended side-view mirror shows the reflection of the boat trailer behind. (PHOTO BY LEN SCHULTE)

**Figure 6-6.** Safety chains attached to a trailer hitch with shackles rather than the standard S-hooks impart an added measure of safety. (PHOTO BY RAY PAGES)

## LICENSE PLATES

Most states require license plates for trailers. Check with your local authorities.

## MIRRORS

Your state may require extended side-view mirrors if the view through your vehicle's standard side mirrors is obscured (Figure 6-5). Even when not required, consider getting these mirrors to make your driving easier and safer.

## SAFETY CHAINS

Safety chains, which run from the tongue of the trailer to the towing hitch, are a legal requirement in most states. The chains should be just long enough to permit free turning and should be crossed under the hitch to form a cradle and then secured to the hitch. If the coupler fails, the cradle may keep the tongue from hitting the pavement and digging in, which could cause the trailer to cartwheel over the back of your vehicle.

If the chains have S-hooks, pass them through the eyes in the hitch from underneath. This way they will be less apt to jump out. Better still, use **shackles** as shown in Figure 6-6. These will not jiggle loose. If you use S-hooks, fasten them on with a piece of wire.

## OTHER LEGAL REQUIREMENTS

There are other legal requirements, such as the type of trailer hitch used. These are discussed in the sections that follow.

# Practical Considerations

In trailering your boat, you should be guided by several practical considerations.

## HULL SHAPE

Your boat's hull shape is a major factor in trailering. The ideal hull for trailering is flat-bottomed, though most small daysailers are easy enough to trailer and to launch. Sailboats with deeper hulls (i.e., having more **deadrise**), those with keel/centerboards, and especially those with fixed keels are the most difficult to support adequately on a trailer, and require deeper water for launching (Figures 6-7, 6-8, and 6-9). Whatever the hull shape, support it evenly on the trailer.

Consider the problem of fitting your boat to a trailer before buying the boat. Fortunately, most small boat designers have standard brands of trailers in mind when they design their hulls. Ask your dealer.

**Figure 6-7.** The West Wight Potter 15 is an easily trailerable pocket-cruising sailboat, great for overnighting on a big lake one day and on sheltered coastal waters the next. Its swing keel and kick-up rudder make it beachable—it draws a mere 7 inches of water with the keel up—and it is also easy to trailer. The keel weighs just 80 pounds, and the entire boat (unloaded) weighs just 475 pounds. Even when the 350-pound skid-type trailer and the motor, gear, and provisions are added in, the GVWR won't much exceed 1,000 pounds. (PHOTO BY JOHN ABREU)

**Figure 6-8.** This boat seems to have a fixed keel, which requires it to ride higher on the trailer than the boat in Figure 6-7. For that reason, this trailer uses height-adjustable pads rather than skids to support the boat. Note the tapered slot on the trailer bed that guides the keel home when the boat is recovered from the water. Like the West Wight Potter 15, and unlike the boat in Figure 6-9, this is a light boat, requiring only a single-axle trailer. (PHOTO BY NORMA LOCOCO)

You may also want to keep launching considerations in mind when you buy your boat. Considering the size and shape of the boat, are there facilities for launching it where you probably will use it? For example, fixed-keel and keel/centerboard sailboats are difficult to launch from a beach or even from a shallow launch ramp. In fact, fixed-

**Figure 6-9.** Trailering a fixed-keel sailboat represents the greatest challenge of all. (PHOTO BY BOB DENNIS)

keel sailboats are most easily launched from a lift. Is the water deep enough at the launch site so a particular boat can be launched? (Note: If you can't float your boat at your local launch ramp without submerging your tow vehicle's rear wheels and/or exhaust pipe, you may be able to solve the problem by buying a tongue extension for your trailer or having one fabricated. The extension—complete with its own hitch coupler—retracts beneath the tongue when not in use; see Figure 6-12. After you arrive at the launch site, extending it will add 5 to 10 feet between your trailer tongue and hitch ball. Do **not** keep the tongue extender deployed while towing.)

## SELECTING YOUR TRAILER

There are also important considerations in selecting a trailer.

### Your Trailer's Size

A trailer's class depends on its own weight and the weight of its load. When considering the load, remember the weight you will add to the boat, including the weight of things such as an outboard motor, gasoline, provisions, and gear. Trailer classes are given in Table 6-1.

Federal law requires that trailers show their GVWR. Add the weight of the boat, its contents, and its motor to that of the trailer. If the sum is within 15% of the GVWR of the trailer, select the next larger class of trailer. On multiaxle trailers, the combined **gross axle weight rating** (GAWR) of all axles must be at least equal to the GVWR.

| TABLE 6-1 | Trailer Classes |
| --- | --- |
| **Class** | **Gross Weight of Trailer and Load (lbs.)** |
| 1 | No more than 2,000 |
| 2 | 2,001–3,500 |
| 3 | 3,501–5,000 |
| 4 | More than 5,000 |

If you are planning to pull a load of 4,000 pounds or more, you will want a multiaxle, tandem trailer. Such trailers have four wheels rather than two. A powerful towing vehicle, most likely with a special towing package (see below), will also be needed.

## Types of Trailers

The three types of boat trailers in use for sailboats are skid, roller-supporting, and screw-pad.

**SKID TRAILERS.** These trailers, also called bunker trailers, have carpet-covered rails, sometimes simple 2 x 4s or 2 x 6s (Figures 6-10 and 6-11), that are called **bunkers.** The boat floats off or onto these when you launch or retrieve it. The simplest type has only two bunkers and is used for small centerboard or daggerboard boats with flat or slightly rounded bottoms (for example, a Laser or Sunfish). Larger bunker trailers for larger, deeper sailboats

**Figure 6-10.** The vertical posts on the rear quarters of this skid- or bunker-type trailer help guide the boat onto the trailer when the trailer is submerged. Some boaters mount their trailer's taillights and brake lights on posts like these to keep them out of the water. (PHOTO BY BOB DENNIS)

have multiple bunkers at various heights (Figure 6-12). Because sailboats are more prone than powerboats to tipping on a trailer, these will almost certainly include a pair of raised bunkers to nestle

**Figure 6-11.** A skid trailer emerging from the water after launch. (COURTESY NATIONAL MARINE MANUFACTURERS ASSOCIATION)

**Figure 6-12.** This bunker-style single-axle trailer for a small keel sailboat shows a tongue extension in its retracted position and the tall winch stand required for a keel sailboat trailer. (COURTESY TRAIL "N" SAIL SAILBOAT TRAILERS)

**Figure 6-13.** This tandem-axle trailer supports most of the boat's weight under its keel, while four screw pads balance and steady the load. A keelboat of this size is not conveniently trailerable. In fact, this one probably has to be hoisted in and out of the trailer—note the absence of a winch stand—which means it must be launched and recovered at a marina or boatyard, not an ordinary launch ramp. (PHOTO BY BRIAN SHENSTONE, COURTESY LOADMASTER TRAILER COMPANY, LTD.)

up under the port and starboard bilges of a fixed-keel or keel/centerboard boat. You may also see a pair of keel-guide bunkers just above the trailer bed to trap the keel and keep it from shifting sideways, and a keel-support bunker in the trailer bed to receive the weight of the keel. When raised bunkers are used they are usually carefully curved to follow the hull curves, and they may be divided into forward and after segments to permit the boat to be lifted in slings by a crane or Travelift. You might be able to adjust the height of the bunkers within modest limits to conform to the slope of your boat bottom and offer maximum support to the hull, but sailboat trailers in general are much more boat specific than powerboat trailers.

Boat hulls can sag or warp if stored on trailers that are not adjusted to give them maximum support. This can cause serious problems such as a warped or jammed centerboard or swing-keel trunk, broken bulkheads, and broken stringers.

It is a good idea to have the dealer fit the trailer to the boat. Adjusting bunkers or rollers with a boat on the trailer is next to impossible if the boat is much larger than a Sunfish, and the dealer will have a hoist to raise and lower the boat while fitting it to its trailer. Check the trailer's fitting bolts from time to time. Are they tight? Take appropriate wrenches with you when towing the boat.

**ROLLER-SUPPORTING TRAILERS.** On a roller-supporting trailer, rollers give support to the boat and aid in launching and retrieving it. Some sailboat trailers incorporate rollers in combination with bunkers, but rollers are much less common in sailboat trailers than in powerboat trailers simply because the hull curves of a sailboat are more conducive to floating than to rolling on and off a trailer.

Some roller-equipped small-sailboat trailers, called tilt trailers, are hinged somewhere along their tongues, and unlocking the hinge allows the trailer to tilt up or down. When it's time to launch the boat, releasing a pin tilts the trailer up, and the boat slides into the water. To retrieve the boat, you tilt up the trailer. As the boat is pulled up on the trailer, the trailer returns to its original position and locks shut. If your trailer has this mechanism, check to see that the pin is in place before pulling your boat up the ramp.

One advertised advantage of a tilt trailer for a very light boat is that you do not have to get your tow vehicle close to the water. In theory, with a small sailing dinghy, you might not even have to back the trailer wheels into the water. This is helpful when a ramp stops at the water's edge, as it sometimes does at deep-water launching sites. It is also good when launching in salt water. Wheel rims immersed in salt water can rust, and when they do, tubeless tires will not hold air. Tilt trailers are less common now than they once were, however, because they've proved less easy to use than advertised.

**SCREW-PAD TRAILERS.** Trailers using screw pads, or poppets, are at least as common as bunker trailers for sailboats larger than 18 to 20 feet, especially for fixed-keel boats (Figures 6-13 and 6-14). When screw pads are used they support the boat only at four or six discrete points rather than distributing the load over the lengths of bunkers, so their placement is critical. The pads must bear against local strong points on the hull—for example, against locations that are reinforced on the interior by bulkheads. A failure to do this could result in damage to hull laminate from long-term flexing or a sudden jolt on a bumpy road.

## Other Considerations

When you're towing a keelboat or a keel/centerboarder, the bunkers or screw pads do not support

**Figure 6-14.** A screw-pad trailer designed to carry a J/24. Note the keel-guide bunkers, the keel support, and the tandem axles—the latter being necessary for any load of over 4,000 pounds or so. The J/24 (perhaps the most popular keel sailboat worldwide) has a designed displacement of 3,100 pounds. This trailer weighs 1,000 pounds and is designed for a GVWR (boat + trailer + gear and provisions) of 5,400 pounds. You would need a powerful tow vehicle and hitch to tow that much weight. (COURTESY TRAIL "N" SAIL SAILBOAT TRAILERS)

most of its weight. Rather, their purpose is to keep the boat upright while the majority of the weight is borne on the trailer frame directly beneath the keel. Obviously, this part of the trailer must be engineered to bear this heavy concentration of weight. If you see any sign of inward flexing where a bunker or pad bears against the bilge, it's a good bet that the support in question needs to be lowered.

In contrast, trailers for sailboats with swing keels or centerboards support the boat in a manner similar to powerboat trailers, with conventional bunkers or rollers bearing most of the hull weight. Even if this is the case, however, the trailer should have a cross member to support the weight of the keel or centerboard, which should be lowered before you hit the highway. Otherwise, the weight of the swing keel or centerboard would rest entirely on a single pivot bolt and on the lifting mechanism, which is often just a single, light-weight cable or line. Towing your boat with the weight of the appendage supported by its pivot bolt and lifting mechanism can easily result in expensive damage to both, and to the fiberglass trunk through which the pivot bolt passes.

It is worthwhile to lower even a light centerboard before towing, although in this instance, if your trailer lacks a centerboard support as an integral part of the frame, you may be able to clamp a piece of 2 x 4 or 2 x 6 across the frame to serve the purpose. Lower the swing keel or centerboard onto its support before towing or storing the boat, taking weight off the pin and pendant, and remember to raise the board before launching.

## CARE OF YOUR TRAILER

Your trailer will last longer and serve better if you care for it properly.

### Wheel Bearings

Bearings exposed to water, especially salt water, may seize up, and when they do they are useless. If they seize up on the road, they create a dangerous situation. A device called a **wheel-bearing protector**, or **Bearing Buddy** (Figure 6-15), is designed to keep water out of the bearings. This plastic cylinder, which you push into place on the wheel hub where the dustcap would otherwise be, contains a

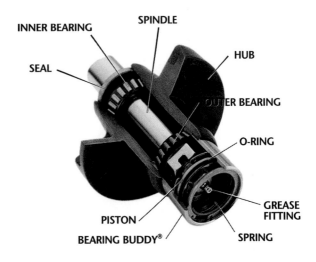

**Figure 6-15.** Cutaway view of a Bearing Buddy pushed into place on a wheel hub. (COURTESY BEARING BUDDY, INC.)

spring-loaded piston and has a grease fitting on its end similar to those used for lubricating automobiles (often called a zerk fitting). Using a small grease gun (that you should carry in your tow vehicle), fill the bearing protectors with grease just before you launch.

Why should you do this? Because when riding down the highway, even well-lubricated bearings warm up. Sometimes they get hot. When immersed in cold water, the hubs cool rapidly and a partial vacuum results. Were it not for the bearing protectors, water would rush into the wheel hubs. With protectors in place, however, the hub will pull in grease instead of water—at least in theory. Even so, some water may enter the hub. It makes good sense to use a good-quality marine wheel bearing grease on your bearings and to keep the hubs out of the water whenever possible, even if you have wheel-bearing protectors. If you must immerse your bearings, let them cool off first. Always carry spare bearings, grease, and tools for replacing bearings when trailering on a highway. It may be impossible on a Sunday afternoon to find bearings to fit your trailer.

### Trailer Lights

If possible, mount the trailer lights on a removable board, and remove it before backing the trailer into the water (Figure 6-16). Boards such as these usually clamp on the boat's transom. No lighting system can tolerate repeated immersion, even lights that supposedly keep water out. "Waterproof"

**Figure 6-16.** Two boaters clamp removable trailer lights to their boat's transom. (PHOTO BY KIM JOHNS)

trailer lights are more water-resistant than waterproof, and this goes double for salt water.

If your trailer lights are not on a removable board, disconnect them before backing down a ramp. Applying the brakes heats the bulbs and they may crack when they contact cold water.

Always carry spare bulbs. Lights on trailers receive rougher treatment than lights on automobiles. If your lights fail and the bulbs seem okay, polish the terminals with a piece of fine sandpaper. Even a small amount of corrosion will keep bulbs from lighting. The same thing applies to the boat's lights.

Always carry highway safety flares, a trouble flag, and trouble lights for use along the road. It is not advisable to store highway flares aboard your boat, however, as they represent a fire hazard there.

## Trailer Tires

Trailer tires require special attention. The chances are good that they will rot of old age before their treads are gone. This comes partially from the conditions under which trailers are stored, and partially from overheating. The number one enemy of tires is heat. Watch for spiderweb cracking on the sidewalls, which is a sign of old age.

**TIRE PRESSURE AND TIRE LIFE.** The portion of a tire in contact with the road surface is continually flexing. Trailer tires are often smaller than those used on automobiles, which means that they spin and flex many more times per mile than a tow vehi-

cle's tires do. When tires flex, they get hot, and eventually they may blow. Therefore, it is important when trailering your boat to check the temperature of the trailer's tires and wheel hubs at rest stops. A hot or excessively warm tire or hub may indicate an impending problem.

Reduce excessive tire wear by keeping trailer tires properly inflated according to the manufacturer's recommendation. Small trailer tires carry high air pressures (60 pounds per square inch is common), which reduces flexing and heating.

The correct pressure for tires is usually stamped on their sidewalls. Inflate them correctly; above all, do not underinflate them. Carry a pressure gauge and check tire pressures often, but be careful. Each time you check a tire's pressure, some air escapes, and you don't have to let much air out of a small tire to reduce its pressure significantly.

Trailer tires normally do not require balancing. If your trailer bounces when being pulled, however, either with or without a load, consider having them balanced.

Your tow vehicle's tires may also need to be inflated for the added load of the boat and trailer. Your vehicle owner's manual should state the correct tire pressure for tires when carrying a heavy load; if it doesn't, the trailer owner's manual may.

**CHANGING A TIRE.** Regardless of how well you care for your trailer tires, sooner or later you may have to change a flat tire. Chances are that this will occur on a weekend when the stores are closed, which is when most people trailer their boats. Be prepared! Always carry a mounted spare tire and wheel, and check to see that it is properly inflated.

A spare tire will not do you any good if you do not have a lug wrench that fits the trailer's lugs. Get one of the correct size with a handle long enough and sturdy enough to loosen the lugs. Since the lugs were probably put on with a pneumatic wrench, they may be more than hand-tight.

In most cases, your car's jack will not work on your trailer. Buy a special jack to take with you and don't forget its handle. You should also carry a strong board or something similar to give the jack support on a soft shoulder.

A scissors-type jack will probably work (Figure 6-17), but make sure that it can be lowered enough to fit under the trailer's axle when a tire is flat.

**Figure 6-17.** A scissors-type jack in use to change a trailer tire. (PHOTO BY RAY PAGES)

If you have a flat tire, drive completely off the road if possible, but not onto soft ground. Gather all your tools, including the mounted spare tire, and check to see that you will not have a problem jacking the trailer. Then, before jacking up the trailer, use the wrench to loosen the lugs slightly since you may find it impossible to loosen them when the wheel is up in the air. Jack up the trailer, put on the new tire and tighten the lugs moderately, and lower the trailer. Then make certain that the lugs are tightened securely.

If you can't get your jack under the trailer's axle for any reason, consider putting the spare tire flat on the ground in front of the blown tire; then pull the trailer up on the spare with your car. You should now have enough room to put the jack under the axle.

## OTHER PRACTICAL CONSIDERATIONS

There are other factors you must consider for your safety and the protection of your load.

### Fire Extinguishers

Keep a fire extinguisher readily available when trailering. Overheated bearings can catch fire, or someone might carelessly throw a cigarette in your boat and cause a fire. If the boat is covered with a tarpaulin, a cigarette could land on it and you would not be able to get to the boat's extinguisher.

Consider mounting an extinguisher on the winch stem or in your car's trunk. Wherever it is, be certain it is readily accessible.

### Winches

A winch is an invaluable aid when retrieving a boat. Two types are available: a manually operated one, which is usually standard equipment (see, for example, Figure 6-13); and an electrically powered one, which is optional. An electrically powered winch operates off the automobile battery and often requires special wiring. The cables to complete this wiring are usually packed with a new winch. Electric winches are recommended for powerboats longer than 16 feet, but since a large sailboat must be floated rather than skidded onto its trailer during retrieval, an electric winch is probably not necessary.

The line on a winch is generally either polypropylene or steel wire, though sometimes it is a web belt. If you have an electric winch, the line will be steel wire. Steel wire is also recommended for any vessel 16 feet or longer, since polypropylene deteriorates in sunlight and may not hold your boat. Nylon stretches too much and is therefore not used on winches.

The primary point of attachment of the boat to the trailer is at the winch. Be certain the winch has a good antireverse mechanism and keep it in good working order. But don't rely on it; after your boat is on the trailer, you should also tie the boat's towing eye to the stem of the winch. The usual ratchet-type antireverse mechanism is small enough that you don't want to trust your boat's security to it.

### Tie-Downs

Use a **tie-down** from the towing eye of your boat (if it has one, as many small sailboats do) to the tongue of the trailer (Figure 6-18) to secure it firmly to the

**Figure 6-18.** Cinching a strap from the towing eye to the trailer frame to prevent sway. This is a powerboat, but the precaution is equally applicable to a sailboat with a towing eye. (PHOTO BY BOB DENNIS)

**Figure 6-19.** A transom tie-down strap, shown here on a powerboat. (PHOTO BY BOB DENNIS)

**Figure 6-20.** A trailer's axle and leaf springs are prime places for rust to form. (PHOTO BY JUNE ESPARZA)

trailer. This way the bow of the boat will still be secure even if the winch stem comes loose.

If there are **lifting rings** on the transom, tie lines from each ring to the trailer (Figure 6-19). If you can't get these lines tight enough, consider buying winching straps made for this purpose.

The best lashing for larger sailboats consists of tie-down straps made of webbing that stretch across the boat and hook to either side of the trailer. These straps are available with ratchet mechanisms that enable you to cinch them tight. If you use straps, place cushioning material under them to keep from marring the boat's varnish or gelcoat. Lash your boat down in this fashion even if it seems to be securely trapped inside its bunkers or screw pads.

### Rust and Breakdowns

If your trailer isn't galvanized, you need to be on the lookout for rust. Iron and steel are subject to rusting, which can be especially heavy if they are exposed to salt water or air. Touch up rust spots as they occur by sanding off the rust with emery cloth and spraying the areas with galvanizing paint or another rust-resistant paint.

Pay special attention to keeping the springs and axles on the trailer rust free (Figure 6-20). If they become rusted, replace the springs or reinforce the axles. Both are subject to heavy strains on the highway and may break, causing serious damage to you, your tow vehicle, and your boat. As with other aspects of trailering, an ounce of prevention is worth a pound of cure.

# The Towing Vehicle

Your vehicle is an important part of the towing package. Most vehicles are not designed, however, to trailer a boat. If yours has front-wheel drive, it is even less capable of trailering.

To steer properly, a vehicle must have enough weight on its front axles, but when weight is added to the rear of a vehicle, the front end lifts, which makes it difficult to control. Weight in the rear also affects the traction of a front-wheel-drive vehicle, as well as the focus of the headlights and the driver's view. In addition, it places a strain on the vehicle's rear tires, shocks, and springs.

The typical front-wheel-drive compact car has a gross weight of about 2,800 pounds. The owner's manual for such a vehicle typically says that it should not pull a trailer weighing more than 800 to 1,000 pounds unless the trailer has brakes. (This maximum tow weight is typically twice as high for a medium-sized car and five or more times higher for a large car, SUV, or pickup.) With trailer brakes and a manual transmission, a compact car can pull 2,200 pounds up hills with less than a 12% slope. It can pull the same 2,200 pounds up a 16% slope if it has an automatic transmission.

Your tow vehicle needs enough power to merge safely with highway traffic when towing its maximum load. It must also be able to climb hills without loss of speed. This usually justifies choosing the largest power package possible when you're buying a vehicle that will be used for towing.

## TOWING PACKAGE

Unless the vehicle is specially equipped, do not tow a trailer that weighs more than the vehicle. Many manufacturers sell towing packages, which are not expensive if ordered with the car. If ordered later, their cost may be prohibitive. Towing packages include several modifications for your car.

### Cooling

When a car is pulling a boat, it uses more energy than usual, which produces more heat. You will need a heavy-duty, high-capacity radiator that has more core tubes to aid heat release. It may also have a special fan shroud. A thermostat-controlled spraying unit may also be available to spray cool water on the radiator if the coolant temperature goes too high.

### Transmission

Towing a trailer places an extra load on a car's transmission. This may thin out its fluid and damage it. A small supplemental radiator to cool the transmission fluid is often available. Be alert to transmission leaks, slippage, or rough shifting.

### Brakes

A towing package also includes oversized brake drums and/or special heavy-duty brake linings for the tow vehicle. Standard auto brakes are too small for towing all but very light trailers. Premium brake linings are essential.

### Suspension System

A tongue weight of 100 pounds has the same effect as putting 400 pounds in the trunk of a car. To avoid sagging and bottoming out, you need heavy-duty springs and extra-large or air-adjustable shock absorbers. These allow the tow vehicle to ride nearly level, which also improves visibility and handling.

### Other Equipment

The trailering package may also contain a larger battery, and a larger alternator for charging it. The tow vehicle probably will have oversized tires and a lower gear ratio in its differential.

# Trailer Hitches

Three types of trailer hitches are available. The first two hold the entire tongue weight of the trailer, while the third distributes the load to all four wheels of the tow vehicle.

## BUMPER HITCHES

*Bumper hitches* are the simplest trailer hitches, merely clamping on the bumper of the tow vehicle. They are illegal in many states, however, because they don't offer enough support for a boat trailer. Modern bumpers, usually made of a lightweight aluminum alloy, are not strong enough for this purpose and may twist out of shape. Most molded bumpers will not accept a bumper hitch in any event, and even if one could, a bumper hitch is not recommended.

Step-bumper hitches, which are mounted on many light trucks (Figure 6-21), are something else again; if your vehicle has one of these, it may be ac-

**Figure 6-21.** A step bumper hitch on a pickup truck. (PHOTO BY JIM FRIJOUF)

ceptable for towing a boat. Check the tow rating in your owner's manual. Some step bumpers are for light duty only and—despite having a hole to accept a hitch ball—do not have tow ratings.

## WEIGHT-CARRYING HITCHES

*Weight-carrying hitches* are available for most vehicle models. They bolt to the vehicle's frame and are rated in parallel with trailer ratings (Figure 6-22). Most are stamped with the total weight they can pull and the tongue weight they can support.

A Class I, or light-duty, hitch attaches to at least two points on the vehicle's frame and may also attach to the bumper, though this is not recommended. The maximum tongue weight on a Class I hitch should not exceed 150 pounds, and for many cars it should not be more than 100 pounds.

**Figure 6-22.** An array of frame-mounted hitches. **Top to bottom:** Class I, Class II, Class III, and Class IV. (COURTESY CEQUENT TOWING PRODUCTS)

Its maximum load is 2,000 pounds, which means it can tow a small daysailer or even one of the smaller trailer-sailing cruisers such as the West Wight Potter 15-footer (475 pounds displacement) or the Precision 18 (1,100 pounds displacement). But if you want to tow a somewhat larger daysailer or trailerable cruiser—say, the Catalina 18 (1,500 pounds) or the Montgomery 17 (1,600 pounds)— you're going to be towing more than 2,000 pounds once the weights of the trailer, outboard motor, gear, and provisions are accounted for.

A Class II, or regular-duty, hitch is entirely frame mounted at multiple attachment points and should be professionally installed. This hitch can pull up to 3,500 pounds and support a tongue weight up to 300 or so pounds. Class II hitches are available with the ball mount built into the hitch frame or as receiver-type models, in which the ball mount is inserted into a square receiver and secured with a pin.

A Class III, or heavy-duty, hitch can tow up to 5,000 pounds and support a tongue weight up to 500 pounds, and will almost certainly need to be mated with a truck or heavy-duty SUV.

A Class IV, or extra-heavy-duty, hitch can tow up to 10,000 pounds of towing weight and support 1,000 pounds of tongue weight. You would probably need a Class IV hitch to tow a J/24.

## WEIGHT-DISTRIBUTING HITCHES

A *weight-distributing hitch*, also sometimes known as a load-equalizing hitch, shifts some of the trailer's tongue weight from the rear axle to the front axle of the tow vehicle, which reduces tow vehicle wear and gives the driver more stability and better handling.

In a weight-distributing system, the standard ball-mount platform is replaced in the hitch receiver by a ball-mount assembly that includes two sockets. Each socket receives the hitch end of a steel bar; the other end of the bar rides beneath the trailer tongue, to which it is attached by a chain (Figure 6-23). Shortening the chain puts tension on the bar, which provides lift at the hitch frame and corresponding downward pressure on the front axle. Many Class III and IV hitch receivers will accept a weight-distributing ball-mount assembly, as will some Class II hitches. If your trailer is depressing

**Figure 6-23.** This weight-distributing (or load-equalizing) hitch from Draw-Tite also has antisway bars. The steel spring bars are sometimes called equalizing bars. Note that both the spring bars and the antisway bars can interfere with surge brake operation. Do not use a weight-distributing and/or antisway hitch without manufacturer or dealer advice and installation. (COURTESY CEQUENT TOWING PRODUCTS)

**Figure 6-24.** A ball-mount platform being slid into its hitch receiver. (PHOTO BY BOB DENNIS)

the back end of your tow vehicle and noticeably impairing its handling, this might seem like the ideal solution, except that a weight-distributing hitch should not be used with hydraulic surge brakes because it can render the brakes inoperative. The hitch manufacturer or the manufacturer of your trailer's surge coupler can advise you further on this.

Some hitches come with antisway bars that help control trailer sway and further improve control. Be aware that these too are likely to interfere with the normal operation of a surge brake coupler. If your trailer has electric brakes (this remains uncommon on boat trailers), ask the manufacturer about the benefits of a weight-distributing hitch and antisway bars.

## TRAILER BALL AND COUPLER

The trailer hitch has a ball-mount platform that the trailer coupler attaches to (Figure 6-24). Balls come in several different diameters; the most common are $1\frac{7}{8}$ inches, 2 inches, and $2\frac{5}{16}$ inches. A $1\frac{7}{8}$-inch ball is used only with Class I (tow weight up to 2,000 pounds) hitches and trailers. A 2-inch ball is limited to Class II (up to 3,500 pounds) or Class III (up to 5,000 pounds) hitches and trailers, depending on the capacity stamped on the ball. Class IV setups require a $2\frac{5}{16}$-inch ball.

You should always use the correct ball for your trailer's load and its coupler. A trailer coupler designed for a larger ball may seem to fit on a smaller one, but it is dangerous to do this since the coupler might come loose on the highway.

It is sometimes possible to put a coupler on a larger ball than it is designed for, but again, don't do this. It will bind, and the trailer will not track

correctly. The threaded shanks of balls vary with the size of the ball. If a smaller ball than required is used, you are also using an undersized shank that could shear.

The trailer's coupler determines the size of the ball, which in turn is determined by the GVWR of the trailer. All couplers manufactured after 1973 have the GVWR they can support stamped on them.

Carry an extra ball with you, and a wrench to install it with, as wear and turning stresses may force a ball out of round. Secure the ball with a lock washer and nut, and then grease it before coupling the trailer to it.

There are two types of couplers—latch or screw (Figure 6-25). If you have a latch coupler,

**Figure 6-25.** Screw-type (top) and latch-type (bottom) trailer couplers. (PHOTOS BY NORMA LOCOCO AND BOB DENNIS)

secure it with a padlock or a pin to keep it from coming loose. A padlock also protects your trailer against theft, an important consideration when leaving your car and trailer at a public ramp.

# Balancing the Load

Balancing the load on your trailer is an important factor in successful towing; 5% to 10% of the total weight of the tow (boat + motor + contents + trailer) should be on the tongue. If you have much more than this, the front end of your tow vehicle may lift up while the rear squats, making the vehicle hard to handle. If you have less than this, the trailer is likely to fishtail, which is dangerous and difficult to control. The wind from a large truck could then cause you to have a serious accident.

Compact cars, and some midsize cars, will not accept more than 100 pounds of tongue weight. Any additional weight will overload the car. Since tongue weight is roughly 5% to 10% of trailer weight, this means that a gross weight of 2,000 pounds is the maximum such a car should tow. Remember that this 2,000 pounds includes the weight of the trailer, boat, motor, and the boat's contents (Figure 6-26). As already mentioned, larger cars, pickups, and SUVs can tow heavier loads.

To measure tongue weight, load your boat with the gear it usually carries. Then stack a couple of cinder blocks in the driveway and put your bathroom scale on the stack. On top of this put something to protect the scale. The total height should be the same as the height of the trailer ball above the ground. Now lower the trailer tongue onto the scale.

You can adjust the weight on the tongue in two ways. The simpler way is to move the load inside the boat. If too little weight is on the tongue, move the equipment forward in the boat. (That may well include moving a bracket-mounted outboard to secure stowage on the cockpit or cabin floor, since you should not, in any case, tow the boat with an outboard mounted on its bracket.) If you have too much tongue weight, move the equipment aft.

More serious weight adjustments entail shifting the boat forward or back on the trailer. The winch stems of most trailers can be moved forward or backward on the tongue if necessary.

Determine the trailer's GVWR by adding the weight of the trailer, the boat and motor, and the equipment. Your dealer can tell you the weight of the trailer, boat, and motor. Estimate the weight of your equipment.

To get a more accurate measure, take the rig to the nearest platform scale, which can be found at highway weighing stations, building supply companies, trucking companies, or junkyards. As a last resort, the local moving company will know where scales are located.

If the tongue weight of the trailer is 70 to 75 pounds or more, consider fixing an accessory jack and dolly wheel to it (Figure 6-27). It will be easier to move the boat, and the jack can be used to

**Figure 6-26.** A rusted trailer tongue broke, causing this mishap. (PHOTO BY BARBARA ESTES)

**Figure 6-27.** A trailer tongue supported above the pavement by a jack and dolly wheel. (PHOTO BY JUNE ESPARZA)

raise or lower the tongue to couple it to your car. You can also raise the jack to its highest point to allow the boat to drain when stored.

# Handling Your Trailer

If you have never handled a trailer before, drive it to a large, empty parking lot some Sunday afternoon and practice backing and parking.

On the way to the parking lot, accelerate slowly from stops and take your vehicle smoothly and gently through gear changes. This will help you get used to your reduced acceleration and longer stopping distances. Think twice before passing another car. If you decide to pass, pick a spot and go. Don't hesitate. Remember that when you turn a corner your trailer will turn inside the arc of your tow vehicle, so be sure to swing wide enough that you don't hit curbs or other cars waiting in the cross street (Figure 6-28). When turning, check traffic behind and alongside and give others plenty of warning with your turn signal.

Underway, remember that you have a long, heavy, awkward "tail" behind you. This is easy to forget, especially when returning to your lane after passing another vehicle.

Remain sensitive to any unusual sounds. If you notice anything at all out of the ordinary, pull over and check. On the highway, check out the entire rig every hour or so. Check the temperature of the wheel hubs and tires by touching them, and check tie-downs, wheel lugs, and trailer bolts. If you are using a heavy-duty flasher, check for burned-out bulbs by turning them on and walking around the car and trailer.

**Figure 6-28.** When pulling a trailer, swing wide in order to take a tight corner. (PHOTO BY BOB DENNIS)

When you reach the parking lot, practice turning. Light poles are excellent for learning how to judge your swing at corners. But be careful—you don't want to buy one!

The main thing to practice is backing up. This can be difficult, especially if you have a short trailer. In fact, the shorter the trailer, the more difficult it is to back. If your trailer is shorter than your automobile, you have a very difficult problem. The trick is to back slowly and not allow the trailer to get much out of line with the towing vehicle.

It is easier to back if you place your hand on the bottom of the steering wheel instead of its top. Then turn your head and watch where you are going. When you want the trailer to go to the left, move your hand on the wheel to the left. To make the trailer go to the right, move your hand to the right.

Work out a set of hand signals with your partner for things such as "continue," "stop," "left," and "right," and rely on these rather than oral directions, which can be hard to hear. The driver can lose sight of the trailer as it starts down many ramps, making a partner indispensable.

# Predeparture Checks

Some things should be done before the day you go. These pertain to the trailer, the boat and its motor, and the tow vehicle.

## CHECK YOUR TRAILER

The two most important items in a predeparture check of your trailer are its wheel bearings and the amount of air in its tires. Have a regular schedule of maintenance for wheel bearings, and clean and repack them at regular intervals or after they have been immersed in water. Before departing, check the air pressure in the trailer's tires.

Assemble the emergency equipment, parts, and tools to take with you. You might want to make a checklist to remind you to do things such as inflate your spare tire and take it along, and to take your jack, lug wrench, spare bearings and grease, spare bulbs, spare fuses, wrenches, trouble flag, and trouble lights.

Before setting out, see that items in your boat are secured, and make certain that no one has tossed in last-minute items that may significantly alter your trailer's balance.

Did you grease the ball before coupling? Is the coupler locked? Are electrical connections made and are the lights and electric brakes, if you have them, working? Are the turn signals working? Are the safety chains in place—crisscrossed under the trailer tongue and hooked securely into the hitch with enough slack to permit turning, but no excess? If your trailer has surge brakes, is the breakaway cable hooked up with enough slack for turns but not so much that it would fail to engage before the safety chains came taut? Have you installed the heavy-duty flasher?

If your boat has a bracket-mounted outboard motor on its transom, have you removed this from the bracket and stowed it securely inboard? A 40- or 50-pound motor bouncing up and down over the road on a bracket is an accident waiting to happen. Are your tie-downs secured? If your trailer has a tilt bed, is the pivot point properly locked? If the trailer has a dolly wheel or tongue jack, is it locked in the "up" position? Is the boat's bow held firmly to the bow stop on the winch stem not just by the winch cable, but also with a line from the boat's towing eye—assuming it has one—to the winch stem and another from the towing eye down to the trailer tongue?

## ✓ TRAILERING CHECKLIST

- ☐ Is boat securely attached to trailer?
- ☐ Is ball locked in socket?
- ☐ Are safety chains in place?
- ☐ Is dolly wheel retracted?
- ☐ Is electrical connection secure?
- ☐ Are brake lights and turn signals working?
- ☐ Are trailer tires properly inflated?
- ☐ Is trailer load properly balanced?
- ☐ Is outboard motor properly secured?
- ☐ Have wheel bearings been checked recently?

The mast and boom should be firmly lashed down, preferably in a padded rack. Some trailerable-boat manufacturers supply just such a fitting, but you can usually rig one yourself. The standing and running rigging should be bundled together and tied to the spar at intervals so as not to work loose. If you travel rough roads or long distances, consider a covering for at least the winch cluster at the base of the spar and the sheave arrangement at the masthead, just to keep out highway dirt. If the mast protrudes aft, it should have a red flag lashed to its end.

If your boat's rudder is removable, it should be removed before trailering. A swing-keel or weighted centerboard should be lowered until it rests on a frame cross member. As mentioned, this will save much wear on the centerboard pendant (the wire rope used to raise the centerboard) and a certain amount of stress on the hull as well.

You may wish to add items to the checklist. Whatever you do, review it thoroughly before you go.

# Preparing to Launch

At the ramp, pull to one side and let your bearings cool down. While waiting, prepare your boat for launching; this way you will hold up other people as little as possible once you've moved to the ramp. Here, again, it is good to have a checklist.

If there is a cover on your boat, remove it and store it in the tow vehicle. Next, undo the tie-downs and put in the drain plug if your boat has one. It is surprising how easy it is to overlook this important item—until your boat slowly sinks into the water after you launch! If your boat is equipped with automatic bailers at the aft end of the cockpit, these too may need to be locked shut before you launch.

When launching a sailboat, you must step its mast (see below). Before doing so, check to see what is overhead. Are there any low power lines? Many municipal ramps were designed for skiffs and small powerboats, not masted vessels. If your mast should fall, are there overhead obstructions it could hit? This is especially important if electrical wires are present, since an aluminum mast and electrified wires are a dangerous mixture. Also check to see that you have a clear overhead path from where you are to the ramp and beyond.

If there is a finger pier, and if your mast is difficult to raise, you may prefer to wait to raise it until you are tied up to the pier, where it will be easier.

Check to see that nothing is protruding from the boat to snag on the trailer frame. Is the daggerboard or centerboard pulled all the way into the well and is the pendant lashed down? If your boat has a kick-up rudder, is it fastened in the "up" position? And if the rudder is removable, is it stowed inboard, as it should be for the launch? If your boat has a transom-mounted outboard motor, you should have stowed it securely inboard while towing. Now is the time to install it on its bracket and hook up the fuel line. Keep the bracket raised and the motor tilted up while launching.

Unplug the trailer's lights, and put the connector from the tow vehicle where it will not dangle into the water. You are now ready to launch your boat.

# Sailboat Trailering: Raising the Mast

Many sailboats have some form of *tabernacle* for raising the mast. This is essentially a mast stepped on a hinge, and most of them are arranged so that the mast swings up from astern. Smaller boats, of course, don't require this kind of fancy gear, and the mast is simply raised by hand and guided into its step by a crewmember, as described in Chapter 4.

Again, before beginning to raise the mast, you should check overhead for wires and obstructions. Check, too, that there is a clear overhead path from the setup area to the actual launching area and beyond.

Masts that pivot up and forward are simple to raise but require a fair amount of muscle power from the crew. With the mast in its hinged tabernacle, attach the upper shrouds and the backstay and tie a pulling line—a good, thick one, comfortable to the hand—to the forestay just above the turnbuckle. As one person stands in the cockpit and raises the spar, the other crewmember at the bow, who should be the stronger of the two, pulls on the forestay extension.

If the boat is very small and light, the person raising the spar should stay out of the boat while doing it, since the unsupported hull might be dam-

aged by the weight of the person inside. As the mast approaches the point where the person aft can exert no more lift, it may be necessary to tie off the forestay extension until the cockpit hand can get around forward to help pull. Until you're used to the stresses involved, don't take anything for granted; even a light mast can exert an enormous pull at certain acute angles.

The mast may, in some cases, swing up and aft from the bow. The spar thus lies flat over the foredeck after being made fast in its tabernacle. In this case, first make fast the upper shrouds and the forestay. Then attach the boom to its gooseneck at right angles to the mast, holding it in place with the topping lift and temporary guys to the deck at either side. To raise the mast, you simply employ the four- or five-part mechanical advantage of the mainsheet tackle system, amplified if necessary by using the genoa sheet winch.

Most times the foregoing is all you need to know about raising a mast, but on some boats it's a little more complicated. If, for example, your mast swings up from the bow and your upper-shroud chainplates are slightly aft of the mast step, the upper shrouds will have to be slacked way off in order to be attached to their chainplates before the mast is raised. If the mast step is on a cabin top—say, 6 inches higher than the chainplates—then the upper shrouds won't prevent the mast from swaying from side to side until it's all the way up. For circumstances like these—or when the mast is simply too heavy to raise without some sort of leverage—you'll need to get creative. Whether the answer involves temporary shrouds, temporary bridles, a tackle, or a temporary ginpole or *sheerlegs* (a brace made from two poles—such as the main boom and a spinnaker pole—lashed together at one end) for leverage, there is always a way. Ask other owners of your class of boat for advice. Often you can find the answer in an online forum for members of the class association.

# Launching

Staying in any boat during launching is unsafe, since boats can tip over when launched. (Personal watercraft—PWC—are the exception; it is common to be aboard a PWC during launch.) Instead, make sure you have a line running from your boat's bow to the shore before launching. Ideally you will have another person to help with the launch. Assuming this is the case, your helper will tend the bow line while you back the trailer down the ramp.

Make certain everyone is out of the way before backing down the ramp, and know where children are at all times. Back the trailer slowly until the boat's stern is in the water (Figures 6-29 and 6-30). There is no prize for backing rapidly, but if you run off the ramp, you may find that there is a penalty! Some people remove the winch line before they are on the launch ramp, but this practice sometimes results in an early launch onto the ramp rather than into the water. Don't remove the winch line until the boat begins to float.

Ramps can be dangerous, and this is particularly true of ramps in tidal waters. Algae grows on ramp surfaces, which can become extremely slick, making it a challenge to walk and sometimes even to prevent your vehicle from following your boat into the water. The steeper the ramp, the more of an issue this can be.

Some bodies of water such as impounded lakes experience periodic changes in their water levels. If the level is low, be careful that you do not back your trailer off the end of the ramp's hard surface into rocks or mud. If you do, you may have a serious problem.

If at all possible, stay in your vehicle while launching your boat and have your bow-line tender remove the winch cable when you request it. That

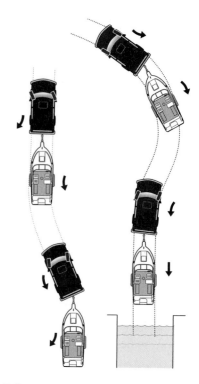

**Figure 6-29.** When backing a trailer, turn the back end of your vehicle to the right in order to make the trailer turn left, and vice versa. Do not oversteer, and begin to straighten your tires somewhat *before* a turn is completed. If the trailer starts to turn too sharply, pull ahead far enough to straighten it out, then try again. Don't get flustered. You'll get the hang of it soon enough.

way, you can keep your foot on the brake pedal, thus applying the brakes to all four wheels of your vehicle. If you leave the vehicle and engage the parking or hand brake, you are applying brakes only to the rear wheels.

If you put an automatic transmission in Park, you have even less braking power than with the parking brake set. In Park the transmission and driveshaft lock, but the vehicle has a differential on its rear axle that allows the rear wheels to turn independently of each other when cornering. Thus, one wheel or the other can turn at any time. This means, in effect, that you are sitting on a steep, slippery ramp depending on the braking power of one wheel. Also, with the engine running and under the strain of the trailered load, the transmission can slip out of Park. It is a horrible feeling to watch your boat, trailer, and vehicle launch themselves. It's even worse if they run you over in the process.

However, don't rely too heavily on your parking brake either. It's not that good. How many times have you backed out of your driveway and then discovered that you hadn't released the brake? In addition to the weight of the vehicle, you have the weight of the trailer, the boat, and its contents to help pull you down the ramp.

If you must leave the vehicle, put the transmission in Park, set the hand brake, and then turn off the engine. If you have a manual transmission, put it in reverse to obtain the lowest gear ratio. Carry wheel chocks with you and have someone put them behind your wheels before you take your foot off the brake.

After launching, pull the trailer up the ramp to the parking area. Don't take unnecessary time and keep others waiting.

While you are parking your vehicle, your crew can pull the boat to the pier and tie it up. Now you are ready to lower the outboard engine into the water, lower the centerboard, install the rudder, finish rigging the boat, attach the sails, and get underway. Remember that starting an outboard engine without the water intake immersed can damage the impeller in the engine's cooling-water pump in a very short time.

Some launch ramps have finger floats or a finger pier along one side of the ramp. In this case you might want to deploy a stern line as well as a bow line from the boat prior to launching. This will give your crew better control of the boat after it's launched, making it easier to pull the boat to the pier.

# Retrieving

Recovering a boat is the inverse of launching it. While it is in the water, store the sails; raise the outboard; raise and secure the daggerboard, centerboard, or swing keel; and remove the rudder or raise it to the traveling position. Then get your trailer and back it down the ramp and into the water.

Float your boat onto the trailer, connect the winch cable to the towing eye of your boat (or through the bow chocks) to secure it, make sure the boat is centered on the trailer, and crank the winch until the bow is firmly seated against the bow stop. If your boat is a fixed-keel or keel/centerboard model, the keel should at this point be squarely seated on the keel support in the trailer

**Figure 6-30.** Launching a trailer-sailer. **1.** Make sure the mast has lateral and aft support—either from shrouds and the backstay or from halyards used as temporary stays—before you raise it. **2.** One crew prevents the mast from falling backward while the other attaches the forestay. **3.** With fenders deployed, the boat is backed into the water until it floats off the trailer, possibly with an assist from the line handler. (PHOTOS BY JOHN POIMIROO)

bed. If the water is clear enough to see the bottom of the keel, make sure this is the case.

With the boat firmly on the trailer, drive up the ramp to the parking area, park, and secure the outboard motor for trailering. Lower the mast and secure it and the boom. Lower the swing keel or centerboard onto the trailer support so that it isn't suspended from its pin and pendant. Lash the boat to the trailer as previously discussed. Then tie down everything that is loose, pull the drain plug, and replace the cover if your boat has one.

Finally, plug the trailer's electrical connection into the tow vehicle's outlet. After checking once more to see that everything is secure, you are ready to roll.

# Storing Your Boat and Trailer

A few simple measures can extend the life of your boat and trailer. If you are going to store your boat on its trailer for an extended period, jack up the trailer and put cinder blocks under its axles. Then check to see that the boat is still evenly supported, since jacking up a trailer can twist it out of shape. Make certain that the whole rig is stable to help prevent strong winds from blowing it over.

Removing the wheels will extend tire life. Put them inside, where they aren't exposed to the sun. Jack up the trailer's tongue so the boat will drain, and make sure the drain plug is removed. Keep the interior of your boat dry to prevent mildew and dry rot.

Cover the boat to keep rainwater out, but let air circulate under the cover to keep it ventilated. Ready-made covers are available, or you can have one custom-made. Be certain that it is secure and will not blow away. Remember, too, that you must prevent puddling of water. Water weighs about 8.3 pounds per gallon and the weight of collected water will stretch the cover, allowing the puddle to grow larger. Eventually, the cover will split and the water will get into the boat. Supporting the cover from below can help prevent puddles.

Before leaving your boat on its trailer for an extended time, check to see that it is still firmly supported. If any rollers or skids have come loose, adjust and tighten them.

If you plan to leave your outboard motor on your boat while it is stored, be certain to flush it and then drain all the water from it by leaving it in a vertical (operating) position. Storing the motor in a vertical position will prevent rainwater from entering the exhaust and possibly cracking the housing during freezing weather. If you plan to store your boat for an extended period, follow the layup procedures recommended in your owner's manual.

One final thought: Replace the heavy-duty flasher on your vehicle with a standard-duty flasher, so that you will be able to tell if a bulb burns out.

# Theft Prevention

Pleasure boats of all sizes, small outboard motors, radios, compasses, binoculars, and other items of boating gear are stolen every year. A few simple measures and some forethought can prevent such thefts. Some of these are things to do at home, and others apply at the launch site.

## BEFORE TRAILERING YOUR BOAT

Permanently mark your boat's hull identification number (HIN) at a second hidden location on your boat. It's already marked on the stern and in another, hidden location, but these numbers can be defaced or altered. Put the HIN in a spot only you know about so that you can identify your boat if it is stolen and recovered.

Mark all your valuable equipment with an identification number. Most police departments recommend using your driver's license number, which is available on most police computers, and can provide an engraving tool for inscribing ID numbers on hard surfaces. Soft materials such as cloth covers, sleeping bags, blankets, and tents can be marked with paint, indelible markers, or invisible ink that shows up under ultraviolet light. Visible markings discourage theft and help law enforcement authorities recover your belongings.

Keep an up-to-date inventory of your boating equipment that includes the name of each piece of equipment and its description and serial number, if any. This will help document any loss. Video or digital recordings, color photographs, or slides can also help identify your equipment and document its condition and that of your boat.

Make sure your insurance covers theft of your boat or its equipment. Homeowners' policies may not provide adequate coverage of marine equipment. Marine coverage for your boat, trailer, outboard motor(s), and equipment is usually worth the low premium charged. Shop around for a reliable company and for the lowest premium.

Stolen vessels can be used for illegal activities that range from reckless joyriding to use in the drug trade. Or your boat may be resold to an unsuspecting victim. Do what you can to protect it and prevent its illegal use.

## AT THE LAUNCH SITE

Keep your valuables out of sight but not in a glove compartment. Don't leave anything in bags or cartons inside the vehicle; a thief may damage your vehicle while trying to see what's inside them. Instead put your gear in the trunk and lock it and the vehicle. It is not difficult to force entry into a locked trunk, but few thieves will do it just on the chance of finding something of value.

Leave your vehicle in a well-lighted area if you expect to be gone until after dark. This enhances personal safety and reduces theft. Do not leave your keys in the vehicle.

Use a trailer-hitch lock, which is difficult to cut loose, to secure your trailer to your vehicle. If you don't lock the trailer to your vehicle, it may disappear at the launch site.

## BACK HOME

At home, secure your trailer by removing a wheel or chaining the trailer to a large tree. Alternatively, you can sink a case-hardened steel eyebolt in concrete and either chain the boat or attach a trailer ball to that. If the latter, lock your trailer on the secured ball with its hitch lock.

But don't be lulled into a false sense of security simply because you have a good hitch lock. Professional thieves carry coupler devices that can be quickly attached to your trailer.

If possible, store your boat in the backyard or in a garage so it won't be seen by passersby. If you have to store it in the driveway, don't leave the hitch facing the street.

Remove all valuable portable equipment from your boat and lock it in a safe place; just don't forget to put it back aboard when you next take out your boat. Above all, don't leave the boat's keys or registration certificate on the boat.

If you have a small outboard motor, it is best to remove it from the boat when not in use. This will protect it from the weather as well as from thieves. If you don't remove it, fasten it with a motor lock across its clamps or a case-hardened chain securely fastened to the boat.

If you keep your boat at a dock or on a mooring buoy, secure it with a case-hardened chain and lock. Remove portable fuel tanks and a vital engine part such as a distributor rotor or ignition wire(s). A hidden switch in the electrical system between the motor and the ignition switch can be a useful deterrent.

Work with your neighbors and fellow boaters to watch for strangers or suspicious activity. Call local law enforcement if you have any doubt whether someone is authorized to work on a boat or trailer. Write down a description of any suspicious people and get their license numbers or the registration numbers and descriptions of their boats.

# Aquatic Nuisance Species

Foreign plants and animals, often called *aquatic nuisance species* (ANS), are invading our waters. Most are thought to come from the ballast water of ships, but once here, the invaders are spread by recreational boaters whenever boats are moved from one body of water to another.

Zebra mussels were accidentally introduced into the Great Lakes region around 1986. Since then, they have spread into the Hudson, Susquehanna, Ohio, Illinois, Tennessee, and Mississippi rivers and many lakes. The economic damage the mussels have caused by fouling power plants and industrial and public drinking water systems, and their damage to boat hulls, engine cooling systems, docks, and navigation buoys, underscore the need to prevent their further spread.

Eurasian water milfoil invades North American lakes so aggressively that, once introduced into a new water body, it quickly outcompetes all indigenous species and spreads across the lake or pond in dense mats that make boating impossible and may even choke all other life out of the lake. Milfoil is readily transported on a boat bottom from one lake to another.

The following are steps boaters can take before moving from one body of fresh water to another to keep zebra mussels and other ANS from spreading to uninfested waters:

- Paint your boat's hull with an environmentally acceptable antifouling paint.
- After boating and before leaving the ramp, flush your boat's engine and hull and your trailer's frame, preferably with hot water (140°F or hotter).
- Empty your bilge and flush it with water containing chlorine bleach.
- Remove any plants, mud, or animals from equipment before leaving all waters.

After flushing, allow your boat and trailer to dry at least two to four days in the sun before moving to another body of fresh water. If you do not perform the flushing procedure at the ramp, drain your engine and bilge and allow them to dry for at least two weeks before launching them in a different body of fresh water.

# Float Plan

Before setting out, file a *float plan*. A copy of a suggested float plan is in Appendix B. Copy it and fill in the descriptive facts about you and your boat.

File your float plan with a friend, relative, or neighbor. The plan tells where you are going, the route you will take, when you will be back, and whom to call if you don't return on time. Most often you will ask that the Coast Guard be notified if you are overdue. The Coast Guard does not accept float plans but will mount a search as soon as you are reported overdue.

When trailering, if you can't find someone to accept your float plan, leave a copy under your windshield wiper. Some police authority will find it, probably soon after dark.

Be sure to cancel your float plan when you return. Otherwise the person with whom you left it, not knowing you have returned, may initiate a needless search.

# Practice Questions

## IMPORTANT BOATING TERMS

In the following exercise, match the words in the column on the left with the definitions in the column on the right. In the blank space to the left of each term, write the letter of the item that best matches it. Do not use an item in the right-hand column more than once.

| THE ITEMS | THE RESPONSES |
|---|---|
| 1. _____ surge brakes | a. secure your boat to its trailer |
| 2. _____ Bearing Buddy | b. includes the weight of the trailer |
| 3. _____ seize | c. bearings immersed in salt water |
| 4. _____ GVWR | d. less than 5% of weight on tongue |
| 5. _____ bumper hitch | e. wheel bearing protector |
| 6. _____ tie-downs | f. automatically applied when towing vehicle stops |
| 7. _____ fishtails | g. circulates water in an outboard motor |
| 8. _____ impeller | h. controls turn signals |
| 9. _____ float plan | i. completed prior to cruising |
| 10. _____ flasher | j. usually illegal |

# Multiple-Choice Items

In the following items, choose the best response:

**6-1.** The widest boat you can trailer on most state roads is

a. 6 feet
b. 7 feet
c. 8 feet
d. 9 feet

**6-2.** The safety chains of your trailer, under the hitch, should always be

a. crossed
b. of open link construction
c. attached to the towing vehicle's bumper
d. short

**6-3.** A bumper hitch is

a. recommended
b. legal in all states
c. the best available
d. illegal in many states

**6-4.** The ball of a trailer hitch and the coupler on the trailer must

a. be free of grease
b. be matched for size
c. be insulated from each other
d. be made of the same material

**6-5.** You should have brakes on your trailer if it is designed for a gross weight of

a. 1,500 or more pounds
b. 2,000 or more pounds
c. 2,500 or more pounds
d. 3,000 or more pounds

**6-6.** Many states require that boat trailers have

a. safety chains
b. license plates
c. lights and turn signals
d. all of the above

**6-7.** Trailer light failure can be reduced by

a. using waterproof lights
b. mounting lights on a high bracket or board
c. unplugging the trailer electrical system before launching or recovering the boat
d. all of the above

**6-8.** Which brakes work from a trailer's momentum?

a. compressed air
b. surge
c. electric
d. none of the above

**6-9.** When trailering, always take along

a. an inflated spare tire
b. a jack
c. spare bearings
d. all of the above

**6-10.** How much of the load should be on the hitch to avoid fishtailing?

a. 2% to 4%
b. 5% to 10%
c. 10% to 15%
d. 12% to 14%

**6-11.** Small trailer tires

a. cost more
b. turn faster and need more air pressure
c. are made with solid cores
d. turn slower and need less air pressure

**6-12.** Winch lines for retrieving boats are made of

a. steel
b. polypropylene
c. webbing
d. all of the above

**6-13.** Dry rot forms most often in

a. salt water
b. fresh water
c. brackish water
d. potable water

**6-14.** It is easier to back a trailer if you place your hand on the bottom of the steering wheel and then move your hand

a. in the direction you want the trailer to go
b. in the opposite direction from where you want the trailer to go
c. clockwise so the trailer will go to the right
d. counterclockwise so the trailer will go to the left

(continued on next page)

# Multiple-Choice Items (continued)

**6-15.** You can increase the life of your trailer's lights if you

    a. mount them on a removable board
    b. keep them out of the water
    c. disconnect them before immersing them in water
    d. all of the above

**6-16.** Before you step the mast of a sailboat

    a. launch the boat
    b. check to see what is overhead
    c. take the boat to the launching ramp
    d. moor the boat securely

**6-17.** Before leaving the dock

    a. check to see that you have enough sandwiches
    b. file a float plan with a friend or relative
    c. be sure the spinnaker is aboard
    d. make certain you have the water skis

**6-18.** If you have too much weight on the hitch, it will cause

    a. the front end of your tow vehicle to lift up
    b. you to lose some steering control
    c. the tow vehicle's rear end to squat
    d. all of the above

**6-19.** An advantage of tilt trailers when towing a small centerboard boat is that

    a. they are cheaper
    b. they can carry a heavier load
    c. you can usually keep the trailer's wheels out of the water
    d. it's easier to balance the load on them

**6-20.** When you buy a trailerable sailboat

    a. buy an inexpensive one
    b. keep launching problems in mind
    c. remember how much trouble it is to maintain it
    d. buy a trailer

**6-21.** Compared with a powerboat trailer, a trailer for a keel or keel/centerboard sailboat is

    a. more likely to be a float-on, float-off variety
    b. likely to have bunkers or screw pads at a greater height above the trailer bed
    c. less easily adapted to fit other models of boats
    d. all of the above

**6-22.** While launching a boat

    a. have someone stay in it to guide you
    b. put the transmission in Park to ensure that your car does not roll down the ramp
    c. if at all possible, stay in your car with your foot on the brake
    d. set the hand brake to ensure that your car does not roll down the ramp

**6-23.** Zebra mussels have been found in

    a. the Great Lakes
    b. the Mississippi River
    c. the Hudson River
    d. all of the above

**6-24.** When filing a float plan, you should

    a. take it with you on the boat
    b. file your plan with a friend, relative, or neighbor
    c. send a copy to the Coast Guard
    d. file it with the local police

# Your "Highway" Signs

## The objectives of this chapter are to describe:

- Aids to navigation (ATONs).
- Cautions in the use of ATONs.
- The meaning of chart symbols.
- The availability of electronic ATONs.
- Reference materials that alert you to changes in ATONs.

THE FIRST SAILORS rarely left sight of land, and their only navigational aids were familiar landmarks. Later mariners began taking long voyages out of sight of land with only the sun, stars, and crude instruments to guide them. To this day we still depend on visible landmarks and

The U.S. Coast Guard buoy tender *Sangamon* heads upstream on the Mississippi River above St. Louis. (PHOTO BY LEN SCHULTE)

151

points of reference, but we also enjoy many more sophisticated aids to navigation.

An *aid to navigation*, or ATON, is any man-made device designed to help you determine your location on the water and plot a safe course to your destination. Short-range ATONs include **buoys**, **daybeacons**, **minor lights**, and **lighthouses**. Long-range electronic aids include **loran**, **satellite beacons**, and **GPS**.

ATONs are shown on nautical charts. With a good chart, a knowledge of ATONs, and proper caution, your boating can be safe and enjoyable.

Although they are not ATONs, prominent structures and natural objects—including church spires, radio towers, water tanks, mountain peaks, promontories, and other landmarks—can also help you navigate. To be useful, landmarks must be visible from the water and appear on charts of the area.

All ATONs are protected by law. It is a criminal offense to damage an ATON or hinder its proper operation. Do not alter, deface, destroy, or move an ATON. Never tie up to one, and avoid anchoring so close to one that it is obscured from the sight of passing boaters.

# Buoyage Systems

Most ATONs are grouped in *buoyage systems*. The United States uses four principal buoyage systems:

1. U.S. Aids to Navigation System
2. Intracoastal Waterway Marking System (ICWMS)
3. Western Rivers System
4. Uniform State Waterway Marking System (USWMS)

We'll discuss each in turn.

## U.S. AIDS TO NAVIGATION SYSTEM

The **U.S. ATON System** is the principal buoyage system used in the United States, and it conforms to the Region B standards of the International Association of Lighthouse Authorities (IALA). The IALA-B system applies throughout North and South America, including Canada, in the Caribbean Sea, and in Japan, Korea, and the Philippines. The rest of the world, however, uses the IALA-A system, which is conceptually similar and uses marks of the same shape but with their colors reversed.

The U.S. ATON System uses buoys, beacons, and minor lights as marks. These mark obstructions, dangers such as wrecks, the edges of navigable channels, and other things of importance to mariners. The U.S. Coast Guard maintains the marks in the system.

There are six types of marks, or ATONs:

1. **Lateral marks**, including **preferred channel marks**
2. **Safe water marks**
3. **Isolated danger marks**
4. **Range marks**
5. **Regulatory marks**
6. **Special marks**

All six are summarized with their chart symbols in Figure 7-1.

## INTRACOASTAL WATERWAY

The **Intracoastal Waterway** (ICW), which is maintained by the U.S. Army Corps of Engineers, runs south from Manasquan Inlet in New Jersey to the Florida Keys. It then runs north along the west coast of Florida and west along the Gulf Coast to Brownsville, Texas. Wherever possible, the ICW runs through protected bays, sounds, and canals, and it also takes maximum advantage of the protection given by offshore islands.

Marks on the ICW, which are maintained by the U.S. Coast Guard, are similar to those of the U.S. ATON System, and are used to show the limits of navigable channels, preferred channels, safe water, and ranges. The system also includes marks with no lateral significance. The aids look the same as the lateral system shown in Figure 7-1, but each includes an additional small yellow symbol (a square for "green" aids, a triangle for "red" aids) designating the ICW markings, as shown in the upper portion of Figure 7-2. There are books and

# U.S. AIDS TO NAVIGATION SYSTEM
## on navigable waters except Western Rivers

### LATERAL SYSTEM AS SEEN ENTERING FROM SEAWARD

**PORT SIDE**
**ODD NUMBERED AIDS**

GREEN LIGHT ONLY

FLASHING (2)
FLASHING
OCCULTING
QUICK FLASHING
ISO

**PREFERRED CHANNEL**
**NO NUMBERS-MAY BE LETTERED**

PREFERRED
CHANNEL TO
STARBOARD
TOPMOST BAND
GREEN

GREEN LIGHT ONLY

COMPOSITE GROUP FLASHING (2+1)

**PREFERRED CHANNEL**
**NO NUMBERS-MAY BE LETTERED**

PREFERRED
CHANNEL TO
PORT
TOPMOST BAND
RED

RED LIGHT ONLY

COMPOSITE GROUP FLASHING (2+1)

**STARBOARD SIDE**
**EVEN NUMBERED AIDS**

RED LIGHT ONLY

FLASHING (2)
FLASHING
OCCULTING
QUICK FLASHING
ISO

"1"
Fl G 6s
LIGHT

G "9"
Fl G 4s
LIGHTED BUOY

GR "A"
Fl (2+1) G 6s

RG "B"
Fl (2+1) R 6s

"2"
Fl R 6s
LIGHT

R "8"
Fl R 4s
LIGHTED BUOY

G
C "9"
CAN

G
"5"
DAYBEACON

GR
"U"
CAN

GR
C "S"

RG
N "C"
NUN

RG
"G"

R
N "6"
NUN

R
"2"
DAYBEACON

### AIDS TO NAVIGATION HAVING NO LATERAL SIGNIFICANCE

**ISOLATED DANGER**
**NO NUMBERS--MAY BE LETTERED**

WHITE LIGHT ONLY

Fl (2) 5s

BR "A"
Fl (2) 5s

A
LIGHTED

C
UNLIGHTED

BR "C"

**SAFE WATER**
**NO NUMBERS--MAY BE LETTERED**

WHITE LIGHT ONLY     MORSE CODE

Mo (A)

N
RW "N"
Mo (A)
LIGHTED
AND/OR SOUND

A
RW "A"
MR

B
RW SP "B"
SPERICAL

N
RW "N"
UNLIGHTED
AND/OR SOUND

**RANGE DAYBOARDS--MAY BE LETTERED**

| KGW | KWG | KWB | KBW | KWR | KRW | KRB | KBR | KGB | KBG | KGR | KRG |

**DAYBOARDS--MAY BE LETTERED**

WHITE LIGHT ONLY

NR
A

NG
A

NB
M

RW
Bn

GW
Bn

BW
Bn

**SPECIAL MARKS--MAY BE LETTERED**

YELLOW LIGHT ONLY
FIXED
FLASHING

A
Y
C "A"
UNLIGHTED

C
Y
N "C"

A
Y "A"
Bn

SHAPE OPTIONAL--BUT SELECTED TO BE APPROPRIATE
FOR THE POSITION OF THE MARK IN RELATION TO THE
NAVIGABLE WATERWAY AND THE DIRECTION
OF BUOYAGE.

B
Y "B"
Fl
LIGHTED

### TYPICAL INFORMATION AND REGULATORY MARKS

INFORMATION AND REGULATORY MARKERS

WHEN LIGHTED, INFORMATION AND REGULATORY
MARKS MAY DISPLAY ANY LIGHT
RHYTHM EXCEPT QUICK FLASHING
AND FLASHING (2)

WHITE LIGHT ONLY

NW
DANGER

W
Bn

EXCLUSION
AREA

RESTRICTED
OPERATIONS

DANGER

5
MPH

Aids to navigation marking the Intracoastal Waterway (ICW) display unique yellow symbols to distinguish them from aids marking other waters. Yellow triangles ▲ indicate aids should be passed by keeping them on the starboard (right) hand of the vessel. Yellow squares ■ indicate aids should be passed by keeping them on the port (left) hand of the vessel. A yellow horizontal band ▬ provides no lateral information, but simply identifies aids as marking the ICW.

Plate 1

**Figure 7-1.**

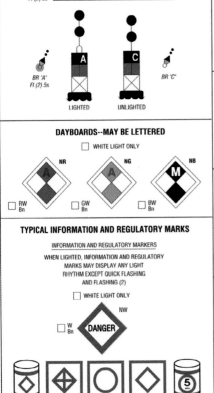

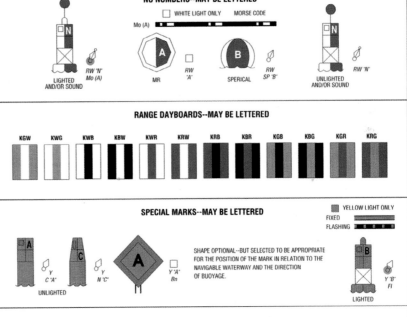

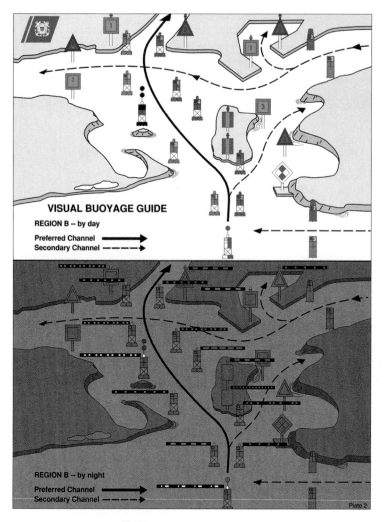

**Figure 7-2.**

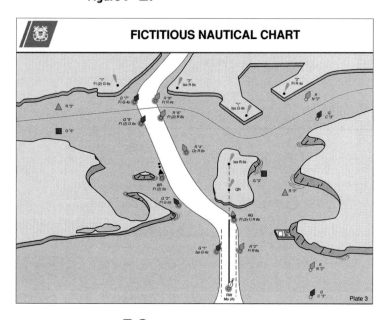

**Figure 7-3.**

charts available specifically to guide you through the ICW.

## WESTERN RIVERS

Officially, the designation **Western Rivers** includes the Mississippi River, its tributaries, South Pass, Southwest Pass, and the Port Allen–Morgan City Alternate Route. It also includes the Atchafalaya River above its junction with the Port Allen–Morgan City Alternate Route, the Old River, and the Red River.

Fortunately, you do not need to know all this unless you are boating along the lower Mississippi River. Otherwise, all you need to know is that the Western Rivers include the Mississippi, its tributaries, and other rivers.

The U.S. Coast Guard maintains the marks on the Western Rivers, and these aids are shown in Figure 7-4.

**WARNING** *Give buoys an adequate berth.* Boaters attempting to pass a buoy close aboard risk collision with a yawing buoy or with the obstruction marked by the buoy.

## UNIFORM STATE WATERWAY MARKING SYSTEM

The marks of the **Uniform State Waterway Marking System** (USWMS) are similar to those of the U.S. ATON System, but with a few significant differences, as shown in the lower portion of Figure 7-4. Until recently, the USWMS was in effect in all waters wholly contained within state boundaries and therefore controlled by state boating authorities. This uniform system was developed in 1966 so that boaters traveling between states would find consistency in the navigation marks maintained by state authorities. By the end of 2003, however, the USWMS was to have been replaced with the U.S. ATON System. As of this writing, there is no confirmation as to whether all states have accomplished the conversion.

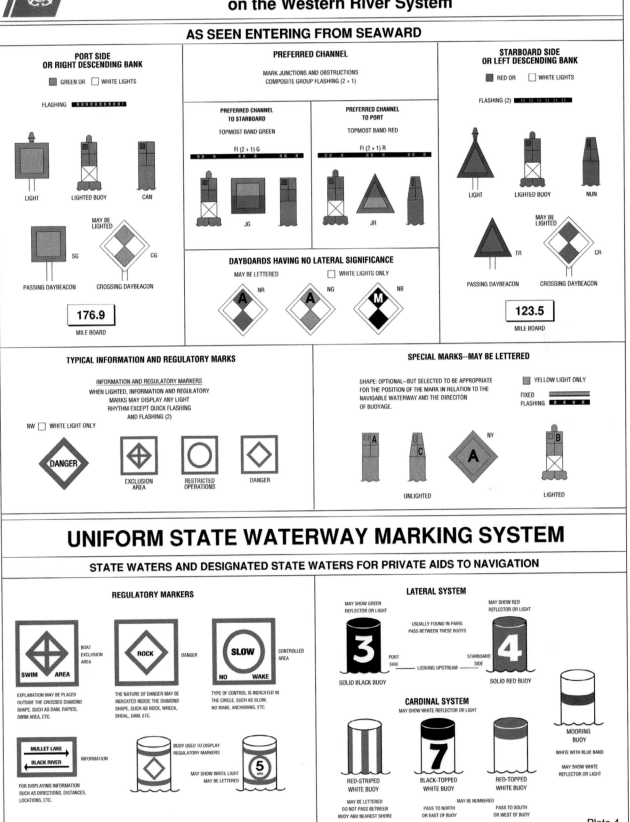

**Figure 7-4.** Note that the cardinal and lateral buoys in the Uniform State Waterway Marking System are being phased out, replaced by U.S. ATONs.

# Waterway Marks

Waterways are marked by a variety of buoys, daybeacons, and fixed structures serving a variety of purposes.

## BUOYS

Floating ATONs, or *buoys*, come in various sizes and shapes and may or may not have lights (Figure 7-5). They mark navigable channels, isolated dangers, obstructions, or shoals. The light, when present, turns on automatically and shines from dusk to dawn. Solar energy charges many of the batteries that power these lights. There are five common types of buoys.

## Pillar Buoys

Pillar buoys vary considerably in shape and function, but most consist of a steel lattice erected on a flat base. The lighted green buoy "3" and the lighted red-and-white bell "LC" in Figure 7-6 are both pillar buoys. The chart symbols for both buoys are also shown in the illustration, and from these we learn that buoy "3" flashes green every 4 seconds, while buoy "LC" flashes the Morse code letter A (one short flash followed by one long flash) that is characteristic of a red-and-white safe water buoy. (We'll discuss light signals later in the chapter.) Pillar buoys range in size from small ones to large, floating lighthouses, and in addition to lights, they may have bells, gongs, whistles, foghorns, or a combination of a light and a sound-producing device.

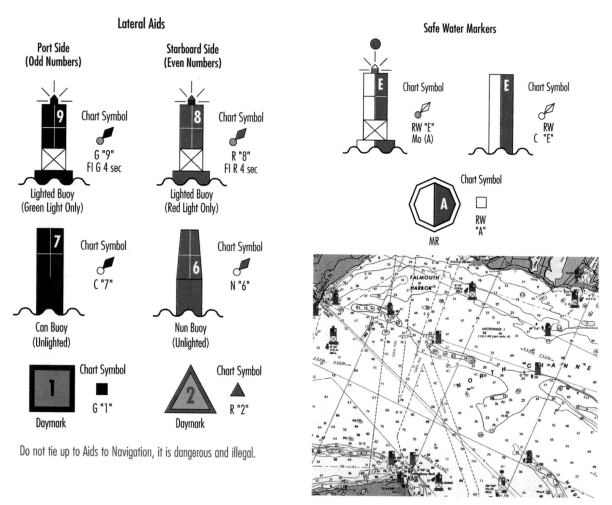

**Figure 7-5. Left and top right:** Buoy shapes and their chart symbols. (REPRINTED WITH PERMISSION FROM "FEDERAL REQUIREMENTS & SAFETY TIPS FOR RECREATIONAL BOATS," U.S. COAST GUARD OFFICE OF BOATING SAFETY) **Bottom right:** Illustrations of selected navigation buoys are superimposed on this chart segment next to their corresponding chart symbols. (REPRINTED WITH PERMISSION FROM *THE WEEKEND NAVIGATOR* BY BOB SWEET)

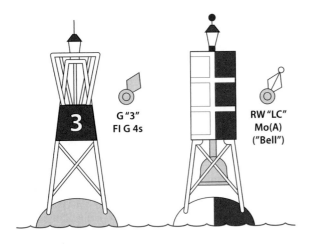

G "3"
FI G 4s

RW "LC"
Mo(A)
("Bell")

**Figure 7-6. Top:** Pillar buoys and their chart symbols. **Bottom left:** A midchannel bell buoy with its single spherical topmark. (PHOTO BY USCG PA3 ROBIN REISLER) **Bottom right:** Two crewmembers from the U.S. Coast Guard cutter *Sycamore*, home port Cordova, Alaska, repair the extinguished light atop a pillar buoy near Spruce Cape on a January day. In the distance, a fishing vessel heads out to sea from Kodiak. (PHOTO BY PETTY OFFICER PAUL ROSZKOWSKI)

**Figure 7-7.** Inspecting a large, multifunctional pillar buoy. (COURTESY NOAA)

The larger structures are multifunctional (Figure 7-7) and may have weather recording and transmitting equipment in addition to lights.

## Spherical Buoys

Spherical buoys are red-and-white striped (Figure 7-8) and are used to mark a *fairway*, or the middle of a channel in *traffic separation schemes* (TSS), which are one-way traffic lanes used in some harbors and other congested areas.

## Nun and Can Buoys

The two most common buoys are *cans* (cylindrical shape) and *nuns* (conical shape; Figures 7-9 and 7-10). In the U.S. ATON System, a can is most often green and bears an odd number, while a nun is most frequently red and bears an even number. Nun and can buoys mark the edges of navigable channels.

## Spar Buoys

Spar buoys look like short, small-diameter telephone poles and may be red with even numbers or

RW
SP "G"

**pass either side**

**Figure 7-8.** A red-and-white vertically striped spherical buoy serves as a fairway or midchannel marker in a traffic separation scheme.

**Figure 7-9.** A red nun buoy being serviced by a Coast Guard buoy tender. (PHOTO BY USCG PA1 JERRY L. SNYDER)

**Figure 7-10.** Can buoys being serviced by the U.S. Coast Guard. (PHOTOS BY USCG AND JONATHAN MCCOOL)

## *Be Cautious Around Buoys!*

When navigating near buoys, use caution. They are at anchor and, like an anchored vessel, they drift around their anchor with wind or current in what is called a **watch circle**. For this reason, the location of a buoy on a chart is sometimes marked "PA," which stands for **p**osition **a**pproximate. A buoy may even drag its anchor out of its charted position due to wind, ice, flooding, or being run down by a vessel. Such a buoy is said to be **off-station**, a condition that may go unreported for some days. In extreme cases a buoy may go missing altogether.

Occasionally the lights on normally lighted buoys will fail for one reason or another, or sound-producing buoys will fail to sound their signals. Waves and swells activate the many whistles, gongs, and bells, but often in a fog the sea is gentle or calm, which means the buoys may be silent.

## DAYBEACONS

*Daymarks* are colored geometrical shapes such as triangles, squares, octagons, diamonds, or rectangles. They are often called **dayboards**, a term in such wide use that it is now accepted. A daybeacon is a daymark plus the pile or *dolphin* (a group of three or more piles, usually fastened together with a wire rope) that holds it.

## *Triangular Daymarks*

A triangular daymark is an equilateral triangle (Figure 7-11) resting on its base. Generally, these daymarks are red and, when numbered, have even numbers—which means that a daymark with an odd number of sides displays an even number.

green with odd numbers. The U.S. ATON System no longer uses spar buoys, nor are they used on the ICW, the Western Rivers, or other navigable waters under U.S. control. You may still see them, however, in state-controlled waters where the USWMS has yet to be replaced by the U.S. ATON System.

**Figure 7-11.** A red daymark on a piling. (PHOTO BY USCG)

## Square Daymarks

Generally, square daymarks are green and, when numbered, have odd numbers (Figures 7-12 and 7-13). Thus, a daymark with an even number of sides displays an odd number.

## Diamond-Shaped Daymarks

There are two kinds of diamond-shaped daymarks. The first is used in the U.S. ATON System and on the ICW, the Western Rivers, and other navigable waters. In this type, two smaller diamonds—which may be red, green, or black—are contained within the outline of the principal diamond (Figure 7-14). These daymarks have no lateral significance—i.e., they do not direct you to pass them on one side or the other. Rather, they are like the Xs on shopping mall maps that show "You are here." When you find the daymark on a chart, you will know where you are. Sometimes, too, they mark underwater hazards; as always, consult your chart to be sure.

The second type of diamond-shaped daymark is called a **crossing daymark** and is found on the Western Rivers and other navigable rivers. These daymarks indicate to upbound and downbound traffic when the channel crosses from one bank of the river to the other.

## LIGHT STRUCTURES

Lighted ATONs, or *light structures*, vary greatly in size, from simple battery-powered lights on wooden piles or dolphins to tall lighthouses with powerful lights (Figure 7-15). Light structures have the same functions as lighted buoys but are used where they are more appropriate.

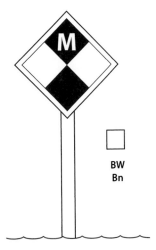

**Figure 7-14.** **Left:** A diamond-shaped daybeacon together with its chart symbol. This mark has no lateral significance, but exists to mark a hazard or to help you locate your position on the water. **Right:** A diamond-shaped daybeacon. (PHOTO BY USCG PA1 RON MENCH)

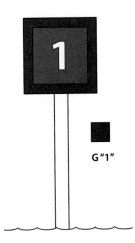

**Figure 7-12.** A green daymark together with its chart symbol.

**Figure 7-13.** This green daybeacon is equipped with a battery-powered light (the battery is recharged by solar panels) and is therefore more properly considered a minor light. The light, like the daymark, is green. (PHOTO BY USCG PA1 TELFAIR H. BROWN)

**Figure 7-15.** The Angel's Gate (Los Angeles Harbor) Lighthouse, built in 1913, is the only lighthouse in the world that emits an emerald-colored light. (PHOTO BY JUNE ESPARZA)

A minor light, for example, may mark the mouth of a channel. *Minor lights* are stationary daymarks equipped with lights, and are either red, green, or white (Figure 7-16). If the light is red, the daymark is a red triangle with an even number. If the light is green, its daymark is a green square with an odd number. And if the light is white, its daymark is diamond or octagonal shaped and may have a letter.

## INFORMATIONAL AND REGULATORY MARKS

*Informational* and *regulatory marks* are white buoys or white daymarks with orange markings, as seen in Figures 7-1, 7-4, and 7-17, top. The buoys are white cylinders, each with an orange band near its top, a second orange band just above its waterline, and an orange diamond or circle between these.

An open diamond on a board or buoy warns of "Danger." If the diamond has lines connecting its opposite corners, it marks an exclusion area for boats. Stay out! This mark frequently guards a swimming area. An open circle on a board or buoy marks an area of restricted operations, such as "slow," "idle speed," or "no wake." The warning is usually printed within the circle.

One informational mark that needs special emphasis is a sign that says "Caution, Manatee Area." South Florida has many such marks (Figure 7-17, bottom), which seek to protect the manatee, an

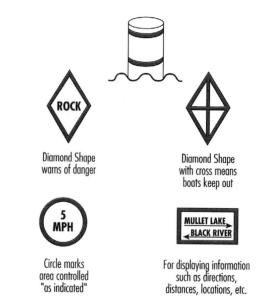

**Figure 7-17.** **Top:** Representative information and regulatory marks. (REPRINTED WITH PERMISSION FROM "FEDERAL REQUIREMENTS & SAFETY TIPS FOR RECREATIONAL BOATS," U.S. COAST GUARD OFFICE OF BOATING SAFETY) **Bottom:** A "Manatee Zone" sign on the Intracoastal Waterway in Florida. (PHOTO BY GENE HAMILTON)

endangered mammal that is especially vulnerable to injury by small boats. If you see the sign, slow to idle speed.

Although other marine mammals do not enjoy the privilege of special informational markers, they are nonetheless endangered and deserving of our protection. Thirty-five species of mammals live near the Atlantic, Pacific, and Gulf coasts, including thirty-two species of whales, dolphins and porpoises, seals, and manatees. At last estimate, there were fewer than 500 northern right whales—the most endangered of the marine mammals—still alive.

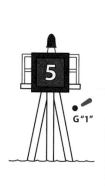

**Figure 7-16.** **Left:** A minor light with a daymark on a dolphin, together with its chart symbol. **Middle:** This minor light has a red daymark, so the light itself is also red. (PHOTO BY USCG PA1 PETE MILNES) **Right:** A minor light erected on a more elaborate shore platform. (PHOTO BY USCG PA1 RON MENCH)

The Marine Mammal Protection Act was passed by Congress in an effort to prevent the extinction of these animals. The act, for example, prohibits vessels from approaching within 500 yards of a right whale. If you sight a right whale, you must change your course and leave the area.

## MARKS FOR SPECIAL PURPOSES

*Special-purpose marks* are yellow and may have letters and amber (yellow) lights. They may be can or nun buoys, diamond daymarks, or small floating structures.

Special-purpose ATONs mark things such as fishnet and anchorage areas, spoil grounds, water intakes, and military exercise zones. They also mark traffic separation schemes when conventional channel marking would be confusing. You can find examples of these special marks in the lower right portion of Figure 7-1.

> **WARNING** **Give beacons and other fixed structures a wide berth.** *Boaters should not pass fixed ATONs close aboard due to the danger of collision with rip-rap or structure foundations, or with the obstruction or danger that is being marked.*

# How Waterways Are Marked

Waterway marks fall into two groups: marks that help you operate in navigable channels, and marks that show special conditions.

## MARKS ON NAVIGABLE WATERS

Marks on the navigable waters of the United States (except Western Rivers and the Intracoastal Waterway) appear in Figure 7-1. Those ATONs that help guide you along channels—i.e., those with **lateral significance**—are shown in the upper half of the illustration. To understand their use, you need to know the principle of "returning from sea," or "red, right, returning."

## Red, Right, Returning

A basic convention of ATON usage is the concept of returning from sea, which is handily summarized in the phrase "red, right, returning." This means that in North America you should always keep red buoys and marks on your starboard side as you return from the sea, while green ones should be on your port side. (In regions of the world where the IALA-A system of lateral buoyage is used, these colors would be reversed.)

When entering a channel that leads from the sea, the meaning of "returning from sea" is obvious. In other cases, however, it is not. By convention, therefore, when traveling in a clockwise direction around the coasts of the United States and Canada, you are returning from sea (Figure 7-18). Thus, traveling south along the east coast of Canada and the United States, north along the west coast of Florida, west along the Gulf Coast, and north along the west coast of the United States and Canada is considered returning from sea.

The situation in the St. Lawrence River and the Great Lakes is less arbitrary. Traveling up the St. Lawrence from its mouth toward its source is considered returning from sea, as is traveling up any river. Similarly, the outlet ends of the Great Lakes are the seaward ends.

Within a body of water such as a bay or sound, channels leading to docking or mooring areas follow the same convention. When returning to a docking or mooring area, you are returning from sea, so you don't even need to have been "to sea" to be considered as returning from it.

Still, in complicated waters with many branching channels, it can be difficult or impossible to

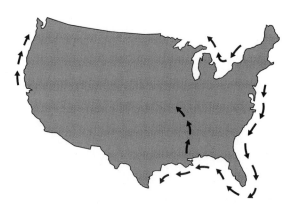

**Figure 7-18.** The "red, right, returning" convention.

determine when you are returning from seaward. Your navigation chart (see Chapter 12) is always the final arbiter; consult it wherever you go.

## Lateral Marks on Navigable Waters

The ATONs that mark the sides of navigable channels are called **lateral marks**. They consist of lighted and unlighted buoys, daybeacons, and minor lights, and they have distinctive colors and numbers as already discussed.

Again, you should leave the red marks with even numbers to starboard when returning from sea. Those you keep to port are green and have odd numbers. When you are going to sea, keep green marks to starboard and red ones to port. When lighted, red marks have red lights and green marks have green lights. The upper half of Figure 7-2 is a channel system as seen entering from seaward.

> **WARNING**  *If a daybeacon appears on your chart but you cannot see it at its charted location, be careful! A collision may have broken it off, and its remains, especially its stump, may still be there. If so, it is a hazard.*

**NUMBERS ON LATERAL MARKS.** The numbers on lateral aids are in sequence, which means that when entering a waterway from seaward, you will see the buoy, daybeacon, or minor light with the lowest number on the waterway. Usually, this is number 1 and it will be a green lighted structure, a green buoy, or a green daybeacon. Keep this mark on your port side as you pass it. Sometimes, however, the first mark is a red ATON with an even number, to be kept to starboard when returning.

Red and green marks occur in pairs only when needed, and such pairs are usually numbered in sequence. Green beacon "5," for example, will stand across the channel from red beacon "6." Though the numbers increase sequentially from seaward, numbers may be missing. For example, a channel may have a long sequence of green marks with no corresponding red marks, simply because there are fewer hazards to mark on the starboard side of the channel. Sometimes a mark will have a letter after

its number, such as "5A"; this indicates that the mark was added after the original sequence was established. At other times the number may have a one- or two-letter prefix denoting the name of the waterway. "MB6," for example, is mark 6 on Mobjack Bay. Your chart will show which numbers mark the waterway and the location of the ATONs.

## Regulatory Markers

There are two kinds of **regulatory markers**: signs and buoys. As mentioned above, both are white with orange markings, and the signs have orange borders. Where letters or numbers appear on the signs or buoys, the lettering is black. Regulatory markers show boat exclusion, danger, and controlled areas and give information or directions.

## Safe Water ATONs

**Safe water ATONs** are spherical buoys, floating structures with balls attached to their tops, or octagonal daymarks. They are red-and-white vertically striped (Figure 7-19) and when lighted, have white lights. Safe water ATONs may have letters, but they never have numbers. The middle portion of Figure 7-1 shows the safe water marks seen in fairways or midchannel.

## Preferred Channel Marks

**Preferred channel marks** (sometimes called "junction buoys"), which are found at junctions of navigable channels (Figure 7-20), show the main or preferred channel, as in Figure 7-2. They may also mark wrecks or obstructions. You may pass on either side, but consult your chart to find the location of the obstruction.

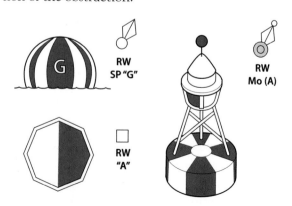

**Figure 7-19.** Vertically striped safe water buoys and their chart symbols.

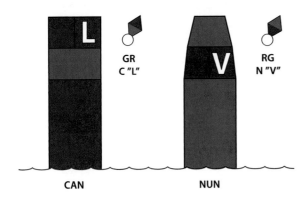

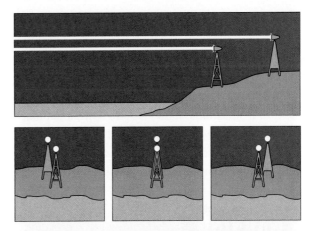

**Figure 7-20.** Buoys marking preferred channels and their chart symbols.

Preferred channel marks include daymarks, nun and can buoys, and floating structures. Their special features are their red and green horizontal color bands. As with safe water marks, these ATONs may have letters but do not have numbers.

The color bands on a preferred channel mark help you know which is the main or preferred channel. The main channel may have the deeper water. When the top band of the mark is red, treat it as if it were a red mark in order to stay in the preferred channel, and leave it to starboard when returning from sea. When the top band is green, treat it like a green mark in order to stay in the preferred channel.

If the preferred channel mark is a can buoy, its top color band will always be green, and if it is a nun buoy, its top color will always be red. So if at a junction point you see the shape of the buoy, you don't even need to see the color of its top band. If it is a can, keep it to port when returning from the sea. If it is a nun, keep it to starboard when you return.

## Ranges

A *range* is a pair of ATONs (Figure 7-21) placed a suitable distance apart. When the more distant one, which is always higher, is directly behind the lower, nearer one from your position, your vessel is in the center of a navigable channel. If you veer to the left of the channel's center, the forward mark will move to the right of the rear one. If you wander to the right of center, the forward one will move to the left of the rear one. To correct your course, steer in the direction of the closer (lower) mark.

Ranges are established to keep a vessel on a course that avoids dangers on either side. While

**Figure 7-21. Top:** Range lights. **Bottom:** Range marks like this pair on the Intracoastal Waterway keep boats and ships in hard-to-follow channels. When the marks get out of alignment, as here, you are wandering toward the edge of the channel. In this case, to get back to the center of the channel, you would steer to port if sighting the range over your bow, or to starboard if sighting it over your stern. (PHOTO BY GENE HAMILTON)

they are most often used by large vessels, they can also be useful to small boats trying to run very narrow channels.

Ranges appear in a variety of colors (see Figure 7-1) and may have letters, but they never have numbers. They often have red, green, or white lights to serve as guides at night. You use the lights in the same manner as the range. Keep them in line and you will be in the middle of the channel.

Always consult your chart when using a range. The marks help you stay in midchannel but do not tell how far you can follow the range before the channel ends or turns. Range marks are often on land, a poor medium in which to operate your boat.

## Directional Lights

A *directional light* may be used where it is impractical to install range lights. A single light is placed at one end of a straight section of a channel, high enough to be seen the full length of the channel. It produces a narrow, intense beam of white light,

> **WARNING** *Red-and-white vertically striped buoys are safe water marks in the U.S. ATON System. In the old USWMS, however, a red-striped white buoy was used to indicate that the boater should not pass between the buoy and the nearest shore. With the states in the process of adopting the U.S. ATON System, a new buoy, colored white with black stripes, has been adopted to replace the red-and-white buoys, but in isolated instances one of the older buoys may still be encountered on state-controlled waters.*

bordered by broader red and green sectors on the red-buoyed and green-buoyed sides of the channel, respectively. Your chart will show the arcs covered by each sector.

When you see only the white light, you are in the center of the channel. If the red light is visible while you are returning from sea, you are to the right of the channel's center. If the green light is visible, you are to the left of the channel's center.

Even though a channel is marked with ranges or directional lights, it may not always be necessary or advisable for you to follow them. In harbors, for example, the water is usually deep enough outside marked channels for small boats to navigate safely. If there is commercial traffic in the channel, or if the channel or harbor is congested, consult the chart to see if you can safely navigate outside the channel.

## INTRACOASTAL WATERWAY MARKS

ATONs on the Intracoastal Waterway are the same as those elsewhere on the navigable waters of North America, with one exception.

## Yellow Triangles, Squares, and Bands

All lateral marks on the ICW have yellow, reflective triangles or squares on them. Generally, red daymarks, buoys, and minor lights have yellow triangles, while yellow squares appear on green marks (Figure 7-22).

When you follow the ICW south from Manasquan, New Jersey, around Florida, and west along the Gulf Coast, keep daybeacons, buoys, and minor lights with yellow triangles to starboard, while leaving ATONs with yellow squares to port.

Nonlateral ICW ATONs, such as safe water marks and ranges, have yellow bands. ICW ATONs can be seen in the upper half of Figure 7-2.

## Dual-Purpose Marks

There are possible points of confusion where the ICW joins or crosses another waterway. There you will find the yellow ICW triangles and squares on

**Figure 7-22.** A can (top) and a red daybeacon (bottom) on the Intracoastal Waterway show the yellow square and yellow triangle, respectively, that are characteristic of ICW ATONs—although, on the red daybeacon, the yellow triangle is mostly obscured by an osprey nest. (PHOTOS BY GENE HAMILTON)

the marks of the crossing waterway. Thus, it is possible to see a yellow triangle on a green, square daymark, a green buoy, or a structure with a green light, and you can find a yellow square on a red, triangular daymark, a red buoy, or a structure with a red light. This is done to avoid duplication of daymarks, which would be even more confusing. When you do encounter this condition, interpret the meaning of these dual-purpose marks as follows: be guided by the yellow markings if you are traveling the ICW; if you are traveling the crossing waterway, ignore the yellow marks and be guided by the colors, shapes, and numbers of the original ATONS.

The upper portion of Figure 7-2 illustrates how you should interpret dual-purpose marks. Note that the ICW is the dashed line going from the upper right to the upper left corner of Figure 7-2. The crossing waterway is shown by the heavy black line.

When traveling on the ICW from right to left in the illustration, you are considered to be returning from sea. As you would expect, red nun buoy "2" has a yellow triangle on it and should be kept to starboard. Green can "3" has a yellow square on it and should be kept to port.

When returning from sea, you might expect to keep red buoy "6" to starboard. Since you are on the ICW, though, and returning from seaward, you are guided by its yellow square and should keep the buoy on the port side. Red buoy "8" has a yellow triangle and should be kept to starboard.

# Light Characteristics

Red ATONs, when lighted, have red lights, and green marks have green lights. ATONs with white lights rarely have lateral significance except on the Western Rivers System above Baton Rouge (see Figure 7-4). Elsewhere, white-lighted ATONS mark safe water (as in midchannel buoys) and ranges, and informational, regulatory, and diamond-shaped marks also have white lights when lighted.

> **TIP** *On the ICW, you should be guided by the yellow square or triangle, not by the colors or shapes of the ATONs on which they are placed.*

## LIGHT PATTERNS

Most lights on ATONs have flashing patterns of illumination to help identify them. Some lights, though, are *fixed*, which mean they shine continuously from sundown to sunup.

Lights flash in a variety of ways. They may flash at regular intervals; a light that flashes every 4 seconds, for example, is said to have a period of 4 seconds. Alternatively, a light may show groups of flashes. It might, for example, flash twice and then remain off for a short period of time. A *quick light* flashes 60 times per minute, making its period 1 second. The lower range light in the middle of Figure 7-2 is a quick light. Figures 7-1 and 7-23 show several of the light patterns in use.

## OCCULTING LIGHTS

A *flashing light* flashes on while an *occulting light* blinks off. Put another way, a flashing light is off more than on, and an occulting light is on more than off. Lights can occult with regular patterns. An *isophase*, or iso, light is on for an interval equal to the time it is off. (**Iso** is from the Greek *isos*, which means equal.) The upper range light in the middle of Figure 7-2 is an isophase light. Red buoy "4" in the middle of Figure 7-2 has an occulting light.

## SAFE WATER ATON LIGHTS

The white lights on safe water marks flash a regular pattern of a short flash followed by a longer one. A period of darkness follows these two flashes. The light is flashing the Morse code letter A (• –) and any light with such a flash is a safe water mark. The light on the red-and-white striped buoy at the bottom of Figure 7-2 is an example.

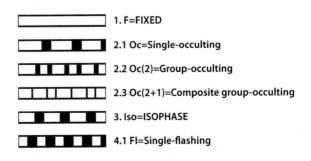

1. F=FIXED

2.1 Oc=Single-occulting

2.2 Oc(2)=Group-occulting

2.3 Oc(2+1)=Composite group-occulting

3. Iso=ISOPHASE

4.1 Fl=Single-flashing

**Figure 7-23.** A selection of light patterns.

## PREFERRED CHANNEL LIGHTS

The light on a preferred channel mark is either red or green; its color matches the color of the top band on the ATON. Whatever its color, it always flashes in a set pattern—two flashes followed by a brief period of darkness, then a single flash—that means "I am a preferred channel light." The period of darkness after the single flash is longer than the one following the two flashes. After this period of darkness, the pattern repeats. Lights that flash in this manner are called **composite group flashing lights**. The particular sequence described here is 2 + 1—that is, two flashes followed by one flash. Note the preferred channel light on Figure 7-2.

## ARTICULATED LIGHTS

An **articulated light** is a combination of a minor light and a buoy. It is a sealed hollow cylinder, up to 50 or more feet long, that attaches directly to the seabed by means of an articulated sinker rather than being anchored with ground tackle. The light remains in a vertical, nearly stationary position, moving only in small circles, thus providing a more precise location than an anchored buoy. The length of the cylinder is equal to the water depth plus the tidal range plus 10 to 15 feet of height above the surface. At its top are daymarks and an appropriate light.

Articulated lights mark positions where more precision is needed than buoys can give, and where water is too deep for a pile or dolphin structure. Since they do not have chains, they are almost always directly over their sinkers and have very small watch circles.

# Chart Symbols

**Chart symbols** help you identify ATONs. The symbol for a buoy, for example, is a diamond with a small watch circle at its tip. If the buoy is lighted, the watch circle is overprinted with a larger, magenta-colored disk. Magenta is used because it is visible under the red lights used in many cockpits and on ships' bridges at night.

When the diamond symbol is green, it represents a green buoy; when red, it represents a red buoy. Letters and figures printed next to the diamond tell you more about the buoy. For example, in the notation G "9" *Fl G 4s*, "G" means green and "9" is the number on the buoy. The buoy has a light that flashes green every 4 seconds, and the italic type indicates that it's a buoy and not a fixed mark. This buoy appears at the left of Figure 7-1.

Suppose a preferred channel buoy has a green top band and its green light flashes in a composite group every 6 seconds. On a chart it would appear as a buoy symbol with the top half green and the bottom half red. It would have a magenta disk overprinted on the watch circle and the notation *Fl (2 + 1) G 6s* such as that for buoy "C" on the left side of Figure 7-1.

## FIXED STRUCTURE LIGHTS

Lights on fixed structures, including minor lights, also have their characteristic chart symbols. These are magenta exclamation marks with black dots that show the locations of the structures. In addition, each light's period, color, number, height, and the distance from which it may be seen appear on the chart. If the position is only an approximation, it is marked PA. The chart symbol and description shown in Figure 7-24 indicate a minor light that flashes green every 6 seconds. It is 12 feet above mean high water and can be seen for 3 miles in clear weather. Note that the printing is roman (not italic), which confirms that it is a minor light, not a buoy.

## SYMBOLS FOR BUOYS

The chart symbol for a can buoy is a green diamond with a small watch circle, with the green color indicating a can. If the buoy is not overprinted in

**Fl G 6s 12ft 3M "5"**

**Figure 7-24.** Chart symbol and description for a light.

magenta, you know that it has no light. If G C "7" was printed next to the diamond, you would know that it is green can number 7. Red nun buoys have symbols that follow a similar pattern. Figure 7-1 shows a complete description of a green can ("9") and a red nun ("6").

## SYMBOLS FOR DAYMARKS

A green daymark appears on a chart as a green square. If the description on the chart is G "1," you know that it is daymark number 1. The symbol for a red daymark is a red triangle, as in Figure 7-1.

You can also tell from a chart if an ATON is a buoy or a fixed structure by the type in which its description is printed. The symbols and descriptions of fixed ATONs are printed in "straight-up" roman type, while symbols and descriptions of floating structures and buoys are printed in italic. You can find additional chart symbols on Figure 7-3.

# Light Structures

Lighted aids to navigation may be as small as minor lights on wooden piles in small creeks or as large as tall lighthouses on the coasts. Their intensities also vary from weak to brilliant. They may be small, battery-powered minor lights or powerful lights with millions of candlepower, such as those in coastal lighthouses. Regardless of their sizes or intensities, they serve the same functions as buoys and daybeacons. Except for lighthouses, they have the same numbering, coloring, light, and sound characteristics as buoys.

## LIGHTHOUSES

Lighthouses are **short-range aids** (SRAs) and are not a part of any buoyage system. Rather, they are built where they will give the most help. While their primary purpose is to mark prominent headlands, harbor entrances, isolated danger areas, and other points, they also serve to support lights at considerable heights above the water. Some have quarters for personnel.

Lighthouse structures vary considerably in appearance, with their designs depending upon their needed heights, their locations, and the geological structures that support them (Figure 7-25). The *Light List*, a Coast Guard publication that lists all aids to navigation, gives a brief description of each lighthouse. For example, the description given for Alligator Reef Light in the Florida Keys says, "White octagonal pyramid skeleton tower enclosing stair cylinder and square dwelling; black pile foundation."

Cylindrical or conical towers may have distinctive color combinations painted on them. The Cape Hatteras Light in North Carolina, for exam-

**Figure 7-25.** **Top:** Marblehead Light. (PHOTO BY USCG PA3 ALLYSON TAYLOR) **Bottom:** Cape Disappointment Light, Ilwaco, Washington, on a stormy day. (PHOTO BY LARRY KELLIS)

ple, has black and white spirals. Each structure and its distinctive colors make up a lighthouse "day-mark" to help navigators identify it during the day since its lights usually shine only at night.

The distance a lighthouse light must be seen is a major consideration in its height and location and the intensity of its light. The higher and the more brilliant the light, the farther away it is visible.

### Lighthouse Sectors

Some lighthouse lights have *red sectors*, which indicate danger. These are created by placing red glass in the beams of light from the lighthouses so that when viewed from areas of shallow water, rocks, or other dangers, the normally white lights appear red. Such red sectors are shown on charts of the area.

The red sectors of Alligator Reef Light are shown in Figure 7-26. The light is normally white, but to a boat between the dotted lines it appears red. The spaces between the dotted lines are the red sectors.

The teardrop-shaped magenta symbol for Alligator Reef Light indicates that it is a light. The light flashes in groups of four flashes every 40 seconds. It is 136 feet above mean high water, and can be seen for 8 miles on a clear night. From its height you can tell it is a major light, one you would expect to be white, which it is except in its red sectors. Charts often include pictures of major lights to aid in identifying them.

## CLASSES OF LIGHT STRUCTURES

Lights on fixed structures include primary seacoast lights, secondary lights, river or harbor lights, and minor lights. The *Light List* gives a description of each light, which include the following:

- name and light rhythm
- location (latitude and longitude)
- nominal range (distance the light can be seen under optimal conditions)

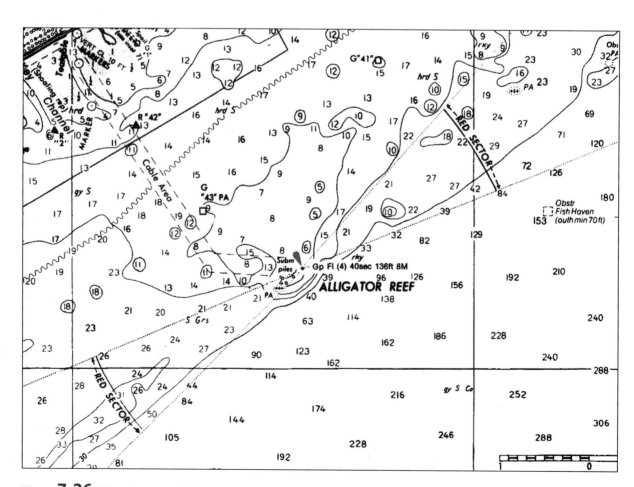

**Figure 7-26.** The red sectors of Alligator Reef Light.

- height above mean high water
- type and appearance of the structure, including height above ground and daymark, if any
- characteristics of sound devices present
- year built

## LIGHT STRUCTURE SOUND SIGNALS

Most lighthouses and major lights, and some minor light structures, have foghorns or other sound-producing devices that warn mariners of danger in periods of poor visibility. On some floating structures, the signals operate either mechanically or electrically, with electrical operation being the most dependable since mechanical operation may depend on wave action.

You can identify a particular structure by the timing of its signals, the silent period between signals, and the tone of the signal, all of which are given on nautical charts. When the number of blasts and the time for a complete cycle are not enough to identify the structure, you may refer to the *Light List*, where the exact length of each blast and silent interval is described.

In some boating areas there may be several active foghorns, each with its own period and tone. When you boat in such an area, you need to be able to recognize each foghorn to help assure safe passage.

# Lights on Bridges

Nautical charts show bridges and describe them and their characteristics. Bridges are described as "fixed" or "draw." Also listed are their horizontal and vertical clearances when closed, the latter given as feet above mean high water. A *bascule* bridge is a type of drawbridge that has a counterweight on one side.

The lights on bridges do not conform to any buoyage system. Red lights mark piers and other parts of bridges and also show that a drawbridge is in the closed position. A corresponding green light on a drawbridge shows that it is open. A green light on a fixed bridge marks the centerline of the channel, while the red lights mark the pilings on the sides.

Sometimes there is more than one safe channel under a bridge, in which case the preferred channel has three white lights in a vertical line above its green light.

# Electronic Aids to Navigation

An array of sophisticated electronic navigational aids is available to assist you. These include Loran-C, satellite navigation systems, radar, and others.

## LORAN-C

*Loran-C* is a once commonly used electronic aid to navigation that has been largely replaced by GPS. Shore-based loran towers transmit precisely timed radio signals, and these are picked up by a shipboard loran receiver that is coupled to a small microprocessor. This unit measures time delays in signals from a master station and two or more secondary stations, and uses these differences to triangulate its position. The unit reports these coordinates as time differences, which can be plotted on Loran-C overprinted nautical charts, or as latitude and longitude coordinates for more convenient chart plotting.

In some areas, positions are accurate to within 100 to 200 feet, but this is by no means universal throughout the loran coverage area. Loran-C is especially notable for its repeatability, which has made it popular among anglers. Once the loran coordinates of a favorite fishing hole are programmed as a waypoint in the receiver, it is possible to return to that spot with great and consistent accuracy. Loran-C units can also be programmed to give an estimated time of arrival based on the vessel's present speed over ground. Loran-C has fallen from wide use due to the enormous convenience, global coverage, and great accuracy of GPS. Nevertheless, the U.S. government is committed to maintaining the Loran-C network, which will continue to provide coverage for the United States and Canada for the foreseeable future.

## GLOBAL POSITIONING SYSTEM

The *global positioning system* (GPS) has become the principal navigation system used worldwide. It employs 24 satellites that maintain circular orbits, and the coverage is such that a shipboard GPS receiver anywhere in the world always has at least six satellites within receiving range. The receiver requires signals from only three satellites to construct a position fix, but additional satellites permit a higher level of confidence in the fix. The system has two levels of accuracy: one for recreational boaters and another, more accurate, one used by the U.S. Department of Defense. The system used by recreational boaters provides accuracy to within 15 meters (49.2 feet) or less 95% of the time.

A supplementary system called *Differential GPS* (DGPS) was created for mariners by the U.S. Coast Guard to work in conjunction with GPS. This system uses precisely located land-based receivers to correct GPS signals for slight distortions due to atmospheric and other factors, then transmits these corrections to appropriately equipped shipboard GPS receivers. This allows users within about 100 miles of a DGPS radiobeacon to realize an accuracy of 5 meters (16.4 feet) or better. These radiobeacons are located at most U.S. harbors, including the U.S. Virgin Islands, Puerto Rico, and most of Alaska. You must have a DGPS antenna and receiver to realize this enhanced precision.

Another new GPS augmentation is called the *wide area augmentation system* (WAAS). It is currently being deployed throughout the United States and will become a standard part of GPS in the near future. This system claims an accuracy of 2.5 meters (8.2 feet). Most new GPS receivers are WAAS capable.

As with Loran-C, GPS receivers can display a boat's present location as latitude/longitude coordinates. You can program your receiver with many latitude/longitude locations, called *waypoints*, which may include buoys, harbor entrances, and other key locations. These waypoints can be linked together to plan a trip, which is called a *route*. Your receiver can give you a compass course to steer for your next waypoint, and it can tell you how far you are from the waypoint and when you will arrive, at your present speed. If wind, current, or inattention causes you to drift off your course line, it will report this to you as *cross-track error*. GPS has truly revolutionized navigation, but it does not relieve you from the need for careful chartwork and "dead reckoning," as discussed in Chapter 12.

Coast Guard *Local Notices to Mariners*, and the website www.navcen.uscg.gov, inform users of forecasted long-term outages of GPS and loran. This website also offers general information about all the navigation systems supported by the U.S. Coast Guard. The mailing address is: Commanding Officer, USCG NAVCEN, 7323 Telegraph Road, Alexandria, VA 22315. The Coast Guard also broadcasts information regarding the systems, as needed, on VHF-FM Channels 16 and 22A.

Shortwave radio station WWV, in Fort Collins, Colorado, also reports the status of GPS at 14 to 15 minutes after the hour. WWVH in Kekaha, Hawaii, reports the same information at 43 to 44 minutes after the hour.

# Navigation Publications

There are a number of publications and charts to aid you (Figure 7-27). Since the location, characteristics, and maintenance status of ATONs change from time to time, obsolete charts can be dangerous and you should be sure yours are up to date.

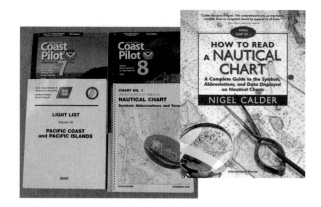

**Figure 7-27.** Assorted navigation publications, including a *Coast Pilot, Chart No. 1*, a *Light List* (PHOTO BY RAY PAGES), and *How to Read a Nautical Chart*.

There are several government and commercial sources of charts, but most of these rely on charts produced by the National Oceanic and Atmospheric Administration's (NOAA) Office of Coast Survey (OCS). In addition, charts of major river systems such as the Mississippi and Ohio are produced by the U.S. Army Corps of Engineers, and charts for the high seas and foreign waters are produced by the National Imagery and Mapping Agency (NIMA), which was recently renamed the National Geospatial-Intelligence Agency (NGA). You can buy charts at marinas, boat stores, and other chart dealers. Reproductions of government charts on waterproof paper or reformatted in bound volumes to cover defined regions are also available from commercial sources, and these will sometimes represent a significant savings or gain in convenience over the government charts. You can also obtain the latest edition of a chart from online print-on-demand services, and download free electronic charts in raster format (for use on a laptop computer or chartplotter) from the Office of Coast Survey website. (This web address, http://chartmaker.ncd.noaa.gov, will also direct you to print-on-demand charts, *Notices to Mariners*, and *Coast Pilots* in print or digital downloadable form.) Note that the latest editions of charts can be several years old and in need of updating.

Each district of the Coast Guard publishes a weekly *Local Notice to Mariners*. Free copies are available online at http://chartmaker.ncd.noaa.gov or www.navcen.uscg.lnm. Use the information in the *Local Notice* to keep your charts and light lists up to date. This publication also includes other important information such as bridge conditions, proposed military operations, and special marine events.

*Chart No. 1, Nautical Chart Symbols, Abbreviations, and Terms*, published jointly by NOAA and the Defense Mapping Agency, is useful in interpreting nautical charts. Though it is no longer available from the government for distribution through commercial chart agents, you can still obtain a print copy of *Chart No. 1* from the U.S. Government Printing Office, or view and download a digital version at http://chartmaker.ncd.noaa.gov. In addition, various commercial publishers offer *Chart No. 1* for sale.

*Light Lists* help you identify aids to navigation, as discussed earlier in this chapter. The Coast Guard publishes it in several volumes as follows:

*Volume I, Atlantic Coast*, describes ATONs in U.S. waters from the St. Croix River, Maine, to Shrewsbury River, New Jersey.

*Volume II, Atlantic Coast*, describes ATONs from Shrewsbury River, New Jersey, to Little River, South Carolina.

*Volume III, Atlantic and Gulf Coasts*, describes ATONs in U.S. waters from Little River, South Carolina, to Econfina River, Florida, including Puerto Rico and the U.S. Virgin Islands.

*Volume IV, Gulf of Mexico*, describes ATONs from Econfina River, Florida, to the Rio Grande, Texas.

*Volume V, Mississippi River System*, describes ATONs on the Mississippi and its navigable tributaries.

*Volume VI, Pacific Coast and Pacific Islands*, describes the ATONs in U.S. waters on the Pacific Coast and Pacific islands. For the convenience of mariners, it includes some of the lighted aids on the British Columbia coast.

*Volume VII, Great Lakes*, describes ATONs maintained by the Coast Guard and some of the aids maintained by Canada on the Great Lakes and the St. Lawrence River above the St. Regis River.

You can order *Light Lists* from the Superintendent of Documents, P.O. Box 371954, Pittsburgh, PA 15250-7954, or call 1-866-512-1800, or go to http://bookstore.gpo.gov. You can download the *Lists* and get the latest information at www.navcen.uscg.gov/pubs/LightLists/LightLists.htm. They are also available from branch offices of the GPO, located in many cities, and from sales agents in most major ports. You can find a sales agent by going to http://www.naco.faa.gov/agents.asp, or get a free catalog by contacting the National Aeronautical Charting Office, Distribution Division (AJW-3550), 10201 Good Luck Road, Glenn Dale, MD 20769-9700, 1-800-638-8972.

# Practice Questions

*IMPORTANT BOATING TERMS*
In the following exercise, match the words in the column on the left with the definitions in the column on the right. In the blank space to the left of each term, write the letter of the item that best matches it. Do not use an item in the right-hand column more than once.

| THE ITEMS | THE RESPONSES |
|---|---|
| 1. _____ daymark | a. mark midchannel |
| 2. _____ lateral marks | b. even numbers |
| 3. _____ red markers and buoys | c. blinks off |
| 4. _____ safe water marks | d. on from sunset to sunrise |
| 5. _____ occulting light | e. mark sides of navigable channels |
| 6. _____ fixed light | f. odd numbers |
| 7. _____ green markers and buoys | g. cylindrical buoy |
| 8. _____ nun | h. flashes on |
| 9. _____ can | i. has a geometrical shape |
| 10. _____ flashing light | j. red buoy, conical top |

# Multiple-Choice Items

In the following items, choose the best response:

**7-1.** To be useful to a boater, landmarks must be visible and

a. appear on a chart of the area
b. well known
c. blend with the background
d. historical in nature

**7-2.** You are "returning from sea" when going

a. counterclockwise around the United States
b. clockwise around the United States
c. downstream on a river
d. east in Lake Erie

**7-3.** Spherical buoys mark fairways and the middles of navigable channels and are

a. green above red
b. all black
c. red above green
d. red-and-white striped

**7-4.** The red buoys used to mark the right side of a channel

a. have white lights
b. have green lights
c. have even numbers
d. are can shaped

**7-5.** Lighted safe water buoys have

a. white lights
b. red lights
c. green lights
d. yellow lights

**7-6.** Going from Manasquan Inlet in New Jersey on the ICW, down the East Coast, up the west coast of Florida, and west across the Gulf of Mexico is considered

a. returning from sea
b. going to sea
c. cruising

## Multiple-Choice Items (continued)

d. going counterclockwise

**7-7.** A preferred channel marker has

 a. green and red lights
 b. green and red horizontal bands
 c. white lights
 d. vertical red-and-white stripes

**7-8.** In the U.S. ATON System, a can is

 a. white
 b. red
 c. black
 d. green

**7-9.** A nun buoy has

 a. a flat top
 b. a conical-shaped top
 c. no letter or number
 d. an odd number

**7-10.** A square daymark with an odd number is the same as

 a. a green can buoy
 b. a red lateral marker
 c. a no-wake zone marker
 d. a midchannel marker

**7-11.** The following special markings are used in the ICW system:

 a. yellow triangles
 b. yellow squares
 c. yellow bands
 d. all of the above

**7-12.** Daymarks on the sides of channels usually have

 a. letters
 b. yellow triangles or squares
 c. numbers
 d. neither letters or numbers

**7-13.** An occulting light is

 a. on more than off
 b. yellow
 c. off more than on
 d. on at all times

**7-14.** On a chart you can tell if an ATON is a buoy from its

 a. gothic type

 b. italic (slanting) type
 c. boldfaced type
 d. large print

**7-15.** You can find a brief description of each light-house in the

 a. *Local Notice to Mariners*
 b. *Chart No. 1*
 c. *Light List*
 d. *Notice to Mariners*

**7-16.** A fixed light is one that

 a. is on from dusk to dawn
 b. has been repaired
 c. shines brightly
 d. is on from sunrise to sunset

**7-17.** The centerline of the navigable channel under a fixed bridge is marked by

 a. amber lights
 b. red lights
 c. green lights
 d. red and green lights

**7-18.** Red daymarks have

 a. three sides and odd numbers
 b. four sides and even numbers
 c. diamond shapes
 d. three sides and even numbers

**7-19.** On a chart, a magenta disk means

 a. a buoy
 b. a lighted aid to navigation
 c. a triangular daymark
 d. a square daymark

**7-20.** A special-purpose mark, such as a yellow buoy, is used to designate

 a. an anchorage
 b. a dredge pipeline
 c. a triangular daymark
 d. a square daymark

**7-21.** If you see a white buoy with an orange diamond, two orange horizontal stripes, and a white center, you should

 a. keep the buoy to your starboard
 b. keep the buoy to your port
 c. keep a safe distance away
 d. slow your speed

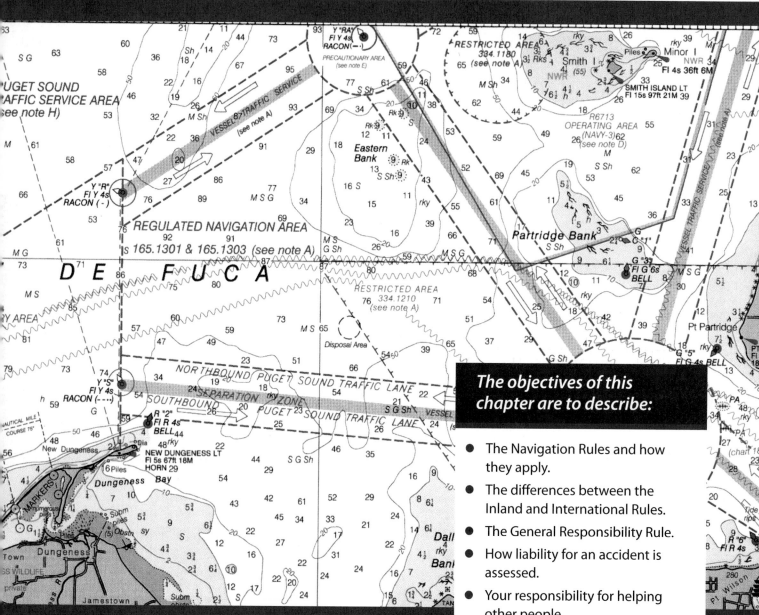

## The objectives of this chapter are to describe:

- The Navigation Rules and how they apply.
- The differences between the Inland and International Rules.
- The General Responsibility Rule.
- How liability for an accident is assessed.
- Your responsibility for helping other people.
- Safe conduct for your vessel.
- Proper sound signals for various situations.
- The proper light configuration for your vessel.
- The rules of operation in restricted visibility.
- What lights and shapes tell you.
- Legal distress signals.

(REPRINTED WITH PERMISSION FROM
*A CRUISING GUIDE TO PUGET SOUND
AND THE SAN JUAN ISLANDS*, SECOND
EDITION, BY MIGAEL SCHERER)

THE DANGER OF collisions has existed since the second vessel was built. Navigation rules exist to help prevent such mishaps. These rules are to vessels what "rules of the road" are to automobiles, and it is the responsibility of a boat operator to know and follow the Navigation Rules.

# Two Sets of Rules

There are two sets of Navigation Rules in force in U.S. waters—the *International Rules* and the *U.S. Inland Rules*. The two are for the most part identical, but the U.S. Inland Rules diverge from international standards in those few instances where necessary to meet the unique needs for safe navigation on U.S. rivers, bays, and other inland waters.

Taken together, the Navigation Rules apply to all vessels on the *navigable waters* of the United States, meaning all U.S. territorial waters (up to 12 miles offshore, generally speaking) and any waters that provide a transportation route between two or more states or to the sea. Further, the International Rules apply to all U.S. vessels on the high seas when not subject to another nation's jurisdiction.

## THE INTERNATIONAL RULES

Rules to prevent collisions have been evolving for the past 150 years. We now use the 1972 International Regulations for Prevention of Collisions at Sea, other names for which are the International Rules and the **72 COLREGS**. These rules were established by international treaty to secure consistency of standards throughout the world.

## THE INLAND RULES

The Inland Navigational Rules Act of 1980, passed by Congress to align U.S. rules with the International Rules, became effective in 1981. Before that time, vessels on inland waters followed several sets of rules, including an older set of Inland Rules, the Western Rivers Rules, the Great Lakes Rules, and parts of the Motorboat Act of 1940. If you think it is confusing to operate under two sets of rules as we do today, imagine what it was like before 1981!

Both sets of Rules appear in *Navigation Rules, International–Inland* published by the U.S. Government Printing Office. You can order a copy from the Superintendent of Documents at P.O. Box 371954, Pittsburgh, PA 15250-7954, call 1-866-512-1800, go to http://bookstore.gpo.gov, or find it at most marine supply stores (Figure 8-1). You can also view them online or download them in PDF

**Figure 8-1.** The *Navigation Rules, International–Inland.*

## More About the Rules

The Rules of the Road presented in this chapter summarize the basic navigation rules for which a boat operator is responsible. There are, however, additional and more in-depth rules regarding various types of waterways and operating your boat around commercial vessels and other watercraft. It is the responsibility of a boat operator to know and follow all the Navigation Rules. For a complete listing of the Navigation Rules, refer to the *Navigation Rules, International–Inland* (COMDTINST M16672.2D), published by the U.S. Coast Guard and available through the U.S. Government Printing Office or on the web at www.uscg.mil/vtm/navrules/navrules.pdf. For state-specific navigation requirements, refer to the state laws where you intend to boat.

format at www.navcen.uscg.gov/mwv/navrules/rotr_online.htm. Any boat 12 or more meters long must have a copy of the Inland Rules aboard. The penalty for failure to carry one can be as much as $5,000.

## YOUR LOCAL WATERS

The Inland or International Rules may not regulate boating on your local lake or other body of water that does not provide a route across a state line or to the sea. Instead, local ordinances or state laws may apply. Nevertheless, when you boat on such waters, you should use the same standards of common sense that underlie the Inland and International Rules.

## DEMARCATION LINES

*Demarcation lines* separate waters on which the Inland Rules apply from those regulated by the International Rules. The Commandant of the U.S. Coast Guard draws these lines, which can be seen as a dashed magenta line on some navigational charts.

In general, the demarcation lines follow the coasts. Across bays and other inlets, they go from one easily described point of land or landmark to another. Seaward of these lines, the International Rules apply (Figure 8-2); landward, the Inland Rules apply. In some areas—along the coast of New England, for example—the line is drawn well into bays and rivers, and a local chart is the best arbiter of where the transition occurs. Exact descriptions of the demarcation lines also appear in the *Navigation Rules*.

# To Whom Do the Rules Apply?

Rule 1 of both the International and Inland Rules answers this question: The International Rules ". . .

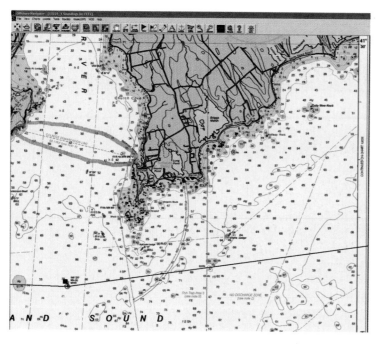

**Figure 8-2.** Seaward of the dashed magenta demarcation line (circled in yellow) on this chart, the International Rules apply. Upriver of the line, the Inland Rules apply. (REPRINTED WITH PERMISSION FROM *THE WEEKEND NAVIGATOR* BY BOB SWEET)

apply to all vessels upon the high seas" and on all connecting waters such as rivers and bays that are navigable by seagoing vessels. The Inland Rules ". . . apply to all vessels on the inland waters of the United States." They apply also to U.S. vessels on the Canadian waters of the Great Lakes unless they conflict with Canadian law.

# Vessel Definitions

Rule 3 tells us that a *vessel* is any type of watercraft, including seaplanes, that can be used for transportation on the water. *Seaplanes* are considered ". . . aircraft designed to maneuver on the water."

The rule further defines *power-driven vessels* as vessels propelled by machinery, and *sailing vessels* as vessels under sail, not using propulsion machinery. When a sailing vessel is using engine power instead of or in addition to sails, it is legally classed as a power-driven vessel. Rule 3 also makes the following distinctions.

## VESSEL UNDERWAY

Some of the Rules require an understanding of the term "underway." A vessel *underway* is not at anchor, nor made fast to a shore or pier, nor aground (Figure 8-3). A vessel *making way* is being propelled through the water. It is **adrift** when it is not being propelled, not at anchor, not made fast to the shore, or aground (Figure 8-4). A **drifting vessel** is underway but not making way.

## FISHING VESSEL

A *fishing vessel* is any vessel fishing with nets, lines, trawls, or other fishing apparatus that restricts its ability to maneuver under the Rules. Vessels fishing with trolling lines are not fishing vessels, and your vessel is not a fishing vessel if you are sportfishing.

## VESSEL RESTRICTED IN ABILITY TO MANEUVER

Some vessels are *restricted in their ability to maneuver,* meaning that their work keeps them from abiding by the Rules and staying out of the way of other

**Figure 8-3.** These vessels are all classified as not underway by the rules. **Top to bottom:** Docked, anchored, and aground. (TOP AND MIDDLE PHOTOS BY BOB DENNIS; BOTTOM PHOTO REPRINTED WITH PERMISSION FROM *SEAWORTHY: ESSENTIAL LESSONS FROM BOAT U.S.'S 20-YEAR CASE FILE OF THINGS GONE WRONG* BY ROBERT A. ADRIANCE)

vessels. Dredges, cable- and pipe-laying vessels, and other such vessels are restricted in their ability to maneuver.

## VESSELS IN SIGHT OF ANOTHER

A vessel is *in sight of another* when it can observe the other vessel or the other vessel's lights visually, without mechanical or optical aids. Other rules apply when one vessel has another in "sight" with radar.

## VESSEL NOT UNDER COMMAND

A vessel is *not under command* when some exceptional circumstance keeps it from maneuvering as required by the Rules. This means that it can't keep

**Figure 8-4.** The 90-foot tall ship *Irving Johnson* lies hard aground only yards from shore near the entrance to Channel Islands Harbor, Oxnard, California. Until it can be refloated, this vessel will be classified under the rules as not underway! (PHOTO BY MIKE BRODEY)

out of the way of other vessels. A drifting boat with an inoperative engine or steering system is not under command.

## VESSEL CONSTRAINED BY DRAFT

The International Rules describe a vessel *constrained by draft* as a power-driven vessel that is severely restricted in its ability to change course because of its draft relative to the depth of water (Figure 8-5). The Inland Rules do not contain such a definition.

**Figure 8-5.** The Law of Gross Tonnage is not listed in the COLREGS, but prudence and common sense dictate that you should keep away from large vessels. Even when not constrained by draft, a ship like this takes a mile or two to stop or turn, and it's moving a lot faster than it may appear to be. (REPRINTED WITH PERMISSION FROM *SEAWORTHY: ESSENTIAL LESSONS FROM BOAT U.S.'S 20-YEAR CASE FILE OF THINGS GONE WRONG* BY ROBERT A. ADRIANCE)

# The General Responsibility Rule

Rule 2 is the General Responsibility Rule, which has two principal aspects.

## THE RULE OF GOOD SEAMANSHIP

Part (a) of the General Responsibility Rule has been called the Rule of Good Seamanship. It says, simply, that nothing in the Rules excuses you from failure to follow the Rules or to practice good seamanship. In situations not covered by the Rules, take the action required by the special circumstances.

## THE GENERAL PRUDENTIAL RULE

Part (b) of the General Responsibility Rule is sometimes called the General Prudential Rule. It directs you to consider all the dangers to navigation when applying the Rules, evaluating and responding to any special circumstances that may make you depart from the Rules to avoid immediate danger. "Immediate danger" means more than just the mere perception of a risk of collision. It means, rather, that a collision is imminent unless you act immediately to avoid it. In such a circumstance, Rule 2(b) says, you *must* depart from the Rules to avoid the collision.

## ASSESSING LEGAL LIABILITY

There are important differences in legal liability between maritime and civil law. Because each skipper must act to prevent a collision and must depart from the Navigation Rules when necessary, all parties usually share responsibility for a marine accident. This does not mean that the shares are equal, however. That is a matter for a court to decide.

If you have a collision, you may be at least partially responsible no matter what the other skipper does. Likewise, skippers operating under the influence of alcohol or drugs are usually held at least partially responsible for an accident no matter what the other skipper may have done. It is not unusual for all parties to be responsible for some act they did or did not do. Only rarely do marine accidents produce a finding of fault on only one skipper.

# General Considerations

The Rules make several important generalizations.

## VESSEL SIZE AND THE RULES

All vessels from the smallest personal watercraft (PWC) to the largest supertanker must obey the Rules. It would be foolhardy, though, for you to demand your "rights" under all circumstances. There are practical limitations on that right. Large vessels are not as maneuverable as small ones. A supertanker, for example, may take several miles to stop even with its engines in reverse. Large freighters throw up high wakes that can swamp or capsize small boats, and you should keep away from them.

You should also keep clear of deep-draft tugs, which can create dangerous currents, especially in shallow water, and sweep small vessels into these currents with serious results.

When a tug is pushing a long line of barges, its operator has a blind spot immediately ahead of the barges. The longer the line of barges, the larger the blind spot. The operator can't see you if you pass in front of the barges, and even when you are seen, the operator can't do anything to avoid hitting you if you come too close.

All vessels, and PWC in particular, should use extreme caution to avoid passing in front of other vessels, including barges and other large vessels. Large vessels move faster than you may think. A deep-draft vessel traveling at a speed of 10 knots covers about 1,000 feet in 1 minute.

It is tempting to jump the wake of another vessel with your PWC, but this can be an extremely dangerous practice, not only because you or a passenger can be thrown off the craft, but also because large vessels operating in shallow waters can often churn up submerged debris, which poses a collision hazard. Various states have passed laws to limit this practice (e.g., no wake jumping within a specified number of feet from the vessel causing the wake).

## MAINTAIN A LOOKOUT

Both sets of Rules require every vessel to maintain a proper **lookout**. The lookout must listen for danger as well as look for it (Figure 8-6), and must also use all means available for watching, including radar, if available. Even if the Rules did not require a lookout, common sense would suggest such a need. **The principal cause of vessel collisions is failure to maintain a lookout!**

Lookouts should have nothing else to do, so don't divide their attention. If you are alone on a vessel and it is underway, serve as your own lookout. Otherwise, appoint someone as lookout who is not responsible for anything else, and change lookouts frequently.

## SAFE SPEED

The Rules require all vessels to proceed at safe speeds so they can stop or take proper and effective action to avoid collisions.

**Figure 8-6.** Always maintain a lookout. (PHOTO BY DUNCAN WILKINSON)

The Rules do not say what a safe speed is, but they do say that a safe speed depends on visibility, traffic density, and maneuverability of your vessel, sea state, current, wind, and other factors. If you were to have a collision, you probably would be judged to have been traveling at an unsafe speed. This can happen even if you were maintaining a proper lookout.

In restricted visibility, you must slow down (Figure 8-7). Fog, mist, falling snow, sleet, heavy rainstorms, sandstorms, smoke, and other conditions restrict visibility. A clear night is not considered an instance of restricted visibility, since navigation lights should be clearly visible at night, but slowing down at night is recommended under the standards of prudent seamanship promoted by the Rules.

## DO YOU HAVE RADAR?

Even if your vessel is fitted with operational radar, you must maintain a lookout and travel at a safe

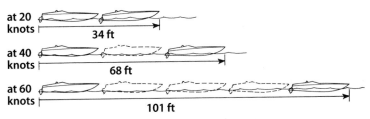

at 20 knots — 34 ft

at 40 knots — 68 ft

at 60 knots — 101 ft

**Figure 8-7.** Given a 1-second reaction time, this is how far your boat would travel at various speeds before you could react to danger ahead—and your boat would go a lot farther still before your reaction could produce its desired effect. In poor visibility, even 10 knots might be an unsafe speed. (ADAPTED FROM *FAST POWERBOAT SEAMANSHIP* BY DAG PIKE)

**WARNING** *Speed and the need for constant vigilance. Many boats are capable of operating at high speeds. PWC, for example, can operate at speeds greater than 60 miles per hour. As speeds increase, the time available to react decreases. According to a recent report by the National Transportation Safety Board, "Operators of two PWC traveling at 40 mph on a head-on course will have a response time of 1.3 seconds to travel 50 yards. Even when the vessels are converging on a 45° angle, the response time is less than 2 seconds. The response time must accommodate perceiving the other vessel, deciding . . . [how] . . . to comply with the rules of the road, determining the risk of collision, and executing a response to alter course." Speed is particularly a problem with small and unstable craft. When these craft are operated at high speeds in other than very calm seas, the operator's attention tends to be focused on the nearest upcoming waves—to the exclusion of other vessels. This tunnel vision may mean that the operator fails to see other traffic and react accordingly. Operators of all fast boats need to adjust their speeds to fit the conditions.*

speed. Having radar may actually increase your responsibility. You must use it whenever it can help you avoid a collision. With it, you may be able to detect another vessel before it sees you. Thus, you may be the first to see that a collision is possible and that evasive action is necessary.

Assess radar information carefully, and do not reach hasty conclusions. Consider your radar's efficiency and limitations. Carefully evaluate the effects of sea state, weather, and other interference on radar reception, and remember that your radar may not be able to detect small vessels or floating objects. Also evaluate the number, location, and movement of vessels shown by your radar. You have responsibility for your radar's proper use and interpretation.

# Conduct in Narrow Channels

All vessels less than 20 meters long and all sailing vessels are required by both the International and Inland Rules to keep to the right in a narrow channel or fairway, and not to impede the passage of a vessel that can navigate safely only within the channel. This means, for example, that you should not cross a narrow channel or fairway when it will impede a vessel that can travel safely only in the channel, nor should you anchor in a narrow channel except in an emergency (Figure 8-8).

**Figure 8-8.** Looking forward from the bridge of a big container ship approaching Port Everglades, Florida. This photo was taken with a telephoto lens. Stick to the edges of a narrow channel and do not impede a vessel like this one. (REPRINTED WITH PERMISSION FROM *SEAWORTHY: ESSENTIAL LESSONS FROM BOAT U.S.'S 20-YEAR CASE FILE OF THINGS GONE WRONG* BY ROBERT A. ADRIANCE)

The Inland Rules have an additional requirement for narrow channels subject to currents. Vessels traveling with the current (downbound) in narrow channels or fairways have the right of way. (Note: This is the only place in the Rules where the term **right of way** appears.) This rule is in effect on the Great Lakes, Western Rivers, and other specified waters. The upbound vessel must yield and allow the downbound vessel to pass. The rule exists because it is easier to control your vessel when you are traveling against the current than when traveling with it.

# Traffic Separation Schemes

The International Rules make provision for *traffic separation schemes* (TSS), a system of one-way lanes used in congested traffic areas, and regulate traffic in them.

Normally, vessels join or leave a TSS at either end. If you enter obliquely, do so at a small angle. You should avoid crossing traffic lanes, but if you must cross, do so as nearly at right angles to the traffic flow as you can. Don't anchor in a TSS unless you have an emergency.

## VESSEL TRAFFIC SERVICES

The Coast Guard maintains *vessel traffic services* (VTS) in several U.S. ports (Figure 8-9). When you are boating in waters subject to a VTS, learn its location and whether it uses TSS lanes. If so, you must be able to recognize the buoys that mark the lanes. Never travel the "wrong way" or anchor in a lane.

# Stand-On or Give-Way?

To interpret the Rules, you must understand the terms "stand-on" and "give-way." The Navigation Rules require that a *stand-on vessel* maintain its course and speed unless a danger of collision is apparent. A *give-way vessel* must take whatever action is necessary to avoid a collision. A stand-on vessel maintains course and speed so that a give-way vessel can predict what the stand-on vessel will do. Conversely, the give-way vessel should show good seamanship and make a significant course change so that the stand-on vessel can easily see that he is responding properly.

It is also important for you to know that the Rules grant no vessel the right of way except when downbound in certain narrow channels of the inland waters, as mentioned above. Instead, when vessels meet, one is usually stand-on while the other is give-way. The fact that no vessel has the right of way explains, in part, the sharing of liability in marine collisions. When driving, one automobile often has the legal right of way over another, but this is not so for watercraft.

## THE DANGER ZONE

Determination of who is stand-on or give-way requires an understanding of how vessels are **sectored**.

On a vessel, three sectors account for the 360° of a circle. As you can see from Figure 8-10, one sector is from dead ahead to 22.5° abaft (behind) the vessel's starboard beam. A second sector is from dead ahead to 22.5° abaft its port beam. Each of these two sectors is 90° + 22.5° or 112.5°. These two sectors

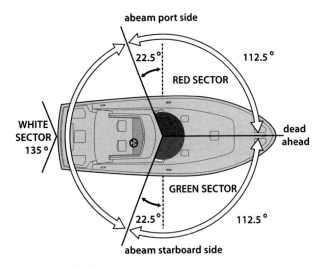

**Figure 8-10.** The red, green, and white sectors of a vessel.

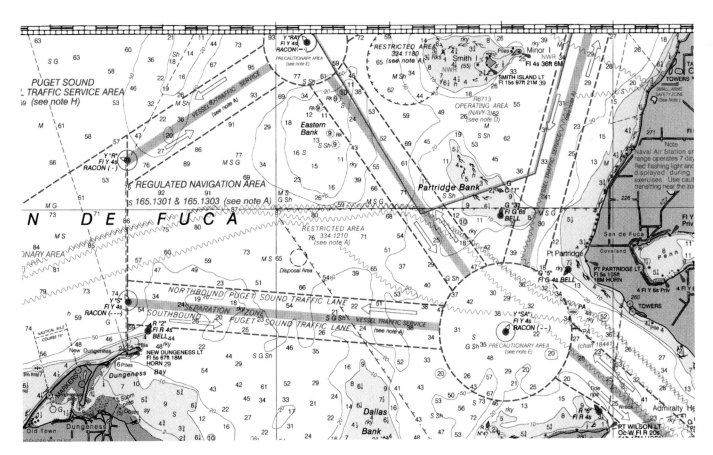

**Figure 8-9.** The lanes of the VTS are clearly shown on this chart of Port Townsend, Washington. (REPRINTED WITH PERMISSION FROM *A CRUISING GUIDE TO PUGET SOUND AND THE SAN JUAN ISLANDS, SECOND EDITION, BY MIGAEL SCHERER*)

account for 2 x 112.5° or 225°. This leaves 360° – 225° or 135° for the third, or stern, sector.

At night, the three sectors are easy to see if a boat's lights are correct. The sector on the starboard side from dead ahead to 22.5° abaft the starboard beam shows a green navigation light and is called the green sector. When an approaching vessel sees your green light, it is required by the Rules to stand on. This sector is your *danger zone* because you are required to give way to any vessel approaching in that sector. The sector on the port side shows a red navigation light and is called the red sector. Together, the red and green lights are the **sidelights**.

Most boats have white **sternlights** with arcs of 135° to cover the stern (white) sector. They also have white **masthead lights** that shine forward over an arc of 225°, covering the red and green sectors combined. Together, masthead lights and sternlights cover 360°. Some small boats have all-round (360°) masthead lights instead of 225° masthead lights and separate sternlights.

## WHO IS STAND-ON?

There are three situations in which the risk of collision exists. First, when you see both the red and green lights of another vessel dead ahead, you know you are on a collision course, meeting **head-on** (Figure 8-11). When the vessels are power-driven, both are give-way, and each must alter its course to starboard. If you have any doubt about whether a head-on situation exists, you must assume that it does and act accordingly.

Second, when another vessel's sternlight draws steadily closer, you are **overtaking** it. You are the give-way vessel and must avoid the other vessel.

Third, when your power-driven vessel approaches another vessel and you see its red light, you know it is in your danger zone and you are the give-way vessel. The other vessel sees your green light and is required to stand on. Alter your course to pass astern of the other vessel. This is a **crossing situation**, and speeding up to pass in front of a stand-on vessel is dangerous.

Whenever a danger of collision exists, be cautious. The other skipper may not see your lights or know what they mean. If the other vessel does not

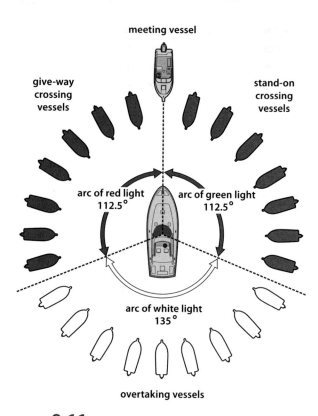

**Figure 8-11.** The three situations.

treat you as stand-on and does not alter its course, you must give the *danger signal*—at least five short and rapid blasts on your whistle—and change your course to prevent a collision. (See Chapter 5 for a description of a boat's whistle.) The change in course is usually to your starboard. When the other vessel is forward of your port beam and you are not overtaking it, do not turn to port. When the other vessel is abeam or abaft the beam on either side of your vessel, do not turn toward it.

## IN THE DAYTIME

In the daytime, although you will not see lights on the other boat, the same three zones exist. The danger zone is still your "green light" zone. When your vessel is power-driven and another vessel approaches you from starboard, you are give-way. You are also give-way if you approach the stern sector of another vessel.

## COURTESY AND COMMON SENSE

Remember, courtesy and common sense are as important as the Rules. Don't use your boat to argue with another skipper. If the other skipper is rude, don't use it as an excuse for rudeness on your part. If the other skipper does not treat you as stand-on, sound the danger signal and yield. The other skipper may not know the Navigation Rules, but winning the argument could ruin your whole day.

## CONSTANT BEARING

If the direction to another vessel stays the same, or nearly so, as you get closer to it, you are on a *collision course* (Figure 8-12). When this happens, take evasive action. Slow down to permit the other vessel to pass in front of you, or change your course, or both.

When you act to avoid a collision, make your change in course or speed large enough that it can be readily seen by the other vessel, either visually or on radar. A change in course should be at least 60°. Even this may not be enough when approaching a large vessel or a tow or when you are close to another vessel.

# Rules for Special Vessels

Some vessels are less maneuverable than others. Because of this, the Navigation Rules give them special stand-on status (Figure 8-13).

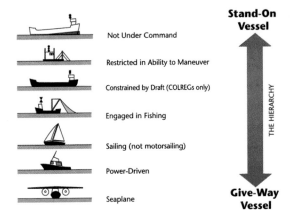

**Figure 8-13.** The "pecking order" for stand-on and give-way vessels. (REPRINTED WITH PERMISSION FROM *RULES OF THE ROAD AND RUNNNING LIGHT PATTERNS: A CAPTAIN'S QUICK GUIDE* BY CHARLIE WING)

## OVERTAKING AND OVERTAKEN VESSELS

For recreational boaters, three special provisions deserve attention. First, an overtaken vessel is stand-on to all other vessels. A sailing vessel that is overtaking another vessel must give way to it even when the overtaken vessel is power-driven.

Second, except when overtaken, a power-driven vessel must give way to a sailing vessel. When a power-driven vessel meets a sailing vessel head-on, the power-driven vessel is the give-way vessel. The same is true in a crossing situation—the power-driven vessel is give-way even if it sees the green sidelight of the sailing vessel.

**Figure 8-12.** When the bearing to an approaching vessel remains constant as its distance off decreases, you are on a collision course. (REPRINTED WITH PERMISSION FROM *SEAWORTHY: ESSENTIAL LESSONS FROM BOAT U.S.'S 20-YEAR CASE FILE OF THINGS GONE WRONG* BY ROBERT A. ADRIANCE)

Third, when on the water, seaplanes are vessels, and should give way to all other vessels except when they are being overtaken.

## SAILING VESSELS

Because of a sailboat's reduced maneuverability, both the Inland and International Rules make special provisions for sailboats in sight of one another. These provisions are the same in both sets of Rules, and apply whenever there is a risk of collision.

In overtaking situations, the overtaken vessel is stand-on, while in meeting and crossing situations, the wind is the deciding factor. When each sailing vessel has the wind on a different side, the vessel with the wind on its port side is give-way (Figure 8-14), and the vessel with the wind on its starboard side is stand-on.

The **windward** side of a vessel is the side from which the wind is blowing. The **leeward** side is the side away from the wind, which is also the side on which the sails are trimmed. For example, when the wind is blowing from the port side of a vessel, this is its windward side, which makes its starboard side its leeward side (sailors pronounce this "loo • ard"). When both sailing vessels have the wind on the same side, the vessel to windward is give-way.

Sometimes you cannot tell if the wind is on the port or starboard side of another sailing vessel. If your sailing vessel has the wind on its port side and you cannot tell if a sailing vessel to windward has the wind on its port or starboard side, you must assume that it has the wind on its starboard side and is the stand-on vessel. Keep out of the way of this other vessel.

Again, for the purposes of the Rules, the leeward side of a sailing vessel is the side on which the mainsail is carried. The windward side is deemed to be the opposite side.

# Risk of Collision

A risk of collision can exist in head-on, crossing, or overtaking situations. The Navigation Rules prescribe the behavior of vessels in these situations and the signals that power-driven vessels exchange.

## HEAD-ON SITUATIONS

Vessels that approach each other on reciprocal (opposite) or nearly reciprocal courses are meeting head-on. At night each vessel sees both the red and green sidelights of the other vessel, and should also see its masthead light or lights if it has them. When it is under sail and without power, a sailboat does not use a white masthead light.

When there are two masthead lights on a vessel and you are meeting head-on, they will be in a vertical line, with the forward one lower than the aft one. Two masthead lights mean that the vessel is 50 or more meters long. Get out of its way!

A small vessel yaws in a heavy chop or in ground swells, which means that another vessel meeting it sees alternating red and green sidelights. When you see this pattern of sidelights, assume that you are meeting another vessel head-on.

It is not as easy to determine when a head-on situation exists in the daytime. If you have any doubt, assume it is a head-on situation. In a head-on or meeting situation involving power-driven vessels, neither vessel is stand-on. Both are give-way.

### Head-On Sound Signals

The usual course of action when two power-driven vessels are meeting head-on is for each vessel to alter its course to starboard. Sound signals are also

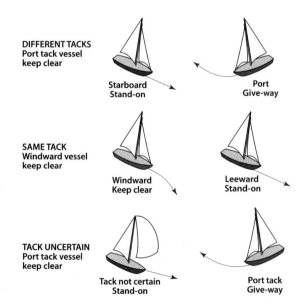

**DIFFERENT TACKS**
Port tack vessel keep clear

Starboard
Stand-on

Port
Give-way

**SAME TACK**
Windward vessel keep clear

Windward
Keep clear

Leeward
Stand-on

**TACK UNCERTAIN**
Port tack vessel keep clear

Tack not certain
Stand-on

Port tack
Give-way

**Figure 8-14.** The International and Inland Rules for sailing vessels. (REPRINTED WITH PERMISSION FROM *RULES OF THE ROAD AND RUNNNING LIGHT PATTERNS: A CAPTAIN'S QUICK GUIDE* BY CHARLIE WING)

given, with a **short blast** of a whistle being a blast of 1 second's duration and a **prolonged blast** lasting 4 to 6 seconds. The term "long blast" is not used in the Navigation Rules.

Whistle signals can be confusing to learn. To make it easier, think of yourself as a vessel's skipper and associate one short blast with the word "port," which has one syllable, and two short blasts with the word "starboard," which has two syllables. Thus, in the head-on meeting situation described above, the other vessel will be on your port side as you pass it so you should sound one short blast. Under the Inland Rules, you may pass another vessel starboard to starboard, in which case you should sound two short blasts.

This rule of thumb is correct in most instances, but as with most rules, there are exceptions. Refer to the *Navigation Rules, International–Inland* for further guidance.

In a meeting situation under International or Inland Rules, when either vessel believes a collision is imminent it must take evasive action. This may consist of trying to stop, signaled by three short blasts. The blasts mean, "I am operating astern propulsion," not "I am backing up." A heavy vessel can operate astern propulsion for some time before it overcomes its headway.

## International Meeting Signals

Under the International Rules, when power-driven vessels meet head-on or nearly so and a risk of collision exists, each vessel turns to starboard as in Figure 8-15. At the same time, one vessel gives a short blast. Thus the vessels pass port to port. Note that under the International Rules, one vessel gives a blast to indicate its intentions, but the other vessel is not required to respond with a signal if it agrees.

## Inland Meeting Signals

Inland meeting signals for power-driven vessels are similar to those used in international waters, but there are significant differences (see Figure 8-15), one of which is that inland signals announce only your *intention* to act—they require a response before you can act. (Except in overtaking situations in narrow channels and near obscured bends in a channel, the International Rules do not require a response from the other vessel.)

**Meeting Head-On or Nearly So Situations**

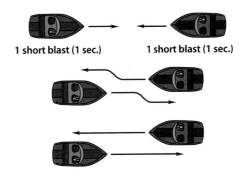

1 short blast (1 sec.)  1 short blast (1 sec.)

**Vessels generally pass port side to port side. On inland waters, however, vessels may pass starboard to starboard if proper signals are given.**

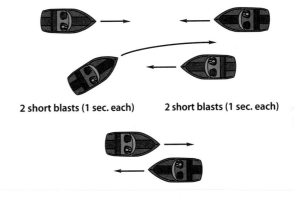

2 short blasts (1 sec. each)  2 short blasts (1 sec. each)

**Figure 8-15.** When power-driven vessels meet, neither vessel is stand-on. Both the International and Inland Rules specify port side to port side passing, and a turn to starboard to accomplish this is signaled with a single short blast (top). On international waters the signal need not be acknowledged before the signaling vessel turns, but on inland waters it must be. On inland waters only, starboard side to starboard side passing is permissible after the proper signal (two short blasts) is made and acknowledged. (REPRINTED WITH PERMISSION FROM "FEDERAL REQUIREMENTS & SAFETY TIPS FOR RECREATIONAL BOATS," U.S. COAST GUARD OFFICE OF BOATING SAFETY)

A second difference is that in inland waters, when power-driven vessels in sight of each other meet head-on or cross within ½ mile, they exchange sound signals even if neither vessel has to change course.

On inland waters in a head-on situation, one short blast means, "I intend to pass you on my port side," and two short blasts mean, "I intend to pass you on my starboard side."

If the other vessel agrees to your intended maneuver, it signals its agreement by returning the same signal. For example, if you sound one short blast and the other vessel agrees, it also sounds one short blast. Each vessel, if necessary, alters its course to starboard and the vessels pass port side to port side.

The other vessel answers a two-blast signal with two short blasts. When necessary, each vessel then alters its course to port and the vessels pass starboard to starboard. When there is no danger of collision, neither vessel changes course.

If the second vessel disagrees or does not understand your intention, it should answer with the **doubt** or **danger signal**, at least five short, rapid blasts.

## CROSSING SITUATIONS

When two vessels meet and each sees either a red or a green light, they are crossing. One vessel is coming toward the other in an area from almost dead ahead to 22.5° abaft either beam. When you are not sure whether you are in a meeting or a crossing situation, assume you are meeting and take appropriate action.

When you are power driven and see a green sidelight on another power-driven vessel, you are stand-on and the other vessel, which sees your red sidelight, is give-way. When a crossing vessel is on your starboard side, you are give-way and must stay out of its way. You can do this by slowing down and letting the other vessel pass in front of you, or by altering your course to starboard and passing astern of it, or both.

### Crossing Signals

Suppose that in inland waters, you meet another power-driven vessel head-on and wish to pass port side to port side. You will sound one short blast. Suppose, however, that the other vessel believes it would be better for your vessels to pass starboard to starboard. It cannot answer your one blast signal with two blasts, because doing so would be to **cross signals**.

Instead, the second vessel must respond with the doubt or danger signal. You can then sound two short blasts to announce your intention to pass starboard to starboard. When this is acceptable to the other vessel, it responds with two blasts. So, the other vessel must respond only with the signal you give or with the danger signal.

### Crossing in International Waters

In international waters, power-driven vessels do not have to give sound signals in crossing situations unless action is needed by the give-way vessel. Of course, either you or the other skipper can give the doubt or danger signal if necessary.

When the give-way vessel finds it necessary to alter course, it sounds one short blast to show it is altering its course to starboard. It will then pass astern of the stand-on vessel, and the stand-on vessel will be on the give-way vessel's port side. The stand-on vessel does not respond. This is a rule in international waters that is generally true; that is, when one vessel gives a signal, and the other vessel agrees with the action, there is no return signal.

### Crossing in Inland Waters

In inland waters, the give-way power-driven vessel announces its intention to pass astern of the stand-on vessel by one short blast (Figure 8-16).

## OVERTAKING SITUATIONS

When you approach another vessel and see only its sternlight, you are overtaking it. This means you are approaching the other vessel from a direction more than 22.5° abaft either of its beams. Whether you are power driven or sailing, you are give-way and must stay clear of the overtaken vessel. If you can't tell if you are overtaking another vessel or

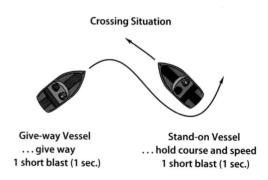

**Crossing Situation**

**Give-way Vessel**
...give way
1 short blast (1 sec.)

**Stand-on Vessel**
...hold course and speed
1 short blast (1 sec.)

**Figure 8-16.** When power-driven vessels cross on inland waters, the give-way vessel announces its intention to pass astern of the stand-on vessel, and the latter responds. On international waters no response from the stand-on vessel is required. (REPRINTED WITH PERMISSION FROM "FEDERAL REQUIREMENTS & SAFETY TIPS FOR RECREATIONAL BOATS," U.S. COAST GUARD OFFICE OF BOATING SAFETY)

crossing its path, assume that you are overtaking and that you are the give-way vessel.

## Overtaking in Inland Waters

In inland waters when you intend to overtake a vessel, you announce your intention to pass it on your port side with one short blast. If this is acceptable to the other vessel, it responds with the same signal—one short blast. You then pass the overtaken vessel on your port side (Figure 8-17).

You state your intention to pass the overtaken vessel on your starboard side with two short blasts. Again, if agreeable to the vessel you are overtaking, it responds with the same signal—two short blasts. It can reject your intention by using the danger signal. Don't give cross signals.

## Overtaking in International Waters

In open waters under International Rules, if one vessel overtakes another from dead astern, the overtaking vessel must alter course. It sounds one short blast to show it is altering its course to starboard, and two short blasts if it alters its course to port.

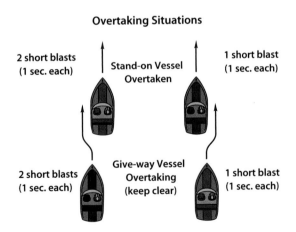

**Overtaking Situations**

2 short blasts (1 sec. each) — Stand-on Vessel Overtaken — 1 short blast (1 sec. each)

2 short blasts (1 sec. each) — Give-way Vessel Overtaking (keep clear) — 1 short blast (1 sec. each)

**Figure 8-17.** When one vessel overtakes another, it is the give-way vessel and must signal its intentions as shown. No response from the overtaken vessel is required on international waters. See the accompanying text for the rules that apply when one vessel overtakes another in a narrow channel on international waters. (REPRINTED WITH PERMISSION FROM "FEDERAL REQUIREMENTS & SAFETY TIPS FOR RECREATIONAL BOATS," U.S. COAST GUARD OFFICE OF BOATING SAFETY)

Under either set of Rules, you remain an overtaking vessel until you are finally past and clear of the overtaken vessel. Any change in bearing of the two vessels does not change your status. Thus, when you are an overtaking vessel, you cannot become a crossing vessel.

## Overtaking in Narrow Channels

The International Rules require sound signals when you are overtaking another vessel in a narrow channel or fairway and the overtaken vessel has to take action to permit safe passage. Sound two prolonged blasts and one short blast to say that you intend to pass the other vessel on your port side. When the other vessel agrees, it should sound one prolonged, one short, one prolonged, and one short blast. If it disagrees, it sounds the danger signal. You cannot pass until there is agreement.

Note that this situation is an exception to the general rule governing sound signals in international waters. In this case, your signal announces intent, not action. It is also an exception in that it requires a response from the overtaken vessel.

When, in a narrow channel or fairway, you intend to pass the other vessel on your starboard side, sound two prolonged and two short blasts. If the overtaken vessel agrees, it responds with one prolonged, one short, one prolonged, and one short blast. It can, of course, respond with the danger signal. You can pass only after there is agreement and should not give cross signals.

The one- or two-short-blast rule still holds: when you overtake a vessel on your port side, sound one short blast, and when you overtake on your starboard side, sound two short blasts. The difference in the rule, as applied here, is that you sound two prolonged blasts before either the one- or two-short-blast signal.

# Bend Signals

In a narrow channel or when nearing a bend, your view may be obscured. Both sets of Rules require you to navigate with "alertness and caution," and to sound one prolonged blast (Figure 8-18). An approaching vessel that hears your signal answers with one prolonged blast.

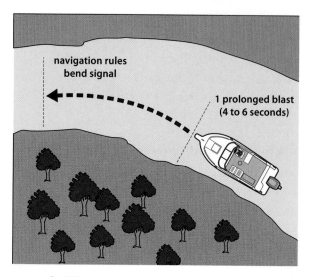

**Figure 8-18.** Approaching a bend.

# Restricted Visibility

Most of the Rules relate to vessels in sight of each other. The rule for bend signals is an exception, and so are the rules that regulate the conduct of vessels in or near an area of restricted visibility. When vessels are not in sight of one another, no vessel is stand-on to any other vessel. Vessels should proceed at a safe speed, adapting to the conditions while continuing to observe the rules for meeting, crossing, and overtaking that pertain to all conditions of visibility. You must take action to avoid a vessel detected by radar, but use of radar is not a justification for operating at an unsafe speed in conditions of reduced visibility, nor is radar an acceptable substitute for a proper lookout. Reduce your speed or take off all way when you hear a vessel forward of your beam, until you deem the danger of collision to be over.

Sound signals in restricted visibility are the same in both sets of Rules. They may be hand-timed and mechanically produced, or automatically produced by electronic means.

## SOUND SIGNALS UNDERWAY

In or near an area of restricted visibility, use the following sound signals when underway:

- When you are power driven and making way, sound one prolonged blast at least every 2 minutes.

- When you are power driven and adrift, sound two prolonged blasts at least every 2 minutes. There should be an interval of about 2 seconds between your blasts.

- Some vessels underway sound one prolonged blast followed by two short blasts at least every 2 minutes. These include vessels not under command, those restricted in ability to maneuver, sailing vessels, vessels towing or pushing other vessels, and fishing vessels.

## SOUND SIGNALS NOT UNDERWAY

When not underway, give the following sound signals in restricted visibility:

- When you are at anchor in open water and your vessel is 12 meters long or longer, ring your bell rapidly for about 5 seconds at least every minute. In a vessel less than 12 meters long, you do not have to give signals with a bell. If you don't, you must make some other efficient sound signal at least every 2 minutes. A vessel 100 meters or more in length sounds a bell in its forepart. Immediately afterward, it sounds a gong for about 5 seconds in its after part. When you hear a bell and a gong, you know you are near a large anchored vessel.

- At anchor you may also sound one short, one prolonged, and one short blast of your whistle. This tells an approaching vessel of your position and warns of the chance of collision. When at anchor, you make more noise than when underway; you can afford to. When underway, you need to listen for sounds from other vessels. Should your vessel be aground, you must give the bell signal given by a vessel at anchor. In addition, give three separate and distinct strokes on your bell immediately be-

**WARNING** *Since PWC are not equipped with lights, it follows that they must not operate at night. To do so violates the Navigation Rules. In addition, many states and localities have laws and ordinances specifically prohibiting the operation of PWC during nighttime hours.*

fore and after the rapid ringing of the bell.

- In special anchorage areas, vessels less than 20 meters long do not need to give sound signals. Nautical charts show these areas. In restricted visibility, if you hear a whistle or a horn, you know it is usually coming from a vessel underway. That vessel may or may not be making way, however. A bell or a gong tells you the vessel is stationary, either anchored or aground.

# Vessel Lights and Shapes

At night, your vessel must have proper navigation lights. Show them from sunset to sunrise and in restricted visibility, and don't show other lights at the same time that might appear to be navigation lights. Also, don't show other lights if they interfere with the vision of your lookout.

Except for searchlights, lights on boats serve different purposes from lights on automobiles. Boat lights do not help you see ahead, but are there to be seen and to communicate vital information to other vessels. Figure 8-20 shows that navigation lights have sectors where they can or cannot be seen, and tells you which way another vessel is facing.

## RANGE OF VISIBILITY

The required intensities of your navigation lights are given in terms of their minimum required ranges of visibility. These required intensities vary with colors and purposes. See Figure 8-21 for the intensities of lights required on your boat. If your vessel is less than 12 meters long, its lights should be visible as follows: masthead, 2 miles; sidelights, 1 mile; all-round lights, 2 miles. (An all-round light shines through an arc of 360°.) Your boat manufacturer probably used properly sized bulbs, so if you need to replace them, use comparable bulbs.

**Figure 8-19.** An at-a-glance summary of the Steering and Sailing Rules (Rules 9–18). (REPRINTED WITH PERMISSION FROM *RULES OF THE ROAD AND RUNNING LIGHT PATTERNS: A CAPTAIN'S QUICK GUIDE* BY CHARLIE WING)

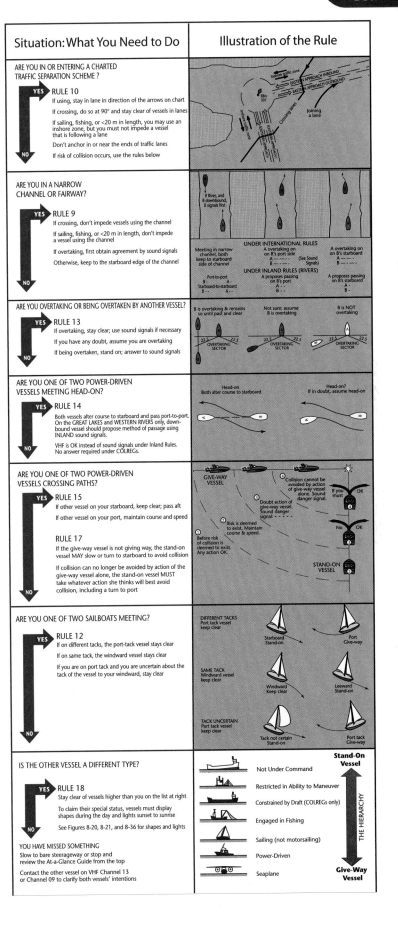

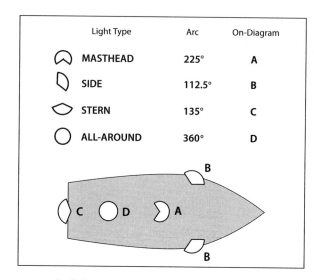

| Light Type | | Arc | On-Diagram |
|---|---|---|---|
| | MASTHEAD | 225° | A |
| | SIDE | 112.5° | B |
| | STERN | 135° | C |
| | ALL-AROUND | 360° | D |

**Figure 8-20.** Navigation lights and their sectors.

| Light Type | Visibility Min. Distance—Nautical Miles | | | |
|---|---|---|---|---|
| | 1 | 2 | 3 | 5 |
| **MASTHEAD** | | ● | ▲ | ◆ |
| **SIDE** | ● | ▲◆ | | |
| **STERN** | | ●▲◆ | | |
| **ALL-AROUND** | | ●▲◆ | | |
| **TOWING** | | ●▲◆ | | |
| **SPECIAL FLASHING** (Inland Rules Only) | | ●▲◆ | | |

● Less than 12 Meters
▲ 12 Meters but Less than 20 Meters
◆ 20 Meters but Less than 50 Meters

**Figure 8-21.** Required light visibilities.

## WHAT LIGHTS TELL YOU

You already know something about vessel lights. You know what sidelights, masthead lights, and sternlights are, and also know how to tell who is stand-on and who is give-way by looking at a vessel's lights.

The lights on another boat answer several questions for you: Is the other boat headed toward you? Is it crossing your course? Are you overtaking it?

The lights on vessels also help you to know something about their size, with larger vessels having more navigation lights than smaller ones. In general, the more navigation lights a vessel has, the greater the danger it poses. Stay clear of vessels with navigation lights you do not understand and vessels with many navigation lights.

As you will see, the special navigation lights of a vessel often tell something about its condition or activity.

## SHAPES ON VESSELS

In addition to lights, vessels show *shapes* to alert you to their special conditions or activities. Shapes are also called "day shapes," since they are the day-time equivalent of special navigation lights. One of the annexes (appendices) to the Navigation Rules describes these shapes, all of which are black. They may be *balls*, *cones*, *diamonds*, or *cylinders*.

## LIGHTS AND SHAPES ON SAILING VESSELS UNDERWAY

At night, a sailing vessel underway must show side-lights and a sternlight as in Figures 8-22 and 8-23, but it does not have a lighted masthead light. Thus, when you see a sidelight but no white light, you are looking at a sailing vessel underway (unless the vessel is improperly lighted). The lights on sailing vessels are the same under either set of Rules.

The sidelights and sternlight of a sailing vessel less than 20 meters long may be combined in one device or fixture carried at or near the masthead, where it is most visible (Figure 8-24). Don't use this light on a sailboat under power. In that case, show the lights of a power-driven vessel (Figure 8-25).

A sailing vessel underway may show, in addition to its sidelights and sternlight, two all-round lights in a vertical line as in Figure 8-26. The upper light is red and the lower is green, and both lights are at or near the top of its mast, where they are most visible. These optional additional lights are not to be used with the three-color light shown in Figure 8-24.

During daylight hours, a sailing vessel that is also under power must show a conical shape with its apex pointed downward (Figure 8-27), and must show this cone where it is most visible. Under the Inland Rules, a sailing vessel less than 12 meters long need not display this day shape.

**Figure 8-22.** A sailing vessel underway with separate sidelights.

**Figure 8-23.** A sailing vessel underway with combined sidelights.

**Figure 8-24.** Alternative light configuration for a sailing vessel less than 20 meters long.

**Figure 8-25.** A sailing vessel under 20 meters long using both sail and power.

**Figure 8-26.** Optional all-round masthead lights for a vessel under sail.

(REPRINTED WITH PERMISSION FROM "FEDERAL REQUIREMENTS & SAFETY TIPS FOR RECREATIONAL BOATS," U.S. COAST GUARD OFFICE OF BOATING SAFETY)

A sailing vessel less than 7 meters long must, if practicable, show the same lights as larger sailing vessels. If it doesn't have lights, it must have an electric torch (flashlight) or lighted lantern with a white light readily available (Figure 8-28), and this light must be shown in time to prevent a collision. Usually, the skipper directs the flashlight against the sail so it is easier to see.

A rowboat may show the same lights as those used on sailboats, including a white flashlight or lantern (Figure 8-29).

## LIGHTS FOR POWER-DRIVEN VESSELS UNDERWAY

Navigation lights on a power-driven vessel underway depend on the vessel's length and whether it is operating on international or inland waters. For small, recreational vessels, the two sets of Rules are practically identical.

There are many rules regulating navigation lights on power-driven vessels. Only those which bear on recreational boating are described here. If you want to learn more about navigation lights, consult the *Navigation Rules*.

Under either set of Rules, a power-driven vessel less than 20 meters long must have sidelights, a masthead light, and a sternlight when underway at night. Its sidelights may be separate or combined in one lantern (Figure 8-30). The masthead light of a vessel 12 meters or more long should be at least 2.5 meters above its gunwale. A power-driven vessel 50 meters or more long is to have a second masthead

**Figure 8-27. (Left)** Day shape displayed by a sailing vessel under both power and sail.

**Figure 8-28. (Middle)** Light for a sailing vessel less than 7 meters long.

**Figure 8-29. (Right)** Light for a rowboat.

(REPRINTED WITH PERMISSION FROM "FEDERAL REQUIREMENTS & SAFETY TIPS FOR RECREATIONAL BOATS," U.S. COAST GUARD OFFICE OF BOATING SAFETY)

light abaft and above the first one. In the Great Lakes, however, a power-driven vessel may carry an all-round light in lieu of the second masthead light stated above.

The masthead light of a vessel less than 12 meters long must be at least 1 meter above its sidelights. It may have an all-round light in place of the masthead light and sternlight (Figure 8-31). On either international or inland waters, if you see a white light and a sidelight on a vessel, the vessel is power driven. At night, you should never see a white navigation light on a sailing vessel when you see a sidelight.

Many small vessels with all-round lights in place of masthead lights carry the lights too low. They are to be at least 1 meter higher than the

**Figure 8-30.** (Left) Navigation lights on a power-driven vessel under 20 meters long.

**Figure 8-31.** (Middle and right) Lights on a power-driven (or power- plus sail-driven) vessel under 12 meters long. (REPRINTED WITH PERMISSION FROM "FEDERAL REQUIREMENTS & SAFETY TIPS FOR RECREATIONAL BOATS," U.S. COAST GUARD OFFICE OF BOATING SAFETY)

sidelights and according to the Rules, must ". . . be placed as to be above and clear of all other lights and obstructions." If the light on your vessel is not high enough, raise it.

In international waters, a power-driven vessel less than 7 meters long needs only an all-round light if its maximum speed is not more than 7 knots (8 miles per hour). Where practicable, it should also have sidelights.

## SPECIAL LIGHTS AND SHAPES

Special lights and shapes announce certain activities or conditions of vessels, and are in addition to the masthead, stern, and sidelights required by the two sets of Rules. Except for towing lights and lights on vessels constrained by draft, the lights are the same in the two sets of Rules, as are the special shapes. Vessels show these special shapes in the daytime, while at night they show their special lights.

### Fishing Vessels

A vessel trawling—that is, dragging a net or some other apparatus—shows two all-round lights in a vertical line, with the upper one being green and the lower one being white. In the daytime, it shows a shape comprising two cones in a vertical line with their apexes touching. In silhouette, these appear as two triangles apex to apex.

A fishing vessel other than one trawling shows two all-round lights in a vertical line, the upper of

which is red, and the lower one white. It shows the same day shape as a trawler. This type of fishing vessel may have long lines extending from it. If fishing gear extends more than 150 meters from the vessel, it must show an additional all-round white light on the side with the gear at night, and an additional cone with its apex upward on the side with the gear by day.

> **WARNING** *Remember, the more lights a vessel has, the larger it is and the more important it is for you to avoid it.*

### Vessels Constrained by Draft

A vessel constrained by draft is recognized only in the International Rules. It shows its condition at night by three red all-round lights stacked vertically. In daylight hours, it displays a black cylinder, which, in silhouette, will appear to be a rectangle.

### Towing Vessels

A towing light is the same as a sternlight except that it is yellow. A power-driven vessel, when towing astern, shows two masthead lights in a vertical line and the yellow towing light above its white sternlight. When the tow is more than 200 meters long, the vessel shows three vertical masthead lights at night and a diamond shape in the daytime.

A sailing vessel could be confused with a vessel being towed at night. Like a sailboat, a boat or barge under tow shows a sternlight and sidelights. Be careful—you may not be able to see the towing cable. Many boats have been destroyed and lives lost when skippers have steered between towboats and their tows. The towing hawsers are not always visible, so be alert for two vessels moving in the same direction and staying the same distance apart. Watch for the two stacked masthead lights and yellow towlight of a towboat at night or the diamond day shape of a vessel with a tow more than 200 meters long.

### Other Special Vessels

Other vessels with special lights include those restricted in their ability to maneuver, those not under command, those engaged in dredging (Figure 8-32) or underwater operations, and those aground.

**Figure 8-32. Top:** A dredge is restricted in its ability to manuever. **Bottom:** Dredge spoils being deposited on a riverbank to build up the shoreline. (PHOTOS BY LEN SCHULTE)

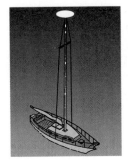

**Figure 8-33.** Vessels less than 50 meters long, anchored at night. (REPRINTED WITH PERMISSION FROM "FEDERAL REQUIREMENTS & SAFETY TIPS FOR RECREATIONAL BOATS," U.S. COAST GUARD OFFICE OF BOATING SAFETY)

There are two kinds of vessels with special lights that you should recognize. Law enforcement vessels when engaged in law enforcement or public safety activities have flashing blue lights. These vessels include those operated by the Coast Guard, marine police, national and state park rangers, conservation officers, and others with police functions.

A vessel engaged in public safety activities may have a flashing red-and-yellow light. The light serves only to identify the vessel as participating in such activities, and does not confer special privileges. Be aware that this vessel may be towing another vessel, and don't cut behind it.

## VESSELS AT ANCHOR

A vessel less than 50 meters long will show an all-round white light at night in its forepart, where it can best be seen when anchored (Figure 8-33). In the daytime, it will show a ball, which will appear to be a black disk. When it is 50 meters long or longer, it will show an additional all-round white light near its stern. This light is lower than the forward light. All anchored vessels may show lights to illuminate their decks, and a vessel 100 meters or more long *must* show these lights.

Under either set of Rules, an anchored vessel less than 7 meters long does not have to show an anchor light or shape. However, when it is in or near a narrow channel, a fairway, an anchorage, or where other vessels normally navigate, it must show a light at appropriate times.

Under the Inland Rules, vessels less than 20 meters long do not need to show anchor lights or shapes when anchored in special anchoring areas. A list of these special anchorage areas appears in Title 33, *Code of Federal Regulations*, Part 110, and they are also shown on nautical charts. This exemption addresses the impracticality of leaving an anchor light burning on an unattended small boat in a designated mooring/anchorage area.

## DIVING OPERATIONS

Under either set of Rules, vessels engaged in underwater operations should show the lights and shapes of vessels restricted in their ability to maneuver, but a vessel has an alternative if its size makes the showing of these lights and shapes impractical. It can, instead, show three all-round lights in a vertical line. The top and bottom lights are red, and the middle one is white (Figure 8-34, left). By day, the boat should fly a rigid replica of the code flag A to show that a diver is down. This **alpha flag** is a white-and-blue swallowtail flag (Figure 8-34, right) and must be at least 1 meter high and visible from any angle (a requirement that can usually be fulfilled only by displaying multiple flags).

The rules about the alpha flag cover "underwater operations," which has left scuba divers and

**Figure 8-34.** Night and day displays for a vessel engaged in diving operations. (REPRINTED WITH PERMISSION FROM "FEDERAL REQUIREMENTS & SAFETY TIPS FOR RECREATIONAL BOATS," U.S. COAST GUARD OFFICE OF BOATING SAFETY)

**Figure 8-35.** Diver-in-the-water flag.

snorkelers confused about which flag to use. As a result, they have informally adopted a red flag with a white diagonal stripe (Figure 8-35). While this flag has legal status in some states, in most places it does not. To be on the safe side, some people use both the red-and-white and the alpha flags. If you see either of these flags, give them a wide berth.

Do not paint or permanently affix a diving flag to your vessel; it should only be used when there is a diver in the water. All vessels should stay clear of diving operations under the rules of good seamanship.

# Distress Signals

Distress signals are described in Rule 37 and in Annex IV. They include (Figure 8-37):

- A gun fired at intervals of 1 minute
- Continuous sounding of a foghorn
- Red star shells
- A Morse code SOS signal ( • • • – – – • • • ) sent by radiotelegraphy, flashing light, or other means
- A radio signal consisting of the spoken word "Mayday"

- Flying international code flags N and C ("November" and "Charlie" in the phonetic alphabet)
- A black square and ball on an orange background
- Flames on the vessel (as from burning tar or oil in a barrel)
- A rocket parachute flare or a hand flare showing a red light

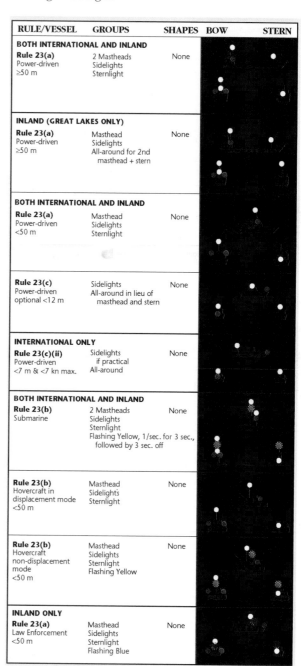

**Figure 8-36.** A summary of navigation lights and day shapes. (REPRINTED WITH PERMISSION FROM *RULES OF THE ROAD AND RUNNING LIGHT PATTERNS: A CAPTAIN'S QUICK GUIDE* BY CHARLIE WING)

- A smoke signal giving off orange-colored smoke
- Slowly and repeatedly raising and lowering your arms outstretched to each side
- An automatic radiotelephone alarm signal
- Signals sent by emergency position-indicating radio beacons (EPIRBs)

In addition, on inland waters, a high-intensity white light flashing at regular intervals of fifty to seventy times per minute is a distress signal. Finally, a searchlight may be directed toward a danger to warn other boaters provided it doesn't cause confusion or embarrassment.

| RULE/VESSEL | GROUPS | SHAPES | BOW | STERN |
|---|---|---|---|---|
| **BOTH INTERNATIONAL AND INLAND** | | | | |
| **24(a)**/Towing astern (Tow 200 m)<br>If vessel 50 m, add | 2 vert. Mastheads<br>Sidelights<br>Sternlight<br>Towlight<br>Masthead aft | None | | |
| **24(a)**/Towing astern (Tow > 200 m)<br>If vessel 50 m, add | 3 vert. Mastheads<br>Sidelights<br>Sternlight<br>Towlight<br>Masthead aft | ◆ | | |
| **24(b)**/Composite (treated as single power vessel)<br>If composite 50 m, add | Masthead<br>Sidelights<br>Sternlight<br>Masthead aft | None | | |
| **24(c)**/Pushing ahead or towing alongside (not composite)<br>If vessel 50 m, add | 2 vert. Mastheads<br>Sidelights<br>Sternlight<br>Masthead aft | None | | |
| **24(e)**/Vessel/object being towed astern (other than 24(g)) (Tow 200 m) | Sidelights fwd<br>Sternlight | None | | |
| **24(e)**/Vessel/object being towed astern (other than 24(g)) (Tow >200 m) | Sidelights fwd<br>Sternlight | ◆ | | |
| **24(g)**/Partly submerged 100 m long (<25 m wide) All-arounds forward & aft<br>(25 m wide) Add all-arounds on beams<br>Partly submerged >100 m long (<25 m wide) All-arounds forward & aft and every 100 m<br>(25 m wide) All-arounds forward & aft Add beam all-arounds every 100 m | | ◆<br><br><br>◆ ◆<br>aft fwd<br>If tow >200 m | | |
| **INTERNATIONAL ONLY** | | | | |
| **24(f)**/Multiple vessels/objects being pushed ahead | Sidelights fwd | None | | |
| **24(f)**/Multiple vessels/objects being towed alongside | Sidelights<br>Sternlight | None | | |
| **INLAND ONLY** | | | | |
| **24(f)**/Multiple vessels/objects being pushed ahead | Sidelights fwd<br>Special flashing | None | | |
| **24(f)**/Multiple vessels/objects being towed alongside | Sidelights<br>Sternlight<br>Special flashing | None | | |
| **24(f)**/Multiple vessels/objects being towed alongside BOTH sides | Sidelights<br>2 Sternlights<br>Special flashing | None | | |
| **INLAND Western Rivers except below Huey Long Bridge** | | | | |
| **24(i)**/Pushing ahead or towing alongside (not composite) | Sidelights<br>2 Towing lights<br>NO mastheads<br>NO sternlight | None | | |

| RULE/VESSEL | GROUPS | SHAPES | BOW | STERN |
|---|---|---|---|---|
| **BOTH INTERNATIONAL AND INLAND** | | | | |
| **Rule 25(a)**<br>Sailing only any length | Sidelights<br>Sternlight | None | | |
| **Rule 25(b)**<br>Sailing only <20 m option | Tri-color | None | | |
| **Rule 25(c)**<br>Sailing only optional any length | Sidelights<br>Sternlight<br>R/G all-around | None | | |
| **Rule 25(d)(i)**<br>Sailing or Rowing <7 m | Sidelights<br>Sternlight | None | | |
| **Rule 25(d)(ii)**<br>Sailing or Rowing <7 m option | All-around or show only to prevent collision | None | | |
| **Rule 25(e)**<br>Motorsailing ≥50 m | 2 Mastheads<br>Sidelights<br>Sternlight | ▼ | | |
| **Rule 25(e)**<br>Motorsailing <50 m | Masthead<br>Sidelights<br>Sternlight | ▼ | | |
| **Rule 25(e)**<br>Motorsailing <12 m | Masthead<br>Sidelights<br>Sternlight | ▼<br>Optional under Inland Rules | | |

**Figure 8-36.** (continued on next page)

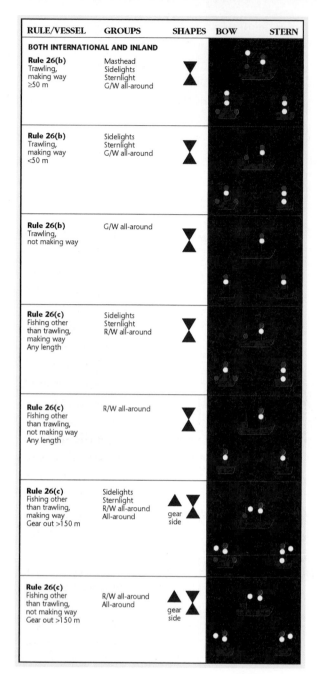

| RULE/VESSEL | GROUPS | SHAPES | BOW | STERN |
|---|---|---|---|---|
| **BOTH INTERNATIONAL AND INLAND** | | | | |
| **Rule 26(b)** Trawling, making way ≥50 m | Masthead Sidelights Sternlight G/W all-around | | | |
| **Rule 26(b)** Trawling, making way <50 m | Sidelights Sternlight G/W all-around | | | |
| **Rule 26(b)** Trawling, not making way | G/W all-around | | | |
| **Rule 26(c)** Fishing other than trawling, making way Any length | Sidelights Sternlight R/W all-around | | | |
| **Rule 26(c)** Fishing other than trawling, not making way Any length | R/W all-around | | | |
| **Rule 26(c)** Fishing other than trawling, making way Gear out >150 m | Sidelights Sternlight R/W all-around All-around | gear side | | |
| **Rule 26(c)** Fishing other than trawling, not making way Gear out >150 m | R/W all-around All-around | gear side | | |

| RULE/VESSEL | GROUPS | SHAPES | BOW | STERN |
|---|---|---|---|---|
| **BOTH INTERNATIONAL AND INLAND** | | | | |
| **Rule 27(a)** Not Under Command Making way | Sidelights Sternlight R/R all-around | | | |
| **Rule 27(a)** Not Under Command Not making way | R/R all-around | | | |
| **Rule 27(b)** Restricted in Ability to Maneuver Making way <50 m | Masthead Sidelights Sternlight R/W/R all-around | | | |
| **Rule 27(b)** Restricted in Ability to Maneuver Making way ≥50 m | 2 Mastheads Sidelights Sternlight R/W/R all-around | | | |
| **Rule 27(b)** Restricted in Ability to Maneuver Not making way | R/W/R all-around | | | |
| **Rule 27(b)** Restricted in Ability to Maneuver Anchored <50 m | R/W/R all-around W all-around | | | |
| **Rule 27(b)** Restricted in Ability to Maneuver Anchored ≥50 m | R/W/R all-around 2 W all-around | | | |
| **Rule 27(d)** Dredging or Underwater Operations Not making way | R/W/R all-around R/R all-arnd obstr. side G/G all-arnd clear side | obstr. side   clear side | | |
| **Rule 27(e)** Diving, but unable to display Underwater Operations lights | R/W/R all-around | Int'l Code Flag "A" | | |
| **Rule 27(f)** Mine-clearing Making way ≥50 m | 2 Mastheads Sidelights Sternlight G △ all-around | | | |
| **Rule 27(f)** Mine-clearing Making way <50 m | Masthead Sidelights Sternlight G △ all-around | | | |

**Figure 8-36.** (continued)

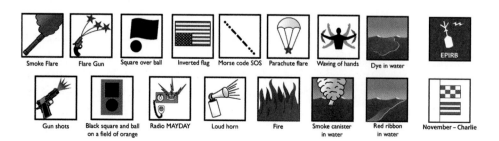

**Figure 8-37.** Distress signals. (REPRINTED WITH PERMISSION FROM *EMERGENCIES ON BOARD: A CAPTAIN'S QUICK GUIDE* BY JOHN ROUSMANIERE)

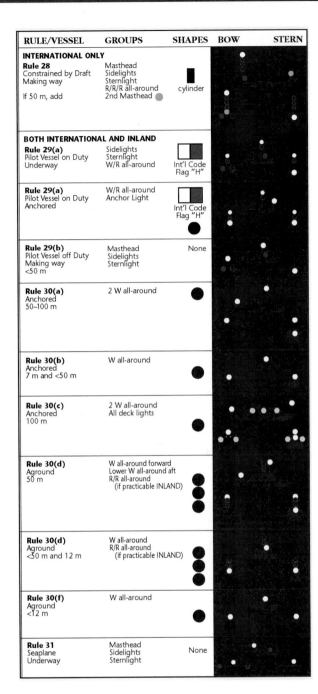

| RULE/VESSEL | GROUPS | SHAPES | BOW | STERN |
|---|---|---|---|---|
| **INTERNATIONAL ONLY** | | | | |
| **Rule 28** Constrained by Draft Making way | Masthead Sidelights Sternlight R/R/R all-around | cylinder | | |
| If 50 m, add | 2nd Masthead | | | |
| **BOTH INTERNATIONAL AND INLAND** | | | | |
| **Rule 29(a)** Pilot Vessel on Duty Underway | Sidelights Sternlight W/R all-around | Int'l Code Flag "H" | | |
| **Rule 29(a)** Pilot Vessel on Duty Anchored | W/R all-around Anchor Light | Int'l Code Flag "H" | | |
| **Rule 29(b)** Pilot Vessel off Duty Making way <50 m | Masthead Sidelights Sternlight | None | | |
| **Rule 30(a)** Anchored 50–100 m | 2 W all-around | ● | | |
| **Rule 30(b)** Anchored 7 m and <50 m | W all-around | ● | | |
| **Rule 30(c)** Anchored 100 m | 2 W all-around All deck lights | ● | | |
| **Rule 30(d)** Aground 50 m | W all-around forward Lower W all-around aft R/R all-around (if practicable INLAND) | ● ● ● | | |
| **Rule 30(d)** Aground <50 m and 12 m | W all-around R/R all-around (if practicable INLAND) | ● ● ● | | |
| **Rule 30(f)** Aground <12 m | W all-around | ● | | |
| **Rule 31** Seaplane Underway | Masthead Sidelights Sternlight | None | | |

**Figure 8-36.**

# Homeland Security Measures

All boats must keep a safe distance away from certain locations that are considered by the U.S. Department of Homeland Security to be at risk to sabotage. The list of these locations is available at local Coast Guard facilities. These locations are typically military installations, commercial port operations, dams, bridges, or any place where massive damage can be inflicted with an explosion or lethal substances. Boaters should report suspicious activities to proper authorities at 1-877-24-WATCH (1-877-249-2824) or 1-800-424-8802.

# Courtesy and Safety

Common courtesy and respect for other boaters underlie most of the Navigation Rules. As one example of this, the person in charge of a vessel is required to give assistance to another vessel that is in immediate danger, though this Good Samaritan obligation does not require you to place your own vessel in danger. Further, you should be sure that the vessel in apparent trouble is willing to accept your assistance. Most states have laws defining proper assistance. Be very cautious about giving assistance where it is not invited.

Sound signals likewise illustrate the spirit of the Rules. A major purpose of sound signals is to alert other vessel operators to the action you are taking or are about to take. The rules concerning the stand-on status of sailboats in relationship to each other and to power vessels serve the same purpose. The rules at first glance seem many and varied, but this spirit of courtesy and common sense informs all of them. If you conduct your boating in this spirit, you will rarely run afoul of the Rules.

Because of courtesy violations, many ordinances and laws have been enacted limiting PWC operations, and the public's reaction to discourteous operators threatens to lead to further curtailments. Weaving in and out of a congested area at high speeds; operating too close to shorelines near residential areas; running too close to people who are fishing; making sharp, unpredictable turns; following water-skiers too closely; cutting behind other vessels when vision is obstructed; failing to respect swimming and other restricted areas; steering toward another vessel or person; and other such actions constitute reckless operation. These actions are also a violation of common courtesy and threaten to give rise to further restrictive legislation. All boaters—powerboaters, sailors, and

PWC operators—need to share the waterways with courtesy and respect.

# Drawbridges

Most drawbridges are normally closed, but they open to permit the passage of vessels. These bridges have bridge tenders. Other bridges—for example, some railroad bridges on infrequently used lines—are usually open, closing only when needed for land transportation. Some drawbridges are always closed and unattended. If you need to pass through an unattended, normally closed bridge, give advance notice of your intention. Nautical charts describe bridges over navigable waterways and tell their horizontal and vertical clearances.

Get information regarding local bridges at a Coast Guard Station or at a marina. If you are planning a cruise and there are drawbridges along the way, you can get information in advance of your trip from a Coast Guard Station in the area. Title 33 of the *Code of Federal Regulations*, Part 117, includes a brief description and the operating regulations for each drawbridge in the United States. Many libraries have the *Code of Federal Regulations*, or you can view it online at www.gpoaccess.gov/cfr.

Because of heavy highway traffic, some drawbridges have scheduled opening times, which are posted on signs near the bridges. Changes in the opening schedules of bridges are published in the *Local Notices to Mariners* (Figure 8-38).

Some bridges do not open during severe weather, such as hurricanes, so they can help pro-vide evacuation routes. Be aware of this and plan ahead if severe weather is approaching.

When bridges have special conditions, such as opening only at specified times, remaining closed during severe weather, or requiring advance notice for opening, a sign announcing the conditions is posted near the bridge. If advance notice must be given, the name, address, and telephone number of the person to contact will be on the sign.

## LIMITATIONS ON DRAWBRIDGE OPENINGS

Federal regulations provide penalties of up to $1,000 for causing a bridge to open unnecessarily. Do not request that a bridge be opened for any purpose other than for you to pass through its opening.

If your vessel can pass under a drawbridge with appurtenances such as antennas and outriggers lowered, and if these are not needed for navigation, you must lower them. Most antennas above the highest fixed point on a vessel are collapsible. Examples of appurtenances not considered lowerable are radar antennas, flying bridges, and sailboat masts.

## DRAWBRIDGE SIGNALS

Signals for requesting the opening of a drawbridge include sound, visual, and radiotelephone. Sound signals are made by whistle, horn, megaphone, hailer, or other device capable of being heard by the bridge tender. When signaling at a bridge with a bridge tender, your signal must be acknowledged, so repeat it until you get an acknowledgment.

If you approach an open draw, give the opening signal. If it is not acknowledged in 30 seconds, proceed, with caution, through the open draw.

### Sound Signals

A whistle or horn sound signal is one prolonged blast of 4 to 6 seconds followed no later than 3 seconds by a 1-second short blast. If the bridge can be opened, the bridge tender will respond with a prolonged blast followed by a short blast no later than 30 seconds after your request. When the draw cannot be opened immediately or must be closed after it has been opened, the bridge tender will signal with 5 short blasts in rapid succession.

**Figure 8-38.** A commercial vessel can request that a drawbridge open outside its scheduled opening times, and if you're nearby you can follow it through. (PHOTO BY GENE HAMILTON)

## Visual Signals

To request the opening of a drawbridge by a visual signal, vertically raise and lower a white flag. If the draw can be opened immediately, the acknowledgment signal is a white flag raised and lowered vertically; a white, amber, or green light raised and lowered vertically; or a fixed or flashing white, amber, or green light or lights. If the draw cannot be opened immediately, the acknowledgment signal is a red flag or light swung back and forth horizontally or a fixed or flashing red light or lights.

## Radiotelephone

If a drawbridge is equipped with a radiotelephone, there will be a sign on each side of the bridge giving its calling and working channels. This sign will be written or will show a symbol of a telephone handset that is often like the symbol at a service station that has a public telephone. In addition to the handset symbol, the sign will show a three-legged lightning slash above the symbol. The preferred calling channel will be shown in the lower left and the working channel in the lower right.

Usually, you call a bridge tender on Channel 16 and then switch to Channel 13 to request the bridge opening, but there are many exceptions to this general rule. In Florida, for example, you call the bridge tender and make your request on Channel 9. At bridges in other states, you may need to call the bridge tenders on other VHF-FM channels. When planning a cruise, you may want to consult bridge tenders via telephone before departing. (Inland waterway charts frequently note who operates a bridge.) Knowing the calling and working channels in advance will prevent delays. When you make a radiotelephone request that a bridge be opened, stay tuned to the working channel until you have cleared the bridge.

# Penalties

If you operate a vessel in violation of the International or Inland Rules, you are liable for a civil penalty of up to $5,000 for each violation. Both the operator and the owner may be held responsible when they are not the same person. When you charter a boat you are liable—not the chartering firm that owns the boat.

If you operate a vessel on U.S. waters in a negligent manner and endanger the "life, limb, or property of a person," you may be liable for a fine of up to $1,000. If you operate a vessel in a grossly negligent manner, you are liable for a fine of up to $5,000 and imprisonment for as long as one year.

Boating accidents occurring in international waters must be reported to the U.S. Coast Guard when the estimated damage is greater than $25,000. This report should be done verbally as soon as possible. There are significant penalties for failing to report.

Accidents occurring in inland waters defer to state reporting requirements, and are reported to the state agency that issued the registration certificate for the vessel. The loss or disappearance of a person must be reported. Also, report any injury that requires medical care beyond first aid. Damage to a vessel estimated to exceed $2,000 should also be reported. The Marine Accident form in Appendix C is a federal form but represents the information that is typically required by state agencies. Damage to any buoy or daymark should be reported as soon as possible to the U.S. Coast Guard.

There are penalties, also, for failure to give help in marine casualties. When you give help, the Good Samaritan clause protects you.

Nothing in the Rules ever requires you to place your own vessel in danger.

# Practice Questions

## IMPORTANT BOATING TERMS

In the following exercise, match the words in the column on the left with the definitions in the column on the right. In the blank space to the left of each term, write the letter of the item that best matches it. Do not use an item in the right-hand column more than once.

| THE ITEMS | | THE RESPONSES |
|---|---|---|
| 1. _____ | head-on situation | a. has an arc of visibility of 135° |
| 2. _____ | lookout | b. black conical shape, apex down |
| 3. _____ | overtaking | c. applies to all boaters at all hours |
| 4. _____ | stay clear of diver | d. at night you see a red or a green light |
| 5. _____ | sternlight | e. red flag with white diagonal stripe |
| 6. _____ | stand-on vessel | f. you see another vessel's sternlight |
| 7. _____ | navigation lights | g. at night you see both sidelights |
| 8. _____ | sailing vessel underway at night | h. maintains course and speed |
| 9. _____ | sailing vessel operating propelling machinery | i. all vessels must display between sunset and sunrise and in restricted visibility |
| 10. _____ | danger zone | j. dead ahead to 22.5° abaft the starboard beam |

# Multiple-Choice Items

In the following items, choose the best response:

**8-1.** The give-way vessel is responsible

    a. to maintain course and speed
    b. to keep astern of all other vessels
    c. to take early and substantial action to keep clear of the stand-on vessel
    d. to use hand signals when ready to pass

**8-2.** The primary purpose of the Navigation Rules is

    a. to establish racing rules
    b. to reduce the number of personal injury suits
    c. to prevent collisions between vessels
    d. to tell you how your boat should be equipped

**8-3.** You may depart from the Navigation Rules when

    a. you are in a marina
    b. you are being overtaken by another vessel
    c. you do not see any other boats
    d. it is necessary to avoid a collision

**8-4.** When underway, every vessel must proceed at a safe speed and maintain a

    a. proper lookout
    b. constant engine watch
    c. straight course
    d. all of the above

**8-5.** When you act to avoid a collision, make your changes in course and speed

## Multiple-Choice Items (continued)

a. at right angles to the course you are steering
b. to port
c. to starboard
d. large enough that they are readily seen

**8-6.** The single white light on a vessel means you are seeing

a. its sternlight
b. a power-driven vessel less than 12 meters long
c. a vessel under oars
d. any of the above

**8-7.** Which vessel is stand-on to all others?

a. a crossing vessel
b. an overtaken vessel
c. an overtaking vessel
d. none of the above

**8-8.** Lines that mark the boundaries between waters governed by the International Rules and those governed by the Inland Rules are

a. lines of position
b. demarcation lines
c. pickup lines
d. shorelines

**8-9.** In an overtaking situation under Inland Rules, you would never expect the other vessel to sound

a. one short blast
b. two short blasts
c. five short blasts
d. one prolonged blast

**8-10.** When in a congested area, you should watch your wake because

a. it should not be more than 3 feet high
b. it could cause personal injury or damage
c. it may be used to estimate speed
d. it can be used to judge clearance from other boats

**8-11.** The sidelight on the starboard side of a vessel is

a. red
b. yellow
c. green
d. white

**8-12.** The color of a sternlight is always

a. red
b. yellow
c. green
d. white

**8-13.** To be environmentally responsible and courteous to other boaters, you should

a. run your boat at slow speeds when close to shore
b. top off the fuel tank to the air vents
c. clean the hull with phosphates
d. empty marine sanitation devices in deep water

**8-14.** Five or more short blasts of the horn is a signal for

a. operating astern propulsion
b. anchoring
c. danger
d. a drawbridge

**8-15.** The appropriate signal for you to give in a head-on, crossing, or overtaking situation when you pass another boat on your port side is almost always

a. one short blast
b. two short blasts
c. one prolonged blast
d. two prolonged blasts

**8-16.** If you are at anchor in restricted visibility and in open water, ring your bell rapidly for about 5 seconds at intervals of no more than

a. 1 minute
b. 2 minutes
c. 3 minutes
d. whenever you think of it

**8-17.** The basic configuration of lights for power vessels less than 20 meters is

a. sidelights and a sternlight
b. masthead light and sternlight
c. sidelights, sternlight, and masthead light
d. a combination lantern at the masthead

**8-18.** In the Navigation Rules, the term "right of way" applies only to a vessel that is

a. being overtaken on coastal waters

**(continued on next page)**

## Multiple-Choice Items (continued)

b. overtaking another on international waters

c. crossing ahead of your vessel from right to left on the Gulf of Mexico

d. downbound in a narrow channel or fairway with a following current

**8-19.** If you are overtaking another vessel, you remain an overtaking vessel until

a. you are abreast of the other vessel

b. it is obvious one of you must change course

c. you are past and clear of the other vessel

d. until the other vessel signals you are clear

**8-20.** If you see both sidelights of another vessel, assume that you are in

a. a crossing situation

b. a head-on or meeting situation

c. an overtaking situation

d. none of the above

**8-21.** Inland meeting sound signals announce

a. action you are taking

b. action you have taken

c. action you intend to take

d. to the other vessel that you are near

**8-22.** When boating in an unfamiliar channel you should

a. maintain speed and stay on plane

b. keep to the port side of the channel

c. stay in the middle of the channel

d. obtain local knowledge

**8-23.** In a crossing situation, the give-way vessel

a. alters course to pass in front of the other vessel

b. increases speed

c. sounds the danger signal

d. turns to starboard and passes astern of the stand-on vessel

**8-24.** In a narrow channel at the entrance to a harbor, which vessel has priority?

a. a deep-draft freighter

b. a kayak

c. a 30-foot sailing vessel

d. a commercial fishing vessel

# Inland Boating

## The objectives of this chapter are to describe:

- The nature of inland waters.
- The navigation rules that pertain on these waters and the aids to navigation used there.
- The nature and meaning of crossing and passing daymarks.
- Some of the hazards of inland waters—including commercial traffic, locks, lowhead and high dams, river currents, dikes, and dredges— and how to avoid them.
- How to read and understand river charts and navigate inland waters.

The face of the water, in time, became a wonderful book—a book that was a dead language to the uneducated passenger, but which told its mind to me without reserve, delivering its most cherished secrets as clearly as if it uttered them with a voice. And it was not a book to be read once and thrown aside, for it had a new story to tell every day. Throughout the long twelve hundred miles there was never a page that was void of interest, never one that you could leave unread without loss, never one that you would want to skip, thinking you could find higher enjoyment in some other thing.

—Mark Twain, *Life on the Mississippi*

MANY BOATERS SPEND their time on the open seas, the gulfs, and other tidal waters. Even more are inland boaters.

Underway on the Intracoastal Waterway. (PHOTO BY GENE HAMILTON)

# Inland Waters

Inland waters include rivers, lakes, and canals, each of which offers unique experiences and challenges.

## RIVERS

There are more than 30,000 miles of **navigable rivers** in the United States, meaning rivers that are subject to tidal influence or are used for interstate or international commerce. These include the Western Rivers and the Tennessee-Tombigbee Waterway (the Tenn-Tom), the Black Warrior, Alabama, Coosa, Mobile, Flint, and Chattahoochee rivers, and the Apalachicola River above its confluence with the Jackson River. The Western Rivers include most of the Mississippi and all its tributaries, including the Missouri, Ohio, Wabash, Green, and Barren rivers. **Navigable waterways** include all navigable rivers as well as the Great Lakes and the Intracoastal Waterway (Figure 9-1).

**Figure 9-1.** Inland waterways provide some of the most beautiful boating areas to be found anywhere. **Top:** Sunset on the Mississippi River at St. Louis, Missouri. (PHOTO BY KITTY NICOLAI) **Bottom:** Sunrise at Strawberry Reservoir, Utah. (PHOTO BY BILL SETZER)

Besides the navigable waterways, many other rivers are used by pleasure boaters, hunters, and anglers. Thus, rivers used for boating range in size and character from the wide Missouri and the muddy Mississippi to small, meandering streams such as the Sipsey and the Cahaba in Alabama. They range also from fast-moving streams such as the Snake River between Idaho and Oregon to slow ones such as the Illinois. Each offers its pleasures and challenges.

## LAKES

Lakes present as much variety for boaters as rivers do. There are large, natural lakes such as the Great Lakes and Lake Okeechobee. There are also large artificial lakes such as Lake Mead between Nevada and Arizona and Lake Sidney Lanier in north Georgia. In between are long, artificial "lakes" made by damming streams for commerce, generation of electricity, irrigation, water supply, and flood control. Besides the large natural and artificial lakes, small lakes and farm ponds are used by boaters, including those who fish and hunt.

## CANALS

Canals are also inland waterways and serve important navigational purposes (Figure 9-2). For example, the Sault Sainte Marie canals connect Lakes Superior and Ontario, bypassing the rapids on St. Marys River. The New York State Barge Canal system is 525 miles long and connects the Great Lakes, Lake Champlain, and the Hudson River.

**Figure 9-2.** The Albemarle and Chesapeake Canal, in Virginia, is part of the Intracoastal Waterway on the U.S. East Coast. (PHOTO BY KEN STANLEY)

The Chesapeake and Delaware Canal is 19 miles long and runs between the head of the Chesapeake Bay and the Delaware River. The Tenn-Tom makes it possible to go from the Tenneessee River to the Gulf of Mexico by way of the Tombigbee and Mobile rivers (Figure 9-3).

## WATCH YOUR SPEED

Artificial waterways are usually narrow. This means that boaters must be especially aware of the effects of their boats' wakes on other boats and on the waterways' shores. Although the Tenn-Tom opened only in the 1980s, wakes have caused serious erosion of its banks and partial blocking of its channel.

Many canals post restricted speeds to reduce wakes. Heavy wakes in narrow waterways echo from the shores several times and create considerable turbulence. Reduced speed is also necessary because of heavy commercial traffic. If you use one of these waterways, yield to barges and other commercial traffic. They can be dangerous, and they have very little ability to avoid you.

# Inland Navigation

Although inland waters are diverse, they require many of the same skills and knowledge needed for boating on tidal waters. Knowledge of radio communication, marlinespike seamanship, boat construction, engines, boat handling, and other subjects can serve you as well on inland waters as on tidal waters.

There are important differences between river and coastal piloting, however. For example, you

**Figure 9-3.** The *Southern Belle* on the Tennessee River in Chattanooga, Tennessee. (PHOTO BY WILLIAM MASON)

seldom need to plot a compass course or maintain a dead-reckoning (DR) plot on a river. You can tell where you are by using a chart of the river and noting the mile markers.

Besides local knowledge and a chart of the river, the river navigator will find that the most useful piloting tool is a good binocular, which is useful for reading mile markers and locating aids to navigation (ATONs).

## INLAND NAVIGATION RULES

The Inland Navigation Rules discussed in Chapter 8 are in force on all navigable waterways. They do not apply on nonnavigable lakes and streams that are entirely within a single state, although state and local regulations may be in effect. Even if the Inland Rules are not in force on a body of water, common sense dictates that you follow them whenever possible. They reflect a large body of experience in avoiding collisions, and you will find that conforming to these rules will usually keep you on the right side of state and local regulations as well.

The need for a lookout, for example, is as great on a lake as on any other body of water. Meeting, crossing, and passing situations are as dangerous on lakes as elsewhere, and proper lighting of vessels at night is equally important wherever boating occurs. The Rules help boaters avoid collisions and you should do your best to observe them.

Where the Inland Navigation Rules apply, the equipment requirements listed in Chapter 5 also apply. Safety practices apply equally on inland and international waters. On large bodies of water such as the Great Lakes and Lake Okeechobee, piloting principles also apply.

## INLAND ATONS

Two ATON systems are in use on inland waters: one marks navigable rivers and is similar to the U.S. ATON System; the other marks waters solely within the control of a state.

### Western Rivers ATONs

The ATONs that appear in the upper part of Figure 7-4 are used on the Western Rivers and other navigable rivers, and are installed and maintained by the Coast Guard. Inland river ATONs differ little from those used in the U.S. ATON System, as described in Chapter 7. Red daybeacons, lights, and buoys mark the starboard banks and limits of channels as vessels "return from sea" or proceed upstream, and green daybeacons, lights, and buoys mark the port banks and limits of navigable channels when going upstream.

**RIVERBANK NAMES.** The banks of rivers are referred to as "left" and "right" from the perspective of a vessel traveling downstream. Thus, the right bank has green ATONs and the left bank has red ATONs. The west bank of the Mississippi is its right bank and has green ATONs.

To avoid confusion, commercial river traffic often calls the right bank the *right descending bank* and the left bank the *left descending bank.* Expressed in this way, it leaves no room for doubt in your mind.

**PASSING DAYMARKS.** In the Western Rivers System, triangular and square *passing daymarks* mark the rivers' banks (Figure 9-4). If you see a triangular red or square green daymark on the bank, you

know that the channel is on that side of the river. You continue past it, since it is a passing daymark.

**CROSSING DAYMARKS.** Because the navigable channels of rivers swing from bank to bank as the rivers bend, the Western Rivers System uses *crossing daymarks* to assist river traffic (Figure 9-5). Crossing daymarks help you know when the channel is changing from one side of the river to the other, and daymarks, buoys, and minor lights help you know where the channel is.

**USING CROSSING DAYMARKS.** The diamond-shaped crossing daymarks, which are always on the opposite side of the river from the channel you have been following, show that the channel is about to cross over to the other side. Thus, you should head for the diamonds!

As you pass a daymark, look back at it. If it has a crossing daymark on its back, you know that the next daymark in your direction of travel will be a crossing daymark on the opposite side of the river. The crossing daymark that you see on the back of a passing daymark is there to guide a vessel traveling in the opposite direction. Looking back at a

**Figure 9-4.** Passing daymarks on inland waterways are like those on coastal waters. **Top:** This green passing daymark marks the right descending bank of the Ohio River. Note the mile marker. **Bottom:** A red passing daymark on the left descending bank of the Cumberland River. (PHOTOS BY JERRY TURLEY)

**Figure 9-5. Top:** A crossing daymark with a mile marker on the right descending bank of the Ohio River. **Bottom:** A crossing daymark on the left descending bank of the Cumberland River. (PHOTOS BY JERRY TURLEY)

passing daymark to see a crossing daymark is particularly helpful at night or in reduced visibility, when the bend in the river may not be visible. It is also easier to spot a green crossing daymark on the opposite bank when you are expecting to see it there.

When you see a crossing daymark, it tells you nothing about what the next daymark will be. It could be a passing daymark or it could be another crossing daymark on the opposite side of the river. Again, look at the back of the crossing daymark you are passing.

In the past, the Western Rivers System has used red or green diamond-shaped dayboards as crossing daymarks. The former has small, darker red diamonds in each of its four corners, and the latter has a small, darker green diamond in each corner.

These older crossing daymarks are being replaced with green-and-white, or red-and-white, diamond-shaped, checkered daymarks like those in the U.S. ATON System (refer back to Figure 7-4). As in that system, the new crossing daymarks have no lateral significance, and indicate only that the channel has crossed over to the other side of the river.

The green-and-white crossing daymarks are easier to see against a background of green foliage, and both the red-and-white and green-and-white ones will be easier to see in dim light. Green passing and crossing daymarks are always on the right descending bank, while red ones are on the left descending bank.

When you look back and see a green crossing daymark, you know that the next daymark will be a red crossing daymark on the left descending bank of the river. Similarly, when you look back and see a red crossing daymark, you know the next daymark is a green crossing daymark on the right descending bank of the river.

**RIVER BUOYS.** Changes in river channels caused by fluctuations in water level, current speed, and shifting shoals make buoy maintenance a continuous task for the Coast Guard. Shifting shoals frequently require adding buoys or taking them out of the system. In wintertime where rivers freeze, river buoys are lost or moved from position, and because of this somewhat temporary nature, do not have letters or numbers and are not usually shown on river charts.

**MILE MARKERS.** Among the most useful markers on a river are the *mile markers*, which are placards attached to daymarks or displayed in other easily seen places. They show distances in statute rather than nautical miles.

With the exception of the Ohio River, mile markers tell you how far it is to the mouth of the river. Ohio River markers start at its headwaters and tell you how far downstream you are. Mile markers help locate your position on a river chart, and also help identify which passing and crossing daymarks you are looking at.

## Uniform State Waterway Marking System

Until recently, states have marked some of their exclusively state waters with markers from the Uniform State Waterway Marking System (USWMS). Due to the confusion this caused, the states agreed to adopt the U.S. ATON System, and the Coast Guard initiated the plan to replace ATONs in state waters in 1998. Until the conversion is complete, however, you will have to find out which system is used on local state waters. See also Chapter 7.

**REGULATORY MARKERS.** Markers that show boat exclusion, danger, and controlled areas, and also give information or directions are called *regulatory markers*. There are two types: signs and buoys, both of which have white backgrounds. The signs have orange borders and orange symbols, while the buoys are white with an orange band near the top and a second band near the water's surface, between which orange symbols appear. Where letters or numbers appear on regulatory signs or buoys, the lettering is black.

Exclusion areas are, for example, areas near dams, rapids, and swimming places, and the markers for such areas have orange diamonds with diagonal marks. They also show the nature of the area in black letters.

Danger area markers have open diamonds, with the nature of the danger often written in black letters.

Controlled area markers have orange circles with the nature of the warnings printed in black letters.

On waters marked with the USWMS, a red-striped white buoy was used to tell you not to pass between it and the nearest shore. Since the states have adopted the U.S ATON System, however, that color combination is used to denote safe water on all sides. Therefore, the states have created a white buoy with black stripes to tell you not to pass between it and the nearest shore.

# Inland Seamanship

One difference between inland and saltwater boating is the constantly changing nature of inland waterways. Saltwater boaters expect the tidal changes that come with predictable regularity. There may be changes due to gradual shoaling near shore, but it is usually not a surprise to local mariners, who prepare for the changes and take them into account while maneuvering and mooring.

## CHANGING WATER DEPTHS

Although some inland waters differ little from day to day, they are the exception rather than the rule. In his book *Life on the Mississippi*, Mark Twain emphasizes the point that rivers are ever-changing. One important feature of this change is the wide range in water depth that occurs in some streams, and another is the speed of their currents.

Rivers and impounded (dammed) waters vary in depth from season to season and day to day, according to the amount of rainfall or melting snow in the area or upstream. Rivers can rise up overnight and overflow their banks, experience droughts and sink to mere rivulets, and even turn from sluggish streams to torrents after rain or snow melts.

The Mississippi River depth at Memphis varies almost 50 feet during an average year; daily changes may be well over a foot. This means that, at times, navigators must use narrow channels, while at other times they have considerable freedom of movement. Continuous monitoring of a river channel's depths is necessary to aid commercial traffic. In many locales, newspapers give daily reports on river and lake levels.

Many rivers have depth gauges posted at important points such as bridges and locks, and a few of these gauges note whether the river is rising or falling. Figure 9-6 depicts two such gauges.

**Figure 9-6.** River stages are noted on gauges (right) up and down many rivers. The river's level and whether the river is rising or falling may also be displayed on signboards (left).

## LAKE HAZARDS

Much of what this chapter says about river boating and its hazards also applies to lakes, especially if the lakes are impounded waters. While all water levels vary from season to season and with local precipitation, the levels of some impounded lakes also vary in response to flood control efforts upstream and to needs for electrical power, irrigation, and community water supplies.

During very high water, boaters need to be aware of overhead power lines that have abnormally low clearance. Sailboaters should be especially cautious.

### Underwater Hazards

If a lake's purpose is to control flooding, engineers may have cleared vegetation only from the shoreline of the normal pool. Entire trees may remain standing, some with their tops close to the water's surface, and in agricultural areas, fences and the remains of farm buildings may be just below the surface, especially when the water level is low.

High water may submerge picnic tables and barbecue grills in recreational areas, making it difficult to get to the shoreline for a landing. And in low water, rocks and shoals, which are not problems during normal water levels, may become hazardous.

In some small reservoirs, and especially downstream of dams, water levels can vary with dangerous speed and little warning. It is important to learn about local conditions and then heed posted warning signs and use extra caution when boating in these areas.

### Other Lake Hazards

The water in spring-fed lakes can be very cold, even in summer, and hypothermia can develop rapidly if you fall overboard. Also, you may not notice that severe weather is approaching, as tree-lined shorelines or high cliffs and hillsides can block the horizon.

The long, narrow profiles of many lakes serve to channel wind down the lakes, and in ones that are shallow, high wind can create severe water turbulence. Be prepared when you round a bend or cross the mouth of a tributary—wind speed and direction may change abruptly.

Anchoring may be a problem in lakes due to debris on the bottom, such as submerged logs and rocks, which can easily foul your anchor. A trip line is good insurance where there is much debris. Because water levels change rapidly in some lakes, it is possible to anchor in a small cove overnight and find yourself aground the next morning. On the other hand, if you beach your boat for the night, you may find it downstream the next morning.

## SERVICES AND FACILITIES

The byword for any trip is planning. If possible, get the telephone numbers of facilities along your route and learn what services they offer ahead of time. You may need to deal with a local service station for fuel and repairs or visit a grocery store ashore for supplies.

Many lakes are far from towns, and emergency responses may be slow. The Coast Guard and the Auxiliary often do not have search-and-rescue capabilities on remote lakes, which means boaters will need to rely on park ranger or sheriff's department rescue teams in such areas. Learn before you go how to contact emergency services, and take a cellular telephone with you if possible.

# River Currents

Most rivers have currents—sometimes powerful ones. These can pose major problems for both recreational and commercial boats.

## RIVER CHANNELS

The river channel is the deepest part of a river. In a way, it is a river within the river. When a river basin floods, either naturally or because of dams, the channel may be lost under the broader river. Since the river may be shallow outside the channel, vessel traffic must know where the channel lies. This is not easy to do, since the channel may meander from bank to bank.

Where charts are available, they can help you locate the channel. ATONs mark the channels on inland rivers where traffic must stay within them.

The river's channel is also the point of concentration of the river's current, which can be a concern for riverboaters. Currents in the Mississippi and other rivers reach velocities of 8 to 10 or more miles per hour. Vessels moving upstream against the current may be making considerable speed through the water while making little progress over the ground, and some low-powered motorboats and sailboats may be unable to make any headway at all upstream.

The current aids movement downstream, boosting both speed and fuel economy, but this economy has its drawback. A vessel carried downstream by a strong current loses some control and is more at the mercy of the current. For this reason, the Navigation Rules give the right of way to vessels headed downstream—the only instance in the Rules where one vessel is accorded right of way over another, as opposed to being designated the stand-on vessel (see Chapter 8).

## BEHAVIOR OF CURRENTS

River currents can be complex, as the flow of the river responds to changes in channel direction and the shape of the bottom. The current at one depth may run counter to that at another depth, which means deep-draft vessels may experience a current moving in one direction while shallow-draft vessels are experiencing a current moving in the opposite direction. Knowledge of these currents, which you can gain through experience and by consulting knowledgeable boaters, is very useful.

## RIVER BENDS

The current usually flows around the outside of a river bend, causing water to pile up there. This deeper water flows faster than water on the inside of the bend, and if it moves fast enough, it scours the channel and sweeps silt downstream. Thus, the water usually moves most rapidly and is deepest on the outside of a bend (Figure 9-7).

On the inside of a bend, where the current moves more slowly, the river deposits silt, and shoaling may occur. Because of the difference in the speed of flow on the inside and outside of a bend, eddies and slack water often occur.

Vessels headed upstream sometimes move to the inside of a bend where the current is weaker or where it may reverse itself and head upstream. If you do this, be careful to avoid running aground. It is good practice to swing wide around points, since they may extend farther out into the streambed than you know.

If you round a bend that obscures your view, sound the bend signal: one prolonged blast (4 to 6 seconds) on your whistle. Any vessel that is entering the bend from the opposite direction should return your signal.

## ENTERING A CURRENT

The effect of a current may be considerable when you enter the main channel from a secondary one. Larger vessels and commercial traffic, such as tows of barges, must anticipate the impact of the change in current. When rounding a bend, tows need to use the current as an aid in maneuvering, so you should be ready to respond to the radical and rapid heading changes tows make as they negotiate such a bend or channel crossing. Tows are like trucks that carry signs saying "This vehicle makes wide turns," and you may suddenly find yourself in the path of the tow (Figures 9-8 and 9-9).

If you run into trouble, try to maneuver out of the channel and away from commercial traffic. Then set an anchor and maintain a lookout until help ar-

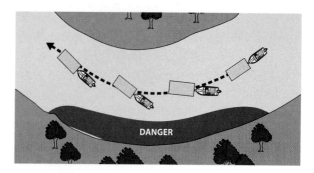

**Figure 9-8.** Do not pass a tow on the outside of a bend. The tow will swing to the outside, and its actual path of travel may be very different from the apparent heading of the tow vessel.

**Figure 9-9.** Rounding a bend on the Black River in Louisiana below the Columbia Lock and Dam. (PHOTO BY JAY J. BRANDINGER)

rives. If you can't get out of the channel, be prepared to warn commercial traffic of your plight by your VHF-FM radio or by visual signals (see Chapter 8).

## RIVER DEBRIS

During periods of high water, debris that has collected on riverbanks, such as brush, tree stumps, entire trees, and discarded trash, floats off. You can usually tell if a river is rising by observing the amount of debris that is floating downstream. As a river crests and the water level begins to lower, less debris will be present. While the debris is moving and after it is deposited, it is a danger to water traffic and can seriously damage small recreational vessels.

In the spring of the year, rising water may break apart sheets of ice that have formed on the northern reaches of rivers. These ice floes, which may travel hundreds of miles downstream before melting, constitute a threat to boat traffic, both moving and moored.

When the water level in a river drops, it leaves debris in the path of boating traffic, and that debris

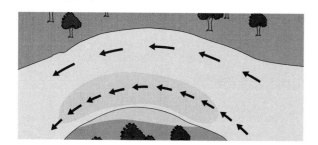

**Figure 9-7.** Currents flow more swiftly along the outside of a river bend. Slower-moving water on the inside of a bend allows silting and the formation of bars there.

is often just below the surface. Boaters should heed Mark Twain's advice and watch for subtle disturbances on the water's surface that may show hazards below. Learn to "read" the water.

# Maintaining Inland Waterways

Rivers, like living organisms, are constantly changing. Channels may change in depth and location, and during flood periods, a river may even change its course in some places. Because of this, channels need to be monitored and controlled continuously.

Maintenance of navigable waterways is the responsibility of the U.S. Army Corps of Engineers (the Corps), whose charge includes containing the wayward streams of the system, maintaining navigable channels, and ensuring channel depths wherever possible. This last charge is a difficult one in some waterways, especially in times of severe drought.

## LEVEES

Rivers flood and may change their courses. This can cause serious problems on many rivers, including the Mississippi, which cuts across bends and shortens its length when unconstrained. Unless some rivers are controlled, river towns can find themselves far from their rivers and without riverfronts following a flood. To control flooding and wandering, and to provide a navigable channel, the Corps maintains systems of levees on major rivers.

At bends in a river, the Corps uses revetments to protect its embankments. A **revetment** is a facing of stone, concrete, or other material that keeps a river from cutting through its embankments and shortening its course.

## OTHER DEVICES

For recreational boaters, a more important function of the Corps is its maintenance of navigable channels, which it does by using **dikes** or **wing dams** built out from the shore toward a river channel (Figure 9-10). These dikes, sometimes called "the works" or some other local name, slow the water flow outside

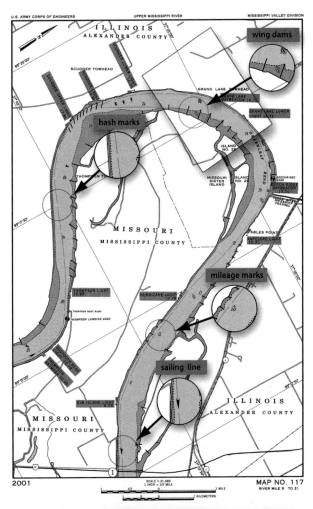

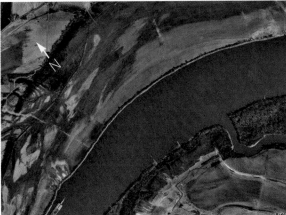

**Figure 9-10. Top:** U.S. Army Corps of Engineers Map No. 117 covers a 13-mile meander of the Mississippi River beginning just 8 miles upriver from the Ohio River confluence. Note the labeled mileage hash marks (statute miles), the sailing line denoted on the map (with arrows pointing downstream), and the numerous wing dams to control silting and erosion and direct the channel. (COURTESY U.S. ARMY CORPS OF ENGINEERS) **Bottom:** This aerial photo shows two of the wing dams quite clearly. The tow at lower left in the photo is headed upriver. He looks perilously close to the Illinois shore, but from the map you can see that he's right on the sailing line. (COURTESY U.S. GEOLOGICAL SURVEY)

the channels, causing silt and sand to accumulate around the dams rather than in the channels.

## Directing a River's Flow

Wing dams and dikes also direct the flow of a river to the center of a channel. This speeds up the flow in the channel and cleanses it of silt and sand, which helps maintain its depth.

On some navigable rivers, the tops of some wing dams are above water, but many are not. While most tops are above water when constructed, older wing dams can be submerged as dams built later raise surrounding water levels. About 95% of the wing dams in the Rock Island, Illinois, District of the Mississippi are below the water's surface all the time. Today, some wing dams have tops about 3 feet below the water's surface at normal water depth.

There are about 1,200 wing dam structures on the Mississippi. Most were built between 1900 and 1927 to maintain 4.5- to 6-foot channels, but today these depths are too shallow for much commercial traffic, so higher dams have been built. The old wing dams are still there and are often hazards for boaters.

## Other Underwater Structures

Wing dams are not the only underwater structures that you must avoid. In many cases the Corps removed only the channel sections of low dams when it built higher ones, meaning the peripheral portions of the low dams remain as hazards.

Wing dams provide calm overnight anchorages downstream, but submerged ones present problems for boaters, as there may not be enough clearance over them to permit the passage of even a small recreational boat. While turbulence may reveal their presence in the daylight, they disappear at night. If river charts are available where you're boating, consult them. Otherwise, get some local knowledge.

## DREDGING

Wing dams seek to "train" the river into channels and control the amount of silt and sand that a river deposits. Even so, silt and sand deposits can make it necessary to dredge the channels (Figure 9-11). For example, in an area below Keithsburg, Illinois, it was necessary for the Corps to dredge the river

**Figure 9-11.** The Memphis District dredge *Hurley* at work dredging the channel along the lower Mississippi River. (COURTESY U.S. ARMY CORPS OF ENGINEERS)

twenty-seven times in 25 years, a period in which the channel was lost several times and closed once. In 1985, however, the Corps built wing dams, and since then, the area has needed dredging only once.

Dredges present problems for boaters. A dredge pumps large volumes of water containing silt and sand, which is then carried through a long pipe and discharged ashore on a **spoil bank**, or into a barge. In the daytime it is easy to see the dredge as well as the pipeline if it is floating or supported on a trestle.

## Lights on Dredge Pipelines

At night, pipelines that are floating or supported must have a row of yellow lights that flash fifty to seventy times per minute. These lights are from 1 meter to 3.5 meters above the water and clearly mark the length and course of the pipeline. Where the pipeline crosses a navigable channel, the lights should be equally spaced and not more than 10 meters apart. There should be two red lights at each end of the pipeline, including the ends in a channel where the pipeline is separated to allow vessels to pass.

## Dredge Lights and Shapes

Knowing on which side of a dredge to pass is not a problem when it is properly marked (Figure 9-12). The Inland Navigation Rules require dredges to carry three shapes in a vertical line during the daytime; the highest and lowest are balls, and the middle one is a diamond. At night a dredge must carry three all-round lights in a vertical line; the highest and lowest are red, and the middle one is white.

**DAY SHAPES**

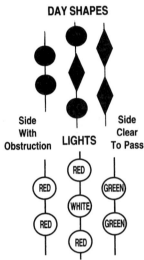

Side With Obstruction

LIGHTS

Side Clear To Pass

RED

RED | WHITE | GREEN

RED | RED | GREEN

**Figure 9-12.** This dredge boat working in the Sacramento River (top) displays the day shapes prescribed by the Navigation Rules (bottom). (COURTESY U.S. ARMY CORPS OF ENGINEERS)

These lights and shapes tell you that the dredge is restricted in its ability to maneuver.

The dredge also carries shapes and lights to tell where the discharge pipe is. Two balls in a vertical line in the daytime, or two red lights at night, show that the pipe is on that side. The side on which you should pass has two green lights or two diamonds in a vertical line. In the daytime, "Go for the diamonds."

# Dams

Over the years, many dams have been built on inland waterways. Some serve to maintain navigable water depths for commercial boating traffic, while others provide water for communities, irrigation, mills, and electrical generation. Some are for flood control.

Dams are seldom, if ever, constructed for recreational boating. While the resulting lakes are often used for this activity, the dams' imposing powerhouses, spillways, and locks are intimidating to many boaters.

## LOWHEAD DAMS

On many small rivers, dams are simply low walls of concrete or stone that remain submerged most of the time. Officially they are "fixed-crest, low-level dams" but they are often called *lowhead dams*. They may be the most dangerous type of dam for boaters, and have been described as "efficient, self-operating drowning machines."

Lowhead dams vary in height from about a foot to several feet and occur frequently in some areas. There are, for example, about 2,000 lowhead dams in the Commonwealth of Pennsylvania. Many serve to impound water for mills, while others provide minimum upstream water levels for water supply systems (Figure 9-13).

### Passing Over Lowhead Dams

Because the drops over some of these dams may appear small, some boaters assume that they can safely pass over them, while others do not know that they are near one of these dams and may accidentally pass over it. If the water level is high enough, this is possible, but boaters should realize that **these dams are extremely dangerous**.

**Figure 9-13.** A drilling rig at work on Dam #2 on the Allegheny River. From upstream, a lowhead dam like this can be hard to see. (COURTESY U.S. ARMY CORPS OF ENGINEERS)

## Lowhead Dam Dangers

There are hazards both in going over a lowhead dam and in the backwash below the dam (Figures 9-14 and 9-15). Anything caught in the backwash circulates around and around, making escape or rescue difficult. A dam does not have to be high to create a backwash, which gets worse during periods of high water and reaches farther downstream.

A person caught in a backwash first encounters tires and logs on the water's surface and rocks and steel bars on the bottom. If you escape these haz-

**Figure 9-14. Top:** An "upstream" view of the lowhead dam adjacent to the Ballard Locks, which connect Lake Union with Puget Sound in Seattle. The vertical drop from Lake Union to the saltwater entrance channel is anywhere from 6 to 26 feet, depending on the tide. **Bottom:** The turbulence below the spillway at the Ballard Locks is clearly visible in this photo from the saltwater side. (PHOTOS COURTESY BOB DENNIS)

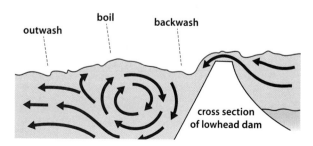

**Figure 9-15.** The hydraulic backwash below a lowhead dam.

ards, the backwash will pull you under and recirculate you back to the dam, where it will catch you again. You can then escape by swimming underwater as far downstream as possible, with the hope of coming up beyond the boil.

Another way to escape is to swim laterally across the stream as you emerge from each cycle. This requires exceptional breathing control and endurance, and your chances of survival are greater if you are wearing a life jacket.

## HIGH DAMS

Conventional dams, with their large structures, present more easily recognized dangers than do lowhead dams. Furthermore, there is usually a greater effort to warn unwary boaters of the presence and dangers of the dams.

Most high dams have "keep out" buoys above them and "danger dam" buoys below them.

## Restricted Areas

Areas immediately upstream and downstream of high dams are restricted and are marked by signs and buoys and, perhaps, by flashing red lights installed in conspicuous places (Figure 9-16). On the upstream side of many high dams there are strong undertows resulting from the rush of water through open gate sections below the water's surface. If a boat approaches the upper side of a high dam too closely, the undertow may pin it against the dam or capsize it.

Dams have gates that open to allow the release of water to the downstream pool, and to control the flow of water during flooding periods or to generate electricity. Most dam operators sound horns or sirens before the gates open, so if you hear such a sound, get out of the way quickly.

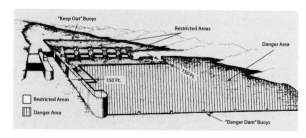

**Figure 9-16.** Dams are dangerous. Stay out of restricted areas. This illustration shows the gravity locks that typically permit upstream and downstream traffic past a dam.

## Dam Gates

There are several types of dam gates in use. **Wicket gates** lower to lie along the bottom of the waterway so that water passes above them, and their principal advantage is that in times of high water, river traffic can pass over the dam. The height of the dam controls the type of wickets used. Wicket dams present potential hazards to small boats, which can be swept over a partially open wicket.

More often, high dams use **tainter gates** (Figure 9-17), which allow water to flow downstream from the bottom of the dam. The advantage of the flow from the bottom is that it flushes sediment downstream. Since the openings are at the base of the dam, boaters cannot tell by looking if the dam gates are open. Open gates mean turbulent water, and this means a dangerous situation for small boats, which can be caught up against the wall of a tainter dam and be held there until rescued if they do not capsize or swamp first.

## FISHING BELOW DAMS

The **tailrace**, or whitewater below a dam (Figure 9-18), is an enticing place to fish, since the moving water churns up food on which fish feed, making them abundant in such an area. Don't succumb to the temptation, however. You may lose your boat and your life.

Many accidents occur when small vessels enter restricted areas, especially those below high dams. If a hydroelectric turbine is turned on, it can send a wall of water 6 feet high that can swamp a boat tied to a short anchor line.

**Figure 9-18.** Top: The tailrace below a high dam is an exceptionally dangerous place for small boats. (PHOTO BY JAY J. BRANDINGER) **Bottom:** The tailrace of the Bonneville Dam on the Columbia River in Oregon. (COURTESY U.S. ARMY CORPS OF ENGINEERS)

As with a lowhead dam, the water coming from a high dam creates a boil and a backwash, with the only difference being that the boil and backwash of a high dam are many times stronger. At the water's surface, a strong current moves toward the dam, and if you get into this current and have an engine failure, the current will push you to the face of the dam and swamp your boat. While getting out of the boil below a lowhead dam is difficult, getting out of the boil below a high dam is probably impossible.

Even if you don't experience engine failure, you may have a problem in the tailrace below a dam. From time to time, dams open for power generation or to lower the water level in the pools behind them. Sirens or horns sound before this happens, but your engine may not start and you may be stuck and swamped when the dam opens. Raise your anchor and hope to be carried downstream, but beware that if you are close enough to the dam, the current may push you to the dam's face.

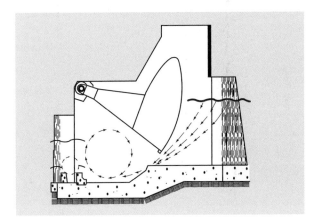

**Figure 9-17.** A tainter gate.

# Locks

Dams built on navigable streams must have some means of passing vessel traffic through them. Locks serve this purpose by raising or lowering vessels to the level of the next pool of water. A lock on a navigable river is a large chamber, most often about 800 to 1,200 feet long and 100 to 120 feet wide, with gates at each end (Figure 9-19). Locks on canals are often smaller.

## LOCK OPERATION

A vessel headed upstream enters the lock chamber through the downstream gates, which then close behind it. Valves in the lock then open to permit water from the upstream pool to enter the chamber, and as the water level rises, the vessel rises with it. When the water level in the lock is even with the level of the upstream pool, the flow of water stops, the upstream gates open, and the vessel moves out of the chamber and continues on its way.

A vessel headed downstream enters the full chamber and the gates close behind it, as in Figure 9-20. The water from the chamber then drains into the lower pool, and this lowers the vessel to the level of the lower pool. When the water inside the lock is at the same level as the water in the lower pool, the lower gates open and the vessel moves on.

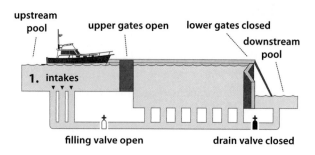

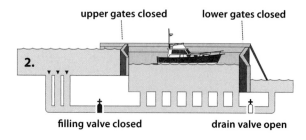

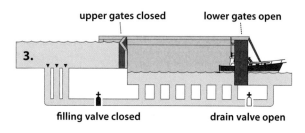

**Figure 9-20.** Lock operations for a vessel headed downstream: **1.** Preparing to lower the vessel. **2.** Lowering the vessel. **3.** Leaving the lock.

**Figure 9-19.** This aerial view of Lock and Dam #25 on the Mississippi River near Winfield, Missouri, shows a string of barges being locked through in sections while other tows wait their turns. (COURTESY U.S. ARMY CORPS OF ENGINEERS)

While gravity powers the entire operation of lifting or lowering a vessel in a lock, electrical power opens and closes most gates. In some small locks, the gates are manually opened and closed.

## PRIORITIES FOR USE

Federal regulations establish priorities for vessels using locks. Military vessels and mail packets have the highest priority, followed by commercial vessels; recreational vessels have the lowest priority.

This is not as bad as it may sound, as there are only a few naval and military vessels on the waterways, mail packets are rare, and passenger-carrying vessels are not common. Usually, the "competition" for lockage is commercial barge traffic.

### Coexisting with Commercial Traffic

On occasion, it is possible to lock through with barges. This depends on the available space in the lock, the nature of the cargo, and the wishes of the towboat operator, whose first responsibility is the safety of the tow. If you do lock through with a tow, use extra caution, as quarters may be tight and you may be moving close to the tow or the lock gates.

Sometimes, when a string of barges is too large to fit into a lock chamber, the operator breaks the tow into two or more parts and locks through in sections. Recreational boats sometimes can lock through in the opposite direction as the chamber is being filled or drained.

Plan on some delay at locks, as long as several hours if commercial traffic is heavy and several tows are waiting. Be patient, but also rest assured that the lockmaster will take you as soon as possible, since few lockmasters want recreational boats loitering near their locks.

## THE LOCKMASTER

While the building, maintenance, and operation of river locks are the responsibility of the Corps, each lock is under the control of a lockmaster, who is entirely responsible for its operation. Whenever possible, a lockmaster will lock you through immediately, but there may be more pressing needs that will cause you to have to wait.

### Communicating with the Lockmaster

You can reach the lockmaster on Channel 16 of your VHF-FM radio; you will then probably be asked to switch to Channel 13. Contacting the lockmaster in advance by radio can be helpful for both of you. When lockmasters know what traffic to expect, they can plan their moves and make more efficient use of their facilities, and if you know what is going on, you can adjust your speed and plans accordingly. Perhaps you can speed up and get into a group locking through, or take a lunch break while a barge or a restricted tow locks through.

Understand that if you are locking through with a tow or several recreational boats, the lockmaster may not be able to respond immediately to your radio call. You may be able to avoid calling the lockmaster by listening to radio traffic and learning what is going on.

Corps-operated locks are equipped with a manual "Small Craft Signal," usually a chain or pull rope located at the outermost end of the lock wall. It will have an explanatory sign, and you should give this signal one pull if you do not have a VHF-FM radio. You may not be able to hear the signal from your location, so stay where you are and wait for the lockmaster to give you instructions.

### Traffic Signals

Light or whistle signals may advise you how to proceed in entering or leaving a lock. Light signals typically resemble traffic signals (Figure 9-21), and you respond to them in much the same way. A red light means "do not approach," and a yellow light, often flashing, means that you should prepare to move

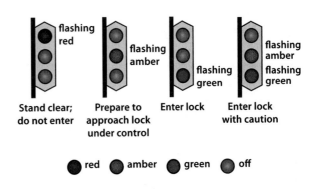

**Figure 9-21.** Light signals at a lock.

into the lock. Don't start toward the lock while the light is yellow; instead wait for the green light to signal that the lock is ready to receive vessels.

Sound signals are of two types: one prolonged blast (4 to 6 seconds) means enter the lock; one short blast (1 second) means leave the lock.

Be careful when you see or hear the signals, since they may not apply to you. If there are other vessels waiting for lockage, the signal could be for them if they have a higher priority than you do.

## LOCKING THROUGH

As you approach the lock chamber, move without a wake, which usually means a fast idle speed. There is a conflict between the need to move quickly and the need to keep your wake down, but avoiding wakes takes priority. A lock is a long, narrow chamber with flat concrete walls, and wakes of boats bounce off these walls. When several boats are moving near each other, be extra careful to avoid damaging boats or gate mechanisms.

All crewmembers should wear life jackets during the locking operation. The lock chamber can be turbulent when filling or emptying, and you and your crewmembers will be moving around, tending lines. It is a dangerous time to fall overboard.

As a precaution against fire, you may be asked to stop your engine and extinguish all flames. Smoking is not allowed. With several boats in close quarters in a closed chamber, a fire could be a disaster.

### *Tying Up in the Lock*

Prepare to tie up to bitts or bollards in the lock using your own lines. Since the walls of locks are often rough and dirty and may have sharp, exposed metal pieces, you will want to make liberal use of fenders. Use boathooks or poles, rather than hands and feet, to keep your boat away from the lock wall. While small boats usually use only one line, boats larger than 25 to 30 feet need lines both forward and aft.

Lock bollards are of two types, fixed and floating. Fixed bollards are usually at the top of the lock wall and require lines more than twice the depth of the lock. On a small boat, tie one end of a line to a bow cleat, loop the line around the bollard, and tend the other end around a stern cleat. If you are

being lowered, let out line from the stern cleat as you progress. If you are being raised, take up line.

In other locks, there is a series of fixed bitts in the lock wall. Ladders sometimes serve the same purpose (Figure 9-22), and in such locks, you should move your line from attachment point to attachment point as you are raised or lowered.

Some larger locks have floating bollards (Figures 9-23 and 9-24), and in these you should secure your line to a bow cleat, take a turn around the bollard, and tend the other end of the line at a stern cleat. With this type of bollard, you neither have to

**Figure 9-22.** A ladder and fixed bitts in a lock wall. (PHOTO BY DEBBIE NEWMAN)

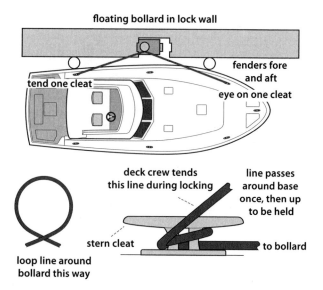

**Figure 9-23.** Tying up to a floating bollard.

**Figure 9-24.** Tending a line on a floating bollard. (PHOTO BY BRIAN DENNIS)

take up nor pay out line. Tend the line carefully, though, and take action in the unlikely event that the bollard jams and does not move up or down, in which case you may need your long line.

Floating bollards can jam from debris snagged in them. If this happens, take your line from the bollard and fasten it to a ladder or to a fixed bitt in the wall. When you retrieve your line from a jammed bollard, be careful, as the bollard may free itself and float to the surface with considerable force.

## Rafting Up

When many small boats lock through together, there may not be enough space along the wall to accommodate all of them. Break out your fenders and lines and raft up with the other boats if requested (Figure 9-25). The lockmaster will tell you where to go on the wall, and may tell you which boats are to raft with you.

## Leaving the Lock

After the water in the lock has reached its desired level, wait for the lockmaster's signal before moving out. Again, move at a no-wake speed, paying close attention to the other boats that are getting underway at the same time.

Please note that the signals and procedures outlined here are general guidelines. Significant

**Figure 9-25.** Rafting up in the Ballard Locks, Lake Union, Seattle. (PHOTO BY BRIAN DENNIS)

variations exist in regulations from waterway to waterway and in lock design from one lock to the next, and it is important that you familiarize yourself with local conditions and procedures before using the installations (Figure 9-26).

**Figure 9-26.** The northernmost of the two locks on the Dismal Swamp Canal, an alternative route to the Intracoastal Waterway for slow-moving sailboats heading south from Norfolk, Virginia, to Elizabeth City, North Carolina. The canal was partly surveyed by George Washington. In this sequence a sailboat is locked in and raised to the higher level. (PHOTOS BY DON LINDBERG)

# River Charts

The Corps makes most of the charts used for river piloting, which differ in many respects from those used in coastal piloting. They are often published as spiral-bound books, with each page containing a chart of a section of the river. In this format, river charts can have large scales and still be handled conveniently aboard recreational boats.

## CHARACTERISTICS

Many river charts are little more than simple sketches that show the principal geographic features of the waterway, the channel and its sailing line, prominent structures, and fixed aids to navigation. Others, such as the chart of the Warrior River in Alabama, are aerial photographs on which symbols have been printed. Some charts, including those of the Mississippi, show the positions of navigation lights but do not show the lights' characteristics. An up-to-date copy of the *Light List* (see Chapter 7) will help you know which light you are viewing.

Depths of water seldom appear on river charts. Since river depths vary greatly from time to time, they would be meaningless. When a chart shows floating aids to navigation, consider their positions approximate and use them with caution. The Coast Guard moves them frequently and it also sets additional buoys during periods of low water to mark shoals that are not of concern when the water is higher.

Unlike coastal charts, landmarks such as smokestacks, water towers, and antennas do not usually appear on river charts. Often, only those structures close to the banks are shown, and then only by symbols and footnotes. Many of these symbols are unlike those on coastal charts, but there should be a key to the symbols on the front pages of the chartbook. It is best to spend some time studying your chart before you begin your voyage.

On most river charts, information about bridges—such as ownership, type of bridge, vertical and horizontal clearances, and location—can be found in the information block, or legend. The horizontal clearances of swing and drawbridges are given for both their open and closed states, vertical clearances are given for some bridges at pool stage and for others for normal high water, and locations are given by mile markers. Most bridge tenders can be reached on VHF-FM Channel 16 or 13.

Some river charts do not show geographical names for areas along their banks. Likewise, most do not include roads other than those that cross the river, so a good road map may be a useful supplement to your river chart.

## A CHART OF A SECTION OF THE MISSOURI RIVER

At first glance, river charts may appear inadequate to boaters accustomed to coastal charts. Careful study will show you, however, that they have most of the features you need for safe boating on the river.

The chart in Figure 9-27 shows a section of the Missouri River. The river flows from left to right, which you can tell from the arrows on the river in the upper left and right corners. North is to the left and south is to the right, as indicated by the arrow with an N on it near the upper right side of the page.

As shown on the lower right of Figure 9-27, it is Chart No. 27. Revetments appear as cross-hatched areas at bends in the river, while dikes and wing dams jut out from the banks and appear as solid and dotted lines.

Mileage numbers are printed on the sailing line that marks the channel, and mileage markers appear at easily seen points such as the daybeacons at Sarpy, Bellevue Reach Upper, and Bellevue Reach. Since the Corps measures the Missouri from its mouth to its source, the mileage numbers decrease as you go downriver.

## DAYBEACONS

As already discussed, daybeacons offer invaluable guidance to riverboaters, especially large commercial craft. They are printed on the chart in the order you see them as you move either up or down the river.

For example, when you pass Manawa at mile 604.6 going downstream (Figure 9-27, upper left), you see a red triangular passing daymark on the left descending bank. On the back of the triangle is a red diamond crossing daymark. If you look back upriver as you pass these daymarks, you see the red diamond, and know that the next daymark will be

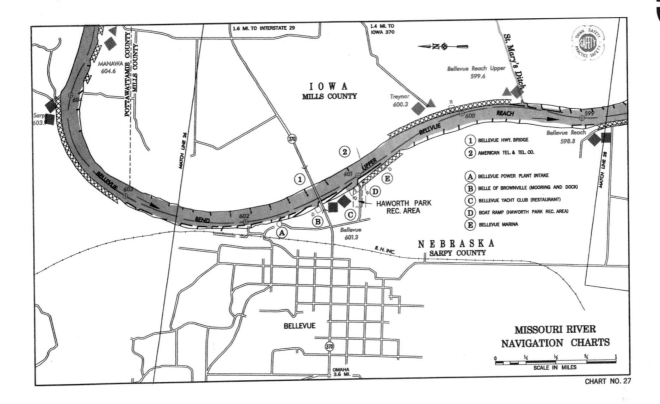

**Figure 9-27.** A portion of a Missouri River chart.

a green diamond on the opposite bank. When you look downriver, you see the green diamond passing daymark at Sarpy and head for it.

Since the diamond at Sarpy has a green square on its back side, you know that the channel continues along the right descending bank. It continues there until Bellevue at mile 601.3, at which point you learn that the channel crosses over to the opposite bank and you head to the markers at Treynor. You can tell the course of the channel by observing the sailing line.

## NAVIGATION LIGHTS

The locations of navigation lights are also shown on some river charts. A red disk between a red triangle and red diamond stands for a red navigation light. Some disks are green to correspond to the green lights they represent. As you would expect, red lights mark the left descending bank and green ones mark the right descending bank.

In some cases a disk has the letter P overprinted on it, indicating a privately maintained light. If it does not have the P, the U.S. Coast Guard maintains it. River charts do not show the

characteristics of navigation lights, such as their colors and periods, but you can tell their characteristics by referring to the *Light List*.

# Commercial Traffic

A variety of commercial traffic uses inland waterways. In some places you can see ships from foreign ports, cruise ships, and floating casinos, but most often, commercial traffic consists of tow boats with strings of barges. Usually, the barges are lashed alongside their tow boats or are pushed ahead of them, and are rigidly connected so that they can be maneuvered as a single unit. A string of barges such as this is a *composite unit*.

## OCEANGOING AND RIVER TOWS

There is an important difference between oceangoing and river tows that recreational boaters should know about. Oceangoing tugs usually tow their loads well behind them, with long steel cables that connect the tugs with their tows and dip just below the water's surface. This presents a dangerous situation for boaters. **Never cut between an ocean-going tug and its tow.**

## You and a River Tow

It takes a long distance for tows to get up speed or to stop. As a result, they stop only to break out a barge, to pass through a dam, or to tie up to the bank because the water is too low or too high. Tenders deliver provisions and fuel to them while they are underway.

An average commercial river tow is about 1,150 feet long with a beam of 105 feet. It draws 8.5 feet and weighs 60,000,000 pounds, and its engines develop as much as 5,600 horsepower.

In contrast, the average pleasure boat is less than 20 feet long with a beam of less than 8 feet. Its draft is 2 feet, and it weighs about 3,000 pounds.

## Watch Out for the Tow

Obviously, commercial tows are big and you are small. It's like comparing a subcompact automobile with a train. The tug has 0.2 horsepower per ton, while you have 133 horsepower per ton and can stop quickly. It may take up to a mile to stop a down-bound tow when the river is running, and the tow also requires a lot of room in which to maneuver.

With your shallow draft, you can go bank to bank almost anywhere, but the tow is limited in where it can go, and cannot turn wherever it wishes due to its draft.

Some tugs have as many as three large propellers. Driven by a tug's large engines, they can produce a prop wash you can feel hundreds of feet behind them (Figure 9-28). The propellers also churn debris from the bottom that may be hazardous to small craft. It makes sense to give tows as wide a berth as possible.

## The Tow's Blind Spot

The operator of a tug pushing a string of barges is in the pilothouse at the after end of the tow, as in Figure 9-29. Although most towboats have high pilothouses, there is always an area immediately in front of the tow that is blocked from view. This blind zone typically extends 600 feet or more ahead of the tow (Figure 9-30).

When boating near a tow, be sensitive to the tugboat operator's field of view, and avoid running

**Figure 9-28. Top:** A towboat on the Lower Mississippi River near Baton Rouge, Louisiana. (PHOTO BY JAY J. BRANDINGER) **Bottom:** The backwash behind the towboat *Rachel* as it pushes its string through a lock on the Colorado River is eloquent testimony to the power of those props. (COURTESY U.S. ARMY CORPS OF ENGINEERS)

**Figure 9-29.** A view from the bridge of the *Christopher M. Parsonage*. The *Parsonage* is pushing the equivalent of 665 railroad cars or 1,820 tractor trailers of grain and coke down the Mississippi River. Don't count on it stopping or turning quickly. (REPRINTED WITH PERMISSION FROM *SEAWORTHY: ESSENTIAL LESSONS FROM BOATU.S.'S 20-YEAR CASE FILE OF THINGS GONE WRONG* BY ROBERT A. ADRIANCE)

into the blind zone. It is tempting to move back to the center of a channel as soon as you pass a tow, but this usually means that you are moving into the blind zone or towing a skier into it. If you have an engine failure, strike a submerged object, lose someone overboard, or drop your skier, the towboat

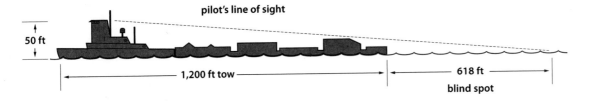

**pilot's line of sight**

50 ft

1,200 ft tow

618 ft

**blind spot**

**Figure 9-30.** A towboat captain's blind spot extends far ahead of his tow. If you can't see him, he can't see you.

operator will never know, and could unwittingly run over you. Even if there is a lookout posted on the bow, the operator cannot stop the tow in time to avoid hitting a stalled boat or someone in the water.

## COMMUNICATING WITH COMMERCIAL TRAFFIC

When you meet or pass a tow, remember that the sound signals for meeting head-on, crossing, and overtaking required by the Inland Navigation Rules are in effect, and you should use them to communicate with the tow and to respond to signals from the tow.

It is very possible that the towboat operator will not hear your sound signals, since there is a high noise level in the pilothouse from the tug's engines, and the pilothouse is often air-conditioned. The towboat operator will probably therefore expect your contact to be by VHF-FM radio.

Call the tow operator on Channel 16 and be ready to switch to Channel 13. Vessels working around docks or barge staging areas where the radio traffic is heavy may direct you to a different working channel. When you talk to a towboat, be certain that it is the towboat you are near and not one farther up or down the river.

If you find yourself in a narrow channel with a tow approaching, move to the edge of the channel. If there is still not room enough for the tow to pass, move out of the channel if the water is deep enough. If not, turn around and retreat to a safe position below the narrow channel. For practical purposes, the responsibility for avoiding a collision is yours.

Avoid meeting tows in a river bend. If you are monitoring your VHF-FM radio, you will know where the traffic is and should wait for the tow to pass through the bend if possible. If a tow catches

you in a bend, move to the inside of the bend, since the towboat will follow the channel, which is most likely on the outside of the bend (Figure 9-31).

Obviously, a VHF-FM radio is essential equipment. Also, consider installing a radar reflector on your vessel, since towboats have radar and a radar reflector can help the towboat operator see you.

# Before You Go

Before you venture out onto a river, study its chart to learn of hazards such as dams and low drawbridges and to gain a general orientation to the river. Being informed is better than being surprised.

If you are moving your boat from one body of fresh water to another, observe the precautions regarding zebra mussels.

Drawbridge signals and regulations are discussed in Chapter 8, which you should review before boating on a river. Although most highway and railroad bridges are high enough to permit the passage of most recreational craft beneath them, you may meet one that is not high enough. This is more likely to be the case if your vessel is a sailboat than if it is a motorboat.

**Figure 9-31.** On the Black River in Louisiana below the Columbia Lock and Dam. (PHOTO BY JAY J. BRANDINGER)

# Practice Questions

## IMPORTANT BOATING TERMS

In the following exercise, match the words in the column on the left with the definitions in the column on the right. In the blank space to the left of each term, write the letter of the item that best matches it. Do not use an item in the right-hand column more than once.

| THE ITEMS | THE RESPONSES |
|---|---|
| 1. _____ navigable waterways | a. left descending bank |
| 2. _____ left bank | b. triangle or square |
| 3. _____ Western Rivers | c. marks channel |
| 4. _____ buoys | d. direct the current into the channel |
| 5. _____ revetment | e. includes navigable rivers, the Great Lakes, and the ICW |
| 6. _____ wing dams | f. the Mississippi and its tributaries |
| 7. _____ tailrace | g. facing of stone, concrete, etc. |
| 8. _____ sailing line | h. diamond |
| 9. _____ passing daymark | i. not usually shown on river charts |
| 10. _____ crossing daymark | j. whitewater below a dam |

# Multiple-Choice Items

In the following items, choose the best response:

**9-1.** Navigable waterways include

a. local lakes
b. the navigable rivers, Great Lakes, and ICW
c. all canals and rivers
d. all inland waterways

**9-2.** Which navigation rules are in force on navigable waterways?

a. U.S. ATON System
b. COLREGS
c. USWMS
d. Inland Navigation Rules

**9-3.** What is the color of the ATONs on the right descending bank of a river?

a. red
b. green
c. yellow
d. white

**9-4.** River buoys are

a. easily located
b. lighted
c. black
d. usually not shown on river charts

**9-5.** The flow of a river's current is often directed by

a. revetments
b. dams
c. locks
d. wing dams

**9-6.** At night you know which side of a dredge the pipeline is on by

a. two red lights
b. two green lights
c. a white and a green light
d. a white and a red light

# Multiple-Choice Items (continued)

**9-7.** Regulatory marks are of two types:

    a. signs and buoys
    b. nuns and cans
    c. dolphins and spherical buoys
    d. spar buoys

**9-8.** River charts have

    a. many details of landmarks
    b. charted water depths
    c. locations of buoys
    d. information about bridges

**9-9.** Lakes include bodies of water that are

    a. natural
    b. impounded
    c. made by damming rivers
    d. all of the above

**9-10.** Which set of ATONs is used on the Western Rivers?

    a. U.S. ATON System
    b. USWMS
    c. ICW
    d. none of the above

**9-11.** Crossing daymarks are

    a. diamond shaped
    b. square
    c. triangular
    d. rectangular

**9-12.** When entering a lock, a red traffic signal means

    a. do not approach
    b. proceed with caution
    c. enter lock
    d. high-priority vessels can enter lock

**9-13.** Maintenance of the federal, navigable, inland waterways is the responsibility of

    a. the U.S. Army Corps of Engineers
    b. the U.S. Coast Guard
    c. state authorities
    d. local authorities

**9-14.** Dredge pipelines are marked by what color lights at night?

    a. blue
    b. green
    c. yellow
    d. white

**9-15.** In locking through, which vessels have the highest priority?

    a. commercial
    b. government
    c. recreational
    d. yachts

**9-16.** Most river charts are made by

    a. the U.S. Coast Guard
    b. the U.S. Army Corps of Engineers
    c. National Oceanic and Atmospheric Administration
    d. National Ocean Service

**9-17.** When communicating with commercial river traffic

    a. call on Channel 16
    b. change to a working channel when you have contact
    c. be sure you know which vessel you are talking to
    d. all of the above

**9-18.** Your speed should be reduced in canals because

    a. they are small and dangerous
    b. you need to watch out for other vessels
    c. your wake will erode the banks
    d. you will miss the scenery

**9-19.** As you travel upstream, which bank is on your port side?

    a. right
    b. left
    c. First National
    d. left descending bank

**9-20.** Crossing daymarks mean

    a. cross over at the next ATON
    b. the river channel continues along the same bank
    c. nothing to you since your vessel is very small
    d. the river channel is on the side with the daymark

**9-21.** Danger areas in the Western Rivers and U.S. ATON systems are marked with

    a. open diamonds

(continued on next page)

## Multiple-Choice Items (continued)

b. diamonds with cross marks
c. circles
d. rectangles

**9-22.** On the inside of a river bend

a. the current scours the channel
b. currents are in one direction at the surface and in the opposite direction below the surface
c. the current moves faster
d. silting and shoaling may occur

**9-23.** Wing dams and dikes

a. appear as solid or dotted lines on charts
b. are not usually shown on charts
c. cause silting
d. provide excellent anchorages

**9-24.** What structures have been described as "efficient, self-operating drowning machines?"

a. wing dams
b. high-rise dams
c. dikes
d. lowhead dams

**9-25.** Call the lockmaster on your VHF-FM radio using

a. Channel 13
b. Channel 6
c. Channel 22
d. Channel 16

**9-26.** River charts seldom show

a. the characteristics of navigation lights
b. locations of passing daymarks
c. locations of crossing daymarks
d. locations of navigation lights

# Sailing Safety

**The objectives of this chapter are to describe:**

- The causes of small boat accidents and how to prevent them.

- How to rescue a person who has fallen overboard.

- The dangers of immersion in cold water, the causes and symptoms of hypothermia, how to prevent hypothermia, and precautions to observe when assisting victims of hypothermia.

- Matters of safety that concern all boaters, including small boat stability, fuel dock safety, and sharing the water with other boats and water-skiers.

- The dangers and symptoms of carbon monoxide poisoning, its causes aboard ship, and its prevention.

- Good sources of weather information.

- Changes in surroundings that indicate a storm is approaching.

I T IS ESTIMATED that there are more than 17 million registered recreational boats in the United States—boats ranging in size and type from small open boats and personal watercraft (PWC) to giant motor yachts and sailboats capable of carrying their crews around the world. This number does not include small sailboats lacking inboard or outboard engines, since most states do not require such boats to be registered. With so many boats sharing the water, operating your boat

The tall ship *Lynx* under full sail makes a lovely sight. In the days of working sail, however, the safety of the sailors was secondary to the profit of the voyage. Not for nothing were long bowsprits like this one called "widow-makers." Today our attitudes toward onboard safety are much less cavalier. (PHOTO BY BOB DENNIS)

227

safely and skillfully is the key to a pleasurable afternoon on the water. That message is woven throughout this book, but in this chapter we take a closer look at a few specific safety concerns that previous chapters have only mentioned.

Boating regulations and safety alerts are constantly changing at the federal and state levels, and it is the responsibility of the boat operator to keep current. The U.S. Coast Guard websites are a good source of information, and also have links to state boating agencies.

# Small Boat Safety

## PASSENGER BRIEFING

All passengers, experienced or not, should be briefed about the locations of life jackets, fire extinguishers, flares, and the first-aid kit, and should understand the procedures for using the boat's toilet, operating the radio in an emergency, handling lines, and recovering a person who has fallen overboard (see below). They should also be briefed on how to help themselves if they fall overboard. Before anchoring or docking, brief your passengers on the procedure. Should you be unlucky enough to face the possibility of a squall or gale that you can't beat back to the dock, brief your passengers on what will happen and what measures you may take. It helps to use a prepared checklist. As mentioned in Chapter 5, non-swimmers, children, and the elderly and handicapped should wear PFDs at all times on a boat, and many states require this. In windy weather and at night, everyone should wear a PFD, and we recommend that everyone do so at all times.

## BOATING FATALITIES

Most boats in use today are less than 16 feet long, and more than 90% are less than 20 feet long. While most are stable and safe when used properly, small boats are more liable than larger ones to become unstable when used improperly. In part for this reason, and in part simply because there are so many more small boats in use, more than half of all boating fatalities occur in boats 12 to 16 feet long. The great

majority of fatalities involve powerboats, not sailboats, but this does not mean that sailboats are inherently safer. Rather, there are simply many more powerboats than sailboats in use. No statistics are kept for fatal accidents per thousand person-hours of use of powerboats versus sailboats, but if there were, the two might be found to be fairly similar.

Contrary to popular opinion, about half of all boating fatalities occur in lakes, ponds, and reservoirs, and not on navigable waterways. More than half of the fatalities occur on weekend afternoons, and about half occur in calm weather and in full daylight. If statistics were kept solely for sailboats, we might see some skewing toward windier weather, when small sailboats are more vulnerable to capsizing, but otherwise the numbers would be much the same.

Of boaters involved in fatal accidents, more than 80% have no training in boat handling and safety. Many probably do not even think of themselves as boaters, since about 25% fish and some hunt in boats. And they are not only young people; almost half are 26 to 50 years old.

These victims have one thing in common with many motorists who do not buckle up: 87% are not wearing life jackets. In addition, a large percentage drink alcohol immediately before their accidents.

Most fatal boating accidents involve people who suddenly and unexpectedly find themselves in the water without life jackets. Most boating fatalities on small boats are due to people falling overboard and drowning. If the victim is in a canoe, skiff, or small powerboat, perhaps he stands up to shoot waterfowl, land a fish, start the engine, or raise the anchor, then either capsizes the boat or falls overboard. If the victim is in a small sailboat, perhaps he capsizes in a sudden gust of wind before he can release the mainsheet or round up into the wind. Sometimes a victim winds up in the water after a collision with another boat or object. Regardless of the cause, being able to swim is not sufficient protection if you find yourself in the water unexpectedly. Nearly 90% of people who lose their lives in boating accidents drown, even though most are "swimmers."

Sadly, most boating fatalities involve people who have life jackets on board but are not wearing them at the time of the accident. A life jacket aboard will not help if you fall overboard without it and your boat floats away, or if you can't reboard the boat. If your boat capsizes and the life jackets are in the cabin, you and your passengers will probably not be able to get to them. Even small boats without cabins often trap life jackets under their thwarts, or seats, when they capsize.

The use of drugs and alcohol accounts for a very large number of boating fatalities, and is no more safe than operating an automobile under the influence. Furthermore, it's illegal to operate a boat under the influence of these substances.

The shock of a sudden plunge into cold water (less than 59°F) can have a severe effect on the body, as we shall see later in the chapter. Good swimmers in good physical condition can be immobilized within a few minutes, and death can occur even after a quick recovery from the water. This is independent of the risks of hypothermia, which involves a more gradual loss of body heat and subsequent loss of body functions even in relatively warm waters.

## SMALL BOAT STABILITY

Obviously, you want to avoid swamping or capsizing if at all possible. You can avoid such accidents in two ways. First, don't go out in a small boat in rough water and strong wind. Second, know how boats float and use this knowledge to your advantage.

When you head out on the water, regardless of the size of your boat, load it according to the weather. The rougher the weather, the more freeboard you need to avoid swamping. A powerboat less than 20 feet long requires a capacity plate, as described in Chapter 5, and you should never exceed the listed capacity even in calm weather. Capacity plates are not required on small sailboats, however.

One rule of thumb offered by the Coast Guard for loading a small boat that has no capacity plate is to limit the number of people aboard to the length of the boat multiplied by its beam in feet, divided by 15. For an 18-foot boat with 5 feet of beam, this would place the upper limit of people aboard at six (18 x 5 ÷ 15 = 6). Six people might be acceptable aboard an 18-foot powerboat—though it seems high—but aboard an 18-foot sailboat they would have no room to move around or handle the sails. Indeed, any more than three or four people would be too many for working an 18-foot sailboat—which

means that the capacity of a sailboat is more likely to be limited by space than by weight.

In Chapter 3 we discussed initial and ultimate stability as properties of hull shape, but the stability of any boat is also affected by its centers of gravity and buoyancy. A boat's *center of gravity* (CG) is the center of its total mass. A sturdy object is stable when its center of gravity is over its base, and unstable when its weight is centered over a point outside the base.

Further, the higher the center of gravity, the less stable the boat. Piling things in a boat, or standing in a boat, raises its center of gravity and lessens its stability. The lower the center of gravity of a boat, the more stable it becomes. This is why a ballasted keel is such an effective way to balance the heeling force of the sails, and it's also why a canoe feels so much more stable when you're sitting down than when you're standing up. The center of gravity of a boat varies with its load and where you place it, as shown in Figure 10-1.

## Attention, Paddlers!

Kayaks and canoes are small boats too, and the information on small boat stability in these pages applies to you. Additional safety measures you should take include:

- Be prepared to enter the water. Wear a properly fitted PFD, and know how to swim.
- Never paddle alone.
- Know your skill level and limits, and avoid bad weather, great distances from shore, rough seas, and strong currents.
- Take a paddling course with hands-on instruction. It will teach you balance, use of stabilizing strokes, safe entry and exit on the water, and rescue and recovery skills.

Another consideration in the stability of a boat is its buoyancy. The buoyant force on a boat is equal to the weight of the water it displaces. The *center of buoyancy* (CB) is the center of the mass of the water the boat displaces. When a boat is at rest, or in equilibrium, the center of buoyancy is vertically aligned with the center of gravity, the former acting upward while the latter acts downward. That equilibrium is disturbed, however, when the center of gravity moves or the boat is heeled by an outside force—usually wind or waves. Small boats

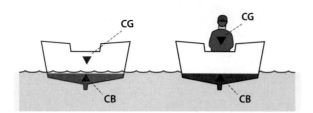

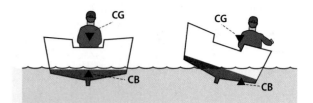

**Figure 10-1.** The centers of gravity (CG) and buoyancy (CB) of a boat when empty and loaded. A boat is in perfect trim when its center of gravity is directly above its center of buoyancy, and the lower the center of gravity, the more stable the boat. When weight is added high in the boat, as by the addition of a passenger and gear in a small boat, the center of gravity rises and stability decreases. When weight shifts outboard or in the fore-and-aft direction, the center of gravity moves accordingly, and the center of buoyancy must likewise move (as in Figure 10-2) to achieve a new alignment with the CG.

**Figure 10-2.** The centers of gravity and buoyancy when a boater leans out in a small boat. The center of gravity shifts outboard, and the center of buoyancy must move outboard to achieve a new equilibrium. In this drawing the centers are back in alignment, but sometimes a careless boater will shift his weight too high and too far outboard to be countered by heeling, and the boat will swamp or capsize.

are more subject to both kinds of disturbance than large boats, so let's look at both in turn.

Figure 10-1 shows two small boats from astern. The first is empty. In the second a person is seated on a raised seat. Notice that only the center of gravity has changed much from the first to the second. It has risen significantly and is farther from the center of buoyancy. If this elevated center of gravity moves off-center, which occurs, for example, if a person stands and leans to one side, it creates a long lever arm with the center of buoyancy, a force acting to heel the boat. In order to counter this, the center of buoyancy must move outboard to the same side as the leaning person, which is exactly what happens when the boat heels as in Figure 10-2. If the boat is small enough relative to the weight of the person, however, the center of buoyancy will not be able to move far enough outboard to get back in vertical alignment with the center of gravity. Put another way, the boat will not be

able to reach a new equilibrium when the person stands and leans to one side, and it will simply continue heeling until either the person falls overboard or the boat swamps or capsizes.

Now let's see what happens when the boat is heeled by a wave or the wind. As Figure 10-3 shows, this time it is the center of buoyancy that moves, while the center of gravity does not change. This shift creates a force on the heeled side of the boat that acts to bring the boat back to a level position.

In either instance—whether the boat is heeled due to a shift in the center of gravity or the action of an outside force—its resistance to that heeling is often called *initial stability*, as we saw in Chapter 3, and that resistance is greater in a flat-bottom boat than a round-bottom one. The bottom line is that a canoe will roll and swamp or capsize with a smaller shift in the center of buoyancy than will a flat-bottom jonboat of similar length, and a smaller boat will roll more easily than a larger boat of sim-

## If You Capsize . . .

- Put on your PFD.
- Account for all your passengers.
- Stay with your boat if at all possible.
- Grab anything that floats.
- Try to attract the attention of other boaters nearby.
- Get people out of the water as soon as you can.

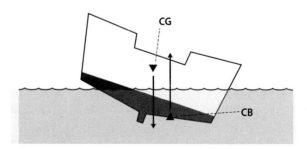

**Figure 10-3.** The centers of gravity and buoyancy in a boat heeled by waves, wind, or a tight turn. This time the center of buoyancy moves, while the center of gravity does not. The resulting lever arm between the CG acting downward and the CB acting upward seeks to restore the boat to its upright position.

ilar hull shape. If you lean out over the side of a canoe, it may roll out from under you.

Boaters who are properly centered and seated low in a small boat do not seriously disrupt the boat's natural stability. However, if a boater stands up in a small boat—say, to reach for a pier—and shifts his weight up and too far to the side, the boat's center of gravity may move outside the gunwale, and if it does the boat will swamp or capsize (Figure 10-4). Small sailboats are less vulnerable to this than many other small boats, but imagine the lever arm you create when you step from a pier onto the gunwale of a centerboard sailboat while grabbing its mast for support. Many sailboats have been capsized this way, right at the dock!

## Maintain Three-Point Contact

Once you take a seat in a small boat, stay seated, and be careful when leaning over the side. When you enter a small boat, step as close to its fore-and-aft centerline as you can, and when you need to move about, keep your profile as low as possible. It is best to maintain three points of contact as in the canoe in Figure 10-5. This will not always be possible when sailing a small sailboat, but the same principle applies: Keep the center of gravity of the boat as low as possible, and be mindful of the impact you have when you shift your weight toward the side of the boat. Moving to windward to help balance the wind in the sails is a part of sailing, but moving to leeward when the boat is already heeled in the wind could prove to be a mistake!

**Figure 10-5.** Maintaining three-point contact for stability. (PHOTO BY DON LINDBERG)

## Stay with Your Boat

Some boats have flotation built in at the factory. This means that if they capsize or swamp, they will stay afloat. However, while positive flotation is required by federal law in powerboats of less than 20 feet, it is not required in small sailboats. Some sailboats have such flotation, but not all do.

Even a boat without such flotation, however, may stay afloat if made of wood or if air is trapped within the hull. As long as your boat remains afloat, even awash, it is usually best to stay with it. Climb on it if possible. The colder the water, the more urgent it is that you get out of it. You may be tempted to swim to shore, but be cautious. It is difficult to judge distances in the water, and the shore may be farther away than you think. Also, if you stay with your boat, it is easier for would-be rescuers to see you.

# Man Overboard

Underway, there is always a risk that someone will fall overboard. That's one of the reasons you wear a PFD. When someone does go overboard, every moment is important, and you and your crew should therefore rehearse ahead of time how to

**Figure 10-4.** Stepping on the gunwale of a canoe or small rowboat is a sure way to capsize it. (PHOTO BY JOE BRITVCH)

react. If you have guests aboard, explain your procedures to them before you go.

The recovery of a person from the water requires the skipper to exercise extreme care. The object is to recover the man overboard (MOB) as quickly as possible while avoiding undue risk to the crew on board. In short, don't make a bad situation even worse.

## SOUND THE ALARM

What is done in the first moments after someone falls overboard may well determine the success or failure of the recovery. The first person to realize that someone has fallen overboard should immediately shout an alarm, point to the location of the victim, and keep shouting until it is clear the skipper has heard. The shouted message should indicate on which side of the boat the person fell. For example, you might shout, "Man overboard, port side!"

If under power, the skipper should immediately get the engine into neutral; if under sail, he should immediately prepare to tack or jibe. Meantime he should assign someone to keep the victim constantly in sight. If you have a GPS, punch in the coordinates of the accident location; most GPS receivers have an MOB button for just this purpose.

Your boat should have a life ring buoy or other Type IV throwable PFD that is kept handy and ready to deploy in just this circumstance. It is advisable to tie a polypropylene retrieval line to the life buoy, because polypropylene floats (Figure 10-6). If the victim is still within range of the boat, throw the buoy to the victim, who can then grab the line or the buoy, at which point your crew should gently but firmly pull the person toward the boat. If a life ring or buoy is not immediately available, throw anything that floats.

**Figure 10-6.** Throwable PFDs. Ideally, the attached retrieval line should be polypropylene.

## RETURNING TO THE VICTIM

If your boat travels well past the person overboard before you can get it stopped or throw him a flotation aid, your first priority is to get back to the victim. If you're under power, make absolutely certain that the victim is nowhere near your propeller, then make a short, hard turn to return to him or her, following the instructions and the pointing finger of the person assigned to keep the victim in constant sight. Take the engine out of gear several yards from the MOB and throw him the buoyancy aid and line.

If you have lost visual contact, return to the MOB coordinates you should have punched into your GPS receiver. If the victim is not located after a short search, make a Mayday call to the Coast Guard on Channel 16, and brief them on the situation.

An alternative way to return quickly to an MOB works under power or sail. Known as the **quick stop**, this method involves turning the boat into the wind, then circling the MOB slowly while towing a buoyancy aid until it or its line is within the victim's grasp. If under sail, keep the sails trimmed tight and don't cast off the jibsheet when tacking or jibing (Figure 10-7). This keeps the sails under control, slows the boat, and allows quick turns.

Yet another alternative when under sail is to sail away from the MOB for a few seconds on a beam reach, tack, reach back below the MOB, then head up into the wind alongside the MOB, drag-

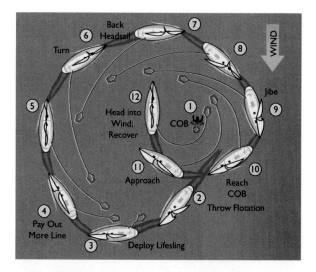

**Figure 10-7.** A quick-stop recovery under sail. (In this maneuver, and in Figure 10-8, COB stands for crew overboard.) (ART BY PAUL MIRTO, REPRINTED WITH PERMISSION FROM *EMERGENCIES ON BOARD: A CAPTAIN'S QUICK GUIDE* BY JOHN ROUSMANIERE)

ging or tossing the buoyancy aid to place it within his grasp. This *figure-eight* approach (Figure 10-8) avoids the need to jibe and may therefore be preferable in a strong wind.

The final approach, whichever you choose, should be very slow, and when you come alongside the victim, be sure to turn off the engine if you are under power. Even in neutral, propellers may continue to spin and could cause serious injury or even death to anyone in the water.

If the victim cannot grab the line or can't keep his or her head above water, make every attempt to recover the person from aboard the boat before allowing someone to go overboard to assist. Anyone who does go into the water should be trained in rescue techniques and should be wearing a PFD with a lifeline. It is common for an MOB to panic and try to climb up the rescuer, increasing the chance that they will both drown. It is the boat captain's responsibility to weigh the risks of every decision and to prevent an emotional crew from taking unwise actions.

## RETRIEVING THE VICTIM

Retrieving someone from the water, even someone who can help him- or herself, is difficult when there is no boarding ladder or special device to assist, especially when your boat's freeboard is higher than about 12 inches. If the victim cannot assist his own recovery, there is a good chance that even strong people aboard the boat may not be able to get him aboard.

If your boat is very small, it is usually advisable to recover a person over the bow or stern to keep from capsizing. On larger boats, the stern is the best recovery point if you have a transom step or swim lad-

der there. Otherwise, make the recovery from the side deck amidships. A secured loop of line extending about 2 feet below the waterline can be used as a "step" to assist a person who has the ability to use it.

If the victim is wearing or can put on a PFD, you can try dunking him just before pulling him up. The inertia from bobbing up after being dunked will assist in the recovery. The victim should be facing the boat so that if the initial recovery gets him only partway on board, he can be held by the torso until the crew can get a new purchase on his legs or belt.

If this fails, turn the victim's back toward the boat and attach a line around his chest and under his armpits, with both parts of the line leading up over his back to the crew on deck to assist in the pulling action (Figure 10-9). The natural roll of the boat may also assist the recovery. Failing this, the only option may be to secure the person so that his or her head is above water, and await additional aid.

Larger sailboats have the advantage of having winches aboard, and can use the boom as a lift point. A *preventer* (a line from the boom to a cleat, toe rail, or other attachment point) should be used to lock the boom in a stationary overboard position.

Practice. Hold impromptu "man-overboard drills" on your boat. Unexpectedly throw a floating object (the "victim") over the side and yell "Man overboard!" Time yourselves from man overboard to recovery and then try to beat your time on the next try. You and your crew will become trained, experienced, and increasingly proficient. If you practice recovery with a live adult you may not be successful in the recovery, so it's important to conduct this in shallow water near shore. Your experience doing this recovery will explain why so much text is devoted to this subject.

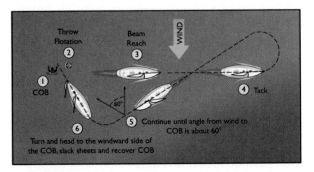

**Figure 10-8.** A figure-eight (reach-and-reach) recovery. (ART BY PAUL MIRTO, REPRINTED WITH PERMISSION FROM *EMERGENCIES ON BOARD: A CAPTAIN'S QUICK GUIDE* BY JOHN ROUSMANIERE)

**Figure 10-9.** Using a line under the arms to help get a person back on board.

# Cold Water

Cold water presents two significant threats to the boater: *cold water immersion*, often called cold shock, poses an immediate life threat; **hypothermia** is the potentially lethal consequence of extended exposure to cold water. Research indicates that certain things happen to anyone who is immersed suddenly and perhaps unexpectedly in cold water:

- There is a gasp response on initial contact with the water, and if the person's face is in the water when the gasp takes place, it is possible that water will be aspirated (inhaled) and rapid drowning will ensue.
- There is an immediate and significant reduction in breath-holding capability.
- There is a very rapid loss of coordination and an early inability to move the hands and feet, followed by a loss of the ability to swim.
- Heart rate, breathing rate and effort, and blood pressure all increase dramatically, accelerating the loss of body heat.

Even among people who are young, in good health, and wearing protective clothing, death from cold water immersion has been known to result within 3 to 5 minutes in water that is 59°F or colder. What can be done to minimize the risks of cold water? First and foremost, make sure that you and everyone on your boat wears a life jacket at all times. With a life jacket on, at least you will remain upright in the water and will be less likely to aspirate water when that first gasp occurs. Wear warm clothes, and select clothing made from fibers that retain warmth after becoming wet.

Hypothermia is the gradual reduction of the body's core, or internal, temperature below the threshold of normal biological functions. Hypothermia is not freezing to death, nor is it frostbite. It can kill at temperatures well above freezing. In hypothermia, the body simply loses heat more rapidly than it can be replenished.

Anytime your body is unable to maintain its normal temperature, you are at least mildly hypothermic. Most people have experienced mild hypothermia from overexposure to winter weather, and it can occur at other times of the year in strong winds, especially if your clothing is wet.

Hypothermia occurs most rapidly when your body is immersed in cold water because water robs your body of heat at least twenty-five to thirty times faster than air of the same temperature. The shivering you may experience is one means your body employs to keep itself warm, but in cold water this stratagem can postpone only for a short time the onset of more serious symptoms. The colder the water, the more rapidly hypothermia occurs, but it can occur even in rather warm water if you are exposed to it for a long enough time. In water of 50°F, your predicted survival time is 1.5 to 3 hours.

## STAGES

Your body metabolizes food to get the energy it needs to operate and to maintain its temperature. Excess heat is eliminated by radiation and the evaporation of perspiration. When the body cools below its normal temperature, however, it responds defensively. Blood flow is redirected from nonvital surface tissues and large muscles to vital organs (brain, heart, lungs), and stored food is burned to generate more heat. One sign of the diversion of blood is the appearance of gooseflesh. Another sign is shivering.

As the core temperature falls and the body's resources decrease, shivering slows, then stops. The body begins a systematic shutdown, abandoning periphery circulation (arms and legs) while it seeks to maintain a constant temperature in its core. If you have been drinking alcohol, your capillaries will be dilated, and you will lose heat more rapidly, speeding the onset of hypothermia.

As cooling continues, speech becomes slurred and incoherent. You become increasingly lethargic and uncoordinated, and your respiration becomes shallow and erratic. You lose consciousness and eventually die.

> **WARNING** *Hypothermia is a serious, life-threatening condition. It is difficult to treat and requires expert care. If you suspect hypothermia, seek prompt and competent medical attention.*

| TABLE 10-1 | Approximate Median Lethal Exposure Times | | |
|---|---|---|---|
| | Time (hours) | | |
| Water Temperature (°F) | Floating with PFD | Treading Water | Swimming |
| 35 | 1.75 | 1.25 | 0.75 |
| 45 | 2.50 | 1.75 | 1.00 |
| 55 | 3.50 | 3.00 | 2.00 |
| 65 | 7.75 | 5.75 | 4.50 |
| 70 | 18.00 | 13.00 | 10.00 |

Hypothermia occurs more rapidly in women than men because of their smaller average body sizes, and more rapidly still in children due to their small sizes and lack of body fat. Table 10-1 gives approximate survival times in water of various temperatures. Note how much survival time increases when you wear a life jacket.

## PREVENTION

The precautions for prevention of hypothermia are well known. Most are "common sense" measures that you would normally take anyway.

### Conserve Your Heat

The simplest thing to do is to avoid situations that promote loss of body heat. This means keeping dry and out of the wind. If you fall overboard, get out of the water as soon as possible.

### Clothing Makes a Difference

The clothing you wear makes a difference in the rate of heat loss. Synthetic fibers are effective in reducing heat loss when they are dry, but afford virtually no protection when wet. Wool retains a higher degree of its insulating properties when wet than most other fabrics.

### Increase Your Energy Reserve

Never go into a potentially hypothermic situation without having eaten a good meal. This is good practice for boating activities and anything that involves working or playing out of doors, especially in the cold.

## ACTIVITY AND HYPOTHERMIA

Your life jacket will help ward off hypothermia, and "jacket" styles offer better protection than "bib" styles. Besides trapping warmed water between it and your body, a life jacket helps you stay afloat with a minimal expenditure of energy. If you are not wearing a life jacket, you may need to tread water to stay afloat, and this uses energy and hastens hypothermia. Tests show that the average rate of heat loss of a person treading water is about 34% faster than for the same person remaining still in a life jacket.

### Floating and Heat Loss

If you aren't wearing a life jacket, try floating with your lungs full of air. Immerse your head in the water and raise it every 10 to 15 seconds to breathe. By this means, even nonswimmers can delay the possibility of drowning for many hours. But this presents problems in cold water, since so much heat is lost through your head. People who use this technique in 50°F water lose heat about 82% faster than if they were floating in a life jacket with their heads out of the water. Better wear a life jacket anytime you are underway!

### Swimming and Heat Loss

If your boat capsizes, your first impulse may be to swim to shore. This is dangerous at any time, and more so if the water is cold. The more you swim, the more heat your body generates, and this heat is lost rapidly in the cold water. In a short time your body may have exhausted its ability to generate heat.

### Get Out of the Water

Studies show that the average person swimming in a life jacket loses body heat 35% faster than when holding still. Instead of swimming to shore, climb onto your boat if possible. This may enable you to balance your heat loss with the heat your body can generate.

**WARNING** *Swimming and treading water cause faster heat loss than remaining still.*

**Treating a Hypothermic Victim**

1. *Rescuers should do all the rescue work (not the victim).*
2. *Dry off the victim, if possible.*
3. *Keep the victim out of the wind.*
4. *Make the victim as comfortable as possible.*
5. *Ask for assistance on the radio.*
6. *Get medical assistance as soon as possible.*
7. *Cover the victim with warm clothing or other material.*

If you find yourself in the water, do what you can to conserve your heat. Keep your clothes on, since they provide some insulation from heat loss, as does the air trapped in them.

Do not struggle or try to swim, either of which will cause you to lose the trapped air in your clothing and thus speed heat loss. Insulated clothing, minimal movement, clear thinking, and a life jacket provide the best possible defenses against cold water.

## THE HELP POSITION

If you are wearing a life jacket, draw your knees up into a **HELP** (heat escape lessening position) posture (Figure 10-10). Make your body as compact as possible. If there are two or three people in the water, huddle together to conserve heat, and move about as little as possible.

If you are wearing a Type III life jacket, however, the HELP position may turn you facedown. Instead, bring your legs tightly together, keep your arms tight against your sides, and lean your head

HELP position

**Figure 10-10.** Conserving body heat. (REPRINTED WITH PERMISSION FROM "FEDERAL REQUIREMENTS & SAFETY TIPS FOR RECREATIONAL BOATS," U.S. COAST GUARD OFFICE OF BOATING SAFETY)

back to keep your face out of the water.

The greatest heat loss from your body is from your head, so keep it above water if possible. The next greatest loss is from your armpits and sides. Thus, in the HELP position, you press your arms against your sides, draw up your legs, and keep your head above water.

## HELPING HYPOTHERMIC PEOPLE

If you try to rescue someone with hypothermia, be careful. The victim's energy resources are minimal, and he or she should do as little as possible to help in the rescue in order to avoid depleting what energy reserves he or she has left. Victims of hypothermia have died after being rescued because of their exertion during the process.

Visible signs of hypothermia are summarized in Table 10-2. If the survivor is rational and responsive, even if shivering dramatically, dry clothes or blankets, shelter from wind and water, and a period of inactivity may be all that is required. Critical hypothermia, however—especially if the victim is unconscious or only semiconscious—requires experienced medical assistance, and your best response is to secure that medical attention as soon as possible. Keep the victim as sheltered, dry, and bundled as possible in the meantime. Remember how fragile a person is when in a hypothermic state. Death for a severely hypothermic individual can occur several hours after rescue.

If you have a VHF-FM radio aboard your vessel, contact the Coast Guard as soon as possible in any life-threatening emergency. Tell them your problem and request that they have an ambulance meet you at the nearest landing place, then ask them to advise you on first-aid methods. The Coast Guard has the specialized knowledge you need and will guide you in rewarming the victim.

# Sharing the Water with Other Boats

One very important Navigation Rule creates an order of precedence for one vessel approaching another. As discussed in Chapter 8 and shown in the

| TABLE 10-2 | Stages of Hypothermia |
|---|---|
| Body Temperature (°F) | Visible Signs and Symptoms |
| 98–96 | Intense, uncontrollable shivering; impaired ability to perform complex tasks |
| 95–91 | Violent shivering; difficulty speaking; sluggish movements; amnesia begins |
| 90–86 | Shivering replaced by muscular rigidity; muscle coordination impaired; erratic movements |
| 85–81 | Irrational; stupor; loss of contact with surroundings; pulse and respiration slow |
| 80–78 | Unresponsive; no reflexes; heartbeat erratic; loss of consciousness |
| Below 78 | Failure of heart and lungs; internal bleeding; death |

SOURCE: *U.S. COAST GUARD BOAT CREW SEAMANSHIP MANUAL*

so that the operator of the powerboat can judge how best to pass you with the least disturbance to both boats.

## Order of Precedence of Vessels

**A vessel is stand-on to all vessels below it in the list:**

- Overtaken vessel
- Vessel not under command
- Vessel restricted in ability to maneuver
- Vessel constrained by draft (International Rules only)*
- Fishing vessel
- Sailing vessel
- Powerboat
- Seaplane

*The Inland Rules do not recognize "vessels constrained by draft."

sidebar, this rule makes sailboats operating under sail alone stand-on to any powerboats that meet or overtake them.

This does not mean you can sail among powerboats without keeping watch or making any attempt to avoid a possible collision. More often than not, when a collision occurs, it is deemed the fault of both boats. The Navigation Rules require even a stand-on vessel to take action when a collision seems imminent. Besides, as Thucydides said, a collision at sea can ruin your entire day.

Moreover, sailing vessels must keep out of the way of vessels not under command, vessels restricted in their ability to maneuver, and vessels engaged in fishing, and a sailing vessel loses its priority when it is overtaking another vessel—even if the other vessel is a powerboat. Also, a sailing vessel operating its engine—even if its sails are hoisted and full of wind—is considered a motor vessel, not a sailboat, and loses its priority over powerboats.

Finally, good seamanship involves courtesy and respect for your fellow boaters. That means not tacking immediately in front of an approaching powerboat if you can help it, and it means holding your course if possible when a powerboat approaches

## PERSONAL WATERCRAFT

The past decade has seen a rapid increase in the number of PWC. Originally the term "personal watercraft" included only those power-driven vessels designed to carry just one standing, kneeling, or sitting passenger, who steered by means of handlebars like those found on bicycles (Figure 10-11). The first sit-down model was introduced in 1987, and by 1993 fully 94% of PWC were sit-down models. The commonly accepted definition of a PWC today is a "vessel that uses an inboard motor powering a water pump as its primary source of power. In addition, it is designed to be operated by a person sitting, standing, or kneeling on the vessel, rather than sitting or standing inside the vessel."

The larger models of PWC on the market can carry as many as four seated people, though they are still steered with handlebars (Figure 10-12). All

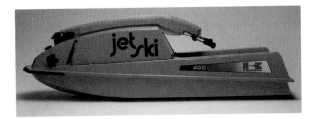

**Figure 10-11.** The first Jet Ski, introduced by Kawasaki in 1973. (COURTESY PERSONAL WATERCRAFT INDUSTRY ASSOCIATION)

**Figure 10-12.** Newer models of PWC can carry as many as four seated passengers and are highly maneuverable. (COURTESY PERSONAL WATERCRAFT INDUSTRY ASSOCIATION)

PWC are Class A motorboats (boats less than 16 feet long), and they are legally obligated to observe the Navigation Rules and all state and local laws and regulations.

Unfortunately, PWC are sometimes operated more like toys than high-performance powerboats, and this can make them an occasional hazard to sailboats. They are small and highly maneuverable, which should make it easy for their operators to stay clear of sailboats, but they are also unstable and are less visible than larger boats. Then too, operating a PWC can be fatiguing, and a fatigued operator can be dangerous to his fellow boaters.

The ability of a fast-moving PWC to accelerate or change direction rapidly can cause passengers or the operator to be thrown from the vessel and possibly injured. A sudden change in direction could place a PWC directly in the path of an on-coming vessel. Whenever you're sailing in the vicinity of PWC, keep a close eye on them so that you can keep out of their way if necessary, and so that you can go to their aid if they're in trouble.

Some PWC have a kill switch that is activated by means of a lanyard that attaches to the opera-tor's wrist or life jacket. If the operator should fall overboard, the engine will be shut off and the boat will stop—at least in theory. If you see a PWC stop suddenly with no one on board, head in their direc-tion to see if help is needed.

## WATER-SKIERS

When sailing in the vicinity of water-skiers, you should keep a sharp lookout and be ready for un-expected maneuvers by the skier or the towing boat. Be prepared to rescue a downed skier who is

in trouble. It is a good idea to learn a water-skier's standard hand signals (Figure 10-13). This will help you interpret what the skier is about to do.

# Fueling Your Boat

Many small sailboats have no engine at all. Oth-ers—especially those in the 16- to 26-foot range—depend for their auxiliary power on a 4- to 10-horse-power outboard installed on a transom bracket and fueled from a portable tank. Larger sailboats with inboard engines are more likely these days to have diesel than gasoline engines—in part because diesel is a safer, less volatile fuel. Nevertheless, plenty of sailboats are still powered by Universal Atomic 4 and other inboard gasoline engines. If your boat has an inboard or outboard gas engine, you need to know the basics of safe fuel management.

## KNOW WHAT YOU ARE DOING!

When fueling, it pays to know what you are doing. For example, people have pumped gasoline into water tanks, and occasionally an error like this re-sults in an explosion or serious injury. Be certain you are pumping gas into your installed tank and not into your bilge.

The law requires electrical parts in an enclosed engine space to be ignition-protected. This means that these parts will not produce sparks that can ignite gasoline fumes. Unfortunately, rebuilt or

**Figure 10-13.** Waterskiing hand signals. (COURTESY NATIONAL MARINE MANUFACTURERS ASSOCIATION)

replaced parts may not be ignition-protected. You could, for example, inadvertently replace a marine alternator with one built for an automobile. Be vigilant on this.

## Keep Fumes Out!

Gasoline vapors are heavier than air and flow to the lowest spot on your boat. Avoid trapping them, since there are many sources of sparks and flames aboard a boat that can ignite such fumes. Close all cabin hatches and ports before fueling. This will keep gasoline vapors from entering your boat. Also, turn off all electrical devices such as ventilating fans, radios, bilge pumps, navigation devices, and lights. Extinguish all open flames, turn off the galley stove, and don't smoke.

To be on the safe side, operate your blower for at least 4 to 5 minutes after fueling. Then, before starting your engine, check all compartments and engine spaces for gas fumes by sniffing. If you don't trust your sense of smell, get an electronic fume detector. Bear in mind, however, that an electronic device is not always as sensitive as your nose.

The need to thoroughly air out the bilge (the lowest part on your boat, and where gas fumes could accumulate) and other compartments after fueling an installed gas tank cannot be overemphasized. It is possible for trapped gasoline vapors to be so rich that a spark will cause an explosion. When you open a hatch or port, or when your boat begins to move, you may introduce enough air to make the vapors combustible. Many vessels have exploded and caught fire after leaving a fueling dock.

## BUILT-IN TANKS

The filler pipe for the gasoline tank should be located so spills do not enter your boat and become dangerous. Clean up any spill that does occur immediately, and get the dirty rags off your boat right away. Spills should be avoided both for the dangers they pose and for environmental protection. Any spill that produces a sheen on the water is a violation of federal pollution laws. When you see one, report it immediately to the nearest Coast Guard station or facility. You can also report a spill to the National Response Center in Washington, D.C., by calling 1-800-424-8802.

Your boat's fuel filler pipe should be connected (grounded) to your boat's electrical grounding system (Figure 10-14). Gasoline passing through the hose line from a pump can generate static electricity, and a spark between the hose nozzle and the filler pipe might then cause an explosion. To prevent this, always keep the hose nozzle in contact with the metal of the fuel filler pipe.

## Fuel Tank Vents

A built-in fuel tank must be vented outside your boat's hull (Figure 10-15). This provides an outlet for gasoline vapors and air so you can fill your tank. It also allows air to enter the tank as you use the gasoline. Without a vent, you could not draw gas from the tank without collapsing it.

Vents are covered with a wire mesh that may become clogged from corrosion, insect nests, etc. When this happens, poor engine performance results.

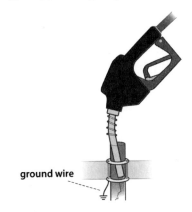

ground wire

**Figure 10-14.** When refueling, keep the nozzle in contact with the filler pipe to prevent static electricity buildup.

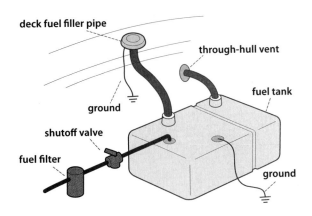

deck fuel filler pipe

through-hull vent

fuel tank

ground

shutoff valve

fuel filter

ground

**Figure 10-15.** The fuel filler deck plate and the tank's air vent must be located outside the hull's enclosed spaces so that fumes do not accumulate in the bilge.

Unfortunately, both the filler pipe and the vent can cause environmental problems. If you overfill your tank, some of the fuel may spurt out of the filler pipe and into the water, and some may leak out of the vent. You can avoid either of these sources of environmental pollution by knowing the capacity of your fuel tank and never filling it to more than 95% of its capacity.

There are devices available that collect fuel spilling from the fuel vent outlet. They attach with a suction cup and can be removed easily.

If you completely fill the tank and then leave your boat in the sun, the fuel will expand and some will leak out of the vent. Any fuel spill, no matter how small or how it occurs, is illegal and can result in a fine from a state regulatory agency or the Environmental Protection Agency (EPA).

The EPA statute on oil spills is unambiguous. Note in what follows that the term "general rule" gives the EPA leeway to impose even higher penalties under special conditions such as not cooperating with the responsible official:

"If your recreational vessel discharges oil into the navigable waters or adjoining shorelines (or what is referred to as the 'exclusive economic zone') of the U.S., then, as a general rule, you are liable for all oil removal costs and certain specified damages resulting from that discharge up to $500,000 or $600 per gross ton, whichever amount is greater."

If a spill occurs and you are in federal waters, it is your responsibility to report it immediately to the Coast Guard. For more information on oil spill liability or compensation questions, contact the National Pollution Funds Center at 202-493-6999, or visit www.uscg.mil/hq/npfc.

## GASOLINE IN YOUR BILGE

If you find raw gasoline in your bilge, don't operate anything electrical and don't disconnect your battery. Turn off all power by using the enclosed, marine-type battery switch. (If you have an open "knife" switch, do not use it!) A marine-type battery switch is ignition-protected and should not produce a spark.

If a sizable spill occurs at a gas dock, call the fire department. You can clean up small amounts of spilled gasoline with a sponge and a plastic bucket. Put the bucket and the sponge ashore. After that,

leave the boat open until you can no longer smell fumes. Then use your blower for at least 4 minutes.

When you don't know where raw gasoline in your bilge has come from, look for its source. But do it after you have cleaned up the mess and before you try to start your engine. A leaking fuel line, for example, could be an invitation to disaster.

## PORTABLE TANKS

Remove portable tanks from your boat before filling them. When filling a portable tank, keep the hose nozzle in contact with the tank to reduce the chance of sparking from static electricity. Portable tanks in the back of a truck can develop a static charge. Touch the fuel nozzle to the side of the tank to dissipate the charge.

# Carbon Monoxide Poisoning

Carbon monoxide (CO) is a colorless, odorless, highly poisonous gas that has about the same weight as air and mixes readily with it. It forms from the incomplete combustion of hydrocarbon fuels, and about 10% to 12% of the exhaust gas of a gasoline engine is carbon monoxide. Carbon monoxide is poisonous because it reduces the ability of the blood to absorb oxygen. Whenever you are operating a gasoline engine (especially an inboard engine, but also an outboard) or generator, you should be alert to the possibility of carbon monoxide buildup in enclosed shipboard spaces. In fact, the American Boat and Yacht Council (ABYC) recommends that boats with enclosed accommodations areas and a gasoline generator or inboard engine have a CO detector installed. (Note that diesel engines produce only 1% to 10% as much carbon monoxide as gas engines and are therefore not covered by ABYC recommendations.)

## SYMPTOMS

Carbon monoxide is toxic in concentrations as small as 1 part per 100 parts of air. The symptoms of carbon monoxide poisoning include drowsiness, headache, dizziness, weakness, nausea, fainting, and coma, with prolonged exposure eventually resulting in death.

Most people know that they should not run their automobile engines in enclosed spaces such as a garage; what they may not know is that the engine in their boat produces the same gas. If you experience any of the symptoms associated with carbon monoxide poisoning, such as constant headaches while you're boating, consider the possibility that you are being exposed to the gas. The early symptoms are not especially alarming and can easily be attributed to heat exhaustion or simply overtiredness. Survivors of near-fatal carbon monoxide poisoning repeatedly describe simply falling asleep, unaware of the danger, before being fortuitously saved (Figure 10-16). Thus, you must be alert to the warning signs.

## CARBON MONOXIDE AND VENTILATION

You may know that it is possible for a moving station wagon to pump exhaust gas in through its rear window. In some instances, people in the back seats of automobiles have died from carbon monoxide drawn into the vehicle from the exhaust.

The same condition can exist in the cockpit of a vessel because the exhaust from the auxiliary engine or generator is traditionally vented through the transom. These gases may be moving forward directly into the cockpit area. Alternatively, carbon monoxide may come from a hot-water heater or from a galley stove. It may even come from a boat in an adjacent slip. One owner of a new powerboat had it equipped with a carbon monoxide detector, which sounded continuously while the engine was operating and for several minutes after it was shut down. A representative of the boat manufacturer suggested that the alarm was faulty, but the headaches, nausea, and disorientation the owners and their children were experiencing all suggested otherwise. The owners surmised that engine fumes might be entering the cabin through the head ventilation exhaust, which was located near the engine exhaust. When the installation was modified, the problem disappeared.

In another case, a boatowner's two young children were poisoned by carbon monoxide from a generator exhaust outlet located under the power-

**Figure 10-16.** Carbon monoxide quickly overcame all four people without warning aboard this boat on Lake Powell, Arizona. One person was killed, and three were unconscious for 14 hours. The boat was moving slowly with the front end closed, and fumes entered the open stern via the station wagon effect. (REPRINTED WITH PERMISSION FROM *SEAWORTHY: ESSENTIAL LESSONS FROM BOATU.S.'S 20-YEAR CASE FILE OF THINGS GONE WRONG* BY ROBERT A. ADRIANCE)

boat's swim platform. The boat was anchored in a Missouri lake on a hot day with the generator running to power the air conditioner, and the children were swimming when they were afflicted. One lost consciousness, and both were hospitalized with high levels of carbon monoxide in their systems. Both recovered fully. Only in retrospect did the owner and his wife piece together what had happened. According to Bob Adriance, author of *Seaworthy: Essential Lessons from BoatU.S.'s 20-Year Case File of Things Gone Wrong*, there have been several similar, well-documented cases (Figure 10-17).

**Figure 10-17.** What's wrong with this picture? In this powerboat at cruising speed, the ensign in the stern is actually flapping forward rather than aft, due to a powerful station wagon effect—a sure indication that the engine exhaust is being sucked aboard over the transom. (REPRINTED WITH PERMISSION FROM *SEAWORTHY: ESSENTIAL LESSONS FROM BOATU.S.'S 20-YEAR CASE FILE OF THINGS GONE WRONG* BY ROBERT A. ADRIANCE)

## PREVENTING CARBON MONOXIDE POISONING

You can prevent carbon monoxide poisoning by making certain that your engine compartment is well ventilated and that the ventilation system is operating properly. And above all, be alert to the symptoms of carbon monoxide poisoning.

### Carbon Monoxide Poisoning Prevention Techniques

1. Provide, maintain, and frequently check adequate engine and generator compartment ventilation.
2. Install a carbon monoxide detector.
3. Be aware of the symptoms of carbon monoxide poisoning.
4. Be aware of any nearby boats that might be sending poisonous fumes your way.

It is a good idea to install a carbon monoxide detector in all enclosed spaces occupied by people. The U.S. Coast Guard recently stated that "Improvements in technology and reliability of carbon monoxide gas detectors have reached the point where their installation in accommodation spaces should be considered by all safety-conscious recreational boaters." Most boats with gasoline engines or generators and enclosed accommodations spaces built since August 1998 have a carbon monoxide detector. If your boat does not have one, you are well advised to install one.

# Weather

Sailors have a special need to know about weather. High winds, lightning, rough seas, and poor visibility are a few of the conditions that can make for uncomfortable boating.

There are two important principles of boating:

1. Know before you go.
2. Update while you are out.

These are particularly true where weather is concerned. Good weather information can be obtained in most locations from AM and FM radio, from television broadcasts after local news, and often from a televised weather channel. Those with Internet access can obtain excellent weather information at www.weather.com, www.nws.noaa .gov/om/marine/home.htm or www.srh.noaa.gov (select a station near you). See www.navcen.uscg .gov for further details. You can also receive National Weather Service broadcasts on inexpensive

### Weather Hazards and Local Knowledge

Dangerous weather conditions come in several varieties. Among the conditions you should watch out for and avoid if possible are these:

- Heavy fog or otherwise reduced visibility can cause you to lose your bearings, increasing the risk of collisions or running aground.
- Thunderstorms bring high winds, reduced visibility, and the danger of lightning strikes.
- Lightning seeks the quickest and easiest path to ground, and when your boat is the tallest thing around, that makes you a target for a strike.
- High winds, no matter what their cause, can churn the water into heavy, breaking seas, increasing the risk of swamping, broaching, or yawing.

See Chapter 15 for more on predicting and avoiding bad weather.

"Local knowledge" means familiarity with the waters in which you routinely do your boating. Developing local knowledge is among the top things you can do to increase your safety—no matter what the weather. Keep yourself up to date on local boating conditions by:

- Reading the *Local Notices to Mariners* regularly (see Chapters 7 and 12).
- Checking with local sources, such as other boaters.
- Becoming familiar with such local hazards as shoals, lowhead dams (see Chapter 9), sandbars, and rocks.

shortwave receiving sets that use either household electrical current or batteries. The broadcasts are also available on the weather channels of your VHF-FM marine radio. In short, there is no reason for a boater to go out without knowing what kind of weather is in store for the day or even for several days.

In some circumstances, local conditions can change suddenly, and the wise sailor is always on the lookout for signs of changing weather. Suppose you embark on a boating trip on a beautiful, sunny summer day, and are then surprised by a late afternoon thunderstorm. Evidence of such storms is readily visible from the following changes:

1. Clouds appear, looking more ominous over an hour or so.
2. Wind comes up or shifts noticeably.
3. Waves appear because of the wind.
4. The air takes on a cool bite.
5. If you are listening to AM radio, static is noticeable.
6. You suddenly realize that other boaters have disappeared.

While you can hope to return home before the storm hits, it may be wiser to find a cove where you can anchor and ride it out. In either case, as a safety precaution, have everyone put on a life jacket, stow or secure all gear so that it cannot blow away, and head for safety. Turn on your navigation lights and review your sound signals for reduced visibility conditions. Controlling a small boat in large waves, with visibility badly reduced by rain, is no fun at all! We will explore the topic of weather more fully in Chapter 15.

## Practice Questions

### IMPORTANT BOATING TERMS

In the following exercise, match the words in the column on the left with the definitions in the column on the right. In the blank space to the left of each term, write the letter of the item that best matches it. Do not use an item in the right-hand column more than once.

| THE ITEMS | THE RESPONSES |
|---|---|
| 1. _____ carbon monoxide | a. a maneuver for returning with maximum speed to an MOB and getting a buoyancy aid to him or her |
| 2. _____ quick stop | b. main cause of boating accidents |
| 3. _____ hypothermia | c. best defense against drowning |
| 4. _____ HELP | d. reduction of a body's core temperature below where normal biological functions can occur |
| 5. _____ wearing a life jacket | e. formed by incomplete combustion of fuel |
| 6. _____ a sailing vessel | f. gooseflesh |
| 7. _____ center of gravity | g. center of the mass of water a boat displaces |
| 8. _____ a first sign of hypothermia | h. a way to reduce loss of body heat in the water |
| 9. _____ human error | i. a sailboat with its sails up and its engine running is not considered one of these |
| 10. _____ center of buoyancy | j. center of a mass |

# Multiple-Choice Items

In the following items, choose the best response:

**10-1.** A major cause of small boat fatalities is

a. being run over by large boats
b. being swamped by waves
c. loading too many people on board
d. falling overboard and drowning

**10-2.** A boat is less stable and more likely to capsize when it

a. is empty
b. is overloaded
c. has an evenly distributed load
d. is in deep water

**10-3.** The percentage of fatalities occurring in lakes and ponds as opposed to navigable waters is about

a. 10
b. 5
c. 90
d. 50

**10-4.** Which of the following fabrics will protect you most from hypothermia when they are wet?

a. synthetic fibers such as nylon
b. cotton
c. wool
d. rayon

**10-5.** The best thing you can do for a hypothermic person is

a. get immediate medical help
b. treat the person yourself
c. give a small drink of whiskey
d. help the person get up and move around to warm up

**10-6.** When sailing in the vicinity of powerboats you should

a. tack and alter course at will, knowing that you are the stand-on boat under the Navigation Rules
b. maintain your course even if a collision seems imminent, since you are the stand-on boat
c. tack only when near shore
d. avoid tacking or making radical course changes immediately in front of an approaching powerboat

**10-7.** Which of the following is correct?

a. about half of all boating fatalities occur in lakes, ponds, and reservoirs and not on navigable waterways
b. over half of boating fatalities occur on weekend afternoons
c. about half of all boating fatalities occur in calm weather and in full daylight
d. all of the above

**10-8.** Standing in a boat raises its

a. center of gravity
b. center of buoyancy
c. blind spot
d. freeboard

**10-9.** A drop in the water temperature from 70°F to 65°F will decrease the median lethal exposure time of a person overboard by

a. 55% to 57%
b. 5% to 10%
c. 20% to 30%
d. 3% to 5%

**10-10.** Which of the following is true?

a. hypothermia occurs more rapidly if you are wet than if you are dry
b. hypothermia occurs more rapidly in women than in men
c. hypothermia can occur in a strong wind even if you are dry
d. all of the above

**10-11.** The best thing you can do to ward off hypothermia if you find yourself in cold water is

a. start swimming to shore
b. keep moving
c. assume the HELP position
d. eat a good meal before you go

**10-12.** Which of the following is not true of cold water immersion?

a. it can cause death within 3 to 5 minutes
b. it is also called cold shock
c. it is the first symptom of hypothermia
d. one of its symptoms, a gasp response, can cause a victim to aspirate water

# Multiple-Choice Items (continued)

**10-13.** The best way to prevent carbon monoxide poisoning is to

    a. install a smoke alarm
    b. burn clean fuel in your engine
    c. keep air flowing through the vessel
    d. stay in the stern area of the boat

**10-14.** What percentage of people who drown in boating accidents are able to swim?

    a. 60
    b. 70
    c. 80
    d. 90

**10-15.** Which of the following is required on small motorboats (less than 20 feet long) but not on small sailboats without engines?

    a. fire extinguisher
    b. capacity plate
    c. installed flotation
    d. registration number
    e. all of the above

**10-16.** If your boat capsizes

    a. have someone swim to shore for help
    b. have someone stay with the boat
    c. have everyone stay in the water and hold on to the boat
    d. climb up on the boat and out of the water, if possible

**10-17.** Which of the following is not true of an MOB rescue?

    a. if possible, one crewmember should do nothing except watch and point to the victim
    b. you must get a Type IV PFD or other buoyancy aid to the MOB as soon as possible
    c. it's okay to leave the engine running when you're alongside the victim, as long as it's in neutral
    d. your chances of a successful recovery will be much higher if you practice the maneuver ahead of time

**10-18.** In comparison with cold air, cold water robs the body of heat

    a. much faster
    b. slower
    c. faster or slower, depending on the humidity of the air
    d. at the same rate

**10-19.** Under which of the following conditions will you lose heat most rapidly in cold water?

    a. swimming
    b. treading water
    c. wearing a life jacket
    d. using the HELP position

**10-20.** Under the Navigation Rules, a boat under sail with its engine running is considered

    a. a sailing vessel
    b. a motorsailer
    c. a power-driven vessel
    d. restricted in its ability to maneuver

**10-21.** Carbon monoxide is

    a. colorless
    b. odorless
    c. poisonous
    d. all of the above

# PART TWO

# More Sailing Skills

(PHOTO BY MIKE BRODEY)

# More on Sail Trim and Boat Handling

**The objectives of this chapter are to describe:**

- How to tune a sailboat's rigging.
- How to recognize and correct lee helm or excessive weather helm.
- How to shape the mainsail for best performance in prevailing conditions.
- How to select and trim a headsail according to wind and sea conditions.
- How to depower the rig when the wind increases.
- How to respond to a knockdown, capsize, or disabled rudder.

IN CHAPTER 4, we discussed basic **rigging** technique. In order to make your boat sail at peak efficiency, however, merely keeping the mast more or less upright isn't enough. Since most beginners' boats have rigid, or non-bendy, masts, let's look first at the proper **tuning** of that type of rig, using Figure 11-1 (which also appears in Chapter 1) for reference.

Reaching along a lee shore with tightly trimmed spinnaker, this boat is making knots. (PHOTO BY MIKE BRODEY)

249

Most small sloops have at least a **forestay**, a **backstay**, and an **upper shroud** on each side. In addition, most boats longer than 16 to 18 feet also have one or two **lower shrouds** on each side. On most boats the upper shrouds pass over the spreader ends and terminate at the masthead (and are therefore sometimes called **masthead** or **cap shrouds**, as noted in Chapter 1). The lower shrouds terminate partway up the mast—usually at the base of the spreaders—and keep the mast from buckling at midheight. In larger craft there are more elements to the rigging system—sometimes including two or more sets of spreaders—but the principle remains the same; every piece of standing rigging exerting tension on the mast must be balanced in some manner, usually by another piece of wire leading to the opposite side of the mast at the same height. Tightening the various pieces of standing rigging to make a balanced system is called *tuning the rig*, and the devices most used in exerting tension on the stays and shrouds are **turnbuckles** (see Figure 1-14).

# Setting Up the Standing Rigging

When tuning the standing rigging, it may be worthwhile to bear in mind the old adage, "the longer the wire, the tauter it should be." Masthead shrouds are set up the most taut because they have the greatest length over which to stretch, and stays and shrouds terminating below the masthead are slightly more slack. The important thing when tensioning the forestay, backstay, and upper shrouds is to set them up evenly, so that the mast looks straight, or *in column*, when you sight upward along the mainsail luff track or groove. If you can, get off the boat and look directly over the stern, checking that the spar is tilted neither to port nor starboard. Chances are the mast should angle aft a little—this is called *rake*, as mentioned in Chapter 4, and the degree is usually specified in your owner's instruction manual. If no literature exists to tell you how many degrees aft to rake the mast, ask some skipper knowledgeable about your class of boat to help you set up the rig the first time.

Masts are often designed to rake aft between 2° and 5°. A rake of 3° will displace the top of a mast approximately 6 inches for each 10 feet of length. Consequently, if the distance from masthead to deck is 20 feet, a 3° mast rake will cause a freely swinging halyard to touch the deck 12 inches aft of the mast. The rake of that same mast could also be determined by measuring down the mast 15 feet from the masthead sheave and making a mark there. When the free-swinging halyard hangs 9 inches aft of that mark, you have a 3° rake in your mast. Check at the same time to be sure the halyard hangs directly behind the center of the mast; if not, your mast may be leaning to one side. Remember, your weight may affect the trim of a small sailboat, so keep your weight centered while checking mast alignment.

## TUNING THE STANDING RIGGING

It's common practice to set your rigging initially with the lower shrouds just taut enough so that there is no visible slack. Bear in mind that the function of the lowers is to keep the bottom half of the spar from buckling when the load of a wind-filled sail pulls it to one side. When there is no side load on the mast, there should be no stress on the lowers.

Now raise the sails, cast off, and sail out to some comparatively traffic-free area. Both main and jib luffs should be taut enough so that there is no sign of scalloping. Put the boat on a close-hauled course on either tack and check the mast (it may be necessary to make these observations from another boat the first time). If the spar is straight as you sight upward, everything is fine. It's quite possible, however, that you'll see one of the following problems:

1. **The mast hooks forward.** The forestay is too taut or—more likely—the backstay is not taut enough.
2. **The mast hooks aft.** The forestay is too slack or the backstay is too taut.
3. **The mast hooks to windward.** The windward-side upper shroud is too taut or the windward lower is too loose.
4. **The mast hooks to leeward.** The windward upper is too slack or the windward lower is too taut.

When adjusting a turnbuckle, do so a little at a time, preferably with the shroud not under load.

When you need to tighten an upper or lower shroud, tack first so that the turnbuckle you tighten is to leeward and therefore slack. Remember to turn the center section of the turnbuckle, holding the upper part to keep it from turning as well. There should always be as much turnbuckle thread showing above the center section as below it.

Tighten (or slacken) no more than a few turns, then tack again to see whether your adjustment has cured the symptom. Once the mast is straight on the original tack, come about to a close-hauled heading on the opposite tack and repeat the adjustment. Do this until the spar is vertical on both close-hauled tacks as well as at rest. Until you get a feel for your rig's proper tension, it may be hard to know whether it's an upper or lower shroud that needs adjusting. As a rule of thumb, proper tension will leave the leeward upper shroud taut at 15° of heel with the crew seated to windward.

You should begin each day's sail by checking the straightness of the mast. Although the stretch of stainless steel shrouds and stays is negligible, the wire has a certain amount of slack in its construction and will loosen a bit, especially early in the sailing season.

When the standing rigging is adjusted to your satisfaction, pin the turnbuckles with **cotter pins** or **split rings** (as in Figure 1-14) to keep them from backing off. Be sure to bend the sharp ends into the turnbuckle to avoid protruding snags. After you've done so, tape over any remaining sharp edges or points on which sails, clothing, or skin might snag. A roll of waterproof tape—sold in any marine supply store—should be a part of your ditty bag. Some skippers use inexpensive plastic tubing instead of tape. It can be employed over and over, but it's another thing to remember when hooking up the turnbuckles.

# Fractional Rigs

The steps involved in tuning a fractional rig (Figure 11-2) are similar but slightly more complicated

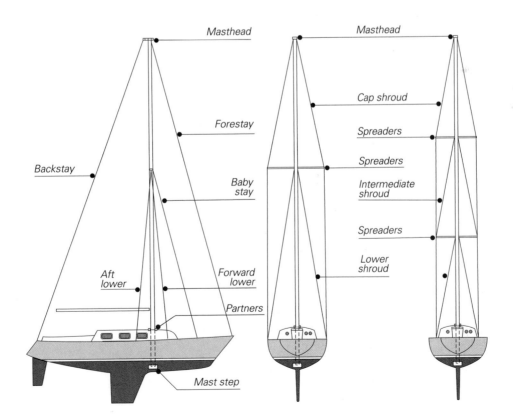

**Figure 11-1.** A masthead-rigged sloop. (REPRINTED WITH PERMISSION FROM *HOW BOAT THINGS WORK* BY CHARLIE WING)

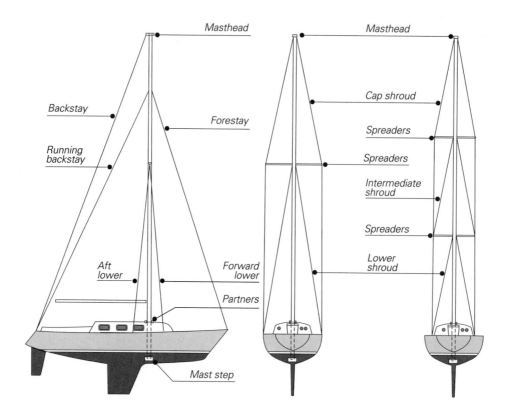

**Figure 11-2.** A fractionally rigged sloop. (REPRINTED WITH PERMISSION FROM *HOW BOAT THINGS WORK* BY CHARLIE WING)

and difficult to generalize. Sometimes the spreaders on a fractionally rigged boat are swept aft, which means that the upper shrouds will affect rake and fore-and-aft mast bend as well as side-to-side lean and bend. Often the backstay can be easily tightened or loosened according to wind strength and point of sailing by means of a tackle or a hydraulic ram. Sometimes there are running backstays to adjust with each tack. The proper balance between shrouds and backstay(s) will vary from boat to boat according to these configurations. Check your owner's manual or ask veteran owners of the same class of boat what is best.

# Lee and Weather Helm

The average modern small sailboat is remarkably well balanced compared with boats of equivalent size from previous periods. Even so, certain adjust-

ments may be required to create the optimum balance of which the boat is capable.

By **balance** we mean a boat's ability—or lack of it—to sail a straight course without pressure on the tiller. A perfectly balanced boat would sail straight with no hand on the tiller when the sails were properly set for the direction and force of the apparent wind. Obviously, waves and weight distribution in the boat can upset the most neutral balance. Not so obviously, a totally neutral balance is not normally considered an asset in a boat.

If you let go of the tiller in an average boat, she will round up into the wind more or less quickly—a centerboard boat will often spin right up, while a long-keeled vessel may take 10 seconds or so. As mentioned in Chapter 3, turning to windward—or to **weather**, to use the old term—when the tiller is released is the mark of a boat with **weather helm**. A slight amount of weather helm is not only advantageous for steering, it is also a safety factor, as the boat will head up into irons and stall out if an emergency causes the skipper to let go of the tiller.

For most skippers, a perfectly balanced helm feels dead and unresponsive. Since most helmspeople sit on the **uphill**, or windward, side of the boat, a degree of weather helm that causes the tiller to pull against them is most comfortable. If you doubt this, try it yourself: Sit first on the low side and try pushing against the average tiller; then switch. Unless you are quite unusual, you'll find the slight pull of a weather helm gives you a better feel for how your boat is progressing through the water.

Some boats have weather helm all the time, and some have it only under certain conditions, as we shall see later. Other boats have the opposite condition, the tendency to head away from the wind when the tiller is released, and this is called **lee helm**. Lee helm is generally considered a negative attribute in a boat, as it makes for tiring steering and is a potential danger. When the tiller is released, a boat with lee helm will head off the wind and into a jibe.

The **center of effort** (CE) of the sails on your boat is a theoretical point calculated by the de-

signer. It represents the single point where all the force of the wind on the sails is concentrated. Think for a moment of trying to balance a dish on a pool cue. If you can find the right point on the bottom of the dish, you can balance the dish. The weight of the dish can be thought of as the force of the wind on your sails, and the point where the cue stick balances the dish is the dish's **center of gravity** (CG), which is analogous to the center of effort of your boat's sail plan.

Similarly, the underwater surfaces of your boat's hull have a **center of lateral resistance** (CLR), which is likewise a point around which forces—in this case the forces seeking to push your boat sideways through the water—are concentrated. This point can also be thought of as the point where the dish is balanced on the cue stick.

Helm balance is affected by the relative location of these two points. The wind tries to rotate the hull around its CLR unless the CE is almost directly above the CLR (Figures 11-3 and 11-4). By applying pressure on the helm, the helmsman

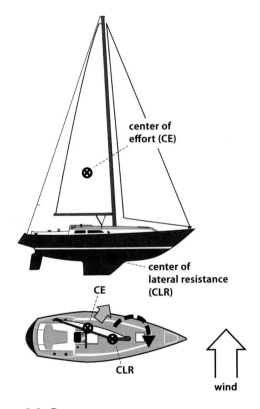

**Figure 11-3.** When the center of effort (CE) is acting aft of the center of lateral resistance (CLR), as here, a boat will display *weather helm*, a tendency to round up into the wind that must be counteracted with the rudder.

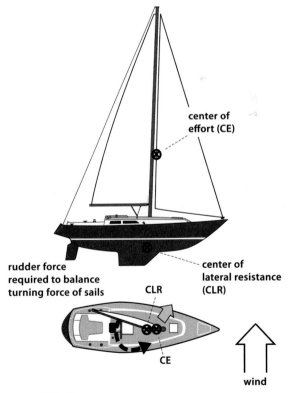

**Figure 11-4.** When the center of effort acts forward of the center of lateral resistance, the boat will tend to turn away from the wind, potentially leading to a jibe or a broach. Fortunately this is rare.

causes the boat's rudder to resist this rotation. The wind also causes the boat to heel over for the same reason: the CE is above the CLR when the boat is under sail.

Helm balance can therefore be changed by moving the CE, the CLR, or both. We can adjust the former by moving the mast forward or aft (an impractical solution in most cases), by changing the rake of the mast, or by changing the relative areas of the headsail and mainsail. We can adjust the CLR by moving an underwater surface such as a centerboard.

## CORRECTION OF WEATHER HELM

Causes of excess weather helm may be temporary or permanent. If your boat's tiller requires uncomfortable amounts of pull underway, or if your rudder angle must be consistently greater than about 5°, your boat probably has too much weather helm.

Temporary causes of weather helm may include any one of the following:

1. The jib is too small or the mainsail is too large for the prevailing conditions.
2. The jib is not trimmed enough or the main is trimmed in too much.
3. The mast is raked too far aft.
4. The centerboard is too far down and forward.
5. There is too much weight forward in the boat.
6. The boat is heeled too much.

The cures for the causes of temporary weather helm are, of course, implicit in the problems themselves. If remedying the above causes doesn't work, then the weather helm may stem from something more basic to the boat. Causes of permanent weather helm include:

1. The foretriangle is too small. (The *foretriangle* is the area bounded by the forestay, the mast, and the deck.)
2. The mainsail is too large.
3. The mast is stepped too far aft.
4. The centerboard drops too far down.

An attempt to correct these problems may or may not prove worthwhile. In most small boats, #2

and #4 can be remedied, while #1 or #3 might be a good reason to sell the boat.

## CORRECTION FOR LEE HELM

Lee helm, too, is either permanent or temporary. Temporary causes tend, reasonably enough, to be the opposites of those that create weather helm:

1. The jib is too large or the main is too small for the conditions.
2. The jib is overtrimmed or the main is not trimmed enough.
3. The mast is raked too far forward.
4. The centerboard is not dropped enough.
5. There is too much weight aft.

Permanent lee helm problems are again the opposites of the conditions causing permanent weather helm:

1. The mainsail is too small or the jib is too large.
2. The mast is stepped too far forward.
3. The centerboard is too small.

# Mainsail Trim and Shape

Adjusting the shape of the mainsail underway is accomplished by altering the tension on its three edges or by bending the mast. The halyard regulates luff tension and—if the main boom is on a sliding gooseneck—sail height off the deck. When sailing on or near the wind—beating or on a close reach—the mainsail luff is normally quite taut, but as the air lightens, more *draft*, or fullness (sail curvature), is required to keep the boat moving. Easing the halyard is one way of gaining fullness.

To prevent your sailboat from becoming overpowered in heavy winds, you must reduce the draft if you wish to sail on a close reach or close hauled. One way to move the draft forward and flatten your mainsail is to use the downhaul under the gooseneck. To get really hard tension along the luff, the main is frequently raised as high as it will go with the halyard, after which tension is applied to the gooseneck downhaul. On a mainsail without a sliding gooseneck, the same effect can be obtained with a *cunningham*—a grommeted hole in the mainsail luff slightly above the foot (Figure 11-5). A hook in the cunningham is pulled downward to exert stress on the luff and flatten the sail.

You can adjust the foot tension on your mainsail with the outhaul. Normally taut, the sail's foot is slackened when sailing off the wind by easing the outhaul. This and easing the halyard cause the main to bag somewhat, creating a more efficient downwind shape.

Primary control over leech tension is exercised by the mainsheet, as discussed below. Figure 11-6 shows the combined effects of these various controls on mainsail shape.

## MAINSHEET

When you trim the mainsail for close-hauled sailing, the boom moves closer and closer to the boat's fore-and-aft centerline. Eventually you reach a point where further trim pulls the boom down

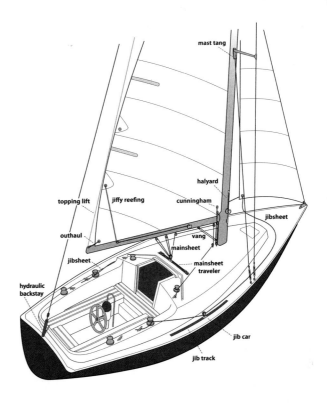

**Figure 11-5.** The principal sail controls.

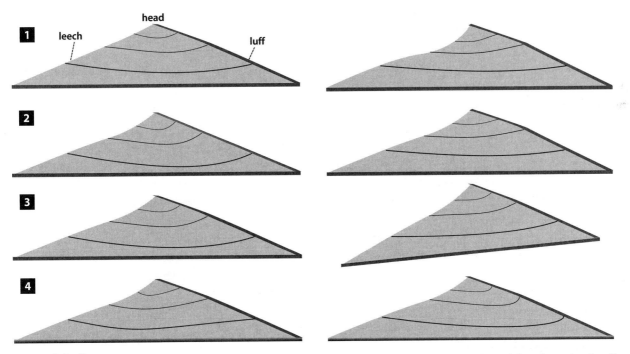

**Figure 11-6.** The effects on mainsail shape of various adjustments. In these illustrations we're looking aloft at the mainsail as if from the cockpit of the boat. **1. Left:** Mainsheet tight for little twist and extra power and pointing. **Right:** Mainsheet eased to add twist and spill power. **2. Left:** Mast straight leaves the sail deep and powerful. **Right:** Mast bend makes the sail flat and depowered. **3. Left:** Traveler up for higher angle of attack and more power. **Right:** Traveler down reduces angle of attack and power. **4. Left:** Little luff tension allows the draft to move aft. **Right:** Luff tension added with halyard or cunningham pulls the draft forward. (REPRINTED WITH PERMISSION FROM *SAIL TRIM AND RIG TUNING: A CAPTAIN'S QUICK GUIDE* BY BILL GLADSTONE)

more than in. When this happens, you are reducing the sail's twist and tensioning its leech. On the one hand, a sail with little twist is more powerful and enables you to point a little closer to the wind, but on the other hand some twist is necessary to keep the wind flowing smoothly over the sail. For a good compromise, trim until the sail's upper batten is approximately parallel with the boom and the leech telltales are streaming aft most of the time. From there, if the sea is smooth, you can try trimming further until the leech is quite straight and the leech telltales are stalling much of the time, and see if that improves your pointing ability without reducing speed. If the sea is choppy, you will probably need to ease the sheet somewhat to increase twist and keep the wind flowing over the sail.

## TRAVELER

A mainsheet traveler is a common feature in a sailboat and enables you to sheet the mainsail to leeward, amidships (as in Figure 11-5), or to windward. When sailing upwind in a light to moderate breeze, move the mainsheet car to windward so that the boom is nearly over the boat's centerline. In a stronger breeze, if the boat is overpowered, ease the mainsheet car to leeward to reduce power and relieve weather helm. Easing the traveler rather than the mainsheet enables you to dump some wind without altering the sail's shape.

## ADJUSTING THE BACKSTAY TENSION

On some boats, as mentioned above, the backstay tension can be adjusted underway—sometimes by a sophisticated hydraulic tensioner, sometimes by a multipart tackle, and sometimes by the simple expedient of putting a wrench to the backstay turnbuckle. Tightening the backstay, especially on a fractionally rigged boat, puts a bow in the spar, flattening the mainsail for upwind sailing and depowering it when the wind is strong. Off the wind, the backstay is eased, the mast straightens, and the main becomes fuller and more powerful. It's worth mentioning that a sail and spar must be properly designed for bending and flattening in this manner; trying to bow a rigid spar will just damage it.

## BOOM VANG

Off the wind, a **boom vang**—a tackle from the boom down to the deck or gunwale—is used to hold down the boom to control leech tension, and rigged to prevent (hence the term **preventer**) an accidental jibe when running directly before the wind. Some boats have permanent vangs rigged from the underside of the boom to a point at the base of the mast, as in Figure 11-5. A four- or five-part tackle can exert tremendous force on a boom, so it's a good idea to go easy with the vang, using just enough pressure to bring the boom down parallel to the water.

One disadvantage of a vang set to the gunwale is that it must be cast off with each jibe and attached to the other gunwale. An accidental jibe using this type of vang could result in a damaged or bent boom.

# Headsails and Headsail Trim

In addition to the average sloop's working sails—her mainsail and jib—she may have any number of light-weather sails. The most common of these is the genoa jib. By definition, a **genoa** is simply a jib that overlaps the mast. Genoas come in all sizes and shapes and in many cloth weights. An offshore racer may have as many as half a dozen such sails, each intended for different weather conditions.

Genoas are often described by numbers that refer to their size and to the weight of the cloth—usually Dacron, but increasingly Kevlar and/or Mylar on high-performance sailboats—from which they are made. A **#1 genoa** is the largest, with a luff running the full length of the forestay and a foot that greatly overlaps the mast and extends just about back to the cockpit (Figure 11-7). A **#2 genoa** is only slightly smaller, but is made from perceptibly heavier cloth. It's hoisted when the wind is strong enough possibly to stretch the #1 out of shape. A **#3** is smaller and heavier still, and the numbers usually run as far as **#5**, which is rather short on the luff but which still has the considerable overlap characteristic of genoas. Tradition-

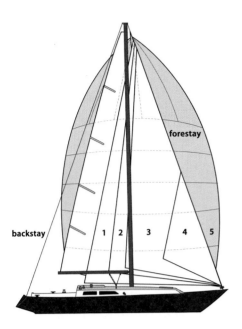

**Figure 11-7.** Headsail choices: **1.** #1 genoa; **2.** #2 genoa; **3.** #3 genoa; **4.** storm jib; **5.** cruising spinnaker.

ally, a boat longer than 30 feet or so would carry at least three headsails—for example, a #1 genoa, a #3, and a working jib—but the widespread adoption of roller-furling headsails on sailboats of this size has lessened the need for headsail changes. A roller-furling genoa can serve as the #1 when fully unrolled and a #3 when partially rolled, and need only be augmented with a working jib, which is often flown from an inner headstay.

## LUFF PERPENDICULAR

A genoa is also sometimes described by its *luff perpendicular* (LP), a term derived from racing (Figure 11-8). Thus, we may hear a sail called a **150% genoa**, which refers to a sail with an LP that is one-

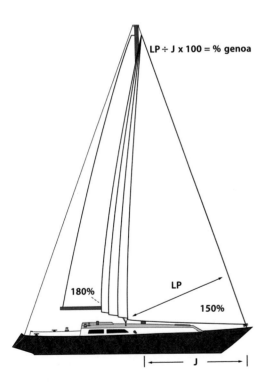

**Figure 11-8.** Sizing a genoa. **Left:** On a 150% genoa the luff perpendicular is 1.5 times the J measurement, which is the length of the base of the foretriangle. **Right:** This solid, comfortable-looking cruiser has two headstays, each fitted with a roller-furling genoa. The bigger headsail, with its head at the top of the mast and its tack at the end of the bowsprit, is used when the wind is light and perhaps mainly when the boat is sailing off the wind—i.e., reaching. The sail is probably awkward to tack, as it will chafe against the inner headstay while coming about; sometimes in a case like this it's easier to roll the sail up, then unroll it on the other tack. The smaller genoa flying from the inner headstay is the better choice when the breeze gets up or the boat is tacking upwind. Not only is it smaller, it moves the center of effort of the sail plan aft, making the boat easier to handle in a stiff breeze. Since both sails can be roller-reefed to smaller sizes, this rig allows flexible responses to varying wind strengths. (PHOTO BY BOB GOLEY)

and-a-half times as long as the distance from the boat's jib tack fitting to the mast. The LP measurement itself is the straight line from the genoa clew to the sail's luff, making a right angle with the luff. The standard #1 genoa, because of handicap rules, is a 150%, but there are sails that come as large as 180% (or even larger; the only limit is the length of the boat).

For maximum efficiency, many genoas are cut to be so-called **deck sweepers**, where the sail's foot is in contact with the deck for nearly its whole length. When close hauled, this kind of sail can cause a blind spot for the helmsman, running from dead ahead to amidships on either side. Some skippers have their sailmaker put a transparent plastic window in the foot of the sail, and this is a help. But there's no substitute for a **lookout**, and one of the crew should be specifically assigned to sit down to leeward or up by the tack to keep an eye out forward.

Tacking with a genoa sometimes causes problems, as the sail drags and whips its way around the shrouds. After a few times out, you will know from exasperating experience which deck or rigging attachments are likely to catch the genoa. These fittings should be taped smooth or relocated if possible. In some large boats, a crewmember is assigned to walk the genoa clew around the shrouds when the boat tacks, but hopefully your boat won't require this.

There are three variants of the genoa worth knowing about. These sails exist for special conditions that are fairly common in some places but may not exist in your home waters.

1. **Lapper.** A cross between a working jib and a genoa. Its luff runs nearly the length of the forestay, but its foot only just overlaps the mast, hence the name. A 110% genoa is often called a lapper.

2. **Reacher.** As big in area as a genoa, but made of lighter fabric, a reacher is usually a 180% LP sail with a very high foot. As the name suggests, it is used for reaching and is normally sheeted right aft to the transom or sometimes to a block at the end of the main boom.

3. **Drifter.** Used for very light airs, when most nonracers will turn on their auxiliary engines.

The drifter is cut like a big genoa, but is made of very light nylon. It often has no snap hooks along the luff, being made fast only at the head, tack, and clew.

## HEADSAIL TRIM

Headsail sheets usually lead to a block that is mounted on a sliding car as in Figure 11-5. The car rides on a track that runs fore and aft on the side deck or gunwale. This arrangement allows a proper lead for nearly any size of headsail simply by moving the car forward or back along the track. The same sheeting rules apply to a genoa as to a working jib. When you hoist the sail, pull the clew aft and set the block at the corresponding position on the track. Now sail the boat close hauled and observe the headsail's foot and leech. If the foot appears loose while the leech is stressed, it means the sheet block is too far forward. If the leech is loose and the foot taut, the block is too far aft. When the leech and foot appear equally tensioned, luff the boat slowly up into the wind. The headsail should begin to ripple all along its luff, and if it does, your sheet lead is correct. If the ripple appears first at the head of the sail, then the leech is still a bit too loose, and vice versa if the sail luffs first toward its foot.

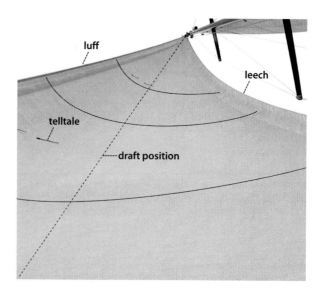

**Figure 11-9.** Looking aloft at a headsail trimmed for close-hauled sailing. Note the telltales streaming aft, the lack of excessive headstay sag in this well-tuned rig, and the line of maximum draft superimposed on the photo. (REPRINTED WITH PERMISSION FROM *SAIL TRIM AND RIG TUNING: A CAPTAIN'S QUICK GUIDE* BY BILL GLADSTONE)

When a genoa is trimmed for close-hauled sailing, it should be close to but not touching the spreader tip aloft and the shrouds at deck level. A headsail should be slightly fuller than the mainsail, and its point of maximum draft (called *draft position*, as in Figure 11-9) should be slightly farther forward than in the mainsail.

The sheet block on the opposite track should be set to match the first one. This will usually be the correct setting, but some slight adjustment may be required. This just means that your boat is imperceptibly out of shape, or the two tracks do not quite match, and is nothing to worry about. In many cases, the headsail sheet is led from the sail's clew through the block to a winch mounted on the cockpit coaming. This mechanical aid is required because of the amount of pull a headsail can create. If your genoa has a very long foot, or if the winch is mounted well forward in the cockpit, you may be faced with a sheet that leads rather abruptly upward from the sheet block to the winch. To prevent this, many boats have a **turning block** mounted well aft of the cockpit winch, and the headsail sheet leads from the sheet block aft to the turning block and then forward again to the winch at the flattest

possible angle. The turning block must be extra strong, as it will be taking stresses nearly twice those on the sheet block.

## THE SPINNAKER

The light-air sail called the *spinnaker* is the queen of the racing sails (Figure 11-10). Shaped like a triangle with two convex sides, the spinnaker is often cut from brightly colored nylon in individualistic patterns. It is often maddening to set, fly, or lower, but no serious racing boat wants to be without one if the sail plan and class rules allow it.

There are a number of ways to arrange the panels of a spinnaker:

1. *Radial head.* A construction consisting of parallel, horizontal panels across the bottom half of the sail and an arrangement of triangular panels at the top. It is suitable for broad reaching and running in light to moderate winds.
2. *Starcut.* A spinnaker that appears to have a three-pointed star superimposed on it. Relatively flatter and smaller than a radial head, it is used downwind in heavier weather or for

**Figure 11-10. Left:** Nothing beats a spinnaker when it comes to moving a boat in the lightest of breezes. These two boats appear to be racing, and since the boats are of different types this is probably a handicapped race, meaning that the first boat over the finish line may not be the winner on corrected time. Under the PHRF (performance handicap racing fleet) rule, the most popular handicapping system, a boat's handicap is determined by the historical performance of similar boats. (PHOTO BY BOB DONALDSON) **Middle:** Note the bow wave and quarter wave on this boat. The distance between the two crests equals the boat's waterline length, which means that the boat is charging along at hull speed. (PHOTO BY MIKE BRODEY) **Right:** The luff of this spinnaker is curling slightly at the shoulder—a good indication that it is neither overtrimmed nor undertrimmed, and the spinnaker pole is horizontal, as it should be. Racing crews like this one often do not wear PFDs during the daytime in nearshore waters, but at night or offshore they certainly should. (PHOTO BY MIKE BRODEY)

beam and close reaching in normal conditions.

3. *Tri-radial cut.* A more recently developed construction that consists of three or four horizontal panels in its midsection, above and below which are triangular panels with their vertices in the corners as in the starcut. It is now the most common cut because it can be flown through a broad range of conditions.

Until the spinnaker is set, the lower edge of the sail is its foot and the two sides are leeches. Likewise, the two lower corners are the clews, and the upper corner is the head. Once a spinnaker is set, the clew that is attached to the **spinnaker pole** becomes the tack, the leech between tack and head becomes the luff, and the sheet attached to the tack is called the *spinnaker guy* (Figure 11-11).

The spinnaker is set *flying*—that is, it's connected to the boat by its halyard and the lines from its clews, but not along any one of its edges. Once the sail is raised, it assumes a position in front of the mainsail. It rides outside all shrouds and stays, including the headstay. With its five attendant lines—halyard, sheet, guy, spinnaker pole topping lift, and spinnaker pole downhaul—the spinnaker adds considerable complexity to any boat. Crews need to be well rehearsed in sail handling, beginning at the dock before you get underway.

Cruising sailboats rarely have the luxury of a large, well-trained crew to handle a spinnaker. *Cruising spinnakers*, also called *gennakers* (Figure 11-12), have been developed for these boats. These asymmetrical sails are set flying like a spinnaker but are tacked to the headsail tack fitting via a short length of line, or pendant. Unlike a spinnaker, a gennaker does not require a pole, and in fact it functions much like a drifter, which it replaces. In a further development, some boats set a larger asymmetrical cruising spinnaker on a retractable bowsprit.

# When the Wind Increases

Up to this point we have been looking at methods and equipment used to make your boat sail at peak efficiency. This assumes that the weather is suitable for efficient sailing. When the weather worsens, efficiency must give way to prudent seamanship.

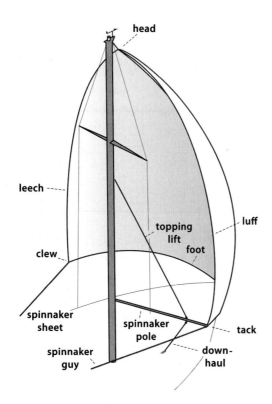

**Figure 11-11.** Spinnaker controls.

**Figure 11-12.** This sloop on San Francisco Bay is flying a gennaker. Judging from the poised, attentive crew and the helmsman's intense focus, this boat is racing. (PHOTO BY MIKE BRODEY)

The time to prepare your sailboat and to learn how to use your equipment in uncomfortable conditions is before you encounter those conditions. Remember, sailing a boat is not like driving an automobile—you cannot pull over to the side and stop when it is no longer pleasant to go on.

Sooner or later you're going to find yourself and your boat caught out when the wind is stronger than you'd like it to be. In such a case remember that your boat was almost certainly built to take a great deal of punishment, and she will come through as long as you keep your head and use proper sailing technique.

## SQUALLS

A sudden squall, whether associated with an approaching cold front or a thunderstorm, can be unnerving simply because it gives you little time to prepare. Even the fastest-moving squall line will nevertheless allow you the few minutes you need to get your boat in shape to handle it. And always remember that a fast-moving squall has one great virtue—it's over in a hurry. Often a squall will last only a few minutes, and seldom more than half an hour.

The first step when it becomes obvious that you're likely to be caught by a squall before you can reduce sail is to have all hands put on a PFD. Not only should every crewmember have a PFD of the proper size capable of supporting his or her weight in the water, but everyone should wear it whenever there's any threat of bad weather. A good PFD will give crewmembers confidence, will conserve body heat, and will absorb the bumps that happen in rough weather. Racing sailors and those sailing offshore make it a habit always to wear a PFD in the cockpit or on deck, and many add a lifeline and harness. (For more on PFDs, see Chapter 5.)

The second step is to luff up into the wind and drop and furl the sails. A serious squall can pack winds over 60 miles per hour and advance as fast as 50 miles per hour, so don't take chances. Until you know the strength of the advancing storm, drop the sails and furl them securely. Drop the centerboard or daggerboard, if it isn't already lowered.

Secure all loose equipment, have a bailer or pump ready to operate, and tell the crew to keep their weight low in the boat. With these precautions you and your boat will be ready to deal with whatever is likely to come. If you're upwind from a beach or shore, it would be well to put your anchor out and set it to avoid being blown ashore.

Squalls are rare, however (see Chapter 15). Much more common is a light breeze that strengthens as the day wears on, and a sailor responds to this first by depowering and then by reefing the sails. Let's see how this works.

## RESPONDING TO A BUILDING BREEZE

Let's say you are sailing close hauled in a light breeze. You have eased the mainsail outhaul and downhaul to get more draft into the mainsail, and you have eased the main- and jibsheets slightly to give their leeches a little more twist. You have the mainsheet leading from near the windward end of the traveler, enabling you to center the boom without too much leech tension. You've moved the headsail sheet blocks forward to add draft in the jib or genoa. If your boat has an adjustable backstay, you have eased its tension to straighten the mast, which adds further draft to the mainsail. In short, you are squeezing all you can from a light breeze with full, powerful sails.

Now the wind begins to freshen. As wrinkles begin to form in the mainsail, you add outhaul and downhaul tension to remove these, which also reduces the mainsail's draft. At the same time you ease the traveler car somewhat to leeward, then trim the main- and jibsheets somewhat to reduce leech twist. You may be able to point higher at this point than you could before—at least until the wind raises a chop. Once that happens, you may need to ease the sheets and bear off slightly in order to power through the chop.

If the wind continues to build, your boat will sooner or later show the symptoms of being overpowered. When your boat develops excessive weather helm, and when it is staggering along with its lee deck awash, it is *overpowered*. It may be exciting to sail **on your ear** in this fashion, but it's actually slower than if your boat were more upright. It's time to *depower* the sails:

Tighten the outhaul further. Tighten the backstay if it is adjustable—this will induce mast bend and flatten the mainsail. Move the jibsheet blocks farther aft; in heavy air you want the upper part of the jib to luff before its lower sections. Lower the mainsheet traveler car to leeward to induce a partial luff in the mainsail. Ease the main- and jibsheets a few inches to induce more leech twist, which depowers the sails aloft, where the heeling force is greatest. And finally, head up slightly in the puffs in order to depower the sails still further.

If the boat still feels overpowered while close hauled and you're not too sure of yourself or the boat, try heading down to a close reach and letting out the sails. A reach is not only the fastest point of sail, it's usually the safest as well; the boat is relatively stable and can head up into the wind, spilling the breeze's force from the sails, or head away as required, without changing tacks.

## REDUCING SAIL AREA

The foregoing measures may be all you need, but eventually, if the wind continues to build, you may require a more drastic response. Then it is time to reduce, or shorten, your sail plan by increments.

The usual first increment is to reduce your headsail area. If you're flying a hanked-on genoa, take it down and put up a smaller genoa or your working jib. If you're flying a roller-furled genoa, roll it up a few turns. Now see how your boat sails. If it's more comfortable, perhaps this is all you need to do. But if the boat still seems overpowered, it's time to *reef* your mainsail—reduce its area.

There are a few ways of accomplishing this on a modern sailboat. One is *roller reefing*, in which the boom is designed so that it can be rolled around its axis, which winds the sail tightly around the boom like an old-fashioned window shade. To roller reef a mainsail, put the boat on a close reach. Now ease the mainsheet just a little, so there's wind in the sail but not the full force of the breeze. Now, while one person eases the main halyard, the other works the crank that turns the boom.

Most roller-reefing gear has the crank located at the forward end of the main boom, which usually means that one person can ease the halyard and turn the boom. In this case, the person at the helm should, if possible, grasp the mainsail leech and pull back, exerting a force parallel to the boom. This

makes for a tighter, more even roll of sail. If you roll a deep enough reef in the sail so that the lower batten becomes twisted, remove it; a wood batten can easily break under this kind of treatment, and even a flexible plastic batten does the sail no good when it's rolled up inside.

Roller reefing used to be common on small sailboats but has fallen from favor. It prohibits a midboom mainsheet attachment (or any other attachments, for that matter), and a roller-reefed mainsail rarely sets well. Much more common these days is what sailors call *jiffy reefing* (Figure 11-13).

Begin jiffy reefing by inducing a partial luff in the mainsail. Then take up on the topping lift so that the boom won't drop when the main halyard is eased. Then ease the mainsheet until it luffs completely.

Now lower the main halyard until the *luff cringle* (the reinforced eye in the luff of the main-

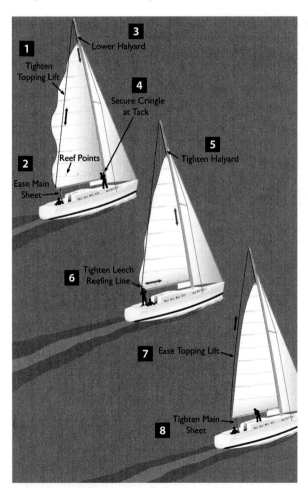

**Figure 11-13.** The standard reefing sequence involves eight steps as shown. (REPRINTED WITH PERMISSION FROM *HEAVY WEATHER SAILING: A CAPTAIN'S QUICK GUIDE* BY JOHN ROUSMANIERE)

sail at its reefing position) can be pulled down to the boom. Secure the luff cringle to the boom with a line or by hooking it over a gooseneck hook that is provided for that purpose, then tighten the halyard until you see tension wrinkles in the luff.

With the sail still luffing, it's time to reef the leech. When you find the leech cringle at the reefing position, there will probably be a reefing line already rove through it. If not, you'll have to **reeve** (pass through) one, and it should run through a cheek block in the boom end. You will have to haul on this line, using a winch if necessary, until you pull the leech cringle down to the boom. Now ease the topping lift, trim the mainsail, and coil your halyard and reefing lines, and your reef is done.

Your sail will have a row of cringles running between the luff and leech cringles, and there may or may not be a pair of short lengths of line called **reef points** hanging from each cringle. If the reefed portion of the sail flogs in the wind or flops about annoyingly, you can tie the reef points around this **bunt** of sail to corral it. If your sail has no reef points, reeving a line through the cringles will accomplish the same thing (Figure 11-14).

**Figure 11-14.** If you practice reefing in a light breeze, you'll be more apt to reef when your boat is overpowered and the maneuver will proceed more smoothly. (PHOTO BY BOB DENNIS)

**Roller-furling mainsails** are a comparatively recent development intended for shorthanded cruising sailors. The sail rolls up around a rod that is mounted inside a specially designed mast or on the aft edge of a standard mast. Typically this is a big-boat adaptation and is quite commonly operated by an electric motor, offering push-button reefing! The downside is that the sail cannot have battens and thus cannot support any roach, so there is a loss of light-air performance.

## STRIKING SAIL

It is possible to reduce sail in a hurry simply by **striking** or **dousing** (lowering) one sail or another, and furling it tightly. Which sail you choose will depend on how your boat balances and what point of sailing you are on.

Boats with mainsails that are much larger than the jib will probably balance better if the main is left raised and the jib is lowered, unsnapped, and bagged (don't leave it on the deck—even if tied down—as it may easily escape over the side to act as an unwanted drag).

If the boat doesn't handle well under main alone, you can try sailing under jib alone, with the main tightly furled around its boom and the boom carefully lashed to prevent its breaking free. Be advised, however, that the mainsail provides much more fore-and-aft support to the mast than the jib, and sailing under jib alone can thus put your mast at risk of breaking if the seas are large.

The only way to find which sail combination works best for your boat is to take her out and try the several variations available to you. The important thing is to try, when possible, to keep the proportion of sail areas ahead and aft of the mast approximately the same. As the wind gets stronger, the relative amount of sail area forward of the mast may increase—the boat will probably balance better for it, a fact which will be reflected in the amount of weather helm felt by the person holding the tiller.

## KNOCKDOWN AND CAPSIZE

When a boat is temporarily overpowered by the wind and heeled over until its mast is nearly level with the water, it is said to be **knocked down**. When a boat is laid over and has shipped so much water that it can't right itself, it is *capsized* (Figures 11-15 and 11-16). Most boats with ballasted keels will right themselves from a knockdown or a capsize even if there's a substantial amount of water in the cockpit, and many of today's small centerboard sailboats are designed to recover from a knockdown. You can aid the process by releasing the sheets and using your weight to bring the boat back up.

In the case of a genuine capsize of a centerboard boat, especially one that is non-self-righting, the situation may be more serious. Several steps should not only be followed by the skipper but also be thoroughly drilled into the crew:

1. Immediately after the capsize, count heads. Make sure all crewmembers have surfaced and swum free of the boat.
2. Stay with the boat as long as it is floating, and put on PFDs if you haven't already done

so. (If you are in this situation you should have already insisted that the crew don PFDs.)

3. Recover the loose gear that will be floating around the boat. Stuff it into a sailbag and tie the sailbag to the boat.
4. Get the sails down or at least make sure the sheets are free to run so the sails will not hold water. This might allow the boat to come upright by itself. More likely you will need to stand on the centerboard, and you may need to have someone help by pushing upward on the mast.
5. Once the boat is upright, lower the centerboard, plug the top of the centerboard trunk if it's open, and bail the boat. You may have to swim alongside and scoop water out until the level is low enough for one crewmember—the lightest—to ease aboard by the stern and finish the job.

If after a couple of tries you see that it will be impossible to empty the boat and sail away, don't use up your energy and body heat with repeated attempts. Turn your attention to signaling for help. Continuous sounding of the foghorn, a smoke signal by day

**Figure 11-15.** The sailor of this capsized single-person Laser will have to use his weight on the daggerboard as leverage to right the boat. (PHOTO BY MOLLY MULHERN)

**Figure 11-16.** Standing on a daggerboard or centerboard will usually get a sailing dinghy back on its feet. If you can't climb onto the board, just hanging from it may do the trick, especially if you lower the sails or at least make sure the sheets are free to run. (PHOTO BY ERIK SKALLERUP AND DOMENIC MOSQUIERA)

or a flare by night, and an International Orange distress flag are all recognized distress signals (see Chapter 5), and all can be purchased in any marine supply store and carried in a waterproof bag (most are sold that way) in even the smallest daysailer. Many skippers equip each PFD with a mouth-operated whistle attached by about 10 inches of lanyard.

If your boat must be towed home while full of water, make sure the towing vessel pulls your boat very slowly—2 to 3 miles per hour at the maximum. Not only are water-filled boats unstable, but the water sloshing back and forth can easily gain such momentum it knocks the transom out. Make sure your boat has an extra-strong cleat or eye bolt on the foredeck, one that is bolted through the deck and through a backing board beneath. This kind of hardware will withstand the great stresses of towing. One crewmember should stay aboard the swamped boat to bail, steer, and keep weight aft so the boat will ride better.

# Disabled Rudder

If you lose your rudder or it becomes jammed, either because of bad weather conditions or a grounding, you can still get home under sail if you fly two or more sails. Naturally, you will want to stop and repair your rudder if you can, but if that is not possible, all is not lost. You can apply the principles of balancing your helm to make your boat sail with a disabled steering system.

Earlier in this chapter we saw that your boat will want to head up into the wind if you sheet in the main and let the jib fly. If you sheet in the jib and let the main go, your boat will fall off. Through a series of adjustments to both sails—trimming the jib and slacking the main if you start to sail above the course you want; doing the opposite if you fall below your desired course—you can keep going in nearly any direction you choose.

Sailing without a rudder is certainly not as easy as sailing with one. Your boat will be far less nimble, and more time and sea room will be needed for any maneuver. You may have to back your jib to come about. Jibing your boat may be difficult because the main can only go out as far as the shrouds. This constraint creates enough of a weather helm on a dead run to prevent an intentional jibe without a rudder. If your boat is small enough, you can shift your crew's weight to leeward to overcome this weather helm; otherwise you may want to sail up into the wind and come about.

A paddle or oar can make a substitute rudder, or a bucket can be trailed on a line over the stern. Moving the bucket to one side or the other will steer the boat in an emergency.

Crew weight can also be used to increase or decrease the helm when you are trying to maintain a steady course without a rudder. When your boat is *out of trim* (all the crew are on one side), the boat will heel. The additional heeling creates more friction between the boat and the water on that side, causing the boat to turn toward the side the weight is on.

You can try out the principles of rudderless sailing by lashing your tiller amidships on a nice day. A little such practice can be a great ego booster. All that theory soon becomes a reality, and you become a more competent skipper.

No sailor is really competent until he or she has faced and matched heavy weather. While it is foolish to take chances, neither should you underestimate yourself or your boat. The best way to find out what heavy weather is all about is to hitch a ride aboard the boat of someone you know to be a top skipper and observe what he or she does. Ask questions anytime the actions aren't obvious. Sooner than you think, you should arrive at the point where you have a healthy respect for the awesome force of the sea, but not an irrational fear of it.

# Practice Questions

## IMPORTANT BOATING TERMS

In the following exercise, match the words in the column on the left with the definitions in the column on the right. In the blank space to the left of each term, write the letter of the item that best matches it. Do not use an item in the right-hand column more than once.

| THE ITEMS | THE RESPONSES |
|---|---|
| 1. _____ reefing | a. permits you to trim the mainsail almost to the centerline without excessive leech tension |
| 2. _____ lee helm | b. center of sail forces |
| 3. _____ weather helm | c. increases luff tension |
| 4. _____ CE | d. lightweight genoa |
| 5. _____ CLR | e. makes sail smaller |
| 6. _____ traveler | f. pulls boom down |
| 7. _____ cunningham | g. boat falls off the wind |
| 8. _____ vang | h. boat turns into the wind |
| 9. _____ drifter | i. boat can't right itself |
| 10. _____ capsized | j. center of forces pushing sideways on the hull |

# Multiple-Choice Items

In the following items, choose the best response:

**11-1.** The device used for adjusting the tension on a shroud or stay is a

a. block
b. pulley
c. turnbuckle
d. pin

**11-2.** Mast rake is the

a. angle aft of the vertical
b. angle forward of the vertical
c. hook to port
d. hook to starboard

**11-3.** Upper shrouds should be tuned to have

a. the same tension as the lower shrouds when not sailing
b. less tension than the lower shrouds when not sailing

c. more tension than the lower shrouds when not sailing
d. more tension on the starboard side

**11-4.** Compared with a masthead rig, a fractional rig permits more

a. shroud adjustment underway
b. mast rake
c. backstay adjustment underway
d. reefing alternatives

**11-5.** If left unattended, a lee helm will cause a boat to turn

a. into the wind
b. away from the wind
c. back and forth around its average course line
d. first slightly downwind, then back to its original course

# Multiple-Choice Items (continued)

**11-6.** The helm characteristic most desired by sailors is

a. balanced helm
b. lee helm
c. heavy weather helm
d. slight weather helm

**11-7.** The center of effort is the

a. geometric center of all hull forces
b. point where crew weight should be concentrated
c. geometric center of all sail forces
d. point where the rudder forces are concentrated

**11-8.** Flattening a sail

a. increases its draft
b. makes it less powerful
c. optimizes its power off the wind
d. gives a boat more power in choppy seas

**11-9.** Mainsail luff tension can be adjusted with

a. the halyard
b. the cunningham
c. the downhaul (if the gooseneck slides)
d. all of the above

**11-10.** Which of the following will not flatten a mainsail?

a. adding cunningham tension
b. adding outhaul tension
c. moving the traveler car to windward
d. adding backstay tension

**11-11.** Moving the headsail sheet block forward will

a. tighten the headsail leech
b. tighten the headsail foot
c. cause the headsail to luff aloft before it luffs at deck level
d. all of the above

**11-12.** A genoa is

a. any headsail
b. any jib
c. a jib that overlaps the mast
d. none of the above

**11-13.** Which of these sails is *not* set free-flying (i.e., with its luff not attached to a stay)?

a. gennaker
b. drifter
c. genoa
d. spinnaker

**11-14.** A #1 genoa is

a. smaller than a #3
b. a good headsail choice in a light to moderate breeze
c. always set from a roller-furling mechanism
d. never set from a roller-furling mechanism

**11-15.** A spinnaker is designed for

a. offwind use
b. heavy air
c. maximum convenience for shorthanded crews
d. beating

**11-16.** The corner of a spinnaker that is attached to the spinnaker pole is the

a. clew
b. head
c. luff
d. tack

**11-17.** The first step in preparing a boat for a squall is to

a. make sure every crewmember is wearing a PFD
b. get a weather report
c. brief the crew on procedures to be followed
d. douse the sails

**11-18.** The second step in preparing for a squall is to

a. get a weather report
b. brief the crew
c. drop and furl the sails
d. set a storm flag

**11-19.** Partially reducing a sail's area is called

a. reefing
b. striking sail

(continued on next page)

## Multiple-Choice Items (continued)

c. securing the rig
d. dropping sail

**11-20.** A boat heeled over so that its mast is nearly level with the water is

a. capsized
b. knocked down
c. swamped
d. turned turtle

**11-21.** A boat that is laid over with its mast in the water and that does not right itself is

a. swamped
b. capsized
c. knocked down
d. turned turtle

**11-22.** Steering a sailboat without a rudder is possible if you

a. trail a bucket over one side or the other of the stern
b. rig an oar over the stern, perhaps by lashing it
c. find the optimum balance of the mainsail and the jib
d. all of the above

**11-23.** Adjustable backstays are often loosened to improve

a. upwind performance
b. offwind performance
c. steering
d. stability

**11-24.** When sailing close hauled in optimum trim, the headsail should be

a. slightly flatter than the mainsail
b. slightly more full than the mainsail
c. luffing slightly but perceptibly at all times
d. pressing against the spreader tip aloft and the shrouds at deck level

# Introduction to Navigation

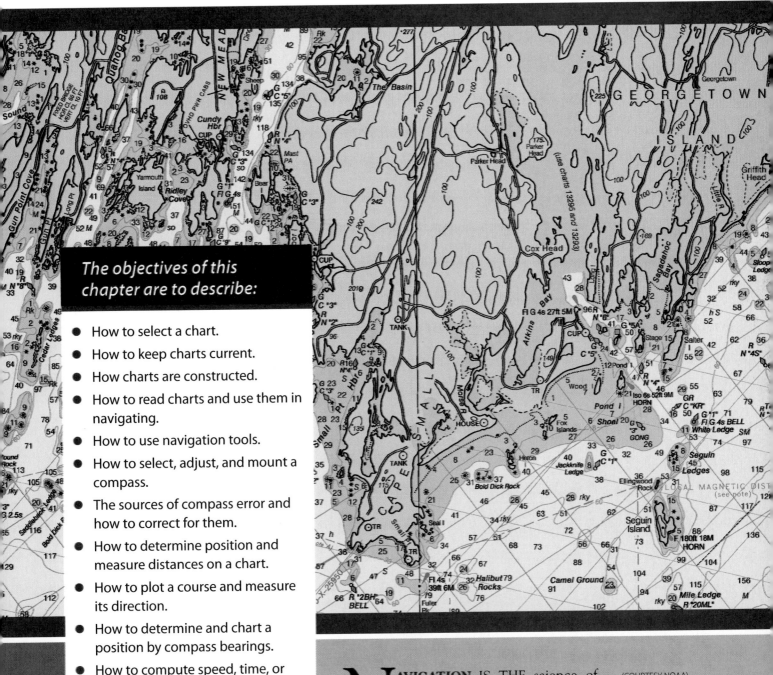

(COURTESY NOAA)

## The objectives of this chapter are to describe:

- How to select a chart.
- How to keep charts current.
- How charts are constructed.
- How to read charts and use them in navigating.
- How to use navigation tools.
- How to select, adjust, and mount a compass.
- The sources of compass error and how to correct for them.
- How to determine position and measure distances on a chart.
- How to plot a course and measure its direction.
- How to determine and chart a position by compass bearings.
- How to compute speed, time, or distance when two of the three are known.
- How to make a dead-reckoning plot.
- The importance and use of *Tide Tables.*
- How to navigate with electronics.

**N**AVIGATION IS THE science of knowing where you are and how to get to where you want to go. In this chapter we introduce you to navigation and give you some useful tools and techniques. If you would like to study navigation in greater depth, the U.S. Coast Guard Auxiliary teaches several classes that will enhance your skills and knowledge. Ask your instructor for more information. Navigational tools vary in complexity and cost. Limit yourself to the basic tools until you have an understanding of what you really need.

Your basic navigational tool kit should include (Figure 12-1):

- **Charts** of the area in which you boat
- A good **magnetic compass** for your boat
- A **course plotter** or **parallel rulers**
- **Dividers** or a **drafting compass**
- A fine-point (0.5 mm) pencil with medium-soft lead
- A good eraser

In addition, you may want to include a binocular, a handheld **bearing compass**, and some means of measuring water depth. You can measure water depth by a calibrated pole, a **lead line**, or an electronic depth sounder. And finally, with handheld global positioning system (GPS) receivers available for as little as $150, more and more boaters are making GPS central to their navigation. And little wonder: The accuracy and reliability of GPS are truly amazing. Remember, however, that use of GPS does not relieve you from chartwork. GPS coordinates mean nothing until you plot them on an up-to-date chart, nor will you know whether the course to your next GPS **waypoint** is a safe one until you find out from the chart whether it takes you across intervening ledges or shoals. And finally, any electronic device can fail at any time, no matter how reliable. It is for this reason that you should continue to maintain a dead-reckoning (DR) plot and keep track of your position by traditional means, despite using GPS.

We will return to the subject of electronic navigation later in this chapter. First, though, we'll explore the time-honored techniques of chart-and-compass navigation.

# Nautical Charts

The word "map" usually applies to a land area, whereas a map of a water area is called a "chart." A *chart* is a representation of a portion of the earth's surface showing information useful to mariners. Quite simply, charts make navigation possible. Charts are printed on paper, though electronic charts are increasingly popular today. (We'll return to the subject of electronic charts later in this chapter.) Usually, charts are drawn *to scale*, which means that the sizes of objects on the chart are proportional to their actual sizes.

Your charts may show both water and land areas, and the land near the water may even show considerable detail. This is especially true if the details can help you pinpoint your location—that is, your *position*. Charts also include details such as the shape of a coastline, harbors, islands, ledges, shoals, water depths, navigation buoys and other aids to navigation, shipping lanes, underwater cables, shoreline topography, and landmarks such as radio towers, church steeples, stacks, large buildings, and other objects. And that's only a partial list.

Charts are technological marvels. If you were to write out all that information, it would take several large books to contain what is on a single nautical chart. Furthermore, the books would be hard to read and interpret.

**Figure 12-1.** The basic piloting tools include a chart, a pair of dividers, a fine-point pencil, and parallel rulers (shown here) or a course plotter (not shown). (PHOTO BY RAY PAGES)

## AVAILABILITY OF CHARTS

The National Ocean Service (NOS) of the National Oceanic and Atmospheric Administration

**WARNING** *Always have up-to-date charts for your current area of operation.* Study *the* Local Notices to Mariners *and enter changes on your charts.*

(NOAA) publishes charts of all U.S. waters other than navigable rivers. You can buy them directly from the NOS or from authorized chart sales outlets such as marinas and marine supply stores. These are the charts prepared by the Office of Coast Survey (OCS), the NOS's sister agency within NOAA.

In addition, as mentioned in Chapters 7 and 9, charts of major river systems such as the Mississippi and Ohio are produced by the U.S. Army Corps of Engineers, and charts for the high seas and foreign waters are produced by the National Imagery and Mapping Agency, or NIMA (recently renamed National Geospatial-Intelligence Agency, or NGA).

Nautical chart catalogs list the available NOS charts. For example, *Nautical Chart Catalog 1* lists all NOS charts that cover the Atlantic and Gulf Coasts, including Puerto Rico and the Virgin Islands. Nautical chart catalogs should be available where charts are sold. In effect, a chart catalog is itself an overview chart of a large region on which the coverage areas of designated navigation charts are outlined.

Don't confuse the nautical chart catalogs with *Chart No. 1: Nautical Chart Symbols, Abbreviations, and Terms.* Although it has the word "chart" in its title, *Chart No. 1* is a book published jointly by NOAA and the Defense Mapping Agency that is useful for interpreting nautical charts. Though it is no longer available from the government for distribution through commercial chart agents, you can still obtain a print copy of *Chart No. 1* from the Government Printing Office, and you can view and download a digital version at http://chartmaker.ncd.noaa.gov. In addition, various commercial publishers offer *Chart No. 1* for sale (Figure 12-2).

Again as mentioned in Chapter 7, reproductions of government charts on waterproof paper or reformatted in bound volumes to cover defined regions are also available from commercial sources, and these will sometimes represent a significant savings or gain in convenience over the government charts. You can also obtain the latest edition

**Figure 12-2.** The government no longer prints *Chart No. 1*, which explains the symbols, abbreviations, and terms used on nautical charts, but various commercial editions are sold, including the one shown here. (REPRINTED WITH PERMISSION FROM *THE WEEKEND NAVIGATOR* BY BOB SWEET)

of a chart from online print-on-demand services, and you can download free electronic charts in raster format (for use on a laptop computer or chartplotter) from the Office of Coast Survey website. (This web address, http://chartmaker.ncd.noaa.gov, will also direct you to print-on-demand charts, *Notices to Mariners*, and *Coast Pilots* in print or digital downloadable form.)

Finally, http://mapfinder.nos.noaa.gov offers interactive mapping tools and links to NOS websites (such as Marine Navigation and Tides and Currents) that provides more information and downloadable data. In some cases, users can view and interact with data.

## DATES OF CHARTS

Information on charts changes from time to time. These changes appear in the *Local Notices to Mariners* published weekly by each Coast Guard District. As the information is outdated, your chart becomes less reliable, so be sure to use up-to-date charts. A new edition of a chart cancels previous editions and such "revisions" contain less significant changes.

You can access the *Local Notices to Mariners* on the Internet at www.navcen.uscg.gov. Click on Local Notice to Mariners, and select your district to get weekly updates.

Charts have dates to help you be certain that you have the most recent versions. The store where you buy your chart should have a copy of the NOS publication, *Dates of Latest Editions* (or view it online at http://chartmaker.ncd.noaa.gov/mcd/dole.htm). Ask to see a copy before buying a chart. Get a current chart and keep it up to date by posting changes as they are reported. When you buy a chart from a print-on-demand source (see above), it will incorporate revisions referenced by *Local Notices to Mariners* through the date the chart is printed for you.

## CHART FEATURES

If the world were flat, chartmaking would be a much simpler process than it is. The central dilemma for all chartmakers is how to represent a curved surface on a flat chart.

### Projections

One way to make a chart is to draw it on the surface of a globe. This accurately represents the earth's surface, but it would not be very useful on a small recreational vessel. It would take a huge globe to show the area where you are boating in any detail, and even if that were possible you'd have a hard time using it for navigation.

Another way to make a chart is by using a mathematical concept called **projection**, which enables a chartmaker to represent a curved surface on a flat sheet of paper. There are several distinct projection types, but only two need concern us here.

**MERCATOR PROJECTIONS.** Most nautical charts use the **Mercator projection**, in which points on the earth's surface are projected onto a cylinder wrapped around a globe as in Figure 12-3. After this, the cylinder is cut open and laid out to make a flat surface.

A chart made by Mercator's method is useful for navigation, although it has limitations. One important feature is that all angles are represented correctly, even in extreme northern and southern waters. This means that you can measure the angle of a course line from one point to another directly on the chart. With this knowledge, you can head your vessel where you want to go.

Unfortunately, Mercator projections introduce distortions both in north-south and east-west directions that become greater the farther north or

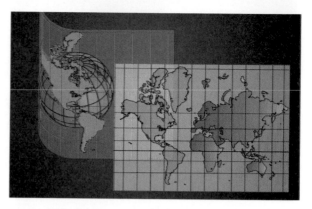

**Figure 12-3.** A Mercator projection shows lines of longitude as vertical, parallel lines, rather than converging at the poles. Compass courses plot as straight lines on a Mercator chart. There is some distortion of landmasses, which becomes progressively greater in the higher latitudes, but for charts of midlatitude local waters this is of no consequence. (REPRINTED WITH PERMISSION FROM *THE WEEKEND NAVIGATOR* BY BOB SWEET)

south you go from the equator. Thus, on a Mercator projection, Greenland appears to cover a much larger portion of the earth's surface than it actually does. This distortion makes Mercator charts nearly unusable in polar or near-polar areas. If the area covered by a chart is small enough, however, the distortion does not present a serious problem where most recreational boating occurs.

**POLYCONIC PROJECTIONS.** Another common way to make a chart is by projecting the earth's surface onto a series of cones, which is called a **polyconic projection** (Figure 12-4). Great Lakes charts are

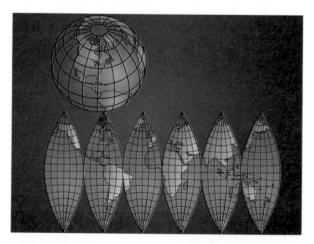

**Figure 12-4.** A map of the world shown as a polyconic projection. Some Great Lakes charts are polyconic projections, but Mercator projections are also available and easier to use for ordinary purposes. (REPRINTED WITH PERMISSION FROM *THE WEEKEND NAVIGATOR* BY BOB SWEET)

most often conic projections, since this projection gives less distortion at high northern and southern latitudes. Mercator projections for the Great Lakes are available, however.

## Chart Scales

A chart can show a small area at a large scale or a large area at a small scale, but showing a large area at a large scale would be impossible on a chart of usable dimensions. A harbor chart, for example, shows a comparatively small area at a comparatively large scale, frequently 1:20,000. At that scale, the drawing of a spit of land, a pier, or other object is 1/20,000th its actual size. Thus, a harbor entrance that is 1 inch wide on the chart would actually be 20,000 inches wide, or about 3/10 of a mile.

If the chart's scale is 1:40,000—as is true of some coastal charts—a 1-inch-wide island is actually about 3/5 of a mile wide. Conversely, the 3/10-mile-wide harbor entrance would be only 1/2 inch wide on this chart (Figure 12-5).

**HARBOR AND COASTAL CHARTS.** Harbor charts sometimes have a scale of 1:10,000, though 1:20,000 is more usual. Such a chart can show detail but cannot cover a large area. Coastal charts, on the other hand, usually have a scale of 1:80,000, which shows larger areas with less detail. Thus, small scales cover large areas, and large scales cover small areas in greater detail.

There are even smaller scales (for example, 1:100,000 or 1:1,000,000) for special purposes such as planning ocean passages. Some charts show an entire ocean on one sheet of paper. Select your charts to give the greatest amount of detail (largest scale) you need for each portion of your cruise. Use small-scale, large-area charts for overall voyage planning, and large-scale, small-area charts for maneuvering in harbors or other difficult areas. Sometimes it's handy to remember that "large scale means large detail, small scale means small detail."

**WHICH CHART IS FOR YOU?** You can get some charts in either of two forms, conventional or small craft. **Conventional charts** are ideal for use on large, flat navigation tables such as you would find on the bridge of a ship or at the nav station of a 40-foot boat, and for many waters, conventional charts are the only alternative the government offers. **Small-craft charts**, on the other hand, feature folded for-

Chesapeake Bay 12280 1:200,000

Chesapeake Bay 12263 1:80,000

Chesapeake Bay 12282 1:25,000

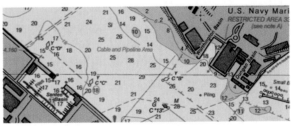

Chesapeake Bay 12283 1:10,000

**Figure 12-5.** A series of chart extracts of the same area, varying in scale from 1:200,000 to 1:10,000. The smaller the second number in the ratio, the larger the scale and the more detailed the chart. (REPRINTED WITH PERMISSION FROM *HOW TO READ A NAUTICAL CHART* BY NIGEL CALDER)

mats for use in the confined navigation spaces of a small boat (Figure 12-6). Several formats are used by NOAA, but they all feature sections of larger, conventional charts printed on smaller panels and enclosed in a folder or booklet. Some are folded accordion style and stored in jackets, while others are printed on both sides of three or four sheets that are folded and bound in a protective cover. They are all designed to be easier to handle on small recreational craft, with each panel giving you access to a small portion of the area.

**Figure 12-6.** A small-craft strip chart.

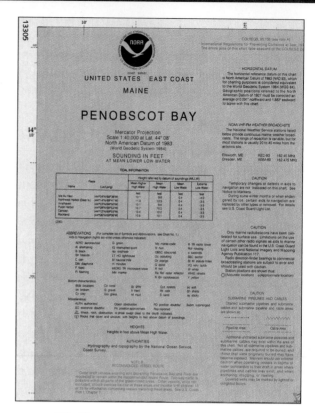

**Figure 12-7.** The general information block of a nautical chart, showing chart number and title, projection, datums, and miscellaneous tide and other information. (REPRINTED WITH PERMISSION FROM *HOW TO READ A NAUTICAL CHART* BY NIGEL CALDER)

Small-craft charts usually have a scale of 1:40,000, but often have insets showing smaller areas at scales of 1:20,000, 1:10,000, or even larger. They also include ancillary information of interest to local boaters such as tide data, public marine facilities, weather information, and more.

NOAA uses water-resistant paper for its charts, but you may want to give your chart additional protection. Encase it in a plastic cover that will allow you to spread it out on a center console or a cockpit seat without worrying about rain, spray, or wind.

## General Information Block

Before you use a chart, read its *general information block* (Figure 12-7). This is sometimes called the *chart block* and will tell you the chart's name. In the lower left corner of the chart you will find the edition number and date of publication.

The general information block will give you information such as the chart's projection, its scale, and its *vertical* and *horizontal datums*—a technical term for the benchmarks from which a chart's vertical and horizontal measurements are made.

**HORIZONTAL DATUM.** Formerly, most North American charts used the North American 1927 horizontal datum, referencing their latitude-longitude grids to a geophysical point in Meade's Ranch, Kansas, from which horizontal measurements were used to locate landmasses and other geophysical

features. With the arrival of space satellites, more precise measurements than those based on the 1927 datum became possible, and many charts were redrawn to the North American 1983 datum. Most nautical charts today use the World Geodetic System 1984 (WGS-84) horizontal datum, which is fundamentally the same as the North American 1983 datum. The differences that result from these datums are very small and for most practical purposes inconsequential. You probably will never know what datum your chart uses unless you read its legend block.

If you are using GPS, however, the chart datum and GPS datum must be the same in order to avoid position error. Your GPS receiver's instruction manual will show you how to change your GPS datum, which is easy to do. This subject will be addressed later in this chapter in the Electronic Navigation section.

**VERTICAL DATUM.** The vertical datum of a chart also has important meaning for you. It helps you know how much water is under your vessel and how much vertical clearance there is under a bridge

(Figure 12-8). NOS charts use **mean high water** (MHW) as the plane of reference for vertical clearances of bridges and high-tension power lines, and **mean lower low water** (MLLW) as the plane of reference for soundings, or depths. These terms are explained below; for the moment, it is enough to know that overhead clearances may be less than indicated on the chart during an extremely high tide, and depths beneath your boat may be less than indicated on the chart during an extremely low tide.

## What Charts Show

Charts show heights and shapes of landforms; depths of water; locations of navigation buoys; locations and characteristics of lighted aids to navigation (ATONs); heights and ranges of fixed lights; and the locations of principal landmarks (including, but not limited to, church spires, water towers, smokestacks, cupolas, and radio towers), harbors, piers and other principal structures within harbors, ledges, sandbars, underwater cables, shipping channels, wrecks and other hazards, and a whole lot more (Figure 12-9). Charts also describe bottom types—such as sand, rock, or mud—using special abbreviations, information that is useful when you are trying to select a place to set an anchor (Figures 12-10 and 12-11). Each chart offers a rich trove of information in shorthand notation, and the key to interpreting the chart's symbology is really quite simple. We'll look at some of the basics here; the symbology used for ATONs (Figure 12-12) is described and illustrated in Chapter 7.

**WATER DEPTHS.** Water depths, or *soundings*, are among the most critical categories of information recorded on a chart. Shallow water is light blue on a chart, whereas deeper water appears as white. Shoal areas that uncover at low tide are shown in green, and areas of land are a gold or tan color. This gives a ready visual reference without having

to look at the numbers that show depth. Remember, though, that the areas of blue and white water vary in depth depending on the scale of the chart. As a rule of thumb, switch to a larger-scale chart when you move into the blue.

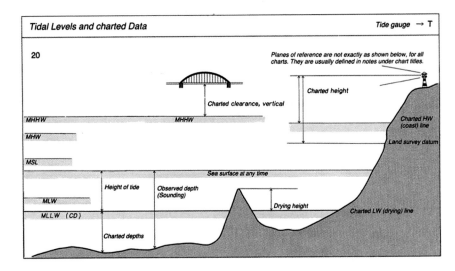

**Figure 12-8.** Vertical datums. NOS charts use mean lower low water (MLLW) as the reference datum for soundings, and mean high water (MHW) as the reference datum for vertical clearances beneath bridges. (REPRINTED WITH PERMISSION FROM *HOW TO READ A NAUTICAL CHART* BY NIGEL CALDER)

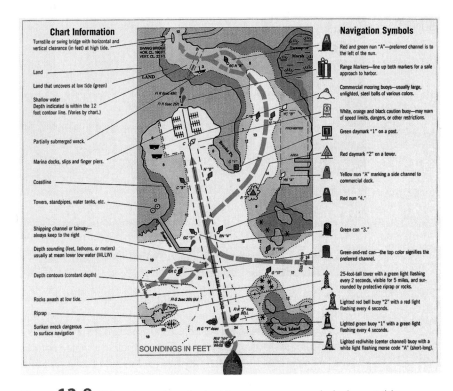

**Figure 12-9.** What charts show. In chart language, some symbols show visible features and others show hazards hidden beneath the water's surface. (COURTESY MAPTECH; REPRINTED WITH PERMISSION FROM *THE WEEKEND NAVIGATOR* BY BOB SWEET)

On most U.S. charts, water depths are in feet. Some charts, though, report depths in **fathoms** (a fathom is 6 feet, or about 2 meters), while some newer charts show depths in meters, and meters are used on charts published by Canada and many other countries. Read your chart's general information block to see what units it uses for reporting depths and heights.

To highlight local trends in water depth, cartographers connect points of equal selected depths with lines known as **contour lines**. These are, in effect, the mirror image of the contour lines that mark points of equal elevation on a topographic map of the land. Most U.S. charts use a 6-foot or 1-fathom interval for depth contours, and you'll see contour lines at depths of 6, 12, 18, 30, and 60 feet. **NOTES.** Charts also contain notes on their borders and in other clear spaces. These give you important safety information and information of a more general nature such as anchoring and precautionary areas. Read them.

For example, page G of Chart 11451 shows "Moser Channel (see note)." The note says, "Moser Channel—Overfalls that may swamp a

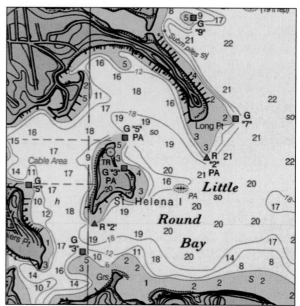

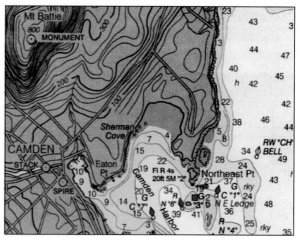

**Figure 12-12.** Selected features of nautical charts. **Top:** PA = position approximate, and TR = tower. Vertical, roman type is used for beacons and land features; slanted, italic type is used for hydrographic features. Soundings are in feet. Labels on depth contours are in italic—in a smaller font and lighter typeface—to distinguish them from spot soundings. Blue denotes shoal water—on this chart, less than 10 feet deep. Note the symbol for a dangerous wreck in the center of the chart. **Bottom:** Contour lines on land are every 20 feet, with every fifth one (100-foot intervals) bolder. The monument, spire, and stack are all accurately charted (positioning dot) and conspicuously visible as landmarks (capital letters). Buoy labels, unlike beacon labels, are italic. (REPRINTED WITH PERMISSION FROM *HOW TO READ A NAUTICAL CHART* BY NIGEL CALDER)

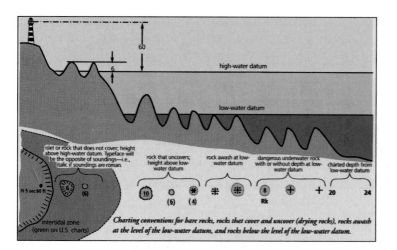

**Figure 12-10.** It is essential to understand the chart symbols for rocks and ledges in order to avoid these hazards. (REPRINTED WITH PERMISSION FROM *THE WEEKEND NAVIGATOR* BY BOB SWEET)

| Grd | Ground |
|---|---|
| S | Sand |
| M | Mud; Muddy |
| Oz | Ooze |
| Ml | Marl |
| Cy:cl | Clay |
| G | Gravel |
| Rk;rky | Rock; Rocky |
| P | Pebbles |
| St | Stones |

**Figure 12-11.** Types of bottoms and their chart symbols.

small boat may occur at the bridge." This means that during certain tidal changes, tidal currents at this point oppose each other and create an overfall. The note warns mariners that their boats may run head-on into an unexpected waterfall. It's much better to know this in advance than to learn it the hard way. **Read the notes on your chart.**

**SHORE DETAILS.** Charted details ashore include easily recognized structures, such as water towers, church steeples, and radio towers. Land contours are often charted, since bold headlands and coastal hills make useful landmarks, and bridges are described in detail.

The shoreline contour is another important feature and, as mentioned, is usually printed a golden color. If the shore is swampy or covers and uncovers with changes in water level, it is light green.

Keep in mind that structures that were once prominent enough to appear on your chart may no longer be there. Sometimes you can't see them because newer, larger buildings screen them from view. This is another reason to keep charts up to date. The U.S. Coast Guard Auxiliary and the U.S. Power Squadrons assist in gathering data to keep charts current.

**AIDS TO NAVIGATION.** These structures, both fixed and floating, serve as signposts, beacons, directional signals, and warnings of danger. They are your most important navigational aids. Refer to Chapter 7 for a discussion of ATONs.

**LOCATION, DISTANCE, AND DIRECTION ON A CHART.** Suppose your GPS receiver tells you that your present position coordinates are 41°31′ north latitude, 70°39′ west longitude (we'll talk more about latitude and longitude coordinates below). You can't use that information to orient yourself to the real world unless your local chart allows you to plot those coordinates; then you'll know right where you are in Vineyard Sound, Massachusetts. Charts therefore include latitude and longitude scales for plotting positions, and the latitude scale can also be used to measure distances on the chart. (The chart may also include a distance scale for the latter purpose, but it's nice to know you can use the nearest latitude scale when the distance scale is folded underneath and not conveniently accessible.)

Now suppose your destination is the channel marker bell off the mouth of Vineyard Haven, but you can't see the bell from your position. You need to know what compass course to steer. The chart gives you directions both in degrees true and degrees magnetic. True directions come from lines of **longitude**, also called **meridians**—that run north to south—and from lines of **latitude**, also called **parallels**—that run east to west. Magnetic directions come from a **compass rose** overprinted in one or several places on the chart (Figure 12-13). We'll discuss all this in greater detail below, but first we'll look at the magnetic compass, which is every bit as important to navigation as the chart.

# Ship's Compass

Select a **compass** to suit your boat. Powerboats need steering compasses built to withstand the vibrations and pounding of boats moving at high speeds or through rough waters. The steering compass of

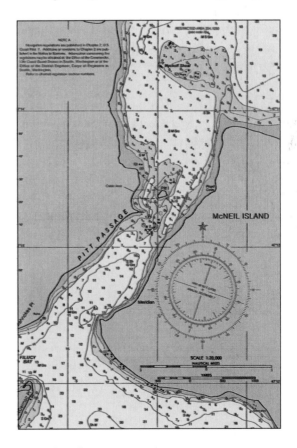

**Figure 12-13.** A segment of Small-Craft Folio Chart 18455, from Puget Sound, showing lines of latitude (parallels), lines of longitude (meridians), and a compass rose. (REPRINTED WITH PERMISSION FROM *A CRUISING GUIDE TO PUGET SOUND AND THE SAN JUAN ISLANDS*, SECOND EDITION, BY MIGAEL SCHERER)

a sailboat must be able to operate satisfactorily at large heel angles (Figure 12-14).

## FEATURES OF A GOOD COMPASS

The bowl of a marine compass is filled with a viscous oil or alcohol-based liquid that dampens vibrations and oscillations and keeps the compass card from swinging rapidly as your boat bounces. The card pivots on a needle point and thus remains more or less level as the boat pitches and rolls. The compass's construction allows for expansion and contraction of the fluid as temperatures change.

Protect your compass from excessive heat and direct sunlight. A compass may leak fluid from a ruptured seal if it overheats, and without its fluid, it is unusable.

You will find it useful to have a light to read the compass at night. A good compass comes with an internal red light, which illuminates the card in darkness yet does not impair night vision.

Large compasses usually are more stable and more finely calibrated than small compasses. Select one that is as large as practical for where it will be mounted.

**Figure 12-14.** An array of small boat compasses. **Top left:** A front-reading powerboat compass. The yellow lubber's line is on the front surface of the glass bowl. Front-reading compasses are a bit counterintuitive and may take some getting used to. **Top right:** A top-reading powerboat compass. **Bottom left and right:** A binnacle-mount sailboat compass and a bulkhead-mount sailboat compass. (COURTESY RITCHIE NAVIGATION; REPRINTED WITH PERMISSION FROM *THE WEEKEND NAVIGATOR* BY BOB SWEET)

## INSTALLING YOUR COMPASS

Install the compass where it will be easily visible from the helm, and so that its central pivot and **lubber's line** are parallel with your boat's keel. Any compass misalignment during installation will give a constant error in readings. Powerboat compasses are often mounted on a dash, a center console, or close by the helm in a pilothouse. Sailboat compasses are typically either binnacle mounted or installed in the cabin's aft bulkhead so as to be clearly visible from the helm. The choice of a front-reading, top-reading, or bulkhead-mount compass will depend on your installation location. Locate the compass as far as possible from radios, other electronic instruments, or masses of ferrous (iron) metal—especially audio speakers. This is not usually a problem on boats with outboard motors, but on inboards it may be a significant problem. Watch your compass card while at a pier. Does it move when you turn on an electric or electronic instrument? If so, move either the compass (or adjust it) or the instrument.

## ADJUSTING YOUR COMPASS

After installing your compass, take your boat to an area with several charted landmarks and one or more **fixed** ATONs (not buoys) that can be aligned with the landmarks to create ranges. Align and point your vessel toward each range and read your compass.

Compare these readings with the magnetic directions measured from your chart (see below). If the compass readings vary no more than 2° or 3° from what they should be, a boater traveling short distances may ignore these errors. Most people can't read such small differences on their compasses or steer a course that accurately anyway. If the differences are greater than 3°, however, make a note of them. You will want to either adjust your compass so as to remove these errors, which are called *deviations*, or compensate for the errors in the courses you steer.

A good compass has internal adjustable magnets that, when appropriately tuned, will counteract the magnetic influences aboard your boat that cause compass error. Don't try to adjust the compass unless you have time, patience, and special knowledge. Local professional compass adjusters can usually be found in the Yellow Pages. Note that electronic compasses automatically compensate for most deviation.

# Fixing Your Position

Navigation involves getting from where you are to where you want to be. To do this, you must be able to locate both your present position and the position to which you wish to move.

## GREAT CIRCLES

Lines of *latitude* (Lat) and *longitude* (Lo) provide a precise means of determining a position on the earth's surface. These lines are made by passing imaginary planes (flat surfaces) through the earth.

### *Parallels of Latitude*

If an imaginary plane passes through the center of the earth, its intersection with the earth's surface is a *great circle*. The great circle formed by passing a plane through the earth's center perpendicular to the earth's axis is the *equator*, which is 0° latitude. Other lines formed by passing planes through the earth perpendicular to its axis are *parallels* of latitude (Figure 12-15). Each is parallel with the equator and every other line of latitude, but only the equator is a great circle.

Latitude lines encircle the earth in an east-west direction and measure angular distances north and south of the equator. These angles are measured in degrees, the symbol for which is °. Each degree can be divided into 60 minutes (60′), and each minute can be divided into 60 seconds (60″). In navigating, however, we most often use tenths of minutes rather than seconds, and you may be required to convert from seconds to "tenths" if the chart displays seconds. To illustrate how parallels of latitude are used, draw a line from the earth's center to the point where it intersects the equator as in Figure 12-16. Next, draw another line from the earth's center to a second point directly above the first and on another line of latitude. The angle between these lines (60°) describes the position of the sec-

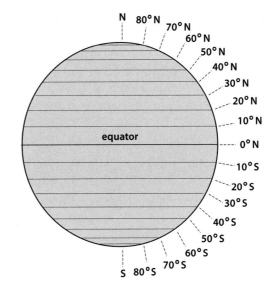

**Figure 12-15.** Parallels of latitude.

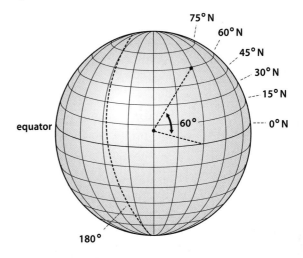

**Figure 12-16.** Measuring latitude.

ond point in relation to the equator. The second point can be either north or south of the equator. In Figure 12-16, the point is at 60°N latitude (abbreviated "Lat"). In Figure 12-17, the angle shows that Greenwich, England, is at 51°28′N latitude.

The angle between the two lines can vary from 0° to 90°, since the equator is 0° and the poles are Lat 90°N and Lat 90°S. A point halfway between the equator and either the north or south geographic pole is at an angle of 45°. It is either Lat 45°N or Lat 45°S, depending on whether it is north or south of the equator.

### *Longitude Lines*

Planes that pass through both geographic poles form great circles on the earth's surface. These are called lines of longitude or *meridians*. On one side of the earth the lines are called the **upper branches,** and on the opposite side they are called the **lower branches.** Meridians run from north to south through the earth's poles and measure angular distances to the east or west of the *prime meridian,* which passes through Greenwich, England, and is designated as 0° longitude. You might ask why the prime meridian was chosen so as to pass through Greenwich. The answer has much to do with England's global dominance of the seas at the time this determination was made.

Note that all meridians are great circles. This is in contrast with lines of latitude, which, with the exception of the equator, are not great circles.

Now imagine a line drawn from the center of the earth to the intersection of the prime meridian with the equator, such as in Figure 12-17. Imagine, too, another line drawn from the center of the earth to a point where a different meridian intersects the equator to form angle "a." Angle "a" between these two meridians tells the position of the point relative to the prime meridian. The position may be east or west of the prime meridian.

If you go west from Greenwich one-quarter of the way around the earth, you are at Lo 90°W. If you go east one-quarter of the way around the earth, you are at Lo 90°E. If you go halfway around the earth, you are at Lo 180°. Lo 180°E and Lo 180°W are the same meridian.

Lo 180° is approximately the international date line (see the line of dashes on Figure 12-17). The date line follows Lo 180° except where it is contorted to exclude or include bodies of land. It is drawn west of Alaska, for example, so that all of Alaska will have the same calendar date.

As with degrees of latitude, degrees of longitude are divided into 60 minutes, and each minute is divided into 60 seconds.

## LOCATING A POINT ON A CHART

You can describe any point on the earth's surface by its latitude and longitude (Figure 12-18). If a vessel's position is 44°00′N, 80°00′W, there is only one place on earth it can be. It is in Lake Huron. Similarly, Greenwich, England, is located at Lat 51°28′N, Lo 0°00′ (Figure 12-17).

Since most charts are Mercator projections, true north is at the top. Parallels of latitude extend horizontally across the page, whereas meridians of longitude run vertically up and down the page. Indeed, one of the defining characteristics of a Mercator projection is its depiction of meridians as vertical lines that are parallel with one another. On a

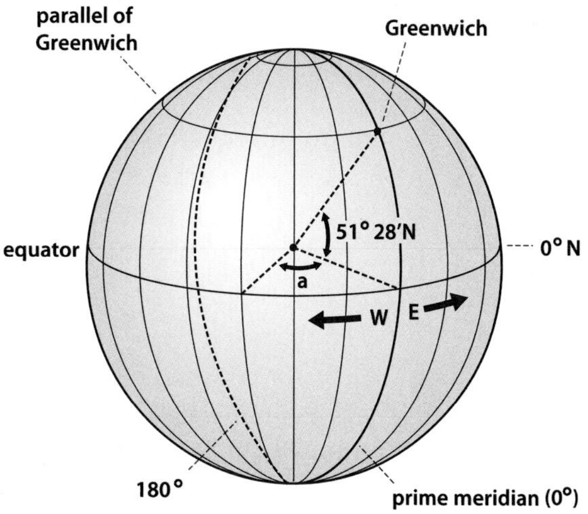

**Figure 12-17.** Meridians of longitude are shown here. The Greenwich or prime meridian is 0° longitude, and longitude is measured east or west from there. The east and west longitudes converge on the opposite side of the globe from the prime meridian, at 180° longitude. Angle "a" in the drawing represents a west longitude.

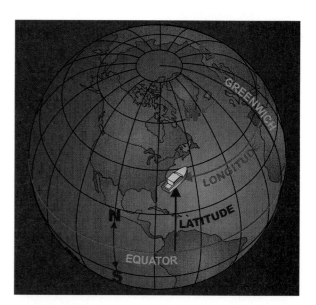

**Figure 12-18.** Together, latitude and longitude measurements provide a coordinate grid system, giving each location on earth a unique "address." (REPRINTED WITH PERMISSION FROM *THE WEEKEND NAVIGATOR* BY BOB SWEET)

round globe, the meridians converge at both poles and thus are not parallel, and this explains why high-latitude landmasses are distorted on a Mercator chart. This feature is also one of the keys to the great utility of a Mercator projection, however, enabling the navigator to plot compass courses and bearings as straight lines on a chart.

Along the margins of a chart are black-and-white scales showing degrees, minutes, and tenths of minutes or seconds. The scales on the left and right margins are latitude scales, while those along the top and bottom are longitude scales.

You can describe any point on a chart using the latitude and longitude scales. Figure 12-19 illustrates their use in determining a position.

## DISTANCE ON THE EARTH'S SURFACE

You have probably heard the term *nautical mile* and wondered why it is used instead of the more common unit of distance, the statute or "land" mile. There is a good reason.

There are 360° in a circle. Each circle therefore has 360° x 60 or 21,600 minutes. The distance described on the earth's surface by 1 minute of arc along a great circle is 1 nautical mile. Thus, the circumference of the earth is 21,600 nautical miles. Since every minute of latitude is a minute of arc along a meridian, and since every meridian is a great circle, 1 minute of latitude is always equal to 1 nautical mile. This makes the nautical mile a convenient measure of distance.

Not all great circles are precisely the same length, however, since the earth is not quite a perfect sphere. In July 1, 1959, the length of 1 nautical mile was set officially at 1,852 meters (about 6,076 feet). This is $1/21,600$th of the distance around the earth at the equator. Since a statute mile is 5,280 feet (about 1,600 meters), 1 nautical mile equals $6,076 \div 5,280$ or 1.15 statute miles. A *knot* is a speed of 1 nautical mile per hour. (Note that "knots per hour" is not a valid expression. Your speed might be 10 knots or 11.15 miles per hour, but it is *not* 10 knots per hour!)

There are two ways to measure the distance between two points on a chart.

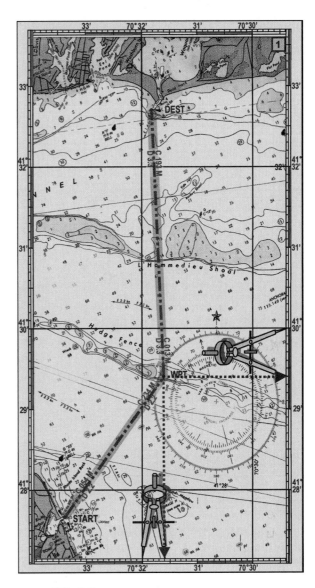

**Figure 12-19.** Locating a position on a chart. Here a boater planning a trip plots a course on the chart that includes a turning point. To find the coordinates of that turning point, he uses dividers to measure its latitude and longitude as shown (and as described in this chapter). If he is using GPS, he can then enter those coordinates into his GPS receiver as a waypoint. (REPRINTED WITH PERMISSION *FROM THE WEEKEND NAVIGATOR* BY BOB SWEET)

## Use the Chart's Scale

Most charts have distance scales, which show distances in nautical miles, statute miles or kilometers, and yards or meters (Figure 12-20). Mariners commonly use nautical miles to measure distance. The fastest and most convenient way to use these scales to measure the distance between two points is with dividers. Set one leg of the dividers on one

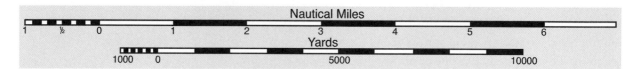

**Figure 12-20.** You will find a distance scale like this one on your nautical chart.

point and the other leg on the second point. Now move the dividers to a scale such as shown in Figure 12-20.

Put one leg of the dividers on one of the whole-number division points—for example, on 1, 2, or 3—such that the other leg of the dividers will fall somewhere within the subdivided portion at the left end of the scale. The whole-number division point is the number of nautical miles, statute miles, kilometers, yards, or meters, and the finer divisions to the left are tenths of a mile, kilometer, yard, or meter. On the "yard" scale, the finer divisions are each equal to 100 yards.

## Use the Latitude Scale

The second way to measure distance on a chart is by use of its latitude scale, since 1 minute of latitude is always 1 nautical mile. Again, set the dividers to extend from one point on the chart to the other whose distance away you want to know (Figure 12-21).

Now, move the dividers to the latitude scale near the midpoint of the latitudes of your points, as in Figure 12-21. Place one leg of the dividers on a minute or a degree mark on the latitude scale. Place the other leg above it on the latitude scale as in Figure 12-21. Now count the minutes and tenths of minutes between the two points. Remember, 1 minute of latitude equals 1 nautical mile.

If the distance between the two points you are measuring is greater than the span of the dividers, set the span of the dividers equal to 1 nautical mile by using the latitude scale of the chart. Now "walk" the dividers from one end of the line joining the two points to the other, keeping count of the number of nautical miles measured. When you get near the end of the line, reduce the span of the dividers to equal the length of the last segment. Apply the dividers to the latitude scale to read the length of this segment in tenths of a mile, and add that to the number of whole nautical miles you counted.

The longitude scales on a chart cannot be used to measure distance. Figure 12-18 shows that, although latitude lines are spaced at equal intervals, longitude lines are closer together near the earth's poles than they are at the equator. Only at the equator does 1 minute of longitude equal 1 nautical mile.

On small-scale polyconic charts, such as those for the Great Lakes, you can measure large east-west distances most accurately by using the distance scale.

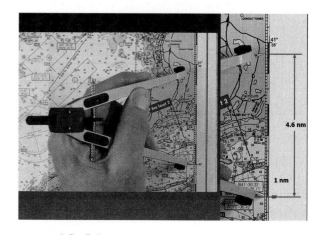

**Figure 12-21.** Using the latitude scale to measure distance. **Top:** Place one point of the dividers on the first location and the second point on the other location. **Bottom:** Without altering that setting, transfer the dividers to the latitude scale on the edge of the chart. One minute of latitude (but not longitude!) is exactly equal to 1 nautical mile. (REPRINTED WITH PERMISSION FROM *THE WEEKEND NAVIGATOR* BY BOB SWEET)

## Use a Piece of Paper

If you don't have dividers, use a piece of paper to make your measurement. Make a mark on the edge of the paper, and place this on one of the points. Align the paper's edge with the two points and put another mark at the second point. Now move the paper to the latitude scale and read the distance.

## COURSE PLOTTING

An important feature of Mercator and large-scale polyconic charts is that angles are represented correctly. Draw a line on a chart from where you are to where you want to go. This is a *course line*. The angle the course line makes with true north is the direction you should go to get where you want to be. In addition, the length of the line represents the distance you have to travel to get there.

### Direction

Direction is measured clockwise from north and expressed in degrees. East is 90°, south is 180°, west is 270°, and north is 360° or 0°. The direction of a course line is its clockwise angle from north.

### Measuring Direction

You can measure the direction of a course line drawn on a chart in several ways, but the two most common use a course plotter or parallel rulers. Whichever method you use, the first step is to *estimate* the direction of the course line. The estimate will help avoid the common error of steering a course exactly opposite the intended one. When making your estimate, remember that a line has two ends, only one of which is in the direction you want to go. The other points in the opposite direction. These two directions are 180° apart, which means they are *reciprocals*.

A direction between north and east is between 0° and 90°. A direction between east and south is between 90° and 180°; between south and west,

180° to 270°; and between west and north, 270° to 360° (0°).

***USING A COURSE PLOTTER.*** A simple way to measure the direction of a course on a small vessel is with a *course plotter* (Figure 12-22). Align any of the lines or long edges of this see-through plastic tool with the course line. Slide it along the line until the bull's-eye is on a meridian or a parallel, and read the direction of the course line from the appropriate protractor scale on the plotter. Complete directions for using a course plotter are in the sidebar on page 284.

One of the great advantages of a course plotter is that you can read the course from any nearby line of latitude or longitude, at least one of which will always be handy on the portion of the chart you happen to be using. You must remember that the course measurement you obtain using this method will be in degrees true, not magnetic. This means that you will have to apply a correction before you can steer the course by your compass, as we'll discuss below.

***USING PARALLEL RULERS.*** You may also measure the direction of a line by using the nearest *compass rose*. Each chart features at least one of these, and often two or three. A compass rose includes two concentric circles, each of which is graduated in degrees. The outer ring is oriented toward "true"

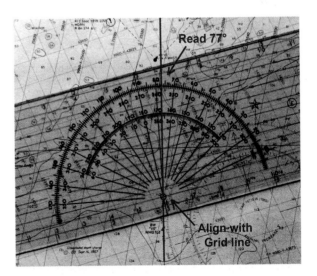

**Figure 12-22.** Using a course plotter to measure direction on a chart. Slide one edge or one of the parallel lines of the plotter along the course line plotted on the chart until the plotter's bull's-eye aligns with a line of latitude or longitude. Then read the course direction in degrees true from the appropriate scale on the plotter. (PHOTO BY RAY PAGES)

or "geographic" north, just like the meridian lines, whereas the inner ring is oriented toward magnetic north—like a compass needle—as discussed below and illustrated in Figure 12-25. Thus, by using a compass rose, you can measure course directions in degrees true or degrees magnetic.

There are several ways to do this, but the easiest is with *parallel rulers*, which are a pair of hinged, articulated rulers designed so that they remain parallel with one another at all times while swinging

## Using a Course Plotter

The **course plotter** is a protractor designed to measure courses and bearings on charts. It is particularly useful in small boats, since it needs little space. To use the plotter, first estimate the direction of the course line as outlined in the text on page 283.

### Measuring Courses and Bearings

To measure a course (or a bearing), place a long edge or a line of the plotter along the course line. Now, slide the plotter along this line until the bull's-eye is over a meridian of longitude or a parallel of latitude. Read the course from the proper scale of the plotter. Note that the plotter has separate dedicated angular scales for measuring latitude and longitude. The scales are very similar, so it's easy to make an error and select the wrong one. Also, the reading may reflect the opposite intended direction, so the reciprocal course must be calculated.

### Drawing a Course or Bearing from a Given Point

To draw a course or bearing from a given point, place the plotter in the general direction of the desired course or bearing. Next, place the point of your pencil on the point. Now, slide the plotter until one of its edges touches the point and the bull's-eye is on a meridian. Then, while keeping the plotter against your pencil and the bull's-eye over the meridian, slide the plotter up or down. When you have adjusted the plotter to the desired angle, draw the course or bearing line along its edge. Again, if your course or bearing is nearly north or south, use a parallel of latitude instead.

### Extending a Course Line

You can easily extend a course line beyond the end of the plotter. First, spread your dividers and place them on the course line. Next, place one edge of the plotter against the dividers. You can now slide the plotter along the points of the divider and draw the extended course line.

apart or together (Figure 12-23). Align one edge of the rulers with the course line, then **walk** the rulers to the nearest compass rose by swinging the leading ruler toward the rose to the full extent of the hinged arms, then anchoring the lead ruler while you swing the trailing ruler so as to catch up. Then repeat. In this fashion you advance by increments across the chart, while retaining the original course direction, until the edge of the lead ruler passes through the center of the compass rose. Then read the direction from the *outer edge* of the compass rose for *degrees true*, or from the *inner edge* for *degrees magnetic*. For more about this choice, see below.

The chief disadvantage of reading directions from a compass rose is that, when you're working in the cramped confines of a small boat, you rarely have room to spread out the entire chart flat. It's common to fold a chart so that the area of immediate interest is the part that shows, but it's also common to find that the nearest compass rose is *not* on the area of the chart that's showing. Therefore, major voyage planning is best done on a large table.

# Sources of Compass Error

Even if you read your compass correctly, the reading may be in error. Two sources of compass error are variation and deviation.

## VARIATION

The earth's core contains ferrous iron, and this creates a magnetic field around the earth, one end of which is the north magnetic pole. Unfortunately, the magnetic north pole is several hundred miles away from the geographic north pole (Figure 12-24), and it also changes gradually over time, wandering around the Canadian Arctic. (Fortunately, the change with time is predictable.) A compass needle points to the magnetic north pole, not the "true" north of the geographic north pole. The resultant error is called *variation*.

It should be noted that marine compasses do not really "point" in the way that hikers' compasses do. Beneath the card of a marine compass is a small

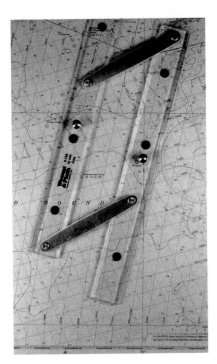
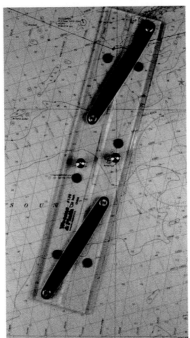

**Figure 12-23.** Using parallel rulers to measure direction. From left to right, a course line is "walked" by increments over to the nearest compass rose, from which direction can be measured in degrees true or magnetic as desired. (REPRINTED WITH PERMISSION FROM *THE WEEKEND NAVIGATOR* BY BOB SWEET)

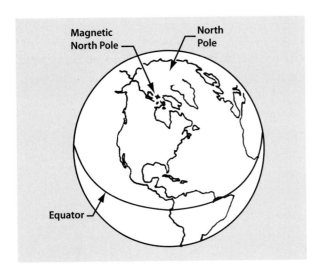

**Figure 12-24.** The relative positions of the true and magnetic north poles.

bar magnet that aligns itself with the earth's magnetic field and remains aligned as the vessel turns. The card to which the magnet is attached *appears* to turn, but in fact it is the vessel that does so, while the card retains its orientation with respect to magnetic north. Thus, the compass is said to "point" toward magnetic north.

Variation is either easterly or westerly—i.e., magnetic north is either east or west of true north, depending on where you are. You can find your local variation by referring to the compass rose printed on your nautical chart. In Figure 12-25, the amount of the variation was 4°15′W in 1985, and at that time it had an annual decrease of 8 minutes. Thus, if you had been using this compass rose in 2005, the local variation would have been 1°35′W rather than 4°15′W. Since variation changes from place to place, a chart with two or more compass roses may show a slightly different variation on each rose. Use the variation noted on the compass rose closest to your position.

Notice that the compass rose has two protractor scales (Figure 12-25). As mentioned above, the outer ring represents directions with respect to true north, whereas the inner ring represents directions with respect to magnetic north after taking variation into account. Thus, another way to calculate the local variation as of the year the chart was issued is to compare magnetic north on the inner ring with true north on the outer ring.

The innermost gradations on a compass rose have more historical interest than practical value for recreational boaters. They are **compass points**. Since there are thirty-two points on the compass, each point represents 11.25°. At one time a prac-

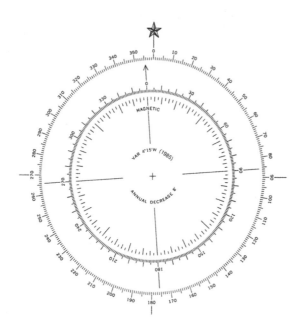

**Figure 12-25.** A compass rose. (REPRINTED WITH PERMISSION FROM *HOW TO READ A NAUTICAL CHART* BY NIGEL CALDER)

> **WARNING** Know the compass variation for your area of operation.

ticing navigator was expected to be able to **box the compass**—name all thirty-two points: north; north by east; north northeast; northeast by north; northeast; northeast by east; etc.

## DEVIATION

Variation is the same for all vessels in an area. **Deviation**, which is compass error caused by magnetic fields aboard the vessel, varies from one vessel to the next. The engine, steering wheel (including its spokes), dashboard instruments, electronic equipment, and bundles of wires may have magnetic fields. A radio speaker has an especially strong magnetic field. These local magnetic fields interact with the earth's magnetic field and the magnetic field of your compass and can cause the compass to deviate from magnetic north.

Some vessels do not cause deviation in their compasses. Outboard motors do not usually influence a compass because they are too far from it and

contain less iron than inboards or stern drives. If your compass is far enough from the electronic equipment and other magnetic fields aboard your vessel, it should have little deviation.

Since your boat carries its local magnetic fields with it, deviation does not change from place to place, but it will change with the heading of the boat. As mentioned above, if the deviation of your compass is no more than 2° or 3° on any heading, and the distance to be traveled on this heading is short, you can safely ignore it. If, however, you find larger deviations after running ranges as described above, you may want to construct a **deviation table** and then use the data in the table to correct your compass courses (Figure 12-26).

Alternatively, again as mentioned above, you can have your compass adjusted by a professional adjuster. In most cases an adjuster can remove most of the deviation from your compass by tuning the compass's internal adjustable magnets. From that point forward you will not need to worry about deviation unless you rewire the boat, install new electronics, relocate your backup anchor to a nearby locker, install a new engine, or make some other change that may affect your boat's magnetic field. At that point you should recheck your compass.

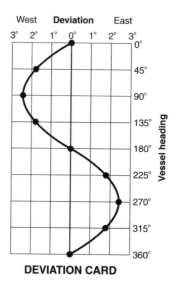

**DEVIATION CARD**

**Figure 12-26.** In theory, the deviation table you construct for your boat's steering compass could be plotted in a symmetrical curve like this one. In reality, your compass deviation may be highly skewed in one direction, east or west. (REPRINTED WITH PERMISSION FROM *BOATER'S BOWDITCH* BY RICHARD K. HUBBARD)

# Correcting a Compass Reading

We've seen how to measure the direction of a course line on a chart as an angle between the course and true north. This is the most convenient way to determine courses on a chart, but steering such a course by your compass without first adjusting it for variation and possibly for deviation can get you into trouble. If the local variation were 18°W and your boat's deviation on the chosen heading were 5°W, you'd be steering off at a 23° angle from the direction you really wanted to go. How can you tell in which compass direction to head your boat?

You can **correct** a compass reading to tell its direction with reference to true north. You can also **uncorrect** a true heading to derive the compass direction in which to head your boat.

## A HELPFUL MEMORY AID

Figure 12-27 shows a memory device that makes correcting or uncorrecting a simple procedure. The letters TVMDC stands for **T**rue, **V**ariation, **M**agnetic, **D**eviation, and **C**ompass. There are several ways to remember TVMDC; one is **T**ele-**V**isions **M**ake **D**ull **C**hildren.

Figure 12-27 has arrows on either side of the memory device. The ones on the left show that when uncorrecting a true heading, you add westerly variations and deviations and subtract easterly ones. The arrow on the right shows that when correcting a compass reading, you add easterly variations and deviations and subtract westerly ones.

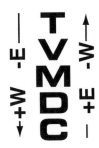

**Figure 12-27.** A memory device for correcting and uncorrecting compass readings.

To simplify, the memory device says, "Tele-Visions Make Dull Children, add Wonder." So, when converting from true headings to compass headings, add westerly variations and deviations. It follows, then, that you would subtract easterly ones. If going from compass to true, do the opposite. Add easterly variations and deviations, and subtract westerly ones. This means that all you need to know is **TVMDC + W** and you can work out the rest.

## SOME EXAMPLES

Let's try an example. In an area in which the variation is 5°W, you measure a course heading on your chart and find it is 047° true. Since you are uncorrecting your heading and converting from true to compass, first add the westerly variation:

$$047° + 5°W = 052°M$$

This is your magnetic heading; use an M to show it.

Then look at your deviation table and find that, for a course of 052°M, your deviation is 8°E. Now subtract the easterly deviation:

$$052°M - 8°E = 044°C$$

This is your compass heading; label it with a C (Figure 12-28).

Here's another example. Suppose the variation in the area where you are boating is 7°W and the compass reads 104°. According to your deviation table the deviation for a compass heading of 104° is 10°W. What is your true heading? This example asks you to correct a compass reading. This means that you will add easterly deviations and variations and subtract westerly ones:

$$104°C - 10°W = 094°M$$

Now subtract the westerly variation:

$$094°M - 7°W = 087°$$

Your true heading is 087°.

It is customary not to label a true course with a T; however, it is customary to label a magnetic course with an M. On some commercial charts, courses in channels are preprinted, and given in magnetic. On many commercially produced charts, directions are given in magnetic. Thus, the mariner can, after dealing with deviation, simply steer the compass course noted on the chart. This works well for short trips, but for longer voyages, convert magnetic to true.

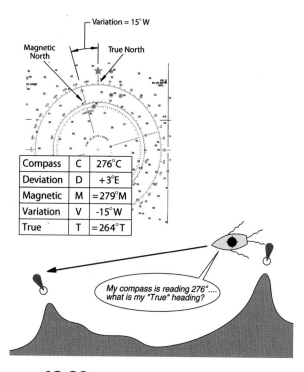

| Compass | C | 276°C |
|---|---|---|
| Deviation | D | +3°E |
| Magnetic | M | =279°M |
| Variation | V | -15°W |
| True | T | =264°T |

*My compass is reading 276°.... what is my "True" heading?*

**Figure 12-28.** Deriving a true course from a compass reading. (REPRINTED WITH PERMISSION FROM *BOATER'S BOWDITCH* BY RICHARD K. HUBBARD)

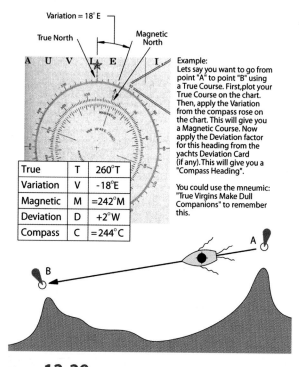

| True | T | 260°T |
|---|---|---|
| Variation | V | -18°E |
| Magnetic | M | =242°M |
| Deviation | D | +2°W |
| Compass | C | =244°C |

**Example:**
Lets say you want to go from point "A" to point "B" using a True Course. First, plot your True Course on the chart. Then, apply the Variation from the compass rose on the chart. This will give you a Magnetic Course. Now apply the Deviation factor for this heading from the yachts Deviation Card (if any). This will give you a "Compass Heading".

You could use the mneumic: "True Virgins Make Dull Companions" to remember this.

**Figure 12-29.** Deriving a compass heading to steer from a true course. (REPRINTED WITH PERMISSION FROM *BOATER'S BOWDITCH* BY RICHARD K. HUBBARD)

# Finding Your Position

The most common navigation problem is pinpointing your position. There are several compelling reasons for knowing where you are. For one, it's the first and most critical step in figuring out how to get where you want to go. Second, you can't be assured of avoiding ledges and other hazards unless you know your position relative to their charted locations. Otherwise, you would just be blundering around out there and trusting to luck. Third, knowing where you are is critical for managing your fuel supply and ensuring that you don't run out before you can refuel. And finally, in the event of an emergency, you need to be able to tell the Coast Guard or a towboat operator where you are.

A *line of position* (LOP) is a line that you draw on a chart such that it passes through your location. A single LOP does not tell you where you are. All you know is that you are somewhere along that line. **Crossing** two lines of position as in Figure 12-30, however, tells you where you are with some degree of certainty; you are at their intersection. You have made a *fix* and have determined your position. You can also get a fix by passing close aboard a charted object such as an aid to navigation. A buoy is not usually used to determine a fix, since it may be

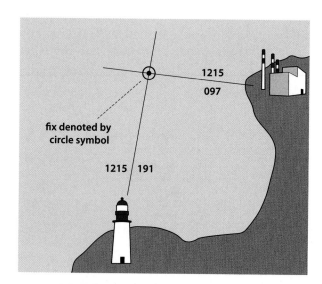

**Figure 12-30.** Position by crossed bearings on two landmarks.

off-station, but a buoy works well enough when precision is not critical, or when the charted hazard it marks is clearly visible and confirms its position, or when no fixed ATON or other landmark is available.

Since LOPs are the key to fixing your position, you need to know how to obtain an LOP. There are several ways.

## Range LOPs

As mentioned in Chapter 7, a **range** offers one way to determine an LOP, and a very precise one at that. If you can line up two charted objects, you can draw a line through the objects toward your vessel (Figure 12-31). You are somewhere along this line, though just where, you can't know without a second LOP. In most coastal waters, opportunities for ranges abound. Line up a daybeacon in front of a church spire, or a prominent half-tide rock in front of the seaward end of a bold headland, or the end of an island in front of a radio tower on the distant mainland. As long as both objects are charted, they qualify as range markers.

Although you may not know where you are from a single LOP, you now know where you are not!

## Bearing LOPs

You will often get your LOPs with a magnetic compass. Using either a handheld bearing compass (Figure 12-32) or the boat's steering compass, select two or more identifiable landmarks or aids to navigation that appear on the chart. Three charted

marks, and thus three LOPs, are preferable to two. If you must use only two marks, select them so that the angle between them, as seen from your position, is as close to 90° as possible.

Take the readings by pointing your handheld compass at each mark in turn. The direction to a mark is its *bearing*. If using your vessel's compass, head your vessel toward each mark and note your compass heading, which is also the bearing to the object.

After you have determined the bearings of two or more marks, the next step is to correct them. If using a handheld bearing compass, assume that its deviation is zero. If using your boat's compass, read the deviation from your deviation table. In either case, determine variation from the compass rose on your chart.

Suppose that at 1215 you took bearings on a tank and a monument by using your boat's compass (refer back to Figure 12-30). Suppose, also, that variation for the area is 12°E, the bearing to the tank is 088°C, and the bearing to the monument is 176°C.

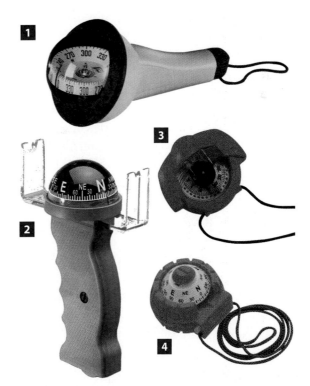

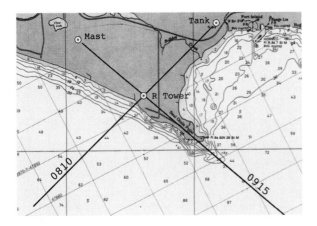

**Figure 12-31.** A range line, obtained when any two charted objects are in line from your position, makes a perfect LOP. Neither compass bearings nor compass correction is necessary. (REPRINTED WITH PERMISSION FROM *BOATER'S BOWDITCH* BY RICHARD K. HUBBARD)

**Figure 12-32.** A selection of hand bearing compasses. **1.** A Plastimo hand bearing compass that can be fix-mounted as well. **2.** A Davis model. **3.** A Plastimo "hockey puck" model. **4.** A Ritchie model for a small boat. (REPRINTED WITH PERMISSION FROM *THE WEEKEND NAVIGATOR* BY BOB SWEET)

Let's also suppose that your deviation table shows that for a heading of 088°C the deviation is 3°W, and for a compass heading of 176°C it is 3°E.

The first step is to correct each compass bearing to a true bearing:

$$088°C - 3°W = 085°M$$

$$085°M + 12°E = 097°$$

The bearing of 176°C must also be corrected:

$$176°C + 3°E = 179°M$$

$$179°M + 12°E = 191°$$

After determining the true directions of the two charted marks, use your parallel rulers and a compass rose to determine where to draw the LOPs. To draw the first LOP, place one edge of the ruler so it passes through the center of the rose and 097° on the outermost scale. Now, walk the ruler to the tank and draw a line back toward your position.

Use the same method to draw the LOP from the monument. Your position is at the point where the two lines cross. This is your fix, and you should label it with a dot with a circle around it. Label the LOPs with the time above the bearing lines and the directions below the lines, as shown in Figure 12-30.

When drawing a line of position, do not run it through the charted mark. Instead, begin seaward of the mark and make the line long enough that it passes through your position. At some later time, you may wish to erase the line. If the LOP runs through the mark, you may destroy it when you erase the LOP.

**CHECK YOUR WORK.** Make an estimate to check your work. From your original sighting, you knew that the tank was in an easterly direction. It had a bearing of 088°C. That means that you are west of the tank and looking east, which is 090°. The true direction of the tank from your position is 097°, which is almost east.

In a similar manner, south is 180°. You observed the monument to be at 176°C, which means you are north of the monument and looking south toward it. The true direction of the monument from your position is 191°, which is a southerly direction.

If you had taken bearings on three marks, the three LOPs would, ideally, cross at a single point. In reality, this seldom happens. More often the intersections of the three lines form a small triangle, which navigators call a **cocked hat** (Figure 12-33). The smaller the triangle, the more exact your position is, since you assume that you are somewhere within the area of the triangle.

Remember, a fix obtained by this method is NOT where you are now if your vessel is moving. It is where you were when you took the sightings. In a fast boat, that could be "way back there."

## Other LOPs

It should be apparent by this time that a range LOP is both simpler and more precise than a bearing LOP. Use range LOPs whenever possible.

There are, in addition, other possible ways of getting LOPs. One is to measure your distance from a charted object and use that to create a **circle of position** (COP). The object will be the center of the circle, and the measured distance will be the radius. It is possible, for example, to measure your distance off a lighthouse or bold headland of known height by measuring the vertical angle of the object with a sextant. You can also, sometimes, get a curve of position from a depth contour where the depth changes rapidly from place to place. Match the depth measured by your depth sounder with, say, the 30-foot depth contour on the chart (making due allowance for tide), and you can be reasonably confident of being somewhere over or near that local contour. Cross that curve of position with an

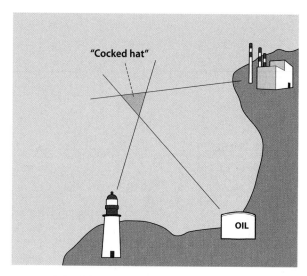

**Figure 12-33.** A "cocked hat" formed by three lines of position.

LOP from another source, and you get an estimated position. Other techniques are possible too, and you can learn more about this in more advanced Coast Guard Auxiliary courses (see www.cgaux.org).

## COMMON CONVENTIONS

When writing bearings on a line of position or a course line, write them using three digits, as in Figure 12-30. In this way, you will not confuse them with units of time or speed. Always write time with four digits using a 24-hour clock. For example, noon is 1200, 9:45 a.m. is 0945, and 3:20 p.m. is 1520.

**Figure 12-34.** Some marine binoculars offer a built-in bearing compass that displays in the bottom of the magnified image (bottom). (COURTESY STEINER; REPRINTED WITH PERMISSION FROM *THE WEEKEND NAVIGATOR* BY BOB SWEET)

Write speed with two digits. Thus, even if you do not identify the units of measure on an LOP or course line, you know what each is. A four-digit number is time, a three-digit number is direction, and a two-digit number is speed. Use leading zeros where necessary to bring the measures to their two-, three-, or four-digit forms.

# Speed-Time-Distance

Suppose you plan to make a fishing trip to a distant point. How long will it take you to get there? You need a measure of your boat's speed and the distance to the fishing hole. When you know any two of these variables—speed, time, or distance—you can calculate the third.

## MEASURING SPEED

Measuring a boat's speed is harder than it sounds. You can install a speedometer on a small boat, but this instrument is not especially accurate (Figure 12-35). Furthermore, it gives measures of speed through the water, and what you need is speed over the bottom, which may differ from speed through the water due to the effects of wind and current. This is one of the many navigation tasks that is performed far more simply and with greater accuracy and reliability by GPS, as we'll see below. But you should know how to work through these problems without GPS.

### Binocular

Most authorities recommend a 7 x 50 binocular, which magnifies objects seven times. In a pitching and rolling boat, it is difficult to steady a binocular stronger than 7 x 50 on an object, although there are binoculars with a stabilizing feature that will assist in steadying the image. The diameters of a 7 x 50 binocular's front (objective) lenses are 50 mm, which is important for nighttime use, since a diameter of less than 50 mm would not admit enough light for good vision in dim light.

Many boaters prefer a binocular with a built-in compass that shows in the bottom of the field of view (Figure 12-34, bottom). These offer a convenient and accurate way to take bearings on landmarks and ATONs, essentially replacing the hand bearing compass.

**Figure 12-35.** A powerboat instrument panel with speedometer display. (PHOTO BY NORMA LOCOCO)

| | Speed Trial Tabulation Over Measured Mile | | | | |
|---|---|---|---|---|---|
| | **N - S** | | **S - N** | | **Average Speed** |
| **RPM** | **Time** | **Speed** | **Time** | **Speed** | |
| 800 | 6m 47s | 8.85 | 8m 32s | 7.03 | 7.94 |
| 1000 | 5m 46s | 10.41 | 7m 31s | 7.98 | 9.20 |
| 1200 | 5m 01s | 11.96 | 6m 46s | 8.87 | 10.42 |
| 1400 | 4m 28s | 13.43 | 6m 13s | 9.65 | 11.54 |
| 1600 | 4m 03s | 14.82 | 5m 47s | 10.38 | 12.60 |
| 1800 | 3m 42s | 16.22 | 5m 01s | 11.96 | 14.09 |
| 2000 | 3m 31s | 17.06 | 4m 53s | 12.29 | 14.68 |
| 2200 | 3m 24s | 17.64 | 4m 41s | 12.81 | 15.23 |

**Figure 12-36.** A table of engine speed versus boat speed.

## The Speed Table

Most small boats have **tachometers**, which measure the speed of your boat's engine in revolutions per minute (rpm). You can use this to construct a **speed curve** or **speed table** to tell your boat's speed through the water at various engine speeds (Figure 12-36).

To make a speed table, find two charted points about a mile apart in navigable waters (two navigation buoys would do, as it won't matter much for these purposes if one or both are slightly off-station), and measure the charted distance between them. If you measure the distance in statute miles, the speed table you construct will be in miles per hour (mph). If you use nautical miles, it will be in knots.

Run the course between the two measured points, and then reverse course, timing your speed each way with a stopwatch. Run the course both ways at the same engine speed to cancel the effects of wind and current. Now, compute your speed in each direction and average the the two speeds. **Do not average times to compute the speed.**

Do this for a variety of engine speeds, averaging the two vessel speeds at each engine speed, and then use these averages to construct a speed table like the one shown in Figure 12-36. Remember, though, that this is your speed through the water, meaning that it is not corrected for wind and most especially not for current. If your speed through the water is 15 knots and you're heading downstream in a 5-knot current, your speed over ground is 20 knots, but if you turn around and head upstream, your speed over ground will fall to 10 knots. To derive speed over ground from speed through the water, you need to know what the current is doing. Later, in our discussion of GPS, you will see an easier method.

## COMPUTING TIME, SPEED, OR DISTANCE

If you know two of the time-speed-distance variables, you can compute the other one. For example, if you travel two hours at 60 statute miles per hour, how far have you gone? You have gone:

$$2 \times 60 = 120 \text{ statute miles}$$

In this formula, time is in hours, speed in statute miles per hour, and distance in statute miles. The formula used was:

$$\text{Distance} = \text{Speed} \times \text{Time}$$
$$\text{or } D = S \times T$$

## Computing Distance

In navigating, we use the same formula, but measure time in minutes, speed in knots or nautical miles per hour, and distance in nautical miles.

Since time is expressed in minutes, it has been multiplied by 60. So we must do the same to the other side of the equation; thus, the formula becomes:

$$60D = S \times T$$
$$\text{or } D = (S \times T) \div 60 \quad (1)$$

## Computing Speed or Time

If you remember your algebra, you can use formula 1, above, to derive two others:

$$T = 60D \div S \quad (2)$$
$$S = 60D \div T \quad (3)$$

Formulas 1, 2, and 3 give you a means of computing distance, time, or speed. Use formula 3 to build your speed table. Again, if you remember your algebra, you need only memorize formula 1 to compute speed, time, or distance.

## Some Examples

Suppose that you drive your boat at a speed of 20 knots for 12 minutes. How far have you gone?

$$D = (S \times T) \div 60$$
$$\text{or } D = (20 \times 12) \div 60$$
$$D = 240 \div 60$$
$$\text{and } D = 4 \text{ nautical miles}$$

How long does it take to travel 4 nautical miles at a speed of 20 knots?

$$T = 60D \div S$$
$$T = (60 \times 4) \div 20$$
$$T = 240 \div 20$$
$$T = 12 \text{ minutes}$$

How fast are you going if you travel 4 nautical miles in 12 minutes?

$$S = 60D \div T$$
$$S = (60 \times 4) \div 12$$
$$S = 240 \div 12$$
$$S = 20 \text{ knots}$$

## An Alternate Method

A graphic representation of the information in the formulas is shown in Figure 12-37. To use this illustration, cover the answer you need. The formula for the answer remains uncovered. For example, if you want to compute speed, cover the S. The formula is 60 x D ÷ T. To find time, cover the T. The formula is 60 x D ÷ by S. To find the distance traveled, cover the 60 x D. You have S and T left. Distance equals S x T. Divide the result by 60.

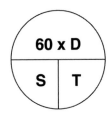

**Figure 12-37.** Speed, time, and distance relationships.

# Dead Reckoning

Navigators plan their voyages on paper charts using *dead reckoning* (DR). It is likely that the term was originally "deduced reckoning," which may have been abbreviated "ded reckoning" and later spelled "dead reckoning." Whatever the origin of the term, DR is used to plot cruises of 30 minutes or more.

A DR plot is a drawing on a chart of the courses you intend to follow (Figure 12-38), and includes notations of directions, intended speed, and DR positions at course changes and at 30-minute intervals. Intended speed is written below the line in two-digit form.

## DRAWING A DR PLOT

Begin your DR plot at a known position or from your last known fix. The mouth of a harbor, an inlet, or a fixed aid to navigation is a good place to begin. Mark it on your course line with a dot and a full circle and the intended departure time.

If there are no obstructions between where you begin your plot and where you intend to go, you can draw a straight line between the two. More often, though, there will be obstructions or hazards that will cause you to travel an irregular course. Use the plotting tools to draw your intended course as a series of straight lines between your turning

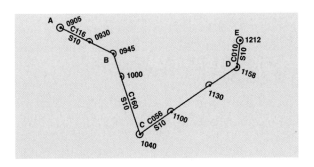

**Figure 12-38.** A typical DR plot.

points. If possible, select turning points where there are suitable landmarks or aids to navigation.

After drawing the legs of your course line, measure their true directions using a course plotter or parallel rulers. Write these directions above the line for each leg using the three-digit form. If you wish, precede each direction with a C (to mean "course"). If you want to add compass directions to the course plot, follow them with a C for "compass."

Make your measurements and calculations carefully. In navigating, neatness and accuracy are essential, and small errors tend to be cumulative.

Now, use the dividers and the latitude scale to measure the lengths of the course legs. Using the part of the scale that is nearest to the midlatitude of each leg, measure carefully to the nearest tenth of a nautical mile.

As you travel over your planned course, you may be able to obtain intermediate fixes from ranges and bearings. Whenever you get the chance, you should do so. If you find this means that your DR course is different from your "real" course, you are most likely being set off course by wind or current. Make the necessary adjustments to your DR plot to compensate for these influences. The farther you travel between fixes, the less accurate your DR plot will become, and the less confidence you can place in it.

## A SAMPLE COURSE

Let's see how this works in practice. In Figure 12-38, the course has four legs. The distance in nautical miles from point A to B is 6.6; from B to C, 9.2; from C to D, 13.0; and from D to E, 2.4.

### Labeling a DR Plot

Since you know where you are at point A, you have a fix. Note this by a dot with a circle around it. A DR position is denoted by a dot with a half-circle around it, and each position is marked with the time.

Now estimate the speed that you intend to use on each leg of your cruise. Write the number below the course line using the two-digit form. You can precede the speeds with an S for "speed." A course line of 116° at a speed of 10 knots would look like:

C116

S10

If you desire to add compass direction to the plot, using a variation of 9°W and a deviation of 0°, it would look like this:

C116     C125C

S10

## Making the Computations

Using the formula T = 60D ÷ S, compute the time needed to get from your departure to your first turning point at your intended speed. Remember, time is always in minutes, rounded off to the nearest whole minute, distance is usually in nautical miles and tenths of a mile, and speed is in knots.

If operating on the Great Lakes, rivers, or other bodies of water where charted distances are in statute miles, speed is in miles per hour. This is perfectly acceptable as long as you do not mix units. Use statute miles and miles per hour or nautical miles and knots. Also, if using statute miles, do not use latitude scales for measuring distances.

As shown in Figure 12-38, you expect your speed on each leg to be 10 knots. The computed times for the four legs are, therefore, 39.6, 55.2, 78.0, and 14.4 minutes. Rounded off, they are 40, 55, 78, and 14 minutes.

After calculating the time that should elapse between your departure and your arrival at the first turning point, add it to your departure time. If you start from point A at 0905, your estimated time of arrival (ETA) at point B will be 40 minutes later, or 0945. Since point B will be a DR position (unless you can fix your position with bearings, ranges, or other means when you arrive there), mark it with a dot and a half-circle. Label this point 0945.

## Compute Each Half-Hour

**Note:** The choice of a 30-minute plotting interval in this illustration is arbitrary. For very slow-moving boats well away from hazards to navigation, 60 minutes might well be appropriate. Operators of fast boats might use a 15-minute interval. DR positions should also be plotted at the time of each course or speed change, and a new DR plot should be started whenever a position fix is obtained.

In our example, your trip to the first turn will include the start of a new half-hour, so calculate your predicted position for that time and plot it on your course line. Mark it with a dot and a half-circle. In this case, use the formula:

$$D = (S \times T) \div 60.$$

The question is, "Where will you be at 0930?" Applying the formula, you find that you will have traveled 4.2 miles. Using the dividers, place a dot and a half-circle at a point 4.2 miles from point A along your DR course line, and label this 0930.

Since you are going to show your predicted position each half-hour, you need to know where you will be at 1000. This is 15 minutes after you pass point B. In that 15 minutes you will travel 2.5 miles. Mark this point with a dot and a half-circle.

If all goes exactly according to predictions, you will arrive at point C at 1040, point D at 1158, and point E at 1212. In reality, of course, the vagaries of wind, tide, waves, and perhaps your own inconsistent steering and throttle control will cause your actual course line, speed, and distances covered to differ from those predicted. Compensating for these vagaries is a good part of the art of traditional piloting. In good visibility and safe waters, the differences won't matter much, but when visibility is poor or there are hazards on either side of your intended track, you'll want to steer as straight as possible, maintain as steady a speed as possible, keep your DR legs between charted landmarks and navigation buoys (preferably ones that are surrounded by safe water and that have easily recognized light or sound signals) as short as possible, and adjust your DR courses for current and leeway to the extent possible.

Most coastal currents are the result of tides, so we'll look at tides next. There are two ways to compensate for a tidal current: either predict what it will be ahead of time and adjust your DR course to cancel the expected influence, or note to what extent your predicted DR position varies from your next fix, and apply that difference to subsequent legs of the trip. Again, a GPS receiver takes all the guesswork out of this process, as we'll see below.

# Tides

**Tides** are the regular rise and fall of coastal waters caused by the gravitational attractions of the moon and sun. The sun dwarfs the moon but is 370 times

more distant, so its effect is subordinate to the moon's. Their effects are additive when both are in line with the earth—that is, at new moon, when the moon is between the sun and earth; and at full moon, when the moon is on the side of the earth opposite the sun. At those times most coastal areas experience the run of higher high tides and lower low tides known as *spring tides*. When the moon is at right angles from the sun—i.e., in its first and third quarters—the sun partially cancels the gravitational attraction of the moon, and we experience the run of lower high tides and higher low tides known as *neap tides* (Figure 12-39).

Tides also vary greatly from place to place, due to complex interactions of local water depths, embayments, and other factors. In some places, such as Alaska and the Bay of Fundy, the mean range of the tides is greater than 30 feet. In others—for example, the Chesapeake Bay—it may be as little as 6 inches.

On the Atlantic Coast there are two high tides and two low tides in each **tidal day** of about 24 hours and 50 minutes. (The tidal day is 50 minutes longer than the solar day because the moon completes about 12.5° of its orbit each solar day, which means that a given spot on the earth's surface must complete slightly more than a full revolution to "catch up" with the moon.) This is a *semidiurnal tide* (Figure 12-40). Both high waters are about equal in height, as are the low waters.

**Figure 12-39.** The spring tide–neap tide cycle. At new moon and again at full moon, the gravitational forces of the moon and sun are additive, and we experience the higher high tides and lower low tides known as spring tides. During the first and third quarters of the moon, the effects of the sun and moon partially cancel each other, and we experience the lesser tides known as neap tides. (REPRINTED WITH PERMISSION FROM *THE WEEKEND NAVIGATOR* BY BOB SWEET)

On the Pacific Coast, there are also two sets of tides each day, but one high tide is higher than the other, and one low tide is lower than the other. Such tides are called *mixed tides*. Along the Gulf Coast and in the Great Lakes, the tides are *diurnal*, with just one high and one low tide each day (Figure 12-41).

Obviously, mariners need some way of knowing how much water is under their keels at any particular time. To meet this demand, the NOS generates and updates tide tables for all of North America. The NOS no longer publishes these tide tables in book form, but they are available from

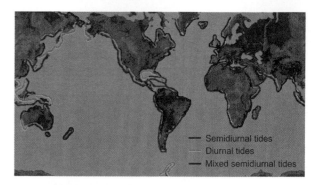

**Figure 12-41.** Areas of the world with semidiurnal, mixed, and diurnal tides. (REPRINTED WITH PERMISSION FROM *THE WEEKEND NAVIGATOR* BY BOB SWEET)

commercial sources and are widely reprinted in smaller editions for local waters.

The datum used on U.S. charts for heights of objects on land and over water is *mean high water* (MHW). This is the average (mean) level of all high tides, and to get this average, all unusual conditions such as storms are excluded. The clearances for bridges that appear on charts are the distances from the water's surface at mean high water to the lowest clearance under the bridge (worst case). Remember, this is the clearance at **mean high water**.

In the past, the datum for charted water depths differed according to the type of tides in an area. On the Gulf Coast and the Great Lakes, where there is only one low tide each day, and on the East Coast, where the two low waters each day are approximately equal, the datum was *mean low water* (MLW). On the Pacific Coast, where the heights of the two low waters each day are unequal, the datum was (and is) the average of the lower of the two. This datum is called *mean lower low water* (MLLW), and all U.S. charts are incorporating it in their new editions. Although the name of the chart datum has changed, indicated water depths will remain the same. On the East and Gulf coasts and the Great Lakes, MLLW will be the average of all low waters. On the Pacific Coast, only the lower of the two daily low waters will be averaged, as in the past. No matter where you are, you should bear

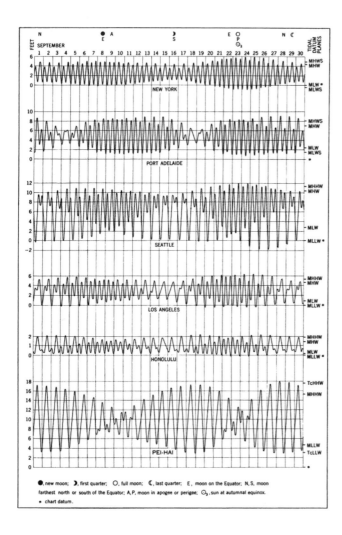

**Figure 12-40.** Tidal variations over 3½ weeks for selected ports around the world. The spring tide–neap tide cycles are clearly visible. New York shows a semidiurnal tide. The other ports show mixed tides to various degrees; there are two highs and two lows in each lunar day, but one of the highs is substantially higher than the other, and one of the lows is lower. (REPRINTED WITH PERMISSION FROM *HOW TO READ A NAUTICAL CHART* BY NIGEL CALDER)

**WARNING** *Remember that datums are averages. At times there will be less vertical clearance under bridges and less water depth over shallows than shown on your chart.*

in mind that actual water depths are likely to be less than charted depths on a spring low tide, and actual vertical clearances under bridges are likely to be less than charted clearances on a spring high tide.

## TIDE TABLES

As mentioned, the NOS compiles data showing the times and heights of predicted tides for the Atlantic, Gulf, and Pacific coasts and for tidal rivers. Local tables made from these data are published in newspapers and are usually available from boating suppliers.

You can also access these data from NOS on the Internet (www.oceanservice.noaa.gov). From the home page, select Tides and Currents, which will guide you through the tide prediction program. Alternatively, go to http://tidesandcurrents.noaa.gov, which will guide you to the NOS's tide predictions as well as Great Lakes water levels and other NOAA products.

Although the NOS data and the tables made from them are dependable, do not follow them unthinkingly. Local conditions such as storms, wind direction and strength, and barometric pressure affect tidal levels significantly.

The depths of water shown on your chart are averages, with some low tides being higher than the charted depths and some being lower. Tide tables tell you when to expect the next high or low tide, and also how much higher or lower than the mean the tide is *predicted* to be. Add or subtract this difference to the charted depth of the water to find out how much water *may* be under your keel at the next high or low tide. While doing so, don't forget to consider the amount of water your boat **draws**, or the distance your boat extends beneath the water's surface (Figure 12-42).

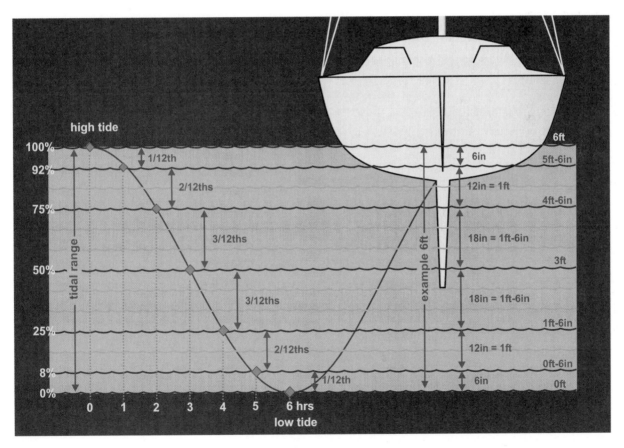

**Figure 12-42.** You can use the Rule of Twelfths to estimate the height of tide at a given place and time. The rule assumes that, from the most recent low (or high) tide, the tide rises (or falls) one-twelfth of its range in the first one-sixth of its rise, two-twelfths in the second sixth, three-twelfths in the third sixth, three-twelfths in the fourth sixth, two-twelfths in the fifth sixth, and one-twelfth in the final sixth. In areas of semidiurnal tide, each sixth of tidal rise or fall is roughly 1 hour. Once you obtain the local height of tide, apply it to the charted depth to obtain a working estimate of actual depth at the time of interest. (REPRINTED WITH PERMISSION FROM *THE WEEKEND NAVIGATOR* BY BOB SWEET)

There are no tide tables for western rivers. NOS *Nautical Chart Catalog 4* lists available bulletins of lake and river pool levels by month, however, and some newspapers give pool levels daily. River pools are the lakes formed by dams.

## TIDAL CURRENTS

In bays, estuaries, gulfs, and other coastal areas with substantial tides, it stands to reason that there must be substantial horizontal movements of water in and out with the tides, and indeed this is true. Where these tidal currents are weak relative to the speed of your boat, you can probably ignore them, but where they are substantial, they must be taken into account. Otherwise, your course over ground will diverge widely from your intended course, and you could navigate your boat into danger. We have already touched upon the two ways of compensating for tidal currents. The first is to observe how your course is being influenced, and counter that effect as you go along. The second is to obtain a prediction of the tidal current and apply a counteracting course adjustment from the moment you begin the affected leg or legs of your journey. The latter approach requires *Tidal Current Tables*, which, like the *Tide Tables*, are prepared but no longer printed by the NOS. These are available from commercial publishers, and in smaller local editions from marine suppliers, or by visiting http://tidesandcurrents.noaa.gov.

# Electronic Navigation

One of the most exciting developments to impact marine navigation is the advent of stand-alone electronic instruments to aid navigation. This movement started during World War II with the invention and implementation of loran (**lo**ng **ra**nge **n**avigation). This system, which was introduced in Chapter 7, enabled vessels and aircraft to fix their positions without reference to surrounding landmarks or celestial bodies and with a precision and accuracy never before attained. After the war, loran became the primary electronic tool for marine coastal navigation. As receiver costs were lowered, the system became attractive to recreational boaters and soon found widespread usage.

With the invention and deployment of GPS (global positioning system), loran has largely been superseded on recreational boats. The U.S. government sees loran as a worthy backup for GPS, however, and intends to keep it usable for some time.

Next in the evolution of electronic navigation came GPS, which became fully functional in March 1994 and has become the navigational tool of choice in the recreational and commercial boating community. GPS receivers continue to improve, adding more and more exciting features and at costs well within the means of most boaters.

There are other electronic navigation tools that won't be covered here, including **radar** (for seeing objects in poor visibility) and **depth sounders** (for plotting assistance when used with charts showing water depths).

Loran and GPS share one central feature in that both systems rely on the establishment of waypoints. Each *waypoint* is a pair of coordinates describing a unique location on the globe—usually either a place we want to go to or come from, or a place we want to be sure to avoid. Both systems enable the mariner to establish routes to follow by the use of one or more waypoints in sequence.

These waypoints are entered into the receiver (and also on the chart). The receiver will then tell the crew the bearing and distance to the waypoint, whether or not you are on course for the waypoint (and what to do to get back on course), your speed over the ground, your ETA, and when you have arrived without doing a calculation.

The one thing neither system will do is tell you what is between you and each waypoint, unless your receiver has a built-in moving map. There may be some very hard stuff in your path, such as rocks, and this is where a chart is needed. To keep good water under your keel at all times, lay out your course, with its waypoints, on the paper chart first, and then transfer the waypoint information into your receiver. Now you can have a pleasant voyage.

## LORAN

Loran is a land-based system that uses radio signals between land-based antennas and shipboard receivers. The land antennas are located mostly along shorelines and are grouped in clusters called **chains**, each chain consisting of one **master** and one or more **slave** antennas. A four-digit **group repetition interval** (GRI) number and a location name, such as Southeast U.S. GRI #7980, identifies each chain. There are nine chains in the United States and Canada.

Each master and slave station broadcasts a precisely timed signal, which is received by the onboard receiver. Since each slave broadcasting station sends its signal at a different time from the master station, each signal arrives at a different time. It is this difference in arrival time that allows the receiver to "locate" just where it is. In other words, each signal presents an LOP from that station to the onboard receiver. As we learned earlier, we need more than one LOP to arrive at a fix, and that is what the multiple loran signals provide. Where they cross identifies the fix.

To better enable the boater to establish this fix, some charts—usually of the 1:80,000 scale—are overprinted with a loran grid. The grid consists of intersecting curves that create small, numbered boxes, and the loran signal from the shore stations is coded with numbers that will match the correct box. The onboard receiver tells which box you are in, thus establishing your fix, or position.

The loran receiver will also show your position using Lat/Lo coordinates. You can then transfer these coordinates to the chart by drawing lines on the chart from the side and bottom Lat/Lo numbers until the two lines cross—and there you are! This method may be used instead of the one above, or in conjunction, as a confirmation.

There are several negative features of loran that recreational boaters should know. First, the loran signal is similar to an AM radio, and we all know what happens to reception from AM radios when thunderstorms are in the vicinity. The signal degrades when you might need it most—in poor weather—and the system may become unreliable or unusable.

Second, not all areas of the world have loran coverage. Indeed, even those that do, such as the U.S. coasts, sometimes have holes in the coverage where reception is not good enough for use. Fortunately, these holes tend to remain the same, so that boaters can quickly learn how their local area coverage works or doesn't work.

Third, loran signals tend to distort as they pass over land, which reduces the accuracy of the fix. Most loran receivers will alert the boater when the signal has degraded enough to make use of the information dangerous.

## GPS

GPS is *everywhere!* This satellite-based system provides extremely accurate navigational information from any place on the globe that has an unobstructed view of the heavens. (But don't expect it to work in the deep valleys of West Virginia!)

There are twenty-four orbiting satellites (and up to five spares) in the system, and they are arranged and programmed to provide continuous worldwide coverage at any time, day or night, no matter what the weather. Your receiver will tell you what satellites it is currently using (the satellites being used change as their usefulness increases and decreases), and where they are in your sky (Figure 12-43).

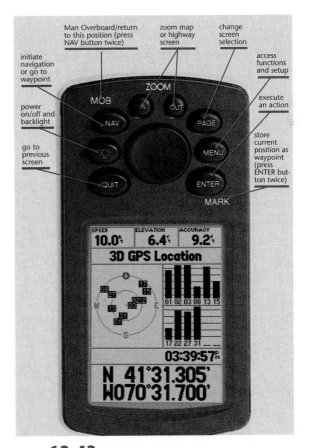

**Figure 12-43.** A handheld GPS receiver and its features.
(REPRINTED WITH PERMISSION FROM *USING GPS: A CAPTAIN'S QUICK GUIDE* BY BOB SWEET)

The system is managed by the U.S. Department of Defense. Prior to May 1, 2000, the system was randomly degraded (called Selected Availability, or SA) to keep enemies of the United States from using our own system to very accurately target their missiles. Since that date, SA is no longer in use. The end result is a public navigational system that is accurate to within 15 meters (49.2 feet) or less 95% of the time. (There is a military-only version that is even more accurate.)

During the period when SA was used, another system, **Differential GPS** (DGPS), was developed and deployed, mostly along the U.S. coasts and the shores of the Great Lakes. DGPS is a land-based supplement to GPS that effectively corrected the errors introduced by SA. This was necessary to provide continuously accurate information around harbors and inlets, where SA degraded the information enough to become dangerous.

DGPS requires a second receiver on the vessel, but it provides super-accurate (errors of less than 5 meters or 16.4 feet) information where it is needed the most—around the hard stuff. Thus, it remains useful even after the termination of SA.

GPS uses the time reception differences between several satellites and the receiver to establish multiple LOPs and, thus, an electronic fix. Usually, there are at least five and as many as twelve usable satellites available at any given time, and the receiver constantly chooses the most accurate satellites to use.

GPS receivers may be permanently installed or handheld. While permanently mounted receivers are likely to have more features and be somewhat easier to operate, the less expensive, lightweight receivers are usually just as accurate. Some of the handheld receivers are extremely feature-rich, and the principle of "more features equal more money" is very much the case. Just know that a unit with many features carries the downside of operational complexity, so the learning curve may be long and only constant practice will enable the operator to retain the skills.

The one operational necessity often overlooked by the user is that the datum used in your GPS receiver must match the datum on your chart. If there is a mismatch, the location you mark on your chart may be inaccurate. It is usually easier to change the datum in your GPS to match that of the chart than to buy new charts.

Simple but very accurate GPS receivers are priced in the $100 to $150 range. These will satisfy the needs, though perhaps not all the wants, of most boaters.

## WAAS

There is another GPS enhancement called the **wide area augmentation system** (WAAS), in which geostationary satellites "parked" over each ocean transmit corrections to GPS signals. Deployed throughout the United States, WAAS has become a standard part of the GPS system. Its usage will ultimately extend to much of Canada and Mexico.

Access to WAAS requires that your GPS receiver be WAAS capable, as most newer units are. The stated horizontal accuracy with WAAS is 2.5 meters or 8.2 feet.

## ELECTRONIC CHARTING

The "moving map" display in a basic GPS receiver is usually in black and white and may be difficult to read due to the size of the screen. In the simplest units, such a map includes only the buoys and other waypoints that you have programmed into the receiver yourself. More sophisticated units, called **chartplotters**, have the capability of storing and displaying multiple color charts in various scales, and these units use their GPS capability to show your real-time location on the displayed chart (Figure 12-44). (There are also chartplotters that lack an in-built GPS receiver and instead accept GPS input from an independent receiver.) Most chartplotters have small, waterproof screens that are sometimes difficult to view in direct sunlight, but in some cases these can be connected with a laptop computer that offers a larger display. Alternatively, you can purchase electronic charts and navigation software for your laptop computer, and run a cable from your GPS receiver to the laptop. Virtually all marine electronic devices can be integrated and displayed on a common screen—usually a large radar screen.

With a chartplotter or laptop-GPS package, your boat is depicted on the chart exactly where it

**Figure 12-44.** A selection of chartplotters. Five- to 10-inch screens are typical, and many models can also display depth sounder and radar information if properly interfaced. (COURTESY RAYMARINE AND GARMIN; REPRINTED WITH PERMISSION FROM *THE WEEKEND NAVIGATOR* BY BOB SWEET)

is in real time, on the course you previously entered into the GPS. Such vital data as your speed over the ground, ETA, and heading are also displayed, and if wind or current is sweeping you off course, the GPS will display your resultant *cross-track error*. Thus, to correct for current or leeway, you have only to adjust your course so as to eliminate cross-track error, making vector diagrams to compensate for current a thing of the past. Always remember, however, that your GPS receiver does not know or care what hazards lie ahead. Whether you're using a simple handheld receiver with paper charts or a chartplotter, avoiding the hazards in your path is still up to you.

Given the data input from relevant sensors, you can also display fuel burn, fuel remaining, weather conditions, radar returns, and depth information on the same screen with your navigation information. So, fellow boaters, stay tuned—it's just begun!

# GPS Operation

The following is a sequence of events for basic operation of a GPS receiver. The use of GPS is quite intuitive as long as you have a good understanding of basic navigation principles—which is why we've saved electronic navigation for the end of this chapter.

Imagine a simple trip in which you leave a marina or launch ramp, go to one or two buoys,

then return to the starting point. With your unit's operating manual at hand, let's see what happens.

When the GPS receiver is turned on, it immediately searches the sky to locate the available satellites, displaying the serial number and relative signal strength of each satellite it locates. The unit selects the optimal satellites, and when it is satisfied that it knows its current location and is ready for use, the screen will change to display your current Lat/Lo coordinates (Figure 12-45). The receiver remembers the satellites it used last, so it may take awhile to find your current location the first time you use it. (It may be looking for the satellites over China, where it probably was built!) Subsequent initializations occur in seconds, however. If it fails to find four satisfactory satellites, it will either continue to search or announce that its accuracy is degraded or that it cannot be used. The GPS antenna requires relatively open access to the sky.

The receiver has a general menu, on which you will find all its main features listed. These include a *setup* feature. The setup menu allows you to adjust screen contrast and select things such as units of measure, audible alarms, and datum. The default settings are usually good enough to become familiar with basic operations.

The next step is to select the feature that allows you to program waypoints (Figure 12-46). There, you can add the waypoints of the trip you're planning. In order to do this, you need to know the Lat/Lo for each waypoint. If you have a chartplotter GPS receiver, and the relevant electronic

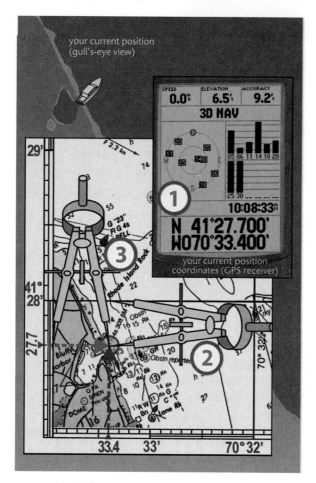

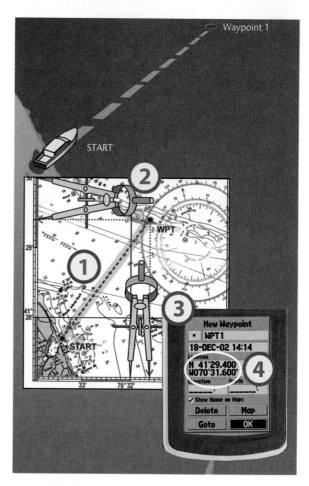

**Figure 12-45.** Using GPS to figure out where you are. Read your latitude and longitude coordinates from your GPS receiver (1), then plot the latitude (2) and longitude (3) on your chart to locate your position. (REPRINTED WITH PERMISSION FROM *USING GPS: A CAPTAIN'S QUICK GUIDE* BY BOB SWEET)

**Figure 12-46.** Using GPS to figure out where you are going. Mark on the chart the position or waypoint you wish to go to, then plot the course from your current position to that destination (1), making sure there are no intervening ledges or other hazards. Next, use dividers to ascertain the latitude (2) and longitude (3) of the waypoint, and enter these coordinates into your GPS receiver (4). Your GPS will now give you the course and distance to the waypoint. (REPRINTED WITH PERMISSION FROM *USING GPS: A CAPTAIN'S QUICK GUIDE* BY BOB SWEET)

chart is loaded for your trip, the waypoints will already be in the waypoint list. The waypoint for your dock or launch ramp will not be there, but you can find it simply by moving the cursor over the relevant point. If you're using a simple GPS without electronic charts, you'll need to pick off the coordinates of your waypoints from the paper chart using dividers.

Once underway, select the first waypoint of the trip from the waypoint list (Figure 12-46). Press the **Go To** button, and the unit will display the course required to get to that waypoint. If your boat wanders off course, the unit provides instructions to get back on course. When you arrive at that waypoint, which might be a buoy or simply a safe water location in midchannel where you wish to change course, you should select the next waypoint from

the list and press Go To again. Repeat this process until you reach your final destination.

Alternatively, you can add all these waypoints to a **Route** file, and when you select that route, the unit will automatically call up each waypoint in its proper sequence and provide the course to steer for the next waypoint. A feature called **Return Course** will reverse the waypoints to provide directions to return home. Many other features augment the ones described here, including ones that provide the distance and time required to complete each leg of the trip. The only difference between this simple exercise and a longer, more complex trip is the number of waypoints to be entered (Figure 12-47). Also, you should review or **prequalify** the trip on an up-to-date chart to be sure the programmed route does not lead you into obstacles or across hazards. If it does, you'll have to program doglegs with additional waypoints to steer the boat around obstructions.

Some skippers with chartplotters bypass the entire process of using waypoints. They simply steer their boats visually, using the marker on the screen that shows their boat's real-time location superimposed on the chart. This technique can invite risks when operating in crowded areas, however, if the skipper spends too much time studying the chart and not enough time watching the helm.

# Practice Your Art

It takes practice to become proficient at navigating. Practice it often, as it can slip away easily. No matter how proficient you become, though, practice the "buddy system." If you move into unfamiliar waters, it is advisable to travel with a companion vessel piloted by someone familiar with the area. Not only will you feel more comfortable, but you will probably have more fun in the process. And that is what it is all about.

# A Further Invitation

See www.cgaux.org for the Auxiliary courses available to enhance your skills in this area.

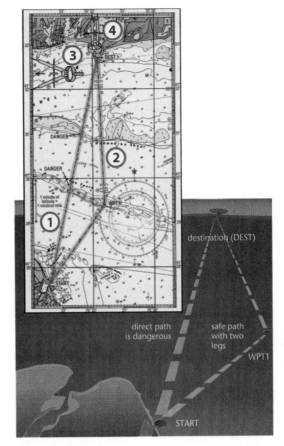

**Figure 12-47.** Using GPS to navigate a route with more than one leg. In this example the direct route to your ultimate destination (1) would take you across a shoal, so you must add a dogleg (2) around the hazard. Once the coordinates of the destination are measured (3 and 4) and entered into your GPS receiver along with the coordinates of the intermediate waypoint (WPT1), you can store this sequence of two waypoints as a route. Selecting this route instructs the GPS receiver to direct you first to WPT1 and then to your destination waypoint. (REPRINTED WITH PERMISSION FROM *USING GPS: A CAPTAIN'S QUICK GUIDE* BY BOB SWEET)

# Practice Questions

## IMPORTANT BOATING TERMS

In the following exercise, match the words in the column on the left with the definitions in the column on the right. In the blank space to the left of each term, write the letter of the item that best matches it. Do not use an item in the right-hand column more than once.

| THE ITEMS | THE RESPONSES |
|---|---|
| 1. _____ datum | a. 1 nautical mile |
| 2. _____ longitude line | b. compass error caused by earth's magnetic field |
| 3. _____ 1 minute of latitude | c. make adjustments for effects of variation and deviation |
| 4. _____ Mercator projection | d meridian |
| 5. _____ latitude line | e. 1.15 statute miles |
| 6. _____ variation | f. benchmark |
| 7. _____ knot | g. parallel |
| 8. _____ correct a compass reading | h. magnetic north |
| 9. _____ direction a compass points | i. 1 nautical mile per hour |
| 10. _____ nautical mile | j. used in most nautical charts |

# Multiple-Choice Items

In the following items, choose the best response:

**12-1.** The best binocular for use on a recreational vessel is

a. 50 x 7
b. 15 x 35
c. 7 x 50
d. 7 x 35

**12-2.** For overall planning on a long cruise, navigators should select a chart with

a. a small scale that shows a large area
b. a large amount of landmass shown
c. a large scale
d. an unknown date of revision

**12-3.** 1 minute of latitude equals

a. 1 statute mile
b. 1 nautical mile
c. 60 nautical miles

d. 60 statute miles

**12-4.** Charts are being revised to use only the following datum for soundings:

a. mean low water
b. low water
c. lower low water
d. mean lower low water

**12-5.** Which of the following measures distances north or south of the equator?

a. a great circle
b. latitude
c. longitude
d. the prime meridian

**12-6.** Which scale of a chart should never be used for measuring distances?

a. longitude scale

# Multiple-Choice Items (continued)

b. latitude scale
c. the chart's distance scale
d. none of the above

12-7. The direction of a course is the angle it makes with a

a. line of position
b. the equator
c. line of latitude
d. meridian

12-8. You can find the amount of variation in your boating area by

a. finding the difference between the direction a magnetic compass points and the direction it should point
b. looking at a compass rose on the chart of the area
c. looking in the chart catalog
d. looking at *Chart No. 1*

12-9. If you measure the direction of a course line from a chart meridian, you have a

a. magnetic direction
b. compass direction
c. true direction
d. line of position

12-10. Variation is the difference between

a. your course heading and your intended heading
b. magnetic north and the direction your compass needle points
c. true north and magnetic north
d. a vessel's heading and its course direction

12-11. Deviation is a compass error caused by

a. the earth's magnetic field at your position
b. a cheap compass
c. proximity to the north geographic pole
d. magnetic influences aboard your vessel

12-12. The technical term for the benchmark from which a marine chart's vertical and horizontal measurements are made is

a. latitude
b. longitude
c. fathom
d. datum

12-13. Direction can be determined on a Mercator chart by using the

a. direction scale
b. variation
c. compass rose
d. chart block

12-14. A speed table is used to

a. determine speed from a tachometer reading
b. measure distances
c. calibrate your speedometer
d. tell you what the maximum legal speeds are

12-15. The vertical datum of a chart

a. helps you know how far apart two points are
b. is the North American 1983 datum
c. helps you know where you are
d. helps you know how much clearance there is under a bridge

12-16. To correct a compass reading

a. add easterly variations
b. add magnetic deviations
c. add westerly variations
d. add westerly deviations

12-17. Mercator projections are made by projecting the earth's surface onto a

a. cone
b. cylinder
c. chart
d. map

12-18. On a chart, shallow water is

a. white
b. light green
c. light blue
d. light yellow

12-19. If you travel at a speed of 12 knots for 10 minutes, you will have gone how far?

a. 2.0 miles
b. 2.0 nautical miles
c. 3.0 miles
d. 3.0 nautical miles

(continued on next page)

# Multiple-Choice Items (continued)

**12-20.** In an area with a variation of 12°E, your heading is 130° by your compass. The deviation for this heading is 3°W. What is your true heading?

a. 121°
b. 145°
c. 115°
d. 139°

**12-21.** A position determined by the intersection of two LOPs is

a. an estimated position
b. a range line of position
c. a fix
d. an advanced line of position

**12-22.** A fix is labeled with

a. a dot and a circle
b. an X
c. a square
d. a half-circle

**12-23.** How long will it take you to go 3 miles at a speed of 20 knots?

a. 60 minutes
b. 6.67 minutes
c. 9 minutes
d. 12 minutes

**12-24.** How fast do you have to go to cover 6 nautical miles in 20 minutes?

a. 6.67 knots
b. 18 knots
c. 3 knots
d. 6 knots

# Engines for Sailboats

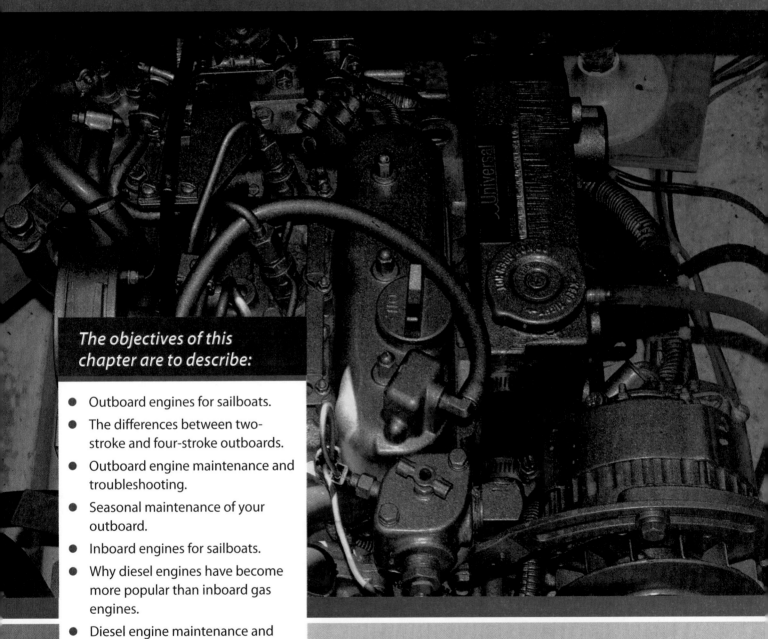

**The objectives of this chapter are to describe:**

- Outboard engines for sailboats.
- The differences between two-stroke and four-stroke outboards.
- Outboard engine maintenance and troubleshooting.
- Seasonal maintenance of your outboard.
- Inboard engines for sailboats.
- Why diesel engines have become more popular than inboard gas engines.
- Diesel engine maintenance and troubleshooting.
- Seasonal maintenance of your diesel.
- Battery and electrical system basics.
- Electrical system dangers.
- Sailboat propellers.
- A basic tool kit.

MOST SAILBOATS handle poorly under power. The sailboat engine is usually described as an **auxiliary**—the main power plant is the sailing rig.

Compared with a powerboat of equal displacement, or weight, a sailboat generally has a very small engine. A cruising sailboat 30 feet

Access to an inboard auxiliary sailboat's engine is almost always restricted, as here. (PHOTO BY DON LINDBERG)

long, with a displacement of perhaps 8,000 to 10,000 pounds, will probably carry an inboard diesel engine of 30 horsepower (hp) or so. A powerboat of similar size will have an engine four or five times as powerful, and even larger if it's a high-speed planing boat. A sailboat 22 feet long with a displacement of 2,000 to 3,000 pounds will probably get its auxiliary power from an outboard motor of 5 hp or 6 hp, whereas powerboats of that size commonly generate 100 hp to 200 hp from single or twin outboard engines.

# Outboard Engines

Although most small sailboats with auxiliary power have outboard motors, the standard outboard designed for high-speed operation is ill suited for sailboat operation. Sailboats work most efficiently with slower-turning, high-torque propellers. They may also need a long shaft on an outboard simply to reach the water from the usual transom-mounting position. Outboard motors designed for sailboat applications work well, and can push displacement-hull sailboats at close to hull speed, or about 4 or 5 knots for a boat with a 20-foot waterline.

Outboard engines are normally found powering sailboats from about 14 feet up to about 27 or 28 feet (and on considerably longer lightweight multi-hulls). As a general rule, outboards up to about 5 hp are adequate for daysailers, while motors from 5 hp to 12 hp are used for small cruisers.

An outboard is usually transom-mounted (Figure 13-1), clamped either to a transom cutout or to an articulated bracket that is bolted to the transom. The former mounting location may or may not require a long-shaft motor, whereas the latter almost always does. Either way, a transom mount offers several advantages:

- The engine, which of course incorporates its own steering, is easy to operate and gives you much better slow-speed maneuverability than you can get from an inboard engine. This is particularly useful when docking or mooring, which is when you're most apt to be using the motor.

- The outboard can be tilted up while sailing or when the boat is moored, which improves sailing efficiency and helps prevent corrosion and marine growth on the lower unit.

- The motor is readily accessible for repair or for removal, and it enables the boat's inboard volume to be devoted to other purposes. An outboard-powered weekend-cruising sailboat of 24 feet offers as much room in its cabin as a 27-footer with an inboard engine.

**Figure 13-1.** **Left:** This 6 hp single-cylinder outboard engine is mounted on a bracket on the transom of a Tanzer 22. This is a four-stroke Nissan motor (model year 2003) yet weighs just 60 pounds and looks no larger than a 6 hp two-stroke, an indication of just how far outboard technology has advanced in recent years. Note that the long shaft for this engine model is 5 inches longer than the standard shaft. (PHOTO BY MOLLY MULHERN) **Middle:** Here's a nice idea—a protective hood for a bracket-mounted outboard. (PHOTO BY DON LINDBERG) **Right:** This Suzuki four-stroke engine is mounted on a transom cutout. Forward of the engine is a well, which prevents a following sea from boarding through the cutout and swamping the cockpit. This uncommon arrangement obviously wouldn't work with a transom-hung rudder. (PHOTO BY DON LINDBERG)

On some boats, however, the shape of the stern prohibits transom mounting or makes it practically inaccessible. Such boats often have outboard wells—usually a lazarette compartment with a hole in the bottom for the outboard lower unit, and a reinforced crossbar for the motor-mounting clamps. An outboard well often looks better than a transom mount, but it frequently requires that the motor stay in the water at all times unless the whole unit is unclamped and removed. In addition, many lazarette-type wells are rather poorly ventilated, causing the engine to run roughly and sometimes to choke on its own exhaust.

## OPERATING CYCLE

Like all internal combustion gasoline engines, an outboard works by drawing in a mixture of fuel and air, compressing it into a smaller volume, igniting it to expand the gases and produce power, and exhausting the spent gases. *Two-cycle outboard engines* combine the intake and compression steps and the expansion and exhaust steps and therefore require just one revolution of their internal parts to complete all four processes. *Four-cycle gas engines* (including all inboard gas engines and an increasing

number of outboard engines) require two revolutions because they complete each of the four steps separately. Two- and four-cycle engines are also called **two-stroke** and **four-stroke engines**, respectively (Figures 13-2 and 13-3).

Inboard engines are almost always four-stroke. Until recently most outboards have been two-stroke, but four-cycle outboards are becoming increasingly popular for reasons outlined below.

## Differences between Two- and Four-Stroke Engines

There are two major differences between engines with two- and four-stroke cycles. First, for a given power rating, two-stroke engines weigh less than four-stroke engines. On a small boat this is an important consideration, and this is the main reason why formerly almost all outboard engines were two-stroke. The difference in weight is much less now than it used to be, however.

The second difference is in the way the engines are lubricated. A four-stroke engine has a **crankcase** that holds oil to lubricate moving engine parts (Figure 13-4). The oil recirculates and is not burned with the fuel. The crankcase of a two-stroke

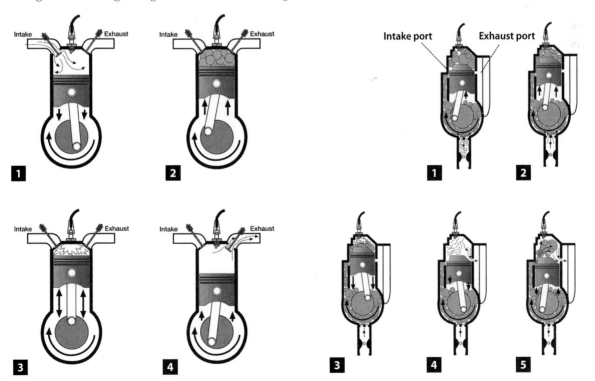

**Figure 13-2. Left:** The four-stroke engine cycle illustrated. **Right:** The two-stroke engine cycle illustrated. (REPRINTED WITH PERMISSION FROM *OUTBOARD ENGINES* BY EDWIN R. SHERMAN)

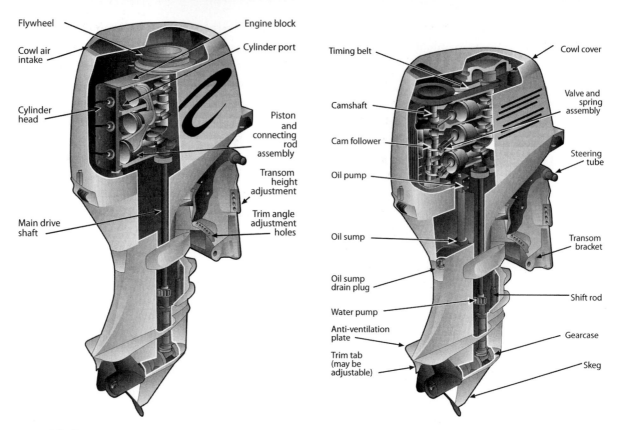

**Figure 13-3.** Cutaway comparisons of a two-stroke (left) and a four-stroke (right) outboard. Note that these are larger motors with shorter shafts than you would typically find on a sailboat. (REPRINTED WITH PERMISSION FROM *OUTBOARD ENGINES* BY EDWIN R. SHERMAN)

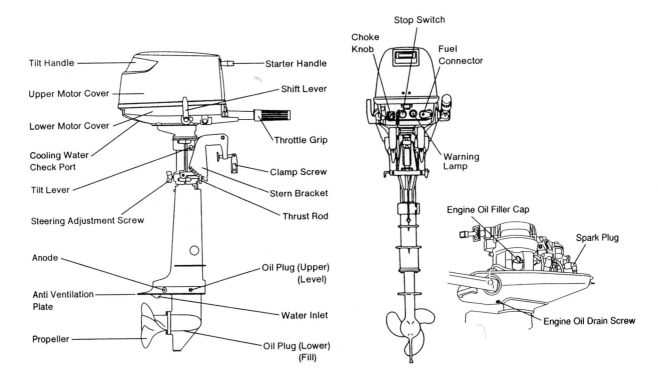

**Figure 13-4.** The Nissan 6 hp single-cylinder four-stroke outboard. The right illustration shows the engine oil filler cap and the drain screw in the bottom of the shallow crankcase. (REPRINTED WITH PERMISSION FROM TOHATSU CORP. OWNER'S OPERATING MANUAL)

gasoline outboard engine, on the other hand, does not contain oil. Instead, it is lubricated from oil mixed with the fuel.

Since two-stroke engines burn fuel less efficiently than four-stroke engines, and since their exhausts contain unburned oil along with unburned fuel, two-stroke engines are a greater source of water and air pollution than are four-stroke engines. This is why small engines such as lawnmower engines, all of which are two-stroke, contribute much more pollution than would be expected based on their proportionate use alone. The least polluting engines are four-stroke engines with fuel injection systems.

Beginning in 1998, the U.S Environmental Protection Agency (EPA) set emission standards for marine engines that will, eventually, cut hydrocarbon emissions by as much as 75%, and this has forced two-stroke engines to become much more efficient. Two-stroke outboard engines with electronic fuel injection (EFI) are more efficient than carbureted engines, and direct-injected two-strokes are more efficient still.

Until recent years, it was necessary to add oil to the fuel in a two-stroke outboard engine's fuel tank or to buy premixed fuel, but most larger two-stroke engines now do this job for you. These engines have special reservoirs for storing oil, which is either metered into the fuel before it enters the engine or injected into the fuel as the fuel is injected into the engine. Motors with **variable-ratio oilers** (VROs) vary the amount of oil mixed with the fuel according to engine speed. In the smaller two-stroke outboards used by most sailboats, however, it is still necessary to mix the oil manually.

Be sure to use the proper oil in your two-stroke engine, one made especially for mixing with your fuel. There are separate types of oil for air- and water-cooled engines. Look at the label on the container. It should say "TC-W," for example, if it is for two-cycle, water-cooled engines.

Four-stroke engines are heavier and more expensive than two-strokes, but their weights have decreased markedly in recent years. Four-stroke outboards first appeared in the higher horsepower ranges but have now migrated into small outboards as their weights have dropped and their efficiency has improved. Not only are four-strokes quieter than two-strokes, they also are proving more reliable and durable, are more fuel-efficient (although direct-injected two-strokes are competitive), and, above all, cause less pollution because no oil is discharged with the exhaust. Their popularity is expanding rapidly as a result.

## LIVING WITH AN AUXILIARY OUTBOARD

Store the fuel for your outboard in its portable tank in a well-ventilated cockpit locker or on deck or on the cockpit sole to prevent the accumulation of explosive vapors (see Chapter 10). Never store gasoline in an unventilated lazarette.

Until fairly recently, only larger outboards were provided with alternators capable of charging a boat's battery. Now, however, many small outboards have alternators, and you can wire these motors to the ship's battery. The generating capacity offered by a small outboard is not great, but it's usually enough to keep a 12-volt battery charged during the season, even allowing for occasional interior lighting and the use of running lights and a VHF radio.

Today's outboards are more reliable than their predecessors of even a few years ago, but the standard outboards are not made to push a sailboat. The special sailboat type of motor is preferred, but even such motors do not thrive on the infrequent slow-speed use typical of sailboat operation. Two common problems with outboard auxiliary engines are **spark-plug fouling** at low speeds and **propeller cavitation**.

Most standard outboards are made to run economically and efficiently at three-quarter throttle or better. Many sailboats achieve hull speed in calm water at about half throttle. Running a standard outboard for extended periods at half throttle or less is an invitation to fouling the spark plugs. While making the fuel-air mixture leaner (less fuel, more air) may help, a certain amount of fouling is inevitable. One answer is to get a motor that's small enough so that it needs to be run near full throttle to attain hull speed in calm water. This solution is only partial, for it means that in rough, windy conditions your engine power may be less than you'd like. But when there is wind, most sailboats are more maneuverable under sail than under power. Learn to maneuver under sail, even in adverse winds, and save the engine for docking and for getting home in a flat calm.

*Cavitation* refers to the bubbles of partial vacuum that may appear around the blades of a propeller that is spinning at excessive speed or under an excessive load. It can also occur if the propeller is not deep enough in the water. Since the propeller blades do not get a good "grip" on the water, the motor overspeeds, causing possible damage to the engine and/or pit marks on the propeller. As mentioned, long-shaft outboard motors are marketed specifically for sailboats with high transoms. The longer shaft permits the propeller to run in deeper water while still giving you access to its controls. These outboard engines often are sold with three-, four-, or even five-bladed propellers for more positive bite and steering at low speeds.

## OUTBOARD ENGINE MAINTENANCE

The modern outboard motor requires about as little maintenance as any piece of marine equipment. Only a small amount of care is needed to keep your motor running smoothly. The precise steps are detailed in the engine owner's manual—a copy of which you should obtain if you do not already have one. If you're mechanically inclined, you can easily perform routine and seasonal maintenance of your engine using this manual, and it will give you the complete parts specifications and advise you on tune-ups and major repairs.

Table 13-1 shows a minimalist routine maintenance schedule for an average small engine.

Modern outboards can operate in either fresh or salt water without harm if cared for properly. Normally, you do not need to flush your engine with fresh water after each use in salt water.

Flushing is helpful, however, in reducing the spread of aquatic nuisance species (ANS; see Chapter 6), such as zebra mussels, from one body of fresh water to another, and can be done using a garden hose and a special adapter. If you are taking your boat from one freshwater lake or river to another, flush your engine.

Consult your owner's manual for instructions on engine operation and care in freezing weather. You will usually want to keep the lower unit of an outboard submerged in freezing weather, as this prevents possible damage—unless the water around the unit freezes.

Figure 13-5 shows the typical points for habitual maintenance for an outboard engine, and Figure 13-6 shows the points for periodic maintenance. Figure 13-7 shows the typical lubrication points.

## OUTBOARD ENGINE TROUBLESHOOTING

Today's outboard engines with complex carburetion and electronic fuel injection are much less accessible to the weekend mechanic than the engines of old, but they are also much more reliable. Most engine failures are caused by one of a short list of problems, and it's surprising how often a little ingenuity will get an engine going again or how a methodical investigation will discover a situation that's easily corrected. Table 13-2 shows the list of

| TABLE 13-1 Routine Outboard Maintenance Schedule | |
| --- | --- |
| **Task** | **Perform** |
| **Exterior Lubrication** | |
| Tilt-lock mechanism | Every two months in fresh water, every month in salt water |
| Clamps | Every two months in fresh water, every month in salt water |
| Throttle-to-shaft gears | Every two months in fresh water, every month in salt water |
| Swivel bracket | Every two months in fresh water, every month in salt water |
| Motor-cover latch | Every two months in fresh water, every month in salt water |
| **Interior Lubrication** | |
| Crankcase (four-stroke engine) | Check the oil level each time you use your boat (before starting the engine) |
| Gearcase (lower unit) | Every 50 hours of operating time or once a season (see below) |
| Fuel tank | Grease fuel line fittings every two months in fresh water and every month in salt water; add fuel conditioner if tank is stored with fuel in it |
| Spark plugs | Replace annually, or sooner as required |

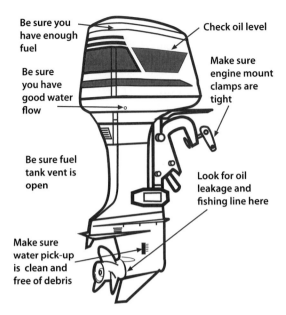

Be sure you have enough fuel

Check oil level

Make sure engine mount clamps are tight

Be sure you have good water flow

Be sure fuel tank vent is open

Look for oil leakage and fishing line here

Make sure water pick-up is clean and free of debris

| Item | Points to Check | Action |
|---|---|---|
| Fuel System | ● Check the amount of fuel in the tank.<br>● Check for debris or water in the fuel filters.<br>● Check the rubber hoses for fuel leakage. | Replenish<br>Clean or Replace<br>Replace |
| Engine Oil | ● Check the oil level. | Fill to the upper level mark on dipstick. |
| Electrical Equipment | ● Check that the stop switch functions normally and make sure the lock plate is there.<br>● Check cords for loose connections and damage.<br>● Check the spark plugs for dirt, wear and carbon build-up. | Remedy or replace<br><br>Correct or replace<br><br>Clean or replace |
| Throttle System | ● Check that the carburetor choke valve functions normally.<br>● Check carburetor linkage is working normally when turning the throttle grip. | Replace<br><br>Correct |
| Recoil Starter | ● Check the rope for wear and chafing.<br>● Check the ratchet engagement. | Replace<br>Correct or replace |
| Clutch and Propeller System | ● Check that the clutch engages correctly when operation the shift lever.<br>● Visually check the propeller for bent or damaged blades.<br>● Check that the propeller nut is tightened and the split pin is there. | Adjust<br><br>Replace |
| Installation of Motor | ● Check all the bolts attaching the motor to the boat.<br>● Check the thrust rod installation. | Tighten |
| Cooling Water | ● Check that cooling water is discharged from the cooling water check port after the engine has started. | |
| Tools and Spares | ● Check that there are tools and spare parts for replacing spark plugs, the propeller, etc.<br>● Check that you have the spare rope. | |
| Steering Devices | ● Check the operation of the steering handle. | |
| Other parts | ● Check if the anode is securely installed.<br>● Check the anode for corrosion and deformation. | Repair if necessary<br>Replace |

**Figure 13-5. Left:** Typical points on an outboard engine that you should check daily. (REPRINTED WITH PERMISSION FROM *OUTBOARD ENGINES* BY EDWIN R. SHERMAN) **Right:** A recommended daily inspection checklist for a small four-stroke engine. Except for the engine oil level, this also applies to a two-stroke outboard. (REPRINTED WITH PERMISSION FROM TOHATSU CORP. OWNER'S OPERATING MANUAL)

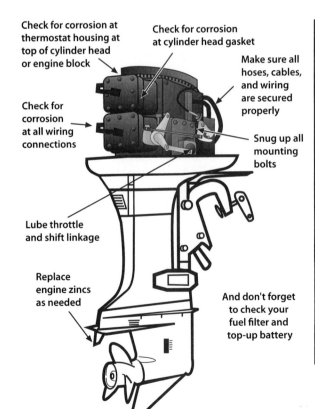

Check for corrosion at thermostat housing at top of cylinder head or engine block

Check for corrosion at cylinder head gasket

Make sure all hoses, cables, and wiring are secured properly

Check for corrosion at all wiring connections

Snug up all mounting bolts

Lube throttle and shift linkage

Replace engine zincs as needed

And don't forget to check your fuel filter and top-up battery

| Item | | Servicing Interval | | | Action | Remarks |
|---|---|---|---|---|---|---|
| | | First 20 hours or 1 month | Every 50 hours or 3 months | Every 100 hours or 6 months | | |
| Fuel System | *Carburetor | | | ○ | Strip, clean, and adjust. | |
| | Fuel filter | ○ | ○ | ○ | Check and clean or Replace. | |
| | Piping | ○ | ○ | ○ | Check and Replace. | |
| | Fuel tank | ○ | | ○ | Clean | |
| Ignition | Spark plug | ○ | | ○ | Check gaps. Remove carbon deposits or Replace. | |
| Starting System | Starter rope | ○ | ○ | ○ | Check for wear or chafing. | |
| Engine | Engine oil | ○ | | ○ | Change | |
| | Valve Clearance | ○ | | ○ | Check & adjust. | |
| Lower Unit | Propeller | ○ | ○ | ○ | Check for bent blades, damage, wear. | |
| | Gear oil | Change<br>○ | ○ | Change<br>○ | Change or replenish oil and check for water leaks. | |
| | *Water pump | | ○ | ○ | Check for wear or damage. | Replace impeller every 12 months. |
| Bolts and Nuts | | ○ | ○ | ○ | Retighten | |
| Sliding and Rotating Parts. Grease Nipples. | | ○ | ○ | ○ | Apply and pump in grease. | |
| Outer Equipment | | ○ | ○ | ○ | Check for corrosion. | |
| Anode | | | ○ | ○ | Check for corrosion and deformation. | Replace |

\* Have this handled by the dealer.

**Figure 13-6. Left:** Typical points on an outboard engine that you should check monthly. (REPRINTED WITH PERMISSION FROM *OUTBOARD ENGINES* BY EDWIN R. SHERMAN) **Right:** A recommended service schedule for a small four-stroke engine. Except for the engine oil, this also applies to a two-stroke outboard. (REPRINTED WITH PERMISSION FROM TOHATSU CORP. OWNER'S OPERATING MANUAL)

### TABLE 13-2 Outboard Troubleshooting

| Problem | Possible Cause/Correction |
|---|---|
| Engine won't start | Fuel tank empty |
| | Fuel tank vent closed (older motors) |
| | Fuel line improperly hooked up—check both ends |
| | Engine not primed |
| | Engine flooded—look for fuel overflow |
| | Clogged fuel filter or line |
| | Spark plug wires reversed or disconnected |
| Starter motor won't work (electric start) | Gearshift not in neutral |
| | Defective starter switch—(sometimes it gets wet and corrodes if motor is mounted too low) |
| | Battery dead |
| | Battery connections loose or dirty |
| Loss of power | Too much oil in fuel mix |
| | Fuel/air mix too lean (backfires) |
| | Fuel/air mix too rich |
| | Fuel hose kinked |
| | Slight blockage in fuel line or fuel filter |
| | Weed or other matter on propeller |
| Motor misfires | Spark plug damaged |
| | Spark plug loose |
| | Spark plug incorrect |
| Poor performance under power | Wrong propeller |
| | Engine improperly tilted relative to transom; engine should be vertical when boat is underway |
| | Bent propeller—usually accompanied by high level of vibration |
| | Improper load distribution in boat |
| | Heavy marine growth on boat bottom |
| | Cavitation |

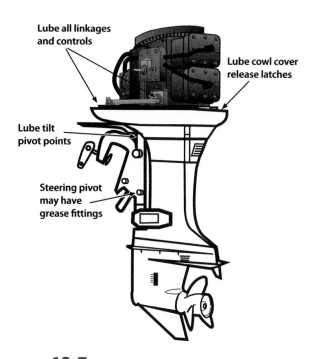

**Figure 13-7.** Typical outboard engine lubrication points.
(REPRINTED WITH PERMISSION FROM *OUTBOARD ENGINES* BY EDWIN R. SHERMAN)

the "usual suspects"; Figure 13-8 summarizes outboard engine troubleshooting.

## OUTBOARD ENGINE SEASONAL MAINTENANCE

An outboard engine will provide reliable service over many boating seasons if you give it a few minutes' attention at the beginning and end of each season. Unless a few simple steps are taken to protect the engine—see the checklists on page 316—more problems may occur during the off-season than when the engine is being used regularly.

# Inboard Auxiliary Engines

Ideally, an inboard engine for a sailboat should meet certain criteria. It should be compact, using

## FUEL SYSTEM

| Engine failing to start | Engine starting but stopping soon | Poor idling | Poor acceleration | Engine speed abnormally high | Engine speed abnormally low | Boat speed low | Overheating of engine | Possible cause |
|:---:|:---:|:---:|:---:|:---:|:---:|:---:|:---:|---|
| • | • | | | | | | | Empty fuel tank |
| • | • | • | • | | • | • | • | Incorrect connection of fuel system |
| • | • | • | • | | • | • | • | Air entering fuel line |
| • | • | • | • | | • | • | • | Deformed or damaged fuel hose |
| • | • | • | • | | • | • | • | Closed air vent on fuel tank |
| • | • | • | • | | • | • | • | Clogged fuel filter, fuel pump, or carburetor |
| | | • | • | | | • | • | Use of improper engine oil |
| • | • | • | • | | | • | • | Use of improper gasoline |
| • | | | • | | | | | Excessive supply of fuel |
| • | • | • | • | | • | • | • | Poor carburetor adjustment |
| • | • | • | • | | • | • | | Spark plug other than specified |
| • | • | • | • | | • | • | | Dirt, soot, etc. on spark plug |

## ELECTRIC SYSTEMS / OTHERS

| Engine failing to start | Engine starting but stopping soon | Poor idling | Poor acceleration | Engine speed abnormally high | Engine speed abnormally low | Boat speed low | Overheating of engine | Possible cause |
|:---:|:---:|:---:|:---:|:---:|:---:|:---:|:---:|---|
| • | • | • | • | | | • | • | No spark or weak spark |
| • | | | | | | | | Short circuit of engine stop switch |
| • | | • | • | | | • | • | Ignition timing incorrect |
| • | | | | | | | | Lock plate not fitted to stop switch |
| • | | | | | | | | Disconnection of wire or loose ground connection |
| • | | • | • | | | • | | Incorrect adjustment of throttle link |
| | | | | | | • | • | Insufficient cooling water flow, clogged or defective pump |
| | | • | | | | • | • | Faulty thermostat |
| | | | | • | • | | • | Cavitation or ventilation |
| | | | • | • | • | • | • | Incorrect propeller selection |
| | | | • | • | | • | • | Damaged and bent propeller |
| | | | | • | | • | • | Improper thrust rod position |
| | | | | • | • | • | • | Unbalanced load on boat |
| | | | | • | • | • | • | Transom too high or too low |
| • | | • | • | | • | | | Low compression |
| | | • | | | | | • | Carbon deposits in the combustion chamber |
| | | Engine makes noise | | | | | | Too much valve clearance |

**Figure 13-8.** Outboard engine troubleshooting. These charts designed for the Nissan 4, 5, or 6 hp single-cylinder four-stroke engine are applicable to any small two- or four-stroke outboard. (REPRINTED WITH PERMISSION FROM TOHATSU CORP. OWNER'S OPERATING MANUAL)

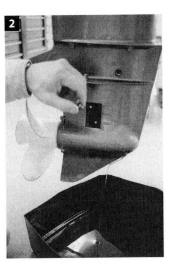

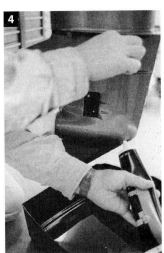

**Figure 13-9.** Changing the gearcase oil in the lower unit of an outboard. **1.** Loosening the gear oil drain screw in the gearcase. **2.** The old gear oil is draining. **3.** Inserting a tube of gear oil into the lower hole for refilling. **4.** Once oil dribbles out of the upper hole, it's time to reinstall the upper screw. When that is tightened, you can withdraw the tube of gear oil. The vacuum in the gearcase will prevent the oil from dripping out while you reinstall the lower screw. (REPRINTED WITH PERMISSION FROM *POWERBOAT CARE AND REPAIR* BY ALLEN BERRIEN)

## ✓ OUTBOARD ENGINE WINTER STORAGE CHECKLIST

☐ **Cooling water system.** Operate the engine for several minutes in fresh water to flush the system, then drain the water completely.

☐ **Fuel system.** Drain all fuel from the fuel hoses, fuel pump, and carburetor, and clean these parts. (Gasoline left in a carburetor over the winter can form gum and varnish, possibly restricting the jets and causing the float valve to stick.) Remove and clean the fuel-filter bowl. Drain and clean the filter elements. Check all gaskets carefully for wear, breaks, or enlarged cutouts. If in doubt, replace the gasket. Empty and clean the fuel tank.

☐ **Ignition system.** Remove the spark plug(s) and spray storage oil (sometimes called fogging oil) through the spark plug holes into the cylinder or cylinders while slowly turning the motor over by pulling on the starter cord.

☐ **Metal surfaces.** Wipe all metal surfaces with a lightly oiled rag. This will keep the surfaces from rusting during the winter months. Remove the propeller and lubricate the propeller shaft.

☐ **Lubrication.** Drain the lower-unit gearcase and refill with the gear oil specified by the manufacturer (Figure 13-9). Also change the engine oil (four-stroke motor only). Apply grease to the propeller shaft and to all sliding parts, joints, nuts, and bolts, and store the engine standing vertically in a dry space.

## ✓ OUTBOARD ENGINE PRESEASON CHECKLIST

☐ **Ignition system.** Regap, clean, or replace spark plug(s) as necessary. If your motor has an electric start, check the battery with a hydrometer to ensure that it has a full charge. Clean and inspect the battery cables. Check the polarity before connecting the cables to the terminals. Clean and lubricate the electric-starter drive mechanism.

☐ **Gear oil system.** Remove the oil-level plug on the lower-unit gearcase and check for the proper gear oil level. If the oil is dirty, change it. (This should have been done at the end of the previous season.)

☐ **Engine oil (four-stroke engine).** Top off as necessary, and change the oil if this was not done at the end of the previous season.

☐ **Fuel system.** Remove and clean the fuel filter. Replace if necessary. Check that the shift and throttle function smoothly. (Be sure to turn the propeller shaft when checking the shift function in order to avoid damaging the shift linkage.) Fill the fuel tank completely. Run the engine at idle for several minutes and at half speed for several additional minutes to burn off the oil that should have been coating the cylinder walls during winter storage.

☐ **Metal surfaces.** Wipe off all surfaces with a clean cloth. Check surfaces for water leaks. When run for the first time, check the operation of the engine's cooling system.

up—with its fuel tank, battery, and wiring system—as little space as possible. It should also be capable of generating sufficient electricity to recharge the ship's battery or batteries and to light the running lights, anchor light, and interior lighting system, and perhaps to operate a radiotelephone, depth sounder, GPS receiver, and radar—and maybe even a refrigerator and other appliances.

It needs to be reliable, as it will get little attention and will often be installed in a compartment too damp and inaccessible for anything else. Still, it should permit as convenient access as possible. The more accessible an engine is, the better it will be maintained. Easy access will be especially appreciated when emergency repairs are required while underway.

The driveshaft bearings should also be accessible, especially the one located where the propeller shaft goes through the hull. This bearing, called a *stuffing box*, does require occasional adjustment so that the shaft can turn easily while admitting as little water as possible (Figure 13-10). The engine should be placed as close to horizontal as possible—something that is frequently overlooked. Lubrication systems within the engine may fail or operate badly if the engine is seated with its forward or aft end too high.

Above all, an engine needs to be safe. Gasoline is volatile; that is, it gives off fumes very easily. These fumes are highly flammable, and, being heavier than air, they can pool in a boat's bilge and other interior spaces, awaiting only a spark for ignition. In a confined area, they are explosive. (In an automobile, gasoline fumes escaping from the fuel tank, fuel line, or engine dissipate into the surroundings rather than pooling within the vehicle.) Many boat fires and explosions—sometimes fatal—have been caused by ignition of gasoline vapors.

Diesel fuel does not give off fumes as readily as gasoline, and the fumes it does give off have a higher

## A SPECIAL WARNING!

*All inboard gasoline engines look like automobile engines, and most use automobile engine blocks, but there are important differences between automobile and marine engines. Most marine engines use special devices for discharging exhaust fumes and cooling water. All marine fuel pumps, alternators, starters, distributors, and other electrical parts are designed specifically to prevent sparks or the release of fumes.*

*Much of this special "marinized" equipment is necessary since, unlike automobile engines, inboard engines operate in enclosed spaces. Gasoline fumes can collect in these spaces, and equipment that can produce sparks may produce disastrous results. **Never repair a marine engine with automobile parts. The result may be a fire or an explosion.***

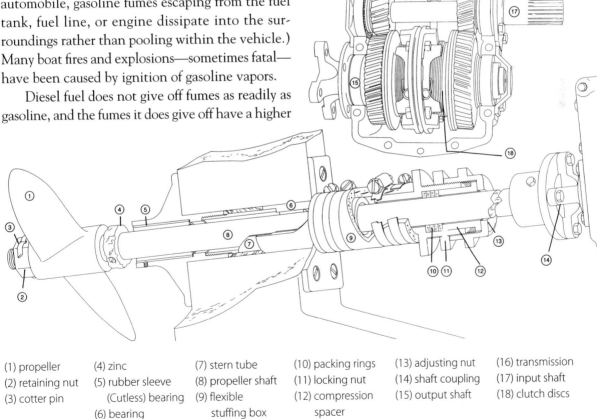

| | | | | | |
|---|---|---|---|---|---|
| (1) propeller | (4) zinc | (7) stern tube | (10) packing rings | (13) adjusting nut | (16) transmission |
| (2) retaining nut | (5) rubber sleeve | (8) propeller shaft | (11) locking nut | (14) shaft coupling | (17) input shaft |
| (3) cotter pin | (Cutless) bearing | (9) flexible | (12) compression | (15) output shaft | (18) clutch discs |
| | (6) bearing | stuffing box | spacer | | |

**Figure 13-10.** A marine transmission (top) and typical driveshaft and stuffing box configuration for a diesel engine (bottom).

(REPRINTED WITH PERMISSION FROM *BOATOWNER'S MECHANICAL AND ELECTRICAL MANUAL*, THIRD EDITION, BY NIGEL CALDER)

flash point. This means that it takes a lot more heat to ignite diesel fuel than it does to ignite gasoline. Thus, diesel fuel has a deserved reputation for being safer than gasoline. This is the biggest reason why diesel engines have largely supplanted gas engines aboard sailboats large enough for an inboard engine (roughly 26 feet and up).

Diesel fuel is not entirely free from risk, however. Any fuel line can rupture and spew its contents onto a hot exhaust manifold, thereby igniting the fuel. If diesel fuel leaks into the bilge, any fire in the bilge will use it as a fuel.

Further, diesel fuel is subject to problems of its own. First, because it is injected into engines, it must be very clean and free of water. To ensure this,

a diesel engine needs additional fuel filters, which should be changed frequently. A second disadvantage is that diesel fuel gels at very cold temperatures. To prevent this (should you ever find yourself boating on a frigid winter day!), add an inhibitor in cold weather. Third, a fuel-eating fungus can form in diesel fuel that clogs fuel injectors. Special antimicrobial agents have been developed as fuel additives to retard fungus formation.

Although no sailboat that we know of has been built with an inboard gasoline engine since the 1980s, there are still plenty of older sailboats getting around perfectly well with gasoline engines such as the Universal Atomic 4, which was once almost universal aboard sailboats with inboard engines. If

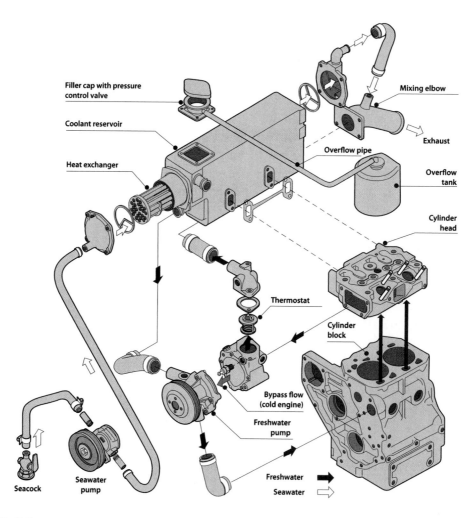

**Figure 13-11.** An exploded view of the cooling system on a freshwater-cooled Yanmar diesel engine. White arrows denote raw-water flow, and solid arrows denote freshwater flow through the closed portion of the cooling system. Raw water enters through the seacock at lower left, then travels through the raw-water pump to the heat exchanger, where it absorbs heat through the walls of the exchanger's many copper tubes. The heated raw water then travels to the mixing elbow (top right) where it is injected into the exhaust. The recirculating fresh water travels through the copper tubes of the heat exchanger, where it passes heat to the raw water, then circulates back to the engine's cooling passages. (REPRINTED WITH PERMISSION FROM *HOW BOAT THINGS WORK* BY CHARLIE WING)

your boat has an inboard gas engine, you can operate it safely by observing the basic fueling, ventilation, and operating precautions outlined in Chapter 10.

## INBOARD COOLING SYSTEMS

The fuel that burns inside an internal combustion engine produces large amounts of heat, making it essential to have some way to cool the engine. Most marine engines are water cooled by one of two methods.

### Open Cooling Systems

Internal combustion engines contain water channels through which water circulates. When that water is pumped into the engine from outside the boat, circulates through the channels, and is then dumped overboard, you have an *open circulation system*, also known as *raw-water cooling*. Raw-water cooling is much less common on recreational boats than it once was, though it is still common on workboats.

Your engine's water intake may become clogged by weeds, trash, or other debris, which can cause the engine to overheat. If this happens, examine the intake and clear out any debris you find. Do not operate your engine if it is overheating, as this can severely damage it.

The engine's cooling system usually has a thermostat that blocks the flow of water through the engine until it warms up. Once the engine is warm, the thermostat opens and allows the cooling water to circulate. A faulty thermostat may stay open all the time and cause the engine to warm up slowly, or may fail to open and cause the engine to overheat. In either case, replace the thermostat.

Most marine engines have an impeller-type water pump. An *impeller* is a propeller-like device made of rubber or neoprene that is turned rapidly by the engine. This device has a relatively short life, one made even shorter if you run your engine without cooling water. If you have to run it when the boat is out of the water, supply water to it through a hose and an adapter.

### Dual Cooling Systems

Most inboard diesel engines on recreational boats have *dual cooling systems*—also called *freshwater cooling*—in which a mixture of water and antifreeze circulates through the engine's water channels. This mixture is circulated by a pump like that on an automobile engine, and as the water circulates, it passes through a heat exchanger that cools it. This is a *closed circulation system*.

The **heat exchanger** serves the same purpose as an automobile radiator, but the exchanger is cooled by water and not by air as in an automobile. Seawater (or raw lake or river water) is pumped into the cooling system, circulated around the exchanger, and discharged out of the boat. In a dual cooling system, only the closed half of the system has a thermostat. As in an open cooling system, the raw-water intake (both strainer and seacock) must be kept clear of weeds and trash, and the impeller in the raw-water pump must be in good condition (Figure 13-11). These are the two most common causes of inadequate cooling water flow.

# Diesel Engine Maintenance and Troubleshooting

## DIESEL ENGINE ROUTINE MAINTENANCE

When preparing to leave the dock, before casting off the lines, check the oil pressure and be sure the cooling water is circulating. If water is not circulating, determine the cause immediately, otherwise overheating may develop and substantial damage could result. To ensure reliable operation of the engine, use the checklist on page 320 before leaving the dock. (Refer also to Figures 13-12 and 13-13.)

## DIESEL ENGINE TROUBLESHOOTING

One reason a diesel engine is so reliable is that it lacks the complex electrical system required to provide a timed spark to a gasoline engine. Since electricity and the dampness of the nautical environment are incompatible, a simple electrical system means fewer breakdowns. Nevertheless, an

## ✓ DIESEL OPERATOR'S CHECKLIST

☐ **Fuel.** Top off the fuel tank; don't run out of fuel at sea.

☐ **Oil.** The dipstick should indicate that the oil level is within the proper operating range. Don't overfill beyond the top level indicator.

☐ **Transmission.** The transmission should be in neutral prior to starting. If the engine has a "stop" device (some but not all diesels do), make sure it's deactivated before you attempt to start the engine.

☐ **Cooling system.** Before starting the engine, check the coolant level in the freshwater expansion bottle. Be sure the raw-water seacock is open and the raw-water strainer is unobstructed. After starting the engine, be sure there is cooling water coming out of your exhaust pipe. (This assumes that your raw cooling water is injected into the exhaust after circulating through the heat exchanger, as is almost always the case.)

☐ **Alternator and pump belts.** Replace belts if frayed or cracked, tighten if loose. Belts should not be too tight as excessive belt and bearing wear may result. Be sure the alternator is charging the battery (i.e., either the ammeter shows a charging current or the light is out) immediately after starting.

☐ **Batteries.** Fill with distilled water to proper level. Check to see that they are fully charged.

☐ **Alarm systems.** There are many alarm systems available for monitoring the items above; however, these systems do not eliminate the need to check the gauges.

☐ **Filters.** Keep filters clean and change them at the frequency recommended by the manufacturer's operating manual. Most diesel engine malfunctions are caused by a failure to ensure clean fuel or a failure to change the oil at the specified intervals.

☐ **Engine.** Allow the engine to warm up slowly. Don't get underway with a cold engine. The result may soon be a breakdown of valves, bearings, etc. It is mandatory that the proper warm-up period be followed so that oil reaches all the moving parts. It is better to warm the engine in gear with propeller loading rather than by prolonged idling, if this can be done without straining deck fittings, etc.

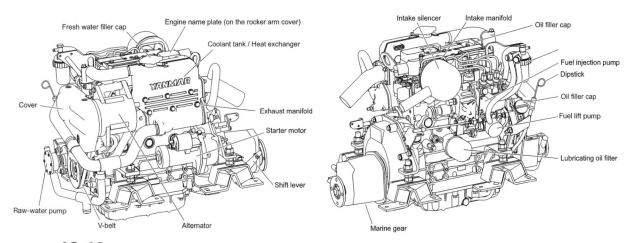

**Figure 13-12.** Location of parts on a Yanmar diesel engine. (COURTESY YANMAR, REPRINTED WITH PERMISSION FROM *DIESEL ENGINE CARE AND REPAIR: A CAPTAIN'S QUICK GUIDE* BY NIGEL CALDER)

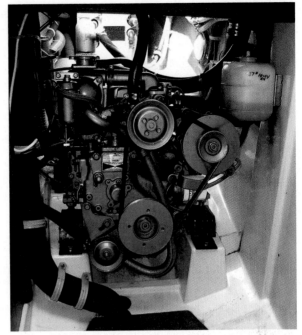

**Figure 13-13. Left:** It's rare to get access like this to the aft end of a sailboat's inboard engine. Here we're looking forward through a hatch in the cockpit sole. You can clearly see the exhaust elbow, where the raw cooling water outflow is injected into the exhaust gases for discharge. Note that all hoses are properly double clamped with stainless steel hose clamps. **Right:** Here's the other end of the same engine, viewed from the cabin. This engine is unusually accessible for servicing. (PHOTOS BY NORMA LOCOCO)

engine that does not crank almost always has an electrical problem, though occasionally the problem is water in the cylinders. An engine that cranks but does not start may not be cranking fast enough to reach ignition compression. If it seems to be cranking at normal speed, suspect an impeded fuel supply, an air intake or exhaust obstruction, or a lack of compression. The latter cause might mean it's time for a rebuild or a new engine.

Figure 13-14 offers a troubleshooting overview. In the text that follows, we focus on a few common problems.

## Fuel Problems

1. Tank empty.
2. Shutoff valve closed.
3. Water in fuel: Open drain cock in bottom of fuel filter. If there is water in the filter, drain it all out and prime system with the prime pump or by cranking the engine.
4. Clogged or dirty filter(s): There are usually at least two filters in a diesel fuel system.
5. Air leak in fuel system: Check connections in the fuel lines from tank to fuel pump. Check gaskets on fuel filter and strainer housing or cap. Disconnect fuel return line and allow fuel to flow until no air bubbles show in the fuel.
6. Fuel not reaching engine: Some engines have electrical fuel shutoffs that operate when the engine is shut down. A short circuit may have closed the switch. Disconnect it and try to start the engine.
7. Air in fuel lines: Use the prime pump to build up fuel pressure and try to restart.

## Electrical Problems

When a diesel has an electrical problem, it is probably associated with the starter motor. The first thing to look for if the starter motor will not operate is a low or dead battery. Turn off all electrical equipment and wait for about 30 minutes. While waiting for the battery to recoup enough power to turn the engine over, remove and clean the battery cable connections and then reclamp them.

If the battery is not at fault, the starter switch may be defective.

## ✓ DIESEL ENGINE POSTSEASON CHECKLIST

☐ **Lube oil system.** Allow the engine to operate until it is warm, then drain the oil and replace it with new oil. If the engine has a filter, replace it with a new one.

☐ **Cooling system.** Most diesels have a closed cooling system in which the freshwater side is cooled by raw cooling water in a heat exchanger. Assuming your diesel is cooled in this fashion, at least every 2 years, drain the freshwater side and fill with fresh ethylene glycol antifreeze solution. The raw-water side should be flushed with fresh water and drained for the winter. Check the water pump carefully for worn gaskets, leaks, cable breaks, worn hoses, or cracked impellers. If you are leaving the raw-water side drained, pull the water pump impeller and plug the exhaust and cooling water lines. Alternatively, you can refill the raw-water side with nontoxic (propylene glycol) antifreeze solution. Remove the raw-water hose from its seacock, dip it into the antifreeze solution, and run the engine until the solution comes out the exhaust.

☐ **Electrical system.** Check the wiring harness and all electrical connections for signs of corrosion or abrasion, and repair or replace as necessary. Spray these components with a corrosion inhibitor. Remove the battery or batteries for off-season storage, or ensure that they get recharged periodically through the off-season.

☐ **Fuel system.** Pump a fuel sample from the base of the tank and check for sediment and water. Remove any found and repeat until none is found. (Use a pump designed for this purpose or hire a commercial fuel-polishing service.) Fill the fuel tank to prevent overwinter condensation.

☐ **Drive system.** Drain the transmission and fill it with the proper lubricant.

☐ **General.** Wipe all exposed metal surfaces with a lightly oiled rag. This should inhibit rusting during the winter. Rinse the valves of any vented loops with fresh water to remove salt crystals. Spray WD-40 or a similar penetrating fluid into the air inlet, and seal the inlet against moisture. (Remember to unseal the inlet the following spring.) Check all hoses for softening, bulging, or deterioration and replace as necessary. Check hose clamps for corrosion and replace as necessary.

## DIESEL ENGINE POSTSEASON AND PRESEASON MAINTENANCE

The information in the checklists above and opposite is adapted with permission from *Diesel Engine Care and Repair: A Captain's Quick Guide* by Nigel Calder.

# Batteries

Unless your outboard engine starts with a pull starter and you use your boat strictly for daysailing, with no need for navigation lights or power to an installed radiotelephone or electronic navigation aid, you need a marine battery. The battery is one of the most important items on your boat. Ideally, a cruising boat should have two 12-volt batteries rated for marine service, one for starting and one for accessories, both charged by the engine's alternator. The batteries should be hooked up to a master switch (see below) that allows current to be drawn from either one or both at once. Batteries should be installed as low as possible, because of their weight, yet above the level of the bilge. They must be secured in their own container or compartment against the most violent heeling the boat may encounter (Figure 13-15), and they

## ✓ DIESEL ENGINE PRESEASON CHECKLIST

☐ **Electrical system.** Before putting the boat in the water, go over the electrical system. Trace each circuit and develop a wiring diagram. Seal the wiring diagram in a plastic bag so that it won't be ruined by moisture.

☐ **Hold-down bolts.** Go over the base of the engine carefully to determine if any of the bolts are loose. This can result in vibration and cause the engine to run improperly. While checking the hold-down bolts, make sure the bolts on the propeller shaft flange coupling are tight. If the boat has been out of the water, this coupling may have been loosened to avoid strain. Check the stuffing boxes on the propeller shaft and rudderpost.

☐ **Alternator belt.** Check the alternator belt carefully. If it is frayed or worn, replace it. If it is loose or too tight, adjust it according to the operator's manual. It should yield no more than ½ inch to thumb pressure at mid-run.

☐ **Cooling system.** Inspect the water hoses thoroughly. Check all clamps; make sure they are tight. Check for leaks. If the hoses are limp or soft, replace them. They may be about to rupture. If the water pump is belt-driven, give the belt the same check as the alternator belt. Check the coolant level in a closed system.

☐ **Batteries.** Replace the batteries if you removed them, but first check the charge level—for example, by measuring specific gravity with a hydrometer—to make sure all the cells are good. Clean the terminals and cover them with grease. Before connecting the battery cables, check the polarity. The cable lugs and battery terminals are marked (+) and (−) or (POS) and (NEG). Just match them. If the batteries have just been charged, allow them to sit for about 30 minutes before installing them. Hydrogen gas is generated by charging, and continues to be released for some time afterward. Hydrogen can be explosive. When you connect the battery terminals connect the "hot" lead first and the grounded lead last.

☐ **Lubrication.** If the oil was changed before storage, check the oil level. If the oil was not changed, do so now, and change the filter, too. Dispose of the old oil and filter properly. Perform all other engine lubrication specified by the manufacturer. Check the transmission oil level as well.

☐ **Other.** Unseal the air inlet if sealed. Replace the raw-water pump impeller if removed.

should also be protected by a cover or shield from accidental short-circuiting caused by dropping a tool across the terminals. The battery box should also be ventilated, as rapid charging builds up explosive hydrogen gas concentrations.

Marine batteries should be **deep-cycle**, meaning they can be completely discharged and recharged through multiple cycles without damage. Automobile batteries are designed for only light discharging while cranking the starter motor. They are not designed to power lights, radios, and other "appliances" while the engine is not running, and will suffer irreversible damage if repeatedly and deeply discharged in this fashion.

## BATTERY SWITCHES

With a **battery isolation switch** you can use either of two batteries or both at the same time. While some of these switches should be operated only when the engine is stopped and the ignition switch is turned off, others can be used to switch from battery 1 to battery 2 or to both while the engine is running. Determine which kind you have before you switch batteries, since failure to do so may damage the alternator.

## CHECK YOUR BATTERY

If your batteries are not "maintenance free," check their fluid levels every month or two and add distilled water if the levels are low. When it is necessary to charge a dead liquid-electrolyte battery, you will probably need to add water. During the charging, some water breaks down into hydro-

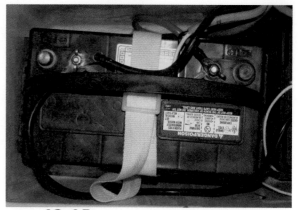

**Figure 13-15.** A secure battery installation is essential. (PHOTO BY DON LINDBERG)

gen and oxygen, and these gases usually escape into the atmosphere. In a confined space, the hydrogen is highly explosive, so keep sparks away from it.

### Checking Your Battery's Charge

You can check a battery's charge with a **hydrometer.** Water has a specific gravity of 1.0. A fully charged battery has a specific gravity of 1.270 or more, while a discharged battery has a specific gravity of 1.150 or less.

If your boat has a **voltmeter,** you have a continuous check on the battery's condition. When the ignition switch is turned on and the engine is not running, a fully charged battery should register about 12.5 volts. If it registers 11 volts or less, it has lost its charge. If your battery is in good condition, the voltmeter will show a reading of about 13.5 to 14.0 volts when the engine is running.

An **ammeter** does not give the same information as a voltmeter, but instead shows the rate at which the alternator is delivering current to the battery when the engine is running. Its charging rate depends on the condition of the battery.

If the battery is low or fails to hold a charge, the ammeter will show a high delivery rate. As the battery charges up, the delivery rate will drop back and may be as little as zero.

You'll know something is wrong with the alternator if the ammeter shows "discharge" when the engine is running. If your alternator has a drive belt, it may be broken. Otherwise, the problem may be with the alternator itself.

**Figure 13-14.** Diesel engine symptoms and their possible causes. (REPRINTED WITH PERMISSION FROM *DIESEL ENGINE CARE AND REPAIR: A CAPTAIN'S QUICK GUIDE* BY NIGEL CALDER)

### Symptom / Possible Causes

| Possible Causes | Seizure | High exhaust back pressure | Hunting | Rising oil level | Excessive oil consumption | Low oil pressure | Knocks | Misfiring | Loss of power | Poor idle | White smoke | Blue smoke | Black smoke | Overheating | Low compression | Lack of fuel | Cranks, but poor starting | Will not crank | Low cranking speed |
|---|---|---|---|---|---|---|---|---|---|---|---|---|---|---|---|---|---|---|---|
| Battery low/loose connections | | | | | | | | | | | | | | | | | | • | • |
| Engine overload/rope in propeller | • | | | | | | | | • | | | | | • | | | | • | |
| Auxiliary equipment engaged | | | | | | | | | • | | | | | | | | | | • |
| Pre-heat device inoperative | | | | | | | | • | | • | | | | | | | • | | |
| Plugged air filter | | | | | | | | • | • | | | | • | | | | • | | |
| Plugged exhaust/turbocharger/kink in exhaust hose | • | | | | | | | • | • | | | | • | | | | • | | |
| Throttle closed/fuel shutoff solenoid faulty/tank empty | | | | | | | | | | | | | | | | • | • | • | |
| Plugged fuel filters | | | | | | | | • | • | • | | | | | | | • | • | |
| Air in fuel lines | | | | | | | • | • | • | • | • | | | | | | • | • | |
| Dirty fuel | | | | | | | • | • | • | • | • | | • | | | | • | | |
| Closed seacock/plugged raw-water filter or screen/plugged cooling system | • | | | | | | | | | | | | | • | | | | | |
| Defective water pump/defective pump valves/air-bound water lines | • | | | | | | | | | | | | | • | | | | | |
| Oil level low | • | | | | | • | | | | | | | | • | | | | | |
| Wrong viscosity oil | • | | | | • | • | | | | | | | | • | | | | | • |
| Diesel dilution of oil | • | | • | | • | | | | | | | | | • | | | | | |
| Lift pump diaphragm holed | | | | | | | | | • | | | | | | | • | • | | |
| Defective injector/poor-quality fuel | | | | | | | • | • | • | • | • | | • | | | | • | | |
| Injection pump leaking | | | | | | | | • | • | • | | | | | | • | • | | |
| Injection timing advanced or delayed | | | | | | | • | | • | • | | | • | • | | | • | | |
| Too much fuel injected | | | | | | | | | | • | | | | | | | | | |
| Piston blowby | | | | | • | | | • | • | • | • | • | | | • | | • | | |
| Dry cylinder walls | | | | | | | | • | • | • | • | | | | • | | • | | |
| Valve blowby | | | | | | | | • | • | • | | | | | • | | • | | |
| Worn valve stems | | | | | • | | | | | | | • | | | • | | | | |
| Decompressor levers on/valve clearances wrong/valves sticking | | | | | | | | • | • | • | | | | | • | | • | | |
| Dirt in oil pressure relief valve/defective pressure gauge | | | | | | • | | | | | | | | | | | | | |
| Governor sticking/loose linkage | | • | | | | | | | | • | | | | | | | | | |
| Governor idle spring too slack | | | | | | | | | | • | | | | | | | | | |
| Blown head gasket/cracked head | • | | • | | | | | | | • | | | | • | • | | • | | |
| Uneven load on cylinders | • | | | | | | | | | | | | | • | | | | | |
| Worn bearings | | | | | | • | • | | | | | | | | | | • | | |
| Seized piston | • | | | | | | | | • | | | | | | | | | | • |
| Water in the cylinders | • | | • | | | | | | | | | | | | | | | | • |

# BATTERY FAILURE

Sometimes, even with fully charged batteries, the starter will not engage and crank the engine. This usually results from loose or corroded battery terminals. If your starter will not operate, check the battery terminals. You may only need to tighten their clamps to correct the problem, or you may need to clean the terminals and clamps. A special brush is available for this purpose.

Crank the engine for a few seconds. Now feel the terminals. If they are more than slightly warm, you have poor or dirty connections.

If the battery cables are worn, or if they get hot when you are starting your engine, replace them. They are doing a poor job of delivering current from the battery, and may also be a fire hazard.

# CORRODED TERMINALS

The easiest way to approach the problem of corrosion on your battery terminals is to prevent it by coating the terminals and their clamps with petroleum jelly, grease, or a spray-on protective coating designed for that purpose.

If you haven't coated the terminals, they will corrode. To remove corrosion, make a solution of 2 tablespoons of baking soda in 1 pint of water. Turn the battery switch to Off and slowly pour the solution over the battery terminals. (Don't let any of it enter the battery.) It will fizz as carbon dioxide is released. Scrub the terminals with a brush if necessary, and then continue the treatment until the fizzing stops. Now, coat the terminals.

Some batteries have side-mounted terminals with wing-nut connectors. While side mounts are not subject to as much corrosion as top-mounted terminals, you may still need to clean them if you haven't coated them.

# SECURE YOUR BATTERY

Keep your batteries in a secured and vented compartment or container with a cover to prevent them from tipping over or tearing loose in rough water or large heel angles.

Covered containers will also help keep batteries from being accidentally short-circuited, which can happen if you drop a tool or some other metal object and it touches both terminals. A shorted-out battery makes a large spark, which can cause a fire or an explosion. Shorting is also hard on the battery and will reduce its life.

A short-circuited battery heats rapidly, and can become hot enough to boil its fluid and explode. This can also happen when you use the starter excessively. Protect yourself and your boat by putting the battery in a vented compartment or properly secured container.

When replacing a battery, remove the negative cable first and install it last. This prevents an accidental sparking if a tool should make contact between the battery's positive terminal and ground.

# USE OF DUAL BATTERIES

Batteries last longer and perform better when used and recharged regularly. If you have two batteries, don't use them both at the same time or use the same battery all the time. Instead switch from one to the other regularly.

If you're on a trip and will be anchored all night, use only one battery for the anchor light. This leaves the other battery for starting the engine the next morning.

# SHORT CIRCUITS

Batteries may be shorted out by anything metallic, such as tools or the jewelry you are wearing. Jewelry can also cause short circuits at electrical junction points, such as a fuse panel, the solenoid on the starter, or any bare wire. Professional mechanics avoid jewelry for this reason. Don't wear necklaces, rings, bracelets, metal watchbands, or the like when working near the battery or any of the electrical connections aboard your boat, and be careful with all tools.

Although the electrical systems on most small recreational boats are 12 volts, short circuits can deliver dangerous amounts of energy for brief periods, and this energy can cause personal injury and pose a fire hazard. The metal causing the short circuit can be melted instantly.

The possibility of a short circuit is another strong argument for a battery isolation switch. The energy present in a short circuit can quickly melt the insulation on a wire and may ignite it or anything in contact with it, and electrical failures of this kind are the leading cause of fires aboard boats. It may be impossible to extinguish an electrically caused fire unless the batteries are disconnected, and even if the fire is extinguished, the fire may be rekindled if the batteries are not disconnected.

The easiest way to disconnect batteries is with a battery isolation switch. If this switch is used to disconnect the batteries from the electrical system of your boat when it is not in use, an electrically caused fire is almost impossible. Just be certain to have the bilge pump wired directly to the battery so that when you leave your boat on the water and turn off the disconnect switch, the pump can operate independently.

## CHARGING YOUR BATTERIES

Many pleasure boats are inactive for long periods, and their batteries lose their charge. This loss may be partial, and there may be sufficient reserve to start the engines. Nevertheless, that battery has experienced a penalty, and repeated loss of charge, small or large, shortens a battery's life. The ideal solution is to keep a low-level maintenance charge on the battery, called a *float charge*. Another, slightly larger charging level is called a *trickle charge*, but this is less ideal for long periods than a float charge. The constant use of carefully regulated charging equipment will most often provide a good payback by lengthening battery life.

The first step in charging your battery, if it doesn't have a built-in charging system, is to turn your battery isolation switch to the Off position. This reduces the possibility of an electrical spark being produced near the hydrogen and oxygen generated during the charging. Also, be careful to see that the area containing the battery is well ventilated so as to disperse the hydrogen and oxygen.

Unless your battery is a "no maintenance" one, before charging it, remove the caps that cover its cells to allow generated gases to escape. Check to

**WARNING** *Read owner's manuals for charging directions on low-maintenance and gel-cell batteries.*

see that the battery's plates are covered with fluid, and add distilled water if necessary—but do not overfill it. Carefully wipe up any spilled battery fluid; it is sulfuric acid, which is corrosive and can burn your skin or eat holes in your clothing. If you come in contact with battery acid, flush the area with water.

## 120-VOLT ELECTRICAL DANGERS

Whenever a boat is connected to a 120-volt alternating current (AC) from ashore or generated aboard, serious dangers may exist. The danger is greatest in a boat with a metal hull, but it is present in any boat with metal fittings or a metal propeller below the waterline.

The most common source of AC problems is the connection between the boat and the power wiring ashore. If the fittings ashore will accommodate only two-prong connectors, the circuit is not grounded and is inherently dangerous. If the fittings accommodate three-prong connectors, a simple, plug-in, three-prong AC circuit tester, readily available at a variety of sources, can be used to test the correctness of the wiring. If the tester shows an incorrectly wired circuit, don't use it since such circuits are dangerous.

Even if the tester shows that the onshore 120-volt source is properly wired, the circuit should be protected with a **ground fault circuit interrupter** (GFCI or GFI). Portable, plug-in GFIs are available, and you should carry one with you and use it whenever a circuit does not have a GFI. Plug it into the source, then plug the cable from your boat into it. Under some circumstances, if a short develops in the circuit, the GFI will immediately disconnect the power source.

All 120-volt appliances on board, such as stoves, refrigerators, and air conditioners, should be grounded to a common ground connection. If the "hot" wire of any of these appliances becomes grounded to its chassis or frame, all grounded metallic components of the boat are energized. A GFI will interrupt the flow of current immediately if this happens, but without one a hazard is present for anyone on the boat or in the water nearby. It is best to stay out of the water if nearby boats are connected to AC current ashore, but if you must go into the water to retrieve something, unplug your boat and nearby boats.

## DIRECT-CURRENT PROBLEMS

The direct current (DC) supplied by your battery can be a source of severe damage to metal parts of your boat. Unless the "hot" wire to your bilge pump is properly sealed from the bilge water, DC current can leak from the wire to metal fittings in the bilge, such as the propeller shaft, through-hull fittings, and other metallic parts of your vessel. It then seeks a ground and takes part of the metal with it, and this electrolytic action can rapidly destroy metal parts of a boat. Although potentially damaging to immersed metal parts, the 12-volt DC system by itself does not present a shock hazard to someone in the water.

## PREVENTING ELECTRICAL PROBLEMS

You can take the following simple steps to reduce the hazards of damage from DC current:

- Keep electrical wiring out of the bilge.
- Use only watertight connections if there is any possibility of immersion in bilge water.
- Install a battery isolation switch.
- Make certain there is a fuse or a circuit breaker in the main distribution line from your batteries and as near to your batteries as possible.
- Use only fuses or circuit breakers of the recommended size in your accessories connection panel.
- If new wiring is added to your boat, be certain it is large enough to carry its intended load without overheating.
- Have any worn or frayed wires replaced by a competent marine electrician as soon as possible.
- Use multistranded, marine-rated wire with copper strands (not aluminum) that have been individually coated with tin.
- Inspect all metal fittings at frequent intervals for electrolytic or galvanic corrosion.

You can also reduce the potential damage and hazards of AC current by doing the following:

- Use a plug-in tester to screen for potential problems in the onshore service line.
- Don't use the onshore service line unless you know it is correctly wired.
- Install a GFI between your vessel and an onshore power source.
- Use a galvanic isolator that has been tested and approved by Underwriters Laboratories to allow AC current to flow to ground while preventing stray DC current from following the same path.
- Each AC circuit should be protected by a fuse or a trip-free circuit breaker.
- Install new wire in your boat for any AC circuit and make certain that it is heavy enough to carry its intended load.

# Sailboat Propellers

Sailboat inboard engines are designed—by and large—to turn a large propeller at a rather slow speed. For this reason, many auxiliary engines are geared down so that the propeller turns at something like one-third the speed of the engine itself. The propeller may be one of several types. On cruising sailboats, where high performance under sail isn't a factor, the propeller is usually three-bladed and large. The skipper accepts the drag penalty under sail in order to have reasonably good performance under power. The sailing cruiser with some pretensions to speed under sail has a two-bladed propeller. While not so efficient for powering as a three-bladed wheel of similar diameter, the two-bladed prop can be made to lie vertically in the space just ahead of, or behind, the rudder, for minimum drag (Figure 13-16).

Racing sailboats frequently use a folding propeller. When moving through the water with the engine off, the prop folds into a flower-bud shape, but when the engine is on and in gear, centrifugal force from the spinning propeller shaft opens the blades and holds them in place, moving the boat forward. Except for boats that will be raced fre-

**Figure 13-16. Left:** On a traditional full-keeled boat like this, a cutout at the aft end of the keel protects the propeller from debris, pot warps, and groundings. (PHOTO BY DON LINDBERG) **Middle:** More common these days, however, is a fin keel and spade rudder, with the propeller exiting the hull forward of the rudder. A folding propeller like this one closes to reduce drag when not in use, increasing speed under sail by an average of 4% over an equivalent fixed-blade prop. The propeller spins open under centrifugal force when the shaft turns. **Right:** This propeller has feathering blades that rotate when not in use until their edges face forward to reduce drag. A feathering prop increases speed under sail by an average of 2½% over an equivalent fixed-blade prop. Note the sacrificial anodes, or zincs, on the propeller shaft. (PHOTOS BY MOLLY MULHERN)

quently, the folding propeller is inefficient for simple propulsion and makes close-quarters maneuvering under power more difficult.

## PROPELLER LOCATION

Generally speaking, a propeller forward of the rudder will steer the boat somewhat more effectively, because the discharge stream from the propeller will impinge on the rudder blade. If a fixed, two-bladed propeller is used, the propeller shaft should be marked to show when the two blades are in an up-and-down position relative to the rudder. This will be the most efficient sailing position from the viewpoint of minimizing prop drag when under sail alone.

Nearly all inboards are installed so that the propeller shaft is in line with the rudder, and most have the propeller just forward of the rudder. Nearly all small engines are right-hand-turning. A right-hand-turning (or right-handed) propeller, when viewed from astern, turns in a clockwise direction to move the boat forward. This means that the boat has a tendency to turn to port when moving either ahead or astern. Going forward, a clockwise prop is more efficient on its starboard side, pulling the stern along with it and, by extension, pushing the bow to port. With the engine in reverse, the counter-clockwise-turning propeller pulls the stern to port as the boat backs. In many cases, this effect—which is often called *prop walk*—is very marked in

reverse, and makes the boat virtually unsteerable; no matter which way the wheel or tiller is turned, the boat backs irresistibly to port. It is always most noticeable when the clutch is first engaged, because the side thrust occurs before the boat begins to move forward or backward so that the rudder is temporarily ineffective.

Eventually you'll learn to live with and even take advantage of prop walk. When docking, for example, approach the dock port-side-to when possible. When you're alongside the dock, a final burst of reverse power will pull the stern into the dock.

## PROPELLER MAINTENANCE

Unless a propeller is damaged, it needs little attention. If it has been damaged, however, even if the damage is slight, you should repair or replace it, since damaged propellers can cause vibration and destroy propeller shaft bearings.

When installing your propeller, grease its shaft with good-quality marine grease. This will make it easier to remove. Propellers are expensive, so protect yours from theft by using one of the propeller locks available.

Keep a wooden plug the size of the shaft tied nearby on a string. If it is ever necessary to remove the shaft (or if it should ever fall out on its own, as has been known to happen on rare occasions!), the plug can be used to stop the hole.

# Galvanic Action

Modern marine engines and lower units use a variety of metals. When you immerse two dissimilar metals in a solution such as salt water, an electrical current flows from the less noble to the more noble metal, and this galvanic current eats away the less noble metal. Although this occurs less rapidly in fresh water than in salt water, it does occur to some degree because of impurities in the fresh water.

## SACRIFICIAL ZINCS

Zinc is one of the least noble of the metals, so zinc plates or bars are used to prevent destruction of metal parts by galvanic action. These zincs are attached to the lower units of outboards, the driveshafts of inboards, and the heat exchangers of many engines with closed cooling systems. Instead of the galvanic action eating away parts of the engine or outdrive, it eats up the zinc, while the engine parts are protected. The zincs should be replaced when they are about half eaten away. If sacrificial metals are not effective, tests can be performed to measure the damaging galvanic currents.

# A Basic Tool Kit

A sailor's tools are generally associated with rigging adjustment. It is a good idea to have a separate set of tools for the boat. In many cases, your owner's manual will suggest special tools for your engine, and many manufacturers offer a prepackaged set of spare parts for their engines—an extra well worth having. Use the following checklist as a good starting point.

---

### ✓ ONBOARD TOOL KIT

**TOOLS**

- ☐ Multimeter—available in hardware stores and essential for diagnosing electrical problems; obtaining one of these and learning how to use it will take you a long way toward getting comfortable with your boat's electrical system and wiring

- ☐ Wrenches—adjustable end wrench (crescent); pipe wrench; box end wrench set (metric or U.S. Standard, to fit the engine and other fittings)

- ☐ Pliers—slip-joint adjustable (insulated) pliers; Vise-Grips; wire-cutting pliers; needle-nose pliers

- ☐ Screwdrivers—assorted regular and Phillips head

- ☐ Hammer

- ☐ Hacksaw

- ☐ File

**SPARE PARTS AND SUPPLIES**

- ☐ Fan belt (and belts for all engine's power takeoffs)

- ☐ Fuel pump

- ☐ Fuel filters for diesel engines

- ☐ Fuel injectors for diesel engines and special tools, if necessary

- ☐ Oil filter

- ☐ Waterproof tape

- ☐ Hose clamps

- ☐ Marine water pump and wheel bearing grease

- ☐ Waterless hand cleaner

# Practice Questions

## IMPORTANT BOATING TERMS

In the following exercise, match the words in the column on the left with the definitions in the column on the right. In the blank space to the left of each term, write the letter of the item that best matches it. Do not use an item in the right-hand column more than once.

| THE ITEMS | THE RESPONSES |
|---|---|
| 1. _____ crankcase | a. formerly missing from small outboards, but now more common; keeps the boat's battery charged |
| 2. _____ fuel injection | b. is replacing carburetors |
| 3. _____ diesel fuel | c. failure to check and replace these causes many diesel engine problems |
| 4. _____ ignition system | d. critical and vulnerable component of a raw-water cooling system |
| 5. _____ alternator | e. drained or filled with antifreeze at end of season |
| 6. _____ fuel filters | f. disconnect negative terminal first |
| 7. _____ removing battery | g. the reservoir of lubricating oil for an inboard or four-stroke outboard engine |
| 8. _____ zinc | h. gels at low temperatures |
| 9. _____ raw-water cooling system | i. a diesel engine does not have one |
| 10. _____ water pump impeller | j. sacrificial metal |

# Multiple-Choice Items

In the following items, choose the best response:

**13-1.** Diesel engines ignite their fuel

    a. by a spark
    b. by an ignition system
    c. the same way as in a gasoline engine
    d. by heat of compression

**13-2.** Diesel fuel has a safety advantage over gasoline because it is

    a. less likely to explode
    b. more efficient
    c. cheaper to use
    d. less odorous

**13-3.** One advantage of a four-stroke outboard over a two-stroke outboard is that it

    a. weighs less, horsepower for horsepower
    b. costs less

    c. uses fuel more efficiently and pollutes less
    d. is easier to replace

**13-4.** Marine engines can be classified by

    a. how they are installed
    b. the number of operating cycles
    c. the type of fuel they use
    d. all of the above

**13-5.** The easiest way to approach the problem of corrosion on battery terminals is to

    a. tighten the terminals
    b. spray them with a mixture of water and baking soda
    c. turn off the switch when the battery is not in use
    d. coat them with grease to prevent corrosion

# Multiple-Choice Items (continued)

**13-6.** Inboard and outboard engines get their names from

a. how they are installed
b. the fuel they use
c. the type of ignition they have
d. none of the above

**13-7.** Which of the following is most accurate?

a. most small marine diesels are raw-water cooled
b. most small marine diesels are air cooled
c. most small marine diesels use a dual cooling system, with recirculating fresh water that is cooled by seawater in a heat exchanger
d. all of the above

**13-8.** If you have two batteries, you should have

a. no battery failure problems
b. a battery isolation switch
c. a ground fault interruptor
d. a voltage regulator

**13-9.** A transom-mounted outboard on a sailboat usually requires

a. power trim
b. a long shaft
c. daily flushing in fresh water
d. a folding propeller

**13-10.** Which of the following is most accurate?

a. a small outboard cannot recharge your ship's battery
b. a small outboard will recharge your ship's battery faster than an inboard engine
c. many small outboards are capable of recharging your battery enough to operate lights, the radio, and other light appliances
d. a small outboard will produce a trickle charge for your battery even when you're not aboard

**13-11.** To protect your battery from accidental short circuits, the terminals should be

a. disconnected whenever the battery is not in use
b. smeared with marine grease
c. protected by a cover
d. allowed to build up a deposit of salts

**13-12.** One feature that you will find on a four-cycle engine that you never find on a two-cycle outboard motor is a

a. crankcase with oil
b. spark plug
c. alternator
d. pull cord

**13-13.** Modern outboard motors require

a. leaded gasoline
b. a lead substitute in the gasoline
c. less lead than a stern-drive engine
d. no lead in the gasoline

**13-14.** Proper lubrication in a two-stroke gasoline outboard engine is provided by

a. oil mixed in the gasoline or injected with the gasoline
b. marine grease packed in the bearings
c. oil pumped throughout the engine
d. oil in the crankcase

**13-15.** The first thing to check if your fully charged battery will not crank your engine is

a. your battery isolation switch
b. your battery terminals
c. the level of fluid in the battery
d. the voltage of the battery

**13-16.** Maintenance procedures include

a. routine
b. winterizing
c. springtime fitting out
d. all of the above

**13-17.** Sacrificial metals are used to keep other metals from eroding. They are made of

a. stainless steel
b. magnesium
c. zinc
d. copper

**13-18.** To prevent most diesel engine problems, keep the following clean:

a. spark plugs
b. fuel and oil
c. ignition system
d. all of the above

(continued on next page)

## Multiple-Choice Items (continued)

**13-19.** To protect against condensation in a diesel fuel tank when your engine is not in use for a long period of time

   a. flush it out with water
   b. run the fuel out of the engine
   c. fill your tank with fuel
   d. pour in a special fuel additive

**13-20.** Most marine engines will start only in

   a. forward
   b. reverse
   c. neutral
   d. idle speed

**13-21.** The newest engines available use what kind of ignition system?

   a. electronic
   b. magneto
   c. distributor
   d. closed

**13-22.** Which of the following is an advantage of an outboard over an inboard engine?

   a. it weighs more
   b. it uses fuel more efficiently
   c. it is easier to winterize, service, and replace
   d. it is quieter

**13-23.** A not-so-obvious advantage of an outboard engine over an inboard engine on a small sailboat is that it

   a. leaves more interior room for storage and passengers
   b. is more reliable
   c. pollutes less
   d. provides more power

**13-24.** To check the gear oil in an outboard lower unit

   a. remove the upper screw cap
   b. remove the lower screw cap
   c. remove both screw caps
   d. see if you can add additional oil

# Lines and Knots for Your Boat

(PHOTO BY DON LINDBERG)

## The objectives of this chapter are to describe:

- The art of handling and working rope known as marlinespike seamanship.
- Rope materials and construction.
- The selection, use, and care of rope.
- How to store rope.
- The rope-handling hardware your boat should have.
- Some useful knots.
- How to secure a boat's lines.

THIS CHAPTER DISCUSSES *marlinespike seamanship*, which is the art of handling and working rope on board. Its name comes from a tapered metal tool, called a *marlinespike*, which is used for working rope. We'll discuss the materials and constructions of rope that is optimized for

333

specific purposes, and we'll look at the uses and care of rope as well as the onboard hardware that helps with line-handling tasks.

# Line or Rope?

The last sentence of the paragraph above mentions line handling instead of rope handling. So when does a rope become a line? Simply put, when you buy it, you ask for **rope**, but when you bring it aboard your boat you call it **line**. Let's look at the few exceptions to this convention.

In traditional terminology, there are times when a rope is a rope. For example, the line used to move a bell's clapper to make the bell ring is a **bell rope**. **Bolt ropes** and **foot ropes** help control sails, while the tillers of sailing ships were once controlled with **tiller ropes**. Today, however, with the exception of the occasional bolt rope sewn into a sail, you won't find ropes in use on a boat.

There are times, though, when the word "line" is too generic for the task at hand. For example, the rope (usually a wire rope) that keeps a sailboat's mast from leaning forward or backward is a **stay**, and the wire ropes that support a mast from side to side are called **shrouds**. Collectively, the stays and shrouds constitute a sailboat's **standing rigging**. The synthetic-fiber or wire ropes used to pull up a sailboat's sails are called **halyards**, and these are part of the boat's **running rigging**. An anchor line and its fittings constitute a **rode**, although you won't be misunderstood if you refer to it as an anchor line. The line that secures a dinghy to a larger boat is a **painter**. A **sheet** is a line that adjusts the trim of a sail.

While sailboats use lines extensively, powerboats use fewer lines and use them less often. Even aboard a powerboat, however, lines serve essential needs.

# Rope Materials

With the exception of the wire rope used in a sailboat's rigging, virtually all modern ropes are made from synthetic fibers. The natural-fiber ropes of earlier generations—manila, sisal, hemp, jute, cotton, and flax—have disappeared from boats and from

| TABLE 14-1 | **Characteristics of Fibers** | | | | | |
|---|---|---|---|---|---|---|
| Material | Breaking Strength[1] (lbs.) | Stretch (%) | Abrasion Resistance | Specific Gravity[2] | UV Resistance | Relative Cost |
| Polypropylene | 1,530 | 18–22 | Fair | 0.91 | Fair | Low |
| Nylon | 2,600 | 30–35 | Excellent | 1.14 | Excellent | Medium |
| Polyester (Dacron) | 3,470 | 15–20 | Excellent | 1.38 | Excellent | Medium |
| High-tenacity polyethylene (Spectra) | 8,160 | 2.3–3.9 | Excellent | 0.97 | Fair | High |
| Aramid (Kevlar) | 8,500 | 1.5–4.5 | Fair | 1.44 | Fair | High |
| High-tenacity copolymer (Technora) | 10,700 | 1.5–4.5 | Fair | 1.44 | Fair | Very high |
| Liquid-crystal polymer (Vectran) | 11,600 | 3.5–4.5 | Very good | 1.40 | Fair | Very high |
| High-tenacity polyethylene (Dyneema) | 12,000 | 2.0–4.0 | Excellent | 0.975 | Very good | Very high |

1. Breaking strength of single-braid ⁵⁄₁₆ in. rope.
2. Floats in fresh water if < 1.00; salt water if < 1.025.

REPRINTED WITH PERMISSION FROM *KNOTS, SPLICES, AND LINE HANDLING: A CAPTAIN'S QUICK GUIDE* BY CHARLIE WING

the shelves of marine supply stores, and for good reason. Synthetic ropes have superior strength either wet or dry, and they can be engineered to optimize certain characteristics for specific jobs. Further, they resist mildew, rot, and damage by acids and alkalis. Heat and sunlight, however, *can* damage *some of* them, as we'll see. The characteristics of various synthetic fibers are shown in Table 14-1. We will mention such high-tech synthetics as Kevlar and Spectra as we proceed, but nylon and polyester predominate on boats and are perfectly satisfactory for every ordinary service.

## Nylon Rope

The most commonly used synthetic fiber is nylon. It does not shrink when wet, and it also resists chafing. Nylon stretches more than any other synthetic or natural fiber rope. Even so, when you remove the stress, it springs back without damage to its fibers or construction.

Nylon's elasticity is both an asset and a liability. When used as an anchor or mooring line, it stretches and helps absorb the shock of a boat's surge. Your anchor is less likely to lose its hold, and the shock loads on your deck hardware are reduced.

On the other hand, since nylon stretches, you should not use it for lines that must stay tight. Thus, you would not use it in the running rigging of sailboats.

Nylon's ability to stretch can make it dangerous if it breaks under strain. In such a case, it may work like an elastic band. A serious accident can result, for example, when one boat is towing another and the hardware comes loose. The line may act as a slingshot and hurl the hardware like a missile.

## Polyester Rope

Polyester rope is manufactured under a variety of trade names, but Dacron is the best known. The stretch rating of a polyester line will vary according to its construction (see below), but polyester in general has substantially lower stretch than nylon and is therefore used widely for sailboat halyards and sheets. Polyester can also be blended with other, even higher-tech synthetics to further increase strength and reduce stretch for specialized applications such as the halyards of racing sailboats. For example, a Spectra, Kevlar, Vectran, or Technora core can make a rope extremely strong and inelastic, while a polyester cover gives that rope better resistance to abrasion and sunlight and makes it easier to handle. Polyester can be formulated to give a rope excellent **hand** (feel)—flexible and soft. Resistance to chafing varies with the formulation but is always much higher than that of Spectra, Kevlar, and other higher-tech fibers.

## Polypropylene Rope

Polypropylene rope is the least costly of the synthetic ropes, which explains its great popularity for lobster trap warps and other commercial fishing applications. Its other major advantage is that it floats, making it useful for ski towlines, painters, and for throwing PFDs to persons in the water. Its ability to float helps keep polyester rope out of a towing boat's propeller.

Polypropylene line deteriorates rapidly in sunlight, however, and it then **parts** (breaks) easily. Don't use it for anchor or mooring lines, or you will risk losing your anchor and, perhaps, your boat.

Polypropylene line also has the disadvantage of a hard, slippery texture. It may slip on a cleat, it can cut your hands, and knots tied in it often work themselves loose.

## Special Ropes

Synthetic fibers are also used to make special types of ropes such as **shock cord**, a multistrand rubber

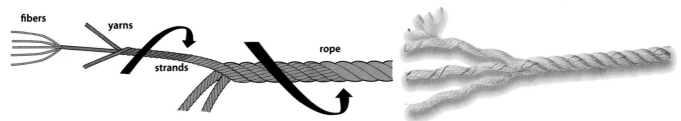

**Figure 14-1.** **Left:** The composition of three-strand line. **Right:** Three-strand nylon line. (COURTESY NEW ENGLAND ROPES)

line with a synthetic cover and hooks or eyes on each end that make connecting it easy.

Shock cord can stretch up to twice its own length. Use it to hold things in place and to prevent halyards from slapping against the mast of a moored boat.

## WIRE ROPE

The standing or permanent rigging on a sailboat is usually *wire rope*, and the running rigging with which sails are hoisted and trimmed is sometimes wire rope as well. Nearly all wire rope used on boats these days is stainless steel, which resists corrosion more successfully than galvanized steel (although, contrary to wide belief, stainless steel *will* corrode). Wire rope provides maximum strength and minimum stretch, which makes it useful also for the davits you see on big boats, by means of which they hoist their tenders clear of the water when making passages.

# Rope Construction

Rope is made in one of three ways: laying, braiding, or weaving.

## LAID ROPE

*Laid rope* (also known as *cable-laid rope*) is made by twisting fibers together to form **yarns**, which are then twisted together in the opposite direction to form **strands**. The strands, in turn, are twisted together in the original direction to form the finished rope.

The direction in which the strands are twisted is called the **lay** of the rope. Thus, rope may be either *right-laid* or *left-laid*. To tell the lay of a line, hold up a length of the line. If the strands spiral upward to the right, the rope is right-laid. Most laid line used on boats has three strands twisted clockwise to form a right-hand lay, and is thus also called *three-strand line*. Three-strand nylon is the most popular choice for mooring pendants and anchor rodes, applications for which high stretch is an asset, not a liability (Figure 14-1).

Sometimes a larger line is desired. In this case, ropes are twisted together to form **cables** or **hawsers**.

Hawsers are used on tugboats and to moor large vessels.

Wire rope is also laid rope in that strands or bundles of wires are twisted together to make it. Figure 14-2 shows a selection of the wire rope constructions in use on boats—primarily sailboats. Wire rope for standing rigging is usually 1 x 19 (spoken as "one by nineteen"). This wire, consisting of nineteen equal elements wound around each other, is strong but not very flexible.

When wire rope is used for running rigging applications (most commonly halyards), 7 x 19 (seven elements, each composed of nineteen individual strands) is the most common choice, followed by 7 x 7 (seven elements with seven strands in each). Wire for running rigging is weaker but more flexible than standing rigging wire of the same diameter.

The 6 x 42 wire rope illustrated in Figure 14-2 has a fiber center, but is rarely seen in use anymore.

## BRAIDED ROPE

A second way to make rope is by braiding, in which fibers are twisted into yarns, two to four yarns are bundled to make a strand, and the strands are then interwoven. *Braided rope* is smooth (like cotton clothesline), which makes it easier on the hands than laid rope. On the other hand, braided line can snag on pilings and other objects, in which case strands may break, weakening the rope.

Braided rope may be *single-* or *double-braid*. A double-braid rope has an outer braided cover over a separately braided inner core (Figure 14-3), whereas a single-braid line has a uniformly braided cross section (Figure 14-4). Double-braid rope is stronger, more durable, more resistant to stretching, and more expensive than single-braid rope of the same diameter and material. Single-braid rope is more supple and easier to handle, especially

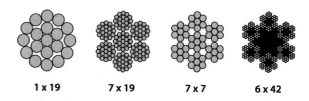

**1 x 19**  **7 x 19**  **7 x 7**  **6 x 42**

**Figure 14-2.** Wire rope cross sections.

**Figure 14-3.** Two examples of double-braid rope, consisting of a braided core inside a braided cover. (TOP PHOTO BY JOE BRITVCH; BOTTOM PHOTO COURTESY NEW ENGLAND ROPES)

when constructed in whole or in part from spun fibers—i.e., from fibers that are a few inches long. Spun nylon or polyester rope is fuzzy, as opposed to continuous-filament rope, which is harder and has a shiny surface.

Small sizes of single-braid ropes, up to ³⁄₈ inch, are used for sailbag ties, flag halyards, and similar special purposes. In larger sizes, single-braid polyester (often spun polyester) is popular for mainsheets, where ease of handling is prized and stretch matters less than it does for headsail sheets. Single-braid nylon is often used for docklines, where some stretch (though perhaps not as much as in an anchor rode) is an asset.

**Figure 14-4.** Two examples of single-braid rope, which is also called solid-braid because it has a uniform braid throughout when seen in cross section. (TOP PHOTO BY DON LINDBERG; BOTTOM PHOTO COURTESY NEW ENGLAND ROPES)

Most other braided rope used on boats is double-braid, which is stronger than laid rope of the same size and material. Single-braid rope is similar in strength but stretches less than laid rope of the same size and material. Braided rope costs more than comparable laid rope.

Various hybrids—both of synthetic materials and of construction methods—have been developed for specific applications. For example, *parallel-core braided polyester rope* consists of a core of parallel, unwoven polyester fibers encased in a braided cover (Figure 14-5). This construction is proving popular for sailboat halyards because it stretches even less than double-braid polyester. On highly competitve racing sailboats this trend is taken even further by substituting Spectra, Kevlar, or some other space-age fiber for the polyester in the parallel core.

Table 14-2 and Figure 14-6 summarize the characteristics of the most popular ropes, and Tables 14-3 and 14-4 show recommended diameters of three-strand or single-braid nylon ropes to use for docklines and anchor rodes on boats of various sizes.

**Figure 14-5.** Parallel-core rope has a core of parallel, unwoven fibers encased in a braided cover. (COURTESY NEW ENGLAND ROPES)

|  |  | Strength | Flexibility | Stretch | Cost |
|---|---|---|---|---|---|
| **THREE-STRAND** |  | Medium | Low | High | Low |
| **SINGLE-BRAID** |  | Medium | High | Medium | Low |
| **DOUBLE-BRAID** |  | High | Medium | Low | Medium |
| **PARALLEL-CORE** |  | Highest | High | Very Low | High |

**Figure 14-6.** The characteristics of various rope constructions. (REPRINTED WITH PERMISSION FROM *KNOTS, SPLICES, AND LINE HANDLING: A CAPTAIN'S QUICK GUIDE* BY CHARLIE WING)

| **TABLE 14-2** | **Approximate Breaking Strengths of Ropes** | | | | | | | |
|---|---|---|---|---|---|---|---|---|
| **Diameter** in inches | 3/16 | 1/4 | 5/16 | 3/8 | 7/16 | 1/2 | 5/8 | 3/4 |
| in millimeters | 5 | 6 | 8 | 9.5 | 11 | 12 | 16 | 19 |
| Polypropylene hollow-braid | 550 | 980 | 1,530 | 2,200 | 2,990 | 3,910 | 6,110 | 8,800 |
| Polypropylene three-strand | 725 | 1,290 | 2,010 | 2,900 | 3,940 | 5,150 | 8,050 | 11,600 |
| Nylon single-braid | 940 | 1,670 | 2,600 | 3,750 | 5,100 | 6,660 | 10,400 | 15,000 |
| Nylon double-braid | 1,090 | 1,940 | 3,040 | 4,375 | 5,950 | 7,770 | 12,100 | 17,500 |
| Nylon three-strand | 940 | 1,670 | 2,600 | 3,750 | 5,100 | 6,660 | 10,400 | 15,000 |
| Polyester single-braid | 1,140 | 1,900 | 3,000 | 4,200 | 5,500 | 7,000 | 11,000 | 15,300 |
| Polyester double-braid | 1,200 | 2,000 | 3,000 | 4,400 | 6,600 | 8,500 | 14,400 | 20,000 |
| with Spectra or Kevlar core | 2,300 | 3,800 | 5,700 | 7,600 | 10,200 | 12,800 | 21,800 | 28,800 |
| with Vectran or Technora core | 2,720 | 4,500 | 8,000 | 10,000 | 15,000 | 18,000 | 31,000 | 42,300 |
| Polyester braid with parallel core | 1,600 | 2,700 | 4,400 | 5,500 | 7,400 | 9,600 | 15,000 | 21,600 |

REPRINTED WITH PERMISSION FROM *KNOTS, SPLICES, AND LINE HANDLING: A CAPTAIN'S QUICK GUIDE* BY CHARLIE WING

## WEBBING

Synthetic fibers are sometimes woven together to form a flat line called **webbing**. Webbing is used for a variety of purposes such as the retrieval line on a trailer, and you may have seen it used for the backs and seats of lawn chairs.

Webbing of woven nylon or polyester is very strong. Use it to tie down a dinghy on a larger boat or to hold a boat on a trailer. Webbing also makes good **sail stops** (ties used to hold a lowered sail to its boom) since it holds knots so well (Figure 14-7), and offshore sailors use webbing for their safety harnesses.

# Measuring Rope

The older, traditional way to measure the size of fiber rope is by its circumference (the distance around the rope). Today, however, most marine suppliers and boaters describe it by its diameter. If you ask for 1/2-inch rope you will get one with a 1/2-inch diameter.

Small lines are suitable for securing small items, but most people have trouble holding onto them. The smallest line most people can conveniently hold has a 3/8-inch diameter. Thus, even

| **TABLE 14-3** | **Docklines** | | |
|---|---|---|---|
| **Boat Length (ft.)** | **Bow/Stern Lines (ft.)** | **Spring Lines (ft.)** | **Rope Diameter (in.)** |
| to 27 | 20 | 25 | 3/8 |
| 28–36 | 25 | 35 | 1/2 |
| 37–45 | 30 | 45 | 5/8 |
| 46–54 | 35 | 50 | 3/4 |
| 55–72 | 40 | 70 | 1 |

REPRINTED WITH PERMISSION FROM *KNOTS, SPLICES, AND LINE HANDLING: A CAPTAIN'S QUICK GUIDE* BY CHARLIE WING

| **TABLE 14-4** | **Anchor Rodes** | |
|---|---|---|
| (recommended rode consists of 15 feet of chain plus 200 feet of three-strand nylon) | | |
| **Boat Length (ft.)** | **Chain Rope Size (in.)** | **Diameter (in.)** |
| to 25 | 3/16 | 1/4 |
| 26–35 | 1/4 | 1/2 |
| 46–54 | 3/8 | 3/4 |
| 55–72 | 1/2 | 1 |

REPRINTED WITH PERMISSION FROM *KNOTS, SPLICES, AND LINE HANDLING: A CAPTAIN'S QUICK GUIDE* BY CHARLIE WING

*Selecting Your Ropes*

*Select each line for its specific purpose.*
*Some characteristics to look for are:*

- *strength*
- *elasticity*
- *resistance to chafing*
- *resistance to sunlight*
- *resistance to slipping*
- *buoyancy*
- *ease in handling*
- *storage conditions*

though a $\frac{1}{4}$-inch-diameter high-tech rope is as strong as $\frac{3}{8}$-inch double-braid polyester, the latter is more likely to be chosen as a mainsheet because it's so much easier to handle (and also because it costs much less!). Choose larger line sizes for sheets, halyards, anchor lines, and mooring lines on anything but the smallest boats.

It is unwise to use small mooring and anchor lines. During a storm, these lines are under heavy stress. The surge of your boat can cause a line to part, and constant chafe can abrade and weaken it. For both these reasons, a thicker line will stand up better and longer than a thinner one, but there are limits. You need to select a line that's appropriate for the size of the cleat you will tie it to. In general, you will want to use the largest dock and anchor lines that will lead fairly through your boat's chocks and tie properly to your boat's cleats and bitts.

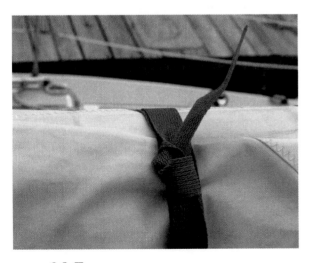

**Figure 14-7.** Webbing used as a sail stop. (PHOTO BY DON LIND-BERG)

Large lines have less stretch per pound of load than smaller lines of the same material and construction. Larger lines also take fewer turns around a winch to raise a sail, and offer more friction on the winch. Regardless of the size of the line, you may wish to wear gloves with palms but without fingers on a sailboat. They are designed to protect your hands from line burn while still keeping your fingers free.

The principal disadvantage of large lines is cost. Large lines cost more than smaller ones, and you will need larger cleats to which to tie them. On a sailboat, larger lines call for larger **blocks** (pulleys), which are also an added expense.

# Care of Rope

All rope requires some care. Stainless steel wire rope needs the least. The time and trouble you take in caring for your lines will be repaid by greater safety and longer rope life.

## UNCOILING ROPE

Proper care begins as soon as you buy your rope. Open new coils carefully. The rope can easily tangle and kink, which makes handling it more difficult and can weaken its fibers.

Both braided and wire ropes usually come on reels or spools. If your rope came on a reel, roll it off. Do not try to uncoil it, as this introduces a kink in the rope with each turn taken off the reel. The same problem occurs if you take rope from a coil in an improper manner.

If you get a kink in the rope, remove it by working it out to the nearest end. You can make a kink disappear by putting a strain on the rope, but don't do it, because some of its fibers will break, weakening the rope at the point of the kink.

## OVERSTRESSED LINES

Never overwork or overstress a line. You may not see it, but too big a load on a line breaks its fibers and weakens it. Check for deterioration by looking inside the rope. If you see a powdery material, replace it. And if the line has decreased in diameter, it has been permanently stretched and weakened.

## DRY YOUR LINES

Stow your lines in dry, well-ventilated places, such as on a shelf or grating, to prevent accumulation of moisture. Do not stow other materials on top of the lines.

You can stow synthetic lines wet, but doing so will introduce moisture into your hold or lockers. Although synthetic fiber will not rot, it will mildew, which makes it look and smell bad.

You should also keep your lines away from sources of heat such as exhaust pipes. Heat is harmful to synthetic fibers, as is battery acid.

## CHAFING

When lines rub against hard surfaces, even highly polished chocks, they will eventually chafe and weaken. Wrap your mooring and anchor lines with canvas or leather to prevent chafing where they pass through chocks or around cleats (Figure 14-8). Where mooring lines contact wooden or concrete piers, pass them through lengths of old garden hose to increase their useful life.

To get the most use out of a mooring or anchor line and to maintain its safety, turn it end for end periodically to distribute chafing at different points. Docklines, too, can be end-for-ended in this manner.

## KEEP YOUR LINES CLEAN

Dirt, sand, salt, and oil are destructive to both natural and synthetic fiber lines. Dirt, sand, and salt crystals cut the fibers, while oil weakens them. To wash a line, put it in a mesh bag or pillowcase and put it in a washing machine. In this way, it won't get tangled up, develop new kinks, or foul up the washing machine. Mild soap or detergent will help get the line clean and will not harm the fibers. If the line is stiff, use a fabric softener.

## FRAYING

The ends of all lines will fray and *unlay* (separate) unless you treat them to prevent it. If you don't

**Figure 14-8.** A canvas sleeve protects this dockline from chafe where it passes around the cleat. (REPRINTED WITH PERMISSION FROM *ROUGH WEATHER SEAMANSHIP FOR SAIL AND POWER* BY ROGER MARSHALL)

care what the end of your line looks like, you can simply tie a knot in it, but this is unsightly and makes the line difficult to use, as the knot will not pass through chocks and blocks easily.

When a synthetic line is cut from a coil by an electric cutter, it does not need care immediately. When it is cut with a knife or otherwise, you can use a match to get the same result as an electric cutter. The heat will melt the end of almost any synthetic line, fusing the strands together and preventing them from unlaying. Eventually, though, the end will begin to unravel.

Another temporary means of treating the end of a line is to tape it with marine, electrical, or adhesive tape. Sooner or later the tape will come off, however, and the line will unravel.

A more permanent way to prevent fraying is by using an air-drying liquid plastic coating (such as Rope Dip) developed for this purpose and sold in marine supply stores. You can even color-code your lines by this means. This is useful on a sailboat, where several lines may end near each other.

*Whipping* the end of a line is another way to keep it from unraveling, one that will look better and last longer than heat-sealing or taping it.

Figure 14-9 shows a *plain whipping*, which is not permanent but will last a long time if done right. Start by forming a loop of whipping twine—which is also called *cord* or *small stuff*, and is most commonly sold in a waxed polyester construction, though nylon twine is also available. Place the apex of the loop about 1/2 inch from the end of the

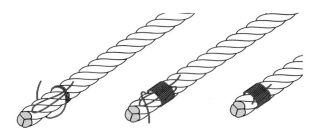

**Figure 14-9.** A plain whipping. (REPRINTED WITH PERMISSION FROM *KNOTS, SPLICES, AND LINE HANDLING: A CAPTAIN'S QUICK GUIDE* BY CHARLIE WING)

rope. Using the long end of the twine, make eight or ten tight turns around the rope, working toward the rope end. Leave the anchored end of the twine exposed, because you will need it in a minute, and stop the turns before you cover the apex of the loop. Pass the working end of the cord through the loop, then pull the anchored end until the loop disappears under the turns. Clip the twine ends flush with the turns, and you're done.

To whip the end of a three-strand line permanently, use a *sailmaker's whipping* as in Figure 14-10. Start by unlaying the rope strands to about 1 inch from the end, then pass a loop of twine around one of the strands so that the apex of the loop points away from the rope end, rather than toward it as in the plain whipping. Then relay the strands back to their original position. Using the long end of the whipping twine, make eight or ten tight turns toward the rope end, leaving a generous bight of the loop exposed under the first turn. Then place the exposed portion of the loop back over its original strand, and pull tight using the anchored end of the twine. Finally, tie the twine ends tightly with a square knot, and trim the ends.

For a more or less permanent whipping that will work on braided as well as laid line, try a *sewn whipping*, as in Figure 14-11. Thread waxed whipping twine through the eye of a heavy needle, then make two stitches through the rope about $1/2$ to $3/4$ inch from the end. Follow with eight to ten tight turns toward the end, then make a stitch through a third of the rope's circumference so that the needle emerges about 120° from its entry point. Pull taut. Now pass the needle and twine back over the turns and make a mirror-image stitch at the beginning end of the whipping. Again pass needle and twine over the turns for a second 120° stitch that begins where the initial stitch emerged. Repeat until you have three double stitches spaced at 120° intervals around the rope end, then take a final stitch and trim the twine ends. Besides being decorative, a whipping like this is very functional.

## CARE OF WIRE ROPE

Wire rope will serve you well if you take care of it. One of the worst things that can happen to it is to get a kink in it, as this weakens it.

Be careful when you run your hand along a wire rope. Under stress, some of the small wires break and then stick out from the rope. Examine wire rope from time to time by running your hand up and down the wire while wearing cotton gloves. If a glove catches on anything, you've most likely found a broken strand, which is often called a *fishhook* or *meathook*.

Any such break indicates that the wire is damaged, and its load-carrying ability has been compromised. If you find more than a few fishhooks, consider replacing the wire. Wire rope ends are usually covered by *swaged terminals*, which are metal

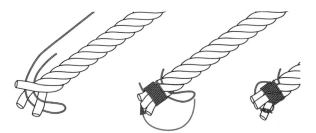

**Figure 14-10.** A sailmaker's whipping. (REPRINTED WITH PERMISSION FROM *KNOTS, SPLICES, AND LINE HANDLING: A CAPTAIN'S QUICK GUIDE* BY CHARLIE WING)

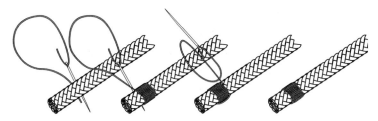

**Figure 14-11.** A sewn whipping. (REPRINTED WITH PERMISSION FROM *KNOTS, SPLICES, AND LINE HANDLING: A CAPTAIN'S QUICK GUIDE* BY CHARLIE WING)

sleeves that are machine-crimped around the wire. The terminal is usually forged with an end fitting by means of which the wire can be connected to a mast tang, a turnbuckle, or other hardware (Figure 14-12). When swaged fittings deteriorate, they usually don't show signs of weakness during inspection. A failure in a sailboat's standing rigging will usually occur during periods of great stress, such as a storm, which is the last time you want this problem to happen. To avoid this, regular, highly critical inspections of your boat's rigging, especially the wire rope, are recommended. Boats exposed only to mild weather and waves should be inspected at least every 10 years, while boats exposed to heavy weather and waves should be inspected at least

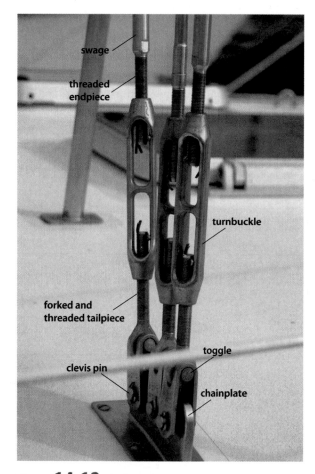

**Figure 14-12.** Sailboat forestays, backstays, and shrouds terminate on deck in swaged end fittings with threads that screw into turnbuckles like these three, which are for a sailboat's starboard shrouds. The turnbuckles are attached to well-anchored chainplates and are used to adjust the tension of the stay or shroud. The wire rope shrouds are not visible in this photo; they're crimped into the swages just above the field of view. (PHOTO BY DON LINDBERG)

every 5 years. All rigging should be inspected thoroughly before any extended offshore passage.

# Making Up a Line

Stow your lines neatly when they are not in use. How you stow lines depends on their intended uses. There are three methods of making up line—coiling, faking, and flemishing.

## COILING A LINE

If you plan to stow a line in a compartment or locker or hang it from a peg, coil it. Coil right-laid rope clockwise, and coil left-laid rope (if you ever encounter any) counterclockwise. Assuming the line is right-laid, start by holding it in your left hand. Run your right hand down the line and sweep the line back to your left hand to form a single loop, then repeat. Continue adding loops until you have coiled all the line.

When you coil the end of a cleated halyard in this fashion, the most convenient place to store the coil is on the halyard cleat. To do so, simply reach through the coil to grasp the line between the cleat hitch and the first bight of the coil. Pull that part of the line through the coil to form a loop, twist the loop once or twice, and hook it over the horn of the cleat (Figure 14-13). There you have it—a neat coil, hung off the deck and out of the way, yet easily loosened when the time comes to lower the sail.

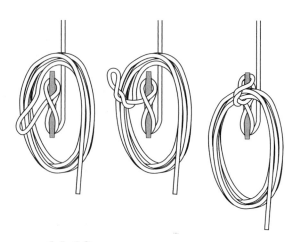

**Figure 14-13.** An easy way to hang a coiled halyard from a mast cleat. This coil will also be quick to undo when it's time to lower the sail. (REPRINTED WITH PERMISSION FROM *KNOTS, SPLICES, AND LINE HANDLING: A CAPTAIN'S QUICK GUIDE* BY CHARLIE WING)

If you are simply coiling an unused line for stowage and wish to hang the coil, release the last loop of the coil and wind the longer end thus created several times around the coil. Then reach through the coil and pull a loop from the last winding you just completed through the coil, then up and over the top of the coil. Pull on the running end to cinch the loop, and you have created a **gasket coil**, which can be hung in a locker or cabin for stowage (Figure 14-14).

## FAKING DOWN A LINE

On a small boat you can usually stow your anchor line by letting it fall into its well. If this is not feasible, try faking it down or flemishing it. **Faked lines** run with less resistance than coiled lines in fast runoffs, and with less chance of tangling or snagging. Mooring lines, anchor lines, heaving lines, lead lines, running rigging, and other lines can all be faked to good advantage. Faking is sometimes known as **flaking**.

Faking down a line consists of laying it onto the deck or into the anchor locker in figure eights called *fakes*, as in Figure 14-15. The fakes may overlap or lie clear of each other. Faking down prepares the line to run out rapidly without fouling or kinking. Keep clear of a line when it is running out, or you could become snarled in it.

## FLEMISHING A LINE

To give a line a neat, ornamental look, **flemish** it. To do so, coil the line flat on a deck or pier like a spring, with each coil encircling the preceding one. Coil right-laid line clockwise. When you have finished, you can tighten the coil by laying both hands flat on the line at the center of the coil. Now, turn your hands in the direction that tightens the coil. The result is a tight, attractive mat (Figure 14-16).

A flemished line looks great. Flemish the ends of your mooring lines, and you will be less likely to

**Figure 14-15.** Faking down a line. (PHOTO BY JOE BRITVCH)

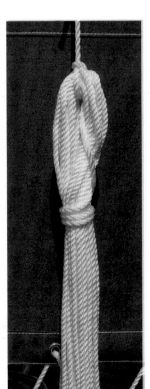 

**Figure 14-14.** A gasket coil is used to coil a line for stowing (left), and is also used for lines on deck that do not need to be adjusted fequently or quickly, such as this boom vang (right). (PHOTOS BY DON LINDBERG)

**Figure 14-16.** Flemishing a line. (PHOTO BY DON LINDBERG)

trip over them. But don't leave a flemished line on a varnished surface very long, especially overnight. The trapped moisture will spoil a varnished finish, and if left for several days on a fiberglass surface, the line may leave a nasty dirt stain.

# Knots, Bends, and Hitches

Lines are used for pulling, holding, lifting, and lowering. Before they can do these things, however, you must fasten them to something.

How you fasten a line depends on what you intend to do with it. In its more general sense, a *knot* is any series of loops, turns, and tucks in a line that modifies the rope itself or that connects it to another line or to some other object. In its narrower sense, however, a *knot* is formed in the line itself, whereas a *bend* ties one line to another, and a *hitch* joins a line to a spar, ring, or other object. There are exceptions to these conventions, as you will see. In any event, knots, bends, and hitches are all known collectively as **knots**.

You can learn something about tying knots by reading about them. If you are to become proficient, though, you must practice. Fortunately, just a few knots will serve all your ordinary needs.

| TABLE 14-5 | **Characteristics of Fibers** | |
|---|---|---|
| How Knots and Splices Reduce Strength of Rope | | Percentage of Breaking Strength Remaining |
| Knots | No knots or splices | 100 |
| | Anchor or Fisherman's Bend | 76 |
| | Timber Hitch | 70–65 |
| | Round turn | 70–65 |
| | Two half hitches | 70–65 |
| | Bowline | 60 |
| | Clove Hitch | 60 |
| | Sheet Bend or Weaver's Knot | 55 |
| | Square or Reef Knot | 45 |
| Splices | Eye Splice (over thimble) | 95–90 |
| | Long Splice | 87 |
| | Short Splice | 85 |

## KNOTS AND LINE STRENGTH

All knots depend on friction created by turns in the line for their holding power. Under strain, friction weakens a line by breaking some of its fibers. Lines also weaken at splices, because these too depend on friction, but splices weaken a line much less than other knots do. You can see how knots and splices weaken lines in Table 14-5.

## CHARACTERISTICS OF GOOD KNOTS

A good knot, bend, or hitch will hold well without slipping. It serves a practical purpose and does what you want it to do. It is easy to tie, and it is also easy to untie. If you can't untie a knot after you have used it, you will lose at least a portion of the line.

## PARTS OF A LINE

The parts of a line have names. These make it easier to describe how to tie knots and to talk about them.

The end of a line in which you're tying a knot is its *working end*. The other end of the line, which is usually tied to the vessel or to a load of some kind, is the *bitter end*. On some boats, you tie the bitter end of an anchor line to a *bitt*—a heavy and firmly mounted piece of wood or metal on the foredeck used for securing lines. On other boats, the bitter end of the anchor rode is tied to a ringbolt in an underdeck anchor locker.

A line has a *standing part*, which is the main part of the line leading away from the knot you are tying and toward the load. Any bend or loop in the line is a *bight*, which becomes a *loop* if the line crosses itself (Figure 14-17). When the bight is around an object or the rope itself, it's a *turn*. When it is wrapped one and a half times around the object to form a complete circle, as in Figure 14-17, it is a *round turn*. An *overhand loop* is a small circle in the standing part of the line made by crossing the working end over the standing part. In an *underhand loop*, the working end crosses under the standing part.

A word of caution in tying knots. Synthetic line is slick, and some knots will pull out of it unless

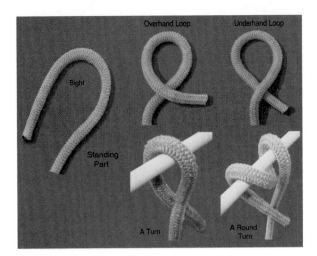

**Figure 14-17.** Some knotwork terminology. (PHOTO BY JOE BRITVCH)

**Figure 14-18.** The overhand knot, shown cinched up and loose. (PHOTO BY DON LINDBERG)

**Figure 14-19.** The figure-eight knot. (PHOTOS BY DON LINDBERG)

you leave an extra amount of line projecting beyond the knot. Pull the knot tight.

## SOME USEFUL KNOTS

The array of available knots can be confusing, but you don't need to know them all. A working familiarity with a few good knots is better than a superficial knowledge of many seldom-used knots.

The knots, bends, and hitches described in this chapter are all functional. They serve many purposes, and, except as noted, are as easy to untie as they are to tie.

### Stoppers

A *stopper knot* is a knot tied in a line to prevent it from running all the way through a block. There are two commonly used stoppers.

**OVERHAND KNOT.** An *overhand knot* can be used not only as a stopper (Figure 14-18), but also to temporarily prevent a freshly cut rope from unlaying or unraveling. It is not a good knot, however, since it jams under tension and is then difficult to untie. Tie it by making an overhand loop in the standing part of the line, then passing the working end up through the loop and pulling it tight.

**FIGURE-EIGHT KNOT.** A *figure-eight knot* (Figure 14-19) makes a better stopper than an overhand knot when heavy loads may occur. It can be untied easily after it has been jammed. Use it on all lines that you want to prevent from running through blocks, but do not use it on spinnaker sheets, which should always be free to run in an emergency. To tie a figure-eight knot, first form an underhand loop, then pass the working end over the standing part, then under and finally up through the loop. Untie the knot by pushing the working end back through the loop.

Note: You can make this knot bulkier by adding one or more round turns of the working end around the standing part before finally passing the working end up through the loop. The knot is then called a *stevedore knot* (Figure 14-20).

## Reef Knot

A *square knot* is sometimes called a *reef knot* because it can be used to secure a reefed sail to a boom. More generally, you can use it whenever you need to tie together two lines of equal diameter or the two ends of a single line, as when tying packages. If you try to use it with lines of unequal size, however, it will probably slip and untie.

A reef knot is useful only when not subject to a heavy or critical load. Under a heavy load it jams and becomes difficult to untie. Further, if you apply unequal tension, such jerking on one side, it is apt to capsize into two half hitches, and when it does it may slip. And if the knot fetches up against an obstacle or restriction, as when running through a pulley, it may come completely undone. For all these reasons, the reef knot should be avoided on a boat except for noncritical applications.

**Figure 14-20.** Take an added turn or two with the working end before you make the final tuck in a figure-eight knot, and you get a stevedore knot, which is bulkier than a figure-eight knot. (REPRINTED WITH PERMISSION FROM *NAUTICAL KNOTS ILLUSTRATED*, REVISED EDITION, BY PAUL SNYDER AND ARTHUR SNYDER)

To tie a reef knot, hold one line in your left hand and the other in your right. Now pass the end in your left hand over and under the line in your right hand. Following this, pass the same end back over and under, this time working right to left. When you finish, it should look like Figure 14-21. The end of each line should emerge from the side it entered and lie parallel to its own standing part. If it doesn't, you have tied a *granny knot*, which will slip under tension.

## Sheet or Becket Bend

The *sheet* or *becket bend* is also called a *weaver's knot*. Use it to join lines of equal or different diameters. There are three forms of the knot: the sheet bend, the double sheet bend, and the slippery sheet bend.

**SHEET BEND.** Tie a *sheet bend* by forming a bight in the larger line. Pass the working end of the smaller line up through the bight, around both parts of the larger line, and back under itself. If you

**Figure 14-21.** The square or reef knot. (PHOTOS BY DON LINDBERG)

are going to stress this knot, tie the ends of both lines to their standing parts with small stuff. If not tied down, alternate loading and unloading of the knot can untie it (Figure 14-22A).

**DOUBLE SHEET BEND.** A *double sheet bend* offers more security than a sheet bend, and is especially needed when one line is considerably larger than the other. Tie a double sheet bend by forming a bight in the larger line. Next, pass the working end of the smaller line up through the bight and around the standing part of the larger line. Now take another turn around the standing part of the larger line with the smaller line and pass it back under itself (Figure 14-22B).

**SLIPPERY SHEET BEND.** A *slippery sheet bend* is a variation of a sheet bend and is tied the same way, except that you don't tuck the line under itself. Instead, form a bight in the end of the smaller line and tuck this bight under the standing part of the smaller line (Figure 14-22C).

A slippery sheet bend is easier to untie than a sheet bend, but it is also less secure. Any knot is "slippery" if it ends in a bight, which makes it easy to untie under tension.

## Clove Hitch

Use a *clove hitch* to tie a line to a piling or bollard or a fender to a rail (Figures 14-23 and 14-24). This knot is wonderfully quick and convenient to tie, but be careful as it will slip if not under constant tension. For example, the loading and unloading of a line caused by a boat surging on its moorings can undo the knot. Thus, a clove hitch is a temporary

**Figure 14-23.** A clove hitch over a post. (PHOTO BY JOE BRITVCH)

**Figure 14-24.** A clove hitch used to store a gasket coil temporarily on a lifeline. (REPRINTED WITH PERMISSION FROM *NAUTICAL KNOTS ILLUSTRATED*, REVISED EDITION, BY PAUL SNYDER AND ARTHUR SNYDER)

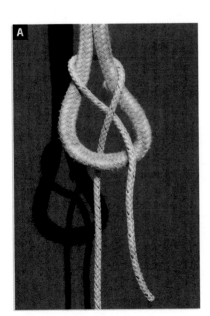

**Figure 14-22. Left to right:** The sheet bend (A), the double sheet bend (B), and the slippery sheet bend (C). (PHOTOS BY DON LINDBERG)

means of securing a boat. It will also jam under load, and if you can't ease the tension on the line, you will find it difficult to untie.

Tie a clove hitch by passing the working end of the line twice around the object to which it is to be tied. The first pass is below the standing part of the line (Figure 14-23). The second is above the standing part. Finish by passing the working end under the second loop.

You can also tie a clove hitch by forming two underhand loops in the standing part of the line, with the second loop on top of the first (Figure 14-25). You can now pass both loops over a bollard or piling.

To make a clove hitch more secure, run the working end over the standing part of the line and then through the loop thus formed (see below). You have now tied a half hitch, which will prevent the working end from slipping out of the clove hitch.

## Two Half Hitches

Two **half hitches** are the same as a clove hitch tied around the standing part of a line (Figure 14-26). To make them, pass the working end of the line around the object to which the line is to be tied.

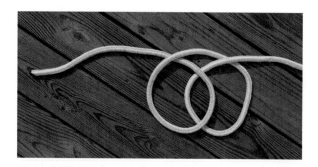

**Figure 14-25.** An alternate way to tie a clove hitch. Make both loops as shown prior to passing them over a bollard or piling. (PHOTO BY DON LINDBERG)

**Figure 14-26.** Two half hitches. (PHOTO BY JOE BRITVCH)

Now, pass the working end of the line over the standing part and through the loop thus formed. This forms the first half hitch.

Form the second half hitch in the same way: pass the working end over the standing part and back through the resultant loop.

You can tie lines to rings, spars, piles, and posts with two half hitches. Under tension, two half hitches are easier to untie than a clove hitch, and they make a more permanent knot than a clove hitch. Under tension, the knot tightens, but even so, it is easy to untie.

To further improve this knot, precede it with a round turn, which distributes the load over a longer length of line, reduces chafe, and makes the knot both secure and easier to untie (Figure 14-27). You'll find numerous uses on board for a **round turn and two half hitches**.

## Anchor or Fisherman's Bend

Use an **anchor** or **fisherman's bend** to tie an anchor line to an anchor fitting such as a ring (Figure 14-28). You can also use it to tie a fishing line or leader to the eye of a fishhook, or more generally for bending a line to any object. It's a wonderfully secure knot, since it develops considerable friction. At the same time, there is less line chafe where it goes around the fitting.

Begin the knot by passing the working end around the object twice, forming a loop and a turn. Then pass the working end over the standing part and through the loop and the turn. Following this, you again pass the end over the standing part and between the standing part and itself.

**Figure 14-27.** A round turn and two half hitches. (REPRINTED WITH PERMISSION FROM *NAUTICAL KNOTS ILLUSTRATED*, REVISED EDITION, BY PAUL SNYDER AND ARTHUR SNYDER)

**Figure 14-28.** The anchor bend. For greater security, seize the working end to the standing part with twine. (PHOTO BY DON LINDBERG)

Actually, the anchor bend is much like two half hitches. Instead of passing around the object once, though, it passes twice. Additionally, you tie the first half hitch through the two loops instead of between the standing part and itself.

To make the knot more secure, seize the working end to the standing part with twine.

## Rolling Hitch

When you tie a *rolling hitch*, you tie one line to the standing part of another (Figure 14-29). Use it to tie a line to the working end of a second line. When tension is put on the first line, it releases the tension on the second. This allows you to adjust the second line. It can be used, for example, to take the strain off a jibsheet while you clear an override from the sheet wraps on a winch or relocate a block (Figure 14-30). You can also use it to adjust fender lines and awning tie-downs, or to adjust the tie-down lines on a dinghy lashing or a rooftop load on your car.

**Figure 14-30.** A rolling hitch can be tied around another line to take the strain off it. Pulling on the braided line will tighten the grip of the rolling hitch around the three-strand line. Sailors sometimes use this technique to take the strain off a jibsheet long enough to clear overrides from a winch drum. (PHOTOS BY JOE BRITVCH)

Tie the knot by passing the working end twice around the line to be held, as in Figure 14-29. In each of these turns, the working end passes over its own standing part. Then take a third turn around the line you want to hold, this time passing the working end under itself to form a half hitch. You must tie the first two turns on the side from which you will apply tension on the standing part.

## Bowline

The *bowline* is a means of forming a temporary loop of fixed size at the end of a line (Figure 14-31). It

**Figure 14-29.** A rolling hitch tied around a rail, as you might do to hang fenders, for example. (PHOTOS BY JOE BRITVCH)

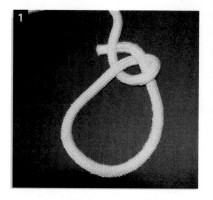
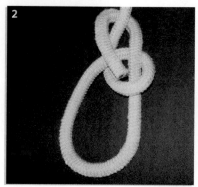
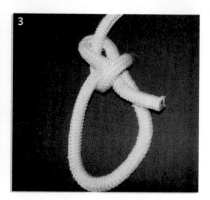

**Figure 14-31.** Tying a bowline. (PHOTOS BY JOE BRITVCH)

is the **king of knots** because of its many everyday uses on boats and elsewhere. A bowline is easy to untie even after being placed under a heavy load. Just push the working end back through the loop around the standing part.

On board, bowlines tie lines to fittings, jibsheets to the clews of sails, and lines to anchors, among many other tasks (Figure 14-32). You can also use them to join lines of unequal sizes, loop to loop. You can even use a bowline as a temporary boarding ladder by lowering it over the side and tying the standing part to a cleat on the opposite side of the boat. If you use a bowline to tie a line to an anchor, consider using a thimble to prevent chafing.

To tie a bowline, first make a small overhand loop in the standing part of the line as in Figure 14-31, leaving enough line at the working end to form a loop of the size you desire. Next, pass the working end up through the small loop, around the standing part, and back down through the small loop. Pull the knot tight. The knot is usually tied with the working end inside the loop.

**Figure 14-32.** Bowlines in jibsheets. (REPRINTED WITH PERMISSION FROM *NAUTICAL KNOTS ILLUSTRATED*, REVISED EDITION, BY PAUL SNYDER AND ARTHUR SNYDER)

# Splices

When you want a more permanent way to join two lines or to form a loop (called an *eye*) in the end of a line, tie a *splice* rather than a knot. Splices are more time-consuming than the knots discussed above, but they cause less reduction in rope strength (see Table 14-5) and hold up remarkably well in long-term use.

You can buy mooring and docklines with eye splices already in place at one or both ends, and sailmakers and marine equipment suppliers sell sheets and halyards with custom splices. Many boating enthusiasts find pleasure in splicing their own lines, however, and the ability to do so is still seen as a sign of competent seamanship.

You can splice any fiber line, though a splice in laid line is simpler. Splicing double-braid line is more difficult, but it can be done.

## SHORT SPLICE

You can join two pieces of laid line of the same size with a short splice (Figure 14-33) or a long splice. A *short splice* increases line diameter by about 40% and is thus inappropriate for any line that will pass through a block. A *long splice*, on the other hand, while it does not increase line diameter, does decrease line strength more than the short splice and is therefore not shown here. When you need a long length of line that will pass through blocks, you would do better to buy new rope than to splice two lengths of line together. For other applications, however, a short splice is a good solution.

**1** Unlay all 6 strands 1" for each 1/16" of rope diameter and tape ends. Tape ropes to prevent further unlaying, and marry the ropes.

**2** Remove one of the rope tapes. Cross a strand end over its adjacent and under the next.

**3** Continue tucking strand over and under for a total of 4 tucks (6 for nylon).

**4** Repeat Steps 2 and 3 for second strand.

**5** Repeat for third strand against the lay.

**6** Remove remaining tape and pull on loose strands to snug splice. Repeat Steps 2–5 going in opposite direction.

**Figure 14-33.** Making a short splice. (REPRINTED WITH PERMISSION FROM *KNOTS, SPLICES, AND LINE HANDLING: A CAPTAIN'S QUICK GUIDE* BY CHARLIE WING)

To practice making a short splice, equip yourself with some laid line about 3/8 to 1/2 inch in diameter. You will need some tape or small stuff—any kind will do, since it is used only until you complete the splice. You will also need a fid or a marlinespike.

Lash or tape both lines about 16 diameters from their ends; if the lines are 1/2 inch in diameter, this means you will tape or lash them about 8 inches from their ends. Unlay the lines to the tapes, then tape or lash the ends of the strands to keep them from untwisting as you make the splice. Next, **marry** the two unlaid ends by alternating the strands of one rope with the strands of the other as shown in Figure 14-33. Then remove the tape or lashing from one of the lines; this is the one you will tuck into first.

Take one of the strands from the line you will be tucking, and cross it over the adjacent strand on the other line, then under the next strand after that, opening a space for the tuck with a fid or marlinespike if necessary. Continue tucking this strand—over one, then under one—for a total of four tucks, or six for nylon. Then repeat this process with each of the other two strands in the line you are tucking.

Remove the tape or lashing from the line you have been tucking, and repeat the process with the three remaining untucked strands, this time working in the opposite direction. When you are done, cut off the ends of the strands to within about 1/4 inch of the standing part, and roll the completed splice between your hands or under your foot to finish it. With practice, you can do the splice quickly and neatly. One way to make a synthetic rope splice tight is by placing it in boiling water, which shrinks the rope.

## EYE SPLICE

Tucking an *eye splice* is much like tucking the first half of a short splice (Figure 14-34). The tucks, though, are made back into the standing part of the same rope on which you are making the eye. To begin, unlay and tape the end of the line much as before, but this time you might unlay a slightly longer length—say, 20 diameters, or 10 inches for a 1/2-inch line. Form the eye to the size desired and lay the unlaid end along the standing part. Make the size of the eye just large enough to pull it over a cleat one horn at a time. *Seize* (lash) or tape the standing part to mark the entry point.

**①** Unlay rope 5" for each 1/4" of diameter. Tape both rope and strand ends to prevent further unlaying. Form the eye and seize rope to mark entry point.

**②** Raise the strand closest to the seizing (use a fid if necessary) and tuck the closest unlaid strand through. Proceeding in the direction of twist, raise the next strand and tuck the corresponding strand through.

**③** Raise the third strand and finish the first series of tucks with the remaining unlaid strand. Remove the seizing and tug on the strand ends to tighten throat.

**④** Following the same order, tuck each strand over and under for a total of 4 tucks (6 for nylon). For a neater appearance, taper the last tuck by removing half of the fibers in each strand.

**Figure 14-34.** Making an eye splice in laid line. (REPRINTED WITH PERMISSION FROM *KNOTS, SPLICES, AND LINE HANDLING: A CAPTAIN'S QUICK GUIDE* BY CHARLIE WING)

## Splicing Double-Braid Rope

Eye splices can also be made in double-braid line (Figure 14-36). The technique involves substituting core for core and cover for cover. This splice is difficult and time-consuming, but it is also extremely useful, and the result is strong and permanent.

To make this splice you need a tubular, hollow fid as shown at the top of page 353, the size of which must be proportional to the line being spliced.

Using a fid or marlinespike if necessary, raise the strand of the standing part closest to the seizing and tuck the closest unlaid strand under it. Next, pass the adjacent unlaid strand over the strand you just tucked the first strand under, and tuck it under the next strand of the standing part. Finally, turn the whole splice over and tuck the last strand under the remaining strand on the standing part. Remove the seizing from the standing part and pull the tucks tight. Continue with the next sets of tucks in the same order and the same manner. Use four sets of tucks in polyester and six in nylon line. To taper the splice for a neater finish, remove half the fibers in each unlaid strand before you make the last tuck. When the tucks are completed, cut the strands about ¼ inch from the standing part, then pound and roll the splice to even it out.

For a chafe-resistant eye, you can tie an eye splice around a *thimble* (Figure 14-35), which is a metal (usually galvanized steel), teardrop-shaped fitting with arms that are concave in cross section to accept a tightly fitted eye splice. The thimble then provides a protective rubbing surface to prevent the line from chafing. A classic application for a thimbled eye is in the end of a mooring pendant that connects to the mooring buoy or chain, or in the end of an anchor rode that connects to the anchor or to a length of chain.

**Figure 14-35.** An eye splice around a thimble, here used in the connection between a nylon anchor rode and a length of chain. The thimble prevents the shackle from chafing through the nylon. (PHOTO BY DON LINDBERG)

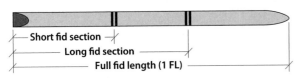

| Short fid section |
| Long fid section |
| Full fid length (1 FL) |

| Lengths of Tubular Fid Sections | | | |
|---|---|---|---|
| Rope Diameter in. (mm) | Short Section in. (mm) | Long Section in. (mm) | Full Length in. (mm) |
| 1/4 (6) | 2 (51) | 3 1/2 (89) | 5 1/2 (140) |
| 5/16 (8) | 2 1/2 (64) | 4 1/4 (108) | 6 3/4 (171) |
| 3/8 (9) | 3 (76) | 4 3/4 (120) | 7 3/4 (197) |
| 7/16 (11) | 3 1/2 (89) | 6 (152) | 9 1/2 (241) |
| 1/2 (12) | 4 (101) | 7 (178) | 11 (279) |
| 9/16 (14) | 4 1/2 (114) | 8 (203) | 12 1/4 (311) |
| 5/8 (16) | 5 (127) | 9 1/2 (241) | 14 (356) |
| 3/4 (19) | 5 3/4 (146) | 11 (279) | 16 (406) |

**Figure 14-36.** Making a double-braid eye splice. (TABLE AND ILLUSTRATIONS REPRINTED WITH PERMISSION FROM *KNOTS, SPLICES, AND LINE HANDLING: A CAPTAIN'S QUICK GUIDE* BY CHARLIE WING)

**1** Tie a slip knot 8 fid lengths (FL) from end. Mark Point "A" 1 FL from end. Form an eye of the desired size (around a thimble if one is used), and mark Point "B" next to Point "A."

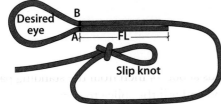

**2** Pry open the cover at "B" and extract a small loop of the core. Mark the core "C." Extract the free end of the core and tape its end. Pinch and tape the end of the cover, as well.

**3** Pull cover back toward slip knot and mark Point "D" 1 short fid length (see table above) from "C." Mark Point "E" 1 short + 1 full fid length beyond "D."

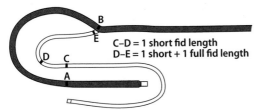

C–D = 1 short fid length
D–E = 1 short + 1 full fid length

**4** Insert the end of the cover into the fid. Insert the fid at "D" and exit at "E." Continue pulling the cover through until "A" just appears. Remove the fid and the tape.

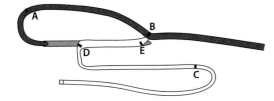

**5** Now taper the exposed cover. Starting at "A" mark every 7th pic (pair of parallel ribs) running at one angle. Then count off 4 pics from "A," and mark every 7th pic running at the opposing angle. Cut one strand at each mark and remove the cut strand ends. Pull the tapered cover back until the end just disappears.

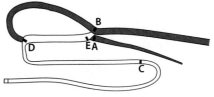

**6** Insert the free end of the core into the fid. Insert the fid at "A" and exit at "B."

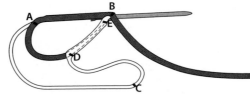

**7** Pull on the core's free end until cover and core eyes match in size.

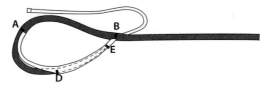

**8** Insert the core end into the fid again, reinsert the fid at "B," and push it as far as you can into the rope's standing part. Pull the fid and core through the cover and cut off the excess core.

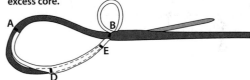

**9** Grip the slip knot and work the cover toward the eye so that "E" and "D" disappear. Continue up to Point "A."

**10** Secure the splice with waxed twine. Take 5 stitches through the throat of the splice, leaving a long tail. Switching the needle to the tail, take another 5 stitches at 90° to the first row of stitches.

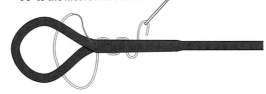

**11** Tie the ends of the twine in a reef knot, and trim the ends.

# Securing Lines

There are many special fittings for securing lines, used both on boats and piers. Fewer such fittings are necessary on powerboats than on sailboats.

## THROUGH-BOLT YOUR FITTINGS

Hardware for securing lines on a boat is attached to the hull or the spars (mast, boom, spinnaker pole, etc.). From time to time, these fittings are subject to considerable stress. For this reason, all deck fittings should be bolted through the deck or gunwales rather than just screwed to them (Figure 14-37).

On all but the smallest boats, the bolts should also go through a backing plate beneath the deck to make the fitting more secure and to distribute the load. If you have a cleat on a gunwale, glue or otherwise attach a metal plate or a piece of 3/4-inch marine plywood under the gunwale. Now, drill holes through the gunwale and the plate and fill them with marine caulking before bolts are inserted in them. (The caulking prevents water from entering and damaging the inner layers of the gunwale.) Secure the bolts of the fitting with appropriate nuts and washers. It's worth the effort, since a fitting that comes loose under severe stress can be dangerous. It is also easier to through-bolt a fitting than to patch a deck after a fitting has pulled loose.

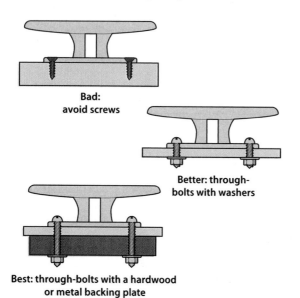

**Bad: avoid screws**

**Better: through-bolts with washers**

**Best: through-bolts with a hardwood or metal backing plate**

**Figure 14-37.** Bad, better, and best ways to install a cleat on deck.

## CLEATS

There are several types of cleats, and each serves a specific purpose.

### Horn Cleats

*Horn cleats* are anvil-shaped fittings, with either open or closed bases. You tie anchor rodes, mooring and docking lines, sheets, and halyards to them, and they are the most common fittings for lines on small boats. Horn cleats are also called *mooring cleats*.

One way to secure a line to a horn cleat is by *belaying* it (Figure 14-38). To do so, take one complete turn around the cleat. Do not make more than one complete turn, as the line may jam on itself under tension or take up too much space on the horns. A lead-in angle of 10° to 20° also helps prevent jamming, and a good cleat installation provides such an angle from a block or chock to the cleat.

After you take a full turn around the cleat, lead the line over the cleat and around its horns to form a figure eight. Make two or more figure eights and pull the line tight. This way of belaying permits you to take the line off the cleat rapidly.

When you belay to a horn cleat and leave your boat unattended, the connection needs to be more secure. To do this, make only one figure eight and finish off with an underhand loop over one of the horns. This hitch is called a *weather hitch* (Figure 14-38). When making a weather hitch, be sure to have the line continue in a fair figure eight as shown to develop maximum friction.

**Figure 14-38.** Belaying a line on a cleat. Note the lead-in angle to prevent the belay from jamming, the full turn around the base of the cleat, and the weather hitch that finishes the belay. (PHOTO BY DON LINDBERG)

**Figure 14-39.** Another way of securing a dockline to a horned deck cleat. The eye of the line is fed through the base of the cleat, then looped over the horns for a secure and quick belay. Notice the seizing on the throat of the eye splice to make it more secure. (PHOTO BY JOE BRITVCH)

## Jam Cleats

A *jam cleat* is similar to a horn cleat, but with one important difference. One of the horns forms a tapered slot into which the line is "jammed" (Figure 14-40). This allows you to secure and release a line quickly, since you need less than a full turn to hold it.

Jam cleats usually secure sheets on sailboats, but they can also be used to secure a centerboard pendant to control its position or depth.

Install a jam cleat so the tapered slot faces the direction from which the line approaches. Thus, the first turn around the base of the cleat will not bind line, but the next turn binds and holds it. A jam cleat accommodates only one line size. If you use either a larger or smaller line than that for which it is specified, it will not function properly.

**Figure 14-40.** A jam cleat (top), showing the tapered slot that "captures" a line of matching diameter (bottom). (PHOTOS BY DON LINDBERG)

## Cam Cleats

A *cam cleat* has two moving, serrated, cam-shaped jaws for holding a line (Figure 14-41). The jaws are spring-loaded and rotate open to release the line when you pull it. When the standing part of the line pulls against the cleat, it tightens.

In use, place the line over the teeth and pull it through and down to open the cams. Tighten the line simply by pulling it in. To ease or release it, first pull the line and lift it out of the cam jaws.

Cam cleats are suited only for small sailboats. They must be installed in the correct direction, since they work only one way, and they can be hard to release when there is a heavy load on the line such as during a high wind. Unfortunately, this may be the time you most want to let the line go quickly.

## TURNBUCKLES

A *turnbuckle* is a threaded fitting that pulls two eyes together (Figure 14-42). On sailboats, turnbuckles are used as terminals on the wire rigging that supports the mast. The threaded bolts enable

**Figure 14-41.** A cam cleat in use. The direction of the load is toward the camera, and pulling the line in this direction only causes the jaws to tighten further. To release the line, a crewmember on the far side of the cleat will have to jerk the line straight upward, out of the jaws, while pulling it toward him or her. (PHOTO BY DON LINDBERG)

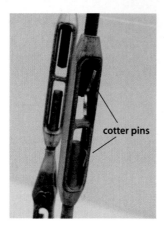

**Figure 14-42.** Cotter pins have been inserted in the turnbuckle in the foreground to prevent the threaded fittings from turning. The pins have yet to be inserted in the turnbuckle in the background. (PHOTO BY DON LINDBERG)

you to tension the shroud or stay. The bolts need to be locked in place to keep them from working loose after they have been adjusted, and there are several ways to do this. Perhaps the most common is to insert cotter pins or split rings through holes in the ends of the bolts.

## SAMSON POSTS

Larger boats have samson posts instead of cleats for anchoring or mooring (Figure 14-43). A *samson post* is a column of wood or metal with a pin or bar inserted through it near the top. To secure a line to the post, first take several turns around its base, then finish with an underhand loop on each pin as if securing to a cleat.

**Figure 14-43.** A line secured to a samson post on the foredeck of a boat. (PHOTO BY JOE BRITVCH)

## BOW BITTS

Large boats may have bow bitts instead of samson posts or cleats (Figure 14-44). *Bow bitts* are a pair of circular metal columns on a common base, and each column has a lip around its top. To secure a line, take a complete turn around the bit or post nearest the standing part of the line, then make a series of figure eights around the bitts.

## CHOCKS

Lines from cleats, samson posts, and bitts are usually led through U-shaped fittings called *chocks* (Figure 14-45), which limit the direction of the pull on a cleat, help prevent chafing of the line, and prevent the line from damaging the boat. Lines are often equipped with chafing gear where they pass through chocks to further reduce chafing.

## OTHER HARDWARE ITEMS

A *winch* helps pull in a loaded line such as an anchor rode, a jibsheet, or a halyard. It consists of a metal drum with a series of gears inside, fastened to a secure base. An anchor winch, called a *wind-*

**Figure 14-44.** A line secured to bow bitts. (PHOTOS BY JOE BRITVCH)

*lass*, may have an electric motor, as might a winch used to help load a boat onto a trailer. Sailboat winches for sheets and halyards are turned manually with a handle.

Drums of winches on sailboats rotate clockwise, as viewed from the top end of the drum. Thus, you must wrap the line clockwise around the drum for the winch to work. The number of wraps depends on the load on the line, since the winch does its work through friction. While four turns are usually the most required for synthetic line, wire rope (as for a halyard) may require six turns.

Some sailboat winches provide two gear ranges to afford more pulling power. Turning the handle clockwise on these winches provides normal power, and turning it counterclockwise changes gears and increases the pulling capability. The drum turns in a clockwise direction in either mode.

On a large sailboat, two people may be needed to operate a winch. One person cranks the winch, while the second keeps a strain on the tail (working) end of the line as it comes off the drum. The second person also secures the line to a cleat after the sail is properly trimmed.

*Self-tailing winches* eliminate the need for the second person to serve as a tailer, which is a great advantage on a shorthanded boat or when working in a confined space (Figure 14-46). The top of the drum contains a notched channel that holds the line as it feeds off the drum. On a self-tailing winch, the notched channel also acts as a cleat to hold the line.

# Lead Lines

A *lead line* is a line weighted with lead on one end that is sometimes used to measure water depths up

**Figure 14-46.** A self-tailing winch. Note that the turns on a winch drum are always clockwise. (PHOTO BY DAVID J. SHULER)

**Figure 14-45.** Chocks like these, on the foredeck of a sailboat, protect lines and the boat from chafe and damage. (PHOTO BY DON LINDBERG)

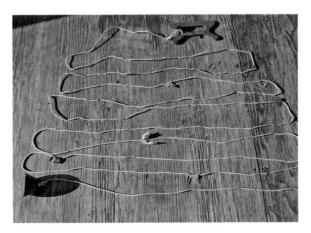

**Figure 14-47.** A lead line, showing the lead itself and the depth-interval markers. (PHOTO BY ED SWEENEY)

to 100 feet (Figure 14-47). At least 5 pounds of lead is recommended on a line of braided cotton, which lays better on the deck than a synthetic line, making it easier to throw. The line should be 150 to 200 feet long so you can throw it out ahead of the boat.

Mark the line at standard depth intervals with strips of tape or leather or with knots. Plastic strips with large numbers are available for this purpose and attach easily to the line. They are difficult to read in the dark, however, and many mariners prefer markings that can be "read" by feel.

In use, you cast the lead forward with an underhand swing while the boat is moving forward slowly. The speed must be slow enough that the lead reaches the bottom by the time the line stands vertically. Subtract the vertical distance from the hand of the person casting the lead to the water from the length of the line paid out to get the water's depth.

Samuel Clemens got his pen name of Mark Twain from a lead line. The name comes from a Mississippi riverboat sounding "by the mark, twain" or 2 fathoms (12 feet).

Some leads have hollowed-out portions in their bottoms, which can be filled with a sticky material such as tallow or bedding compound. This material will collect a small sample of the bottom sediment on contact. Since nautical charts usually note the character of the bottom, the sample may help you confirm your position, and it can also tell you whether the bottom will provide good holding for an anchor.

# Dipping the Eye

At times you must put the eye of your mooring line over a piling on which there is already a line. It is poor etiquette to place your line on top of one that is already there, and it may also be dangerous. If the other boat leaves before you do, the owner is likely to remove your line so that he can cast off, and he may or may not return your line to the piling.

To avoid the problem and to be courteous, *dip the eye* of your line by passing it up through the eye of the first line before dropping it over the piling (Figure 14-48). The other line can then be removed first. If you leave first, simply reverse the process. In this way you can free your line without removing the other line.

**Figure 14-48.** To *dip the eye*, pass your dockline through the eye of your neighbor's line before dropping the loop over the post. That way, if your neighbor leaves first, he can cast off without untying your line. (PHOTO BY DON LINDBERG)

# Practice Questions

## IMPORTANT BOATING TERMS

In the following exercise, match the words in the column on the left with the definitions in the column on the right. In the blank space to the left of each term, write the letter of the item that best matches it. Do not use an item in the right-hand column more than once.

| THE ITEMS | THE RESPONSES |
|---|---|
| 1. _____ nylon | a. polypropylene |
| 2. _____ ski rope | b. fisherman's bend |
| 3. _____ standing part | c. polyester |
| 4. _____ Dacron | d. main part of a line |
| 5. _____ turn | e. forms a temporary loop |
| 6. _____ hitch | f. will slip if not under tension |
| 7. _____ bend | g. ties one line to another |
| 8. _____ anchor bend | h. elastic |
| 9. _____ bowline | i. line attached to an object |
| 10. _____ clove hitch | j. bight around an object |

# Multiple-Choice Items

In the following items, choose the best response:

**14-1.** Which of the following types of line will float?

a. polypropylene
b. polyester (Dacron)
c. nylon
d. all of the above

**14-2.** Most boatowners prefer ropes made from

a. natural fiber
b. wire
c. synthetic fiber
d. a mixture of synthetic and natural fibers

**14-3.** Which of the following types of line stretches the most?

a. manila
b. polypropylene
c. nylon
d. polyester

**14-4.** Whipping a line is done to

a. make it easier to manage
b. reduce stretching
c. cover a damaged spot
d. keep it from unraveling

**14-5.** Wrap your mooring and anchor lines with canvas or leather to prevent

a chafing
b. soiling
c. bleaching from the sun
d. whipping

**14-6.** A square knot is useful

a. for most purposes
b. when you are in a hurry
c. if it is not subject to a heavy load or critical load
d. for mooring a boat

(continued on next page)

## Multiple-Choice Items (continued)

**14-7.** A bowline is useful when you want

    a. a temporary, fixed-size loop in the end of a line
    b. to tie two lines together
    c. to tie a line to a cleat
    d. to tie up to a mooring

**14-8.** The "king of knots" is the

    a. square knot
    b. half hitch
    c. clove hitch
    d. bowline

**14-9.** Protect synthetic and natural fiber lines from

    a. kinks
    b. mildew
    c. dirt
    d. all of the above

**14-10.** The best knot for tying different-size lines together is the

    a. sheet bend or becket bend
    b. square knot
    c. bowline
    d. clove hitch

**14-11.** Make an eye splice in a manner similar to a

    a. short splice
    b. back splice
    c. long splice
    d. dual splice

**14-12.** One of the most secure knots for attaching a line to an object is the

    a. weaver's knot
    b. sheet bend
    c. clove hitch
    d. anchor bend

**14-13.** Pulleys on a boat are called

    a. blocks
    b. sheets
    c. winches
    d. hitches

**14-14.** A horn cleat is

    a. used to hold up a boat's rail
    b. a device through which a line is passed
    c. a means of warning nearby vessels
    d. an anvil-shaped fitting

**14-15.** Which of the following is used to moor a vessel?

    a. a cleat
    b. a bitt
    c. a samson post
    d. all of the above

**14-16.** Lead lines are used

    a. to pass a line from one boat to another
    b. where strength is important
    c. to measure the depth of the water
    d. all of the above

**14-17.** The half hitch you use as the last step in securing a line to a cleat is called a

    a. clove hitch
    b. weather hitch
    c. anchor bend
    d. wedding hitch

**14-18.** If you tie a line to itself, it is called a

    a. bend
    b. hitch
    c. knot
    d. reef

**14-19.** The tool used in working rope is called a

    a. splicer
    b. awl
    c. pick
    d. fid

**14-20.** The best type of line for anchoring and mooring is

    a. nylon
    b. Orlon
    c. Dacron
    d. polypropylene

**14-21.** The end of a line tied to a vessel is the

    a. working end
    b. standing end
    c. bitter end
    d. whipped end

**14-22.** To make a clove hitch secure, finish tying it by adding a

    a. half hitch
    b. square knot
    c. reef knot
    d. bowline

# Weather and Sailing

**The objectives of this chapter are to describe:**

- Weather information sources.
- Basic weather patterns.
- Storm forecasting and precautions.
- Go, no-go decision making.
- A personal weather equipment and experience checklist.

BOATERS HAVE A special need to know about weather. The effects of storms can be devastating on land, but at sea they can be even worse. High winds, lightning, rough seas, and poor visibility may accompany storms on the water. If you are caught unprepared by a severe storm, your

A fast-moving storm blankets the Strawberry Reservoir in Utah. (PHOTO BY MART GARDNER)

recreational outing can end in disaster, but it doesn't have to.

The first rule for avoiding weather problems is to "know before you go." There are many readily available sources for good weather information. If bad weather is in the offing, don't go out.

The second rule is to recognize that weather is always changing, and that forecasts are not always accurate. This chapter will cover the chief indicators of impending adverse weather that you can observe on board.

The third rule is to implement defensive measures in a timely fashion when caught in unexpected weather conditions. There are well-tested tactics that can see you and your boat through severe weather and sea conditions.

# Weather Information

The science of weather observation and forecasting has made incredible advances in the past decades. With satellite imagery, radar, and other methods of information gathering, accurate weather data are produced for almost every place in the world—certainly everywhere in the United States.

The distribution of these weather data has also undergone immense improvement. Television, from both national and local stations, offers weather reporting and forecasting programs throughout the day and night. Of course, The Weather Channel gives incredibly accurate weather summaries for the entire country, and the national forecast is usually followed by local weather reports and forecasts (Figure 15-1).

Likewise, both FM and AM radio stations broadcast almost continuous local weather information, which is highly useful though not specifically targeted to mariners. Near the coasts and large inland waterways, TV and radio stations often provide regional marine weather broadcasts.

Thus, there is little excuse for not knowing what the weather is doing and will do. Boaters need not be surprised unless they are boating in remote areas. Even there, timely weather information is available using shortwave (see below), marine single-sideband, or ham radio.

Having said that, a forecast *can* be inaccurate. Therefore, boaters should get their information

**Figure 15-1.** A newspaper weather map showing low- and high-pressure areas along with fronts and areas of precipitation associated with the lows. (COURTESY NOAA)

from more than one source—the more the better. Experienced boaters also depend on their own weather knowledge to make "go, no-go" decisions, but the proper context for your own observations is provided by the regional weather forecasts you obtain before you head out and perhaps update while you're on the water. Note that "skipper error" in failing to seek out available weather information is what dooms most boats and crews to the ravages of bad weather.

## TELEPHONE INFORMATION

In some locales, principally large metropolitan areas, recorded telephone marine weather forecasts are available. If you use them, call while you are planning your cruise, then call again just before you leave to get the latest update. Check with the service to see how often it updates its forecasts.

## NATIONAL WEATHER SERVICE

The National Weather Service (NWS) continuously broadcasts weather information over its network of FM weather stations. Its forecasts focus on specific locales and give marine weather conditions where applicable. The NWS updates its forecasts as soon as new information is available. If severe weather develops, the NWS immediately broadcasts the information. (Note, however, that sometimes the development is so fast that the NWS can't keep up with it.)

You can receive NWS broadcasts on inexpensive, narrow-band FM receiving sets that use either household electrical current or batteries. The broadcasts are also available on the weather channels of your VHF-FM marine radio. You should be able to receive NWS broadcasts on one or more of their broadcasting frequencies. If you have a VHF-FM radio or a narrow-band receiving set aboard your vessel, you can receive the latest information while you cruise. See Chapter 16 for more on NOAA's VHF-FM frequencies.

## INTERNET

The Internet now provides a wide array of weather information, ranging from historical weather recitals to the current conditions any place on the globe. Boaters may obtain long- and short-range forecasts and detailed weather maps depicting reported conditions. There are also websites that provide both basic and advanced weather education. With the recent advent of wireless technology, it is often possible to access the Internet from a boat, while underway, using a PC or fax machine.

A good place to start for weather information is the Coast Guard site www.uscg.mil/news/stormcenter. This site provides essential storm information, as well as providing links to:

- Tides and storm surge information
- Boating safety issues
- Tropical storms worldwide
- The Weather Channel Online (with site-specific information)
- NOAA marine weather information web page
- NOAA's United States *Coast Pilot* publications
- And many others

National Weather Service predictions are also available at www.nws.noaa.gov. For other links, see www.navcen.uscg.gov.

## OTHER INFORMATION SOURCES

For those who cruise long distances and for commercial shipping interests, coded weather data are broadcast by shortwave radio, and facsimile weather maps are also available from shortwave broadcasts. You can detect an electrical storm by the static on an AM radio tuned to a broadcast station. You can detect a storm even if it is so far away that you can't see or hear it. Static is an irritation for landlubbers but a timely warning for mariners.

### Some Sources of Weather Information

AM and FM radio stations
Local TV
National TV, including the Weather Channel
The Internet, including www.weather.com (The Weather Channel), www.uscg.mil/news/stormcenter (Coast Guard Storm Center), and www.nws.noaa.gov (the National Weather Service)
Marine VHF radios, Channels 1 through 10 (see Chapter 16)
Shortwave and marine SSB radio, as well as ham radio (for those who are qualified)
Newspapers
Telephone (recorded messages)
CB radio (you can ask others, nearer the bad weather, about conditions)

# Wind and Boating

Fog, heavy rain, sleet, and snow create problems for boaters by reducing visibility. In severely reduced visibility you become more vulnerable to collisions and groundings. You may be unable to navigate back to port. Serious though these problems are, however, they are often mild in comparison with those created by wind.

We all know that vicious winds accompany gales, thunderstorms, tornadoes, waterspouts, tropical storms, hurricanes, and other extreme weather conditions. But the wind does not have to be gale force or stronger to create dangerous boating conditions. Even fairly mild winds can create rough seas.

Storm winds cause indirect as well as direct problems. Strong winds blowing onshore will pile up water ahead of a storm system or hurricane, and this effect is amplified by the water's rise in response to falling atmospheric pressures. This so-called **storm surge** may raise local sea levels as much as 18 to 20 feet ahead of a hurricane, and the results can be particularly destructive when the peak surge coincides with local high tide. Hurricane surges may extend inland for hundreds of miles.

Winds do not have to be of hurricane force to create a surge that will inflict significant damage. In strong winds such as the northeasterly gales that sometimes strike the Northeast coast, the water levels of bays and sounds rise beyond those of normal tides. Moored boats may rise as far as their mooring lines will permit and will sink if the water rises farther. Docked boats may rise above the pilings to which they are tied and be impaled on them as the water level falls (Figure 15-2). Boats in covered slips may be crushed against the roofs.

## WIND AND WAVES

The most common wind-related problem faced by boaters, however, is rough water. Large breaking waves can overturn or swamp small boats, and as we have already seen, breaking waves can make small boats yaw, broach, or pitchpole.

Most waves are caused by wind and continue to grow from it. Up to a point, the longer the wind blows from a constant direction and the greater the uninterrupted expanse, or **fetch**, over which it blows, the higher the waves will build. Eventually, the waves reach a maximum height for the given fetch and wind speed, at which point the seas are said to be **fully developed** (Table 15-1).

## Swells

*Swells* are waves that have traveled a long way from the storm that created them. As they travel, their heights decrease, the distance between them increases, and they assume the rounded shape of a sine curve. Even large swells are not dangerous to

| TABLE 15-1 | **Beaufort Wind Scale** | | | | | |
|---|---|---|---|---|---|---|
| Beaufort Number | Wind Description | Mean Wind Speed Equivalent (knots) | Sea Conditions | | Mean Wave Height | |
| | | | | | meters | feet |
| 0 | Calm | < 1 | The sea is like a mirror. | | — | — |
| 1 | Light air | 1–3 | Ripples without foam crests. | | 0–0.1 | 0–0.3 |
| 2 | Light breeze | 4–6 | Small wavelets. Crests look glassy but do not break. | | 0–0.2 | 0–0.6 |
| 3 | Gentle breeze | 7–10 | Large wavelets; crests begin to break; a few whitecaps. | | 0–0.6 | 0–2 |
| 4 | Moderate breeze | 11–16 | Small waves becoming longer; frequent whitecaps. | | 1 | 3.3 |
| 5 | Fresh breeze | 17–21 | Moderate waves with a more pronounced long form; many whitecaps. A little spray. | | 2 | 6.6 |
| 6 | Strong breeze | 22–27 | Large waves begin to form; extensive whitecaps. Some spray. | | 3 | 9.8 |
| 7 | Near gale | 28–33 | Sea heaps up, and white foam blows in streaks in the direction of the wind. | | 4 | 13 |
| 8 | Gale | 34–40 | Moderately high waves of greater length; edges of the crests begin to break into spindrift; streaks of foam. | | 5.5 | 18 |
| 9 | Strong gale | 41–47 | High waves; crests begin to tumble; dense streaks of foam. Spray may affect visibility. | | 7 | 23 |
| 10 | Storm | 48–55 | Very high waves with long toppling crests. The sea appears white as foam is blown off in dense bands. Spray affects visibility. | | 9 | 29.5 |
| 11 | Violent storm | 56–63 | Exceptionally high waves limit visibility. The edges of the wave crests are blown into froth. The sea is covered with blowing spray. | | 11.5 | 38 |
| 12 | Hurricane | 64+ | Seas tumultuous. The air is filled with foam. The ocean is totally white with driving spray. Visibility seriously reduced. | | 14 | 46 |

boats, though they may be uncomfortable for boaters.

## Breaking Waves

As waves approach shore, they begin to "feel" the rising seabed, and this friction slows the speed of each wave's bottom. At the same time, the crests, which are not slowed by friction, begin to overrun their bases. As the water continues to shoal, the crests eventually become unstable and spill or plunge forward as **breakers**. A series of breakers approaching a shore constitutes surf, but breakers can also occur in navigable waters in the right circumstances. For example, when incoming waves encounter an ebb current—such as in the entrance to an inlet—the seas will rise and steepen and may begin to break. In a breaker, the energy that has been locked inside a deep-water wave is translated into the violent momentum of white, breaking water. In a big breaking sea, tons of seawater may be hurled forward at speeds approaching 40 miles per hour. Breaking seas are a real danger to small boats.

**Figure 15-2.** The storm surge from Hurricane Katrina made a mess of this New Orleans marina, leaving some boats on floats, some on top of their neighbors, and some submerged. (COURTESY FEMA)

## Wave Height

A prediction of "seas 3 to 5 feet" means that 70% of the waves are expected to be between 3 and 5 feet high. This is what is known as the **significant wave height**. Of those, 15% will be less than 3 feet high, and 15% will be more than 5 feet. Be prepared for the occasional wave that may be 7 or more feet high. Never anchor from the stern of your boat. Your boat may be swamped by an "occasional" wave or severe wake. It can happen in fairly calm seas.

In large bays, lakes, sounds, and at times in coastal areas, wave heights can change abruptly with a change in weather (see Table 15-2). Waves

### TABLE 15-2 Wave Height

**Significant wave heights as a function of wind speed, duration, and fetch**

| Fetch in n. miles | Force 4 (11-16 knots) time in hours | height in feet | period in seconds | Force 5 (17-21) time | height | period | Force 6 (22-27) time | height | period | Force 7 (28-33) time | height | period |
|---|---|---|---|---|---|---|---|---|---|---|---|---|
| 10 | 3.7 | 2.6 | 2.4 | 2.2 | 3.5 | 2.8 | 2.7 | 5.0 | 3.1 | 2.5 | 6.0 | 3.4 |
| 20 | 6.2 | 3.2 | 2.9 | 5.4 | 4.9 | 3.3 | 4.7 | 7.0 | 3.8 | 4.2 | 8.6 | 4.3 |
| 30 | 8.3 | 3.8 | 3.3 | 7.2 | 5.8 | 3.7 | 6.2 | 8.0 | 4.2 | 5.8 | 10.0 | 4.6 |
| 40 | 10.3 | 3.9 | 3.6 | 8.9 | 6.2 | 4.1 | 7.8 | 9.0 | 4.6 | 7.1 | 11.2 | 4.9 |
| 50 | 12.4 | 4.0 | 3.8 | 11.0 | 6.5 | 4.4 | 9.1 | 9.8 | 4.8 | 8.4 | 12.2 | 5.2 |
| 60 | 14.0 | 4.0 | 4.0 | 12.0 | 6.8 | 4.6 | 10.2 | 10.3 | 5.1 | 9.6 | 13.2 | 5.5 |
| 70 | 15.8 | 4.0 | 4.1 | 13.5 | 7.0 | 4.8 | 11.9 | 10.8 | 5.4 | 10.5 | 13.9 | 5.7 |
| 80 | 17.0 | 4.0 | 4.2 | 15.0 | 7.2 | 4.9 | 13.0 | 11.0 | 5.6 | 12.0 | 14.5 | 6.0 |
| 90 | 18.8 | 4.0 | 4.3 | 16.5 | 7.3 | 5.1 | 14.1 | 11.2 | 5.8 | 13.0 | 15.0 | 6.3 |
| 100 | 20.0 | 4.0 | 4.4 | 17.5 | 7.3 | 5.3 | 15.1 | 11.4 | 6.0 | 14.0 | 15.5 | 6.5 |
| 120 | 22.4 | 4.1 | 4.7 | 20.0 | 7.8 | 5.4 | 17.0 | 11.7 | 6.2 | 15.9 | 16.0 | 6.7 |
| 140 | 25.8 | 4.2 | 4.9 | 22.5 | 7.9 | 5.8 | 19.1 | 11.9 | 6.4 | 17.6 | 16.2 | 7.0 |
| 160 | 28.4 | 4.2 | 5.2 | 24.3 | 7.9 | 6.0 | 21.1 | 12.0 | 6.6 | 19.5 | 16.5 | 7.3 |
| 180 | 30.9 | 4.3 | 5.4 | 27.0 | 8.0 | 6.2 | 23.1 | 12.1 | 6.8 | 21.3 | 17.0 | 7.5 |
| 200 | 33.5 | 4.3 | 5.6 | 29.0 | 8.0 | 6.4 | 25.4 | 12.2 | 7.1 | 23.1 | 17.5 | 7.7 |
| 220 | 36.5 | 4.4 | 5.8 | 31.1 | 8.0 | 6.6 | 27.2 | 12.3 | 7.2 | 25.0 | 17.9 | 8.0 |
| 240 | 39.2 | 4.4 | 5.9 | 33.1 | 8.0 | 6.8 | 29.0 | 12.4 | 7.3 | 26.8 | 17.9 | 8.2 |
| 260 | 41.9 | 4.4 | 6.0 | 34.9 | 8.0 | 6.9 | 30.5 | 12.6 | 7.5 | 28.0 | 18.0 | 8.4 |
| 280 | 44.5 | 4.4 | 6.2 | 36.8 | 8.0 | 7.0 | 32.4 | 12.9 | 7.8 | 29.5 | 18.0 | 8.5 |
| 300 | 47.0 | 4.4 | 6.3 | 38.5 | 8.0 | 7.1 | 34.1 | 13.1 | 8.0 | 31.5 | 18.0 | 8.7 |
| 320 | | | | 40.5 | 8.0 | 7.2 | 36.0 | 13.3 | 8.2 | 33.0 | 18.0 | 8.9 |
| 340 | | | | 42.4 | 8.0 | 7.3 | 37.6 | 13.4 | 8.3 | 34.2 | 18.0 | 9.0 |
| 360 | | | | 44.2 | 8.0 | 7.4 | 38.8 | 13.4 | 8.4 | 35.7 | 18.1 | 9.1 |
| 380 | | | | 46.1 | 8.0 | 7.5 | 40.2 | 13.5 | 8.5 | 37.1 | 18.2 | 9.3 |
| 400 | | | | 48.0 | 8.0 | 7.7 | 42.2 | 13.5 | 8.6 | 38.8 | 18.4 | 9.5 |
| 420 | | | | 50.0 | 8.0 | 7.8 | 43.5 | 13.6 | 8.7 | 40.0 | 18.7 | 9.6 |
| 440 | | | | 52.0 | 8.0 | 7.9 | 44.7 | 13.7 | 8.8 | 41.3 | 18.8 | 9.7 |
| 460 | | | | 54.0 | 8.0 | 8.0 | 46.2 | 13.7 | 8.9 | 42.8 | 19.0 | 9.8 |
| 480 | | | | 56.0 | 8.0 | 8.1 | 47.8 | 13.7 | 9.0 | 44.0 | 19.0 | 9.9 |
| 500 | | | | 58.0 | 8.0 | 8.2 | 49.2 | 13.8 | 9.1 | 45.5 | 19.1 | 10.1 |
| 550 | | | | | | | 53.0 | 13.8 | 9.3 | 48.5 | 19.5 | 10.3 |
| 600 | | | | | | | 56.3 | 13.8 | 9.5 | 51.8 | 19.7 | 10.5 |
| 650 | | | | | | | | | | 55.0 | 19.8 | 10.7 |
| 700 | | | | | | | | | | 58.5 | 19.8 | 11.0 |
| 750 | | | | | | | | | | | | |
| 800 | | | | | | | | | | | | |
| 850 | | | | | | | | | | | | |
| 900 | | | | | | | | | | | | |

Note that fully developed seas exceed the wave heights shown in Table 15-1, from which you can extrapolate estimated wave heights for winds stronger than Force 7.

can go from 2 to 4 feet to 6 to 10 feet in just a few minutes.

## Waves in Shallow Water

Waves are influenced not only by wind speed, wind duration, and fetch, but by water depth as well. Wind over shallow water generates steep waves that are close together. Two- to 4-foot waves in shallow water can present a serious hazard for small boats, while in deep water, waves of the same height have more gradual slopes and are farther apart.

# Understanding Weather

The knowledge that wind causes waves begs the question, "What causes wind?" To answer this question, you need to understand a few things about weather.

There is also another reason you need to know something about weather. You have learned how to get good weather information. Now you need to be able to answer the question, "Does what I see mean the weather is changing?" If it is, you may want to change your plans. If you are on the water, you may wish to seek shelter.

Knowing something about weather can help you avoid some of its perils such as high winds, thunderstorms, lightning, heavy rain, fog, and other hazards to boating. It can also help you anticipate and know how to react to conditions such as squall lines, microbursts, and wind shear.

## WEATHER AND HEAT

Heat from the sun warms the air, and this in turn causes wind and weather. There are two basic facts at the heart of this dynamic: warm air is lighter than cold air, and warm air can hold more moisture than cold air. Because it is lighter, warm air rises. As it rises, warm, moist air expands and cools and must therefore lose some of its moisture in the form of clouds, rain, hail, or snow.

## Heat and Air Pressure

When land or water is heated, some of that heat radiates into the air above, which expands and becomes less dense when warmed. The heated air rises, which reduces the air pressure locally.

Cooler air from surrounding areas then flows into the low-pressure area caused by the rising air. Like water, air always flows from areas of high pressure toward areas of low pressure. This moving air is **wind**. The greater the difference in pressure between areas overlaid by warm and cool air, the stronger is the wind.

## Land and Sea Breezes

Unequal heating of land and water causes land or sea breezes. During the daytime, land heats more rapidly than water. Thus, air rises over the land, and the air over the water flows in to take its place. This is a **sea breeze** (Figure 15-3). At night, the land loses heat more rapidly than the water. The cooler air over land then moves under the warmer

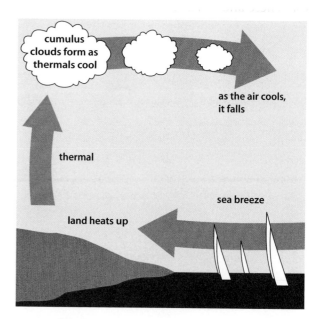

**Figure 15-3.** Sea breeze dynamics. Heated air rises over land as the day advances, to be replaced by cooler air flowing in from seaward, as shown here. When a land breeze forms at night, this process is reversed. The air over land cools more rapidly than the air over the sea, and the resultant wind blows from the land toward the sea. A nighttime land breeze is rarely as strong or steady as a daytime sea breeze. (REPRINTED WITH PERMISSION FROM *GARY JOBSON'S CHAMPIONSHIP SAILING* BY GARY JOBSON)

ocean air in what is called a **land breeze**. This diurnal movement of air is often conducive to the formation of fog.

## Heat and Temperature Changes

Other factors affect the temperature changes in an air mass. Thick vegetation or swampy land is slower to warm and slower to cool than arid, barren land. Thus, the dry air above a desert gets hotter by day and cooler overnight than the air over a rainforest. These and other factors cause differences in air pressure, amounts of moisture in the air, and the strength of the resulting wind.

## Global Air Circulation

The ultimate engine for earth's weather is the unequal distribution of heat over the planet's surface. Simply put, the tropics receive more heat energy from the sun than the poles, and the result is a continual poleward transport of heated air (and heated water in the form of ocean currents) from the equatorial regions. Heated air rises in a broad band called the **doldrums** between roughly 15°N and 15°S—an area of light and baffling winds punctuated by violent thunderstorms—and when it reaches the upper troposphere it flows poleward both north and south. At roughly 30° north and south of the equator—the latitude of St. Augustine, Florida, in the northern hemisphere—some of the air has been cooled enough to subside, forming a band of high pressure and light and variable winds called the **horse latitudes**. The rest of the upper-atmosphere air from the tropics continues poleward, subsiding over arctic and Antarctic areas.

This poleward movement of air aloft must be balanced by an equatorward movement of air at the surface, and so it is. Part of the air that sinks at around 30° north and south flows back toward the low-pressure doldrums region to replace what has risen aloft there. In the northern hemisphere this north-to-south surface flow is deflected to its right by the spinning of the earth, and in the southern hemisphere the south-to-north movement is deflected to its left. The result is the northeast and southeast **trade winds**, respectively (Figure 15-4).

The rest of the air that sinks at 30° north and south flows poleward at the surface, and is deflected to the right in the northern hemisphere and to the left in the southern hemisphere to form the **prevailing westerlies** that characterize the circulation patterns of the middle latitudes, including most of the United States.

Along the polar front, at about 60° north and south, the prevailing westerlies run into high-latitude **easterlies** flowing from the poles toward lower latitudes, which forces the comparatively warm, moist air of the westerlies aloft. Rising air always causes instability—this is why bad weather is associated with low pressure—so it comes as no surprise that the polar front is a zone marked by frequent severe storms.

## THE CORIOLIS FORCE

The **Coriolis force** affects anything that moves over the earth's surface, through the air, or through water, including birds, missiles, aircraft, ocean and air currents, and submarines. Though called a "force," it is

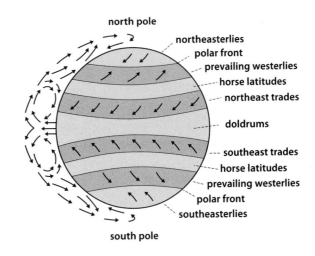

**Figure 15-4.** Global atmospheric circulation patterns.

in fact a complex response to the earth's rotation, and so is more properly called the **Coriolis effect**. For the purposes of understanding weather, it is sufficient to recognize that the Coriolis force/effect does exist, and that it causes both winds and ocean currents to be deflected to the right in the northern hemisphere and to the left in the southern hemisphere. This is why surface air flowing toward the equator from the horse latitudes becomes the northeast and southeast trade winds, and it's why surface air flowing poleward from the horse latitudes becomes the prevailing westerlies of the middle latitudes.

## COLUMBUS AND WIND PATTERNS

Columbus took advantage of the northeast trade winds and the prevailing westerlies when he came to the "new world." His square-rigged sailboats were best at sailing before the wind. He sailed down the coast of Africa to the belt of the northeast trade winds, then turned west. No wonder his crews were upset. Day after day the wind blew from astern. How were they going to get home?

But Columbus understood the trade winds. When he left the West Indies, he sailed north until he came to the prevailing westerlies. He then sailed east. Is it any wonder that St. Augustine became a replenishing port for food and water for Spanish ships returning from the New World? It is on the Florida coast at 29°53′N latitude, 7 nautical miles south of 30°N latitude.

## TEMPERATURE AND HUMIDITY

One more factor is necessary to explain weather. As has already been stated, warm air can hold more moisture than cool air. You see the result of this on a summer day when you mix a cool drink: the glass cools the warm, moist air that contacts it, the air can't hold as much moisture as when it was warmer, and some of it condenses on the glass.

The temperature at which moisture begins to condense on the glass is the **dew point**. The more moisture the air contains, the more **humid** it is. If there is no change in temperature, the more humid the air, the higher its dew point. In other words, moisture condenses out of saturated air when the temperature is lowered only slightly.

Contrary to popular belief, moist air is lighter than dry air. When it's warm, moist air is even lighter, and it therefore rises rapidly. Cold, dry air descends. Warm air over cold ground or water is stable; cold air over warm ground or water is unstable.

## Moisture and Energy

It takes enormous amounts of energy to change water from a liquid to a vapor. When water vapor condenses back to a liquid, this energy is released. When you heat water, it takes relatively little heat to raise its temperature to the boiling point, but it takes many more times that amount of heat to change it into steam. When the steam changes back into a liquid, that same amount of heat is released. This is why steam burns flesh so badly, and it also accounts for the violence of some storms. In a storm, the moisture in the air changes back to a liquid and releases its pent-up energy.

## AIR MASSES

In the temperate regions between roughly 30° and 60° north and south—that is, between the horse latitudes and the arctic regions—weather systems move generally west to east, steered by the prevailing westerlies at the surface and by east-flowing jet streams aloft.

These upper-atmosphere jet streams, which average more than 50 knots and can reach 200 knots or more, are concentrated around 30° north and south (the **subtropical jet stream**), where air is subsiding, and over the polar fronts around 60° north and south (the **polar jet stream**), where air is rising. These boundary zones in the planetary atmospheric circulation are regions of rapid horizontal temperature change, and horizontal temperature gradients are what cause wind both aloft and on the surface. The jet streams migrate poleward and equatorward with the seasons. In the northern hemisphere winter, for example, the subtropical jet stream may disappear entirely from North American weather maps, while the polar jet stream dips far south, sometimes steering arctic air all the way to Florida.

Middle-latitude weather is dynamic and constantly changing, dominated by an endless, generally west-to-east parade of distinctive air masses.

For purposes of this book we'll put aside the complex atmospheric mechanics that form these systems and just accept their existence, so familiar to mariners.

These air masses move over the earth's surface and determine much of our weather. As they move they tend to retain the moisture, pressure, and temperature characteristics they acquired upon formation. As we might expect, air masses with high pressure, called *highs*, contain cool, dry air. Low-pressure areas, or *lows*, are characterized by warm, moist air.

Air pressure is a function of the weight or mass of the atmosphere above us. At sea level the air pressure is approximately 14.7 pounds per square inch (psi). We call 14.7 psi *one atmosphere* of pressure. On weather maps or synoptic charts, areas of low and high pressure are delineated by *isobars*, generally concentric circles that connect points of equal atmospheric pressure and show how air masses are moving. Air masses move as the atmosphere tries to erase its horizontal pressure gradients, with the air in high-pressure areas flowing toward low-pressure areas and creating wind in the process.

A high-pressure area contains cooler air, and the higher the altitude, the cooler the air. This cooler air above weighs more than warmer air below. Gravity causes the cooler air to sink, causing higher barometric pressures. High-pressure cells generally are areas of clear and stable weather.

The lows denote areas where air is rising, which is why barometric pressures are lower there. Since rising air will cool and will eventually become supersaturated, low-pressure cells are areas of instability marked by precipitation and often by strong winds.

Isobars are usually more closely spaced around lows than highs, denoting stronger winds in the lows. A high might be 1,000 or more miles across, while a low tends to be more tightly coiled—typically 400 or fewer miles across. Simply put, good weather is associated with highs, bad weather with lows.

Surface winds spiral inward toward the center of a low, counterclockwise in the northern hemisphere and clockwise in the southern hemisphere. The winds spiral outward from a high, clockwise in the northern hemisphere and counterclockwise in the southern hemisphere (Figure 15-5). The characteristics of highs and lows can be summarized as in Table 15-3.

It is useful to know where the high and low pressure areas are in relation to you. Lows are a source of bad boating weather, and the highs that are moving toward them may be preceded by strong

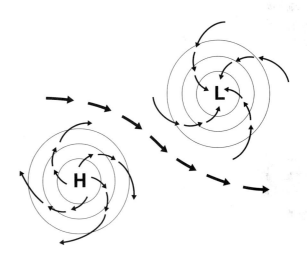

**Figure 15-5.** Air circulates clockwise around highs and counterclockwise around lows in the northern hemisphere. Where a high is close to a neighboring low, you may see strong winds between the two systems.

| TABLE 15-3 **Characteristics of Midlatitude High- and Low-Pressure Systems** | High | Low |
|---|---|---|
| Weather | Generally fair | Stormy, precipitation |
| Temperature | Stable—long periods | Cool to warm changing to colder |
| Average motion (west to east) | Winter: 565 nm/day | Winter: 660 nm/day |
| | Summer: 390 nm/day | Summer: 430 nm/day |
| Winds | Moderate, rising near edge | Strong and changing with possible high seas |
| Pressure (typical) | Rapid rise on approach, slow decline on retreat | Rapid fall on approach, slow rise on retreat |
| Clouds | Sparse, near periphery | Wide variety, all altitudes |

winds that create waves and bad boating conditions. The area between a high and a nearby low may have stormy weather.

To locate highs and lows in the northern hemisphere, stand with your back to the surface wind (Figure 15-6). Now turn 45° to your right. This aligns you with the wind aloft. The high-altitude wind is always rotated from the surface wind in this

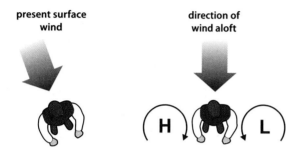

**present surface wind**

**direction of wind aloft**

**Figure 15-6.** Using Buys Ballot's Law to determine the direction of a low-pressure system.

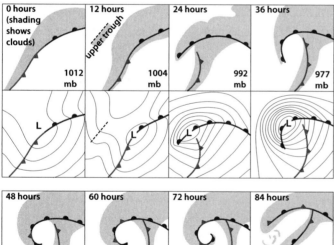

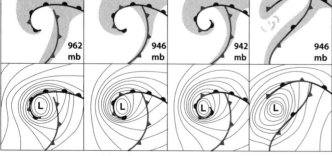

0 hours (shading shows clouds) — upper trough — 1012 mb | 12 hours — 1004 mb | 24 hours — 992 mb | 36 hours — 977 mb

48 hours — 962 mb | 60 hours — 946 mb | 72 hours — 942 mb | 84 hours — 946 mb

**Figure 15-7.** Typical life cycle of a northern hemisphere low. It begins as a kink in the isobars, with cold air advancing on warm air. As more isobars close around the low, winds increase. After 84 hours and perhaps thousands of miles from the point of its formation, this low is dissipating. (ADAPTED FROM *BOATER'S BOWDITCH* BY RICHARD K. HUBBARD)

fashion unless the surface wind is affected by local conditions such as buildings. After you have turned 45° to your right, the closest low is normally to your left, and the high is to your right. The low- or high-pressure area to the west is usually the one that will reach you. The one to the east has already passed. If low pressure is to the west, your local weather conditions may deteriorate.

In practice, you listen to what the weatherperson tells you, but you also weigh this with local circumstances, since local conditions can often vary dramatically from those indicated by the "big picture." Learning your local conditions can make your sailing or boating much easier and safer.

## FRONTS

The lows that drive our middle-latitude weather form along the boundaries between adjacent air masses—for example, between the cold, dry air mass that persists over Canada and the warm, moist air mass that recurs over the southern United States (Figure 15-7). A low is born when a kink forms along this boundary and begins a counterclockwise rotation (northern hemisphere). East of the kink, southerly warm air starts to override colder air to the north and east, while to the west, northerly cold air pushes south and east, displacing the warmer air ahead of it. The resultant frontal zones (called *fronts*) separating regions of cool or colder air from warm assume the shape of an inverted V, with the low at the apex. Across a frontal zone, temperature, humidity, air pressure, and wind often change abruptly over a short distance. Fronts are the sites of most large-scale weather conditions such as winter rainstorms, sleet, and snow. They are also the source of many boating problems.

The newly formed system migrates eastward, steered by the overhead jet stream that follows and defines the air mass boundary, until the low dissipates several days later. The isobars surrounding the low show distinct bends along fronts, marking abrupt shifts in wind direction there.

## TYPES OF FRONTS

Fronts are named for the type of air that is arriving. When a mass of cold air catches up with a mass of warmer air, a *cold front* forms. If the overtaking air mass is warmer than the overtaken mass, the front is a *warm front*. When neither air mass is overtaking the other, the front is *stationary*.

A cold air mass may approach a warm air mass and form a cold front. If the cold air mass then slows to a stop, a stationary front forms. If the cold air mass then moves back toward where it came from, a warm front forms. The air behind a warm front is warmer than the air ahead of it.

On a weather map, commonly recognized symbols designate each of these three fronts (Figure 15-8). A heavy line with pointed barbs on the advancing side represents a cold front. (As a memory aid, think of the pointed barbs as icicles.) A warm front is denoted by a heavy line with rounded barbs on its advancing edge. (Think of the rounded barb as suns.) A stationary front is indicated with alternating rounded and pointed barbs. The pointed barbs point toward the warm air, while the rounded barbs point toward the cold air.

If the map is in color, such as on TV, cold fronts are blue, warm fronts are red, and stationary fronts have blue and red segments.

## Changes as Fronts Pass

When a front passes, there are noticeable changes in air properties. If the overtaking air mass is moving rapidly, the zone between the air masses is narrow and the changes are abrupt. If the zone is wide and diffuse, the changes are more gradual. When the change is abrupt, the weather is more violent.

**TEMPERATURE DIFFERENCES.** As a front passes, the changes in temperature are usually pronounced. The air behind a cold front is always colder than the air in front of it. In a warm front, the overtaking air is warmer than the air it is overtaking.

**MOISTURE.** The moisture content of air in the two masses is usually significantly different. Behind a cold front the air is drier than the air in the overtaken mass. The air behind a warm front has more moisture than the air in front of it. When a cold front passes in the winter, you expect clear, cold, dry air to follow. Ahead of it, you expect rain or sleet. You expect moist air and probably fog when a warm front passes. Ahead of it may be snow, rain, or fog.

**WIND.** Wind always changes across a front. The change may be in direction or in speed or both. The wind shift as a front passes in the northern hemisphere is almost always clockwise. For example, if it is blowing from the southwest before the front passes, it will change to northwest after it has passed. The shift is usually abrupt, and higher winds occur. These may pose a danger for small craft. If you are on the water when such a shift occurs, head your vessel into the wind.

**PRESSURE.** Pressure is higher in the cold air. Thus, when a frontal passage ushers in colder air, the air pressure usually rises abruptly. When a front brings warmer air, the pressure usually falls until the front passes. It then remains steady or may decrease slightly. The important thing to remember is that when a front passes, a change in pressure occurs. If you have a *barometer*, you can measure the change in air pressure.

A barometer is most useful for predicting changes in weather. A falling barometer means that a low-pressure system is approaching; a rising barometer means that the low is passing and a high is approaching. Not all changes in barometric pressure are significant, but a rise or fall of 0.02 inch or more per hour usually indicates changing weather. The more rapid the rise or fall, the greater the expected change.

## Cold Fronts

Cold fronts move at speeds of 10 to 30 knots, depending on the time of year (Figure 15-9). They are two to three times as fast in winter as in summer.

**WARNING** *If a cold front is approaching, or has arrived, use extreme caution. This includes not boating or returning to port.*

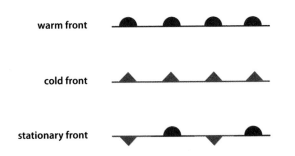

**Figure 15-8.** Representations of fronts on weather maps.

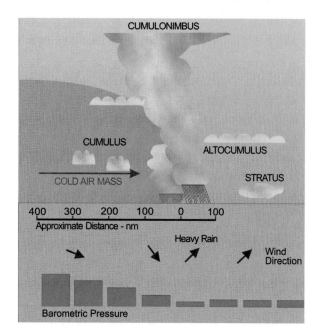

**Figure 15-9.** An idealized cross section through an advancing cold front shows the characteristic northern hemisphere sequence of cloud types, wind changes, and barometric pressure changes. (REPRINTED WITH PERMISSION FROM *ONBOARD WEATHER FORECASTING: A CAPTAIN'S QUICK GUIDE* BY BOB SWEET)

If a cold front is moving fast, the zone between it and the warm air mass in front of it will be narrow, and the changes in weather will be abrupt. Thus, if a cold front is moving fast, there will probably be a line of strong winds in front of it called a *squall line*. Wind speeds in squall lines are often as high as 30 to 60 miles per hour, with gusts as high as 80 to 100 miles per hour. Squall lines present dangerous boating conditions. In and behind them, typically, there is heavy rain, followed by clearing.

The air behind a cold front is denser than the air in the warm mass it is overtaking. This is so because dry air is heavier than wet air, and cold air is heavier than warm. As a result, the cold air wedges in under the warm, moist air it is overtaking, and this forces the warm air to rise.

If the air temperature difference on the two sides of the front is small, the slope of the warm air rise is gradual. The frontal area is broad and its stormy weather is not severe. If the temperature difference is large, however, the warm air rises rapidly. The frontal zone is narrow and the resulting weather is severe.

When the warm, moist air in the mass preceding a cold front rises, it cools, and can no longer hold all its moisture. Some of it condenses to form clouds. If it condenses still further, precipitation occurs. As the moisture condenses, it releases the energy it absorbed in changing from a liquid to water vapor. This gives the storm its energy.

When a cold front passes, the abrupt shift in wind direction may create **wind shear**, in which strong circular wind currents (eddies) occur along the mixing zone. If the zone is very narrow, the eddies may be strong.

A vessel passing across the mixing zone is subject first to strong winds from one direction, and a short time later to equally strong winds from the opposite direction. Wind shear has caused airplane crashes, and sailboats have been dismasted by it. Powerboats may be subjected to severe yaw and may capsize.

If the difference in temperature between the two air masses is small, the precipitation is usually light. If the difference is larger, more violent storms occur. Frequently, the storms that occur are thunderstorms that may include strong winds, wind shear, lightning, heavy rain, hail, and sometimes tornadoes. Needless to say, this is not good boating weather.

## Warm Fronts

Warm fronts travel much more slowly than cold fronts (Figure 15-10). The zones between warm fronts and the cold air that precedes them are wider and more diffuse than those that precede cold fronts. Thus, the changes as warm fronts approach are more gradual and less violent.

As a warm front approaches, air pressure starts to fall steadily and winds increase. A steady rain begins to fall. The temperature begins to rise. Air pressure falls slightly but steadily.

The air in a warm air mass is warmer and holds more moisture than the air in a cold air mass. Warm, moist air is lighter than cold, dry air. As a result, the warm, moist air rides up and over the cold air in front of it. The slope of the rise is very gradual, however, and the frontal area may be hundreds of miles wide. Some fog will probably form.

The rising warm, moist air cools and its moisture condenses. Since the slope of the rise is gradual, clouds are formed well in advance of any precipitation, which is gentle. Rain or snow may occur, but you would not expect violent weather

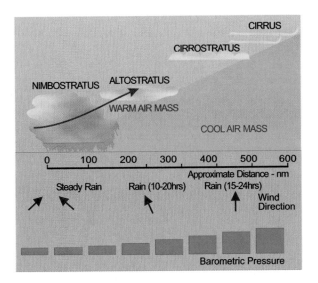

**Figure 15-10.** The characteristic cloud, wind, and barometric pressure changes that accompany an advancing warm front. (REPRINTED WITH PERMISSION FROM *ONBOARD WEATHER FORECASTING: A CAPTAIN'S QUICK GUIDE* BY BOB SWEET)

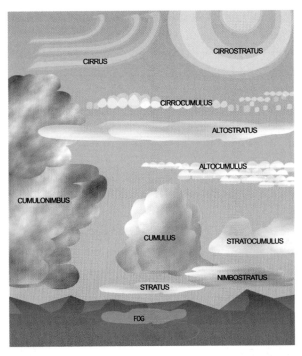

**Figure 15-11.** Principal cloud types and their relative altitudes.

such as in a thunderstorm. Warm front weather seldom presents violent boating conditions, but the fog that may accompany it can be a problem. Be alert for fog near a warm front.

## Clouds and Fronts

Three types of clouds accompany fronts—cirrus, stratus, and cumulus (Figure 15-11). All are the result of moisture-laden air carried aloft. As air rises, it cools, and some of its moisture condenses to form a cloud. The rapidity with which warm, moist air

ascends determines the structure of the cloud. In general, clouds get their names from their shapes and their altitudes.

High-level clouds have a prefix of *cirro-*. In Latin, *cirro* means "curl," which often describes their appearance. These clouds have altitudes of 20,000 feet or higher. **Cirrus clouds** are thin, high-level clouds made of ice crystals (Figure 15-12).

 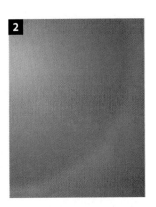 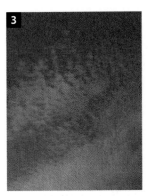 

**Figure 15-12.** High-altitude clouds are either cirrus or begin with the prefix *cirro*. Composed mainly of ice crystals, these clouds have a bright, wispy appearance. **1.** The highest of the group, cirrus, may be isolated tufts, streaks, feather-like plumes, or curved lines called *mares' tails*. Cirrus can be the first indicator of an approaching warm front, sometimes thickening at such times. **2.** Cirrostratus clouds form a thin veil that can produce a halo effect around the sun or moon. When these replace cirrus, they may indicate that the precipitation of an approaching warm front is about 24 hours away. **3, 4.** Cirrocumulus clouds are thin and patchy, and are sometimes called *mackerel sky*. When more fully developed, as in (4), their wavy appearance indicates turbulent air but not necessarily the approach of bad weather. (PHOTO #4 BY JAY BRANDINGER)

They are often called **mares' tails** and may be as high as 50,000 feet. **Cirrostratus clouds**, the lowest of the high-level clouds, are flat. Their altitudes vary from 20,000 to 30,000 feet. They cause halos around the sun, and hint at lower clouds to come.

Middle-level clouds have the prefix *alto-*. Their average altitude is about 10,000 feet (Figure 15-13). They may be **altocumulus** or **altostratus**, depending on whether they are puffy or flat.

**Stratus clouds** are flat and frequently layered (Figure 15-14).

**Figure 15-13.** Midlevel clouds begin with the prefix *alto* and have altitudes between 6,000 and 20,000 feet. **1.** Altostratus clouds form a sheetlike layer. They may result from thickening and lowering of cirrostratus clouds, and when they do, they may indicate the closer approach of a warm front. **2, 3.** Altocumulus clouds are common late in the day and can give us beautiful sunsets—the "red sky at night" that suggests a fine day tomorrow. (PHOTO #2 BY MIKE BRODEY; PHOTO #3 BY BOB DENNIS)

**Figure 15-14.** Low-level clouds (under 6,500 feet) acquire a thick, ominous look. **1, 2.** Sheetlike, stratified clouds known as stratus often result from a lowering and thickening of altostratus. They look more threatening the lower and darker they get. **3.** Stratocumulus clouds are lumpier than stratus and hold a lot of moisture. **4.** Nimbostratus clouds are low and dark and almost always accompanied by precipitation, often in association with a warm front.

*Cumulus* clouds are the fluffy, piled-up clouds often seen in summer skies (Figures 15-15 and 15-16). They are usually "fair weather" clouds but they can develop into towering *cumulonimbus* clouds (Figure 15-17) in the right circumstances. Thunderstorms are produced from cumulonimbus clouds.

The importance of clouds lies in what they can tell you about weather. Cumulonimbus clouds tell you that thunderstorms are forming. Altostratus clouds tell you that a warm front is approaching. Small cumulus clouds are a harbinger of fair weather. In general, as a front approaches, clouds become progressively lower and thicker.

**WEATHER CLUES FROM CLOUDS.** Clouds carry other weather clues as well (Table 15-4). When you see clouds moving in a leisurely fashion across the sky, you can expect continued fair weather. You can look for wind and rain when they scud rapidly overhead. When small clouds decrease or melt away to-

ward sunset, expect fair weather. Increasing and lowering clouds mean unsettled weather ahead.

**COLD FRONT CLOUDS.** About 150 miles ahead of the usual cold front are high sheets of altocumulus clouds. In the summer, the front is probably about

**Figure 15-17.** Cumulonimbus clouds result when cumulus clouds build up to great heights (2 to 5 miles) as a result of extreme instability and violent thermal activity. These are thunderclouds, and when fully formed show the characteristic anvil top (bottom). Expect heavy showers, strong wind gusts, and lightning when these approach. (TOP PHOTO BY BOB DENNIS)

**Figure 15-15.** When not vertically developed, cumulus clouds are the innocent puffballs that mark fair weather in the summer sky.

**Figure 15-16.** Cumulus clouds often form over islands at sea.

| TABLE 15-4 | **Weather Clues from Clouds** |
|---|---|
| **Clouds** | **Precipitation** |
| Cumulonimbus—*vertical, developed cumulus* | Rain, possible thundershowers, possible hail, tornadoes |
| Cirrus—*thin, high level* | None |
| Stratus—*flat, often layered* | Possible light drizzle |
| Cumulus—*white, puffy* | None (but may be windy) |
| Altocumulus—*puffy, middle level* | None |
| Altostratus—*flat, middle level* | Light rain or snow possible |
| Nimbostratus—*flat, low level* | Heavy, steady rain |
| Nimbus—*lowest of clouds* | Rain is falling |

12 hours away, but in the winter, the front may be only a few hours away.

As the front nears, *nimbus* and, perhaps, cumulonimbus clouds appear (Figure 15-17). Nimbus clouds are those from which rain is falling. They are the lowest of the clouds.

As the cold front passes, the clouds rise and become stratocumulus or altocumulus and possibly cumulus. The storm is over. You can probably expect at least two to three days of cool or cold or less cloudy dry weather.

**WARM FRONT CLOUDS.** High, thin cirrus clouds extend as much as 1,000 miles ahead of a warm front. These are clouds formed from warm, moist air that has risen up and over the retreating cold air mass. As the front slowly advances, the clouds thicken and lower. High-level cirrostratus clouds become midlevel altostratus clouds, and rain or snow begins to fall.

After the warm front passes, rain or snow may continue to fall while the clouds gradually rise. The wind direction veers, or shifts clockwise—for example, from southeast to southwest. Rain, mist, or fog may linger. Some clearing begins.

# Deck-Level Forecasting

## Approaching Low

Clouds: high cirrus, gradually lowering and thickening to altostratus
Wind: backing to southeast and possibly increasing
Barometer: begins to fall (2 to 10 mb in 3 hours)
Offshore: swell increases, with decreasing period

**What to Expect:**

Rain: Within 15 to 24 hours
If low is west to northwest and passing to your north, you will see fronts.
If low is west to southwest and passing to your south, you will not see distinct fronts, but wind will shift from southeast to east, northeast, then north to northwest.

## Approaching Warm Front

Cirrus or cirrocumulus clouds: front is more than 24 hours away
Lowering, thickening clouds (cirrostratus to nimbostratus): front is less than 24 hours away
Rain: begins lightly, then becomes steady and persistent
Barometer: falls steadily; a faster fall indicates stronger winds
Wind: increases steadily, stays in the southeast
Visibility: deteriorates, especially in rain

## Passing Warm Front

Sky: lightens toward western horizon
Rain: breaks

Wind: veers from south to southwest and may increase
Barometer: stops falling
Temperature: rises

## Within Warm Sector

Wind: steady, typically from the southwest, will strengthen ahead of cold front
Barometer: steady—may drop shortly ahead of cold front
Precipitation: mist, possible drizzle
Clouds: variety of cumulus clouds

## Approaching Cold Front

Wind: southwesterly, increasing; line squalls possible up to 100 miles ahead of front
Barometer: begins brief fall, could be rapid
Clouds: cumulonimbus build to the west
Temperature: steady
Rain: begins and intensifies, but duration is short (1 to 2 hours typical)

## Passing Cold Front

Wind: veers rapidly to west or northwest, gusty behind front
Barometer: begins to rise, often quickly
Clouds: cumulonimbus, then nimbostratus, then clearing
Temperature: drops suddenly, then slow decline
Rain: ends, gives way to rapidly clearing skies, possibly with leftover altocumulus or stratocumulus

## DECK-LEVEL FORECASTING

You can synthesize what we've covered so far to create your own deck-level forecasts, either to confirm or interpret what region-wide forecasts are telling you. You should log your observations at regular intervals. Record wind direction and speed, cloud type and direction, and how much of the sky is cloud-covered. The directions and relative speeds of the mid- and high-level clouds will give a hint of the direction of the approaching low. See the sidebar opposite for how to refine a regional forecast with your own observations.

## FOG

*Fog* is a cloud in contact with the earth's surface. It consists of water droplets or ice crystals, which form when air is cooled below its dew point. Fog is the most frequent cause of limited visibility and also the most common weather hazard (Figure 15-18). The speed with which fog can form makes it especially hazardous; it is not unusual for visibility to drop to less than 1 mile in a few minutes.

### Conditions Favoring Fog Formation

Moisture-laden air is essential for fog formation, which means that the conditions are especially conducive to fog in coastal areas. Fog can and does occur anywhere, however. It usually forms around microscopic particles such as dust, soot, and chemicals, and thus occurs frequently in industrial areas.

### Advection Fog

Of the several types of fog, the one of greatest concern to boaters is *advection fog*, which occurs in coastal waters and is caused by warm, moist air blowing over cold water. It is a concern for boating since it moves rapidly in dense fogbanks that can overtake and surprise unwary boaters.

**WARNING** *Advection fog can reduce visibility to a few feet in a matter of minutes.*

**Figure 15-18.** The thicker the fog, the more slowly and carefully you should progress. (PHOTO BY JOE BRITVCH)

## Fog Precautions

1. Mark your position prior to entering the fog area.
2. Reduce speed.
3. Assign lookouts to both look AND listen.
4. Consider anchoring if out of shipping channels.
5. Give appropriate (bell and/or whistle) sound signals.

### Predicting Fog

Fog can be forecast with a moderate degree of accuracy. Factors that aid predictions are historical, wind strength, air temperature, air moisture, the air temperature–dew point difference, and other information such as sky appearance (Figure 15-19).

Historical predictions are based on questions such as "Did fog form last night?," and "Are the conditions the same tonight?" If the answers are yes, then it is likely that fog will form again tonight.

Wind strength is important in fog formation. A warm, damp, gentle, steady wind without gusts favors the formation of fog. This is especially true if the wind is warmer than the water.

**Figure 15-19.** A morning fog, like this one on the Strawberry Reservoir in Utah, will often dissipate as the day progresses. (PHOTO BY MART GARDNER)

If the air temperature and the dew point in early evening are within 10° of each other, you can expect fog. The air is carrying almost all the moisture it can hold. Any lowering of its temperature will cause the formation of water droplets.

A variety of other factors aid in predicting fog. A hazy sky that is not very blue is a forerunner of fog. When the sky is like this, the horizon is poorly defined. At night, halos around lights mean high air moisture content. Finally, is the time of the year right for fog?

### Fog Precautions

As with other bad weather, it is advisable not to boat in fog; if it's foggy, don't go!

If you are on the water and fog settles in, take note of your position. Record it and the time. If you do not know where you are before the fog settles in, you will not know later on.

The next important thing is to reduce your speed. Assign lookouts at the bow and stern to watch and to listen. Listening in a fog is even more important than watching. The direction of sound is difficult to determine since the water droplets distort it. If you need to hear better, stop your engine and **listen**. If you are out of shipping lanes and other frequently traveled waterways, consider stopping and anchoring. You can hear better under these conditions.

Above all else, remember the sound signals you must give when underway or anchored in fog. If you have forgotten them, refer to Chapter 8 to refresh your memory.

# Nonfrontal Weather

Stormy weather can also occur in the absence of lows or fronts. Nonfrontal weather includes thunderstorms, tornadoes and waterspouts, and tropical storms.

## THUNDERSTORMS

As already discussed, thunderstorms may accompany cold fronts, but they can also occur in nonfrontal weather. Summer thunderstorms are usually of this type. Regardless of its cause, a thunderstorm is probably the storm most feared by boaters. A thunderstorm may arise in a short time and produce powerful winds. Cumulus clouds in the morning may mean thunderstorms later in the day. Boaters should listen to National Weather Service radio broadcasts or other forecasting media.

The winds, heavy rains, and lightning in thunderstorms are dangerous. The National Weather Service calls a thunderstorm **severe** if its winds are 50 knots or greater and/or if it contains hail that is ¾ inch or larger. And when a tornado is embedded in a thunderstorm, it is especially severe.

Thunderstorms form in rising, moist air. The advancing edge of a cold front or surface heat can provide the lift. There are usually three stages in the formation of any thunderstorm (Figure 15-20).

### Stage One

In the first stage, the land or water surface heats, and the air above it heats and rises. If the air is moist, some of its moisture condenses and light, fluffy cumulus clouds form. Cloud development may not stop with small cumulus cloud formation, however. If there is enough heat, the air will continue to rise, and towering cumulus clouds will develop vertically. They may rise in a column 15,000 to 25,000 feet high at this stage. In rising to these heights, the air temperature may cool as much as 80°F to well below freezing at the top of the cloud. Even so, the air is still warmer than the surrounding air. As the air cools, its moisture condenses, releasing large amounts of heat. This heat energy is the power behind the developing storm.

### Stage Two

In the second stage, the storm matures. At this point, clouds often reach a height of 40,000 feet, but heights of up to 80,000 feet have been recorded. The higher the cloud, the greater the release of energy and the more severe the storm.

As the air rises, its water vapor condenses and precipitation occurs at the outer edges of the column. The falling rain or hail further cools the air in the column, creating downdrafts and heavier rains. Air is still rising in the center of the column, bringing in more moisture. This air may reach a speed of as much as 6,000 feet per minute.

The rising air may catch descending hailstones, if there are any, and carry them back up the col-

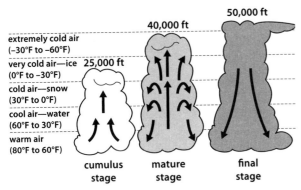

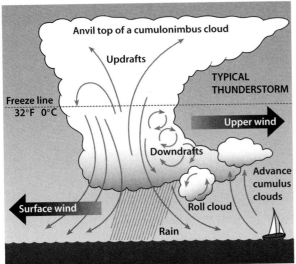

**Figure 15-21.** Clouds like these indicate the approach of a squall line and are often associated with a thunderstorm embedded in or preceding a cold front. Expect rapid wind shifts and strong gusts. (COURTESY NOAA)

**Figure 15-20. Top:** The three stages of thunderstorm development. **Bottom:** A maturing storm. The anvil top points in the storm's direction of travel. (BOTTOM ILLUSTRATION REPRINTED WITH PERMISSION FROM *BOATER'S BOWDITCH* BY RICHARD K. HUBBARD)

umn. During the trip up the column, more moisture forms on the hailstones and freezes. Thus, the hailstones grow in size. If the updrafts are strong enough, a hailstone may make several trips up and down the column, growing in size with each trip.

The cold, descending air accelerates and may reach speeds of as much as 2,500 feet per minute. When it reaches the surface it spreads outward. This produces strong, gusty winds, a sharp temperature drop, and a rapid rise in pressure. The surface wind is a called a *plow wind*, and its leading edge is the *first gust*.

Wind shear occurs frequently in squall lines that appear before thunderstorms. A squall line is a row of black, towering clouds that may reach heights of 40,000 or more feet, and they often develop ahead of cold fronts in moist, unstable air (Figure 15-21). They may also develop in unstable air far from any front. As the squall line passes, there is an abrupt change in wind direction—a wind shear. Squall lines present a serious weather hazard for boaters.

### Stage Three

In stage three the storm continues to move. You may be able to tell the direction of its movement from the anvil-shaped top of the cloud. The anvil points in the direction toward which the cloud is moving.

At this point, the falling air cools the earth's surface and the storm loses part of its energy source—hot air. The entire cloud becomes sinking air. With no ascending air to cool, rain stops. The storm dies.

## WHEN THUNDERSTORMS FORM

On some summer days, afternoon cumulus clouds are capable of turning into thunderstorms if there is enough moisture in the air. Keep an eye on growing cumulus. You may be able to run for safety before there's any danger.

In hazy weather, however, you may not see the thunderstorms forming. Haze limits visibility and is ideal weather for thunderstorms. On such hot, muggy, hazy afternoons, you should be alert for static on your AM radio, the sound of distant thunder, and/or the flicker of lightning. Stay close to port so you can run in if necessary. If you are sailing and do not have auxiliary power, be especially alert, and perhaps shorten sail. The winds may die shortly before the storm begins. This is no time to be becalmed. If there is a threat of bad weather, have all hands don their life jackets, batten your hatches, and tie down all loose equipment. Considerer anchoring.

## Lightning

Lightning is a serious boating hazard. It is a giant electrical spark arcing between clouds, within clouds, and between clouds and the ground. Never take shelter under a tree when you are on land, because lightning usually strikes the tallest object around. When you are out on the water, *you* may be the tallest thing for miles around (Figure 15-22).

The best way to escape the dangers of lightning is to avoid it. This is a strong argument in favor of understanding weather. The more "weather-wise" you become, the less likely you are to be caught out on the water in a thunderstorm.

**HOW FAR AWAY IS THE STORM?** Lightning heats air. This makes it expand rapidly and creates a partial vacuum. It then cools rapidly and rushes back in to fill the vacuum. The sound of the air rushing into the vacuum is thunder. For practical purposes, you can consider that lightning and thunder occur at the same time.

You will see the lightning before you hear the thunder. Sound travels much more slowly than light, about 1,100 feet per second. It takes sound about 5 seconds to travel 1 statute mile or 1.7 kilometers, whereas light travels 186,000 miles per second.

**GROUND YOUR BOAT?** You can lessen the danger of a lightning strike by staying off the water during thunderstorms. You can also lessen it by having a **grounding system** installed, similar to those found on buildings and other land structures. A grounding system may prevent a lightning strike or it may provide lightning a path to reach ground (water) without causing damage or injury to you or your boat.

Most physicists believe that a good grounding system serves to lead lightning into the water by the most direct means. They also believe that a good grounding system can prevent or lessen lightning strikes.

According to physicists, a good grounding system neutralizes the difference in electrical potential between the water and the air and prevents static buildup. This is the reason farmers put lightning rods on buildings such as barns. There are, though, no guaranteed safeguards against lightning. It is very unpredictable and powerful.

The installation of a grounding system is a job for a professional. Don't try it yourself, and don't assume that the builder of your boat provided any lightning protection for it.

## Microbursts

In 1976 the U.S. government identified microbursts as possible hazards to landing aircraft and to pleasure boats. The downdrafts from thunderstorms

**Figure 15-22.** Lightning over the shore. (COURTESY NOAA)

> **WARNING** When you see a flash of lightning, count slowly, "one thousand and one, one thousand and two, one thousand and three . . ." Each five counts tells you the lightning is about 1 mile away. Be careful that you relate the sound to its appropriate flash. This may be difficult if the lightning is nearly continuous.
>
> Any heavy weather, tornadoes, or waterspouts that appear not to change their position relative to you may be moving toward you.

act in the same manner as the downdrafts in front of squall lines. Cold downdrafts meet warm air and cause wind directions to change suddenly. These downdrafts radiate out from the thunderheads where they hit the surface in what is called a *microburst*. A microburst is strongest in the direction in which the thundercloud is moving, and its winds may exceed 100 knots (Figure 15-23). Microbursts may occur even when there is no rain below a thunderhead. A *dry microburst* occurs when falling rain in a thunderhead evaporates before it reaches the earth's surface. Because there is no visible sign of wind shear, it is difficult to predict.

Microbursts can occur several miles away from an associated squall line. Even if it is not raining, be alert for a possible squall. Near a thunderstorm, these may be from a direction different from the prevailing wind.

### If You Are Caught

If you are boating and find yourself in a thunderstorm, have each person aboard don a life jacket. Next, pinpoint your exact location before the storm arrives. Heavy rain will reduce your visibility.

Reduce your boat's speed or reduce sail, and keep a sharp lookout for other boats and obstructions. Secure all hatches and ports. Strap down or stow in lockers all loose gear on or belowdeck.

Once the storm hits, try to take the first (and heaviest) gusts of wind on your bow, not abeam. Heading into the wind is the most seaworthy position for most small boats. Approach waves at a 45° angle. This will keep your propeller under water, and it also reduces pounding and provides a safer and more comfortable ride.

Stay low in the boat. Don't make yourself the tallest target. Keep away from all metal objects. Lightning does not have to strike a boat directly for strong electrical charges to be aboard. If it strikes the water near your boat, it may affect the metal parts on the boat.

## A Few Pointers on Lightning

- The more frequent the lightning, the more severe the storm.
- Lightning strikes increase in number as the storm grows.
- Decreasing lightning means the storm is dying.
- At night, frequent distant flashes along a large sector of the horizon suggest a probable squall line.

### ✓ STORM-AT-SEA SAFETY CHECKLIST

- ☐ Have ALL aboard don life jackets.
- ☐ Close ports and hatches, and stow gear.
- ☐ Pinpoint and write down your exact location.
- ☐ Reduce speed.
- ☐ Keep a sharp lookout for boats, floating objects, shallow water, and the shore.
- ☐ Head into the wind.
- ☐ Approach waves at a 45° angle.
- ☐ Stay low in the boat.
- ☐ Keep away from all metal objects.

**Figure 15-23.** A microburst. (COURTESY NOAA)

### Tornadoes

A *tornado* is a whirlpool of air with a relatively small diameter that extends downward from a cumulonimbus cloud. It has a funnel-like appearance. The average diameter of the funnel is about 750 feet, and the wind speed at its center may exceed 250 knots.

Tornadoes are usually spawned in the squall lines ahead of cold fronts (Figure 15-24). They also occur frequently in hurricanes, however, and can even occur in calm, sunny weather.

**Figure 15-24.** A tornado. (COURTESY NOAA)

Tornadoes usually form over land and then sometimes move out over water. A tornado over water is different from a similar-appearing phenomenon called a waterspout (see below).

Tornadoes always have a counterclockwise circulation and almost always move from southwest to northeast, although they sometimes move in the opposite direction. If a tornado appears to be standing still or growing larger, watch out! It is moving toward you. Move at right angles to its path as fast as you can, and you may avoid it.

## Waterspouts

Waterspouts come from two different sources. The first is a tornado that has gone out to sea, which is not a true waterspout. Since it is over water, though, it may contain large quantities of water. Both the water and the tornado's wind make it dangerous for boaters (Figure 15-25).

True waterspouts, unlike tornadoes, do not develop in weather fronts. They usually occur in fair weather and always over water. Their winds may circle either clockwise or counterclockwise, almost more like dust devils over land than tornadoes. Waterspouts may have diameters of 20 to 200 feet

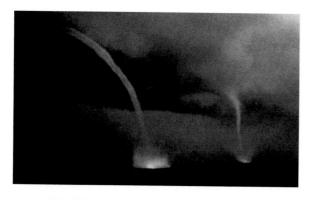

**Figure 15-25.** Twin waterspouts. (COURTESY NOAA)

and are more common in the tropics than in the middle latitudes.

Unlike tornadoes, which form in clouds and grow downward toward the earth (and may or may not reach the earth), waterspouts form close to the water's surface and grow upward. They are usually small, of short duration, and less dangerous than tornadic waterspouts.

Although waterspouts are less violent than tornadoes, they are a danger to boats. They may last from 10 minutes to half an hour, and as they subside, they dump large quantities of water that can swamp a small boat.

## TROPICAL STORMS

**Tropical storms** are nonfrontal storms that form in the tropics. They have counterclockwise circulation in the northern hemisphere.

### Tropical Waves

Tropical storms usually begin as tropical waves of low pressure and move from east to west in the trade wind belt. Good weather precedes tropical waves and extensive cloudiness follows them, often accompanied by rain and thunderstorms. Tropical waves occur in all seasons, but they are more frequent and stronger in summer and early fall. Tropical waves can develop into tropical cyclones.

### Tropical Cyclones

A *tropical cyclone* is a general term for any low-pressure area that forms over warm, moist, tropical waters. The strength of tropical cyclones comes from the heat of the water over which they form. Over cold water, they lose strength.

Tropical cyclones are classed according to their intensities based on average 1-minute wind speeds. Wind gusts may be as much as 50% higher than the average wind speed.

There are three classes of tropical cyclones: **tropical depressions, tropical storms,** and **hurricanes** or **typhoons.** Additionally, hurricanes are called different names, depending on where they occur. An intense tropical cyclone in the Atlantic and eastern Pacific is a hurricane; in the western Pacific Ocean, it is a typhoon; and in the Indian Ocean, it is a cyclone. No matter what their names, they are serious storms. Among other factors, hurricanes require water temperatures of at least 79°F for their formation as they absorb tremendous amounts of energy from the water over which they form.

**WINDS IN TROPICAL CYCLONES.** The sustained winds in tropical cyclones are:

- Tropical depressions: up to 34 knots
- Tropical storms: 35 to 63 knots
- Hurricanes or typhoons: 64 knots or more

## Hurricanes

On land, the greatest property destruction and loss of life in a hurricane usually results from the storm surge. Hurricane-force winds pile up the sea before them—in effect, the entire sea rises up—and this surge may extend for up to 100 miles along the coast to the right side of the storm's path of advance. Storm waves then roll ashore on top of this surge, resulting in storm surge heights from about 4 feet to over 18 feet.

Your boat will probably need more protection from the storm surge than from the wind. Even so, protection from the wind is not unimportant because windblown objects may damage it. There are many suggested ways to protect your boat in a hurricane, but none of them is completely satisfactory. If you live in a hurricane-prone area, get advice from seasoned boaters. Weigh the advice, then make up your own mind.

Well-developed hurricanes average 300 miles in diameter. At the center or *eye* of a hurricane is a low-pressure area that may be 15 to 25 miles in diameter. Since the winds of a hurricane rotate strongly, the center is a very low-pressure area of light winds. Although the sea below the eye is heavy and confused, the wind in the eye seldom reaches 15 knots.

The Atlantic Ocean hurricane season is June through November, although hurricanes also occur in other months (Figure 15-26). Early- and late-season hurricanes usually form in the Gulf of Mexico and the Caribbean Sea and develop rapidly. The mid-season storms of August and September may begin as tropical waves coming off the coast of Africa, and they develop slowly.

Hurricanes also begin off the west coast of Mexico. These usually do not present threats to the

**Figure 15-26.** Hurricane Hugo bearing down on South Carolina, September 21, 1989. (COURTESY NOAA)

**WARNING** *Above all, do not stay on your boat during a hurricane, even a minimal one!*

continental United States, but may reach the Hawaiian Islands and beyond.

The National Weather Service is a continuous source of information for tropical storms and hurricanes. Keep abreast of its warnings and heed them.

Don't wait until the last minute, though, to take measures to protect your boat. You may find safe harbors filled and storm equipment no longer available. Besides, you may find your time occupied in taking care of your family and home.

The Weather Channel on cable and satellite TV offers excellent coverage of hurricanes and other serious storms.

## WATER AND AIR TEMPERATURE

Water and air temperatures are also important to the comfort and safety of recreational boaters. Cold air temperatures require boaters to wear additional clothing. Cold air temperatures also mean that it is more difficult to start engines—or to restart them after a day of fishing. Cold water temperatures increase the risk of cold shock and hypothermia in the event of falls overboard. U.S. Coast Guard recreational boating accident statistics indicate that the risk of fatalities associated with accidents increases dramatically as a function of water temperature.

## THE JET STREAM

The winds that are experienced at the earth's surface throughout the middle latitudes are caused by the interactions of low-pressure and high-pressure air masses. These surface air masses are steered by strong, high-altitude winds (18,000 feet or higher) that move west to east around the earth in sinusoidal paths. What we call a *jet stream* is a narrow, especially strong concentration of this upper-altitude flow. A complete explanation of the effects of jet streams on surface weather is beyond the scope of this chapter and is unnecessary for the deck-level forecasting presented above.

# The Go, No-Go Decision

Where you boat is of great importance to your boating safety and enjoyment as it relates to weather. Your boat type and size, its equipment, and your ability to operate it also weigh heavily on your personal go, no-go decision making.

If you have a small boat and are boating on a small lake, with the shore nearby, your need for navigational equipment is minimal. You won't need much beyond a handheld compass and a VHF radio. After all, if fog develops, you can simply steer a steady compass course and land will appear sooner or later; maybe not exactly where you want it to be, but dry land will happen! On the other hand, if a squall line develops with attendant high winds and waves, you and your passengers should be wearing life vests, have a communication device to ask for assistance, and have a plan B for escape, at the very least.

A trip south along the California coast in a 42-foot cabin cruiser, however, presents the skipper and crew with a wholly different set of concerns and requirements. The chances of encountering fog are excellent! Is your vessel equipped with radar and loran or GPS? If not, and if you encounter fog, drop the hook or, perhaps, just don't go in the first place.

Regardless of the size of your boat or where you intend to take it, before you make the go, no-go decision, ask the following questions: Do you and your crew know how to use the equipment you have? Do you regularly practice using foul weather equipment in good conditions, so that when the bad stuff arrives it is a natural process to transition from visual cruising to marginal visual cruising? If

you and your crew cannot answer such questions positively, then leave your ego at the dock—and probably your boat, also.

## CREATING YOUR PERSONAL GO, NO-GO CHECKLIST

It is next to impossible to provide an all-encompassing go, no-go decision-making framework that will serve for all situations. There are too many variables of environment, weather, equipment, and skipper experience and comfort level.

The following checklist may be helpful, however. Personalize and expand it to suit your boat and the type of boating you do, and have a safe, pleasant day (or month!) on the water.

| ✓ | GO, NO-GO CHECKLIST |
|---|---|
| ☐ | Is the forecast and current weather suitable for the planned cruise? |
| ☐ | Does my boat have the equipment necessary for safe operation under any situation that might arise? |
| ☐ | Do my crew and I have confidence that we can successfully operate such equipment in the expected conditions? |
| ☐ | Do my crew and I have the necessary clothing, food, water, first-aid equipment, and training appropriate to the voyage? |
| ☐ | Do I understand how to ask for weather information while underway? |
| ☐ | Is my boating knowledge of all safety aspects, such as the Rules of the Road, up to date? |
| ☐ | Can I successfully navigate to safety if my electronic equipment fails? |
| ☐ | Do I have a plan B in case the original plan won't work? |
| ☐ | Have I filed an appropriate float plan with a responsible person? |
| ☐ | What is my comfort level in this situation? |

# Practice Questions

*IMPORTANT BOATING TERMS*

In the following exercise, match the words in the column on the left with the definitions in the column on the right. In the blank space to the left of each term, write the letter of the item that best matches it. Do not use an item in the right-hand column more than once.

| THE ITEMS | THE RESPONSES |
|---|---|
| 1. _____ high | a. small cumulus clouds |
| 2. _____ front | b. rain clouds |
| 3. _____ dew point | c. alto- |
| 4. _____ fair weather clouds | d. zone between two air masses |
| 5. _____ cirrus clouds | e. cool or cold, dry air |
| 6. _____ nimbus clouds | f. waves that have traveled a long way |
| 7. _____ swells | g. cumulonimbus |
| 8. _____ thunderstorm | h. water vapor condenses |
| 9. _____ middle-level clouds | i. ice crystals |

# Multiple-Choice Items

In the following items, choose the best response:

**15-1.** A condition favoring fog formation is

    a. a cold front
    b. moisture-laden air
    c. nonfrontal weather
    d. air moving over warm water

**15-2.** The temperature behind a cold front is

    a. higher than that in front of it
    b. lower than that in front of it
    c. about the same as that in front of it
    d. none of the above

**15-3.** The air pressure behind a cold front is

    a. higher than that in front of it
    b. lower than that in front of it
    c. about the same as that in front of it
    d. none of the above

**15-4.** The majority of weather systems in the United States come from a(n)

    a. easterly direction
    b. southerly direction
    c. westerly direction
    d. northerly direction

**15-5.** Which one of the following is the best source of marine boating weather information?

    a. National Weather Service
    b. TV broadcasts
    c. newspapers
    d. telephone

**15-6.** In the northern hemisphere, winds flow around and into a low in what direction?

    a. westerly
    b. easterly
    c. clockwise
    d. counterclockwise

(continued on next page)

# Multiple-Choice Items (continued)

**15-7.** Warm air

a. rises
b. falls
c. is very dry
d. is present in high-pressure areas

**15-8.** Warm moist air, in comparison with dry, cool air is

a. heavier
b. lighter
c. higher pressure
d. about the same weight

**15-9.** Stand with your back to the surface wind and then turn 45° to your right. A low-pressure area will be

a. in front of you
b. behind you
c. to your right
d. to your left

**15-10.** A high-pressure air mass is characterized by

a. warm, moist air
b. counterclockwise rotation
c. calm winds
d. cool, dry air

**15-11.** The fastest-moving fronts are usually

a. warm fronts
b. stationary fronts
c. cold fronts
d. occluded fronts

**15-12.** A hurricane is a tropical storm with sustained winds

a. greater than 50 knots
b. less than 64 knots
c. 64 knots or greater
d. blowing from the south

**15-13.** A tropical cyclone is

a. a whirling, funnel-shaped wind
b. a low-pressure area over warm, tropical waters
c. a local storm
d. a thunderstorm over the Caribbean

**15-14.** Clouds from which rain is falling are called

a. stratus
b. cirrus
c. nimbus
d. cumulus

**15-15.** The main problem in thunderstorms, tornadoes, tropical storms, etc., is

a. heavy rain
b. wind
c. lightning
d. reduced visibility

**15-16.** Which of the following poses the most serious problem for boaters?

a. fog
b. wind
c. rain
d. sleet

**15-17.** The height of wind-created waves depends on

a. how long the wind has been blowing
b. the extent of the fetch
c. the strength of the wind
d. all of the above

**15-18.** Fog occurs most often near a

a. warm, dry surface
b. cold front
c. large body of cold water
d. warm front

**15-19.** A particularly dangerous phenomenon that can occur several miles away from a thunderstorm and a squall line is a

a. willy-willy
b. microburst
c. cyclone
d. fetch

**15-20.** Fronts are named for the kind of air that is

a. in front of them
b. behind them
c. being displaced
d. being cooled

**15-21.** Thunderstorms form ahead of

a. cold fronts
b. warm fronts
c. stationary fronts
d. occluded fronts

## Multiple-Choice Items (continued)

**15-22.** On a colored weather map warm fronts are

    a. blue
    b. red and blue
    c. red
    d. orange

**15-23.** Weather is caused by

    a. wind
    b. rain
    c. heat
    d. all of the above

**15-24.** Thunderstorms are produced by

    a. cumulus clouds
    b. stratus clouds
    c. cirrus clouds
    d. cumulonimbus clouds

**15-25.** The clouds in front of a warm front are

    a. cumulus
    b. stratus and cirrus
    c. nimbus
    d. cumulonimbus

## The objectives of this chapter are to describe:

- The types of radios in use on recreational boats.
- The functions of marine radios and their proper use.
- The necessity for, and how to obtain, a station license.
- When a radio operator's license is needed and how to get one.
- What to look for when buying a radio.
- The limits of VHF-FM radios.
- How to select an antenna.
- How to make a radio check.
- How to make distress, urgency, and safety calls.

A Coast Guard Auxiliarist uses a fixed-mount VHF radio on his boat on the Washington, North Carolina, waterfront.
(PHOTO BY DON LINDBERG)

YOUR BOAT'S RADIO is your link to the outside world. It enables you to get weather information, learn of hazards to navigation, communicate with other boats and shoreside facilities, and get help if you need it. Boats carrying six or more passengers for hire, as well as many other commercial vessels, must have radio equipment. Although most privately operated boats are not required to have radios, it is nevertheless advisable to carry one or two.

# Communications on the Water

When you're on your boat, you can communicate with other boats or with people onshore in several ways. These include VHF-FM radio, single-sideband (SSB) radio, amateur (ham) radio, citizens band (CB) radio, and cellular telephone. SSB and ham radio are not often used by coastal and inland boaters but come into their own beyond VHF and cell phone range. Offshore boaters are well advised to carry, in addition, an emergency position-indicating radio beacon, or EPIRB.

## COASTAL AND INLAND

### VHF-FM Radios

VHF-FM radios are the most commonly used marine radios and also the most useful. Two types are available: full-sized, fixed-mount radios (Figure 16-1), which typically offer the legal maximum transmitting power of 25 watts, and handheld portables (Figure 16-2), which offer 5 or 6 watts of peak power and are limited to close-range communications. You can use VHF-FM radios to call for help, to arrange for a marina berth, to get weather information, to call home, or to talk with other boaters. A handheld set is a good standby if your fixed-mount radio fails. Note that it is against Federal Communications Commission (FCC) rules to transmit from a handheld VHF-FM radio onshore.

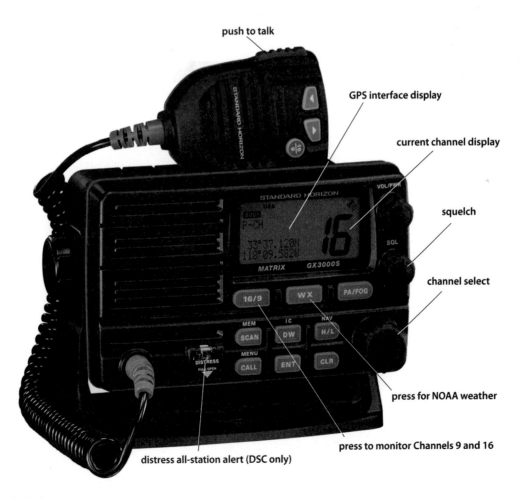

push to talk

GPS interface display

current channel display

squelch

channel select

press for NOAA weather

press to monitor Channels 9 and 16

distress all-station alert (DSC only)

**Figure 16-1.** A fixed-mount VHF-FM radiotelephone with digital selective calling (DSC) capability. The advantages of a DSC-equipped radio are discussed in this chapter. This radio is interfaced with a GPS receiver and thus displays the boat's latitude and longitude coordinates. In the event of an automated distress call (see DISTRESS button at lower left), these coordinates will be transmitted with the call. (COURTESY STANDARD HORIZON)

**Figure 16-2.** A handheld VHF-FM radio offers a maximum communications range of 3 to 5 miles. (COURTESY STANDARD HORIZON)

VHF communications are essentially limited to line-of-sight between the transmitting and receiving antennas, which means that the average maximum ship-to-ship range of a fixed-mount VHF-FM radio is about 10 to 15 miles, depending on the height of its antenna. A masthead antenna, or one installed high on a powerboat's flybridge, might reach up to 20 miles at 25 watts in ideal conditions. The ship-to-shore range may be 20 to 30 miles, depending on the height of the onshore antenna as well as the shipboard antenna. A handheld VHF-FM radio has not only less power but less antenna height (with its stubby, integral antenna) than a fixed-mount unit, and thus offers a maximum range of 3 to 5 miles.

## Citizens Band Radios

CB radios are inexpensive and popular. In many inland areas CBs are common on boats, and often are the only radios on board. They serve useful functions on lakes and rivers where the Coast Guard does not maintain a presence, and are the only radios many river marinas have. A CB can serve as an emergency backup for your VHF-FM.

CBs have several limitations, however, such as their short range. Also, there are so many sets in use that the channels are often overcrowded, and many CB owners fail to exercise discipline and proper radio etiquette and overpower other stations. In addition, there is no common distress channel. Furthermore, CBs are AM radios and, therefore, susceptible to static caused by lightning, which means that in a storm, when you might need them most, they are least reliable.

Channel 9 is the channel most often used for emergency calling, but the Coast Guard does not monitor it. For all these reasons, the Coast Guard does not encourage the use of CBs as the first or only means of radio communication for boaters.

## Cellular Telephones

In recent years, the use of cell phones has gained popularity, and receiving stations are widespread. Although cell phones are not marine radios, they may serve in an emergency. You may be able to use your cell phone to call for help on rivers and lakes where the Coast Guard does not maintain a presence, and some Coast Guard stations will answer when "*CG" is pressed.

There are drawbacks to the use of cell phones in an emergency, however. First, you may be too far from the nearest relay tower for your signal to be received, although the proliferation of cell towers has reduced this problem enormously in recent years. Second, the time required to relay your call from a 911 operator to the Coast Guard might be critical, and if the call is dropped, the Coast Guard might not be able to call you back. Further, although the locations of SSB and VHF-FM radios can be pinpointed by means of radio direction finders, this is not true of cell phones. Newer cell phones incorporate a GPS chip so their location can be tracked, but that feature is limited over water, so if you don't know where you are, your telephone signal may not help rescuers locate you. Additionally, an emergency call by cell phone does not alert nearby boaters to your distress and may thereby deny you the most immediate assistance available.

## OFFSHORE

## Single-Sideband Radios

For boats operating beyond VHF range, an SSB radio provides a valuable link to shoreside communications and emergency help. The range of an SSB radio varies with time of day, season, and the frequency used, from as little as 25 miles to worldwide. Specific information on frequency selection can be found in the operator's manual that comes with the radio.

SSB radios cover the marine portion of the medium-frequency (MF) band (2.0 to 3.0 MHz) and the international marine channels in the high-frequency (HF) band (3.0 to 23.0 MHz). These radios include distress, safety, and calling channels; ship-to-ship channels; and public correspondence channels that can connect you through a High Seas marine operator to the land-based public telephone system. With an SSB radio you can also access worldwide weather forecasts and limited e-mail messaging far at sea.

Four Coast Guard stations within the continental United States, and one in Hawaii, monitor the SSB distress and calling frequency of 2,182 kilohertz (kHz).

Since few recreational boaters have SSB radios, we will not discuss them at length in this chapter. You probably do not need one unless you are planning an offshore passage or a voyage to a foreign port.

## Amateur (Ham) Radios

If you are a shortwave amateur operator, called a **ham**, you might use a shortwave radio aboard your boat. Many ham operators have found their sets useful in marine and other emergencies, such as severe storms and other disasters. These radios operate in eight medium- and high-frequency bands that are interweaved with SSB frequencies and can reach around the globe. There are 420,000 licensed ham operators in the United States, more than 100,000 of whom may be on the air at any time and willing to assist you.

Before using the amateur radio service, you must pass an FCC examination and obtain a license and an assigned call sign. There are eighteen amateur maritime networks throughout the world, and they cover international as well as coastal waters. These networks operate 24 hours a day, with operators trained to handle emergency traffic and to provide the licensed amateur with an excellent communications network. A shore-based ham can patch you through the telephone lines to your home without the fees charged by SSB High Seas marine operators. Many amateur radio operators are listed in telephone directories. For all these reasons, ham

radio remains popular among long-distance cruisers as a way to maintain contact with their homes.

You should be aware, however, that the Coast Guard does not monitor ham frequencies as it does VHF and SSB emergency frequencies. Because ham radio is of limited use for near-shore boating, this chapter will not discuss it in depth.

## Emergency Position-Indicating Radio Beacons

An EPIRB is a portable transmitter that can be activated manually or automatically (by immersion) to summon help offshore. Several types are available, but the best transmit a coded signal at 406 MHz that is received by orbiting satellites and relayed to search-and-rescue personnel in the nearest ground station (Figure 16-3). Since the EPIRB is registered, rescue personnel will know the identity of the vessel in distress, and the receiving satellites will pinpoint its location—especially if the EPIRB incorporates a GPS unit.

An EPIRB is only a transmitter; it does not receive, and it does not permit voice communications. In contrast with a VHF or SSB emergency call, search-and-rescue personnel cannot tell the nature of the distress. Nevertheless, an EPIRB

**Figure 16-3.** A 406 MHz EPIRB. (REPRINTED WITH PERMISSION FROM *ROUGH WEATHER SEAMANSHIP FOR SAIL AND POWER* BY ROGER MARSHALL)

transmission is effective for quick response, and every boat venturing offshore should carry an EPIRB for use as a last resort.

# Functions of Radiotelephones

VHF-FM and SSB marine radios serve three important communications functions—sending and receiving safety, operations, and commercial messages. No other type of message is permissible.

## SAFETY MESSAGES

There are three types of safety messages: distress, urgency, and safety. Use **distress messages** when you face or are witness to grave or imminent danger to life or property and you need immediate help. Use **urgency messages** when there is a chance that a dangerous situation may become life threatening. **Safety messages** relay important information about weather or safety of navigation. We'll look at the protocols for each type of message later in the chapter.

## OPERATIONS MESSAGES

Operations messages deal with exchange of information about navigation or the movement or management of vessels. For example, you can call a lockmaster for instructions, or you may call a bridge tender to open a drawbridge (Figure 16-4). You may also call a marina to secure a berth or arrange for boat repairs, and you can exchange information about fishing or scheduling a rendezvous with other vessels.

Don't chitchat on your marine radio, however. Idle chatter is against the rules because it clutters up important channels and interferes with essential communications.

## COMMERCIAL MESSAGES

These messages concern the business in which a commercial vessel is engaged. Recreational boaters should not use the radio channels designated for commercial communications.

**Figure 16-4.** One example of a VHF-FM operations message is calling a bridge tender. The Figure Eight Island bridge on the Intracoastal Waterway in North Carolina, at Mile 278, is a single-pivot swing bridge with a vertical clearance of 20 feet. It opens on the hour and half-hour, but you can follow commercial traffic through at other times. Bridge tenders in Virginia, North Carolina, and Georgia monitor VHF Channel 13, whereas in South Carolina and Florida they use Channel 9. (PHOTO BY GENE HAMILTON)

# Licenses

VHF-FM radios, EPIRBs, and radar units do not require station licenses when used on most recreational vessels. Power-driven recreational vessels that are 20 meters (65 feet) or more long do require station licenses, however, and you'll need a station license for your VHF-FM station if you travel to a foreign port or communicate internationally. Under some circumstances, you may also need an operator's permit.

Additionally, a VHF-FM radio equipped with **digital selective calling** (DSC) should be registered with an entity that will assign a **Maritime Mobile Service Identity** (MMSI) number, which will automatically identify your boat when you transmit over the radio (see below). There is a charge for this registration when you apply through the FCC, but there is no charge when you apply through BoatU.S. or Sea Tow Services International. Note also that although EPIRBs operating at 406 MHz don't require a license, they do require registration.

## STATION LICENSE

You must have a **ship station license** for an SSB radio. Furthermore, if you have an SSB radio, you also need a VHF-FM radio. To get a license for an SSB from the FCC, you must show a need for the radio.

Apply to the FCC using FCC Form 605. You may be able to get a copy of this form from a marine radio dealer or you can get it on the Internet at www.fcc.gov/formpage.html. If you buy an SSB radio, the form may be packaged with it. You can also get forms from the FCC, Forms Distribution Center, 9300 East Hampton Drive, Capital Heights MD 20743, or by calling 1-800-418-3676, if you can't get them elsewhere. Be certain the form is current.

Submit your application with the required fee (upward of $200) to the Federal Communications Commission, Wireless Bureau Applications, P.O. Box 358130, Pittsburgh, PA 15251-5130.

Use Schedule F of FCC Form 605 for temporary authority to operate your ship's SSB and VHF-FM radio stations after you have mailed in your application. Until you get your station license, use your boat's registration number for your call sign. You must post the temporary permit near the ship's radio, and it is good for 90 days, by the end of which time you should have received your permanent license.

If you change your mailing address, your legal name, or the name of your boat, and if you are required to have a station license, let the FCC know in writing. Also tell the commission in writing if you sell your boat, and return your license. If you replace your SSB radio or its companion VHF-FM radio with another set that operates on the same frequencies, you do not need to do anything.

Even though you may not be required to have a station license, you are responsible for complying with all FCC regulations on the proper use of marine VHF-FM radios. Those regulations of importance to recreational boaters are described in the sections that follow.

## OPERATOR'S PERMIT

An operator's permit is not needed to use your VHF-FM radio in domestic or international waters if your vessel is less than 20 meters. If you plan to dock in a foreign port, however, you must have a **restricted radiotelephone operator's permit** (RP). Also, if you leave a foreign port to enter and dock at a U.S. port, you must have an RP. Use FCC Form 605 (which is a multipart form) to apply for your

RP. The fee was $60 in 2007 but is subject to change. The RP is good for your lifetime.

# Selecting Your VHF-FM Radio

All marine radios must be acceptable to the FCC, which means they meet required minimum technical standards. Such radios carry labels certifying compliance.

VHF-FM radios differ widely in price and basic characteristics, so shop around to see what is available before you buy. When looking at sets, ask about their sensitivity, selectivity, audio output, signal strength, available channels, type of channel selector and readout, and the amount of current they use.

## GLOBAL MARITIME DISTRESS AND SAFETY SYSTEM

GMDSS is a relatively new worldwide emergency communications system that will, when fully implemented, allow recreational boaters to send automated digital distress messages that include the boat's identity and location, leaving the boater free for emergency actions while the message transmits. To use GMDSS, your radio must be equipped with DSC capability. All fixed-mount VHF radios (Figure 16-5) manufactured since 1999 are DSC-capable, but most handheld VHFs (Figure 16-6) are not.

While all marine transceiver radios, including HF and SSB, can be equipped with DSC, the VHF-DSC radio will be the combination used by the great majority of recreational boaters. Don't forget that VHF radios have a limited range, no more than 30 to 50 miles and quite possibly less. If your cruising takes you farther than that from land stations or possible ship stations, you may want to consider an SSB.

Channel 70 is the frequency reserved for digital distress calls on a VHF radio. Each DSC radio must be programmed with its own data relating to the boat and owner, and these data are encoded in a unique nine-digit number, your MMSI number. When the DSC distress button or switch is activated, an automated signal is sent out with the identity of the boat, its position (assuming the radio is interfaced with a GPS receiver), the current time, and (if selected by the user) the nature of the distress. Any ship or land station that is within range and monitoring Channel 70 will receive the signal. Both transmitter and receiver may then switch to Channel 16 or another VHF working channel for voice communications.

As of early 2006, the Coast Guard is monitoring Channel 70 DSC calls out to 50 miles offshore between Maine and Maryland, and expects to institute similar coverage throughout the East Coast and Gulf of Mexico by the end of 2007. West Coast coverage may not be operational until 2009. In the interim, Sea Tow Services International monitors Channel 70 near shore, though its towers do not give it the range of Coast Guard towers. (This is the same company that now handles maritime phone calls, a service formerly provided by MariTEL.) Because its Channel 70 monitoring program is taking longer than expected to roll out, the Coast Guard will continue to monitor Channel 16, the voice-only distress channel, through at least 2010.

To begin using GMDSS, first make sure your VHF radio is DSC-equipped. You will then need to obtain an MMSI number. This can be done for a fee by contacting the FCC directly as described above, or without a fee by contacting BoatU.S. at BoatU.S. MMSI Program, 880 South Pickett Street, Alexandria, VA 22304; 1-800-563-1536; MMSI@BoatUS.com; or online at www.boatus .com/mmsi. The same service is provided by Sea Tow online at www.seatow.com/boating_safety/ mmsi.asp. As of 2006, MMSI numbers obtained from BoatU.S. or Sea Tow are not included in the FCC database, which feeds the international database. What this means is that unless your MMSI is obtained directly from the FCC, it will not properly identify your boat in international waters. Hopefully this will be rectified, but the deficiency makes little difference to boaters operating in U.S. coastal and inland waters.

After obtaining the MMSI number, program your radio with the number and other information, following the radio manufacturer's instructions. Then familiarize yourself with DSC radio procedures, which include the requirement to monitor Channel 70 (along with Channel 16) when at sea with the radio on.

For more information on DSC and GMDSS, consult the U.S. Coast Guard website at www.nav cen.uscg.gov/marcomms.

## SENSITIVITY

The *sensitivity* of a radio helps determine its ability to pick up distant signals. The less microvoltage a set needs to reach the 20-decibel (dB) sound level, the more sensitive it is. Thus, a radio using 0.5 microvolt is more sensitive than one using 2.5 microvolts. If a set is too sensitive, however, it may "talk" continuously when close to shore. If possible,

**Figure 16-5.** A Coast Guard Auxiliarist uses a fixed-mount VHF radio on his boat on the Washington, North Carolina, waterfront. (PHOTO BY DON LINDBERG)

**Figure 16-6.** A Coast Guard Auxiliarist using a handheld VHF. (PHOTO BY JOE BRITVCH)

sample several radios on friends' boats and select the model that performs best.

## SELECTIVITY

*Selectivity* is a measure of how well a receiver rejects signals from other channels close to the channel you are using. The units for selectivity are also decibels, but selectivity is expressed in negative decibels. A set with a –0.75 dB selectivity will do a much better job than one rated at –0.55 dB.

## AUDIO OUTPUT

Audio output measures the loudness of the radio. Your radio needs to be loud enough to be heard over the sound of your engine.

Small radios usually have small speakers and do not produce loud sounds. Thus, handheld VHF-FM radios usually do not produce sounds as loud as fixed-mount ones. If the radio has an outlet for an external speaker, you can use one to improve the sound level and audio quality.

## SIGNAL STRENGTH

Your VHF-FM set must be able to transmit on a power of 1 watt. Most fixed-mount VHF-FM radios provide, in addition, a maximum power setting of 25 watts, while most handheld sets transmit on a "low" power of 1 watt and a "high" power of 5 watts. One watt is more than enough power for short distances, and it is mandatory to use the 1-watt setting when transmitting in a harbor. Make it a point to evaluate the signal strength of a VHF-FM radio before buying it.

## SIGNAL SUPPRESSION

When two VHF-FM radios are transmitting on the same channel in the same area, the stronger one "steps on" or suppresses the weaker. Unlike AM radios, which can receive two stations at the same time, an FM radio receives only the stronger station. Limit your signal distance by using the lowest power needed for your communication, and don't reach out of your area and, perhaps, inadvertently suppress an important communication from another vessel.

## LINE-OF-SIGHT TRANSMISSION

VHF-FM is essentially a line-of-sight system (Figure 16-7 and Table 16-1), reaching only slightly beyond the antenna's horizon. This is sufficient for most marine communications. Important land stations, such as a Coast Guard station, are equipped with high antennas, and these increase

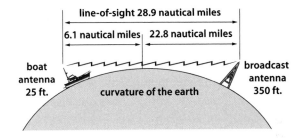

**Figure 16-7.** Since VHF range is limited to a line-of-sight between the transmitting and receiving antennas, antenna height makes a big difference in effective range. In this example, a boat 29 miles at sea with an antenna height of 25 feet can receive transmissions from a U.S. Coast Guard 350-foot broadcast tower onshore. Communications between two boats with 25-foot antenna heights, however, would be limited to about 12 miles.

| TABLE 16-1 | **VHF Communications Range** | | | | |
|---|---|---|---|---|---|
| **Range (in nautical miles) as a function of transmitting and receiving antenna heights** | | | | | |
| **Transmitting Antenna Height** | **Receiving Antenna Height** | | | | |
| | 5 ft. | 10 ft. | 25 ft. | 100 ft. | 250 ft. |
| 5 ft. | 5 | 7 | 9 | 15 | 23 |
| 10 ft. | 9 | 10 | 11 | 18 | 25 |
| 30 ft. | 10 | 12 | 13 | 20 | 28 |
| 60 ft. | 12 | 14 | 15 | 21 | 30 |

the Coast Guard's range of reception and transmission. Whenever one antenna can "see" another, communication is possible.

With 25 watts of power, an installed VHF-FM radio is limited by antenna height rather than power, and it will reach as many stations as it could reach with more power. A more powerful radio would only send its signal farther out into space.

## AVAILABLE CHANNELS

The VHF-FM frequency band includes 73 channels, of which 55 are in use in the United States. Modern marine radios have all the channels required and needed. Even low-priced radios are full-channel capable. There are, however, eight channels that are blocked and reserved for government use: 3, 21, 23, 61, 64, 81, 82, and 83. Any of these can be unblocked with proper justification.

### U.S. and International Channels

Your VHF-FM radio may have a two-position switch labeled "USA" and "International." This is because the channel frequencies used in the United States differ, in some instances, from those used in foreign countries. Where there is a difference, the USA channel number includes the letter A.

For example, one of the channels used by the Coast Guard is Channel 22. Since the U.S. Channel 22 has a different frequency than a foreign Channel 22, the Coast Guard channel is 22A, which you say as "22 alpha." If the Coast Guard tells you to shift to 22 alpha, be certain that your switch is in the USA position.

## CHANNEL SELECTOR

During a transmission to another vessel or a coastal station, it is necessary to switch from the calling channel to a working channel. On many older sets this is done with a rotary dial, which may have small numbers that are difficult to read, especially in poor light.

Newer sets have number pads for channel selection and digital readouts, making them easier to use. The digital readout is even easier to read in dim light than in good light, and a good set includes a dimmer switch for nighttime operation.

You can buy a scanning set that will scan as few as two channels or as many as the total available, though it will not scan the weather channels. Just be certain that the scanner you purchase includes Channel 9 as well as Channel 16. If a message comes in on a preset channel, the set automatically switches to that channel.

## POWER USAGE

The amount of electrical current a radio uses is important. The **amp draw** is a measure of the power a radio uses when sending or receiving that also shows how much drain is imposed on your battery. For handheld radios, it gives some idea of how long you can operate the radio before recharging the battery. The batteries of most handheld sets need charging after about 3 hours of use.

While efficient handheld radios draw as little as 0.02 amp on standby and 0.8 amp when sending, efficient fixed-mount radios require as little as 0.2 amp on standby and about 5.0 amps when transmitting.

# Installation

You can install a fixed-mount VHF-FM radio yourself, but you cannot repair or adjust it, since this might change its transmitting characteristics. Only FCC-licensed General Class commercial operators can make repairs or adjustments.

Improper power and antenna connections can impair performance or cause equipment damage. When you install your radio, keep it and its speaker as far away from your compass as practicable, and be sure that the power connections are secure and correct. The positive lead from the battery should go to the positive terminal of your radio. On a 12-volt system, the positive lead is usually red and the negative lead, which goes to the negative terminal, is usually black. There should also be a fuse somewhere in the positive (red) lead. Installation is not difficult.

## YOUR RADIO ANTENNA

Select a good-quality antenna in the right frequency band for your radio (e.g., a CB antenna should be used only for a CB transmitter, and SSB antennas are designed only for SSB transmitters). If you use the wrong antenna, you will greatly reduce your ability to transmit and receive. You may also damage your transmitter if you attempt to transmit without an antenna.

Place the antenna as high in your boat as you can. Sailors often place their antennas at the masthead, thus increasing their range, and most powerboats use 8-foot-long antennas. When you install one, allow enough room to lay it down for trailering and passing under low bridges.

The *ferrule* is the nylon or metal fitting at the bottom of the antenna. Nylon is good and will serve you well on lakes and in calm to moderate seas. If you plan to fish or cruise in rougher weather, however, a metal ferrule is advisable.

Nylon or metal (usually stainless steel) mounts connect antennas to boats. You should match the mount to the ferrule—if the ferrule is nylon, use a nylon mount, and use a metal mount with a metal ferrule.

*Gain* is a measure of an antenna's effectiveness. The higher the gain, in theory, the farther you can communicate within the line-of-sight envelope for VHF transmissions. It is tempting to select a higher-gain antenna than needed, but don't do it. Theory aside, with a high-gain antenna, you may not be able to communicate at all.

Figure 16-8 shows why, illustrating the radiation patterns of 3 dB, 6 dB, and 9 dB gain antennas.

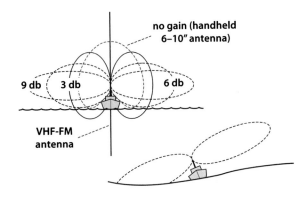

**Figure 16-8.** Typical radiation patterns of VHF-FM radio antennas. A 9 db gain antenna, which might be 24 feet long, offers greater potential range but also a vertically compressed signal. When the boat rolls, you might be transmitting down into the sea on one side of the boat and up into space on the other side. Many powerboaters choose a 6 db, 8-foot antenna as a good compromise.

On land or in a very stable boat you might select a 9 dB antenna. In a pitching and rolling vessel, though, the flat, vertically compressed signal of a 9 dB antenna sometimes will point at the sea and sometimes will point up in the air, so much of its signal is wasted. Most small boats should avoid antennas with gain ratings above 6 dB.

When installing your antenna, keep it away from masts, shrouds, stays, or other metal that might shield it. If the antenna cable is 25 feet long or less, you can use the cable that came with the antenna, but if a longer cable is needed, use a low-loss cable. Keep the cable as short as possible.

# Operating Your VHF-FM

Before you turn your radio on, check that the **high power–low power switch** is in the 1-watt position. This is where you will operate most of the time. Check, also, to see that the **USA/International switch** is in the USA position.

Your VHF-FM radio is a *transceiver*, which means that it is both a transmitter and a receiver, but it can only perform one of these functions at a time. When you turn on the radio, it is ready to

## Radio Usage Caveats

- Do not send false distress and emergency messages.
- Do not use obscene, indecent, or profane language.
- Observe the confidentiality of others' messages (except in emergency situations or broadcasts of general use).
- Do not use your radio when the boat is on land.
- Listen on your selected channel before transmitting your message, so as not to "step on" a communication in progress.
- Shift to a working channel immediately after contact has been made on the calling channel (except in an emergency situation).
- Learn and practice the correct radio usage techniques and language. Rehearse your message (to yourself) **before** making the transmission.
- Think through your responses **before** responding. (Responses don't have to be given immediately. You can simply say "Wait." Think through your response, then respond.)
- Speak slowly and distinctly.

receive. To send, press a button or a switch. You will usually find a **push-to-talk button** on the microphone.

The volume control usually doubles as the **On/Off switch**. When you turn it, it first turns the radio on, then increases the receiving volume. It has no impact on your transmission strength, however; the high power–low power switch controls that.

Another important switch, the **squelch control**, stops the constant noise you hear when not receiving a signal from another radio. Turn it up until the static just disappears, but no farther. Too much squelch lowers the ability of your radio to receive signals, so set it just high enough to make the static disappear and to screen out signals that are so far away that you can't understand them.

## MAINTAIN A RADIO WATCH

You do not have to keep your radio turned on whenever you're boating. When it *is* on, however, and when it's not being used for messages, you should keep it tuned to Channel 16 (unless it's a scanner model, in which case you should include Channel 16 in the scan pattern).

You will do far more listening than talking. Your radiotelephone is a busy party line with many users, and it is also vital for emergency communications. Always listen carefully before transmitting to see if someone else is using the channel or if there is an emergency condition in effect. When you listen, adjust the squelch so you can understand distant signals.

## RADIOTELEPHONE STATION LOG

A radio log is a record of calls made and received by a station, as in the accompanying sample. Each page of the log should be numbered, should include the name of the vessel and its call sign, and should be signed by the operator. Entries should show the time each watch began and ended using 24-hour military time.

If your boat is less than 65 feet long, you do not need to keep a radio log, but you must record as completely as possible all emergency signals and communications you hear and keep this log for at least 3 years. Keep it for a longer time if it concerns commu-

**WARNING** *Be careful about giving credit-card information over a radio channel. It is NOT secure.*

nications under investigation by the FCC or against which claims or complaints have been filed.

## CHANNELS HAVE SPECIAL PURPOSES

Each VHF-FM channel has an assigned frequency. For example, Channel 16 has a frequency of 156.800 MHz for receiving and sending. We will not discuss VHF-FM frequencies, though, since you do not need them. Use channel numbers, which are keyed to frequencies by the radio, to tune your set. (SSB radios use frequency settings, not channels. The SSB distress and calling frequency is 2182 kHz.)

Table 16-2 summarizes the VHF-FM channels and their uses. Begin most calls on Channel 16, and begin all distress, urgency, and safety messages on Channel 16 unless you're using Channel 70 with a DSC radio.

Channel 9 is both an intership and ship-to-shore channel, and is often used by marinas and yacht clubs. Boaters often switch to Channel 9 after contacting another boat on Channel 16, and Channel 9 is an alternate calling channel as well.

Shift to Channel 6, the intership safety channel, for ship-to-ship safety messages. If you have an emergency and the Coast Guard or the Auxiliary comes to your aid, it may communicate with you on Channel 6.

If you call the Coast Guard, it may request that you switch to one of its working channels, such as Channel 22A (USA setting), the Coast Guard Liaison channel. You should initiate your call on Channel 16, however.

A message on any noncommercial channel must be about the needs of your vessel. Typical uses include fishing reports, rendezvous, repair scheduling, and berthing. Channel 72 is only for ship-to-ship messages.

Public correspondence channels connect your ship's radio with a telephone operator ashore. Through these channels, you can call any telephone. This service was formerly provided by Mari-

# RADIOTELEPHONE STATION LOG

Vessel Name:_____     Vessel Call Sign:_____     Page #_____

| Date | Local Time Symbol | | Channel or Frequency Used | Station Called or Calling | Message | Operator's Signature |
| | Time Begun | Time Ended | | | | |
|---|---|---|---|---|---|---|
| | | | | | | |
| | | | | | | |
| | | | | | | |
| | | | | | | |
| | | | | | | |
| | | | | | | |
| | | | | | | |
| | | | | | | |
| | | | | | | |
| | | | | | | |
| | | | | | | |
| | | | | | | |
| | | | | | | |
| | | | | | | |
| | | | | | | |
| | | | | | | |
| | | | | | | |
| | | | | | | |
| | | | | | | |
| | | | | | | |
| | | | | | | |
| | | | | | | |
| | | | | | | |
| | | | | | | |
| | | | | | | |
| | | | | | | |
| | | | | | | |
| | | | | | | |
| | | | | | | |
| | | | | | | |
| | | | | | | |
| | | | | | | |
| | | | | | | |
| | | | | | | |
| | | | | | | |
| | | | | | | |
| | | | | | | |
| | | | | | | |

TEL on a charge-per-call basis, and is now (after a 2-year service lapse) provided by Sea Tow on a subscription basis. The primary channels for this service are 26, 27, and 28, and as of 2006, in the near future Sea Tow expects to be operational nationwide. If you plan to use ship-to-shore telephone service, find out which channel to use in your area, and arrange your subscription in advance. Since marine telephone conversations can be heard by anyone with a VHF-FM marine radio, you would not want to broadcast your credit-card number. Consult your telephone directory for information on how to call a marine operator using a public correspondence channel. There are no restrictions on the content of public correspondence calls. Remember, though, that your call is over public airways and is not secure.

In some ports, vessel traffic service systems use Channels 11, 12, and 14. The port operations channels are for directing the movement of ships in or near ports, locks, or waterways, and messages must be about the handling, movement, and safety of ships.

Channel 13 is the working channel at most locks and drawbridges. The navigational channels are bridge-to-bridge channels. These "bridges" are ships' bridges, the places from which they are controlled. Navigational channels are available to all ships, but the messages must be about vessel navigation—for example, passing or meeting other vessels. Keep your message short. No communication between two ships should exceed 3 minutes after the ships have made contact, and your transmission power should not be more than 1 watt.

You can talk to ships and coast stations operated by state or local governments on the maritime control channel, Channel 17. Your message must be about regulation and control, boating activities, or assistance to ships.

Channel 70, the digital selective calling channel, is an alternative channel for distress, safety, and general-purpose calling with a DSC-capable VHF radio. **Do not use this channel for voice transmissions.** Assuming both boats have digital radios, you can call a fellow boater's MMSI number on Channel 70 much as you dial a cell phone number. His radio will sound an alarm to alert him to the incoming call, and when he presses a button to acknowledge, both radios will switch automatically to a working channel for a voice conversation. This is the chief advantage of a digital radio for routine communications.

In addition to the primary three weather frequencies given in Table 16-2, there are as many as seven other VHF receive-only weather frequencies. Some have special applications, however, and some carry regional weather only in certain locations. Scanning the frequencies will show you which weather channels are available in your waters.

| TABLE 16-2 | VHF-FM Channels Used for Various Noncommercial Messages |
|---|---|
| **Type of Message** | **Suitable Channels** |
| Distress, Urgency, Safety, and Calling | 16 |
| Boater Calling Channel | 9 |
| Intership Safety | 6 |
| Coast Guard Liaison | 21A, 22A |
| Noncommercial[1] | 68, 69, 71, 72, 78A |
| Public Correspondence (Marine Operator) | 24, 25, 26, 27, 28, 84, 85, 86, 87, 88[2] |
| Port Operations | 1, 5[3], 11, 12, 14, 20[4], 63, 65, 66, 73, 74, 77[5] |
| Navigational | 13 |
| Maritime Control | 17 |
| Digital Selective Distress and Calling | 70 |
| Weather[6] | WX1 (162.550 MHz) WX2 (162.400 MHz) WX3 (162.475 MHz) |

1. Working channels for recreational boats only. Other channels are reserved for working vessels.
2. Only for use in the Great Lakes, the St. Lawrence Seaway, and Puget Sound and its approaches.
3. Available only in the Houston and New Orleans areas.
4. Channel 20 used only for ship-to-coast messages.
5. Channel 77 is limited to intership communications to and from pilot boats.
6. Weather channels are "receive only."

## SOME NO-NOS

**Do not send false distress or emergency messages.** Hoaxes can lead to loss of life. The Coast Guard answers every distress call regardless of the weather or other conditions. These calls often are sent by children who do not realize the seriousness of their hoaxes.

The Coast Guard works closely with the FCC to identify offenders. Both the Coast Guard and the FCC have direction-finding equipment available, which means that when you are in waters where the Coast Guard has a presence, it is very likely that the location of your broadcast can be pinpointed. The misuse of Channel 16 is serious enough that it is a Class D felony; offenders are liable for a $5,000 fine plus all costs the Coast Guard incurs as a result of the hoax. So guard your radio against unauthorized use, because you are responsible for it.

### Obscenity, Indecency, and Profanity

When using your radio, you are using an extensive party line and can assume that other people are listening. You therefore have a compelling moral obligation as well as a strict legal responsibility to watch your language. It is a criminal offense to use obscene, indecent, or profane language, and the penalty is a fine of up to $10,000, imprisonment for up to 2 years, or both.

### Secrecy of Communication

The Federal Communications Act protects the secrecy of radio communications. You must not communicate the contents of any radio message to anyone other than the addressee or the addressee's agent or attorney unless you are authorized to do so. If you intercept a message, you must not use its contents for your own benefit or the benefit of other people.

This secrecy requirement does not apply to distress messages, however, nor does it apply to radio broadcasts meant for general use.

### Using Your VHF-FM Radio on Land

Do not use your radio to transmit when your boat is on land—while it is on a trailer, for example. Also, do not make general calls except in an emergency or when your radio is being tested. Instead, direct your calls to a particular station.

# Copies of the Rules

Recreational boaters do not need to keep copies of the FCC rules aboard their vessels. You can get a copy, however, by writing to Superintendent of Documents, P.O. Box 371954, Pittsburgh PA 15250-7954, or call 1-866-512-1800, or go to http://bookstore.gpo.gov.

## RULES VIOLATIONS

If the FCC believes that you have violated the rules, it may send you a written notice of the violation. A violation notice that covers a technical radio standard will require you to stop using your radio until the problem is fixed. You may be required to have your radio tested and the results sent to the FCC, and the commercial operator who conducted the test must sign the results.

If the FCC finds that you have willfully or repeatedly violated the Federal Communications Act or the rules, it may revoke your license if you have one. You can also be fined or even sent to prison, as mentioned above.

# Calling Another Station

To call another station, first turn the radio on and make sure it is on low power. Tune it to your chosen calling channel—often Channel 16—and listen for a few moments to make sure no one else is using it. Next, press the microphone button and speak directly into the microphone. Hold the microphone 2 to 4 inches from your mouth, use a normal tone of voice, and speak clearly. Switch to high power if you suspect that the other station is too far away to hear you.

Call the other station by saying the name of the vessel or station you are calling, followed by your vessel's name. An example is: "*Sundown*, this is *Rusty Nail*."

Do not add unnecessary words such as "Come in, Bob," or "Do you read me?" These only add to the traffic on the channel. Also, calling in reverse, with your vessel's name first, is improper and confusing.

After you have called the other station, release the microphone button. If you continue to press the button, you won't be able to hear the other station's response. When you send, press the button, but when you want to listen, release it.

Do not call the same station for more than 30 seconds at a time. If you do not get a reply, wait at least 2 minutes before calling again. After three attempts, wait at least 15 minutes before calling again.

When the other station answers, immediately request that it switch to a working channel. Table 16-2 lists the channels to use for the kind of message you wish to send. Know which channel you want to switch to before you call.

After reaching the other station, switch to a working channel and send your message. If you expect an answer, end your transmission with the word "Over." If you do not expect an answer, say "Out." Do not say "Over and out."

Be sure to identify your station by giving your FCC call sign (if one has been issued) at the beginning and end of each message. You must do this in English.

Keep your communication brief, and when you are through, give your vessel's name and call sign. The other station should also give its name and call sign. After this, switch back to the calling channel.

## PUBLIC CORRESPONDENCE CALLS

If you want to place a telephone call, first turn the radio on. Next, switch to a public correspondence channel and listen to be sure it is not currently in use. Then press the microphone button and say, "[Name of coast station], this is [your call sign or vessel's name]."

When the marine operator answers, say, "This is [name of boat, call sign, and billing number assigned], placing a call to [city and telephone number]." Except for distress calls, you need to be a subscriber to the service from the company that owns the coast station.

## SHIP-TO-SHIP CALLS THROUGH A COAST STATION

Although you usually make a call to another ship by calling it directly, you can do it through a coast station as well. Use the same procedure as you do for ship-to-shore calls. You might make such a call if the vessel you are calling is too far away for you to

reach directly. Remember, the coast station has a high antenna.

## SHORE-TO-SHIP CALLS

To call a vessel from a shore telephone, you need to know where the vessel is. Then dial 0 (zero) and ask the operator to connect you to or give you the phone number of the marine operator nearest the vessel. Tell the marine operator the name of the vessel you are calling, and also the call sign of the vessel's radio station, if you know it.

Once connected with the vessel, remember that the ship station operates using a push-to-talk radio. Don't try to break in while the ship station is transmitting, but wait until you hear, "Over." When you are through, hang up.

## LIMITED COAST STATIONS

Limited coast stations serve the operational and business needs of vessels. Some, such as those operated by a harbormaster or at a drawbridge, also serve a safety function. Limited coast stations are not open to public correspondence.

Yacht clubs with docking facilities, marina operators, boaters, dockside restaurants, marine police, towing services, and others operate limited coast stations. There is no charge for communications services incidental to their business.

Call a limited coast station on its working channel. If that doesn't work, try the local calling channel, but be ready to switch to a working channel. A limited coast station calls vessels on the local calling channel, so you do not need to monitor its working channel if you are expecting a call.

# Procedure Words

A key to efficient use of radiotelephone time is the use of *procedure words*, or *prowords* for short. These words are a form of shorthand, and you can see from Table 16-3 how much they reduce transmission time.

Don't be sensitive about using prowords. No one will think you are showing off by using terms such as "wilco" if you use them correctly.

## TABLE 16-3  Procedure Words (Prowords)

| Procedure Word | Meaning |
|---|---|
| OUT | This is the end of my transmission to you. No answer is required or expected. |
| OVER | This is the end of my transmission and a response is expected. Go ahead, transmit. (Omit when it is clearly not needed.) |
| ROGER | I received your last transmission okay. |
| WILCO | Your last message has been received and understood, and will be complied with. |
| THIS IS | This transmission is from the station whose name and call sign follows immediately. |
| FIGURES | Figures or numbers follow; for example, "Vessel length is FIGURES 2 3 feet." |
| SPEAK SLOWER | Your transmission is difficult to understand. Speak slower. |
| SAY AGAIN | Repeat. |
| WORDS TWICE | It is difficult to understand you. Give each phrase twice. |
| I SPELL | I shall spell the next word phonetically. (Used when a proper name is important in the message; for example, "Boat name is *Martha*. I spell—Mike, Alfa, Romeo, Tango, Hotel, Alfa.) |
| WAIT | I must pause for a few seconds; stand by for further transmission. |
| WAIT OUT | I must pause for longer than a few seconds. I will call you back. |
| AFFIRMATIVE | You are correct, or what you have transmitted is correct. |
| NEGATIVE | No. |

Beware of other words in common use that sound like prowords, but accomplish nothing. For example, following several unanswered calls to a boat on Channel 9, you may hear something such as, "Negative contact. This is [boat name], out." This is meaningless. Anyone listening knows there was no contact, and, worse still, the unnecessary announcement could have masked another call.

# Phonetic Alphabet

When radio signals are weak and reception is poor, you may need to spell words or to express numbers in clear ways. The phonetic alphabet and its pronunciation appear in Table 16-4. In use, the person sending the message says, "I spell," and then gives the phonetic spelling of the word or words. The proper use of the phonetic alphabet reduces misunderstandings.

## NUMBERS

Closely allied to the phonetic alphabet is the manner of pronouncing numbers. In a message, if you spell out a number, you precede it by saying, "Figures . . ." The correct pronunciations of the numbers are given in Table 16-5.

If your vessel is in distress and you can't give its exact location, the Coast Guard may request that you

## TABLE 16-4  Phonetic Alphabet

| Letter | Phonetic Equivalent | Pronunciation |
|---|---|---|
| A | Alfa | *Al* fah |
| B | Bravo | *Brah* voh |
| C | Charlie | *Char* lee |
| D | Delta | *Dell* tah |
| E | Echo | *Eck* oh |
| F | Foxtrot | *Foks* trot |
| G | Golf | Golf |
| H | Hotel | Ho *tell* |
| I | India | *In* dee ah |
| J | Juliet | Jew lee *et* |
| K | Kilo | *Key* loh |
| L | Lima | *Lee* mah |
| M | Mike | Mike |
| N | November | No *vem* ber |
| O | Oscar | *Oss* cah |
| P | Papa | Pah *pah* |
| Q | Quebec | Keh *beck* |
| R | Romeo | *Row* me oh |
| S | Sierra | See *air* rah |
| T | Tango | *Tan* go |
| U | Uniform | *You* nee form |
| V | Victor | *Vik* tah |
| W | Whiskey | *Wiss* key |
| X | X-ray | *Ecks* ray |
| Y | Yankee | *Yang* key |
| Z | Zulu | *Zoo* loo |

1. Emphasis is on the **bold**, *italic* part of the word.

make a "long count" during which it will home in on your signal with a radio direction finder to determine where you are. If the Coast Guard asks you to give a long count, say slowly, "Wun, Too, Thuh ree, Fo wer, Fi yiv, Six, Seven, Ate, Niner, Zero, Zero, Niner, Ate, Seven, Six, Fi yiv, Fo wer, Thuh ree, Too, Wun." A short count goes from Wun to Fi-yiv, repeats Fi-yiv, and goes back down to Wun.

| TABLE 16-5 | Pronunciation of Numbers |
| --- | --- |
| **Number** | **Pronunciation** |
| 0 (Zero) | Zero |
| 1 (One) | Wun |
| 2 (Two) | Too |
| 3 (Three) | Thuh ree |
| 4 (Four) | Fo wer |
| 5 (Five) | Fi yiv |
| 6 (Six) | Six |
| 7 (Seven) | Seven |
| 8 (Eight) | Ate |
| 9 (Nine) | Niner |

# Routine Radio Check

You can't tell if your radio is transmitting unless you talk to another station. Direct your call to a station you know is operating.

Begin your request on the local calling channel, then switch to a working channel. Before calling, listen long enough to be sure that the calling channel is not busy, then call a specific station or vessel. Include the phrase "Request a radio check" in your initial call.

If you make a general radio check request ("in the blind") on a calling channel, keep the request short and on low power, and do not endlessly repeat the request. The lack of a response may mean your radio really isn't working.

# Distress, Urgency, and Safety Calls

If your vessel is in distress, you may use any means, in addition to your radio, to attract attention and get help. Often visual signals such as flags, flares, lights, and smoke or audible signals such as your horn or a whistle will get the attention and help you need.

If you can't use visual or audible signals, use your VHF-FM radio. Initiate your call on Channel 16, but remember, you can use it or any other channel, including the public correspondence channels, to request emergency help.

## SPOKEN EMERGENCY SIGNALS

There are three spoken emergency signals that show the degree of severity of the emergency. All three signals are initiated on Channel 16. Distress and urgency messages are then given on Channel 16, while safety messages are given on a working channel.

### Distress Signal: Mayday

The distress signal, **Mayday**, precedes a distress message about a grave and imminent danger and a request for immediate help, and this signal has priority over all other calls. The word "mayday" comes from the French expression, *m'aidez*, which means "Help me." If you use it, speak the word three times, "Mayday, Mayday, Mayday."

***SENDING A DISTRESS CALL.*** You send a voice distress signal and message on Channel 16. During the emergency, remain on that channel. Provided you are being received on Channel 16, you do not want to risk losing contact by switching to another channel.

After the initial contact, the following message sequence should be broadcast slowly and distinctly:

1. The distress signal **Mayday**, spoken three times.
2. The words **This is**, spoken once.
3. The **name of your vessel**, spoken three times, and **your call sign**, spoken once.
4. The distress signal **Mayday**, spoken once.
5. The **name of your vessel**, spoken once.
6. The **position of your vessel** either by latitude and longitude or by a bearing (either true or compass) and distance from a well-known landmark. You can give it any way that will assist in locating you.
7. The **nature of your distress**: for example, taking on water, sinking, or fire.
8. The **kind of help needed**.

9. Any **other information** that might help. This might include the length or tonnage of your vessel, the number of people on board, and the number of people needing medical attention. It helps to give a description of your vessel, including the color of its hull, deck, cabin, and masts.

10. When you are through, say, **"I will be listening on Channel 16."**

11. End your message by saying, **"This is [your boat name and call sign], over."**

Release the microphone button and listen. Someone should answer. If you do not receive an answer, repeat your call beginning at #1 above.

To help you recall the above steps in an emergency, refer to the accompanying Distress Communication form. Copy it, fill it in except for items 6 through 9, and post it near your radio.

***ACKNOWLEDGING A DISTRESS MESSAGE.*** If you hear an unanswered distress message, you must answer on Channel 16. You can wait a short time for others to acknowledge if you are reasonably certain that the distressed vessel is not in your vicinity. Wait, also, in waters where there are reliable communications with the Coast Guard.

After you acknowledge receipt of the distress message, wait a short time. There may be others in a better position to help than you are, and they should also acknowledge receipt.

## DISTRESS COMMUNICATION FORM

**Instructions:** Complete this form now (except for items 6 through 9) and post near your radiotelephone for use if you are in distress.

### SPEAK: SLOWLY—CLEARLY—CALMLY

1. Make certain your radio is turned on.
2. Select **VHF-FM Channel 16** or **2182 kHz for your SSB.**
3. Press microphone button and say: **MAYDAY—MAYDAY—MAYDAY.**
4. Say: **THIS IS**_____
   (Your boat name, repeated three times, and your call sign.)
5. Say: **MAYDAY**_____
   (Your boat name)
6. **TELL WHERE YOU ARE.** (What navigational aids or landmarks are you near? What direction and distance are you from a landmark? What is your latitude and longitude? What are your loran coordinates?)
7. **STATE THE NATURE OF YOUR DISTRESS.**
8. **GIVE NUMBER OF PEOPLE ABOARD AND CONDITIONS OF ANY INJURED.**
9. **ESTIMATE CURRENT SEAWORTHINESS OF YOUR BOAT.**
10. **BRIEFLY DESCRIBE YOUR BOAT:** _____ FEET; _____
    (Length)                                                          (Type)
    _____ HULL; _____ TRIM; _____ MASTS;
    (Color)                      (Color)                        (Number)
    _____
    (Anything else you think will help rescuers find you.)
11. Say: **I WILL BE LISTENING ON CHANNEL** _____16/2182_____
    (Cross out one that does not apply).
12. End message by saying: **THIS IS**_____, **OVER.**
    (Your boat name and call sign)
13. Release microphone button and listen. Someone should answer. **IF THEY DO NOT, REPEAT CALL, BEGINNING AT ITEM #1 ABOVE. IF THERE IS STILL NO ANSWER, CHECK TO SEE IF YOUR SET IS TURNED ON, IS ON HIGH POWER, AND IS ON CHANNEL 16 IF IT IS VHF-FM OR 2182 kHz IF IT IS SSB.**

When you are sure you are not interfering with other distress-related communications, contact the vessel in distress and tell them what assistance you can give. If the vessel is in your area, you are obligated to render any possible assistance. Make sure the Coast Guard knows about the distress and relay the distress message if necessary.

If you can't reach the Coast Guard directly, call the nearest marine operator. This is especially important if the distressed vessel is beyond reach of the Coast Guard and you are between the Coast Guard station and the distressed vessel.

You acknowledge receipt of a distress message by saying the name and call sign of the distressed vessel three times. Follow this by saying, "This is" and your vessel's name and call sign. Do this three times, then add, "Received Mayday."

After a momentary pause to ensure that you are not interfering with a vessel better situated to help, send the following: Start with the "Mayday," then give the name and call sign of the distressed vessel. Continue with "This is," and give your vessel's name and call sign. Tell where you are, your speed, and how much time it will take you to reach the other vessel.

A vessel or shore station that learns a vessel is in distress should send a distress message when the vessel in distress can't send the message itself. It may also do so if more help is needed. If it hears an unacknowledged distress message and is not able to assist, it should send a distress message.

In such a case, the transmission consists of the radiotelephone alarm signal (if available) followed by "Mayday relay, Mayday relay, Mayday relay." You then say, "This is," and give the name and call sign of your vessel or shore station three times. If you send a distress message under these conditions, contact the Coast Guard.

***IMPOSING SILENCE.*** The vessel in distress or the station in control of distress communications may impose silence on any station that interferes by sending "Seelonce Mayday." ("Seelonce" is the French pronunciation of the word "silence.") Any other station that believes it is essential to impose silence may do so by sending "Seelonce Distress," followed by the name and call sign of the station imposing the silence.

After distress communications have ceased, or when silence is no longer necessary, the station in control ends the silence. It does so on Channel 16 by sending the following: "Mayday, to all stations, to all stations, to all stations, this is [name and call sign of station ending the distress], [the time], [name and call sign of vessel in distress], Seelonce Feenee." ("Seelonce feenee" is the French pronunciation of *silence fini*, meaning "silence finished.")

## Urgency Signal: Pan-Pan

The urgency signal, **Pan-Pan**, announces that an urgent message follows. "Pan" (pronounced PAHN) comes from the French word *panne*, which means urgency, and should be used when the safety of a vessel or person is in jeopardy. Only a distress signal has a higher priority.

Urgency signals and messages are sent on Channel 16 in situations such as the following:

- Loss of a person overboard, but only when help is needed.
- Repeating an urgent storm warning from an authorized shore station.
- Loss of steering or power in a shipping lane.

# Distress Calls on a DSC-Capable VHF-FM Radio

If your radio is DSC-capable—as all fixed-mount VHF radios manufactured since 1999 are—and if the radio is properly registered, properly interfaced with your boat's GPS receiver, and programmed with the proper MMSI for emergency calling, a distress call is largely automated. The procedure is as follows:

1A. Lift the cover and press the Distress button. If the display reads "Undesignated," press the button for 3 to 5 seconds. The radio transmits a single "Mayday" alert in a digital signal containing your identity and location over Channel 70 to the Coast Guard, Sea Tow, and/or nearby ships.

1B. If the display provides a choice between "Undesignated" and "Designated," selecting "Designated" calls up a menu that allows you to specify the trouble you are in. Then press the button for 3 to 5 seconds to send the signal.

2. When the call is acknowledged digitally by another DSC-equipped radio, you will hear a tone.

3. If your radio does not switch automatically to Channel 16 for voice transmission, press the Cancel/Clear button.

4. On Channel 16, send a voice message concerning your situation (see above), and talk to rescuers and other vessels.

***SENDING AN URGENCY CALL.*** The urgency signal and message usually include the following:

1. The urgency signal **Pan-Pan**, spoken three times.
2. **To all stations** (or a particular station).
3. The words **This is**.
4. The **name of your vessel**, spoken three times, and your call sign, spoken once.
5. The **urgency message** (describe the problem).
6. The **position and description of your vessel** and any information that will help responding vessels.
7. The words **This is**.
8. The **name of your vessel** and its **radio call sign**, spoken once.
9. The proword **Over**.

## Safety Signal: Sécurité

The safety signal announces a message about safety of navigation or an important weather warning. It is the French word *sécurité*, pronounced "say-cur-ee-tay," and is said three times. Safety signals have higher priorities than any other messages except distress and urgency messages.

Most safety messages are initiated by the Coast Guard, and are announced on Channels 9 and 16 and given on a Coast Guard working channel, usually Channel 22A. If you have a safety message to send, announce it on Channel 16 and give it on a working channel.

Any message headed by one of the emergency signals has priority over other messages. Continue to listen but don't transmit, and be prepared to help if you can.

The decision about which emergency signal to use is the responsibility of the person in charge of the vessel, and sometimes there is no clear line to separate one signal from the other. Also, what starts as a routine problem might develop into a serious one. Running out of gasoline is not an emergency; running out of gasoline in a shipping lane might be an urgency situation, however, and running out of gas in a shipping lane with large ships headed toward you is more serious still.

***SENDING A SAFETY MESSAGE.*** Initiate the safety call on Channel 16. The following is an example of a safety message from the vessel *Barbara Ann*, which has radio call sign WX 3456: "Sécurité, sécurité, sécurité. This is *Barbara Ann*, Whiskey X-Ray 3456. Shift to Channel [local working channel] for safety message. This is *Barbara Ann*, Whiskey X-Ray 3456. Out."

On the working channel the message might be as follows: "Sécurité, Sécurité, Sécurité. This is *Barbara Ann*, Whiskey X-Ray 3456. A log approximately 20 feet long, 2 feet diameter is adrift off Haines Point in the Potomac River. This is *Barbara Ann*, Whiskey X-Ray 3456. Out."

Many skippers prefer to contact the Coast Guard and let them give the Sécurité call.

**Note:** If you have not been assigned a call sign by the FCC, use only your boat name.

# Crew Training

More than one person on board should know how to operate your vessel and your radio. Give your guests a brief introduction to your radio when you describe your vessel's operation and safety features, and fill out a Distress Communication Form and post it so that anyone on board can summon help in an emergency.

This may seem too cautious, but many emergencies could have had better outcomes if someone aboard other than a stricken skipper knew how to operate the radio or start the boat's engine. Many emergency broadcasts fail to summon help because the rattled operator does not turn on the power, or calls on the wrong channel, or forgets to depress the press-to-talk button. Others fail because the squelch is too high or the press-to-talk button isn't released and the return message isn't received.

# Practice Questions

## IMPORTANT BOATING TERMS

In the following exercise, match the words in the column on the left with the definitions in the column on the right. In the blank space to the left of each term, write the letter of the item that best matches it. Do not use an item in the right-hand column more than once.

| THE ITEMS | THE RESPONSES |
|---|---|
| 1. _____ distress signal | a. Sécurité |
| 2. _____ VHF-FM | b. I am through but I expect a response |
| 3. _____ urgency signal | c. I am through and I do not expect a response |
| 4. _____ safety signal | d. Pan-Pan |
| 5. _____ Public correspondence channels | e. message received, will comply |
| 6. _____ Out | f. distress, urgency, and safety |
| 7. _____ I spell | g. Mayday |
| 8. _____ Channel 16 | h. most commonly used marine radio |
| 9. _____ Wilco | i. use phonetic alphabet |
| 10. _____ Over | j. public telephone system |

# Multiple-Choice Items

In the following items, choose the best response:

**16-1.** VHF-FM licenses are issued by the

a. Coast Guard
b. state in which you live
c. FCC
d. marine patrol

**16-2.** You will need an operator's license for your VHF-FM if you

a. broadcast on your station
b. plan to dock in a foreign port
c. want to communicate with the Coast Guard
d. all of the above

**16-3.** If a VHF-FM channel number has the letter A attached to it, this means the channel is

a. an alternate one
b. already in use
c. available
d. USA only

**16-4.** Before you transmit

a. listen to see if someone else is using the channel
b. write out what you want to say
c. review the correct procedure
d. give your station call letters

**16-5.** At the beginning and end of each message, you must

a. state your name
b. give your call sign
c. turn your radio on and off
d. tell who you are calling

**16-6.** The most important purpose of a marine radiotelephone is

a. to arrange for boat repairs
b. to contact other skippers to find out where the fish are biting
c. to keep in touch with your home so

# Multiple-Choice Items (continued)

they will know everything is okay

d. safety

**16-7.** Radios equipped with digital selective calling (DSC)

a. use Channel 70 to transmit its digital information

b. have a seven-digit MMSI number assigned

c. can transmit location data without using any external equipment

d. are designed to have voice communication on the same channel as digital data

**16-8.** If you set your squelch control too low you will

a. reduce your ability to receive signals

b. lower your transmission power

c. interfere with weaker stations

d. receive too many stations

**16-9.** The distress signal that is used to indicate grave and imminent danger and to request immediate assistance is

a. Pan-Pan (said three times)

b. Sécurité (said three times)

c. Mayday (said three times)

d. radio check (said three times)

**16-10.** Which channel is the Coast Guard liaison channel?

a. 6

b. 16

c. 22A

d. 83

**16-11.** When you have completed your radiotelephone communication and do not require a reply, use the proword(s)

a. over and out

b. over

c. wilco

d. out

**16-12.** If you hear "Seelonce Mayday" on your marine radio, you know that

a. a Mayday is in progress

b. you are not supposed to use your radio

c. radio silence is requested

d. all of the above

**16-13.** The range of your VHF-FM radio depends on

a. the height of your antenna

b. the height of the receiving antenna

c. the gain of your antenna

d. all of the above

**16-14.** Keep a watch on the calling channel at all times except when

a. you are communicating on another channel or when your radiotelephone is not turned on

b. you are underway

c. no one is using the calling channel

d. you are maintaining a watch on another channel

**16-15.** A radio message concerning weather or safety of navigation is preceded by the word(s)

a. Mayday

b. Pan-Pan

c. Now hear this

c. Sécurité

**16-16.** Do not call a Coast Guard Station on Channel 16 to request

a. a radio check

b. assistance

c. a tow

d. a message be relayed

**16-17.** Although you may install your VHF-FM radio, any repairs or internal adjustments must be made by

a. a Coast Guard Auxiliarist communication specialist

b. a qualified electrician

c. a shortwave ham

d. an FCC-licensed general class commercial operator

**16-18.** Although a CB radio may be useful, it should not be seen as a means of

a. getting fishing information

b. contacting the Coast Guard

c. chitchat with other operators

d. calling home

(continued on next page)

# Multiple-Choice Items (continued)

**16-19.** When calling another vessel, the preliminary call must not exceed

a. 10 seconds
b. 30 seconds
c. 1 minute
d. 2 minutes

**16-20.** If you can't reach a limited coast station on its working channel, call it on

a. Channel 6
b. the local calling channel
c. Channel 16
d. Channel 22A

**16-21.** If another station answers your call, and you identify yourself, then

a. wait 10 seconds before talking
b. ask the other station to identify itself
c. request that it switch to a working channel
d. give your message

**16-22.** If you do not get a reply to your call to another station wait

a. at least 1 minute before trying again
b. at least 2 minutes before trying again
c. at least 3 minutes before trying again
d. at least 5 minutes before trying again

**16-23.** After you have tried three times to call another station, wait at least

a. 10 minutes before calling again
b. 15 minutes before calling again
c. 20 minutes before calling again
d. 30 minutes before calling again

**16-24.** An urgency message is preceded by the urgency signal

a. Sécurité
b. Mayday
c. Pan-Pan
d. all of the above

**16-25.** If you willfully or repeatedly violate the communications act or the FCC rules, you may

a. have your license revoked, if you have one
b. be fined
c. be sent to prison
d. any of the above

# Your Responsibilities as a Boat Operator

CHAPTER 5 FEATURED the items required by federal law for safe and enjoyable boating. Those are just part of the responsibilities you have as a boat operator. This section will discuss responsibilitites to your passengers, to other boaters, to Homeland Security, and your environmental obligations. In addition, we'll discuss the unique aspects of operating a PWC, as well as considerations when hunting or fishing from a boat.

## Responsibilities to Your Passengers and Others

In most states you are responsible for any damage your boat may cause other boats or for injuries suffered by your passengers or others. Under federal law, reckless and negligent operation of a boat is a crime and punishable by law. For grossly negligent operation, you may be fined up to $5,000 or imprisoned for 1 year, or both. You are responsible for anything your boat does or anything that happens to or on your boat—if you are present or if it is used with your express or implied consent. For example, if your wake rocks another vessel and breaks dishes in its galley, you are responsible. If this happens when hot food is being prepared or served, you are liable for any personal injury. The courteous thing to do when passing another vessel is to slow down enough that you do not create a large wake.

Federal law requires you to provide whatever assistance you can to anyone at sea in need of help. However, it does not require you to endanger your passengers, your vessel, or yourself while doing so.

If you render assistance, you are protected by the "Good Samaritan" clause of the Federal Boat Safety Act of 1971. This act says that if you "gratuitously and in good faith" render assistance and there is no objection, you cannot be held liable for anything you do or don't do, provided you act as an ordinary, reasonable person would have acted under the same or similar circumstances.

### SUBSTANCE ABUSE

Recreational boating is an activity that people engage in for fun. Many people focus their entire social lives around boats. Some of these social activities include consumption of alcohol and other mood-altering substances.

Unfortunately, as with automobiles, alcohol is a contributing factor in many boating accidents and deaths. Legal issues aside, drugs and alcohol have no place on a boat. Operating a boat is usually a simple, relaxed affair. But a single wrong choice, a single moment of inattention, can turn an afternoon outing into a disaster. The sea can be very unforgiving.

Over 700 people a year die in boating accidents. A large number of these deaths involve alcohol, used either by the victim or by another person involved in the incident. Add to this number the thousands who are injured each year, and a frightening picture emerges of needless suffering and expense directly related to the use of alcohol and other drugs. The federal minimum blood alcohol concentration (BAC) at which a person is considered "under the influence" has been lowered recently from 0.10% to 0.08%, which reinforces the concerns regarding alcohol abuse.

Boating, pleasant as it is, can be a stressful activity. After only a few hours on the water, a normal, healthy boat operator's perceptions and judgment are impaired even without alcohol or drugs. Unaccustomed exposure to fresh air, glare, ultraviolet light, motion, and noise can impair you as much as if you were legally intoxicated.

If you doubt that these factors can alter behavior, spend a couple of hours at a launching ramp. See how otherwise rational people try to load their boats on trailers. Add a few drinks or substance use and you have an explosive situation.

If you have been drinking or using drugs, your chances of surviving an accident are greatly reduced. Alcohol causes your physical reactions to slow, and alcohol and depressant drugs lower your resistance to hypothermia, a serious medical problem. Intoxicated people who fall into the water are much more likely than sober ones to become disoriented. They may swim downward rather than toward the surface. Just when good judgment and mental sharpness are needed most, they are muddled by the intoxicants.

Illegal drugs are just that—illegal. If you or guests on your boat are found in possession of or using illegal drugs, the results may be devastating for all involved. At the least, under the zero tolerance rule, you stand to lose your boat and other personal assets. You may also lose your freedom.

Even legal drugs may impair physical ability and judgment. Antihistamines, "seasickness" pills, sedatives, tranquilizers, etc., can all affect you adversely.

## SPEED REGULATIONS

Most speed regulations are local ordinances or state laws or regulations. You must respect all no-wake and speed restriction areas. Federal regulations require that you proceed at a safe speed so you can take proper and effective action to avoid collision. You must be able to stop in a distance appropriate to the circumstances and conditions. To determine safe speed, things such as visibility, traffic density, maneuverability of your vessel, and wind and sea state are considered.

A speed limit and no-wake sign at a marina entrance. (PHOTO BY BOB DENNIS)

## STATE AND LOCAL REGULATIONS

You are responsible for obeying all state and local regulations. Their purpose is to protect you and other people. They vary from location to location but include things such as: (1) using a kill switch on a PWC, which shuts off the engine if the operator falls away from the helm or overboard, (2) speed and wake regulations, (3) operator's license, (4) a requirement for a rearview mirror and observer if towing skiers, (5) age restrictions for operating or renting boats, and (6) laws regulating the operation of personal watercraft. You can consult your local police department or marine patrol for further information.

In most states, a PWC must have a kill switch unless the PWC is designed to circle back to its operator when the operator falls overboard. The kill switch is to be fastened to the operator by means of a lanyard whenever the vessel is in operation.

## BOATING ACCIDENT REPORTS

The operator of a vessel involved in an on-the-water accident must stop, render assistance, and offer identification. Notify local authorities immediately if a person disappears from a vessel or a death occurs.

A written accident report is required within 48 hours if a person dies, disappears from a vessel, or requires treatment beyond first aid. A written report is to be filed within 10 days if a vessel is lost or damage to it or other property exceeds $2,000. File the report forms with the state authorities that have jurisdiction over the waters on which the accident happened. Accident reports are used to compile safety data. Information contained in them is not made public.

A generic Boating Accident Report form, which includes most state requirements, can be found in Appendix C.

# Law Enforcement and Homeland Security

## BOARDINGS

Federal regulations require that vessels underway, when hailed by the Coast Guard, heave-to or maneuver in such a way that an officer can come aboard. Other federal, state, and local law enforcement officials may also come aboard and examine your boat. With the exception of customs, you can recognize such boats by their markings, their blue lights, and the uniforms the personnel wear.

## HOMELAND SECURITY

As a recreational boater, you share in keeping our waterways, marinas, and harbors safe and secure. It is important to know and observe security zones or restricted areas. Be aware that naval vessels (including Coast Guard vessels) maintain security zones. Within 500 yards of a naval vessel you must slow your boat to a minimum speed, and you must main-

tain a 100-yard distance from the naval vessel. If you must pass within 100 yards, hail the naval vessel on VHF-FM Channel 16 to get permission to pass.

Do not tie up to or obstruct any aid to navigation, and never anchor under bridges.

The Coast Guard's America's Waterway Watch program is a way for you as a recreational boater to assist in Homeland Security. Because you know your own harbors and marinas, you know what is ordinary and what is not. If there is immediate danger to someone's life or property, call 911. Report any suspicious activity to the National Response Center's Hotline, 1-877-24-WATCH.

# Environmental Concerns

## CLEANSERS, CHEMICALS, AND PAINTS

Purchase the least toxic product able to do the job and use lots of elbow grease. Clean spills with a rag, not a hose. Share leftover boat cleaning and painting supplies with other boaters or dispose of them safely onshore. Conduct all sanding, scraping, and painting away from the water and use a vacuum sander and tarps to collect particles.

## DISCHARGE OF FUEL AND OIL

All vessels under 100 gross tons are to have a fixed or portable means of discharging oily bilge slops into a container. A bucket or bailer is acceptable. Any discharge that causes a sheen on the water is a violation of the Federal Water Pollution Control Act.

When spilled, a single quart of motor oil can create a 2-acre slick (three football fields), fouling the water's surface and impacting marine life. Every year Americans spill or throw away more than thirty times the oil that was spilled from the *Exxon Valdez*. Use absorbent wipe "bilge pillows" to remove oily water from your bilge. Recycle used oil at a local recycling facility. Learn how to gauge when your tank is almost full and don't "top it off." Keep your engine or engines well tuned and check frequently for possible oil or grease leaks.

If your vessel is 26 feet or more in length, you must post a placard stating the federal oil discharge requirements. The placard shall be at least 5 by 8 inches and made of durable material. Post it in the machinery spaces or at the bilge and ballast pump control station.

The sumps of oil-lubricated machinery or the contents of oil filters, strainers, or purifiers are not to be emptied into the bilge of any U.S. vessel.

## Discharge of Oil Prohibited

The Federal Water Pollution Control Act prohibits the discharge of oil or oily waste into or upon the navigable waters and contiguous zone of the United States, if such discharge causes a film or sheen upon, or discoloration of, the surface of the water, or causes a sludge or emulsion beneath the surface of the water. Violators are subject to a penalty of $5,000.

# DISCHARGE OF OIL PROHIBITED
## The Federal Water Pollution Control Act

prohibits the discharge of oil or oily waste into or upon the navigable waters of the United States, or the waters of the contiguous zone, or which may affect natural resources belonging to, appertaining to, or under the exclusive management authority of the United States, if such discharge causes a film or discoloration of the surface of the water or causes a sludge or emulsion beneath the surface of the water. Violators are subject to substantial civil penalties and/or criminal sanctions, including fines and imprisonment.

Report all discharges to the
National Response Center at 1-800-424-8802
or to your local U.S. Coast Guard office
by phone or VHF radio, Channel 16.

## Oil Pollution Act

As a recreational boater, be aware of your potential liability under the Federal Oil Pollution Act of 1990. You may be assessed the cost of actions taken to prevent a spill, to remove oil, or to pay for damages resulting from an oil spill for which you are responsible. If your boat runs aground, sinks, or spills oil in some manner, you could be liable for prevention or cleanup costs of up to $500,000.

You can protect yourself from circumstances beyond your control, such as an accidental sinking, through liability insurance. Most recreational boat insurance policies will not protect you from liability under the Oil Pollution Act. If your policy does not have an oil pollution clause or if the clause is vague, consider purchasing pollution insurance.

Also help ensure that others obey the law. You are encouraged to report any polluting discharge you

see to the nearest U.S. Coast Guard office. Report its location, source, size, color, substance, and the time you saw it. Do not take samples of any chemical discharge. If you are uncertain of what the discharge is, keep flames away. Avoid physical contact and inhalation of vapors. The Coast Guard oil spill and pollution telephone number is 1-800-424-8802.

## PLASTICS AND GARBAGE

On July 31, 1990, a new federal regulation went into effect that applies to all vessels. Vessels 26 feet or more in length must post one or more 9-by-4-inch placards that list all at-sea garbage restrictions (see accompanying graphic). Place them in the cockpit, galley, or other areas where people on board gather. A boat 40 feet and over with a galley and berths must have a written trash disposal plan, and name the person in charge of the plan.

It is illegal for any vessel to dump plastic trash anywhere in the oceans or in the navigable waters of the United States. Plastic includes, among other things: plastic bags, Styrofoam cups and lids, six-pack holders, bottles, caps, buckets, shoes, milk jugs, egg cartons, stirrers, straws, synthetic fishing nets, ropes, lines, and "bio- or photodegradable" plastics.

On recreational boats, garbage includes all kinds of food. It also includes maintenance waste such as oil and grease, and domestic waste, which we usually call "trash." It does not include fresh fish or fish parts. On the Great Lakes and their connecting or tributary waters, the discharge of ALL garbage is prohibited.

"Dishwater" is the liquid residue from manual or automatic dishwashers. Its definition assumes that the dishes and cooking utensils have been pre-cleaned to remove food particles that would interfere with the operation of automatic dishwashers. If they haven't been pre-cleaned, the water they are washed in is considered garbage.

"Gray water" is water from a dishwasher, shower, laundry, bath, or washbasin. It does not include waste from toilets or urinals. It is not classed as garbage.

"Dunnage" is cargo-associated waste. It includes lining and packing materials that float. It also includes the containers and boxes your fish bait came in.

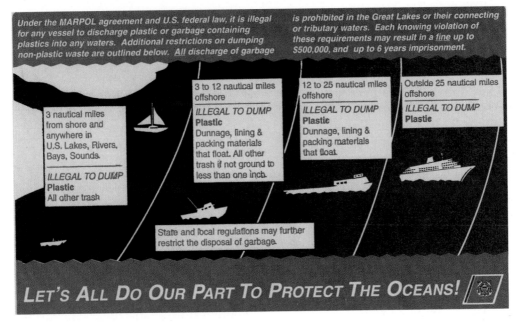

Under the MARPOL agreement and U.S. federal law, it is illegal for any vessel to discharge plastic or garbage containing plastics into any waters. Additional restrictions on dumping non-plastic waste are outlined below. All discharge of garbage is prohibited in the Great Lakes or their connecting or tributary waters. Each knowing violation of these requirements may result in a _fine_ up to $500,000, and up to 6 years imprisonment.

3 nautical miles from shore and anywhere in U.S. Lakes, Rivers, Bays, Sounds.

ILLEGAL TO DUMP
Plastic
All other trash

3 to 12 nautical miles offshore

ILLEGAL TO DUMP
Plastic
Dunnage, lining & packing materials that float. All other trash if not ground to less than one inch.

12 to 25 nautical miles offshore

ILLEGAL TO DUMP
Plastic
Dunnage, lining & packing materials that float.

Outside 25 nautical miles offshore

ILLEGAL TO DUMP
Plastic

State and local regulations may further restrict the disposal of garbage.

LET'S ALL DO OUR PART TO PROTECT THE OCEANS!

**DUMPING OF GARBAGE _PROHIBITED_ IN THE GREAT LAKES**
and connecting or tributary waters

Violators are subject to a civil penalty of up to $25,000, a criminal fine of up to $500,000 and imprisonment for up to 6 years for each violation.

Report marine pollution incidents to the National Response Center at 1-800-424-8802 or to your local Coast Guard office by phone or VHF radio, channel 16.

**Help keep the Great Lakes great!**

This placard meets the requirements of 33 CFR 151.59 for vessels operating solely on the Great Lakes and their connecting or tributary waters.

If a recreational boating facility can provide wharfage or other services for ten or more vessels, it has to have a means of garbage disposal. Facilities include marinas, yacht clubs, and attended launching ramps. Vessels that are conducting business with the facility or marina qualify for the service. The terminal or marina can charge reasonable fees for its service.

Violators of this federal regulation are liable for a civil penalty not to exceed $25,000 for each violation. Criminal penalties, not to exceed $50,000 and/or imprisonment up to 5 years, may be imposed.

# Operating a Personal Watercraft

You may never have occasion to operate a personal watercraft (PWC), but in case you do, here's what you should know about the unique attributes of PWC. This section will also help you make sense of PWC maneuvers when you're sailing in their vicinity.

As stated in Chapter 10, PWC are indeed boats, and must follow all rules and regulations that govern the waterways.

PWC must observe the Navigation Rules and all state and local laws and regulations. They should be properly registered and numbered, and their certificates of number must be aboard when they are underway. PWC are required to carry fire extinguishers.

Operators need both physical capability and maturity of judgment to operate these craft safely and responsibly.

Each person aboard must wear a life jacket. Inflatables are not suitable for this purpose because of their inflating mechanisms. Furthermore, inflatable life jackets are incapable of providing resistance to impact. Printing on your life jacket should indicate its degree of impact resistance. Wear your life jacket and have your riders wear theirs when underway, since chances are good that all of you will spend some time in the water. If the weather is cold, consider wearing a wet suit, as hypothermia can occur more rapidly than you may think. Learn the procedures for righting and reboarding a PWC before you head out, and if you can't swim, don't drive or ride on a PWC.

It is advisable to wear some kind of shoes or protection for your feet. This helps you keep your footing and avoid scrapes and bruises from underwater objects. You may also want to consider wearing gloves to protect your hands and to aid in moving your watercraft during docking and loading.

As with any vessel, the responsibility for what happens to or on a PWC rests with the skipper. The skipper has responsibility for any damage the PWC may cause, including damage from its wake, and must see that the PWC is operated legally. Among other things, this means not operating your PWC at night and observing all the Navigation Rules for overtaking, crossing, and meeting situations.

Operating any vessel can be stressful, but handling a PWC can be even more so. Be aware that wind, glare, sun, and water can be fatiguing. To boat safely, stay alert, and don't exceed your limitations.

## BE RESPECTFUL OF OTHERS

Quite apart from your legal responsibilities, you should operate your PWC in a safe and courteous manner, with due regard for the rights of the swimmers, boaters, water-skiers, and anglers with whom you're sharing the water. Irresponsible operators have caused state and local agencies to enact restrictive laws controlling PWC. Don't add to the need for more laws, and be sure to obey the laws of the state in which you are boating.

Be mindful that noise carries farther over water than over land, particularly when there are no other noises around. Since people place an especially high value on "peace and quiet" in the early

**WARNING** *Some of the "don'ts" for operating a PWC (they may even be against the law) include:*

- *Don't speed in a congested area.*
- *Don't speed in fog or stormy conditions.*
- *Don't operate in a swimming area.*
- *Don't operate close to dams.*
- *Don't cut through a regatta or marine parade.*
- *Don't cut across flats where people are fishing.*
- *Don't jump boat wakes.*
- *Don't race up to something and swerve at the last moment.*
- *Don't operate in very shallow water, and be aware of environmental issues.*
- *Don't go alone; cruise with at least one other PWC.*

morning and late afternoon, watch where you boat at those times. Stay away from homes, campgrounds, or other places where people retreat for peace and quiet.

Never operate a vessel while or immediately after drinking. A PWC is an agile and responsive craft, and operating conditions change with every wake or wave. Even small amounts of alcohol reduce your ability to respond effectively. You must be alert and in control.

## STEERING A PWC

PWC are fun boats—quick, exciting, fast, and highly maneuverable. Some can reach speeds of well over 60 miles per hour. Their power comes from a two-stroke inboard engine that may develop as much as 40 to 80 (or more) horsepower and that pumps in large amounts of water and ejects it at high speed through a special nozzle.

The nozzle turns to one side or the other to steer the boat. The operator and passengers also help steer by leaning and shifting their body weights much as they might do on a bicycle. Some PWC reverse direction by lowering a clamshell barrier behind the nozzle. This redirects the force of the jet forward, causing the vessel to reverse direction. Do not use reverse for braking. It is advisable to shift to neutral and to stop before reversing.

This arrangement of a relatively high-powered inboard engine, jet propulsion, and light weight means that PWC can accelerate rapidly and stop quickly. Since their pivot points are roughly 14 to 20 inches forward of their engines, they can also turn sharply.

## SOME SAFETY CONSIDERATIONS

The high speed and maneuverability of PWC create special safety issues. For example, if a PWC is moving at fast speed, its operator may not see an object in the water ahead in time to avoid hitting it.

Even at slow speeds, a PWC creates a lot of spray. This may blind its operator and cause an accident, so most PWC manufacturers recommend that operators wear goggles or wraparound eye protectors.

The ability of a fast-moving PWC to accelerate or to change direction rapidly can cause passengers or the operator to be thrown from the vessel and possibly injured. A sudden change in direction could place a PWC directly in the path of an oncoming vessel. Operators should always look carefully for other boats and objects before starting and before making quick maneuvers.

Do not operate a PWC at high speed unless you are thoroughly familiar with its operation. A beginning operator needs to learn that releasing the throttle or turning off the engine causes loss of directional control by stopping the flow of water through the steerable nozzle. Thus, reducing power to avoid a collision—which may be your automatic reflex—can cause you to run into the very object you are trying to avoid. Consult your owner's manual or an experienced operator on how best to avoid obstacles.

If your PWC is not of the type that circles back when you fall off, it will have a lanyard and a kill switch. Be certain to fasten one end securely to your wrist or life jacket and the other to its appropriate place on the ignition switch. When (not if) you fall overboard, this will shut off the engine and stop the boat. If you don't connect the lanyard, your vessel may continue on without you, or it may circle back and run over you.

## LEARNING TO OPERATE A PWC

If you are learning how to operate a PWC, be cautious. Read the manual carefully and be sure you understand it fully. Pay particular attention to procedures for reboarding in deep water.

Before starting up, make certain the water is deep enough to avoid drawing sand into the jet-drive intake, since doing so can damage the impeller and possibly injure someone when the sand is ejected from the nozzle. Try not to operate your PWC in water less than 2 feet deep, and before starting up, check to see that there are no objects in the water that might enter the intake.

If the intake becomes clogged, stop the engine before you try to clear it. Do not reach into the noz-zle when the engine is running and keep your hands, feet, hair, and clothing away from the intake.

Start slowly and get a feel for the vessel. A PWC responds differently to a lighter person than a heavier one, and differently with a full load than with a sole operator. When pulling a skier (which is illegal in some places) or another PWC, it may respond in a sluggish manner, and the resulting loss of control can create a hazardous condition.

A beginning operator has to concentrate on learning how to control the boat, and as a result is not fully aware of nearby swimmers, other vessels, and immovable objects close at hand. It makes sense to operate slowly until you master control of the vessel.

Some PWC are self-righting, while others require special techniques to right them after they turn over. Operators should be thoroughly familiar with the procedures outlined in their manuals before operating the vessels, and rental boat operators should see that renters know the procedures.

It makes good sense to stay within sight of land, whether you are alone or not, and to watch your gasoline use. Many PWC do not have fuel gauges. Instead, they have reserve tanks. If you run out of fuel while underway, flip the fuel selector switch from On to Reserve, and refuel as soon as possible. Observe the One-Third Rule of fuel management: Use no more than a third of your fuel on the trip out, save a third for the trip back, and keep the other third in reserve.

PWC provide an enjoyable form of watersport activity, and like all other types of boating, are best enjoyed when the operators know his or her vessel, observe the nautical Rules of the Road, and share the waterways with respect.

# Using Boats for Hunting and Fishing

As a sailor, you are perhaps even less likely to use a boat for hunting or fishing than you are to operate a PWC. In case you do, however, here's what you should know.

Anglers and hunters often times do not consider themselves boaters, but they should. As boaters, they are subject to the same rules and regulations as recreational boats, and should also understand basic boating safety. Victims of boating accidents frequently belong to the "sportsman" category.

People who fish or hunt frequently use small boats of 12 to 14 feet or less in length. Such boats are generally safe but can be unstable and may be dangerous under some circumstances. If you stand up in one, it may capsize. If it is overloaded, it may easily swamp, especially in adverse weather and water conditions.

Although the boat may be unstable, its occupants may stand up and move about to land a fish, shoot a duck, exchange positions in the boat, relieve themselves, or for other reasons. One of them may fall overboard, or their movements may cause the boat to capsize and everyone may end up in the water. If these boaters are not wearing PFDs, they may find themselves in serious trouble. Hunters and fishermen may be wearing waders, which can fill with water and make swimming impossible.

Many people who drown under such circumstances are good swimmers, but a sudden plunge into cold water is disorienting. Sometimes an injury occurs during the fall—a head is hit on the side of the boat, or a hand is caught in the propeller. These sorts of accidents are always unexpected, so a PFD should be worn at all times. The smaller the boat, the more important it is to observe this rule.

Hunters often overload their boats and fail to get weather checks to learn water and wind conditions. A safe load in favorable weather may not be safe with approaching poor weather, and hunting seasons often coincide with periods of changing weather that may turn suddenly violent.

In a fatal accident that occurred several years ago, two duck hunters launched a small aluminum boat at a ramp in a sheltered cove about an hour before sunrise, when the wind was calm. They carried two shotguns, ammunition, twenty decoys with lead weights, lunches, a thermos of hot coffee, a 50-pound Labrador retriever, two PFDs (which they were not wearing), extra fuel, and a 15-horsepower outboard. Each man weighed about 180 pounds.

Although heavily loaded, the boat was not overloaded for the water and wind conditions in the cove. As they turned into the river and headed upstream, however, they met a brisk breeze. Since this stretch of the river was short and the wind was blowing across it, surface conditions were fairly calm.

At the first bend in the river, they headed directly into the wind. The combination of the river current and the wind blowing downstream raised considerable spray. Suddenly, they found themselves in a dangerous situation. They turned the boat to return to the cove. Unfortunately, when the boat's beam turned to the waves and the wind, it swamped. One man drowned.

Many other incidents could be cited, but they all teach the same lessons:

- If you move about in a small boat, keep as low as possible; better still, avoid moving about.
- Wear your PFD under all conditions.
- Get a weather report before you launch your boat.
- Keep a weather eye peeled for changing conditions.
- Load your boat with current and anticipated weather conditions in mind, but never overload it.

# FLOAT PLAN

INSTRUCTIONS: Complete this plan before you go boating and leave it with a reliable person who can be depended upon to notify the Coast Guard, or other rescue organization, should you not return or check-in as planned. If you have a change of plans after leaving, be sure to notify the person holding your Float Plan. For additional copies of this plan, go to: **www.floatplancentral.org**

nws.cgaux.org

**Do NOT file this plan with the U.S. Coast Guard**

www.uscgboating.org

## VESSEL

**IDENTIFICATION:**

Name & Home Port_____

Doc/Registration No._____

Year & Make_____

Length _____(ft/M) Type _____ Draft _____(In/CM) Hull Mat._____

Hull Color(s)_____

Prominent Features_____
_____

**PROPULSION:**

Primary - Type _____ No. Eng.____ Fuel Capacity_____(gal/L)

Auxiliary -Type _____ No. Eng.____ Fuel Capacity_____(gal/L)

**TELECOMMUNICATIONS:**

Radio Call Sign _____

DSC MMSI No. _____

Radio-1: Type _____ Ch./Freq. Monitored _____

Radio-2: Type _____ Ch./Freq. Monitored _____

Cell Phone No. _____

Pager No. _____

**NAVIGATION: (Check all on board)**

☐ Maps  ☐ Charts  ☐ Compass  ☐ GPS / DGPS
☐ Radar  ☐ Loran C  ☐ Sounder  ☐ _____

## SAFETY & SURVIVAL

**VISUAL DISTRESS SIGNALS:**

☐ Day Only type

☐ Night Only type

☐ Day & Night type

**PFDs: (Do not count Type IV devices)**

_____ Quantity On Board

**AUDIBLE DISTRESS SIGNALS:**

☐ Horn / Whistle

☐ Bell

☐ _____

**GROUND TACKLE:**

☐ Anchor: Line Length_____(ft/M)

**OTHER GEAR:**

☐ Life boat / Life raft  ☐ Flashlight / Searchlight

☐ Dinghy / Skiff  ☐ Signal Mirror

☐ Food & Water  ☐ Drogue / Sea Anchor

☐ EPIRB _____  ☐ _____

☐ Foul Weather Gear  ☐ _____

## PERSONS ON BOARD

**OPERATOR:**

Name _____

Address _____

City _____ State ____ Zip Code _____

Vehicle (Year, Make & Model):_____

Trailer will be parked at:_____

|  | Age | M/F | Notes (Special medical condition, Can't swim, etc.) |
|---|---|---|---|
| OPERATOR | _____ | _____ | _____ |

Has experience: w/Boat ☐  w/Area ☐

Home phone: _____

Vehicle License No.: _____

Trailer License No.: _____

**PASSENGERS/CREW:**  Name & Address

| # | Name & Address | Age | M/F | Notes (Special medical condition, Can't swim, etc.) |
|---|---|---|---|---|
| 1. | _____ | ____ | ____ | _____ |
| 2. | _____ | ____ | ____ | _____ |
| 3. | _____ | ____ | ____ | _____ |
| 4. | _____ | ____ | ____ | _____ |
| 5. | _____ | ____ | ____ | _____ |

Attach "Supplemental Passenger List" if additional passengers or crew on board.

## ITINERARY

|  | DATE | TIME | LOCATION | MODE OF TRAVEL | REASON FOR STOP | CHECK-IN TIME |
|---|---|---|---|---|---|---|
| Depart |  |  |  |  |  |  |
| **Arrive** |  |  |  |  |  |  |
| Depart |  |  |  |  |  |  |
| **Arrive** |  |  |  |  |  |  |
| Depart |  |  |  |  |  |  |
| **Arrive** |  |  |  |  |  |  |
| Depart |  |  |  |  |  |  |
| **Arrive** |  |  |  |  |  |  |
| Depart |  |  |  |  |  |  |
| **Arrive** |  |  |  |  |  |  |
| Depart |  |  |  |  |  |  |
| **Arrive** |  |  |  |  |  |  |

Attach "Supplemental Itinerary" if space for additional destinations is needed.

Contact 1: _____  Phone Number _____

Contact 2: _____  Phone Number _____

If you have a genuine concern for the safety or welfare of any persons on board the Vessel described above, who have not returned or checked-in in a reasonable amount of time, then follow step-by-step instructions on the **Boating Emergency Guide™** included with this plan, or on the World Wide Web at:

## www.floatplancentral.org/help/BoatingEmergencyGuide.htm

Rev 2007.05.11

1 of 2

# BOATING EMERGENCY GUIDE™

You will need the following items before you begin: 1) the **Float Plan** if one was given to you, 2) **Pen** or **Pencil**, 3) Clean sheet of **paper** or **Writing Tablet**, and 4) your local **Telephone Directory**.

### Step 1

Do you have a genuine concern for the safety or welfare of any persons on board the Vessel described above, who have not returned or checked-in in a reasonable amount of time?

If YES, then continue with **Step 2**, otherwise STOP, no further action is required.

### Step 2

Were you given a prepared Float Plan by anyone on board the vessel?

If YES, then continue with **Step 3**, otherwise got to **Step 5**.

### Step 3

On the Float Plan, locate the two Contact lines below the Itinerary at the bottom of the Float Plan. Call Contact number 1...

| IF | THEN |
|---|---|
| A person answered the phone... | Take notes during your conversation. 1. Let the person know you are responding to a late return or check-in by the individuals designated on the Float Plan. 2. Determine if the person you are talking to or anyone else at that location, has recently had contact with anyone on the vessel, and when and where that contact occurred. 3. Are you still concerned about the safety or welfare of any persons on board the vessel? |
| | IF / THEN: Yes — Continue with **Step 4**. No — STOP. No further action is required. |
| Otherwise... | Continue with **Step 4**. |

### Step 4

Call telephone number for Contact number 2...

| IF | THEN |
|---|---|
| A person answered the phone... | Take notes during your conversation. 1. Let the person know you are responding to a late return or check-in by the individuals designated on the Float Plan. 2. Determine if the person you are talking to or anyone else at that location, has recently had contact with anyone on the vessel, and when and where that contact occurred. 3. Are you still concerned about the safety or welfare of any persons on board the vessel? |
| | IF / THEN: Yes — Continue with **Step 6**. No — STOP. No further action is required. |
| Otherwise... | Continue with **Step 6**. |

### Step 5

Take a moment to jot down the facts you know about each item in the checklist below.

> Do NOT speculate. Speculation about a detail may mislead Search And Rescue (SAR) personnel, and add to the overall search and rescue time, adversely affecting the outcome.

- ❑ Period of time the vessel has been overdue.
- ❑ Purpose of the trip or voyage.
- ❑ Description of the Vessel (type, size, color, features, etc.)
- ❑ Vessels departure point and destination.
- ❑ Places the Vessel planned to stop during transit.
- ❑ Navigation equipment on board (such as GPS, Loran C, Radar, Compass, Sounder, etc.)
- ❑ Number of people on board the Vessel, as well as personal habits e.g. dependability, reliability, etc.
- ❑ Was the Vessel already moored, or did a vehicle tow it to the launch point?
- ❑ License plate number and description of the tow vehicle, and/or passenger transport vehicle.
- ❑ Communications equipment on board, including type of radio and frequencies monitored, cellular telephone numbers of any persons on board.
- ❑ Additional points of contact along the vessels planned route.
- ❑ Where there any pending commitments e.g. work, appointments, etc.

Continue with **Step 6**.

### Step 6

1. Contact your local Law Enforcement agency (Police or Sheriff).
2. Let the dispatcher know that you are responding to a late return or check-in by the persons on board the vessel.
3. The dispatcher will instruct you from here.

> **Note:** The dispatcher will provide you with the necessary contact or agency connection (*if one was not provided for you on the Float Plan*) to get a Search And Rescue mission started. This is usually handled this way because it puts you closest to the agency conducting the actual search and rescue, eliminating an unnecessary middleman.
>
> If the dispatcher would like a follow-up call from you on the outcome of the rescue, they will let you know.

4. Continue with **Step 7**.

### Step 7

Be patient... you've done everything you can possibly do for now. It is important to stay off the telephone, so emergency personnel can contact you with additional information and/or questions concerning the search and rescue effort.

STOP--End of Guide

Float Plan Central™ is a service of the U.S. Coast Guard Auxiliary
www.floatplancentral.org

# Boating Accident Report Form

## BOATING ACCIDENT REPORT

*States have different requirements for accident reporting. Each state specifies what conditions require you to report an accident (for example: death, injury or property damage exceeding $500), how soon the report must be filed after an accident occurs, and to whom the accident must be reported. Most states have their own Accident Report form, but the information collected will be very similar to that shown below. All reports are confidential. Indicate those not applicable by "NA"* **Complete all blocks and both sides.**

### INFORMATION ABOUT BOAT OPERATOR

Name and address of operator

Operator's phone #

Name and address of owner

Age of operator
Date of birth

Owner's phone #

Is this boat rented? ☐Yes ☐No

Number of persons on board

Operator's experience

This type of boat
☐ Under 20 hours
☐ 20 to 100 hours
☐ 100 to 500 hours
☐ Over 500 hours

Other type of boat
☐ Under 20 hours
☐ 20 to 100 hours
☐ 100 to 500 hours
☐ Over 500 hours

Formal instruction in boating safety
☐ None  ☐ State  ☐ USCG Auxiliary
☐ U.S. Power Squadrons  ☐ American Red Cross
☐ Other (specify) _____

### INFORMATION ABOUT OPERATOR'S BOAT

Boat registration # | Boat name | Boat make | Boat model | Hull I.D. #

Type of boat
☐ Open motorboat
☐ Cabin motorboat
☐ Auxiliary sailboat
☐ Sailboat
☐ Row boat
☐ Canoe
☐ Other (specify)

Hull material
☐ Wood
☐ Aluminum
☐ Steel
☐ Fiberglass
☐ Rubber/Vinyl
☐ Other (specify)

Engine
☐ Outboard
☐ Inboard gasoline
☐ Inboard diesel
☐ Inboard-outboard
☐ Jet
☐ Other (specify)

Propulsion
☐ Number of engines
☐ Total horsepower
☐ Type of fuel

Construction
Length _____

Year built _____

Has boat had a safety examination? (specify)
☐ None  ☐ State/local examination  ☐Other
☐ USCGAux/USPS Vessel Safety Check
For current year? ☐ Yes  ☐ No

### ACCIDENT DATA

Date of accident | Time _____ ☐ am ☐ pm | Body of water | Precise location

State | Nearest city or town | County

Weather
☐ Clear  ☐ Rain
☐ Cloudy  ☐ Snow
☐ Fog  ☐ Hazy

Water conditions
☐ Calm (waves less than 6")
☐ Choppy (waves 6" to 2')
☐ Rough (waves 2' to 6')
☐ Very rough (greater than 6')
☐ Strong current

Wind
☐ None
☐ Light (0-6 mph)
☐ Moderate (7-14 mph)
☐ Strong (15-25 mph)
☐ Storm (over 25 mph)

Visibility
Day
☐ Good
☐ Fair
☐ Poor

Night
☐ Good
☐ Fair
☐ Poor

Estimated temperature
Air _____ ° F
Water _____ ° F

Operation at time of accident
(check all applicable)

☐Commercial activity
☐Cruising
☐Maneuvering
☐Approaching dock
☐Leaving dock
☐Water skiing
☐Racing
☐Towing
☐Paddling
☐Drifting

☐At anchor
☐Tied to dock
☐Fueling
☐Fishing
☐Hunting
☐Skin diving/ swimming
☐Being towed
☐Other (specify)

Type of accident

☐Collision with boat
☐Collision with fixed object
☐Collision with floating object
☐Grounding
☐Capsizing
☐Flooding/ swamping
☐Sinking
☐Hit by boat or propeller

☐Fire or explosion (fuel)
☐Fire or explosion (other than fuel)
☐Fallen skier
☐Falls overboard
☐Falls in boat
☐Other (specify)
_____
_____

What, in your opinion, contributed to the accident? (check all applicable)

☐ Weather
☐ Excessive speed
☐ No proper lookout
☐ Restricted vision
☐ Overloading
☐ Improper loading
☐ Hazardous waters
☐ Alcohol use

☐ Drug use
☐Fault of hull
☐Fault of machinery
☐Fault of equipment
☐Operator inexperience
☐Operator inattention
☐ Other (specify)
_____

### FIRE EXTINGUISHERS

Were fire extinguishers used? ☐No ☐Yes
Type(s) _____ Quantity: _____

### PERSONAL FLOTATION DEVICES (PFDs)

Was the boat adequately equipped with U. S. Coast Guard-approved personal flotation devices? ☐ Yes ☐ No
Were they accessible? ☐ Yes ☐ No Were they serviceable? ☐ Yes ☐ No
Were they used by survivors? ☐ Yes ☐ No Were they adjusted? ☐ Yes ☐ No
Were PFDs properly used? ☐ Yes ☐ No What type? ☐ I ☐ II ☐ III ☐ IV ☐ V

Were they sized? ☐ Yes ☐ No
Was the boat carrying non-approved PFDs? ☐ Yes ☐ No
Were they accessible? ☐ Yes ☐ No
Were they used? ☐ Yes ☐ No If yes, indicate kind: _____
(include any comments on PFDs under Accident Description on other side)

### PROPERTY DAMAGE

Describe property damage

Name/address of owner of damaged property

Estimated amount of property damage
This boat $ _____ Other boat $ _____
Other property $ _____

| | | DECEASED | | | | |
|---|---|---|---|---|---|---|
| Name | Address | Date of birth | Was the victim... ☐ Swimmer ☐ Non-swimmer | Death caused by ☐ Drowning ☐ Other ☐ Disappearance | Was a PFD worn? ☐ Yes  ☐ No What type? |
| Name | Address | Date of birth | Was the victim... ☐ Swimmer ☐ Non-swimmer | Death caused by ☐ Drowning ☐ Other ☐ Disappearance | Was a PFD worn? ☐ Yes  ☐ No What type? |
| Name | Address | Date of birth | Was the victim... ☐ Swimmer ☐ Non-swimmer | Death caused by ☐ Drowning ☐ Other ☐ Disappearance | Was a PFD worn? ☐ Yes  ☐ No What type? |

| | | INJURED | | |
|---|---|---|---|---|
| Name | Address | Date of birth | Nature of injury | Was medical treatment required? ☐ Yes  ☐ No |
| Name | Address | Date of birth | Nature of injury | Was medical treatment required? ☐ Yes  ☐ No |
| Name | Address | Date of birth | Nature of injury | Was medical treatment required? ☐ Yes  ☐ No |

### ACCIDENT DESCRIPTION

*Describe sequence of events. If it applies, include any information about failure of equipment, use or non-use of PFDs, influence of drugs or alcohol, etc. If diagram is needed attach it separately. Continue this description on additional sheets if necessary.*

### VESSEL # 2

| | | |
|---|---|---|
| Name of operator | Address | Boat # |
| Phone # | | Boat name |
| Name of owner | Address | |

### WITNESSES

| | | |
|---|---|---|
| Name | Address | Phone # |
| Name | Address | Phone # |
| Name | Address | Phone # |

### INFORMATION ABOUT PERSON COMPLETING THIS REPORT

| | | |
|---|---|---|
| Name | Address | Phone # |
| Signature | | Date submitted |

Qualification *(check one)* ☐ Boat operator   ☐ Boat owner   ☐ Investigator   ☐ Other *(specify)*

### TO BE FILLED OUT BY REPORTING AUTHORITY ONLY — *USE AGENCY DATE STAMP*

| Causes based on *(check one)* ☐ This report  ☐ Investigation ☐ Could not be determined ☐ Investigation and this report | Name of reviewing office | | Date received |
|---|---|---|---|
| | Primary cause of accident | Secondary of accident | Reviewed by |

# Digital Selective Calling (DSC) Radio Fact Sheet and MMSI Registration Form

## Fact Sheet

United States Coast Guard Auxiliary
**America's Volunteer Lifesavers**℠

## DIGITAL SELECTIVE CALLING RADIOS

Digital Selective Calling (DSC) is a VHF radio technology that provides recreational boaters with two unique features that will be discussed below. To be fully functional three items must be available:

- A DSC radio
- A Maritime Mobile Service Identity (MMSI) number
- A compatible GPS or Loran unit

The MMSI is a unique nine (9) digit number that is assigned to a DSC radio station. If the boater has a valid Federal Communications Commission (FCC) station license or plans to operate in international waters they need to contact the FCC to get an MMSI. Otherwise, they can register with BoatU.S. or SEA TOW Services by obtaining an MMSI Assignment form. Forms are available on the BoatU.S. website **www.BoatUS.com/mmsi** or by calling 1-800-563-1536 and the SEA TOW Services website **http://www.seatow.com/boating_safety/mmsi.asp**.

Some important points to consider are:

- Each vessel you own needs to have a discrete MMSI to be properly identified.
- The boater needs to keep their MMSI Assignment data current.
- Depending on the make and model of the DSC radio, it may limit the number of times you can try to program your MMSI number into the radio. Typically the radios offer you two (2) chances before locking out future attempts, forcing you to send the radio back to the manufacturer.

DSC technology makes a VHF radio function more like a telephone. It allows boaters to send a digital call directly to another DSC-equipped vessel or shore station.

- In an emergency, one push of a button and the DSC radio will send an automated digital distress alert consisting of your identification (MMSI), and position (if the radio is connected to a GPS or loran unit) to other DSC-equipped vessels and rescue facilities.
- You can privately hail another DSC-equipped vessel, or shore station, if you know their MMSI. It is similar to having a VHF phone number that "rings" the radio called and then automatically switches you to a predetermined working channel.

Rescue 21 is the Coast Guard system that will provide the Mayday response capability described above. For more details on the Rescue 21 System and its availability in your area visit **www.uscg.mil/rescue21**.

The Global Maritime Distress and Safety System (GMDSS) is the international system governing safety radio equipment on commercial ships. For more information on GMDSS visit **www.NAVCEN.USCG.gov/marcomms/gmdss**.

Rev 1

# MMSI Registration Form

*Denotes a required field. These fields must be completed in order to receive an MMSI #.

*OWNER'S FIRST NAME:_____ *OWNER'S LAST NAME:_____
OR COMPANY NAME:_____

* STREET ADDRESS:_____ * CITY:_____ * STATE:_____
* ZIP CODE:_____ PROVINCE, MAIL CODE, COUNTRY: _____ *OWNER'S HOME PHONE:_____
OWNER'S WORK PHONE:_____ EMAIL ADDRESS:_____ (Confirmation will be sent to email
address, if provided)

*NAME OF PRIMARY EMERGENCY CONTACT ASHORE:_____ *PRIMARY CONTACT HOME
PHONE:_____ PRIMARY CONTACT WORK PHONE:_____
NAME OF ALTERNATE CONTACT ASHORE:_____ ALTERNATE CONTACT HOME PHONE:_____
ALTERNATE CONTACT WORK PHONE: _____

VESSEL NAME: _____ RADIO CALL SIGN:_____
VESSEL WIRELESS PHONE 1: _____ WIRELESS 2: _____
VESSEL WIRELESS PHONE 3: _____ WIRELESS 4: _____
INMARSAT TELEPHONE #: _____
VESSEL FLAG STATE (Usually USA): _____

*SHIP CLASSIFICATION (SEE TABLE BELOW):_____
EX-SHIP NAME (IF KNOWN): _____
EX-CALL SIGN (IF KNOWN) :_____ EPIRB ID CODE: _____
*VESSEL REGISTRATION NUMBER:_____ OR *DOCUMENTATION NUMBER:_____

*VESSEL HOME PORT: (Marina Name or Residence)_____
PORT CITY: _____ PORT STATE: _____
ALTERNATE VESSEL HOME PORT:_____

*CAPACITY (# OF PERSONS EXPECTED TO BE ON BOARD): _____
SHIP'S RADIO INSTALLATION (VHF, DSC, MF/HF WITH DSC, MF/HF W/O DSC,
AIS TRANSPONDER, CELL PHONE, ETC.):_____

REMARKS (BOAT LENGTH, COLOR, TYPE, ETC.):_____

*SHIP CLASSIFICATION TABLE

| | |
|---|---|
| DUN - KETCH | MTB - MOTOR BOAT |
| SLO - SLOOP | YAT - YACHT |
| GOL - SCHOONER | VLR - SAILING SHIP |
| SAE - RESCUE VESSEL | XXX - UNSPECIFIED |

*Note: If XXX-Unspecified, please be sure to describe the vessel in the remarks section

**WHEN COMPLETE, FAX THIS FORM TO:**
**703-461-2840**

**OR SUBMIT BY MAIL TO:**

**BoatU.S. MMSI Program**
**880 S. Pickett St.**
**Alexandria, VA 22304**

# Metric Conversion Tables

| English to Metric* | | | | Metric to English | | |
|---|---|---|---|---|---|---|
| When you know | Multiply by | To find | | When you know | Multiply by | To find |
| 1 inch (in) | 2.54 | centimeters (cm) | | 1 centimeter (cm) | .39 | inch (in) |
| 3 feet (ft) | 91.44 | centimeters (cm) | | 1 centimeter (cm) | .03 | feet (ft) |
| 1 yard (yd) | .91 | meters (m) | | 1 meter (m) | 39.37 | inches (in) |
| 1 mile (mi) | 1.61 | kilometers (km) | | 1 meter (m) | 1.10 | yards (yd) |
| | | | | 1 kilometer (km) | .62 | mile (mi) |

## Some Common Equivalents

| English | Metric | Metric (approximate) | English (approximate) |
|---|---|---|---|
| | | 1 kilometer (km) | 3280 ft  9.6 in |
| 1 statute mile (mi) | 1.61 km | 1000 meters (m) | 3280 ft  9.6 in |
| | | 500 m | 1640 ft  5 in |
| .62 statute mile | 1 km | 200 m | 656 ft  2 in |
| 1000 ft | .2 km | 150 m | 492 ft  1 in |
| 5 ft | 1.5 m | 100 m | 328 ft  1 in |
| 8 ft | 2.4 m | 75 m | 246 ft  1 in |
| 10 ft | 3.0 m | 60 m | 196 ft  10 in |
| 12 ft | 3.6 m | 50 m | 164 ft  0 in |
| 16 ft | 4.8 m | 25 m | 82 ft  0 in |
| 20 ft | 6.0 m | 20 m | 65 ft  7 in |
| 24 ft | 7.2 m | 12 m | 39 ft  5 in |
| 30 ft | 9.0 m | 10 m | 32 ft  10 in |
| 40 ft | 12.0 m | 8 m | 26 ft  2 in |
| 50 ft | 15.0 m | 7 m | 23 ft  0 in |
| 60 ft | 18.0 m | 6 m | 19 ft  8 in |
| | | 5 m | 16 ft  5 in |
| | | 4.5 m | 14 ft  10 in |
| | | 4 0 m | 13 ft  1 in |
| | | 3.5 m | 11 ft  6 in |
| | | 2.5 m | 8 ft  2 in |
| | | 2.0 m | 6 ft  7 in |
| | | 1.5 m | 4 ft  11 in |
| | | 1.0 m | 3 ft  4 in |
| | | .9 m | 35.4 in |
| | | .6 m | 23.6 in |
| | | .5 m | 19.7 in |
| | | 1 centimeter (cm) | .39 in |
| | | 300 millimeters (mm) | 11.8 in |
| | | 200 mm | 7.9 in |

*Approximate conversions from English to Metric measures and Metric to English measures.

# Vessel Safety Check

## U.S. COAST GUARD AUXILIARY

### BE A SAFER BOATER, LEARN FROM THE BEST.

### *Benefits of a Vessel Safety Check*

For over 50 years, members of the Coast Guard Auxiliary have been especially trained to provide free safety checks of recreational boats. The safety checks are conducted with the boater's consent to verify equipment compliance with all federal, state, and local boating regulations.

During the safety check, the Auxiliary's vessel examiner will explain both the value and function of your boat's safety equipment, plus discuss "Best Boating Practices" to ensure a safe, fun day on the water for you and your family and friends.

For more information, call the Coast Guard Auxiliary Public Information Hotline at 1-877-875-6296.

Take a Virtual Vessel Safety Check or Sign up for a VSC online! Visit our website: www.safetyseal.net

A Vessel Safety Check can reduce the potential for accidents and injury by educating you as to the value and use of marine safety equipment, and other best on-the-water safety practices.

A Vessel Safety Check may save you money by preventing citations due to noncompliance with federal, state, and local regulations, by identifying safety equipment–related insurance discounts, and by increasing awareness of "best practices" to avoid costly breakdowns or accidents.

- Personalized One-on-One Education
- An Informed Boater Is a Safer Boater
- It's FREE
- It's Fast
- It's NOT a Law Enforcement Activity
- Up-to-Date Federal, State, and Local Boating Regulations
- Other Safety Suggestions

# Join the Coast Guard Auxiliary

*DO YOU WANT TO*
*Be a Better Boater,*
*Learn from the Best,*
*Be Part of the Action . . .*
**THEN, VOLUNTEER TO
MAKE A DIFFERENCE!**

Consider furthering your boating knowledge and safety on the water by joining the U.S. Coast Guard Auxiliary.

## WHO WE ARE

The U.S. Coast Guard Auxiliary is the uniformed, volunteer civilian component of the Coast Guard team. Created by an Act of Congress in 1939, the Auxiliary directly supports the Coast Guard in all their missions, except military and law enforcement actions. Auxiliary membership is open to U.S. citizens 17 years of age and older.

## HOW YOU CAN HELP MAKE A DIFFERENCE

As a member of the Coast Guard Auxiliary, you will be able to choose from many exciting opportunities for service:

- Help Save Lives—Through boating safety instruction in the classroom, through Vessel Safety Checks, or in on-the-water operations.
- Increase Your Skills—Take advantage of advanced training on the water, in leadership, or through many courses available through the Auxiliary and Coast Guard. As a member of the Auxiliary, there are no fees for any of these courses.
- Support the Coast Guard—Become qualified to serve at Coast Guard units in radio watchstanding,

Saving lives through education is a satisfying mission! (PHOTO BY JOSEPH CIRONE)

Vessel Safety Checks provide the opportunity to engage in individual safety education. (PHOTO BY BOB DENNIS)

One benefit of on-the-water training is assisting the Coast Guard in search-and-rescue missions. (PHOTO BY KEN SOMMERS)

marine environmental protection, Homeland Security, and other operational and administrative support.

- Fun and Fellowship—Enjoy the company of fellow Auxiliarists, whether during training missions, at meetings, or social events. We enjoy our work and we enjoy each other's company!

Join the over 30,000 men and women who have volunteered to make a difference!

Call the Coast Guard Auxiliary Public Information Infoline at 1-877-875-6296 or visit our website at www.cgaux.org and select "Join the Auxiliary."

Harbor patrol is another important function of the Auxiliary. (PHOTO BY MICHAEL BRODY)

Auxiliarists gather together for dinner after a day of Vessel Safety Checks. (PHOTO BY NOREEN FOLKERTS)

# Become an Associate Member

## Interested in Supporting the U.S. Coast Guard Auxiliary?

### *You can help by . . .*

Your tax-deductible financial contribution to and/or Associate Membership in the Coast Guard Auxiliary Association, Inc., the financial support organization of the Auxiliary, can help in tremendous ways.

One-hundred percent (100%) of your contribution supports the activities, programs and missions of the United States Coast Guard Auxiliary—*America's Volunteer Lifesavers* ®!

Go to www.cgauxa.org for information on donating or becoming an Associate Member of the

**Coast Guard Auxiliary Association, Inc.** CGAuxA

*The Coast Guard Auxiliary Association, Inc. is a 501(c)(3) Non-profit Corporation under the laws of the District of Columbia for the purpose of supporting the U.S. Coast Guard Auxiliary and its missions with funds, support functions, and business management.*

Coast Guard Auxiliary Association
9449 Watson Industrial Park
Saint Louis, MO 63126
314-962-8828
www.cgauxa.org

# Preventive Boat Maintenance Checklist

These are suggested items for a typical small boat and trailer checklist. It is not all inclusive, and it may contain items that are not applicable to your boat. It is designed to assist in the preparation of your personalized checklist. (It does not include items to be checked before every departure, such as fuel.)

## BOAT

- [ ] Anchor/rode
- [ ] Battery connections
- [ ] Battery tie-downs
- [ ] Bilge cleanliness
- [ ] Bilge pump
- [ ] Boathook
- [ ] Canopy
- [ ] Cockpit drains
- [ ] Compass
- [ ] Deck railing
- [ ] Emergency flares/light
- [ ] Engine controls
- [ ] Engine tune-up
- [ ] Fire extinguishers
- [ ] First-aid kit
- [ ] Fuel filter
- [ ] Fuel vents
- [ ] Gauges
- [ ] GPS/loran
- [ ] Halyards
- [ ] Horn
- [ ] Hoses
- [ ] Hull condition

- [ ] Hull lettering
- [ ] Life ring
- [ ] Lower unit condition
- [ ] Lower unit oil
- [ ] Mast step
- [ ] Navigation lights
- [ ] Propeller
- [ ] Radar
- [ ] Radio
- [ ] Registration
- [ ] Rub rails
- [ ] Sails
- [ ] Searchlights
- [ ] Seats
- [ ] Sheets and sheet winches
- [ ] Shrouds
- [ ] Spare parts/storage
- [ ] Steering
- [ ] Tools
- [ ] Transducer
- [ ] Turnbuckles
- [ ] VHF-FM radio/antenna
- [ ] Wiring/terminals

## TRAILER

- [ ] Brakes/fluid
- [ ] Hitch
- [ ] Jack
- [ ] Lights
- [ ] Rollers
- [ ] Safety chains
- [ ] Springs

- [ ] Tie-downs
- [ ] Trailer tires
- [ ] Wheel bearings
- [ ] Winch
- [ ] Winch cable
- [ ] Wiring

| Chapter 1 | | Chapter 2 | | Chapter 3 | | Chapter 4 | | Chapter 5 | | Chapter 6 | | Chapter 7 | | Chapter 8 | |
|---|---|---|---|---|---|---|---|---|---|---|---|---|---|---|---|
| 1. | i | 1. | j | 1. | f | 1. | b | 1. | h | 1. | f | 1. | i | 1. | g |
| 2. | d | 2. | e | 2. | a | 2. | f | 2. | f | 2. | e | 2. | e | 2. | c |
| 3. | h | 3. | i | 3. | b | 3. | d | 3. | c | 3. | c | 3. | b | 3. | f |
| 4. | j | 4. | c | 4. | g | 4. | a | 4. | j | 4. | b | 4. | a | 4. | e |
| 5. | g | 5. | d | 5. | e | 5. | e | 5. | a | 5. | j | 5. | c | 5. | a |
| 6. | a | 6. | g | 6. | c | 6. | c | 6. | b | 6. | a | 6. | d | 6. | h |
| 7. | b | 7. | a | 7. | d | 7. | j | 7. | d | 7. | d | 7. | f | 7. | i |
| 8. | e | 8. | h | 8. | j | 8. | g | 8. | e | 8. | g | 8. | j | 8. | d |
| 8. | f | 9. | b | 9. | h | 9. | i | 9. | i | 9. | i | 9. | g | 9. | b |
| 10. | c | 10. | f | 10. | i | 10. | h | 10. | g | 10. | h | 10. | h | 10. | j |

| Chapter 1 | | Chapter 2 | | Chapter 3 | | Chapter 4 | | Chapter 5 | | Chapter 6 | | Chapter 7 | | Chapter 8 | |
|---|---|---|---|---|---|---|---|---|---|---|---|---|---|---|---|
| 1-1 | d | 2-1 | c | 3-1 | a | 4-1 | d | 5-1 | d | 6-1 | c | 7-1 | a | 8-1 | c |
| 1-2 | c | 2-2 | c | 3-2 | b | 4-2 | b | 5-2 | b | 6-2 | a | 7-2 | b | 8-2 | c |
| 1-3 | a | 2-3 | a | 3-3 | d | 4-3 | c | 5-3 | c | 6-3 | d | 7-3 | d | 8-3 | d |
| 1-4 | d | 2-4 | c | 3-4 | b | 4-4 | b | 5-4 | b | 6-4 | b | 7-4 | c | 8-4 | a |
| 1-5 | b | 2-5 | c | 3-5 | c | 4-5 | a | 5-5 | d | 6-5 | a | 7-5 | a | 8-5 | d |
| 1-6 | d | 2-6 | b | 3-6 | d | 4-6 | d | 5-6 | c | 6-6 | d | 7-6 | a | 8-6 | d |
| 1-7 | b | 2-7 | a | 3-7 | b | 4-7 | c | 5-7 | b | 6-7 | d | 7-7 | b | 8-7 | b |
| 1-8 | a | 2-8 | b | 3-8 | b | 4-8 | b | 5-8 | c | 6-8 | b | 7-8 | d | 8-8 | b |
| 1-9 | b | 2-9 | d | 3-9 | d | 4-9 | d | 5-9 | b | 6-9 | d | 7-9 | b | 8-9 | d |
| 1-10 | c | 2-10 | d | 3-10 | d | 4-10 | a | 5-10 | d | 6-10 | b | 7-10 | a | 8-10 | b |
| 1-11 | d | 2-11 | b | 3-11 | c | 4-11 | c | 5-11 | c | 6-11 | b | 7-11 | d | 8-11 | d |
| 1-12 | c | 2-12 | a | 3-12 | b | 4-12 | c | 5-12 | a | 6-12 | d | 7-12 | c | 8-12 | d |
| 1-13 | c | 2-13 | c | 3-13 | a | 4-13 | c | 5-13 | a | 6-13 | b | 7-13 | a | 8-13 | a |
| 1-14 | a | 2-14 | c | 3-14 | b | 4-14 | a | 5-14 | d | 6-14 | a | 7-14 | b | 8-14 | c |
| 1-15 | c | 2-15 | c | 3-15 | c | 4-15 | c | 5-15 | c | 6-15 | d | 7-15 | c | 8-15 | a |
| 1-16 | c | 2-16 | b | 3-16 | b | 4-16 | a | 5-16 | b | 6-16 | b | 7-16 | a | 8-16 | c |
| 1-17 | d | 2-17 | d | 3-17 | a | 4-17 | b | 5-17 | b | 6-17 | b | 7-17 | c | 8-17 | c |
| 1-18 | a | 2-18 | b | 3-18 | b | 4-18 | d | 5-18 | d | 6-18 | d | 7-18 | d | 8-18 | d |
| 1-19 | a | 2-19 | d | 3-19 | a | 4-19 | c | 5-19 | c | 6-19 | c | 7-19 | b | 8-19 | c |
| 1-20 | b | 2-20 | b | 3-20 | a | 4-20 | b | 5-20 | a | 6-20 | b | 7-20 | a | 8-20 | b |
| 1-21 | c | 2-21 | d | 3-21 | b | 4-21 | a | 5-21 | b | 6-21 | d | 7-21 | c | 8-21 | c |
| 1-22 | a | 2-22 | d | 3-22 | a | 4-22 | a | 5-22 | a | 6-22 | c | | | 8-22 | d |
| 1-23 | a | 2-23 | d | 3-23 | a | 4-23 | d | 5-23 | d | 6-23 | d | | | 8-23 | d |
| 1-24 | a | 2-24 | a | 3-24 | c | 4-24 | c | 5-24 | c | 6-24 | b | | | 8-24 | a |
| | | | | | | | | 5-25 | d | | | | | | |

| Chapter 9 | | Chapter 10 | | Chapter 11 | | Chapter 12 | | Chapter 13 | | Chapter 14 | | Chapter 15 | | Chapter 16 | |
|---|---|---|---|---|---|---|---|---|---|---|---|---|---|---|---|
| 1. | e | 1. | e | 1. | e | 1. | f | 1. | g | 1. | h | 1. | e | 1. | g |
| 2. | a | 2. | a | 2. | g | 2. | d | 2. | b | 2. | a | 2. | d | 2. | h |
| 3. | f | 3. | d | 3. | h | 3. | a | 3. | h | 3. | d | 3. | h | 3. | d |
| 4. | i | 4. | h | 4. | b | 4. | j | 4. | i | 4. | c | 4. | a | 4. | a |
| 5. | g | 5. | c | 5. | j | 5. | g | 5. | a | 5. | j | 5. | i | 5. | j |
| 6. | d | 6. | i | 6. | a | 6. | b | 6. | c | 6. | i | 6. | b | 6. | c |
| 7. | j | 7. | j | 7. | c | 7. | i | 7. | f | 7. | g | 7. | f | 7. | i |
| 8. | c | 8. | f | 8. | f | 8. | c | 8. | j | 8. | b | 8. | g | 8. | f |
| 9. | b | 9. | b | 9. | d | 9. | h | 9. | e | 9. | e | 9. | c | 9. | e |
| 10. | h | 10. | g | 10. | i | 10. | e | 10. | d | 10. | f | | | 10. | b |
| | | | | | | | | | | | | | | | |
| 9-1 | b | 10-1 | d | 11-1 | c | 12-1 | c | 13-1 | d | 14-1 | a | 15-1 | b | 16-1 | c |
| 9-2 | d | 10-2 | b | 11-2 | a | 12-2 | a | 13-2 | a | 14-2 | c | 15-2 | b | 16-2 | b |
| 9-3 | b | 10-3 | d | 11-3 | c | 12-3 | b | 13-3 | c | 14-3 | c | 15-3 | a | 16-3 | d |
| 9-4 | d | 10-4 | c | 11-4 | c | 12-4 | d | 13-4 | d | 14-4 | d | 15-4 | c | 16-4 | a |
| 9-5 | d | 10-5 | a | 11-5 | b | 12-5 | b | 13-5 | d | 14-5 | a | 15-5 | a | 16-5 | a |
| 9-6 | a | 10-6 | d | 11-6 | d | 12-6 | a | 13-6 | a | 14-6 | c | 15-6 | d | 16-6 | d |
| 9-7 | a | 10-7 | d | 11-7 | c | 12-7 | d | 13-7 | c | 14-7 | a | 15-7 | a | 16-7 | a |
| 9-8 | d | 10-8 | a | 11-8 | b | 12-8 | b | 13-8 | b | 14-8 | d | 15-8 | b | 16-8 | a |
| 9-9 | d | 10-9 | a | 11-9 | d | 12-9 | c | 13-9 | b | 14-9 | d | 15-9 | d | 16-9 | c |
| 9-10 | a | 10-10 | d | 11-10 | c | 12-10 | c | 13-10 | c | 14-10 | a | 15-10 | d | 16-10 | c |
| 9-11 | a | 10-11 | c | 11-11 | a | 12-11 | d | 13-11 | c | 14-11 | a | 15-11 | c | 16-11 | d |
| 9-12 | a | 10-12 | c | 11-12 | c | 12-12 | d | 13-12 | a | 14-12 | d | 15-12 | c | 16-12 | d |
| 9-13 | a | 10-13 | c | 11-13 | c | 12-13 | c | 13-13 | d | 14-13 | a | 15-13 | b | 16-13 | d |
| 9-14 | c | 10-14 | d | 11-14 | b | 12-14 | a | 13-14 | a | 14-14 | d | 15-14 | c | 16-14 | a |
| 9-15 | b | 10-15 | e | 11-15 | a | 12-15 | d | 13-15 | b | 14-15 | d | 15-15 | b | 16-15 | d |
| 9-16 | b | 10-16 | d | 11-16 | d | 12-16 | a | 13-16 | d | 14-16 | c | 15-16 | b | 16-16 | a |
| 9-17 | d | 10-17 | c | 11-17 | a | 12-17 | b | 13-17 | c | 14-17 | b | 15-17 | d | 16-17 | d |
| 9-18 | c | 10-18 | a | 11-18 | c | 12-18 | b | 13-18 | b | 14-18 | c | 15-18 | d | 16-18 | b |
| 9-19 | d | 10-19 | a | 11-19 | a | 12-19 | a | 13-19 | c | 14-19 | d | 15-19 | b | 16-19 | b |
| 9-20 | d | 10-20 | c | 11-20 | b | 12-20 | d | 13-20 | c | 14-20 | a | 15-20 | b | 16-20 | c |
| 9-21 | a | 10-21 | d | 11-21 | b | 12-21 | c | 13-21 | a | 14-21 | c | 15-21 | a | 16-21 | c |
| 9-22 | d | | | 11-22 | d | 12-22 | a | 13-22 | c | 14-22 | a | 15-22 | c | 16-22 | b |
| 9-23 | a | | | 11-23 | b | 12-23 | c | 13-23 | a | | | 15-23 | c | 16-23 | b |
| 9-24 | d | | | 11-24 | b | 12-24 | b | 13-24 | a | | | 15-24 | d | 16-24 | c |
| 9-25 | d | | | | | | | | | | | 15-25 | b | 16-25 | d |
| 9-26 | a | | | | | | | | | | | | | | |

**abaft:** Toward the rear (stern) of the boat. Behind.

**abeam:** At right angles to the keel of the boat, but not on the boat.

**adjusting a compass:** A good compass has internal magnets to adjust it for magnetic influences aboard a boat that cause compass error. Otherwise adjusting should be done by a professional.

**adrift:** Floating loose, not on moorings or a towline.

**advection fog:** A type of fog that occurs when warm air moves over colder land or water surfaces; the greater the difference between the air temperature and the underlying surface temperature, the denser the fog.

**aft:** At the stern or back of a vessel.

**aground:** A vessel touching or fast to the bottom.

**ahead:** In front of the boat. Opposite of astern.

**aid to navigation (ATON):** Lighthouses, lights, buoys, sound signals, racon, radiobeacons, electronic aids, and other markers on land or sea specifically intended to help navigators determine position or safe course, or to warn them of dangers or obstructions to navigation.

**air-cooled engine:** A motor such as a small outboard that is cooled by having air blown over it.

**alternating current (AC):** An electric current, usually 120 volts, that reverses its direction at regularly recurring intervals.

**alternator:** An electric generator for producing alternating current.

**altocumulus clouds:** "Piled up" clouds at middle altitudes.

**altostratus:** A cloud formation similar to cirrostratus but darker and at a lower level.

**amateur radio:** Shortwave radio useful in marine and other emergencies. Operates in eight frequency bands and can often reach around the globe.

**amidships:** In or toward the center portion of the vessel.

**ammeter:** An instrument for measuring electric current in amps.

**amp draw:** The amount of electrical current a radio set uses when sending or receiving a message.

**anchor:** Device used to secure a boat to the bottom of a body of water.

**anchor bend:** The most secure knot for bending a line to an object.

**antifreeze:** A substance added to a liquid, such as the water in an engine, to lower its freezing point.

**apparent wind:** The combination of a boat's wind of motion and the true wind—the wind experienced by an observer in motion.

**aquatic nuisance species (ANS):** Foreign plants and animals that are invading U.S. waters.

**articulated beacon:** A beacon-like buoyant structure, tethered directly to the seabed and having no watch circle. Called "articulated light" or "articulated daybeacon," as appropriate.

**astern:** Behind the vessel. Opposite of ahead.

**athwartships:** Across or at right angles to the centerline of a boat; rowboat seats are generally placed athwartships (thwarts).

**audio output:** Tells the loudness of a radio.

**available channels:** The VHF-FM frequency band includes 73 channels of which 55 are in use in the United States.

**babystay.** See *inner forestay.*

**backfire flame arrester:** A part of an engine that prevents a fire or explosion when the fuel ignites and a backfire occurs.

**back splice:** A method of splicing rope that is an alternative to whipping the rope end; it increases rope diameter by 40% and provides a handle.

**backstay:** Standing rigging that keeps the mast from falling forward over the bow.

**backwind:** When a sail takes the breeze on its forward side, braking the boat's forward motion.

**balance:** A boat's ability—or lack of it—to sail a straight course without pressure on the tiller.

**band:** A range of radio frequencies, such as the medium-frequency band or the high-frequency band.

**bare poles:** When a sailboat has no sails set.

**barometer:** An instrument for measuring the air pressure.

**barometric pressure:** The pressure of the atmosphere; usually expressed in terms of the height of a column of mercury.

**batten:** A wood or plastic strip used to support and extend the leech, or free edge, of a mainsail.

**beam:** The greatest width of a boat.

**beam reach:** Sailing with the apparent wind blowing more or less at right angles to the boat. It combines excellent lift over the leeward side of the sail with good thrust on the windward side, and thus is usually a boat's fastest point of sailing.

**bearing:** The direction to an object, given as a horizontal angle from a line of reference.

**bearing compass:** A handheld compass used to take bearings and determine your position.

**beat.** See *close hauled.*

**becket:** A looped rope, hook and eye, strap, or grommet used for holding ropes, wires, or spars in position.

**belay:** To make a line fast. Also, a command to stop.

**bend:** To attach a line to another line. Also, to attach a line to a spar or stay.

**bight:** A long and gradual bend or recess in the coastline that forms a large, open receding bay. Also, a curve made in a rope by doubling it back on itself.

**bilge:** The lowest spaces in a vessel's hull.

**bilge pump:** Pump used to clear water or liquid from the bilge.

**binocular:** A tool used to magnify objects that is particularly useful in piloting.

**bitt:** A heavy and firmly mounted piece of wood or metal used for securing lines.

**bitter end:** The inboard end of a rope or cable.

**blanket:** To deprive a sail of the wind, as when one sail blocks another.

**block:** A device consisting of a case enclosing one or more sheaves through which a line may be led to increase mechanical advantage or to change direction.

**boathook:** A pole with a hook or spike at the end, commonly used to facilitate line handling.

**bollard:** A heavy post set into the edge of a wharf or pier to which the lines of a ship may be made fast.

**bolt rope:** Line attached to the foot and luff of a sail to give it strength or to enable it to be attached to the spars.

**boom:** A spar attached horizontally to the mast for extending the foot of the sail.

**boomkin:** A short spar or structure projecting from the stern of a vessel to which the mizzen sail is sheeted.

**boom vang:** A tackle from the boom down to the deck or gunwale. Off the wind, it is used to hold down the boom to control leech tension, and rigged to prevent an accidental jibe when running directly before the wind.

**boottop/bootstripe:** A stripe painted along and above the waterline. Serves as a useful reference to determine if the boat has been properly loaded.

**bottoms, types of:** The types of ocean bottom materials such as sand, clay, and mud that are described on nautical charts.

**bow:** Forward end of a vessel.

**bow bitt:** A post fixed on the deck of a ship near the bow for securing lines.

**bow line:** A docking line leading from the bow.

**bowline:** A knot used to form a temporary eye in the end of a line.

**bowsprit:** A spar extending forward from the bow.

**braided rope:** A rope made by interweaving individual fibers or by weaving three or four strands of fiber.

**branch:** The upper or lower half of a line of longitude or meridian that passes through both geographic poles.

**breaking wave:** A wave cresting with the top breaking down over its face.

**bridge clearance:** Vertical datum of a chart tells how much vertical clearance there is under a bridge.

**broach:** The uncontrolled turning of a boat parallel to the waves, subjecting it to possible capsizing.

**broad on the bow:** A direction midway between abeam and dead ahead.

**broad reach:** Sailing with the apparent wind coming over either quarter.

**bulkhead:** A vertical partition separating one part of the boat from another.

**bunt:** Reefed portion of a sail.

**buoy:** A floating aid to navigation of defined shape and color, which is anchored at a given position and serves as an aid to navigation.

**cable:** A large line made by twisting ropes together. Cables are used on tugboats and to moor large vessels.

**call sign:** Unique letter-and-number vessel identifier issued to vessels that are required to carry radio equipment and also to voluntary vessels calling at foreign ports.

**calling channel:** The designated channel for station-to-station contact and distress calling.

**camber ratio:** The relationship between the depth of the draft at a given height and the straight-line distance between the luff and leech of the sail at that height.

**cam cleat:** A cleat with two moving, serrated cam-shaped jaws for holding a line. The spring-loaded jaws rotate open to release the line when you pull on it, and the cleat tightens when the standing part of the line pulls against it.

**cap shrouds.** See *upper shrouds.*

**capsize:** To turn a vessel bottom side up. When a boat is laid over and has shipped so much water that it can't right itself.

**carbon dioxide:** A heavy colorless gas that does not support combustion and is formed in animal and human respiration.

**carbon monoxide:** A colorless, odorless, and highly poisonous gas that has about the same weight as air and mixes readily with it.

**carry:** The distance a boat requires to lose momentum when headed into the wind from a close-hauled course.

**catamaran:** A twin-hulled boat.

**catboat:** A sailboat with a single sail attached to a mast stepped well forward.

**caulk:** To stop up and make watertight by filling with a waterproof compound or material.

**cavitation:** The bubbles of partial vacuum that may appear around the blades of a propeller that is spinning at excessive speed or under an excessive load. It can also occur if the propeller is not deep enough in the water. Since the propeller blades do not get a good "grip" on the water, the motor overspeeds, causing possible damage to the engine and/or pit marks on the propeller.

**centerboard:** A retractable bottom appendage that retracts by pivoting sternward. It pivots around a pin in its forward corner and thus can be fully raised or lowered.

**centerline:** An imaginary line down the middle of a vessel from bow to stern.

**center of buoyancy (CB):** The center of the mass of the water a boat displaces.

**center of effort (CE):** The single point where all the force of the wind on the sails is concentrated.

**center of gravity (CG):** The center of a boat's total mass. Point in a vessel where the sum of all moments is zero. With the vessel at rest, the center of gravity and the center of buoyancy are always in a direct vertical line.

**center of lateral resistance (CLR):** The point on a boat's hull around which forces seeking to push the boat sideways through the water are concentrated.

**chafing:** The wearing away of lines as they rub against hard surfaces, which weakens them. Chafing can be prevented by wrapping lines with canvas or leather where they pass through chocks.

**chain:** A cluster of land antennas located usually along a shoreline that are part of loran. A chain consists of one master and one or more slave antennas.

**chainplate:** A heavy metal strap bolted and/or fiberglassed to the hull or its principal bulkheads.

**channel selector:** The dial or button used on any of several possible pieces of equipment to switch from the calling channel to a working channel during a transmission to another vessel or a coastal station.

**chart:** A printed or electronic geographic representation generally showing such things as depths of water, aids to navigation, dangers, and adjacent land features useful to mariners.

**chine:** The intersection between the side and bottom of a boat.

**chock:** A metal fitting through which anchor or mooring lines are led. May be open or closed.

**circuit breaker:** A switch that automatically interrupts an electric circuit under an infrequent abnormal condition.

**cirrostratus:** A fairly uniform layer of high stratus clouds darker than cirrus.

**cirrus:** A wispy cloud usually of minute ice crystals formed at altitudes of 20,000 to 40,000 feet.

**citizens band radio:** A range of radio wave frequencies that in the United States is allocated for private radio communications.

**cleat:** A fitting to which lines are made fast. The classic cleat to which lines are belayed, approximately anvil-shaped.

**clew:** The after, lower corner of a sail.

**close hauled:** Sailing at approximately 45° to the true wind, or as close to the source of the wind as possible. Also referred to as sailing upwind or on the wind, beating to windward, or beating.

**close reach:** Sailing with the sheets slightly eased and the apparent wind forward of the beam.

**clove hitch:** A hitch for temporarily fastening a line to a spar, ring, post, or piling.

**coaming:** A raised lip around the edge of a boat's cockpit that serves to deflect water.

**coast station:** The radio station at a land-based post; for example, a U.S. Coast Guard unit, a tugboat company, or a fishing company.

**coil:** To lay a line down in circular turns.

**cold front:** An advancing edge of a cold air mass.

**cold water immersion:** The sudden exposure to cold water that can result in death within 3 to 5 minutes in water that is 59° F or colder. Also called cold shock.

**color-code lines:** Using a material such as an air-drying plastic to make the end of each line a different color. This is particularly useful on a sailboat where several lines end near each other.

**COLREGS 72:** The 1972 International Regulations for Prevention of Collisions at Sea, commonly called the International Rules.

**commercial messages:** Messages that concern economic and commercial matters directly related to the use of a boat.

**compass:** Instrument for determining direction.

**compass rose:** A circle graduated in degrees, clockwise from 000 at true north to 360. It may also be graduated in points. It is printed on nautical charts for determining directions.

**cooling system:** Any of several systems used to cool an internal combustion engine by using things such as air or water.

**Coriolis force:** The deflective effect of the earth's rotation on an object in motion that causes it to divert to the right in the northern hemisphere and the left in the southern hemisphere.

**correcting a compass:** You can correct a compass reading to tell its direction with reference to true north.

**corrosion:** To wear metals away gradually, usually by chemical action.

**course line:** The horizontal direction in which a vessel is steered or intended to be steered, expressed as angular distance from north.

**course plotting:** Drawing a line on a chart from where you are to where you want to go.

**crankcase:** A case in an engine that holds oil to lubricate moving engine parts.

**cringle:** A circular metal reinforcement for attaching hardware.

**cruising spinnaker:** An asymmetrical sail that is set flying like a spinnaker but is tacked to the headsail tack fitting via a short length of line. Also called a gennaker.

**cuddy:** A small shelter cabin in a boat.

**cumulonimbus:** A cumulus cloud often spread out in the shape of an anvil extending to great heights.

**cumulus clouds:** Clouds with vertical development.

**cunningham:** A grommeted hole in the mainsail luff slightly above the foot. A hook in the cunningham is pulled downward to exert stress on the luff and flatten the sail.

**current usage:** The amount of electrical current a radio set uses, or the amp draw.

**cutter:** A single-masted sailboat with its mast stepped anywhere from 40% to 50% of the deck length back from the bow.

**cyclone:** A storm that rotates about a system of low atmospheric pressure, advances at a speed of 20 to 30 mph, and often brings heavy rain.

**daggerboard:** A retractable bottom appendage that retracts straight upward.

**Danforth anchor:** A lightweight anchor with long narrow twin flukes that pivot about the stock.

**datum:** The technical term for the baseline from which a chart's vertical measurements are made (i.e., heights of land or landmarks, or depths of water).

**davits:** Mechanical arms extending over the side or stern of a vessel, or over a seawall, to raise or lower a smaller boat.

**daybeacon:** A fixed structure having one or more daymarks, which is used in shallow water.

**daymark:** A signboard attached to a fixed structure to convey navigational information presenting one of several standard shapes (square, triangle, rectangle, diamond, octagon) and colors (red, green, orange, yellow, or black). Daymarks usually have reflective material indicating their shapes.

**dead ahead:** A relative bearing of 000°.

**dead reckoning (DR):** The practice of estimating position by advancing a known position for course and distance run. The effects of wind and current are not considered in determining a position by dead reckoning.

**decibel (dB):** A unit of measure for expressing the relative intensity of sounds.

**deck sweeper:** A genoa cut so that its foot is in contact with the deck for nearly its whole length.

**deep-cycle battery:** A kind of battery used in a marine engine that can be discharged and then recharged.

**depower:** Reduce a boat's angle of heel and slow it down by easing the sheets or heading closer to the wind.

**depth sounder:** An electrical device used with charts showing water depths to plot courses.

**deviation:** The effect of the vessel's magnetic fields upon a compass. Deviation is the difference between the direction that the compass actually points and the direction that the compass would point if there were no magnetic fields aboard the vessel.

**dew point:** The temperature at which a vapor begins to condense.

**Differential GPS (DGPS):** A land-based supplement to GPS, which corrected the error introduced by Selected Availability (SA). This was necessary to provide continuously accurate information around harbors and inlets, where SA degraded the information enough to become dangerous.

**digital selective calling (DSC):** A technique using digital codes that enables a radio station to establish contact with, and transfer information to, another station.

**dike:** A man-made structure projecting from the shore into a waterway to control shoaling and to maintain a navigable channel.

**dinghy:** A small open boat. A dinghy is often used as a tender for a larger craft.

**dip the eye:** To bring the eye of a line up through the eye of a line that is already on a piling and then drop it over the piling. This way the line already there can be removed first.

**direct current (DC):** A constant electric current that flows in only one direction.

**directional light:** A light illuminating a sector or very narrow angle and intended to mark a direction to be followed.

**direction finder:** Equipment used by search-and-rescue services and salvage operators to locate the approximate source of radio emissions.

**displacement:** The weight of water displaced by a floating vessel; thus, a boat's weight.

**displacement hull:** A type of hull that pushes through the water displacing a weight of water equal to its own weight, even when more power is added.

**distress communication form:** A form for boaters to complete and post near the radiotelephone to help them remember the steps to take in an emergency.

**distress signal.** See *Mayday*.

**distress system:** The system of emergency visual, audible, and radio signals used to attract attention and get help.

**distributor:** An apparatus for directing the secondary current from the induction coil to the various spark plugs in an engine in the proper firing order.

**diurnal:** Having a period or cycle of approximately one tidal day. Thus the tide is said to be diurnal when only one high water and one low water occur during a tidal day, and the tidal current is said to be diurnal when there is a single flood and single ebb period in the tidal day. A rotary current is diurnal if it changes its direction through all points of the compass once each tidal day.

**dividers:** An instrument consisting of two pointed legs joined by a pivot, and used principally for measuring distances or co-ordinates. An instrument having one pointed leg and the other carrying a pen or pencil is called a "drafting compass."

**documentation:** A special federal license or registration for a vessel. A vessel of 5 or more net tons, owned by a U.S. citizen, may be documented as a yacht. The process is administered by the U.S. Coast Guard.

**dolphin:** A structure consisting of a number of piles driven into the seabed or riverbed in a circular pattern and drawn together with wire rope. Used for mooring and to protect other structures.

**double-braid rope:** Braided rope that has an outer braided cover over a separate inner braided core.

**double sheet bend:** A secure knot used to tie together two lines of unequal diameter.

**douse:** To lower the sails quickly.

**downhaul:** A line attached to the boom at the tack area of the sail in order to pull the luff of the sail downward.

**draft:** The vertical depth from the bottom of a boat's keel to the top of the water. In other words, the depth of water required to float a boat. Also, a sail's belly or curvature.

**draft position:** A sail's point of maximum draft.

**drag:** The forces opposing the direction of motion due to components such as friction and profile.

**drifter:** A sail cut like a big genoa, but made of very light nylon. It often has no snap hooks along the luff, being made fast only at the head, tack, and clew. Used for very light airs.

**dual cooling system:** A system used in most inboard diesel engines in which a mixture of water and antifreeze circulates through the engine's water channels. Also called freshwater cooling.

**ease:** To slacken or relieve tension on a line.

**electronic charting:** Charting a course using tools such as GPS (global positioning system).

**emergency call:** A call made using a radiotelephone to get help during an emergency.

**emergency position-indicating radio beacon (EPIRB):** A device that emits a continuous radio signal alerting authorities to the existence of a distress situation and leading rescuers to the scene.

**engine, diesel:** An engine that burns diesel fuel and operates more efficiently than a gasoline engine.

**engine, four-cycle:** An engine that requires two revolutions of its internal parts to complete the internal combustion process. Also known as a four-stroke engine.

**engine, gasoline:** An engine that burns gasoline.

**engine, two-cycle:** An engine that requires one revolution of its internal parts to complete the internal combustion process. Also known as a two-stroke engine.

**engine power:** As of September 1, 1989, all measures of engine power are made at their propeller shafts except for inboard engines sold without transmissions.

**equator:** Great circle formed by passing a plane perpendicular to the axis of rotation of the earth at a point 90° from the north and south poles.

**eye of the wind:** The direction from which the true wind is blowing. Also called the wind's eye.

**eye splice:** A permanent loop spliced in the end of a line.

**fairway:** The main thoroughfare of shipping in a harbor or channel.

**faking:** Laying out a line in long flat bights that will pay out freely without fouling or kinking.

**fall off:** Turning the bow of a boat away from the wind.

**fathom:** A nautical measure of length (1 fathom = 6 feet) used for measuring water depth and length of anchor rode.

**Federal Communications Commission (FCC):** The federal government organization that manages the radio spectrum within the United States.

**fender:** A cushion placed between boats, or between a boat and a pier, to prevent damage.

**ferrule:** A nylon or metal fitting at the bottom of an antenna.

**fetch:** The unobstructed distance over which the wind blows across the surface of the water.

**fetch the mark:** Head a boat on a course to the intended destination.

**fiberglass:** Resin reinforced with fibrous glass (or glass-reinforced plastic) used in boat construction. Its forms are mat, cloth, woven roving, and chopped strands.

**fid:** A tapered, pointed tool used to separate strands of rope when splicing.

**figure-eight knot:** A knot in the form of a figure eight usually tied at the end of a line as a stopper to keep the end of the line from passing through a block or fairlead.

**fisherman's bend:** A hitch for making fast to a mooring buoy or spar or to the ring of an anchor.

**fitting:** Generic term for any part or piece of machinery or installed equipment.

**fix:** A geographical position determined by passing close aboard an object of known position determined by the intersection of two more lines of position (LOPs) adjusted to a common time, determined from terrestrial, electronic, and/or celestial data. The accuracy, or quality, of a fix is of great importance, especially in coastal waters, and dependent on a number of factors.

**fixed light:** A light showing continuously and steadily, as opposed to a rhythmic light. (Do not confuse with "fixed" as used to differentiate from "floating.")

**flashing light:** A light in which the total duration of light in each period is clearly shorter than the total duration of darkness, and the flashes of light are all of equal duration. This term is commonly used for a light that exhibits only single flashes that are repeated at regular intervals.

**flemish:** A decorative method of coiling a line flat on the deck or dock.

**floating aid to navigation:** A buoy that is secured in its assigned position by a mooring.

**float plan:** A document that describes the route(s) and estimated time of arrival for a particular voyage. The float plan generally includes description of the vessel, radio and safety equipment carried, planned stops, names of passengers, and other pertinent information.

**flood current:** The horizontal movement of a tidal current toward shore or upstream in a tidal river or estuary. In the mixed type of reversing tidal current, the terms "greater flood" and "lesser flood" are applied respectively to the flood currents of greater and lesser speed of each day. The terms "maximum flood" and "minimum flood" are applied to the maximum and minimum speeds of a flood current having a speed that alternately increases and decreases without coming to a slack or reversing.

**fluke:** The flat palm-shaped or shovel-shaped part of an anchor that digs in to prevent dragging.

**flying:** Said of a sail when it is connected to the boat by its halyard and the lines from its clews, but not along any one of its edges.

**foot:** The lower edge of a sail.

**foot rope:** A rope used to help control sails on a sailboat.

**forestay:** Standing rigging that runs from the bow of the boat to the top of the mast, or near the top of the mast, to keep the mast from falling over the stern.

**foretriangle:** The area of a boat bounded by the forestay, the mast, and the deck.

**forward:** Toward the bow of the boat.

**fouled:** Said of any piece of equipment that is jammed or entangled.

**fraying lines:** When the ends of lines begin to come apart, which can be prevented through treatments such as tying, heating, or taping the ends.

**freeboard:** The vertical distance from the surface of the water to the gunwale.

**frequency setting:** A frequency is the number of vibrations or radio waves per unit of time. It determines the pitch of a sound and is reckoned in cycles per second with one up-and-down vibration or oscillation equaling one cycle, called a Hertz.

**freshwater cooling.** See *dual cooling system.*

**front:** The juncture or boundary between two air masses of different temperatures.

**gaff:** A spar that supports the head of a gaff sail.

**gain:** Antennas differ in gain; the higher the gain, the farther you can communicate.

**galley:** The kitchen area of a boat.

**galvanic action:** An electrical current that passes between two dissimilar metals when they are immersed in a solution such as salt water and that will eat away one of the metals.

**general information block:** A block of information on a nautical chart that gives information such as the chart's projection, its scale, and its vertical and horizontal datums, or benchmarks from which a chart's vertical and horizontal measurements are made.

**gennaker.** See *cruising spinnaker.*

**genoa:** A jib that overlaps the mast. Genoas are often described by numbers that refer to their size and to the weight of the cloth from which they are made.

**give-way vessel:** A term from the Navigation Rules used to describe the vessel that must yield to another in a situation where risk of collision exists. (Formerly called the burdened vessel.)

**Global Maritime Distress and Safety System (GMDSS):** A worldwide system for dealing with distress situations at sea.

**global positioning system (GPS):** A satellite-based radio navigation system that provides precise, continuous, worldwide, all-weather, three-dimensional navigation for land, sea, and air appplications.

**gooseneck:** A kind of universal joint that connects the mast and the boom and allows the boom to pivot up, down, or sideways.

**government channels:** Eight radio channels that are blocked and reserved for government use: 3, 21, 23, 61, 64, 81, 82, and 83.

**grapnel anchor:** A straight-shank anchor with four or five curved claw-like arms and no stock; used mostly for recovering lost articles or objects.

**ground fault circuit interrupter (GFCI):** A device intended to protect people by interrupting an AC circuit whenever its current limit is exceeded.

**ground tackle:** A collective term for the anchor and its associated gear.

**gudgeon:** The socket on the transom of a boat into which the pintle, or pin, of the rudder fits.

**gunwale:** The upper edge of a boat's sides.

**half hitch:** The simplest kind of hitch; a knot made by passing the end of the rope around the rope and then through the loop just made.

**halyard:** A line or wire used to hoist a spar, sail, or flag.

**"ham."** See *amateur radio*.

**handheld radio:** A portable type of VHF-FM radio commonly used on boats.

**harbor chart:** A chart that shows the features of the harbor, anchorages, and protection for ships.

**"hard alee":** The command given before putting the helm (tiller) to the lee side of the boat when coming about.

**hatch:** An opening in a boat's deck fitted with a watertight cover.

**hawser:** A heavy rope or cable used for mooring or towing.

**head:** A marine toilet. Also, the upper corner of a triangular sail.

**header:** A wind change that moves the eye of the wind away from the bow. This means that, to hold the same course relative to the wind, the boat will have to head away from its objective.

**heading:** The instantaneous direction of a vessel's bow. It is expressed as the angular distance relative to north, usually 000°, clockwise through 359°. "Heading" should not be confused with "course." A heading is constantly changing as a vessel yaws back and forth across the course due to the effects of sea, wind, and steering error. It is expressed in degrees of either true, magnetic, or compass direction.

**headsails:** Sails set forward of the mast.

**headstay:** A forestay that runs from the very bow of the boat to a position at or near the top of the mast.

**head up:** Turning the bow of the boat into the wind.

**headway:** The forward motion of a boat through the water.

**heat exchanger:** A part on an engine that cools water passing through it.

**heave-to:** To stop a boat without mooring it, usually by bringing a vessel close to the wind, trimming the jib and mainsail tight, and tacking without releasing the jibsheet.

**heel:** When a boat is sailing to windward, the sideways force developed by the wind on the sails that both pushes the boat to leeward and causes it to tip, or heel. Heeling can be controlled by hull shape, by a ballast keel, by crew weight, or by sail trim. Also, the base of a spar.

**helm:** The wheel or tiller controlling the rudder.

**helmsperson:** The person who steers the boat. ("Helmsman" is the traditional name.)

**hike out:** Sitting along the windward gunwale to reduce excessive heeling.

**hitch:** A knot used to secure a rope to an object or to another rope.

**hold:** A compartment belowdeck in a large vessel, used solely for carrying cargo.

**horn cleat:** An anvil-shaped fitting used for tying up anchor rodes, mooring and docking lines, sheets, and halyards.

**horse latitudes:** Either of two belts or regions near 30°N and 30°S latitude characterized by high pressure, calms, and light baffling winds.

**horsepower:** A unit of power equal, in the United States, to 746 watts.

**hull:** The load-carrying part of a vessel.

**hull identification number (HIN):** A number that includes the manufacturer's identification code, hull serial number, date of certification, and model year, displayed on the boat's hull.

**hull speed:** A boat's maximum displacement speed.

**humidity:** Moisture in the air.

**hurricane:** A large, tropical storm, measuring hundreds of miles in diameter, having steady winds in excess of 64 knots. It is called a typhoon on the Pacific Ocean and a cyclone on the Indian Ocean.

**hydrometer:** An instrument used to determine the specific gravity of a liquid and hence its strength.

**hypothermia:** A lowering of the core body temperature due to exposure to cold water or air resulting in a subnormal body temperature that can be dangerous or fatal.

**impeller:** A rubber or neoprene device within a water pump that pumps water and circulates it throughout a marine engine, or through the nozzle of a jet drive.

**imposing silence:** A vessel in distress or the station in control of distress communications may impose silence on any station that interferes by sending "Silence Mayday."

**inboard:** Inside the boat's hull. Opposite of outboard.

**inboard engine:** An engine toward the center of a ship, inside the hull.

**inboard-outboard powered:** A propulsion arrangement that places the engine inside the boat against the transom. The driveshaft passes through the transom and into a stern-drive unit that resembles the lower half of an outboard motor and contains the reduction gear and propeller shaft.

**inboard-powered:** A propulsion arrangement in which the engine and reduction gear are mounted inside the hull, and power is transmitted to the propeller through a driveshaft that penetrates the hull.

**in column:** Straight; the way a mast should look when you sight upward along the mainsail luff track or groove.

**induction system:** A system in a gasoline-powered internal combustion engine that brings fuel and air together and then mixes them in the proper proportion, vaporizes the mixture, and delivers it to the engine.

**in irons:** When a sailboat stalls halfway through a tack with its bow facing directly into the wind and its sails luffing.

**initial stability:** A boat's ability to resist the first few degrees of heeling.

**inner forestay:** Standing rigging that runs from a point on the foredeck midway between the bow and the mast to a landing point some two-thirds of the way up the mast, permitting a smaller jib to be flown in strong winds. Also called a babystay.

**international channels:** The channels used in foreign countries that in some instances have different frequencies than those used in the United States.

**intership safety channel:** The internationally defined frequency (VHF Channel 6, 156.300 MHz) for search-and-rescue and salvage operations.

**Intracoastal Waterway (ICW):** An inland waterway that runs parallel to the Atlantic and Gulf coasts from Manasquan Inlet on the New Jersey shore to Brownsville, Texas.

**isolation switch:** A switch used to disconnect batteries from the electrical system on a boat.

**jam cleat:** Similar to a horn cleat, but one of its horns forms a tapered slot into which the line is jammed.

**jet drive:** A propulsion arrangement in which an inboard engine is used to drive a high-capacity pump that forces water through a nozzle to achieve thrust. Steering is achieved by changing the direction of thrust.

**jet stream:** A long narrow current of high-speed winds blowing from a generally westerly direction and often exceeding a speed of 250 mph.

**jib:** The sail in front of the mast.

**jibe:** The downwind equivalent of tacking. Occurs whenever you turn the stern through the eye of the wind in order to bring the breeze onto the other side of the sail.

**jibsheet:** The line, usually paired, that controls the athwartships movement of the jib.

**jiffy reefing:** A reefing method in which you induce a partial luff in the mainsail, take up on the topsail so the boom won't drop when the halyard is eased, and ease the mainsheet until it luffs completely.

**keel:** The main structural member of a vessel running fore and aft; the backbone of a vessel.

**ketch:** A two-masted sailboat in which the forward mast, called the mainmast, is the larger, and the after mast, the mizzen, is stepped forward of the rudderpost.

**"king of knots":** Another name for the bowline because of its many everyday uses on boats and elsewhere.

**knocked down:** When a boat is temporarily overpowered by the wind and heeled over until its mast is nearly level with the water.

**knot (kn or kt):** A measure of speed equal to 1 nautical mile (6,076 feet) per hour.

**knot:** A fastening made by interweaving rope to form a stopper, to enclose or bind an object, to form a loop or noose, to tie a small rope to an object, or to tie the ends of two small ropes together.

**laid rope:** Rope made by twisting fibers together to form yarns.

**land station:** A radio station on land, such as a Coast Guard station.

**lapper:** A cross between a working jib and a genoa. Its luff runs nearly the length of the forestay, but its foot just overlaps the mast.

**latitude:** Angular distance north or south of the equator expressed in degrees from 0 to 90, and labeled north or south to indicate the direction of measurement; e.g., Lat. 35°N.

**lay:** To "lay a mark" is to be able to reach it without tacking. The lay of a line is the direction in which its strands are twisted, usually to the right.

**layline:** The course line a sailboat needs to reach.

**lead line:** A weighted line used to measure the depth of the water.

**leech:** The after edge of a triangular sail.

**lee helm:** The tendency of a boat to head away from the wind when the tiller is released. Generally considered a negative attribute, as it makes for tiring steering and is a potential danger.

**leeward:** The direction away from the wind. Opposite of windward.

**leeway:** The sideways slippage of a boat caused by either wind or current.

**length at the waterline (LWL):** The length of a boat measured on the horizontal plane where the hull floats on the water.

**length overall (LOA):** The length of a boat along its deck from bow to stern.

**liaison channel:** Channel 22A, a working channel of the U.S. Coast Guard.

**lie-to:** Lying more or less beam-to the wind with all sails luffing to leeward.

**lift:** Negative pressure perpendicular to the sail surface created when air passing over the leeward side of a sail (the upper side of a wing) is moving faster than the flow on the opposite side. Also, a wind change in a boat's favor that enables it to sail closer to its objective than anticipated.

**light:** The signal emitted by a lighted aid to navigation. The illuminating apparatus used to emit the light signal. A lighted aid to navigation on a fixed structure.

**lighthouse:** A lighted beacon of major importance that assists the mariner in determining his position or safe course, or warns of obstructions or dangers to navigation.

**line of position (LOP):** A line of bearing to a known origin or reference, upon which a vessel is assumed to be located. An LOP is determined by observation (visual bearing) or measurement (RDF, loran, radar, etc.). An LOP is assumed to be a straight line for visual bearings, or an arc of a circle (radar range), or part of some other curve such as a hyperbola (loran). LOPs resulting from visual observations (magnetic bearings) are generally converted to true bearings prior to plotting on a chart.

**line-of-sight transmission:** Communication when one antenna can "see" another. VHF-FM is a line-of-sight system that reaches only a little way beyond the horizon.

**lines:** A general term for rope used aboard a boat, but especially rope used for a specific function.

**line whipping:** Treating the end of a line with Dacron or nylon whipping twine to keep it from unraveling temporarily.

**list:** Permanent leaning of a vessel to one side.

**longitude:** Distance east or west of the prime meridian expressed in degrees from 0 to 180 east or west; e.g., Long. 123°W.

**long splice:** A method of joining two ropes without increasing the diameter of the rope. Normally used when line must pass through a block or over a fairlead without jamming.

**loran:** An acronym of **lo**ng **ra**nge **n**avigation; an electronic navigation system that uses a chain of transmitting stations to allow mariners and aviators with specialized receivers to determine their geographical positions.

**lower shrouds:** Shrouds that run from the sides of the hull to the mast just beneath the intersection of the spreaders. Also called lowers.

**lubber's line:** An index mark or permanent line on a compass, which is used to read the compass heading of a vessel.

**luff:** The leading edge of a triangular sail. Also, the shivering or fluttering of the luff that occurs when the angle at which the wind hits the sail's leading edge is much too small. Also, to head up into the wind, causing the sail to flutter.

**luff cringle:** The reinforced eye in the luff of the mainsail at its reefing position.

**magnetic compass:** A compass for indicating any horizontal reference direction relative to the earth's magnetic field and magnetic north. It is equipped with a graduated compass card (which is balanced and is free to turn in a horizontal plane), and a lubber's line, which serves as a reference point for direction indication.

**magnetic north:** The northerly direction of the earth's magnetic field indicated by the north-seeking pole of a compass needle.

**mainsheet:** The sheet controlling the athwartships movement of the mainsail.

**major lights:** A light of high intensity and reliability exhibited from a fixed structure or on a marine site (except range lights). Major lights include primary seacoast lights and secondary lights.

**marconi rig:** A rig on a sailboat in which triangular sails are flown in a fore-and-aft plane. Also known as a Bermudan or jib-headed rig.

**maritime control channel:** Channel 17, used to talk to ships and coast stations operated by state or local governments. The message must be about regulation and control, boating activities, or assistance to ships.

**Maritime Mobile Service Identity (MMSI) number:** A unique serial number that identifies an individual vesssel, a group of vessels, or a coast station. Required for use with digital selective calling equipment.

**marlinespike:** A spike for opening the strands of a rope while splicing. The art of handling and working rope.

**masthead shrouds.** See *upper shrouds*.

**mast partner:** A hole in the deck or in a seat that helps brace the mast both athwartships and fore and aft.

**mast step:** A socket shaped so that the spar's heel cannot slide off.

**Mayday:** Spoken international distress signal, repeated three times, given to indicate that a mobile station is threatened by grave and imminent danger and requests immediate assistance.

**mean high water (MHW):** A tidal datum that is the average of all high water heights observed over a specific 19-year cycle.

**mean lower low water (MLLW):** A tidal datum that is the average of the lowest low water heights of each tidal day observed over a specific 19-year cycle.

**measuring rope:** Once done by a rope's circumference, but now usually done by its diameter.

**Mercator projection:** The projection technique most commonly used in the production of navigational charts. This is a cylindrical projection ingeniously modified by expanding the scale at increasing latitudes to preserve directions and to maintain the correct relationships between the latitude and longitude scales.

**meridian (geographic meridian):** A great circle of the earth passing through both the geographic poles and any given point on the earth's surface.

**minor lights:** An automatic unmanned light on a fixed structure usually showing low to moderate intensity. Minor lights are established in harbors, along channels, along rivers, and in isolated locations.

**mixed tide:** Type of tide with a large inequality in the high or low or both water heights, with two high waters and two low waters usually occurring each tidal day. Actually, all tides are mixed, but the name is usually applied to the tides intermediate to those predominantly semidiurnal and those predominantly diurnal.

**mooring:** Chain or synthetic line that attaches a floating object to a stationary object (e.g., dock, mooring buoy).

**mooring cleat.** See *horn cleat*.

**mooring line:** The line, often made of nylon, used to secure a boat to a mooring buoy or pier.

**mooring pendant:** A heavy nylon rope with a large eye spliced in its foredeck end attached to the surface buoy of a mooring rig.

**mushroom anchor:** A stockless anchor with a cast-iron bowl at the end of the shank; used principally in large sizes for permanent moorings.

**National Ocean Service (NOS):** An agency of the National Oceanic and Atmospheric Administration that publishes charts of all U.S. waters other than those used on navigable rivers. It also makes data available showing the times and levels of predicted tides for the Atlantic, Gulf, and Pacific coasts and for tidal rivers.

**National Weather Service (NWS):** A division of the National Oceanic and Atmospheric Administration that gives accurate weather forecasts.

**natural fiber rope:** Rope made of natural fibers such as manila, sisal, hemp, jute, cotton, and flax.

**nautical chart:** Printed or electronic geographic representation of waterways showing positions of aids to navigation and other fixed points and references to guide the mariner.

**nautical mile (nm):** Length of 1 minute of latitude, approximately 6,076 feet compared to 5,280 feet per a statute mile.

**navigable waters:** Coastal waters, including bays, sounds, rivers, and lakes, that are navigable from the sea.

**navigation:** The art and science of locating your position (knowing where you are) and how to get where you want to go (plotting a course).

**navigational channel:** A bridge-to-bridge radio channel available to all ships; the messages must be about vessel navigation.

**Navigation Rules:** Regulations governing the movement of vessels in relation to each other, formerly the Rules of the Road.

**nimbus:** A rain cloud or thunderhead.

**noncommercial channel:** A channel used to send messages about the needs of a vessel, such as fishing reports, rendezvous, repair scheduling, and berthing.

**no-wake zone:** An area where you must slow your vessel so it does not make either a bow or stern wake; usually this means the vessel is off plane and level in the water.

**nylon rope:** Rope made of the synthetic fiber nylon does not shrink when wet, stretches more than any other synthetic or natural fiber rope, and resists chafing.

**occulting light:** A light in which the total duration of light in each period is clearly longer than the total duration of darkness and in which the intervals of darkness (occultations) are all of equal duration. (Commonly used for a single occulting light that exhibits only single occultations, which are repeated at regular intervals.)

**open circulation system:** A system in which water is pumped into an internal combustion engine from outside the boat, circulates through its water channels, and is then dumped overboard. Also called raw-water cooling.

**operating cycle:** The cycle by which a marine engine operates, either two- or four-cycle.

**operations message:** A message about navigation or the movement or management of vessels.

**outboard:** Toward or beyond the boat's sides. Opposite of inboard.

**outboard engine:** A detachable engine mounted on a boat's stern.

**outboard-powered:** A propulsion arrangement in which the engine is mounted outside the hull on the transom.

**outdrive:** The system of engine gears mounted outside the boat on the transom.

**outhaul:** A carriage riding on the boom that extends the foot of the sail.

**out of trim:** When all the crew are on one side of a boat, causing it to heel.

**overhand knot:** Used as a stopper or to prevent a freshly cut rope from unlaying or unraveling. Tied by making an overhand loop in the standing part of the line, then passing the working end up through the loop and pulling it tight.

**overpowered:** When a boat develops excessive weather helm.

**overstand:** Waiting too long to tack.

**painter:** A line attached to the bow of a small boat for use in towing or making fast.

**Pan-Pan:** Spoken urgency signal, repeated three times, used when the safety of a vessel or person is in jeopardy.

**parallel of latitude:** Any of the imaginary lines parallel to the equator and representing latitude.

**parallel rulers:** An instrument for transferring a line parallel to itself, used in chartwork for drawing and measuring courses or bearings.

**part:** To sever or otherwise break apart, as a line.

**pay out:** To ease out a line, or let it run in a controlled manner.

**pendant:** A line by which a boat is made fast to a buoy.

**pennant:** A small flag, most often a signal flag.

**personal flotation device (PFD):** A life jacket that, when properly used, will support a person in the water. Available in several sizes and types.

**personal watercraft (PWC):** A small motorized vessel powered by a jet-drive engine.

**phonetic alphabet:** Used when radio signals are weak and reception is poor to express words by saying each letter in a clear and particular way.

**phonetic numbers:** Used when radio signals are weak and reception is poor to express numbers in a clear and particular way.

**pile (piling):** A long, heavy timber driven into the seabed or riverbed to serve as a support for an aid to navigation or dock.

**piloting:** Navigation involving frequent or continuous reference to charted objects and landmarks, ATONs, and depth soundings.

**pintle:** The pin on the forward edge of a rudder that goes into a corresponding socket, or gudgeon.

**pitchpoling:** A boat being thrown end over end in rough seas.

**pivot point:** A point somewhat aft of the bow, somewhere forward of the midpoint. To an observer on board, a vessel appears to turn about its pivot point.

**planing hull:** A type of hull that, when moving fast enough and with the right weight distribution, can ride on top of the water.

**point:** To sail toward the eye of the wind. Most boats cannot point closer than 45° to the true wind.

**points of sailing:** Running, close hauled, and reaching.

**polyconic projection:** A map or chart projection in which the earth is projected on a series of cones concentric with the earth's axis and tangent to the sphere of the earth. Charts of the Great Lakes are typically based on the polyconic projection.

**polyester rope:** A synthetic fiber rope often used for sheets and halyards; aka Dacron, Terylene, etc.

**polypropylene rope:** The least costly of the common synthetic ropes; the major advantage is that it floats.

**port:** The left side of a boat looking forward. Also, a harbor.

**port operations channel:** A radio channel used to direct the movement of ships in or near ports, locks, or waterways.

**port tack:** Sailing with the wind coming over the boat's port side and the main boom extended out to starboard.

**position:** On the earth this refers to the actual geographic location of a vessel defined by two parameters called coordinates. Those customarily used are latitude and longitude. Position may also be expressed as a bearing and distance from an object, the position of which is known.

**preferred channel mark:** An aid to navigation that indicates a channel junction or bifurcation between a main (preferred) and a subordinate channel. Its color scheme and its light characteristics or its shape assist the navigator in identifying the preferred channel.

**preventer:** A line from a sailboat's main boom to a belay point forward of it. Can help prevent an accidental jibe.

**prime meridian:** The meridian passing through Greenwich, England, from which both east and west longitude are measured; i.e., the 0° meridian.

**procedure words (prowords):** An oral shorthand used to express common words and phrases in radiotelephone communication.

**propeller:** A device consisting of a central hub with radiating blades forming a helical pattern that when turned in the water creates a discharge that drives a boat.

**prop walk:** When a counterclockwise-turning propeller pulls the stern to port as a boat backs up.

**public correspondence:** Ship-to-shore radiotelephone communications through a public coast radio station.

**pulpit:** A platform built forward of a vessel's bow currently used to assist in raising or lowering an anchor but formerly the place where a harpooner stood.

**push-to-talk button:** A button on a microphone that you press to begin sending a radio message.

**quarter:** The corner of the transom.

**quick light:** A light with more than 50 but less than 80 flashes per minute. (Previously called quick flashing light.)

**radar:** Self-contained navigation and collision avoidance system consisting of a shipboard transmitter and receiver. The transmitter transmits briefly, then shuts off to permit the receiver to "listen" for the reflected transmission or echo.

**radial head:** A spinnaker construction that consists of parallel, horizontal panels across the bottom half of the sail and an arrangement of triangular panels at the top. Suitable for broad reaching and running in light to moderate winds.

**radiobeacon:** Electronic apparatus that transmits a radio signal for use in providing a mariner a line of position.

**radio check:** Spoken test call by a boater asking what the strength and clarity of the transmission is; a response indicates the radio is working.

**radio direction finding (RDF):** Older short-range radio navigation system consisting of a series of land-based stations broadcasting in the LF/MF band and onboard receivers with directional antennas.

**radio language:** Special words used to transmit radio messages quickly and clearly.

**radio station log:** A record of calls made and received by a radio station.

**rake:** The fore-and-aft tilt of the mast.

**range:** The distance in nautical miles that a vessel can travel with the available fuel on board. The range may or may not include an allowance for a fuel reserve. Range is a function of throttle setting and other factors.

**ranges:** A pair of ATONs placed a suitable distance apart, with the far daymark mounted higher than the near one. When the range marks are in line, the vessel is in the channel. Ranges can also be established by any charted objects.

**raw-water cooling.** See *open circulation system*.

**reach:** Sailing with the wind blowing more or less perpendicular to the boat's course.

**reacher:** A sail that is as big in area as a genoa, but made of lighter fabric used for reaching.

**"ready about":** The preparatory command, given before "hard alee," to get ready to tack.

**reciprocal bearing or course:** A bearing or course that differs from the original by 180°.

**reciprocal direction:** Corresponding but reversed direction.

**red, right, returning:** Saying to remember which aids you should be seeing off the vessel's starboard side when returning from seaward.

**red sector:** A sector of the circle of visibility of a navigational light in which a red light is exhibited. Such sectors are designated by their limiting bearings, as observed at some point other than the light. Red sectors are often located such that they warn of danger to vessels.

**reef:** To reduce the area of the sail exposed to the wind.

**reef knot:** A square knot used to secure a reefed sail to a boom.

**reeve:** To pass a line through a block or similar device.

**regulatory mark:** A white and orange aid to navigation with no lateral significance. Used to indicate a special meaning to the mariner, such as danger, restricted operations, or an exclusion area.

**restricted visibility:** Any condition in which visibility is restricted by fog, mist, falling snow, heavy rainstorms, sandstorms, or other similar causes.

**rig:** The collective term for the various elements that form a sailboat's power system—the spars, the rigging, and the sails.

**rigging:** The general term for all the lines of a vessel. Standing rigging stays put; it supports the mast under tension. Running rigging runs through blocks to raise, lower, ease out, or trim in the sails; it requires frequent adjustment.

**roach:** Convex curve of the leech of a sail.

**rode:** The line and chain of an anchor.

**roller furling:** Reefing by rolling a sail around a rod mounted inside a specially designed mat or on the aft edge of a standard mast.

**roller reefing:** A method of reefing in which the boom is designed so that it can be rolled around its axis, which winds the sail tightly around the boom like an old-fashioned window shade.

**rolling hitch:** A hitch made by tying one line to the standing part of another; used to tie a line to the working end of a second line.

**rope:** Cordage made of natural or synthetic fibers; can also be made of steel wire.

**rudder:** A vertical plate or board that can be pivoted to steer a boat.

**running:** Sailing with the wind more or less directly astern.

**running backstays:** Standing rigging that provides aftward tension to balance the forestay if the forestay doesn't end near the masthead.

**running lights:** Lights required to be shown on boats between sundown and sunup.

**running rigging:** Rigging—sheets, halyards, topping lifts, downhauls, vangs, etc.—that runs through blocks to raise, lower, ease out, or trim in the sails; it requires frequent adjustment.

**sacrificial zincs:** Zinc plates or bars used to prevent destruction of metal parts on engines by galvanic action.

**safety call:** A DSC alert to all stations to warn of hazards to normal waterway use.

**safety signal.** See *Sécurité*.

**sails:** Flexible vertical airfoils, generally made of cloth, that use wind pressure to propel a boat.

**sail stop:** Lengths of sail fabric or rubberized shock cord used to bundle a lowered sail to its boom.

**schooner:** Usually a two-masted vessel of some size with the mainmast aft and the smaller foremast forward.

**scope:** Length of anchor line or chain. The ratio of the length of the anchor rode to the vertical distance from your bow chock to the seabed (i.e., the depth of the water plus the distance from the water surface to the bow chock).

**seacock:** Valve in the ship's hull through which seawater may pass.

**sea trial:** A short cruise to test the mechanical and handling characteristics of a boat.

**seaworthy:** Refers to a boat capable of putting to sea and meeting any usual sea conditions.

**secrecy of communication:** The Federal Communications Act protects the secrecy of radio communications and requires that a person not communicate the contents of any radio message to anyone other than the addressee or the addressee's agent or attorney unless authorized to do so.

**Sécurité:** Spoken safety signal, repeated three times, used to warn others of hazards to normal waterway use.

**seelonce.** See *silence*.

**selectivity:** A measure of how well a radio receiver rejects signals from other channels close to the channel you are using.

**self-tailing winch:** A winch that has a notched channel in the top of its drum that holds the line as it feeds off the drum; the notched channel also acts as a cleat to hold the line.

**semidiurnal:** Having a period or cycle of approximately half a tidal day. The predominating type of tide throughout the world is semidiurnal, with two high waters and two low waters each tidal day. The tidal current is said to be semidiurnal when there are two flood and two ebb periods each day.

**sensitivity:** The ability of a radio set to pick up distant signals.

**72 COLREGS.** See *COLREGS 72*.

**shackle:** A U-shaped connector with a pin or bolt across the open end.

**sheave:** The rolling part of a block.

**sheet:** The line used to control the forward or athwartships movement of a sail.

**sheet bend:** A bend used to join two ropes of unequal size. Functionally different from a square knot in that it should be used between lines of different diameters.

**ship station license:** An FCC license required to operate marine VHF radio equipment aboard a vessel.

**shock cord:** A multistrand rubber line with a synthetic cover and hooks or eyes on each end.

**short splice:** A method of permanently joining the ends of two ropes.

**shortwave radio:** Operates in eight frequency bands and can often reach around the globe.

**shrouds:** Standing rigging that supports the mast at the sides of the boat.

**signal strength:** The power on which a radio transmits; a VHF-FM set must be able to transmit on a power of 1 watt and may have a maximum power of 25 watts.

**silence:** The word (pronounced "seelonce") used by a vessel in distress or the station in control of distress communications to impose silence on any radio station that interferes. "Silence distress" is a command to maintain radio silence during a Mayday, issued by other vessels in the vicinity of the rescue.

**single-braid rope:** One braid of rope made by interweaving individual fibers or by weaving three or four strands of fiber. Used for things such as sailbag ties and flag halyards.

**single-sideband radio (SSB):** A radio that varies in range depending on the time of day, the season, and the frequency of the channel being used. Covers the marine portion of the medium-frequency band and the international marine channels in the high-frequency band.

**skiff:** A flat-bottom utility boat with either straight or slightly flared sides.

**slippery sheet bend:** A variation of the sheet bend that is easier to untie. Tie it by forming a bight in the end of the smaller line and tucking this bight under the standing part of the smaller line.

**sloop:** A vessel with a single mast and two sails, one set ahead of the mast and one behind.

**spar:** A general term for masts, yards, booms, etc.

**speed curve:** A curve relating the vessel's speed through the water to the engine's throttle setting expressed in revolutions per minute (rpm).

**spinnaker:** A large, light-air headsail used for running or reaching.

**spinnaker guy:** The sheet attached to the tack once a spinnaker is set.

**splice:** A method used to tie two pieces of line together or to form a permanent loop, called an eye, at the end of a line.

**spoken emergency call:** Any of the three spoken emergency signals—distress, urgency, and safety—initiated on Channel 16.

**spreaders:** A pair of horizontal spars fitted about two-thirds of the way up a mast used to widen the angle at which the shrouds reaches the masthead, giving a more effective sideways angle of pull.

**spring line:** A fore-and-aft line used in docking and undocking, or to prevent the boat from moving forward or astern while made fast to a dock.

**square knot.** See *reef knot.*

**squelch:** A radio control that suppresses background interference.

**standing part:** That part of a line that is made fast. The main part of a line as distinguished from the bight and the bitter end.

**standing rigging:** Standing rigging—wires, terminals, and fittings—that stays put; it supports the mast under tension.

**stand-on vessel:** The vessel that continues its course in the same direction at the same speed during a crossing or overtaking situation, unless a collision appears imminent. (Formerly called the privileged vessel.)

**starboard:** The right side of a boat when looking forward.

**starboard tack:** Sailing with the wind coming over the boat's starboard side and the main boom extended out to port.

**starcut:** A spinnaker that appears to have a three-pointed star superimposed on it. Used downwind in heavier weather or for beam and close reaching in normal conditions.

**stay:** Standing rigging that supports the mast from forward and aft.

**staysail:** A sail (usually triangular) set on one of the stays.

**steerage:** The act or practice of steering. A ship's steering mechanism.

**steerageway:** The lowest speed at which a vessel can be steered.

**stem:** The foremost upright timber of a vessel to which the keel and ends of the planks are attached. The forwardmost part of the bow.

**stern:** The after part of the boat.

**stern drive:** An engine that is mounted inside a boat, near its stern.

**stopper knot:** A knot at the end of a line to keep the line from slipping through a hole or a block.

**stratus clouds:** Air masses that are lifted gently and evenly form clouds that are even, flat, and layered.

**strike:** To lower the sails quickly.

**stuffing box:** The driveshaft bearing that is located where the propeller shaft goes through the hull of a boat.

**swamp:** To fill with water, but not settle to the bottom.

**swells:** Relatively long wind-generated waves that have traveled out of the generating area. They exhibit more regular and longer periods (distances between swells) and flatter crests.

**swing keel:** A heavy, retractable keel that looks and operates like a centerboard.

**synthetic rope:** Rope made from materials such as nylon, polyester, and polypropylene.

**tabernacle:** A hinged fitting at the base of the mast to enable the mast to be easily raised or lowered.

**tack:** To come about. Also, sailing with the wind on a given side of the boat, as in starboard or port tack. Also, the lower forward corner of a sail.

**tacking:** Turning a boat's bow through the wind's eye from close hauled on one tack to close hauled on the other tack. Also known as coming about or going about.

**tackle:** A combination of blocks and line to increase mechanical advantage.

**tack pendant:** A length of wire running from the jib tack to the deck.

**telltale:** Lengths of yarn, ribbons, or strips of fabric tied to shrouds that indicate wind direction. Also known as woolies, streamers, or wind tallies.

**thimble:** A horse collar–shaped metal or plastic device that is inserted in the eye splice at the end of an anchor line. Also, a grooved metal loop around which a rope or wire rope may be spliced, thus making the spliced eye more chafe resistant.

**through-bolt:** A bolt that is used to fasten a fitting to the deck. It goes through the deck and backing plate (located belowdeck).

**thwart:** A seat or brace running laterally across a boat.

**tidal current:** Horizontal motion of water caused by the vertical rise and fall of the tide.

**tide:** Periodic vertical rise and fall of the water resulting from the gravitational interactions between the sun, moon, and earth.

**tiller:** A bar or handle for turning a boat's rudder or an outboard motor.

**toggle:** A small casting that allows the turnbuckle to lie in the same straight line as the stay or shroud to which it is fitted.

**topping lift:** Running rigging that is used to support a boom when its sail is not raised.

**transceiver:** A radio set such as a VHF-FM set that is both a transmitter and a receiver.

**transom:** The stern cross section of a square-sterned boat.

**traveler:** A device that enables you to sheet the mainsail to leeward, amidships, or to windward.

**trimaran:** A three-hulled boat.

**tri-radial cut:** A spinnaker construction that consists of three or four horizontal panels in its midsection, above and below which are triangular panels with their vertices in the corners as in the starcut. Now the most common cut because it can be flown through a broad range of conditions.

**true wind:** Air in motion.

**tuning the rig:** Tightening the various pieces of standing rigging to make a balanced system.

**turn:** A bight, or the middle part of a slack line, that is around an object or the rope itself.

**turnbuckle:** A threaded fitting to pull two eyes together for adjustment of standing rigging.

**twin propellers (screws):** A boat equipped with two engines and two propellers.

**two half hitches:** The same as a clove hitch tied around the standing part of a line.

**ultimate stability:** A boat's resistance to capsize.

**underway:** A vessel not at anchor, made fast to a pier or wharf, or aground.

**Uniform State Waterway Marking System (USWMS):** A system of marks to supplement the federal system in marking of state waters. A system of regulatory markers to warn a vessel operator of dangers and to provide general information and directions.

**upper shrouds:** Shrouds that run over spreaders to the masthead. Also called uppers, or masthead or cap shrouds.

**urgency signal.** See *Pan-Pan.*

**U.S. Aids to Navigation System:** The principal buoyage system used in the United States. Conforms to the Region B standards of the International Association of Lighthouse Authorities (IALA). The U.S. ATON System uses buoys, beacons, and minor lights as marks. These mark obstructions, dangers such as wrecks, the edges of navigable channels, and other things of importance to mariners. The U.S. Coast Guard maintains the marks in the system.

**USA-International switch:** A two-position switch on a VHF-FM radio used to choose channels in the United States and those in foreign countries.

**utility outboard:** A boat specifically designed for outboard motors.

**vang.** See *boom vang.*

**variation:** The angular difference between the magnetic meridian and the geographic meridian at a particular location.

**very high frequency (VHF) radio:** A radio system with a frequency of 30 MHz to 300 MHz that is essentially a line-of-sight system limited in range to just beyond the horizon.

**vessel traffic service (VTS):** A shore-based service to control movements of large ships in harbors.

**visual distress signal (VDS):** A signal to attract attention and to guide rescuers in a search-and-rescue situation.

**wake:** Disturbed water astern of a moving vessel.

**warm front:** An advancing edge of a warm air mass.

**waterline:** The line of intersection of the water surface with the boat's hull.

**wave:** A periodic disturbance of the sea surface, most often caused by wind.

**wave height:** The height from the bottom of a wave's trough to the top of its crest, measured in the vertical, not diagonal.

**waypoint:** A place established on the globe that represents fixes that boaters want to go to or come from.

**weather:** Windward side of a boat.

**weather channel:** Any of three radio channels in the United States used to give weather forecasts.

**weather helm:** The tendency of a boat to round up into the wind when its tiller is released.

**weather hitch:** A hitch made by making a figure eight and finishing it off with an underhand loop over one of the horns of a cleat.

**weaver's knot.** See *sheet bend.*

**webbing:** A flat line formed by weaving together synthetic fibers.

**wharf:** A man-made structure bounding the edge of a dock and built along or at an angle to the shoreline, used for loading, unloading, or tying up vessels.

**whipping:** The act of wrapping the end of a piece of rope to prevent it from fraying.

**whisker pole:** A portable spar used to extend the jib.

**winch:** A device to increase hauling power when raising or trimming sails, adjusting tows, or weighing anchor.

**wind of motion:** The wind created by a moving vehicle, whether on land or sea, as it moves through the air.

**wind's eye.** See *eye of the wind.*

**windward:** Toward the direction from which the wind is coming. Opposite of leeward.

**wing and wing:** Running with the mainsail set on one side of the boat and the jib set on the other side.

**wing keel:** A keel with horizontal winglets at its lower end.

**wire rope:** A kind of rope used on boats that is nearly always stainless steel, which provides maximum strength and minimum stretch. The standing or permanent rigging on a sailboat is usually wire rope, and running rigging is often wire rope.

**working channel:** A radio channel used for voice communications.

**working end:** The end of a rope opposite the bitter end that can be attached to an anchor or a cleat.

**working sails:** Previously, sails employed in everyday business. Currently, smaller, stronger cruising sails.

**yaw:** Rotary oscillation about a vessel's vertical axis in a seaway. Sheering off alternately to port and starboard.

**yawl:** A two-masted sailboat with the small mizzen stepped aft of the rudderpost.